Systematic Investing in Credit

The Frank J. Fabozzi Series

Systematic Investing in Credit

ARIK BEN DOR
ALBERT DESCLÉE
LEV DYNKIN
JAY HYMAN
SIMON POLBENNIKOV

WILEY

For general information on our other products and services or for technical support, please contact our Customer Care Department within the United States at (800) 762-2974, outside the United States at (317) 572-3993 or fax (317) 572-4002.

Wiley also publishes its books in a variety of electronic formats. Some content that appears in print may not be available in electronic books. For more information about Wiley products, visit our web site at www.wiley.com.

Library of Congress Cataloging-in-Publication Data is Available:

Hardback: 9781119751281
Adobe PDF: 9781119751304
ePUB: 9781119751298

10 9 8 7 6 5 4 3 2 1

Acknowledgments

The authors would like to thank their colleagues at Barclays Research – Vadim Konstantinovsky, Jingling Guan, Mathieu Dubois, Xiaming Zeng and Stephan Florig for their contributions to the book and help in reviewing and editing the manuscript.

The authors would also like to acknowledge former colleagues Carlo Rosa, Bruce Phelps, Anando Maitra, Jason Xu and Kwok Yuen Ng for their past contributions to the group's research.

The authors are very grateful to Jeff Meli – Head of Barclays Research – for his support of the group's work.

The authors would like to recognize Laurent Caraffa, Richard Cunningham, Steve Lessing, Paul Degen and Ellis Thomas for their consistent support of our work and for including us in their dialog with institutional investors who motivated many of the studies contained in this book.

Finally, the authors would like to thank their families for bearing over the years the sacrifices of family time necessary to produce the research in this book and prepare it for publication.

Contents

Foreword

I first met Lev Dynkin and other members of the Barclays Quantitative Portfolio Strategy (QPS) Group at one of their esteemed annual investment councils. The experience brought back fond memories of the intimate conferences from my prior academic life in physics. The focus of the QPS council was not to sell or promote but rather to expand the knowledge of attendees and seek understanding of complex market phenomena. Evident throughout the day was the team's sincere desire to help investors achieve better outcomes.

For over 25 years, the QPS team has been at the forefront of research into methods to guide investors in making better decisions in their fixed income portfolios. This book is another milestone for this respected team. Here they compile their past and present research for the benefit of a broader investment community. The focus is not simply on innovation for its own sake. Rather it is to share and educate readers, thereby advancing the field and adding to the core knowledge of all market participants.

Why does this collection of insights deserve your attention? Because systematic approaches—and, more broadly, scientific approaches—are the future of credit investing. Scientific problem solving is the primary means of tackling data-rich complexity in virtually any field, investment related or not. In the field of investing, such approaches utilize the best of the human mind's natural ability to design processes and methodologies while avoiding the cognitive and behavioral biases inherent within traditional discretionary asset management.

Scientific approaches in fixed income credit are the exception rather than the rule and have lagged those in equity markets. This is because the successful implementation of a scientific investment approach generally requires four primary inputs: rich and relevant data availability, high breadth of investable instruments, sophisticated markets enabling long and short positioning, and a growing body of research, built on a foundation of prior knowledge, from which to find new and workable insights.

Credit markets in recent years have seen these four conditions met for the first time. This was not the case 20 years ago when today's homogeneous European credit market was born, nor when the first credit default swap was traded in the 1990s. Scientific credit investing stands today where scientific equity investing stood at the turn of the century: in an uncrowded space and on the threshold of considerable secular growth. This suggests significant and durable alpha generation possibilities for those investors capable of grasping the opportunity at hand.

It's not easy, however: Credit is complex, heterogeneous, and illiquid relative to equities. Scientific credit investing requires not only predictive insights but also the analysis and incorporation of bespoke liquidity, risk, and transaction cost considerations. Growing issuer breadth further demands high data capture. If success is achieved, the prize is enormous: the intellectual property of a scientific approach sits at an organizational level rather than in the minds of star traders. This lasting form of knowledge management can be built upon to create further iterative improvement—a powerful incentive.

Necessarily, this book covers only a small, yet important, part of the annals of current research in the field. A book could be written on each component of the investment process: selection of the traded universe, data management and application, creation and utilization of predictive insights, and the crucial step of portfolio construction—where insights must optimally and realistically meet risk management, trading costs, and liquidity considerations specific to credit. Each part of the process stands to benefit from a rigorous approach.

A collaborative spirit runs through the scientific investment community that is generally in contrast to the siloed mindset of traditional active management. This positive knowledge sharing is evident across a number of scientific firms and their practitioners, who publish insights and share best practices with investors. It is in this spirit that the QPS team has compiled the contents herein. I know nothing will make the QPS team happier than if readers benefit from, and build upon, QPS's research in the context of their own portfolios.

May this book inform and guide you on your own scientific journey, even as the QPS team tackles new frontiers of research.

Alex Khein
Chief Executive
BlueCove Limited

Preface

For over two decades, Barclays Research's Quantitative Portfolio Strategy (QPS) group has been recognized as a leading source of innovative insights into the fixed income markets. In the 1990s, the team was involved in the development of what was then known as the Lehman Brothers Global Family of Indices, providing an essential foundation for quantitative analysis of fixed income markets: high-quality data, available systematically. Today, the Bloomberg Barclays fixed income indices remain an integral part of the active and passive global portfolio management processes.

In its early years, the QPS team made use of fixed income data to create some of the first risk and return analytics for corporate bond portfolios, coded in C for Windows 1.0 and shipped to clients by mail every month on floppy disks. Client requests for data analysis beyond the scope of the software platform led to bespoke research projects and, ultimately, to the shift in the QPS team's focus toward a broad range of quantitative topics in portfolio management. Over the years, the group cemented its reputation among fixed income professionals, collecting many accolades along the way, including being repeatedly top ranked in *Institutional Investor* surveys in the United States and Europe.[1]

The QPS team has always paired a relentless focus on relevant, implementable findings in response to questions from practitioners with a sophisticated and rigorous approach. Many of the ideas behind the team's research projects come from interactions with a broad range of investors, through one-on-one meetings as well as various seminars and councils organized by Barclays. This has enabled the team to expand its research beyond its traditional fixed income focus. One important example is the group's development of cross-asset signals, where information from credit is applied to equities, and vice versa. While simple in concept, mapping bonds to equities requires a deep understanding of corporate bonds, which the team has developed over decades. Several of the approaches detailed in this book draw on these cross-asset insights.

The QPS group also remains closely connected with Barclays Research's fundamental analysts. This connectivity has helped the team incorporate fundamental data alongside prices and risk metrics in its products; several of these are discussed in detail in this volume. Going forward, the team remains committed to evolving its approach. Recently it has begun to partner with Barclays Research's data science team, with a view to incorporating modern data techniques and new, and at times larger, datasets into its analysis.

It is rare to find a group that has had such consistent success with its core mission over the years, yet remains so committed to innovation and creativity. Collaborating with the QPS team has been a great privilege.

—Jeff Meli, Head of Barclays Research

NOTE

1. The team ranked #1 in the Quantitative Analysis category in the *Institutional Investor* All-America Fixed Income Research Team Survey (2006–2008) and in 2017 and #2 in 2018. From 2009 to2016, this category was not included. The team ranked #1 in the Quantitative Analysis category in the All-Europe *Institutional Investor* Fixed Income Research Survey (2013–2015 and 2018).

Introduction

A systematic approach to investing in corporate bond portfolios is becoming more widely used by investors as a result of the increased availability of fixed income data, improved price transparency, and the influence of established quantitative insights from the equity markets. This book is focused on new research in this area covering a broad spectrum of algorithmic credit investing: exploiting inefficiencies of benchmark indices, investing based on factors constructed using a combination of fundamental and market data as well as extending quantitative equity methodologies and signals to credit.

The authors are long-term members of the Quantitative Portfolio Strategy (QPS) group, which has been a part of Barclays (and, previously, Lehman Brothers) Research for nearly three decades. The group has a unique focus on working with major institutional investors across the globe on all issues of portfolio management that are quantitative in nature. As a result of this focus, research results produced by the group are practical and implementable. The group's publications target portfolio managers and other investment practitioners as well as research analysts and academics. Past involvement by the QPS group in the creation and replication of Bloomberg Barclays Fixed Income Indices and its expertise in quantitative research in both equities and bonds further help it to produce innovative portfolio construction methodologies and timing signals.

This is the fourth book published by the QPS team. The group's prior books—*Quantitative Credit Portfolio Management* (Wiley, 2012) and *Quantitative Management of Bond Portfolios* (Princeton University Press, 2007)—were focused on QPS original risk measures, benchmark customization and replication, and other aspects of the investment process. The 2012 book was dedicated to credit investing while the 2007 book also included our research related to mortgage-backed securities and rates portfolio management. One of our risk measures for credit securities—Duration Times Spread (DTS)—was broadly adopted by institutional investors since its introduction in 2005 and is the sole subject of another QPS book, *A Decade of Duration Times Spread (DTS)* (Barclays, 2015). Given the broad use of DTS, we continue to monitor its validity in different market regimes and credit asset classes.

In this book, we focus on our original research into systematic strategies—fully rules-based algorithmic methodologies aimed at improving credit portfolio performance by generating alpha. Some of the strategies fall into "smart beta" category and take advantage of inefficiencies in conventional market-value-weighted benchmarks. Others harvest risk premia associated with risk factors, both traditional and new, and are formulated as scorecards—ranking methodologies for credit securities, issuers, and industry sectors by measures that are informative of future performance. Most of these scorecards are produced by Barclays Research on a periodic basis and are shared with clients.

All the materials included in the book reflect QPS research as it was originally published for Barclays clients*. We decided against going back and updating individual chapters to avoid any possibility of hindsight tainting the results.

Credit portfolio management was originally, and still mostly is, discretionary in nature. Managers form views on issuers, industry sectors, and credit spread curves based on fundamental bottom-up analysis and seek to implement those views using securities available in the market subject to liquidity constraints. However, there is a growing trend toward incorporating systematic (algorithmic) approaches into this process, either as additional filters of the eligible investment universe or as checks on the discretionary choices made by the fundamental manager or even—in some cases – as stand-alone strategies. This trend is helped by the increasing availability of bond-level index data and of large datasets that require a quantitative approach to be useful in the investment process as well as by the migration of rich, highly developed systematic equity methodologies into credit management.

Over the years, we have often heard investors question whether credit is an independent asset class or can be replaced in a portfolio by an appropriately weighted combination of Treasury bonds and equities. Part I addresses this fundamental question head-on with a thorough empirical analysis of the role of credit in a Treasury/equities portfolio. We analyze the underlying sources of the performance difference between a credit portfolio and a risk-matched and issuer-matched portfolio of equities and Treasuries. To ensure that the corporate bond portfolios and the Treasury/equity portfolios in this study are exposed to the same corporate entities, we rely on an issuer-level historical mapping between bond issuers and the associated equity tickers built by our team over time. This very detailed mapping process required that we correctly reflect all corporate events that can cause this mapping to

---

*Fixed income index data used in this book is sourced from Bloomberg Barclays Indices.

change as well as address several technical challenges of the differences between the two markets. We rely on this mapping throughout this book for all studies and models that analyze corporate bonds using stock market data or fundamental issuer information.

Credit investing is often an index-centric process subjecting managers to index rules and constraints. The continued popularity of low-fee passive management, coupled with the need for pension consultants to have a basis for comparison among different managers, ensures that it will remain this way going forward. In Part II we discuss ways of exploiting index inefficiencies to generate alpha. Empirical evidence of a particular methodology generating outperformance is never sufficient for us to call it "smart beta" or systematic alpha. We always insist on economic intuition explaining which market inefficiency allows for the outperformance and whether there is a reason to expect it to persist or to mean-revert. In this sense, index inefficiencies are among the most reliable sources of outperformance, as they stem from the rules of inclusion and elimination of securities built into the index definition. These rules, which are predefined and independent of market pricing, lead to strong demand for debt being added to the index increasing allocations to large borrowers and strong selling pressure on issuers being dropped from the index. These dynamics can often cause bonds to trade at levels that diverge from their financial fair value. We further look at the performance impact of other liquidation constraints based on rating downgrades in a credit portfolio beyond the traditional index constraints. We demonstrate their impact on portfolio performance and on the optimal allocation in a portfolio to different rating categories. This forced liquidation is one of the reasons long-horizon investors do not always significantly overweight credit during various crises and wait for the spreads to mean revert to generate alpha. The liquidation rule may trigger a realized loss before spreads recover.

In Part III we proceed with research on the performance implications of bond portfolio characteristics: both traditional ones, such as coupon level and maturity distribution, and those that came into focus more recently such as environmental, social, and governance (ESG) rankings. We show that low-coupon bonds offer a performance advantage over their high-coupon peers at the time of significant changes in Treasury yields due to better price protection provided by the recovery value. We also explain the causes of the outperformance of short-dated corporates over long-dated peers and attribute it to market factors. Our study of the impact of an ESG tilt on credit portfolio performance was first undertaken to see whether it leads to reduced returns. Like so many of our studies, it was prompted by a large US asset manager seeking to understand whether such tilt is justified in its pension mandate, given the return maximization objective. The concern was that high-ESG bonds might be overbought, which could lead to lower returns. We were surprised to find in a series of studies that, all else equal, an ESG tilt led to improved performance in both investment-grade and high-yield markets in both the United States and Europe. This finding held true using ESG rankings from different providers and over different time periods. We analyze the reasons for this outcome, both for the markets overall and for specific industry sectors.

The traditional approach to building a credit portfolio is based on allocations to industry sectors, credit ratings, spread duration buckets, and, of course, issuer selection based on fundamental bottom-up analysis. Most institutional investors measure these allocations in terms of contribution to Duration Times Spread (DTS)—a new measure of credit risk introduced by our group in 2005. These allocations may or may not reflect priced factors in credit markets: categories of risk that is compensated by corresponding return. Also, these allocations may contain biases, such as issue size or coupon level, which may affect performance. Finally, they can be correlated. In Part IV of this book we present two priced factors in credit markets that have risk premia associated with them—value and momentum—and analyze the role of issuer size as a factor. Again, we use our proprietary mapping between bonds and equity of a given issuer to access fundamental data and equity market information. We construct two value measures based on the combination of bond market data and fundamental data, one for monthly time horizon—excess spread to peers (ESP)—and the other for annual horizon—SPiDER (*SP*read per un*i*t of *D*ebt to *E*arnings *R*atio). ESP rankings are relative in nature and are meant to be used within a peer group. SPiDER scores are absolute and can be used across sectors as well as at the aggregate market level. Both are shown to be informative of future bond returns on their respective horizons. Our momentum factor for a given issuer, constructed based on the recent momentum of its equity rather than its bonds, equity momentum in credit (EMC), is shown to be highly informative of future bond returns on a monthly horizon. Diversified strategy portfolios based on both ESP and EMC are shown to deliver excellent performance. We find that performance of value portfolios is positively correlated with market returns, while momentum portfolios have negative market correlations. We explain the reasons for these results. We then introduce OneScore, which combines these two signals. Portfolios formed of bonds with strong positive scores for both value and momentum have outperformed those with strong negative scores in both dimensions in most market regimes with a significant information ratio, in both historical back-tests and since going live.

Quantitative investing in equities has been in place for decades and is well represented in hedge fund offerings as well as in exchange-traded funds and long-only funds. One reasons it has attracted significantly more attention than quantitative credit investing is the broad availability of equity market data based on definitive pricing from the exchanges. Much of the academic work on factor investing and systematic signals was done in equity space. Until recently, fixed income market data was produced mostly by index providers—investment banks that traded bonds over the counter and were in a position to price broad market segments. In the last few years, the task of producing fixed income indices and data moved to data vendors and pricing of bonds became increasingly transparent, making it possible to develop algorithmic credit strategies. However, quantitative bond analysts can learn a lot from the methodologies, signals, and techniques well established in systematic equity investing. Since both the equity and the credit of a given issuer are claims on the same underlying company, there is reason to expect that some equity models may also apply to credit. In Part V we give examples of using equity methodologies in credit markets to produce informative credit performance signals. In particular, we research whether the post-earnings-announcement-drift (PEAD) exists for corporate bonds and whether equity short interest is informative of the future performance of an issuer's credit securities.

We would like to thank our clients for stimulating questions and continuous dialogue that led to many results covered in this book, our colleagues who provided invaluable help with the analysis and preparation of the manuscript, and the senior management of Barclays for their continuous support and encouragement of our work. We hope that credit managers, research analysts, and academics in the field of systematic investing will find these chapters useful. As always, we welcome inquiries and challenges to our work.

Investing in Credit vs. Investing in a Combination of Treasuries and Equities

CHAPTER 1

Can a Combination of Treasuries and Equities Replace Credit in a Portfolio?

INTRODUCTION

The corporate bond market is one of the largest markets in the world. According to the Security Industry and Financial Markets Association (SIFMA), $1.38trn worth of new corporate bonds were issued in the United States alone in 2018, while total equity issuance that year was only $0.22trn.[1] Since equity and bonds of the same issuer represent claims to the same underlying operating cash flows and are affected by the same set of firm fundamentals, their valuations are innately related, as formalized in Merton (1974).[2] The economic link between firms' corporate bonds and equity has led some investors to consider the possibility of replacing credit with a simple "barbell" combination of equities and Treasuries that will result in similar returns with the added benefit of higher liquidity. Studies examining this idea offered varying conclusions, partly because of the differences in approach and sample period. Asvanunt and Richardson (2017), for example, argued that corporate bonds carry a positive premium for bearing exposures to default risk using a long time series of corporate bond index returns since 1926 after properly adjusting for the bond exposures to Treasuries. In contrast, Norges Bank (2017) found that in an asset allocation framework, corporate bond indices did not offer any benefit to an equities/Treasuries portfolio in a more recent sample period from 1988 to 2017.

Given the central role played by credit in asset allocation, we conduct a comprehensive two-part study spanning almost three decades and leveraging our unique access to the Bloomberg Barclays Indices pricing and analytics data as well as a proprietary firm-level capital structure mapping developed by Barclays. Similar to most studies, we start with an asset-allocation-level analysis and examine the effect of including an allocation to a broad credit index (consisting of investment-grade [IG] and high-yield [HY] bonds) in various equities/Treasuries portfolios. Although very simple conceptually, great care should be taken in the implementation phase to control for the reallocation effect. This effect is caused by the possible difference between the equities/Treasuries mix in the portfolio and the one implied by the introduction of the allocation to credit. To demonstrate this issue, note that credit returns can be seen as a combination of equities, Treasuries plus some credit-specific returns. If the credit index equivalent mix of equities and Treasuries is different from that of the equities/Treasuries in the benchmark that the credit allocation is added to, the introduction of credit will effectively change the mix of equities and Treasuries in the original benchmark and thus affect performance. For example, in a portfolio with an initial large allocation to equities (relative to Treasuries), adding credit indirectly increases the weight of Treasuries. If Treasuries happened to rally on average during the sample period, adding an allocation to credit is likely to increase the risk-adjusted returns of the portfolio. Interpreting such a result as a confirmation of the benefit provided by credit may be incorrect if the improvement is due mostly to the increased weight of Treasuries in the portfolio rather than to the contribution of the credit-specific component of credit performance. The existence of the reallocation effect explains, at least in part, why different studies came up with opposing conclusions when using different time periods in the analysis.

We explicitly neutralize the reallocation effect in our analysis by finding the equivalent combination of equities and Treasuries that would best mimic the month-to-month return fluctuations of the credit index. The performance improvement from including the equivalent equities/Treasuries combination instead of the credit index captures the reallocation effect. We find that an allocation to credit improved the risk-adjusted performance of the benchmark regardless of the original mix of equities and Treasuries, controlling for the reallocation effect. For the period 1993 to 2019, for example, adding an allocation to a (market capitalization weighted) credit portfolio comprised of IG and HY indices increased the Sharpe ratio of a 60/40 equities/Treasuries portfolio from 0.71 to 0.86.

The latter result is not sufficient, however, to conclude that the barbell approach has no merit because our analysis has not taken into account a second element we term the "mismatch effect." This effect emanates from the differences between commonly used bond and equity indices in terms of issuer composition and sector weights. A nonnegligible number of bond issuers do not have publicly traded equities, especially issuers with ratings below investment grade. Similarly, many small capitalization firms (especially in sectors such as technology) do not have public debt outstanding. Furthermore, even if a company is represented in both indices, the weights (or size relative to other issuers) of its bonds and stock are likely to differ, causing a mismatch at the issuer level and possibly at the sector level as a result of difference in the typical financing channels across industries (i.e., some industries traditionally use more debt or equity to finance their operations). The results of the analysis can therefore be affected when stocks of companies with no corporate bonds earn extreme returns during the sample period or when sectors with a larger representation in the credit indices (relative to the equity indices) perform differently from other sectors.

Isolating the true contribution of credit requires explicitly controlling for the mismatch effect. This, in turn, cannot be done at the aggregate level (i.e., index) and requires an issuer-level analysis that allows a comparison of bonds with a risk-equivalent combination of Treasuries and equity from the same company. To reduce interference from idiosyncratic risk, we aggregate the issuer-level returns to portfolios and compare the performance of the corporate bond portfolio and replicating portfolio with matched issuers, weights, and risk. Since both reallocation and mismatch effects are absent in this case, any return difference between an issuer's corporate bonds and the combination of its risk-matched equity and Treasuries would represent the unique contribution of credit.

After careful issuer and risk matching, we find that corporate bonds achieved better risk-adjusted performance than a combination of Treasuries and equities of the same companies with similar risk exposures, in both IG and HY, regardless of the weighting schemes used. From 1993 to 2019, the corporate bond portfolio outperformed the risk-equivalent combination of Treasury and issuer-matched equity portfolio by more than 1.5%/yr and 3%/yr for IG and HY, respectively. The information ratios of the bond-over-replication portfolio were all relatively large and ranged from 0.47 to 0.84, depending on the portfolio weighting schemes. The results were qualitatively similar across subperiods, ratings, sectors, and geographies.

To make sure our findings do not reflect simply our choice of the risk-matching method, we consider two alternative approaches: matching based on total volatility and using analytical hedge ratios based on the Merton (1974) model. We find that the bond portfolio still delivered outperformance over the replication portfolios and that the bond outperformance was not driven by outliers, underweighting equity risk, or illiquidity. Taken together, the evidence suggests that corporate bonds offered a clear return benefit over a risk-matched combination of equities and Treasuries that was not driven by any specific industry, time period, rating, or our choice of risk matching approach, and could not be explained by risk or liquidity considerations.

What accounts for credit's return advantage over the matched combination of equities and Treasuries? The persistent nature of our results points to the existence of systematic drivers, perhaps certain risk premia or market anomalies that benefit bondholders rather than idiosyncratic and transient effects. To test various possible explanatory variables, we regress the monthly performance of the bond portfolio in excess of the replication portfolio against the returns of a host of commonly used risk factors and market anomalies. The regression results suggest that two in particular are responsible for the majority of credit return outperformance over the replicating portfolio: equity and bond volatility risk premia (VRP) and the low risk anomaly. Investors in corporate bonds earn the equity VRP, since holding a corporate bond is akin to owning a risk-free bond coupled with a short put option on the firm's assets (Merton 1974), which creates a short exposure to the volatility of the firm's underlying assets.[3] The impact of the bond VRP (i.e., exposure to interest rate volatility) is a result of both possible rate convexity mismatch between the bond portfolio and the replicating portfolio of equities and Treasuries, which we did not directly control for, as well as the existence of call provisions.[4] Choi, Mueller, and Vedolin (2017) show that a short rates volatility exposure (via selling delta-hedged calls and puts on Treasury futures) generates on average a positive risk premium (termed the bond variance risk premium). Israelov (2019) finds that corporate bond returns have a significant positive exposure to short interest rate volatilities strategies.

The second driver of corporate bond outperformance over the replicating portfolio is related to a manifestation of the low-volatility phenomenon well documented across asset classes. A substantial body of research documents that in both equities and fixed income markets, less volatile securities earned higher risk-adjusted returns compared with securities that experienced higher volatility (Ambastha, Ben Dor, Dynkin, Hyman, and Konstantinovsky 2008; Chapter 11; Ang, Hodrick, Xing, and Zhang 2006, 2009; Frazzini and Pedersen 2014). The main explanation for this phenomenon is that most investors are leverage-constrained and therefore have a bias toward riskier securities that offer higher absolute returns as they are unable to generate similar returns investing in the lower-risk securities. This dynamic bids up prices for riskier securities and drives down their returns relative to otherwise similar, less risky, securities (Asness, Frazzini, and Pedersen 2012; Frazzini and Pedersen 2014). The evidence we find indicates that this phenomenon is also present across the capital structure of a firm for which bonds and stocks play the role of the low- and high-volatility securities, respectively. In other words, investors who hold a favorable view on a firm have incentive to express it via the firm's stock rather than a leveraged (risk-matched) position in the firm's bonds. As a result, on average, bonds will outperform stocks of the same firms on an ex ante risk-matched basis.

It is important to emphasize that while the VRP premia and the low-volatility factor jointly are able to *explain* most of the corporate bond outperformance, they are not easily accessible directly in practice. Capturing the two VRPs requires trading equity and interest rate derivatives daily, while the equity low-volatility factor requires buying and shorting a large number of individual stocks with leverage. Harvesting the VRPs and equity low-volatility factor is therefore challenging for several reasons. First, capacity constraints in derivatives and stock loan markets limit the ability to implement these strategies on the scale needed in aggregate. For example, given the current size of the US corporate market (as of April 2020, the total market value of the Bloomberg Barclays corporate bond indices [IG and HY] was approximately $7trn), it would take more than a decade to execute trades in the Treasury option market to replicate the interest rate volatility exposure of the corporate bond indices without imposing any significant price impact. Second, most institutional investors face explicit or implicit limitations on their ability to invest in derivative markets or short stocks. Third, transacting on a daily basis in these markets requires different knowledge and infrastructure from that needed to invest in equities, Treasuries, and corporate bonds over longer horizons. Fourth, investors attempting to capture these factors directly would incur significant trading costs. The VRP strategies require daily hedging with futures, and the equity low-volatility factor requires shorting, which imposes additional shorting costs. Our results, however, imply that investors in corporate bonds should take into account the existing exposures embedded in their corporate bond portfolios from a risk management perspective, especially when considering direct allocations to short volatility strategies or equity low-volatility strategies.

Taken together, our results suggest that using a Treasury-equity barbell as a substitute for a credit allocation with the added benefit of higher liquidity is not trivial to implement and requires care to control for the reallocation and mismatch effects. In addition, even with careful implementation, investors will be missing out on important sources of returns and on average will end up underperforming an otherwise similar portfolio with an allocation to credit.

The rest of the chapter is organized as follows. The first section examines the role of credit in an asset allocation framework, while the next section presents an issuer-level analysis. It reviews in detail the construction methodology and performance of the corporate bond portfolio and its risk-matched equity/Treasury replication portfolio. The third section investigates additional alternative risk-matching approaches to understand to what extent our results are sensitive to the exact specification we use. The fourth section investigates various possible drivers that explain the performance difference between the bond and equities/Treasuries portfolios. The last section concludes and outlines some possible directions for future research.

BENEFIT OF CREDIT IN AN ASSET ALLOCATION CONTEXT

To evaluate the effect of adding credit to an equities/Treasuries portfolio, we perform a simple asset allocation exercise, starting with a portfolio composed of equity and Treasury indices, and examine whether increasing the allocation to credit improves the Sharpe ratio of the portfolio. We use the S&P 500 Index (total return including dividends) and the Bloomberg Barclays Treasury index to represent the Equity and Treasury allocations and the combined Bloomberg Barclays IG and HY Corporate Bond Indices (weighted by market value) to capture the performance of credit (based on total returns). The sample spans the period from January 1993 to December 2019.

Figure 1.1 plots the Sharpe ratios of different equities/Treasuries benchmarks (20/80, 40/60, 60/40, and 80/20 equities/Treasuries mixes) as a function of the percentage of credit allocation added. The allocation to credit replaces a mix of equities and Treasuries with the same ratio as in the original benchmarks, respectively. The Sharpe ratios display a hump-shaped pattern as a function of the weight allocated to credit for all benchmark

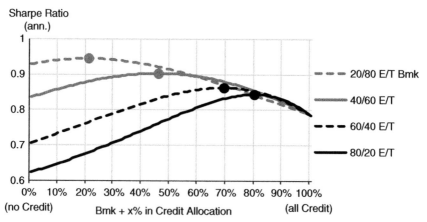

FIGURE 1.1   Sharpe Ratios of Equities/Treasuries Benchmarks with Credit Allocation
Note: The added credit allocation replaces a mix of equities/Treasuries with the same ratio as in the original benchmark.
Source: Bloomberg, Barclays Research

portfolios. The portfolio's Sharpe ratios always increased once some credit was allocated to the original benchmarks; then the ratios reached a maximum and started decreasing. The patterns suggest that having an allocation to credit improves the Sharpe ratio of an equities/Treasuries benchmark regardless of the original mix.

Decomposing the Effects of Including Credit

Does the improvement from credit allocation mean that credit cannot be replaced by a combination of equities and Treasuries? Not necessarily, as there are several effects stemming from the inclusion of credit. Some of them are unique to credit as an asset class, while others can be replicated by equities and Treasuries alone. The first is a reallocation effect, caused by the fact that the inclusion of credit may alter the original equities/Treasuries mix in the new portfolio, given the sensitivity of credit to the Treasury and equity markets. This reallocation effect is illustrated in Figure 1.2. For example, if we start with a 60/40 equities/Treasuries portfolio and replace 40% of it with a credit index, the credit index could be equivalent to, for example, a 20/80 equities/Treasuries mix, and thus the inclusion of credit effectively increases the Treasury weight in the portfolio and will change its performance. Therefore, a positive impact from the reallocation effect does not mean that credit cannot be replaced by equities and Treasuries, because this effect could have been replicated by changing the mix of equities and Treasuries in the original portfolio.

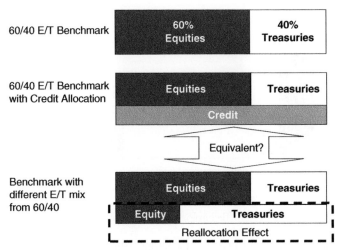

FIGURE 1.2   Illustration of Reallocation Effect
Source: Barclays Research

The second effect stems from issuer and weight mismatch between bond and equity indices. For example, there are a number of private issuers in the HY bond index with no publicly traded equities and, similarly, there are a number of public companies with no outstanding corporate bonds, especially in certain sectors, such as technology. Even if the same company is included in both indices, the weights of the bonds and the stock of the same issuer could be different, which would cause a weight mismatch at the issuer and eventually at the sector level. Figure 1.3 illustrates this by comparing the weights of the information technology and communications sectors in the S&P 500 and Bloomberg Barclays Corporate and High Yield Indices as of the end of December 2019. The weight of the tech sector is seven times as large in the equity index (21%) compared to that in the bond indices (3% each). The pattern is reversed when it comes to the communications sector. The benefit of including the credit index could therefore come from the fact that it had overweighed issuers and sectors that happened to outperform on a relative basis. This mismatch effect cannot be replicated explicitly by investing in equity and Treasury indices, but any benefit resulting from it is likely to be temporary and not structural.

The third contributor is the component of credit return profile that is either a compensation for the risk embedded in corporate bonds due to their specific payment structure or results from some market anomalies. This effect, if it exists, is unique to credit as an asset class and is more likely to persist since it is structural.

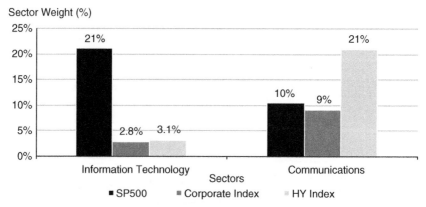

FIGURE 1.3   Sector Weight of Technology and Communications Sectors in Equity and Bond Indices (as of December 2019)
Note: Sector weights are calculated using market value at the end of the month.
Source: Bloomberg, Compustat, Barclays Research

Out of the three effects, the reallocation effect can be mitigated by changing the mix of equity and Treasury indices directly in the original portfolio, whereas the mismatch effect and the unique benefit of credit are specific to the credit index. Therefore, without teasing out the reallocation effect, evaluating the effect of including credit could be misleading. In this section, we decompose the overall effect of including the credit index into the reallocation effect vs. credit index–specific effects, which include the mismatch effect and the unique benefit of credit as an asset class.

To estimate the reallocation effect, we construct a replication portfolio composed of equities (S&P 500), Treasuries (Treasury index), and cash (3m T-bills) that minimizes the monthly return differences (tracking error volatility) relative to the credit index. To determine the weights of equities and Treasuries, we estimate each month a regression of trailing 36m credit returns against the S&P 500 and the Treasury index returns. The coefficients on the S&P 500 and the Treasury index are their respective weights in the replication portfolio in the coming months, and any excess is allocated in T-bills.[5] Figure 1.4 plots the historical weights of equities and Treasuries in the replication portfolio. On average, the replication portfolio allocates 16% to equity, 81% to Treasuries, and 3% to 3m T-bills.

To estimate the reallocation effect associated with an equities/Treasuries benchmark with an x% allocation in credit, we merely need to look at the performance of the same original benchmark with an x% allocation in the replication portfolio. Its performance would capture the reallocation effect. The difference between the benchmark with credit and the benchmark with the replication portfolio would capture any credit-specific effect.

To illustrate how we separate the reallocation and the credit-specific effects, we first start with a 60/40 equities/Treasuries benchmark portfolio and vary the allocation to credit. The x% allocation in credit replaces the

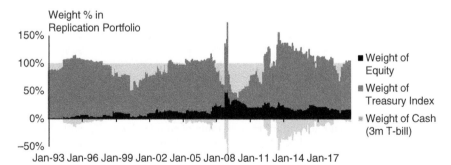

FIGURE 1.4 Historical Weights of Equities/Treasuries in the Replication Portfolio
Source: Bloomberg, Compustat, Barclays Research

original mix of equities/Treasuries (e.g., 0.6*x% equities and 0.4*x% Treasuries in this case). Figure 1.5 plots the portfolio Sharpe ratios when we increase the credit allocation to a 60/40 equities/Treasuries portfolio. The dotted line plots the Sharpe ratio of the benchmark portfolio (no credit), which had a Sharpe ratio of 0.71 from January 1993 to December 2019. The solid line plots the Sharpe ratios with x% in credit, and the distance of the solid line and the dotted line captures the net effect of including credit. The dashed line in the middle plots the Sharpe ratios with x% allocation in the replication portfolio, and the distance between the dashed line and the dotted line captures the reallocation effect. The distance between the solid line and the dashed line then identifies the credit-specific effect. The credit index-specific effect is positive for all allocation levels in credit in this case, achieving the maximum Sharpe ratio of 0.86 with 69% allocation in credit. The overall effect of including credit is also positive for all allocation levels, while the reallocation effect stays positive for most levels.

In reality, the fractions of equity and Treasury allocation in investors' portfolios depend on a number of factors, such as the investors' objectives, risk preferences, historical evaluation periods they use, and strategic outlooks on each asset class. This chapter does not intend to prescribe an

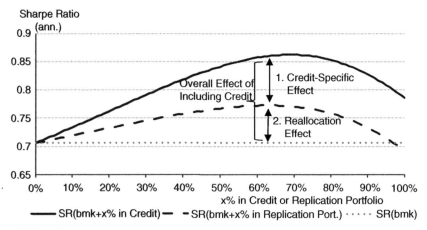

FIGURE 1.5 Performance of 60/40 Equities/Treasuries Portfolio with x% Credit Allocation
Note: The added credit allocation replaces a mix of equities/Treasuries with the same ratio as in the original benchmark. The monthly returns used are from January 1993 to December 2019.
Source: Bloomberg, Compustat, Barclays Research

optimal asset allocation recipe. Our objective is to assess the additive value of credit to an equities/Treasuries portfolio. In order to examine whether the unique benefit of credit is present for a wide range of E/T mixes or is specific to certain E/T allocations only, we repeat the previous analysis for different equities/Treasuries benchmarks. The results are shown in Figure 1.6, with Panel A, B, and C for the 20/80, 40/60, and 80/20 equities/Treasuries benchmarks, respectively. The reallocation effect can be positive or negative depending on the original benchmark. For example, the reallocation effect in Panel C for the 80/20 E/T benchmark is positive. This is because the optimal allocation in this period was 22/78 E/T, and including the credit index effectively increased the allocation in Treasuries, which moved the portfolio closer to the optimal allocation and thus created a positive reallocation effect. Another thing worth noting is that in a simple exercise of adding credit allocation to an equities/Treasuries benchmark, the effect on the Sharpe ratios is sensitive to what asset the credit allocation replaces. For example, when adding the same credit index to a 60/40 equities/Treasuries benchmark, the portfolio Sharpe ratio will increase if credit replaces equities but will decrease if credit replaces Treasuries. This is precisely because of the reallocation effect. When credit replaces equities, it effectively adds more Treasuries to the portfolio and moves the E/T allocation closer to optimal, and vice versa when credit replaces Treasuries. Evaluating the effect of credit without controlling for the reallocation effect could thus be misleading.

In contrast, the credit index-specific effects are positive regardless of the original mix of E/T in the benchmark. We also repeat the analysis using the IG and HY indices separately as the credit portfolio, instead of the IG and HY combined index as in the previous analysis. Overall, we find qualitatively similar results with all the variations.

Next we want to understand how the effects of including credit vary over time, especially during crisis and noncrisis periods. We divided our sample period into crisis periods (the tech bubble: January 2000–December 2002; and the financial crisis: January 2008–December 2009) and noncrisis periods and repeated the analysis for each subperiod. The Sharpe ratios of the 60/40 E/T benchmark with different credit allocations are shown in Figure 1.7, with the results in the crisis and noncrisis periods in Panel A and B, respectively. We find that allocating to credit increased the Sharpe ratios substantially in the two crises (tech bubble and financial crisis) during our sample period, while the benefit of credit was much smaller during the noncrisis months.

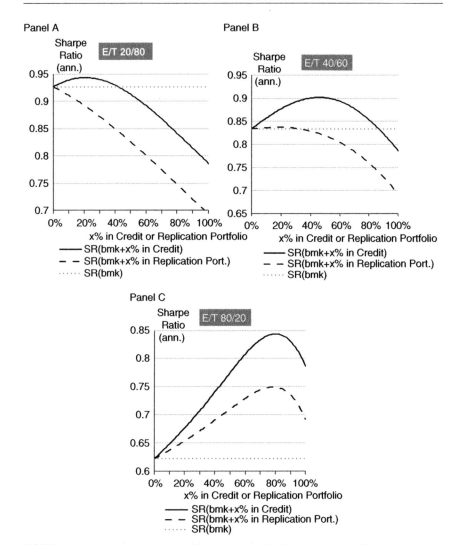

FIGURE 1.6 Sharpe Ratio of Adding x% Credit Allocation to Different Mixes of Equities/Treasuries

Note: The added credit allocation replaces a mix of equities/Treasuries with the same ratio as in the original benchmark. The monthly returns used are from January 1993 to December 2019.

Source: Bloomberg, Compustat, Barclays Research

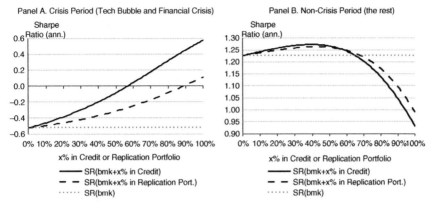

FIGURE 1.7   Sharpe Ratio of Adding x% Credit Allocation to the 60/40 E/T Benchmark in Crisis and Noncrisis Periods

Note: The crisis periods include the tech bubble (January 2000–December 2002) and the financial crisis (January 2008–December 2009). Noncrisis period are the rest of the months in the January 1993–December 2019 period. The added credit allocation replaces a mix of equities/Treasuries with the same ratio as in the original benchmark.

Source: Bloomberg, Compustat, Barclays Research

CAN A CORPORATE BOND BE REPLICATED BY TREASURIES AND SAME-ISSUER EQUITY?

The results in the previous section suggest that credit improves the risk-adjusted performance of an equities/Treasuries benchmark controlling for the reallocation effect irrespective of the original equities/Treasuries mix. Does that mean that credit cannot be replaced by a combination of equities and Treasuries in a portfolio? Not exactly, because there are two components in the credit index–specific effect that we already pointed out: (1) issuer and weight mismatch and (2) the unique benefit of credit as an asset class.

To separate the two effects, we perform an issuer-level comparison of corporate bonds to a combination of the issuer's equity and Treasuries in such a way that it matches the systematic risk exposures of the corporate bonds to make sure that the risk differences in bonds and equities are correctly accounted for. We begin by defining the universe of securities used in the analysis comprising matched bonds and stocks at the company level. We then explain how we construct the bond portfolio and form replication portfolios using Treasuries and equities from the same companies.

Sample Construction and Methodology

The first challenge in our analysis is constructing a company level bonds-to-equities mapping. Bonds and equities have different security identifiers and usually lack a common company identifier. Moreover, companies typically have a single class of common shares traded at any point in time but may have multiple outstanding bonds differing in terms of maturity, seniority, rating, coupon rates, and other structural differences (e.g., callability). A company may also have several different subsidiaries in different industries that issue corporate bonds. Corporate actions often have different effects on outstanding bonds and equities. Bonds issued by the acquired company often continue to trade after the acquisition, while their equities normally cease to do so. The bond-to-equity mapping should also take into consideration the fact that stock and bond identifiers may change over time. We rely on the proprietary mapping algorithm developed by Ben Dor and Xu (2015) to construct the historical matching of corporate bonds to equities.

To create the universe of mapped bonds and equities at the company level, we start with all issuers in the Bloomberg Barclays US Corporate and High Yield indices from January 1990 to December 2019 and link each issuer to equity data from Compustat.[6]

In addition, we have several filters to make sure that bonds and equities in the final sample are tradable. First, we exclude bonds with prices less than $40 because these bonds typically trade on recovery value and have very thin trading. Prices of these bonds may not be representative of actual executable prices.[7] Second, if the mapped equities are ADR, traded OTC or outside of the United States, we remove the company (both equity and bonds) from the universe. This ensures that exchange rate dynamics do not affect stock returns. Third, we remove from the sample penny stocks with beginning-of-month prices less than $1. These stocks usually are thinly traded and could be very volatile.

We perform all analyses separately for IG and HY universes. Conceptually they are all corporate bonds and differ only in rating. In practice, because of restrictions from investment mandates, there is market segmentation between the two markets that results in distinctive market dynamics among the two. For example, see Ambastha, Ben Dor, Dynkin, and Hyman (2010) on the jump in the ratio of a bond's analytical/empirical duration going from Baa (IG) to Ba (HY), and see Chapters 2 to 4 on the forced selling/price pressure when IG bonds get downgraded to HY. To account for the different dynamics in the IG and HY universes, we present all analyses separately for IG and HY in case any result is specific to only one universe. The separate analyses also provide results more relevant to readers interested in only one universe.

TABLE 1.1 Percentage of Bloomberg Barclays US Indices Included in the Sample by Market Value

Year-End Statistics	Corporate Index							High-Yield Index						
	1994	1999	2004	2009	2013	2017	1994	1999	2004	2009	2013	2017
Index Population ($Billion)	513	900	1,691	2,548	3,703	5,172	133	353	599	704	1,260	1,321
% Mapped	91%	94%	95%	96%	96%	97%	71%	72%	82%	71%	67%	81%
% Included in Final Sample	78%	84%	77%	81%	80%	80%	47%	50%	69%	62%	57%	72%

Note: To calculate the index coverage, we look at the issuer constituents in the return statistics universe at the end of December of the reported years.
Source: Bloomberg, Compustat, Barclays Research

Table 1.1 displays the proportion of Bloomberg Barclays US Corporate and High Yield indices covered by the final sample. The coverage ratio by market capitalization reaches 97% for the IG index and 81% for the HY index at the end of the sample. The coverage ratio is lower for the HY index because a higher percentage of HY issuers are private companies, which do not have publicly traded equities. The difference between the numbers in the rows of "Mapped" and "Included in Final Sample" are due to the three filters we mentioned earlier.

Despite the partial coverage of the two indices, the final sample is very similar to each respective index in terms of key analytics. Figure 1.8 shows that the time series of value-weighted averages of bond-level option-adjusted spreads (OAS) and option-adjusted spread durations (OASD) are very much aligned between the sample and the index. Therefore, any dynamics we observe are unlikely to be driven by the differences between our sample and the indices.

To reduce the effect of idiosyncratic risk, we aggregate issuer-level returns for both corporate bonds and equities to the portfolio level for comparison. In particular, we follow two steps to build a replication portfolio that has the same constituents and issuer weights with systematic risk exposures similar to the bond portfolio. In the first step, we build a bond portfolio and an equity portfolio with the same constituents and the same weight assigned to each issuer's bonds and equity in their respective portfolios to make sure that there is no issuer and weight mismatch. In the second step, we use the equity portfolio together with a Treasury portfolio to construct a replication portfolio that has the same systematic risk exposures as the bond portfolio. The steps are illustrated in Figure 1.9 and discussed in detail next.

Step 1: Constructing Mapped Bond and Equity Portfolios   As shown in Panel A of Figure 1.9, each month we construct two portfolios: a bond and an equity portfolio, with identical sets of issuers, and each issuer receiving the same weight in its bonds[8] and its equity, respectively. To allocate the weights among different issuers in the portfolios, we use four intuitive weighting schemes: equal weighting, value weighting using bond market value, equity market value, and total market value (the sum of a company's bond and equity market value), henceforth denoted as EW, Bond-VW, Equity-VW, and Total-VW, respectively. We performed our analysis using all four weighting schemes to ensure that the results were not specific to the choice of weights.

Step 2: Constructing a Replication Portfolio Using Sensitivity Matching   Corporate bonds consist of exposures to two key risk factors: a significant Treasury component with exposures to interest rate risk and a credit component driven by firm fundamentals with exposures to market risk that is highly correlated with

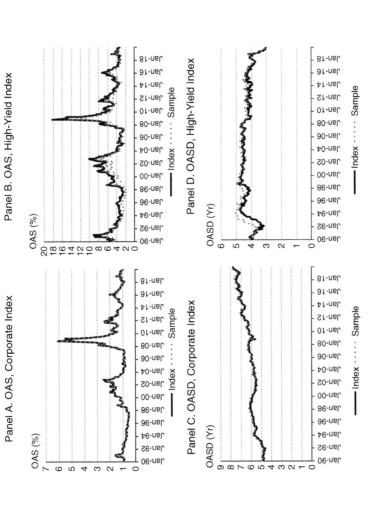

FIGURE 1.8 Characteristics of the Sample vs. Corresponding Indices

Note: OAS and OASD are aggregated bond-level averages weighted by the bond's market value at month-end.

Source: Bloomberg, Compustat, Barclays Research

equities. Equities may have negligible or even negative exposures to interest rate risk and much higher exposure to market risk. Comparing the performance of the bond and equity portfolios directly without any risk matching would yield misleading results. To account for the different risk exposures between bonds and equities, we construct a replication portfolio using a Treasury portfolio and the issuer-matched equity portfolio such that its risk sensitivities match that of the bond portfolio. Panel B of Figure 1.9 illustrates the idea: We vary the weights in the Treasury and the equity portfolios (two unknowns) such that the replication portfolio's sensitivities to the two key risk factors equal that of the bond portfolio (two equations). We solve for the two unknowns in the two equations, and any excess weight (two unknowns may not necessarily add up to 1) is allocated in cash (3m T-bills).

The portfolio weights are calculated monthly in two steps. First, we proxy for the market risk factor using the S&P500 index total returns and the interest rate risk factor using returns of the 10-yr on-the-run (OTR) Treasury portfolio. We also construct the replication portfolio with the Bloomberg Barclays Treasury Index instead of the OTR 10-yr Treasury portfolio. The results are qualitatively similar (included in Appendix 1.1).[9] We estimate the sensitivities (betas) of the bond and equity portfolios to these two factors through monthly ordinary least squares (OLS) regressions with exponential decay weighting using trailing 36m data to avoid any look-ahead bias.[10] In the replication portfolio we use the 10-yr OTR treasury portfolio, which by construction has a beta of 1 to the interest rate risk factor and a beta of zero to the S&P 500 returns. Second, we solve for the weights on the equity portfolio and 10y Treasuries of the replication portfolio (two unknowns) such that its two factor sensitivities match those of the bond portfolio (two equations).[11] Any extra weight is allocated to 3m T-bills.

Table 1.2 reports the average factor sensitivities across all 36m-calibration periods and the percentage of the calibration periods in which the respective sensitivities are statistically significant. Consistent with our expectation of a considerable Treasury component in bond returns, 97% (IG) and 40% (HY) of the time the bond portfolios had statistically significant sensitivities to Treasuries within all trailing 36m calibration windows with an average sensitivity of 0.60 for IG and 0.09 for HY. The bond portfolios also had a credit component with significant sensitivities to the S&P 500 index 72% of the time for the IG index and 85% for the HY index. The equity portfolios had significant sensitivities to the same market factor 100% of the months. On average, the equity portfolio has no sensitivity to Treasury returns for the IG index and negative sensitivity to Treasury returns for HY and is significant only 12% (IG) and 29% (HY) of the time.

Panel A. Step 1: Construct mapped bond and equity portfolios

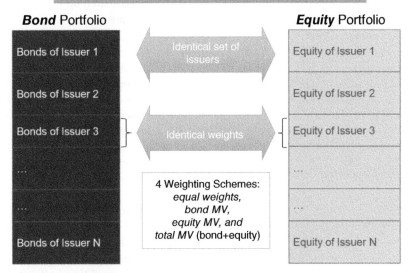

Panel B. Step 2: Build a replication portfolio through multidimensional risk matching

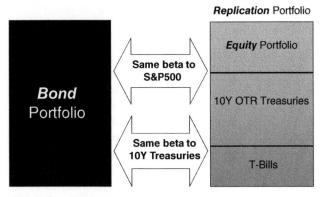

FIGURE 1.9   Illustration of Risk-Matching Steps
Source: Barclays Research

TABLE 1.2   Pre-Formation Average Sensitivities

Portfolio		$\beta_{S\&P\ 500}$	% of mth w. 5% sig.	$\beta_{10y\ Treasury\ ret.}$	% of mth w. 5%-sig.	Average Adj. R^2
IG	Bond	0.09	72%	0.60	97%	75%
	Equity	0.94	100%	0.00	12%	86%
HY	Bond	0.25	85%	0.09	40%	43%
	Equity	1.28	100%	−0.39	29%	67%

Note: The pre-formation sensitivities each month were estimated from trailing 36m regression and then averaged across the time series from January 1993 to December 2019. All individual issuer returns were equally weighted, and bond total returns were used.
Source: Bloomberg, Compustat, Barclays Research

Figure 1.10 reports the average weights in each asset for the replication portfolio. The replication portfolio in IG has 9% of its weight in equities, 60% in Treasuries, and the rest in cash. The replication portfolio in HY has twice the weight in equities (19%) and much smaller weights in Treasuries (18%), consistent with what we would have expected.

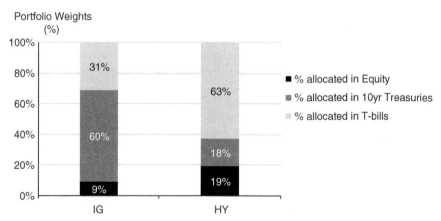

FIGURE 1.10   Average Portfolio Weights
Note: The corresponding weights were estimated from trailing 36m regression and then averaged across the time series from January 1993 to December 2019. All individual issuer returns were equally weighted, and bond total returns were used.
Source: Bloomberg, Compustat, Barclays Research

Did the ex ante factor matching succeed in matching the two sources of risk in the bond portfolio? To examine this question, we look ex post whether the difference portfolio (bond-over-replication portfolio) had any exposures to the equity and Treasury factors. If the risk matching approach did a good job, we would expect the difference portfolio to have no significant exposures to the two factors. Indeed, that is the case. Table 1.3 shows the regression results of the post-formation portfolio returns on the S&P 500 and Treasury return factors. The difference portfolio (bond over replication) had no exposures to both factors with small insignificant beta coefficients in the −0.02 to −0.01 range and still a significant alpha in both IG and HY. The adjusted R^2 for the difference portfolio is very small (−0.2% for IG and −0.5% for HY) compared to that for the bond and the replication portfolio, respectively, which are in the 33 to 84% range. The adjusted R^2s indicate that the bond and replication portfolios themselves have significant exposures to the two factors, but the replication portfolio does a good job replicating the systematic risk of the bond portfolio as the factor exposures have been neutralized in the difference portfolio.

Portfolio-Level Performance

Table 1.4 shows the performance statistics of the bond, the replication, and the bond-over-replication portfolios for the four weighting schemes in both IG and HY. The last column shows the correlation between the bond and the replication portfolios in each weighting scheme for IG and HY,

TABLE 1.3   Post-Formation Portfolio Return Sensitivities

	Portfolio	Intercept	t-stat.	$\beta_{S\&P500}$	t-stat.	$\beta_{10y\ Treasury\ Ret.}$	t-stat.	adj. R^2
IG	Bond over Replication	0.15	2.54	−0.01	−0.44	−0.02	−0.65	−0.2%
	Bond	0.12	1.90	0.12	4.35	0.56	14.72	61%
	Replication Portfolio	−0.03	−0.87	0.13	8.44	0.59	22.91	84%
HY	Bond over Replication	0.30	2.73	−0.01	−0.25	−0.01	−0.17	−0.5%
	Bond	0.26	2.27	0.28	5.42	0.03	0.41	33%
	Replication Portfolio	−0.03	−0.53	0.29	11.31	0.04	0.89	55%

Note: The post-formation portfolio returns are from January 1993 to December 2019.
Source: Bloomberg, Compustat, Barclays Research

TABLE 1.4 Performance of Bond-over-Replication Portfolios

Portfolio		Weighting Scheme	Avg. Ret. (%/yr)	Volatility (%/yr)	Sharpe (Inf.) Ratio (Ann.)	Worst Monthly Ret. (%)	Max. Drawdown (%)	Corr. w. Bond Portfolio
IG	Bond	EW	6.48	5.02	0.81	-8.22	-13.80	
		Bond-VW	6.20	5.18	0.73	-6.84	-14.23	
		Equity-VW	6.37	5.04	0.79	-6.54	-11.61	
		Total-VW	6.35	5.05	0.78	-6.42	-11.99	
	Replication Portfolio	EW	4.85	4.55	0.54	-5.81	-9.04	0.82
		Bond-VW	4.64	4.78	0.47	-8.53	-15.93	0.78
		Equity-VW	4.81	4.70	0.51	-6.93	-10.07	0.85
		Total-VW	4.78	4.71	0.51	-7.26	-10.58	0.84
	Bond over Replication	EW	1.63	2.93	0.56	-3.11	-13.52	
		Bond-VW	1.56	3.35	0.47	-5.67	-9.61	
		Equity-VW	1.56	2.70	0.58	-3.59	-8.11	
		Total-VW	1.57	2.79	0.56	-3.90	-8.10	

(Continued)

TABLE 1.4 (*Continued*)

Portfolio		Weighting Scheme	Avg. Ret. (%/yr)	Volatility (%/yr)	Sharpe (Inf.) Ratio (Ann.)	Worst Monthly Ret. (%)	Max. Drawdown (%)	Corr. w. Bond Portfolio
HY	Bond	EW	7.99	6.71	0.83	−15.58	−25.13	
		Bond-VW	7.62	6.59	0.79	−13.51	−24.80	
		Equity-VW	8.03	5.55	1.01	−13.36	−19.98	
		Total-VW	7.95	5.83	0.95	−13.40	−21.28	
	Replication Portfolio	EW	4.56	5.48	0.40	−8.94	−22.69	0.68
		Bond-VW	5.20	5.49	0.51	−10.42	−22.06	0.72
		Equity-VW	4.68	4.32	0.53	−8.47	−16.79	0.70
		Total-VW	4.88	4.62	0.54	−9.01	−17.96	0.71
	Bond over Replication	EW	3.43	5.04	0.68	−6.64	−17.10	
		Bond-VW	2.42	4.65	0.52	−4.50	−13.52	
		Equity-VW	3.34	3.97	0.84	−4.90	−8.20	
		Total-VW	3.07	4.10	0.75	−4.40	−9.41	

Note: The post-formation portfolio returns are from January 1993 to December 2019.
Source: Bloomberg, Compustat, Barclays Research

respectively. The numbers suggest that the replication portfolios have high correlations with the bond portfolios, around 0.80 for IG and 0.70 for HY. The high correlations are consistent with the results in Table 1.3 that the replication portfolios successfully mimicked the factor exposures of the bond portfolios post-formulation. Despite the similarity in risk between the two portfolios, the bond portfolios produced much higher average returns than the replication portfolios, regardless of the weighting schemes and in both IG and HY. The bond portfolios outperformed the otherwise similar replication portfolios by over 1.5%/yr in IG and around 3%/yr in HY. The bond portfolios also had better risk-adjusted performance in terms of higher Sharpe ratios than the replication portfolios in both IG and HY. The information ratios of bond-over-replication portfolios ranged from 0.47 to 0.84 across different weighting schemes.

Moreover, the bond outperformance was not limited to a single period. Figure 1.11 Panel A compares the Sharpe ratios of bond vs. the replication portfolios in five-year subperiods for both IG and HY. The bond portfolios had higher Sharpe ratios than the replication portfolios in most subperiods except 1998 to 2002 for HY. The subperiod performance comparison was similar in all weighting schemes. Moreover, Panel B of Figure 1.11 shows more detailed time-series dynamics of the bond outperformance by plotting the cumulative returns and information ratios of the bond-over-replication portfolios in trailing windows (12m for cumulative returns and 36m for information ratios) over the sample period. The bond portfolio outperformed the replication portfolios in most periods, but in some periods, the replication portfolio did outperform bonds.

Performance Dynamics in Subsamples and European Markets

We also examine the consistency of bond outperformance, both in and out of sample. Within the original US sample, we find that the bond-over-replication outperformance was consistent across ratings and GICS sectors. Many anomalies with significant in-sample results became insignificant after their initial publication. (See, e.g., Linnainmaa and Roberts 2018.) For this reason, out-of-sample performance is often viewed as strong validation of any in-sample findings. As out-of-sample test, we evaluate whether the bond outperformance is present in the European markets. We find that in European markets, bond portfolios also had higher average returns and Sharpe ratios than the equity-treasury-replication portfolios constructed using the same risk-matching approach. The information ratios of bond over replication portfolios are about 0.4 for IG and 0.67 for HY. All detailed results are included in Appendix 1.2.

Panel A: Sharpe Ratios of Bond vs. Replication Portfolios in Subperiods (EW)

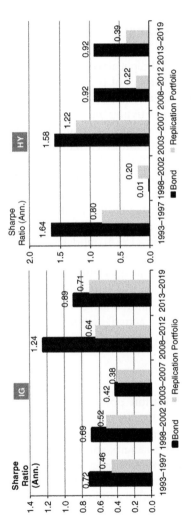

Panel B: Average Returns and Information Ratio of Bond-over-Replication Portfolios in Trailing Windows (EW)

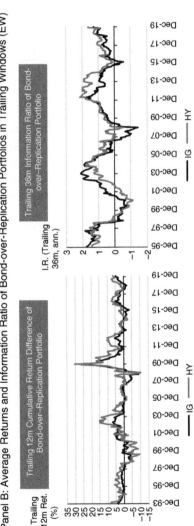

FIGURE 1.11

Note: The post-formation portfolio returns are from January 1993 to December 2019. Portfolio returns are formed from equal-weighting issuer returns.

Source: Bloomberg, Compustat, Barclays Research

Overall, we find that across subperiods, subsamples, and geographies, corporate bonds offer greater return benefit than a portfolio of Treasuries and equities with similar systematic risk. The additional return benefit that corporate bonds offer suggests that they cannot be replaced by a combination of Treasuries and equities.

RISK MATCHING USING ALTERNATIVE APPROACHES

Risk matching is one key element in creating a good replication portfolio for the bond portfolio in order to make a fair comparison of performance. In practice, investors may have different views on which risk exposures are the most important for them besides the factor risk sensitivities we used for risk matching (sensitivity matching). In this section, we consider two alternative approaches of risk matching. The first is simple and intuitive: matching by total volatility of the bond and the equity portfolio. Total volatility captures both systematic risk and idiosyncratic risk of a portfolio altogether and might be an important concern for some investors. We also need to bear in mind that total volatility captures only one aspect of risk and might not be sufficient for a good replication. The second approach we consider is using the analytical hedge ratios implied by the Merton (1974) model for the credit component of bonds and the analytical durations for the Treasury component. The analytical hedge ratios are appealing since they take into consideration an individual company's characteristics, have theoretical underpinning, and may be more forward looking than the hedge ratios calculated from trailing regressions. However, their actual hedging ability could be sensitive to the assumptions made in the theoretical models.

Risk Matching Using Total Volatility

For each bond portfolio, we construct a replication portfolio using its respective equity portfolio and cash. To make the volatility of the replication portfolio match that of the bond portfolios, we scale the equity portfolios by relative historical portfolio-level volatility of bond to equity and allocate the rest of the portfolio in 3m T-bills (cash).[12] Each month, the volatilities of bond and equity portfolios are calculated from respective portfolio returns in the trailing 36m window. The results using alternative window length are similar. The scaled equity portfolio with cash is denoted as volatility-matched replication portfolio.

Table 1.5 shows the performance statistics of the bond, the volatility-matched replication, and the bond-over-replication portfolios, as well as the correlations between the bond portfolio and the volatility-matched

TABLE 1.5 Bond vs. Volatility-Matched Equity/Treasury Portfolio Performance

Portfolio		Weighting Scheme	Avg. Ret. (%/yr)	Volatility (%/yr)	Sharpe (Inf.) Ratio (Ann.)	Worst Monthly Ret. (%)	Max. Drawdown (%)	Corr. w. Bond Portfolio
IG	Bond	EW	6.48	5.02	0.81	-8.22	-13.80	
		Bond-VW	6.20	5.18	0.73	-6.84	-14.23	
		Equity-VW	6.37	5.04	0.79	-6.54	-11.61	
		Total-VW	6.35	5.05	0.78	-6.42	-11.99	
	Volatility-Matched Replication Portfolio	EW	6.25	5.30	0.73	-6.52	-21.56	0.26
		Bond-VW	5.66	5.69	0.58	-7.50	-30.62	0.26
		Equity-VW	5.90	5.39	0.66	-6.71	-23.51	0.18
		Total-VW	5.86	5.45	0.64	-6.87	-24.80	0.20
	Bond over Replication	EW	0.24	6.30	0.04	-5.01	-33.19	
		Bond-VW	0.53	6.64	0.08	-5.68	-31.86	
		Equity-VW	0.47	6.68	0.07	-4.94	-34.45	
		Total-VW	0.50	6.67	0.07	-4.91	-34.16	

(Continued)

TABLE 1.5 (*Continued*)

Portfolio		Weighting Scheme	Avg. Ret. (%/yr)	Volatility (%/yr)	Sharpe (Inf.) Ratio (Ann.)	Worst Monthly Ret. (%)	Max. Drawdown (%)	Corr. w. Bond Portfolio
HY	Bond	EW	7.99	6.71	0.83	-15.58	-25.13	
		Bond-VW	7.62	6.59	0.79	-13.51	-24.80	
		Equity-VW	8.03	5.55	1.01	-13.36	-19.98	
		Total-VW	7.95	5.83	0.95	-13.40	-21.28	
	Volatility-Matched Replication Portfolio	EW	5.06	7.06	0.38	-8.87	-29.50	0.69
		Bond-VW	5.42	7.04	0.43	-9.88	-28.76	0.65
		Equity-VW	4.95	5.69	0.45	-7.66	-25.26	0.57
		Total-VW	5.14	6.07	0.45	-8.33	-26.11	0.60
	Bond over Replication	EW	2.93	5.45	0.54	-6.71	-15.38	
		Bond-VW	2.21	5.72	0.39	-7.66	-18.97	
		Equity-VW	3.08	5.24	0.59	-5.70	-14.84	
		Total-VW	2.82	5.32	0.53	-5.25	-16.04	

Note: The sample period is from January 1993 to December 2019.
Source: Bloomberg, Compustat, Barclays Research

replication portfolio for each weighting scheme in both IG and HY. In IG, total volatilities were matched well ex post, but the correlations between the bond and replication portfolios were low (around 0.22), suggesting that risk was matched inappropriately using the volatility-matching method. This is because IG bonds have a significant Treasury risk exposure, which is not included in equity volatilities. When risk was matched properly, as in the case of sensitivity matching, the correlations were much higher at around 0.80. Because of the inappropriate risk mismatch between the bond and the replication portfolio in IG, their performance may not be directly comparable.

In HY, the volatility-matched replication portfolios did a decent job in mimicking risk of the bond portfolio. First, the correlations between the bond and the volatility-matched replication portfolios were fairly high at around 0.63, only slightly lower than the correlations using sensitivity matching (around 0.70). Second, the ex-post portfolio volatilities of the bond and the volatility-matched replication portfolios were very similar, as shown in Table 1.5. Moreover, the time-series of trailing 36m vol. of the bond and the volatility-matched replication portfolios were similar at each point in time throughout the sample (not reported for brevity). With similar volatilities, the HY bond portfolios still had higher average returns than the volatility-matched replication portfolios, regardless of the weighting scheme. Moreover, the HY bond portfolios had higher Sharpe ratios than the volatility-matched replication portfolios. The information ratios of bond-over-volatility-matched-replication portfolios ranged from 0.39 to 0.59 across different weighting schemes. The volatility-matching results were very similar in European markets as well.

Analytical Risk Matching Using Hedge Ratios

One drawback of both sensitivity- and volatility-matching methods that we looked at is that they are inherently backward looking, as the weights are calculated from trailing statistics. In reality, the weights might be time-varying and very dynamic. Another approach is to use analytical hedge ratios based on the characteristics of each individual issuer. For the credit component of each bond issuer in our portfolio, we use the analytical hedge ratios implied by the Merton model (1974) to determine the weights on equity. For the Treasury component of each bond issuer, we use the ratio of analytical duration of the issuer's bonds (value-weighted average at the issuer level) to the analytical duration of the OTR 10y Treasury portfolio as the weights on Treasuries. Any excess weight is allocated in T-bills.

Research has shown that analytical equity hedge ratios based on the Merton model make reasonably accurate predictions of how corporate bond returns vary given the corresponding equity returns (Schaefer and Strebulaev 2008). Based on Merton, a corporate bond (D) is short a put on the underlying asset (V) plus a risk-free asset, while the equity (E) is equivalent to a call option on V. Overall, V=D+E. The hedge ratio (change in bond return with respect to change in equity return) can thus be derived analytically.[13]

Table 1.6 shows the distribution of the equity hedge ratios implied by the Merton model by rating. As the rating worsens, the average hedge ratio increases, which is what we would expect for two reasons. First, bonds with lower ratings are closer to default, and their stock valuations are also driven more by the downside as with the bonds. Second, for bonds with lower ratings, the credit component plays a bigger role in their returns than the Treasury component. In addition, the averages were higher than the median in all ratings, suggesting that the equity hedge ratios had some large positive outliers. However, when we compare the average analytical hedge ratios to the empirical hedge ratios calculated using sensitivity matching (last column of Panel A), the analytical hedge ratios were lower by about 5% in both IG and HY.

As the first quartile and five-percentile cut-offs indicate (4.36% and 0.25%, respectively), some HY companies had low hedge ratios, lower than one would expect for a typical HY company. A closer look at the data reveals that some of these firms are internet companies, such as Netflix, which have low levels of debt but also low profitability. Because of their low profitability, they were rated HY initially. Their equity market value may be high, based on expectations of future revenues. High equity market value, together with low debt levels, leads to low leverage ratios. In the Merton model, low leverage ratios are translated into low hedge ratios. As a result, we observe the conceptual inconsistency of HY companies with low hedge ratios. These observations highlight one limitation of the Merton model: Essentially, it uses the leverage ratio as one of the few inputs to determine a firm's hedge ratio and ignores other important aspects of a firm's operations, such as cash flows and profitability. The sensitivity matching method, which relies on past data to extract the empirical hedge ratios, has the advantage of being model free and takes into consideration all aspects of a firm's operations that affected its asset value.

To examine whether the bond outperformance still exists using the analytical hedge ratios, we construct a replication combination for each company using its analytical hedge ratios and then aggregate the company-level replicated returns into a portfolio using the four weighting schemes discussed earlier. Table 1.7 reports the performance of the replication portfolios using analytical hedge ratios and compares it with those using OLS-based empirical hedge ratios (last two columns). Similar to using empirical hedge

TABLE 1.6 Summary Statistics of Merton Hedge Ratios by Rating

Rating	Mean	Median	Std.	Q1	Q3	5 %tile	95 %tile	Avg. Empirical HR (EW) from Sensitivity Matching
All	7.89%	3.39%	10.64%	0.25%	12.66%	0.00%	27.37%	
Aaa/Aa	1.67%	0.03%	4.12%	0.00%	0.93%	0.00%	10.25%	
A	2.80%	0.49%	4.70%	0.01%	3.50%	0.00%	13.44%	
Baa	4.83%	1.55%	6.93%	0.12%	7.08%	0.00%	19.47%	
Ba	8.92%	6.19%	9.37%	1.59%	14.02%	0.04%	25.87%	
B	15.61%	14.49%	12.08%	6.76%	21.89%	0.85%	34.24%	
Caa and below	26.66%	23.83%	17.06%	16.85%	32.10%	6.48%	55.07%	
IG	3.90%	0.90%	6.17%	0.04%	5.27%	0.00%	17.12%	9.28%
HY	14.28%	12.29%	12.92%	4.36%	20.93%	0.25%	34.78%	19.49%

Note: The sample period is from January 1993 to December 2019.
Source: Bloomberg, Compustat, OptionMetrics, Barclays Research

TABLE 1.7 Portfolio Performance and Risk Sensitivities using Analytical vs. Empirical (OLS-Based) Hedge Ratios

Panel A. Portfolio Performance using Analytical vs. Empirical (OLS-Based) Hedge Ratios

	Bond Portfolio	Using Analytical Hedge Ratios (Merton Model)		Using Empirical Hedge Ratios (OLS Based)	
		Replication Portfolio	Bond over Replication	Replication Portfolio	Bond over Replication
IG Avg. Ret. (%/yr)	6.59	5.17	1.42	4.96	1.64
Volatility (%/yr)	5.06	5.43	3.44	4.52	2.93
Sharpe (Inf.) Ratio (Ann.)	0.82	0.51	0.41	0.57	0.56
Corr. w. Bond Portfolio Ret.	1.00	0.79		0.82	
Avg. Weights in Equities		4%		9%	
Avg. Weights in 10Y Treasury		78%		60%	

(Continued)

TABLE 1.7 (Continued)

Panel A. Portfolio Performance using Analytical vs. Empirical (OLS-Based) Hedge Ratios

	Bond Portfolio	Using Analytical Hedge Ratios (Merton Model)		Using Empirical Hedge Ratios (OLS Based)	
		Replication Portfolio	Bond over Replication	Replication Portfolio	Bond over Replication
HY Avg. Ret. (%/yr)	8.03	5.90	2.12	4.92	3.11
Volatility (%/yr)	6.83	6.21	5.81	5.72	5.14
Sharpe (Inf.) Ratio (Ann.)	0.82	0.56	0.37	0.44	0.60
Corr. w. Bond Portfolio Ret.	1.00	0.61		0.68	
Avg. Weights in Equities		15%		19%	
Avg. Weights in 10Y Treasury		52%		18%	

Panel B. Portfolio Ex Post Factor Exposures using Analytical vs. Empirical (OLS-Based) Hedge Ratios

Dependent Variables: Bond-over-Replication Portfolio Ret.	Intercept	Beta on S&P500	Beta on 10Y Treasury	Adj. R^2
IG Using analytical hedge ratios	1.673**	0.042	−0.199***	21.7%
Using empirical hedge ratios (OLS)	1.761**	−0.009	−0.017	−0.3%
HY Using analytical hedge ratios	3.457***	−0.01	−0.428***	25.9%
Using empirical hedge ratios (OLS)	3.413**	−0.02	−0.047	0.0%

Note: ***/**/* indicate significance at the 1%/5%/10% levels. The portfolio returns are from January 1993 to December 2019. All Issuers are equally weighted in the portfolios. The analytical hedge ratios use the Merton (1974) implied hedge ratios for equities and the ratio of bond analytical duration to the 10yr Treasury analytical duration as the hedge ratio for Treasuries. The empirical hedge ratios use the hedge ratios that match the 2-factor (S&P 500 and 10yr Treasury) sensitivities of the bond portfolio where the sensitivities are calculated from trailing 36m regressions.
Source: Bloomberg, Compustat, OptionMetrics, Barclays Research

ratios, the bond portfolios had higher average returns and Sharpe ratios than the replication portfolios using analytical hedge ratios in both investment grade and high yield. The bond-over-replication portfolios had information ratios of 0.41 in IG and 0.37 in HY with EW. The bond outperformance was similar across weighting schemes.

Another interesting observation is that the correlations between the bond and the replication portfolios were slightly lower when using analytical hedge ratios than when using empirical hedge ratios (0.79 vs. 0.82 in IG and 0.61 vs. 0.68 in HY). The lower correlations suggest that the analytical hedge ratios were less effective at replicating the bond portfolios compared to the empirical ones. To understand why, we regress the bond-over-replication portfolio returns using each type of hedge ratios on the market (S&P 500) and 10y Treasury return factors. The results are shown in Panel B of Table 1.7. The regression results show that the bond-over-replication portfolios using analytical hedge ratios had significantly negative exposures to the Treasury factor, which suggests that the analytical hedge ratios overweight Treasuries. This is to be expected, as prior research shows that the empirical durations (the realized sensitivity of bonds to Treasury returns) of corporate bonds are lower than their analytical durations, especially true in HY and to a less extent in IG (Ambastha et al. 2010). This explanation is also consistent with our findings that the bond-over-replication portfolio in HY had a more negative Treasury exposure than that in IG.[14]

Overall, we find that corporate bonds still offered additional return benefit over a combination of Treasuries and equities constructed using alternative risk matching approaches that properly replicate the bond portfolios. This evidence suggests that corporate bonds cannot be replaced by a combination of Treasuries and equities, regardless of the risk-matching methods.

DRIVERS OF CREDIT NONREPLICABLE RETURNS COMPONENT

In this section, we investigate potential drivers of the return differences between the bond portfolios and their replication portfolios. We examine a number of possible explanations for bond outperformance, such as (1) outliers, (2) underweighted equity risk in the replication, (3) higher bond performance as a compensation for low liquidity, (4) the backward-looking trailing window we used in sensitivity matching is insufficient to capture the time-varying sensitivities between bonds and equities, and (5) the higher Sharpe ratio in bonds is due to their serial correlation in returns. We perform empirical tests to evaluate these possible explanations, and the results ruled out all of the above explanations. The test details and results are included in Appendix 1.3.

Next, we investigate whether the bond outperformance can be explained by risk factors or known risk premia. Besides the Treasury return factor and a host of commonly used equity risk factors (Fama–French five factors on market, size, value, investment, and profitability; momentum), we also include three other factors that can potentially explain the bond outperformance. The first two stem from the nonlinear payoff features in corporate bonds, and the third comes from the low-volatility phenomenon across the capital structure. We first discuss the economic intuition of why these factors might be related to the bond outperformance. Then, to verify whether these factors can indeed explain the bond outperformance, we regress the monthly bond-over-replication returns on these three factors while controlling for a host of other commonly used risk factors.

Risk Factor 1: Equity Variance Risk Premium

In the Merton model (1974), a corporate bond is a short put on the underlying asset plus a risk-free asset, while the company's stock is a call option on the underlying asset. The short put on the underlying asset also can be decomposed into a stock (call) plus a short straddle (a call and put at-the-money (ATM)) position on the underlying asset. Therefore, holding a corporate bond creates the similar exposure to holding a risk-free bond, the stock of the same company, as well as shorting a straddle on the same underlying asset. In our earlier analysis, we accounted for the stock and the risk-free bond (Treasury) in the replication portfolio but did not account for the short straddle exposure that corporate bonds offer. Shorting a straddle is essentially selling volatility, and previous research shows that selling volatility on equities generates a positive premium, termed the equity variance risk premium (VRP). The equity VRP is positive because the option implied volatility is consistently higher than realized volatility (Bakshi and Kapadia 2003; Carr and Wu 2009), so selling equity volatility generates a premium on average. A corporate bond has a short straddle position on the underlying asset, which is essentially a short position on the asset volatility. This short straddle position could have payoffs similar to a short position on the equity volatility, since equity volatility makes up a substantial component of asset volatility of the same company. As shorting equity volatility carries a positive premium (equity VRP), it is possible that the bond outperformance over the replication portfolio is simply capturing the equity VRP. Previous research has also found evidence that credit returns benefit from the equity VRP (Israelov 2019). In our later regression test, the equity VRP is proxied using the returns of shorting a 1m expiry ATM straddle (call + put) on the

SPX (hold to maturity) and daily delta hedged with SPX futures[15] to take out return variations due to the market's directional movements.

Risk Factor 2: Bond Variance Risk Premium

A second source of nonlinearity in corporate bond payoffs is the callable features common in bonds. A considerable fraction of corporate bonds have callable features that allow issuers to repurchase the bonds at a preset redemption price. For issuers, the call feature offers them the option to benefit from declining interest rates (similar to the payoffs of a put on Treasury futures). For bondholders, the embedded call feature is equivalent to selling a put on interest rate futures. Similar to equity VRPs, research has also documented a positive VRP on Treasury rates; that is, the option-implied volatilities are often higher than realized volatilities for Treasury rates, and an investor can collect a positive premium by selling hedged calls and puts on Treasury futures (Choi, Mueller, and Vedolin 2017). Since the call features on the corporate bonds give their holders an embedded short position on interest rate options, part of the bond outperformance may come from the premium of selling volatility on interest rates. Because bond issuers are more likely to call their bonds when interest rates are low, bond returns should be more sensitive to downward volatility than upward volatility. In this case, a short position on Treasury puts should better capture bondholders' exposures instead of a short position on a straddle (a call and a put) in the equity case.

Another source of exposures to interest rate volatility is convexity mismatch. When we constructed the replication portfolios, we carefully matched the sensitivity to interest rates to that of the bond portfolios. However, we did not match convexity of the bond and the replication portfolio. The convexity mismatch between the two could lead to exposure to interest rate volatility.

To test whether either type of exposure is actually the case, we proxy for the call feature premium and convexity exposure using the hold-to-maturity returns of shorting 1m expiry ATM puts and calls separately on the US 10y Treasury futures and daily delta hedged with 10y Treasury futures.[16] The reason that we use puts and calls separately on Treasury futures instead of straddles (a put plus a call combined) in the usual case of proxying for a bond VRP (Israelov 2019) is to distinguish between the call feature premium and the convexity mismatch. With the former, since corporate bonds usually are called when interest rates fall and their market prices are above their predetermined call prices, the payoffs to the embedded call features are equivalent to holding a put option on the Treasury futures for the issuers (shorting a put for the bondholder). Thus, we expect the bond returns to be more sensitive to a short position on an ATM Treasury put than a Treasury call. With the convexity mismatch, bond returns could have exposures to both a call and a put on Treasury futures.

Risk Factor 3: Low-Volatility Phenomenon across the Capital Structure

The low-volatility (low vol.) phenomenon—the tendency of lower-risk stocks to outperform high-risk stocks on a risk-adjusted basis—is widely documented (Ang et al. 2006, 2009; Frazzini and Pedersen 2014). A similar pattern was also detected within credit: Short-maturity bonds had better risk-adjusted and even non-risk-adjusted performance than long-maturity bonds (Ambastha et al. 2008, Chapter 11). One underlying theory behind the low-volatility phenomena is that investors with leverage constraints chase risky assets as a form of taking on leverage and, thus, bid up the prices and drive down the expected returns of risky assets (Asness et al. 2012; Frazzini and Pedersen 2014). As a result, holders of low-volatility assets receive a premium paid by the other leverage-averse investors.

Could the bond outperformance over the replication portfolio made of equities and Treasuries be a manifestation of the low-volatility phenomenon across asset classes? Bonds and stocks represent two extremes of a company's capital structure, with different claims to the same fundamental cash flows of the firm. Bonds are the low-volatility assets, while stocks are the high-volatility assets. According to the low-volatility hypothesis, bonds as the low-volatility assets should have better risk-adjusted performance than stocks, which is consistent with our findings.

In our regression test, we proxy for the low-volatility phenomenon using the BAB (betting-against-beta) factor,[17] which was proposed by Frazzini and Pedersen (2014). This factor longs low-beta stocks and shorts high-beta stocks. It also leverages up the low-beta leg to make the strategy market neutral. This strategy, as it longs the low-volatility stocks and shorts the high-volatility stocks, is designed to capture the time dynamics of the low-volatility phenomenon across equities. The low-volatility dynamics are time-varying because the underlying elements that make investors favor risky over low-volatility assets, such as investor risk aversion and investors' financing constraints, are time-varying. These same underlying dynamics are likely to drive both the within-equity and the cross-capital-structure low-volatility phenomenon. Therefore, the BAB factor, even constructed from equities, might be able to capture, at least partially, the time dynamics of the cross-capital-structure low-volatility phenomenon.

Empirical Tests on Risk Factors

To verify whether these factors can indeed explain the bond outperformance, we regress the monthly bond-over-replication returns on these three factors while controlling for a host of other commonly used factors. If these factors can explain the bond outperformance, the intercept of the regressions should disappear after we include them.

We start with a baseline model that includes two main risk factors that we used earlier: S&P 500 and Treasury (OTR 10y) excess returns over the risk-free rate (3m T-bill). The first (IG) and sixth (HY) columns of Table 1.8 show the regression results for the baseline model using the S&P 500 and Treasury factors (Specification 1). The coefficients are consistent with earlier results. The bond-over-replication portfolio returns had no significant exposures to either factor, indicating that the sensitivity-based risk-matching did a good job neutralizing the bond portfolio's exposures to the two factors in the replication portfolio. The intercept terms were 1.806%/yr for IG and 3.495%/yr for HY, and both were statistically significant, suggesting that the bond portfolios delivered significant outperformance over the replication portfolio when we controlled for any residual S&P 500 and Treasury risk. The adjusted R^2s for the baseline regressions were small at 0.2% for IG and –0.5% for HY, indicating that the majority of the time variation of bond-over-replication portfolio performance cannot be explained by the baseline factors.

As an additional control, we add the commonly used equity risk factors (Specification 2): the Fama–French five (FF5) factors [market (S&P 500 over rf, already in baseline model), value (HML), size (SMB), investment (CMA), and profitability (RMW)] and the momentum (MMT) factor. The market, size, and value factors have been staples of modern asset pricing models used in the literature since Fama and French (1993). The momentum factor has also been used extensively for many years (Jegadeesh 1990; Jegadeesh and Titman 1993). The investment and profitability factors are proxies for the quality factors and have been proposed more recently (Fama and French 2015). The intercepts were still statistically significant after including the commonly used equity factors, which indicates that the bond portfolios still significantly outperformed the replication portfolios after controlling for these common equity risk factors. All together, the Fama–French five factors and momentum factor increased the adjusted R^2 by around 4–5% to 5.71% in IG and 3.57% in HY.

Next, we add the Equity VRP factor (Specification 3) to the host of the control factors. Consistent with our hypothesis, the coefficient on the equity VRP was positive and significant, suggesting that exposures to the equity VRP might be one of the drivers of the bond-over-replication return

TABLE 1.8 Regression Coefficients of Bond-over-Replication Portfolio Monthly Returns on Common Factors

Specification		IG					HY			
Variables	1	2	3	4	5	1	2	3	4	5
	Baseline	+ FF5 + MMT	+Equity VRP	+Bond VRP	+BAB (Low-Volatility Factor)	Baseline	+ FF5 + MMT	+Equity VRP	+Bond VRP	+BAB (Low-Volatility Factor)
Intercept (%/yr)	1.806**	2.145***	1.673**	1.12	0.801	3.495**	4.153***	3.404***	2.557*	2.108
S&P 500 over rf	−0.013	−0.021	−0.02	−0.027	−0.025	−0.015	−0.032	−0.031	−0.042	−0.039
Treasury over rf	−0.037	−0.032	−0.024	−0.025	−0.014	−0.026	−0.046	−0.034	−0.036	−0.02
SMB (size)		0.01	0.011	0.017	0.016		−0.039	−0.038	−0.029	−0.03
HML (value)		−0.053	−0.052	−0.034	−0.035		−0.081	−0.079	−0.053	−0.055
RMW (profitability)		−0.014	−0.015	−0.022	−0.021		−0.014	−0.016	−0.029	−0.027
CMA (investment)		−0.006	−0.006	−0.027	−0.024		−0.052	−0.052	−0.084	−0.08
MMT (momentum)		−0.029**	−0.029**	−0.037**	−0.037**		−0.018	−0.018	−0.029	−0.029
Equity VRP			0.224**	0.196**	0.148**			0.355***	0.312**	0.244**

(Continued)

41

TABLE 1.8 (*Continued*)

Specification	IG					HY				
	1	2	3	4	5	1	2	3	4	5
Bond VRP (puts)				1.502***	1.368***				2.121***	1.933**
Bond VRP (calls)				−0.046	−0.179				0.106	−0.081
BAB (low vol.)					0.107***					0.151***
adj. R^2	0.15%	5.71%	10.66%	16.14%	29.02%	−0.47%	3.57%	7.85%	12.05%	20.76%
Δ in adj. R^2 from previous model		6%	5%	5%	13%		4%	4%	4%	9%
Δ in Intercept from previous model (%/yr)		0.34	−0.47	−0.55	−0.32		0.66	−0.75	−0.85	−0.45

Note: */**/*** indicates 10%/5%/1% level of significance. The portfolio returns are from January 1996 to December 2019 due to availability of equity option data.
Source: AQR, Bloomberg, CME, Compustat, Ken French data library, OptionMetrics, Barclays Research

difference. Including the equity VRP in the regressions also decreased the intercepts by 47bp in IG and 75bp in HY. Overall, adding the equity VRP increased the adjusted R^2 by 4 to 5% in both IG and HY.

In Specification 4, we add the Bond VRP puts and calls factors to the list of factors in the prior step (including Equity VRP). The coefficients were significant on the Bond VRP puts, but not on the calls, indicating that collecting the call feature premium may be a major contributor to the bond outperformance, while the convexity mismatch may play only a small role. The coefficients on Treasury puts in HY (2.121) were 1.4 times the size of the coefficient in IG (1.502), suggesting that HY bonds benefited more from selling puts on Treasury rates, which is to be expected since there are a higher fraction of callable bonds in HY than in IG. Overall, adding the bond VRP factors decreased the intercepts by 55bp in IG and 85bp in HY and increased the adjusted R^2 by 5% in IG and 4% in HY.

The last regressions (Specification 5) add the BAB factor, which proxies for the low-volatility phenomenon. The coefficients on the BAB factor were positive and significant in both IG and HY, suggesting that the time variation of bond outperformance over the replication portfolio had significant exposures to the low-volatility dynamics in equity. Adding the BAB (low-volatility) factor decreased the intercept by another 32bp in IG and 45bp in HY and increased the adjusted R^2 by 13% in IG and 9% in HY. It is quite a surprising finding that a cross-asset class return difference (bonds over equities and Treasuries) was significantly related to a purely within-equity dynamic. The common return dynamics are driven by investor preferences for riskier assets with higher returns, both across and within asset classes. When macroeconomic conditions change over time, such as when leverage is more stringent, or investor risk aversion is low, investors' preferences for risky assets may become stronger, leading to bigger bond outperformance and bigger equity low-volatility effect at the same time.

The final intercepts after controlling for Treasury risk, the commonly used equity risk factors, equity VRP, bond VRP, and the low-volatility factor were 80bp in IG and 211bp in HY, not statistically significant. In the end, the nonlinear payoff features (equity and bond VRP) and the equity low-volatility effect jointly explained the bond outperformance. It is important to note that these results do not mean that, in practice, corporate bonds are redundant and that an investor can replicate the returns of corporate bonds by selling equity and interest rate volatilities and investing in the equity low-volatility factor together with equities and Treasuries. Harvesting the VRPs and equity low-volatility factor is challenging for several reasons.

First, from an equilibrium perspective, the corporate bond market may be too large for investors to replicate its volatility exposures using derivatives. To illustrate the relative size, we took a snapshot on May 4, 2020: The

Bloomberg Barclays Investment Grade and High Yield Corporate indices have a total market value of more than $7trn, as reported in Table 1.9. In contrast, the SPX options and the 10yr Treasury options have a total open interest of about $4,463bn and $329bn in terms of notional, about 62% and 4% of the market value of the corporate indices. Aside from the size, the liquidity in the options markets may also be limited to support large trades that replicate the existing volatility exposures in the entire corporate bond markets. Daily trading volumes of the SPX and 10yr Treasury options are shown in the second row of Table 1.9. To obtain a rough estimate of the dollar amount of the corporate bonds whose volatility exposures the option strategies are able to replicate subject to their current liquidity, we assume that up to 5% of the daily trading volumes can be allocated to the replication trades without causing any negative price impact. We also assume that the corporate bond's average exposures to short-volatility strategies are roughly 0.196 for equity and 1.65 for interest rates based on regression coefficients in Table 1.8.[18] Given current daily volumes, in one day we would be able to replicate the volatility exposures of $35bn and $1bn of corporate bonds with SPX and Treasury options, respectively, representing only 0.48% and 0.02%, respectively, of the total bond market value.[19] To replicate the overall volatility exposures in the bond indices, it would take 208 trading days (nine months) and 5,273 trading days (21 years) in the SPX and Treasury option markets, respectively, to implement the trades with current liquidity. In reality, the replicating trades collectively can be more than 5% of daily volume, but the negative price impact that they might cause could also wipe out the profit of the trades. Overall, the numbers suggest that the option markets might have limited capacity to absorb trades that replicate the exposures in corporate bonds on a large scale.

Second, selling equity and interest rate volatilities requires trading options and futures, which is not allowed in a lot of traditional type of mandates. Capturing the equity low-volatility factor requires shorting stocks, which is also prohibited in many mandates, such as for mutual funds and pension funds. Moreover, all the returns in the regression including returns for the bond portfolios and the risk factors are gross of transaction costs. In reality, trading the BAB factor requires buying and selling a good number of small-cap stocks on a monthly basis, where the transaction costs could potentially be high on top of the shorting costs. Capturing the VRPs requires daily delta hedging using SPX or Treasury futures, which could also be costly. In contrast, the bond portfolio is fairly inexpensive to trade as its average holding period is four to six years per bond. Another aspect to

TABLE 1.9 Size of Corporate Bonds vs. Option Markets

		Corporate Bond Index	SPX Options	10yr Treasury Options
Total Market Value ($bn)		$7,323	$4,563	$329
Daily Volume (in notional, $bn)			$276	$92
Corporate bond positions that can be replicated in 1 day in each derivative market with 5% DV trading limit	Market value ($bn)		$35	$1
	% total bond market value		0.48%	0.02%
# days to replicate entire corporate market			208	5273

Note: The data was taken as a snapshot at the market close of May 4, 2020. The market value reported for SPX options and 10yr Treasury options (June expiry) are the notional for each contract multiplied by the total open interest of contracts for each type of security. For details of calculation, see notes 18 and 19.
Source: Bloomberg, OptionMetrics, CME, Barclays Research

consider is that the dynamics of volatilities are very different from traditional asset returns in bonds and equities. Therefore, trading volatilities would require building one or more teams with special expertise, and additional infrastructure may be needed for daily trading.

Overall, the equity and bond VRPs, as well as the equity low-volatility factor, help us understand the source of the bond outperformance over equities and Treasuries. Given the limited capacity of derivatives markets, mandate constraints, and explicit and implicit trading costs, it might be difficult for investors to capture the VRPs and the equity low-volatility strategy directly. Corporate bonds, however, provide a single instrument to gain exposures to a variety of risk premia without the need of frequent rebalancing at little additional cost. These findings have important implications for investors seeking exposures in the volatility and equity low-volatility strategies: Existing corporate bondholders should be aware of their effective exposures from their bond portfolios, and nonbondholders should consider buying corporate bonds as an alternative to gain such exposures.

CONCLUSION

We conduct a comprehensive two-part study spanning almost three decades and leveraging our unique access to the Bloomberg Barclays Indices pricing and analytics data as well as a proprietary firm-level capital structure mapping to examine a key fundamental question for any investor who has or considers having an allocation to credit: Can it be replaced in a portfolio by a combination of equities and Treasuries?

We explicitly address two major pitfalls related to the reallocation and mismatch effects, which led to contradictory results in previous studies, and find that introducing an allocation to credit improves the risk-adjusted performance of a host of equities/Treasuries portfolios. At an issuer level, corporate bonds achieved better risk-adjusted performance than a combination of Treasuries and equities of the same companies with similar systematic exposures, in both IG and HY, regardless of the weighting scheme used. Such outperformance was persistent in subperiods, ratings, industries, in both the United States and European markets, and using alternative risk-matching approaches.

Our cross-sectional results suggest that for a majority of issuers, on average, their bonds outperformed their stocks on a risk-adjusted basis, but there were still a nonnegligible proportion of issuers with stocks outperforming their bonds. Based on these results, an interesting future area of research may be to understand what characteristics make it more likely for a company to have bonds that outperform their stocks after adjusting for risk, and vice versa. Portfolio managers with the flexibility of combining corporate bonds and equities in their portfolio could benefit from this line of research by adding another source of alpha to their portfolios.

The nonreplicable component of corporate bond performance was largely explained by credit having exposure to equity and bond VRPs because of the options embodied in corporate bond payoffs and the low-volatility phenomenon across the capital structure where corporate bonds represent the low-risk asset compared to equities. Various constraints facing investors, however, prevent them from realistically replacing credit with a proper combination of Treasuries and equities with an overlay of these strategies. Thus, credit offers an efficient channel to gain exposures to these risk premia.

Even if the ability to replicate credit returns improves because of increased liquidity and capacity in derivatives markets, for example, we would expect from an equilibrium standpoint a repricing in credit such that it continues to offer a unique benefit to investors. From a supply-side perspective (i.e., corporations), issuing corporate bonds is an important financing channel that offers several benefits compared to equity issuance, such as preferential tax treatment. Given the strong demand for bond financing, corporations have incentives to lower bond prices to make spreads attractively high for investors. Given the strong benefits that corporations enjoy from issuing corporate bonds, supply and demand will ensure that corporate bonds will not be replaceable by a combination of equities and Treasuries or by other instruments.

REFERENCES

Ambastha, M., A. Ben Dor, L. Dynkin, and J. Hyman. 2008, March. "Do Short-Dated Corporates Outperform Long-Dated Corporates? A DTS-Based Study." Global Relative Value, Lehman Brothers Fixed Income Research.

Ambastha, M., A. Ben Dor, L. Dynkin, J. Hyman, and V. Konstantinovsky. 2010. "Empirical Duration of Corporate Bonds and Credit Market Segmentation." *Journal of Fixed Income* 20(1): 5–27.

Ang, A., R. J. Hodrick, Y. Xing, and X. Zhang, 2006. "The Cross-Section of Volatility and Expected Returns." *Journal of Finance* 61(1): 259–299.

Ang, A., R. J. Hodrick, Y. Xing, and X. Zhang. 2009. "High Idiosyncratic Volatility and Low Returns: International and Further US Evidence." *Journal of Financial Economics* 91(1): 1–23.

Asness, C., A. Frazzini, and L. H. Pedersen 2012. "Leverage Aversion and Risk Parity." *Financial Analysts Journal* 68(1): 47–59.

Asvanunt, A., and S. Richardson. 2017. "The Credit Risk Premium." *Journal of Fixed Income* 26(3): 6–24.

Bakshi, G. and Kapadia, N., 2003. "Delta-Hedged Gains and the Negative Market Volatility Risk Premium." *Review of Financial Studies* 16(2): 527–566.

Ben Dor, A., J. Guan, and X. Zeng. 2018, April 23. "Using Credit Signals to Enhance Equity Momentum Strategies (BEAM): An Application to European Markets." Barclays Research.

Ben Dor, A., and J. Xu. 2015. "Should Equity Investors Care about Corporate Bond Prices? Using Bond Prices to Construct Equity Momentum Strategies." *Journal of Portfolio Management* 41(4): 35–49.

Carr, P., and L. Wu. 2009. "Variance Risk Premiums." *Review of Financial Studies* 22(3): 1311–1341.

Choi, H., Mueller, P. and Vedolin, A., 2017. "Bond Variance Risk Premiums." *Review of Finance* 21(3): 987–1022.

Fama, E., and K. French. 1993. "Common Risk Factors in the Returns on Stocks and Bonds." *Journal of Financial Economics* 33(1): 3–56.

Fama, E., and K. French. 2012. "Size, Value, and Momentum in International Stock Returns." *Journal of Financial Economics* 105(3): 457–472.

Fama, E., and K. French. 2015. "A Five-Factor Asset Pricing Model." *Journal of Financial Economics* 116(1): 1–22.

Frazzini, A., and L. H. Pedersen. 2014. "Betting against Beta." *Journal of Financial Economics* 111(1): 1–25.

Israelov, R. 2019, April 10. "Give Credit Where Credit Is Due: What Explains Corporate Bond Returns?" http://dx.doi.org/10.2139/ssrn.3293357

Jegadeesh, N. 1990. "Evidence of Predictable Behavior of Security Returns." *Journal of Finance* 45(3): 881–898.

Jegadeesh, N., and S. Titman. 1993. "Returns to Buying Winners and Selling Losers: Implications for Stock Market Efficiency." *Journal of Finance* 48(1): 65–91.

Konstantinovsky, V., K. Y. Ng, and B. D. Phelps. 2016. "Measuring Bond-Level Liquidity." *Journal of Portfolio Management* 42(4): 116–128.

Korwar, A. N., and R. W. Masulis. 1986. "Seasoned Equity Offerings: An Empirical Investigation." *Journal of Financial Economics* 15(1/2): 91–118.

Linnainmaa, J. T., and M. R. Roberts. 2018. "The History of the Cross-Section of Stock Returns." *Review of Financial Studies* 31(7): 2606–2649.

Merton, R. C. 1974. "On the Pricing of Corporate Debt: The Risk Structure of Interest Rates." *Journal of Finance* 29(2): 449–470.

Myers, S., and N. Majluf. 1984. "Corporate Financing Decisions When Firms Have Investment Information that Investors Do Not." *Journal of Financial Economics* 13(2): 187–221.

Norges Bank. 2017, September 4. "Corporate Bonds in a Multi-Asset Portfolio." Discussion notes.

Schaefer, S. M., and I. A. Strebulaev. 2008. "Structural Models of Credit Risk Are Useful: Evidence from Hedge Ratios on Corporate Bonds." *Journal of Financial Economics* 90(1): 1–19.

APPENDIX 1.1

Using Treasury Index as the Treasury Portfolio

When we use the Bloomberg Barclays Treasury Index as both the Treasury Portfolio and the Treasury risk factor, the performance of the replication portfolio increased slightly, as shown in Table 1.10, because the Treasury Index had better performance to duration ratio than the 10yr Treasury Portfolio. However, the qualitative results remain the same as the bond portfolio still outperformed the replication portfolio with higher average returns and higher Sharpe ratios. Notice that the magnitude of the bond-over-replication outperformance decreased in both IG and HY, but the decrease was much smaller in HY because Treasury returns make up a much smaller component for HY bonds.

TABLE 1.10 Performance Statistics of Bond vs. Replication Portfolio (Using Treasury Index)

Portfolio		Weighting Scheme	Avg. Ret. (%/yr)	Volatility (%/yr)	Sharpe (Inf.) Ratio (Ann.)	Worst Monthly Ret (%)	Max. Drawdown (%)	Corr. w. Bond Portfolio
IG	Bond	EW	6.48	5.02	0.81	-8.22	-13.80	
		Bond-VW	6.20	5.18	0.73	-6.84	-14.23	
		Equity-VW	6.37	5.04	0.79	-6.54	-11.61	
		Total-VW	6.35	5.05	0.78	-6.42	-11.99	
	Replication Portfolio	EW	5.53	4.59	0.68	-6.10	-9.44	0.82
		Bond-VW	5.34	4.84	0.61	-9.22	-17.21	0.77
		Equity-VW	5.54	4.73	0.67	-7.57	-10.57	0.84
		Total-VW	5.51	4.74	0.66	-7.91	-11.09	0.83
	Bond over Replication	EW	0.95	2.93	0.33	-3.34	-14.72	
		Bond-VW	0.85	3.43	0.25	-5.87	-11.87	
		Equity-VW	0.83	2.74	0.30	-3.85	-10.11	
		Total-VW	0.84	2.85	0.30	-4.15	-10.13	

(Continued)

TABLE 1.10 (Continued)

Portfolio		Weighting Scheme	Avg. Ret. (%/yr)	Volatility (%/yr)	Sharpe (Inf.) Ratio (Ann.)	Worst Monthly Ret (%)	Max. Drawdown (%)	Corr. w. Bond Portfolio
HY	Bond	EW	7.99	6.71	0.83	-15.58	-25.13	
		Bond-VW	7.62	6.59	0.79	-13.51	-24.80	
		Equity-VW	8.03	5.55	1.01	-13.36	-19.98	
		Total-VW	7.95	5.83	0.95	-13.40	-21.28	
	Replication Portfolio	EW	4.69	5.48	0.42	-8.93	-23.35	0.67
		Bond-VW	5.63	5.54	0.58	-10.39	-22.09	0.72
		Equity-VW	5.07	4.38	0.61	-8.51	-17.69	0.70
		Total-VW	5.27	4.67	0.62	-9.04	-18.53	0.72
	Bond over Replication	EW	3.30	5.06	0.65	-6.65	-17.02	
		Bond-VW	2.00	4.61	0.43	-4.29	-15.28	
		Equity-VW	2.96	3.98	0.74	-4.85	-9.70	
		Total-VW	2.68	4.09	0.65	-4.37	-11.00	

Source: Bloomberg, Compustat, Barclays Research

APPENDIX 1.2

Bond Outperformance in Subsamples

This section examines the consistency of bond outperformance, both in sample and out of sample. Within the original US sample, we examine the bond outperformance by rating and by industry. Many anomalies with significant in-sample results became insignificant after their initial publication (e.g., Linnainmaa and Roberts 2018). For this reason, out-of-sample performance is often viewed as strong validation of any in-sample findings. As an out-of-sample test, we evaluate whether the bond outperformance is present in the European markets.

By Rating

Figure 1.12 compares the annualized Sharpe ratios of the bond with the replication portfolio and shows the information ratio of the bond-over-replication portfolio for each rating. In all rating categories, the bond portfolios have higher Sharpe ratios than their replication portfolios. The returns difference of the bond-over-replication portfolios also have positive information ratio ranging from 0.50 to 0.73. The results hold regardless of weighting schemes.

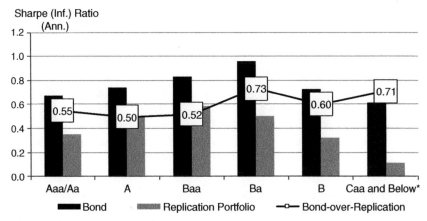

FIGURE 1.12 Sharpe (Information) Ratios of Bond vs. Replication Portfolios by Rating
* The statistics shown for Caa and below are from January 2002 to December 2019 due to lack of observation in this rating bucket from 1993 to 2001.
Note: The portfolio returns are from January 1993 to December 2019. All portfolios are equally weighted.
Source: Bloomberg, Compustat, Barclays Research

By Industry

Figure 1.13 shows the information ratio of the bond-over-replication port-folios by industry (GICS 2-digit sector) for equally weighted portfolios. The results for other weighting schemes are similar and omitted for brevity. In all industries, the bond portfolios outperform the respective replication portfolios in both IG and HY, generating positive information ratios in all sectors, and the results are similar regardless of weighting scheme. The results indicate that the bond outperformance we observed is present in all industries and not driven by a small number of industries.

In European Markets

Is the bond over equity outperformance we found in fact a persistent phenomenon across asset classes, or is it spurious and only a product of data mining? One way to answer this question is to perform the same analysis on a different sample to see if the results hold. Similar to the United States, we construct a sample of mapped bonds and equities at the company level for bonds in the Bloomberg Barclays Pan Euro Corporate and HY indices.[20] Panel A of Table 1.11 reports the percentage of bond market value of the

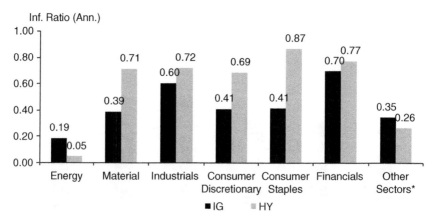

FIGURE 1.13   Annualized Information Ratio of Bond-over-Replication Portfolios by Industry

Note: The portfolio returns are from January 1993 to December 2019. All portfolios are equally weighted. Industries are classified using GICS 2-digit sector. "Other sectors" include utilities, health care, information technology, and telecommunications. These sectors did not have enough observations on their own, so they were grouped together.

Source: Bloomberg, Compustat, Barclays Research

TABLE 1.11 Mapping Coverage and Portfolio Performance in European Markets

Panel A. Mapping Coverage Ratio of Pan Euro Corporate and High-Yield Index Constituents to Compustat (by Bond Market Value)

Year-End Market Value	Pan Euro (€bn)					
	2003	2007	2011	2014	2017
Corporate Index	1,003	1,205	1,607	1,930	2,330
Mapped	77%	90%	86%	87%	88%
HY Index	67	77	154	348	330
Mapped	56%	67%	66%	74%	73%
Agg. Universe (IG+HY)	1,065	1,282	1,761	2,279	2,660
Mapped	76%	89%	84%	85%	86%

(Continued)

TABLE 1.11 *(Continued)*

Panel B. Bond vs. Replication Portfolio Performance in European Markets

Portfolio		Weighting Scheme	Avg. Ret. (%/yr)	Volatility (%/yr)	Sharpe (Inf.) Ratio (Ann.)	Worst Monthly Ret. (%)	Max. Drawdown (%)	Corr. w. bond portfolio
IG	Bond	EW	3.75	3.42	0.77	-3.87	-8.23	
		Bond-VW	3.67	3.52	0.74	-4.74	-7.14	
		Equity-VW	3.87	3.17	0.88	-3.07	-5.17	
		Total-VW	3.85	3.19	0.87	-3.20	-5.32	
	Replication Portfolio	EW	2.87	2.60	0.69	-2.29	-5.00	0.68
		Bond-VW	2.77	2.82	0.60	-2.79	-6.74	0.65
		Equity-VW	2.79	2.48	0.70	-2.06	-3.46	0.69
		Total-VW	2.81	2.50	0.70	-2.08	-3.72	0.68
	Bond over Replication	EW	0.88	2.51	0.35	-3.25	-8.68	
		Bond-VW	0.91	2.73	0.33	-4.52	-6.68	
		Equity-VW	1.07	2.32	0.46	-3.13	-5.52	
		Total-VW	1.04	2.35	0.44	-3.24	-5.54	

(Continued)

TABLE 1.11 (*Continued*)

Panel B. Bond vs. Replication Portfolio Performance in European Markets

Portfolio		Weighting Scheme	Avg. Ret. (%/yr)	Volatility (%/yr)	Sharpe (Inf.) Ratio (Ann.)	Worst Monthly Ret. (%)	Max. Drawdown (%)	Corr. w. bond portfolio
HY	Bond	EW	6.85	7.96	0.72	−15.45	−31.11	
		Bond-VW	6.30	7.42	0.70	−13.22	−26.96	
		Equity-VW	6.55	7.47	0.73	−14.46	−26.86	
		Total-VW	6.50	7.43	0.73	−14.33	−26.78	
	Replication Portfolio	EW	2.44	6.62	0.21	−8.29	−29.79	0.61
		Bond-VW	2.12	6.93	0.16	−8.39	−29.70	0.58
		Equity-VW	2.20	5.60	0.21	−6.40	−23.39	0.58
		Total-VW	2.23	5.79	0.21	−6.51	−24.10	0.58
	Bond over Replication	EW	4.41	6.54	0.67	−8.93	−14.83	
		Bond-VW	4.18	6.59	0.63	−6.88	−13.21	
		Equity-VW	4.34	6.24	0.70	−8.62	−13.82	
		Total-VW	4.27	6.21	0.69	−8.25	−13.44	

Note: The portfolio returns include the period May 2005 to December 2019.
Source: Bloomberg, Compustat, Barclays Research

bond indices that was successfully mapped to equities in Compustat at multiple points during the sample period with an interim of three to four years. The mapped percentage has increased over the year and reached over 80% at the end of 2017 for IG and HY combined.

Following the same methodology of sensitivity matching, we constructed replication portfolios using the equity portfolio, euro 7–10y Treasury index, and cash based on factor sensitivities calculated from trailing 36m regressions.[21] Panel B of Table 1.11 reports the performance of the bond, the replication, and the bond-over-replication portfolios in European markets. The performance numbers show a similar pattern of bond outperformance over the replication portfolios. Returns of the bond and their replication portfolios also have similarly high correlations as in the US market, ranging from 0.58 to 0.69. Despite the high correlations, the bond portfolios have higher average returns and Sharpe ratios than the replication portfolios, similar to the US markets. Moreover, the information ratios of bond-over-replication portfolio are positive at about 0.4 for IG and 0.7 for HY. The results are consistent across different weighting schemes. Overall, the results suggest that the bond outperformance also is present in European markets.

APPENDIX 1.3

Tests for Other Explanations of Bond-over-Equity Outperformance

This appendix provides detailed analysis of a few tests on some possible explanations for the bond-over-equity outperformance we documented.

Are Outliers Driving the Bond-over-Equity Outperformance? A Look at the Cross-Section

In the portfolio analysis, we find that the bond portfolios outperformed the replication portfolios with similar risk exposures. It is possible that the average bond outperformance was driven by a small number of firms but was not prevalent in the cross-section. To assess whether this is the case, we conducted pairwise comparisons on performance of bonds and the risk-matched-equity returns from the same company. The risk-matched-equity returns for each company are a combination of the 10yr Treasury, cash, and the equity from the same company. We determine the weights on Treasuries, cash, and the same-company equity in two approaches. In the first, we use the same weights from the portfolio analysis with trailing OLS regressions calculated each month from IG and HY portfolios, respectively (empirical hedge ratio[22]). One caveat of this approach is that each month it applies the same set of weights across the board for all companies in IG and HY, respectively, while in reality there are cross-sectional differences in the exposures to equity and Treasuries across bonds from different issuers. To incorporate the cross-sectional differences in risk sensitivity, we look at a second approach that takes into consideration each individual issuer's characteristics. In the second approach, for weights on equities we use the analytical hedge ratios based on the Merton model, and for weights on Treasuries we use the ratio of the average analytical duration of an issuer's bonds[23] to the duration of the 10y Treasury index as weights. Although the second approach incorporates individual companies' characteristics, earlier analysis such as Table 1.7 suggests that, at the portfolio level, the empirical hedge ratios are more effective than the analytical hedge ratios as the empirical hedge ratios lead to more volatility reduction and create more risk exposures similar to the bond portfolio. To balance out the trade-off between the hedge ratio efficacy and lack of cross-section variation, the subsequent analysis presents results using both approaches.

Table 1.12 shows the fraction of companies whose bonds had higher average returns compared with their risk-matched equities in the whole sample period as well as in each of the five-year subperiods. In the cross-section from 1993 to 2019, using empirical hedge ratios, 81% of IG and 77% of HY companies have bonds outperforming their risk-matched equities. In the subperiods, the fraction of companies with bond outperformance ranged from 55% (2003–2007 IG, 1998–2002 HY) to 88% (2008–2012 HY). The numbers suggest that across the sample, the majority of companies had bonds that outperformed their risk-matched equities, indicating that the bond outperformance at the portfolio level was unlikely to be driven by a handful of outliers.

Are We Underweighting Equity Risk?

Another possible explanation of the bond outperformance over the risk-matched equities is that the risk was not matched properly and bonds have higher returns as a compensation for the higher risk they carry. To examine whether this is the case, we look at the cross-sectional distribution of the pairwise volatility ratio (bond over risk-matched equity) for each company and its relation to the pairwise return differences. If the higher returns in bonds are a compensation for their higher risk (proxied by volatility), then we should expect to see a positive relation between the pairwise return difference and volatility ratio, as relatively riskier bonds (higher volatility ratio) should have more outperformance over the risk-matched equity from the

TABLE 1.12   Percentage of Positive Pairwise Return Differences (Bond-over-Risk-Matched Equities)

		Using Empirical Hedge Ratios (OLS Based)		Using Analytical Hedge Ratios (Merton Model)	
	Period	IG	HY	IG	HY
Whole Sample	Jan. 1993–Dec. 2019	81%	77%	84%	73%
Subperiod	Jan. 1993–Dec. 1997	82%	79%	84%	68%
	Jan. 1998–Dec. 2002	71%	55%	65%	55%
	Jan. 2003–Dec. 2007	55%	71%	71%	68%
	Jan. 2008–Dec. 2012	87%	88%	78%	70%
	Jan. 2013–Dec. 2019	75%	72%	93%	81%

Note: The returns are from January 1993 to December 2019. The analytical hedge ratios use the Merton (1974) implied hedge ratios for equities and the ratio of bond analytical duration to the 10yr Treasury analytical duration as the hedge ratio for Treasuries. The empirical hedge ratios use the portfolio-level hedge ratios that match the 2-factor (S&P500 and 10yr Treasury) sensitivities of the bond portfolio (EW) where the sensitivities are calculated from trailing 36m regressions.
Source: Bloomberg, Compustat, Barclays Research

same issuer (higher return difference). Panel A of Table 1.13 shows the summary statistics of the cross-sectional volatility ratio. The average volatility ratios are indeed slightly higher than one, but the median volatility ratios are fairly close to one, except IG companies using empirical hedge ratio. Panel B of Table 1.13 shows the results of regressing pairwise average return differences of bond over risk-matched equity on the pairwise volatility ratios in the cross-section. Contrary to the hypothesis, we see either a negative or an insignificant coefficient on the volatility ratio, which suggests that in the cross-section, companies with a higher volatility ratio of bond over risk-matched equity do not have a higher return difference, suggesting that the bond outperformance is not compensation for their higher risk.

Is Liquidity Driving the Bond Outperformance?

Credit markets are known to be relatively illiquid compared to equity and Treasury markets. Is it possible that the bond outperformance we find is a compensation for its illiquidity? We try to address this question in three ways. In the first approach, we perform the same set of analysis on a more liquid subsample: companies with stocks in the S&P 500. In the second

TABLE 1.13 Summary Statistics and Regression Results of Pairwise Volatility Ratios

Panel A. Cross-Sectional Summary Statistics of Pairwise Volatility Ratio (Bond over Risk-Matched Equity)

Statistic in Cross-Section	Using Empirical Hedge Ratios (OLS Based)		Using Analytical Hedge Ratios (Merton Model)	
	IG	HY	IG	HY
Average	1.27	1.10	1.09	1.10
Standard Deviation	0.49	0.59	0.26	0.43
25%tile	0.97	0.72	0.93	0.80
Median	1.18	0.96	1.02	1.03
75%tile	1.47	1.30	1.17	1.30
% of Companies w. Vol. Ratio <=1	29%	55%	44%	47%

(Continued)

TABLE 1.18 (Continued)

Panel B. Cross-Sectional Regression of Pairwise Average Monthly Return Difference on Pairwise Volatility Ratio (Bond over Risk-Matched Equity)

Independent Variables	Using Empirical Hedge Ratios (OLS Based)		Using Analytical Hedge Ratios (Merton Model)	
	IG	HY	IG	HY
Intercept	0.245***	0.715***	0.218***	0.327***
Volatility Ratio (Bond/Risk-Matched Equity)	−0.11***	−0.458***	−0.09*	−0.097*
Adj. R²	6%	17%	2%	0%

Note: The returns are from January 1993 to December 2019. The analytical hedge ratios use the Merton (1974) implied hedge ratios for equities and the ratio of bond analytical duration to the 10yr Treasury analytical duration as the hedge ratio for Treasuries. The empirical hedge ratios use the portfolio-level hedge ratios that match the 2-factor (S&P500 and 10yr Treasury) sensitivities of the bond portfolio (EW) where the sensitivities are calculated from trailing 36m regressions. Companies with less than 24 months of observations are eliminated from the sample of volatility ratio calculation. Individual volatility ratios are winsorized at 99%tile to eliminate the impact of outliers on the regression.

Source: Bloomberg, Compustat, Barclays Research

approach, we sort companies into different buckets based on the liquidity of their bonds and test whether there is any difference in bond outperformance in different liquidity buckets. In the third approach, we take into consideration transaction costs of trading bonds and examine whether the bond portfolio still has any outperformance over its replication portfolio made of equities and Treasuries. In all three approaches, we find similar bond outperformance.

Test 1: Performance in the S&P 500 Subsample

In the first approach, we focus on a subsample with liquid bonds and equities: S&P 500 companies with publicly traded bonds included in the Bloomberg Barclays Corporate and HY index. We perform the similar analysis of bond vs. replication portfolio comparison for this subsample. If bond illiquidity is a main driver behind its outperformance, we would expect this liquid sample to have very limited bond outperformance. Figure 1.14 shows the percentage of S&P 500 market capitalization that have mapped index bonds. The coverage ratios indicate that the majority of the S&P 500 have mapped index bonds, with the percentage covered approximately 90% in 2014 and onward. Table 1.14 shows the performance of the bond-over-replication portfolios for this subsample. The last column shows the correlation between the bond portfolio and its replication portfolio, respectively, for each weighting scheme. The correlations are fairly high, ranging from 0.71 to 0.80, depending on the weighting scheme, indicating that our

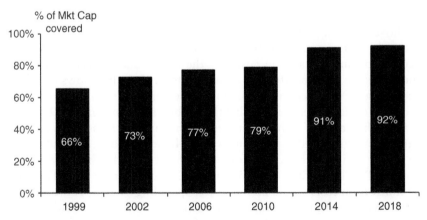

FIGURE 1.14   Percentage of Market Cap of S&P 500 Stocks Having Mapped Index Bonds
Source: Bloomberg, Compustat, Barclays Research

risk-matching methodology does a decent job for this subsample as well. Regardless of the weighting scheme, the bond portfolios outperformed the replication portfolios, delivering higher average returns by 1.70 to 1.90% per year with information ratios between 0.49 and 0.57. As the numbers suggest, the bond portfolios outperform their replication portfolios in the S&P 500 subsample with a magnitude similar to the IG universe.

Test 2: Rank Companies by Their Bond Liquidity

In the second approach, we used Liquidity Cost Score (LCS)[24] as a proxy for bond liquidity. Each month, we divided all issuers into low and high LCS categories and tracked their performance in a similar way as in earlier analysis. If bond liquidity is the reason for bond outperformance, we would expect the bond portfolio in the low-liquidity bucket to have greater outperformance over the replication portfolio than the bond portfolio in the high-liquidity bucket. Table 1.15 shows the performance of bond-over-replication portfolios by LCS ranking. In low and high LCS buckets, bond-over-replication portfolios have similar information ratios in both IG and HY and across weighting schemes. The similar magnitude of bond outperformance across LCS buckets suggests that liquidity is not likely to be a reason for bonds' outperformance over equities.

Test 3: Incorporating Bond Transaction Costs

In the third approach, we take out transaction costs in the bond portfolios, using LCS as a proxy for transaction costs.[25] Panel A of Table 1.16 compares the gross with the net performance of the bond portfolio and the bond-over-replication portfolio, and Panel B reports the average transaction cost and holding period for the bonds in the bond portfolio. We did not account for any transaction costs for the equity and Treasury portfolio, which puts the bond portfolio at a disadvantage. The table shows that after accounting for transaction costs in bonds, the bond-over-replication portfolio outperformance deteriorates slightly, but by a small magnitude (9bp/yr in IG and 50bp/yr in HY). The results suggest that average transaction cost per year is small compared to the returns of the bond portfolio. This is because the securities in the bond portfolio have fairly long holding periods, as shown in Panel B of Table 1.16 (5.9 yr for IG and 3.5 yr for HY). The average transaction costs would be small after spreading over the entire holding period. As a result, incorporating transaction costs in bonds made only a very small difference in the bond outperformance over equities. The information ratios of the net returns of bond-over-replication portfolios remain strong at 0.51 for IG and 0.73 for HY. Results are similar across weighting schemes.

TABLE 1.14 Performance of Bond over Replication Portfolio for S&P 500 Subsample

Weighting Scheme	Avg. Ret. (%/yr)	Volatility (%/yr)	Inf. Ratio (Ann.)	Worst Monthly Ret. (%)	Max. Drawdown (%)	Corr. (Bond, Replication Portfolio)
EW	1.90	3.38	0.56	-2.93	-10.98	0.73
Bond-VW	1.85	3.77	0.49	-5.43	-8.26	0.71
Equity-VW	1.70	2.96	0.57	-3.35	-7.95	0.80
Total-VW	1.74	3.09	0.56	-3.68	-7.85	0.79

Note: The portfolio returns are from January 1993 to December 2019. Weights on equity, 10y Treasury, and T-bills calculated monthly from EW bond and equity portfolios using sensitivity matching of two factors (S&P 500 and 10y Treasury Ret).
Source: Bloomberg, Compustat, Barclays Research

TABLE 1.15   Performance of Bond over Replication Portfolios by LCS Ranking

	LCS Ranking	Avg. Ret. (%/yr)	volatility (%/yr)	Inf. Ratio (Ann.)	Worst Monthly Ret. (%/m)	Max. Drawdown (%)
IG	Low LCS (high liquidity)	1.45	1.74	0.83	−1.12	−2.40
	High LCS (low liquidity)	2.45	3.08	0.79	−1.99	−7.05
HY	Low LCS (high liquidity)	3.86	2.87	1.35	−1.73	−3.70
	High LCS (low liquidity)	5.41	4.98	1.09	−3.92	−6.66

Note: Portfolios returns are from January 2010 to December 2019. Analysis starts in 2007 due to availability of LCS data. All portfolios are equally weighted among individual securities.
Source: Bloomberg, Compustat, Barclays Research

Overall, accounting for bond liquidity, by focusing on a liquid subsample such as S&P 500 firms, by ranking issuers by the liquidity of their bonds, or by taking out bond transaction costs, seems to have limited effect on the bond outperformance over replication portfolios. These sets of results suggest that bond liquidity is not likely to be a driving force for bond outperformance.

Using Moving Average and Forward-Looking Window in Calibrating Weights for Replication Portfolios

Some are concerned that the correlations between bond and equities are higher during recessions. As a result, using a trailing window to calibrate the weights for equities may underweight equities in the replication portfolio during recessions and lead to overall bond outperformance. To rule out this hypothesis, we reconstruct the replication portfolio using two alternative windows to calculate the weights for equities and Treasuries:

1. A moving average window centered on the calibration month (denoted as centered)
2. A forward-looking window starting on the calibration month (denoted as forward)

TABLE 1.16 Transaction Costs and Net Performance

Panel A. Gross and Net Performance of Bond-over-Replication Portfolios

| | IG | | | | | | HY | | | | | |
| | Bond | | | Bond-over-Replication Portfolio | | | Bond | | | Bond-over-Replication Portfolio | | |
	Avg. Ret. (%/yr)	Volatility (%/yr)	Sharpe Ratio (Ann.)	Avg. Ret. (%/yr)	Volatility (%/yr)	Inf. Ratio (Ann.)	Avg. Ret. (%/yr)	Volatility (%/yr)	Sharpe Ratio (Ann.)	Avg. Ret. (%/yr)	Volatility (%/yr)	Inf. Ratio (Ann.)
Gross	5.90	5.03	0.95	2.02	3.76	0.54	7.40	8.03	0.78	4.69	5.73	0.82
Net of Transaction Costs	5.81	5.04	0.94	1.93	3.75	0.51	6.89	8.15	0.71	4.18	5.76	0.73

Panel B. Average Bond Transaction Cost and Holding Horizon

	Annualized Bond Transaction Cost (%)	Average LCS (%)	Average Bond Holding Period (Yr)
IG	0.09	1.02	5.9
HY	0.50	1.56	3.5

Note: Portfolios returns are from January 2007 to December 2019. Analysis starts in 2007 due to availability of LCS data. All portfolios are equally weighted among individual securities.
Source: Bloomberg, Compustat, Barclays Research

TABLE 1.17 Performance Statistics of Bond-over-Replication Portfolio Return Differences by Replication Window in Calibrating Weights on Equities and Treasuries

	Replication Window	Avg. Ret. (%/yr)	Volatility (%/yr)	Inf. Ratio (Ann.)	Worst Monthly Ret. (%)	Max. Drawdown (%)
IG	Trailing (Original)	1.60	3.06	0.52	−3.11	−13.52
	Centered	1.88	2.55	0.74	−3.37	−8.28
	Forward	1.72	2.46	0.70	−3.69	−10.13
HY	Trailing (Original)	3.37	5.27	0.64	−6.64	−17.10
	Centered	4.00	4.32	0.93	−7.10	−13.37
	Forward	3.84	4.14	0.93	−7.37	−12.21

Note: Return periods are from January 1993 to January 2017 for an overlapping sample between three types of replication windows.
Source: Bloomberg, Compustat, Barclays Research

TABLE 1.18 Portfolio Performance Adjusted for Autocorrelations in Volatilities

Portfolio	Weighting Scheme	Avg. Ret. (%/yr)	Volatility (%/yr)	Sharpe (Inf.) Ratio (Ann.)	Worst Monthly Ret (%)	Max. Drawdown (%)	Corr. w. Bond Portfolio
IG Bond	EW	6.48	5.74	0.70	−8.22	−13.80	
	Bond-VW	6.20	5.86	0.64	−6.84	−14.23	
	Equity-VW	6.37	5.59	0.71	−6.54	−11.61	
	Total-VW	6.35	5.63	0.70	−6.42	−11.99	
Replication Portfolio	EW	4.85	4.79	0.52	−5.81	−9.04	0.82
	Bond-VW	4.64	4.98	0.45	−8.53	−15.93	0.78
	Equity-VW	4.81	4.86	0.50	−6.93	−10.07	0.85
	Total-VW	4.78	4.87	0.49	−7.26	−10.58	0.84
Bond over Replication	EW	1.63	3.27	0.50	−3.11	−13.52	
	Bond-VW	1.56	3.56	0.44	−5.67	−9.61	
	Equity-VW	1.56	2.99	0.52	−3.59	−8.11	
	Total-VW	1.57	3.07	0.51	−3.90	−8.10	

(Continued)

TABLE 1.18 (Continued)

Portfolio	Weighting Scheme	Avg. Ret. (%/yr)	Volatility (%/yr)	Sharpe (Inf.) Ratio (Ann.)	Worst Monthly Ret (%)	Max. Drawdown (%)	Corr. w. Bond Portfolio
HY Bond	EW	7.99	8.46	0.65	-15.58	-25.13	
	Bond-VW	7.62	7.99	0.65	-13.51	-24.80	
	Equity-VW	8.03	6.75	0.82	-13.36	-19.98	
	Total-VW	7.95	7.09	0.77	-13.40	-21.28	
Replication Portfolio	EW	4.56	6.29	0.35	-8.94	-22.69	0.68
	Bond-VW	5.20	6.41	0.44	-10.42	-22.06	0.72
	Equity-VW	4.68	4.82	0.48	-8.47	-16.79	0.70
	Total-VW	4.88	5.25	0.48	-9.01	-17.96	0.71
Bond over Replication	EW	3.43	5.18	0.66	-6.64	-17.10	
	Bond-VW	2.42	5.06	0.48	-4.50	-13.52	
	Equity-VW	3.34	4.56	0.73	-4.90	-8.20	
	Total-VW	3.07	4.64	0.66	-4.40	-9.41	

Source: Bloomberg, Compustat, Barclays Research

Besides the positioning of the window relative to the calibration month, other aspects of the calculation methods are similar to the original specification: Both windows have the same length (36m), exponentially decay weighting with a half-life of 9m, and assigning the calibration month the most weight.

Results are shown in Table 1.17. The performance statistics cover the sample period of January 1993 to January 2017, when the time series of the replication portfolio returns overlap among the three calibration windows.[26] The patterns of return comparisons are very similar to the original results, indicating that the time dynamics of the correlations between bonds and equities are not a driving force behind the bond outperformance.

Adjusting for Autocorrelation in Computing Portfolio Returns Did Not Account for Higher Sharpe Ratio in Bonds

There might be high autocorrelation in bond monthly returns, which increases volatilities of the bond portfolios. We adjust for possible serial correlation in the volatilities in the bond, replication, and the bond-over-replication portfolios (results shown in Table 1.18).[27] Bond portfolios still have considerably higher Sharpe ratios than the equity portfolios in both IG and HY, regardless of the weighting schemes used.

NOTES

1. Capital market information provided by SIFMA can be found at www.sifma.org.
2. Merton (1974) lays out a framework where the payoffs to bonds and stocks are driven by the same underlying asset value and derives the link between the two types of securities. Merton's model implies that a corporate bond is represented by a risk-free bond and a short put position on the underlying assets of the firm while the company's stock is represented by a call option on the firm.
3. Studies such as Bakshi and Kapadia (2003) and Carr and Wu (2009) found that a short volatility position on equities generates on average a positive risk premium, termed the equity variance risk premium.
4. Call provisions are more likely to be exercised when interest rates decline and bond prices rise. Hence, the impact of call features is similar to holding put options on interest rates for bond issuers and vice versa equivalent to shorting put options on interest rates and having a short exposure to interest rate volatility for bondholders.
5. Each month *s* we run the following regression using trailing 36m data with exponentially decayed weighting (half life=9m, but results are robust to use equal weighting or other half lives):

Credit Index Total Ret$_t$

$$= \alpha + w_E * \mathrm{Re}\, t_t^{S\&P\ 500} + w_{Treasury} * \mathrm{Re}\, t_t^{Treasury\ Index} + \varepsilon_t, where\ t$$

$$= s - 36, \ldots, s - 1$$

Any access weight is allocated in T-bills: $w_{T-Bills} = 1 - w_E - w_{Treasury}$

6. The process of creating the bond–equity mapping is discussed in great detail in Ben Dor and Xu (2015).

7. The results have no material difference from the results when we include all bonds with no price filters.

8. All index bonds of the same issuer are aggregated to issuer level using bond market value as weights.

9. The results using the Treasury Index are qualitatively similar to that using the 10-yr OTR but the replication portfolio performed slightly better when it uses the Treasury index than when it uses the 10-yr Treasuries. This is because the Treasury index outperformed the 10-yr Treasuries on a duration-matched base.

10. The results are similar using 48m or 60m trailing window and using equal-weighting instead of exponential decay weighting. The results are also similar using different half-life (currently 9m) of the exponential decay weighting. The exponential decay weighting is to ensure that we don't have big monthly changes in the weights when certain months with large effects are suddenly dropped out of the trailing window.

11. Step1: Estimate factor sensitivities in month t using regressions and trailing 36m data:

$$Ret_s^{Bond} = Intercept_{Bond,t} + \beta_{Bond,t} * SP500_s + \gamma_{Bond,t} * 10yTreasury_s + \varepsilon_{Bond,s}$$

$$Ret_s^{Equity} = Intercept_{E,t} + \beta_{E,t} * SP500_s + \gamma_{E,t} * 10yTreasury_s + \varepsilon_{E,?}$$

$$where\ s = t - 36, .., t - 1$$

Step 2: Solve for weights on equities, 10-yr treasuries, and 3m T-bills:

$$Replication\ Portfolio = W_{E,t} * Equity + W_{T,t} * 10yTreasury + W_{RF,t} * 3mTbill,$$

We solve for the two unknowns $(W_{E,t}, W_{T,t})$ in two equations: 1) $\beta_{Bond,t} = W_{E,t}\beta_{E,t}$, 2) $\gamma_{Bond,t} = W_{E,t}\gamma_{E,t} + W_{T,t}$, and any excess is allocated in the 3m T-bills: $W_{RF,t} = 1 - W_{E,t} - W_{T,t}$.

12. Vol.-Matched Replication Portfolio = HR * $Equity\ Portfolio$ + $(1 - HR)$

$$* 3mTbillRet, where\ Hedge\ Ratio\ HR = \frac{Vol\left(Bond\ Portfolio\ Ret\right)_{t-36,t-1}}{Vol\left(Mapped\ Equity\ Portfolio\ Ret\right)_{t-36,t-1}}$$

13. The analytical hedge ratio is:

$$
Hedge\ Ratio_{equity} = \frac{\frac{\partial D}{D}}{\frac{\partial E}{E}} = \left(\frac{\partial D}{\partial V}\right)\frac{E}{D} = \left(\frac{1-\frac{\partial E}{\partial V}}{\frac{\partial E}{\partial V}}\right)\frac{E}{D} = \left(\frac{1}{\frac{\partial E}{\partial V}}-1\right)\frac{E}{D}
$$

where $\dfrac{\partial E}{\partial V} = N(d1), N(.)$ *is the normal cdf function*

$$
d1 = \frac{\ln\left(\dfrac{V}{book\_debt}\right)+\left(rf+\sigma^2/2\right)T}{\sigma\sqrt{T}}
$$

book_debt: long-term debt from Compustat; D: market value of long-term debt, cal-

ibrated as $\dfrac{MV\_index\ bonds}{AmtOutstanding\_index\ bonds}$ * book_debt; E: market value of equity;

V = D+E; rf: 3m Libor; σ^2: asset volatility =

$$
\left(\frac{E}{V}\right)^2\sigma^2_{E(option\ implied,\ ATM)} +\left(\frac{D}{V}\right)^2\sigma^2_{D(DTS)} + 2\left(\frac{E}{V}\right)\left(\frac{D}{V}\right)Corr_{DE}\sigma_E\sigma_D
$$

14. Alternatively, we could estimate empirical durations as a function of analytical durations, as suggested in prior QPS studies, but such a method would estimate bonds' sensitivity to interest rate risk in isolation of their sensitivities to the market factor. The market factor in reality has a negative exposure to treasuries on average, but positive in a small number of months. Similarly, the credit component in HY bonds, which has high correlation with the market factor, on average should have a negative sensitivity to yield changes, which is partly the reason why empirical durations of HY bonds are much lower than their analytical durations. To dynamically account for both the market risk and interest rate risk in an unbiased manner, we should include both risk factors simultaneously in the OLS regressions, which is exactly what we did in sensitivity matching.

15. SPX option data is from OptionMetrics and available since January 1996. Option returns are calculated as:

Option Return$_t$

$$
= \frac{OptionPrice_t - OptionPrice_{t-1} - Delta_{t-1}\left(SPXFuture_t - SPXFuture_{t-1}\right)}{SPX\ Spot_{t-1}}
$$

16. Treasure option data is from CME. Treasury option returns are calculated as:

Option Return$_t$

$$
= \frac{OptionPrice_t - OptionPrice_{t-1} - Delta_{t-1}\left(TreasuryFuture_t - TreasuryFuture_{t-1}\right)}{Treasury\ Future_{t-1}}
$$

17. The BAB factor longs low-beta stocks and shorts high-beta stocks and makes the factor market-neutral by leveraging up the low-beta leg.
18. The exposure estimates are based on the regression coefficients on the Equity VRP and Bond VRP (puts) reported in Table 1.8. The reported numbers are the average coefficients of IG and HY to simplify the illustration. For example, coefficient 0.5 means that for each $1 value change in a $100 notional position in the short volatility strategy (e.g., equity VRP or Bond VRP), the value change in a $100 market value position in bonds would be $0.50. In other words, to replicate the exposures in a $100 market value position of bonds, we would need $100*0.5 =$50 in the underlying notional for each short volatility strategy.
19. To calculate the $ amount of the corporate bonds whose volatility exposures the option strategy can replicate (call it x), for each option market we solve for x from the equation: Exposure coefficient*x = 5%*Daily volume/2. We divide the daily volume by 2 because the daily volume accounts for both calls and puts, and the replication strategy would require one of each.
20. Ben Dor, Guan, and Zeng (2018) provides details on the European mapping.
21. For European markets, we proxy for the market risk factoring using the Stoxx 600 index returns and the interest rate risk using the Bloomberg Barclays Euro 7–10yr Treasury index.
22. We used the weights calculated from equally weighted bond and equity portfolios. Results using other weighting schemes are similar.
23. Each month, returns of all index bonds of the same company are aggregated into one return number using bond market values as weights.
24. Liquidity Cost Score (LCS) measures the cost of an immediate, institutional-size, round-trip transaction, expressed as a percentage of the bond's price. LCS is computed based on bond-level quotes. (See Konstantinovsky, Ng, and Phelps 2016 for more details.)
25. LCS is expressed as a percentage of a bond's price and is taken out from a bond's return when the bond leaves the portfolio.
26. Since the forward window requires the subsequent 36m to calibrate for the current month, the last observation for the replication portfolio is January 2017, 36 months before the end of the sample period (December 2019). Since this sample period is 36m shorter than the original sample period, the performance for the trailing window is also slightly different from originally reported in Table 1.4.
27. To account for first-order autocorrelation in monthly returns, the annualized volatility is calculated as volatility in monthly returns multiplied by the squared-root of $(12+2*11*AR1)$, where AR1 is calculated from regressions of monthly returns on the lagged one-month returns: $r_t = a + AR1 * r_{t-1} + \varepsilon_t$.

Two

Capitalizing on Index Inefficiencies

A number of years ago, investors asked us to investigate a seeming anomaly in the returns of investment-grade (IG) corporate bonds. Option-adjusted spreads (OAS) provide a forward-looking measure of the additional yield of corporate bonds over duration-matched Treasuries, while excess returns give an ex post measure of the additional return that is ultimately realized. Surely market fluctuations cause the two measures to diverge in the short term, with excess returns exceeding the spread carry in market rallies and underperforming in market downturns. However, over the long term, one might expect the two measures to converge, with average annual excess returns slightly below the average OAS due to a small amount of losses due to defaults. This is not the case. Long-term average excess returns have been substantially less than average spreads. For example, from June 1989 through December 2019, the average excess return of the Bloomberg Barclays US IG Corporate Bond Index was 73bp per year, while the average OAS of this index was 132bp. Thus, only 56% of the additional yield promised by the OAS was ultimately realized by index investors. Our investigation of this anomaly, detailed in Ng and Phelps (2011), led us to the conclusion that this performance was not necessarily an innate characteristic of the asset class but rather the result of strict adherence to index rules. In particular, we focused on the role played by the rule restricting index membership to IG bonds.

The life cycle of a bond index is usually fairly straightforward. Each qualifying bond enters the index immediately upon issuance (or shortly thereafter); and it exits the index shortly before maturity (for Bloomberg Barclays indices, when the remaining time to maturity falls under one year). When bond portfolios are managed in this hold-to-maturity fashion, the long-term return that a bond delivers to the portfolio (assuming it does not default) is roughly equal to its yield at issuance. This orderly existence can be disrupted by various events that can cause bonds to depart an index prior to maturity or enter an index at a later date. Chief among such events are defaults and changes in credit ratings. In particular, bonds whose ratings changes from investment-grade (IG) to high-yield (HY), known as fallen angels (FA), exit the IG index and join the HY index at the end of the downgrade month; the "rising devils" whose ratings improve from HY to IG change index memberships in the opposite direction. These events can have a major impact on index performance.

When a bond is downgraded from IG to HY, it suddenly becomes an ineligible asset, or a core-plus asset, in portfolios that already own it. Managers of passively indexed IG portfolios, whose goal is to replicate index returns, will generally be forced to sell these bonds as close as possible to the end of the downgrade month, at which time they exit the index. Managers of other IG portfolios will have an incentive to sell at this time as well, because after this time these bonds will be out-of-index securities, and holding them will entail greater tracking error (return difference) vs. the index. Managers of HY portfolios will need to buy these bonds as they enter HY index. However, as the total market value invested in HY corporate bonds is far less than that in IG, the number of natural sellers tends to far outweigh the number of natural buyers. This dynamic creates selling pressure that often causes the prices of FA to decrease by far more than justified simply by their fundamentals. Very often, this mispricing is followed by their recovery to fair value over the subsequent months.

In our investigation of the above-described credit index return anomaly, we found that forced selling of FA bonds was a major cause for the surprisingly low long-term excess returns of IG corporate bond indices. This reaction to downgrades tends to lock in the losses and reduce long-term performance. We showed that some of these losses can be recouped by holding on to FA bonds for a longer period of time—from 12 to 24 months after the downgrade. However, holding these HY bonds in an IG portfolio is not always possible; many mandates require that they be sold within three months of a downgrade. Even where allowed to remain in a portfolio, these high-risk out-of-benchmark securities inevitably raise its tracking error volatility vs. the IG index. We therefore suggested that when a plan sponsor and manager agree on a policy of longer holding periods for downgraded bonds, they reflect this by adopting a downgrade tolerant benchmark. Such an index includes new issues only when they carry an IG rating, but if they subsequently are downgraded to HY, they remain in the index for a prespecified amount of time.

In our research, we have addressed the FA phenomenon from the viewpoints of different types of investors. From the perspective of IG investors, the selling pressure on FA bonds represents a huge long-term loss of value. For HY investors, they provide a nice boost to long-term returns. For alpha-seeking investors, a wave of fallen angels can represent a prime buying opportunity. In Chapters 2 through 4, we study fallen angels in detail, primarily from this opportunistic point of view.

The FA phenomenon can be seen as a notable example of a more general effect. By their very nature, standardized indices create biases, or inefficiencies. Institutional portfolio mandates typically use combinations of constraints to define the intended investment universe. A mandate will also specify the benchmark against which portfolio performance will be compared. The need for a benchmark to appropriately mirror the constraints of a portfolio mandate has encouraged the ecosystem of portfolio mandates and standard benchmarks to evolve together in a sort of chicken-and-egg cycle: Index providers design index rules to match common market practice, and plan sponsors are motivated to assign mandates linked to standard benchmarks. Certain conventions have become almost universally accepted within this ecosystem. For example, IG and HY bonds are managed in separate portfolios, with separate benchmarks; and benchmark indices are typically constructed as market-weighted averages of bonds that satisfy all of the constraints.

This rules-based approach to performance measurement has many advantages. A market-weighted index is a fair and objective measure of the performance of the asset class, based on the performance of all eligible securities available to the portfolio manager. It is fully transparent, allowing managers the ability to prepare in advance for anticipated changes in index composition. It is owned collectively by investors and therefore carries a risk premium.

However, while rules-based indices fulfill their mission of providing objective and transparent benchmarks of asset class performance, they are not necessarily optimal investment strategies. Especially as more and more money piles into passive strategies, the need for all indexed investors to execute the same transactions at the same time can expose a portfolio to inefficiencies of various types. These inefficiencies can represent a drag on performance for passively indexed investors but sometimes offer performance-enhancing opportunities for market participants not bound by index rules. In this part of the book, we explore a number of such phenomena in corporate bond markets.

The first three chapters in this section focus on FA bonds. Chapter 2 starts with an event study of fallen angels and meticulously documents both the selling pressure that tends to accompany a downgrade event and the recovery that tends to follow. We investigate a number of variations on a strategy of systematically buying fallen angels and show that these can generate attractive returns. One potential challenge for this strategy is that the supply of fallen angels is not steady, as downgrade rates tend to increase in economic downturns and decrease in market upswings. Chapter 3 examines the capacity of the strategy in light of these issues, modeling the extent to which portfolios of different sizes would have been able to remain fully invested in FA bonds, and how this would affect the achievable performance. It also presents a strategy variation in which credit default swaps (CDS) are used to hedge the issuer-specific risk of the strategy while continuing to reap the benefits of the price pressure on FA bonds via the cash-CDS basis. In Chapter 4, we further develop and refine the strategy of buying fallen angels. We construct rules to efficiently determine which FA to buy to maximize the outperformance resulting from their recovery and how to optimally time the entry and exit points to achieve the best risk-adjusted strategy returns.

In the following chapters, we investigate other index inefficiencies. Whereas the focus of the FA phenomenon is on when bonds drop out of the IG index, one can also examine the rules that control how bonds come into the index or, more specifically, how they get purchased into indexed portfolios: What bonds should be purchased, exactly when, and in what amounts? In Chapter 5, we highlight an unfortunate fact of passive bond index investing: By buying all index-eligible bonds, at market weight, upon issuance, passive investors cede control over the decision of what to buy to a group of market participants whose interests are diametrically opposed to their own—the issuers. As issuers manage their debt through the cycle, they will aim to borrow more, at longer maturities, when rates are low, and borrow less and at shorter maturities when rates are high. In addition, the more a company (or industry) needs to borrow, the greater the allocation their debt will receive in passive portfolios. The result is a steady drag on the performance of passively indexed investors—and an opportunity to outperform, for example, by overweighting the bonds of more moderate issuers against those of companies that have been borrowing aggressively.

Another question facing portfolio managers is exactly when to buy a newly issued bond. A typical convention in Bloomberg Barclays bond index construction is that bonds issued within a given calendar month enter the index at the following month-end date. For portfolio managers benchmarked to the index, tracking error is minimized by matching this timing precisely and buying the new bonds as close as possible to month-end on the secondary market. Chapters 6 and 7 investigate alternatives to this approach, taking very different viewpoints. Chapter 6 starts with the premise that bonds tend to be most liquid immediately after they are issued. If so, buyers of new issues must presumably be paying a liquidity premium on a regular basis. For investors who do not have a specific need for liquidity, might it be more efficient to systematically buy new issues a few months after issuance, once the bonds become more seasoned, at slightly more favorable levels? Upon investigation, we find that this strategy can indeed improve long-term performance but that the main driver of this effect is not liquidity. Rather, we find that a lot of negative credit events occur within the first year or two of a new issue coming to market, and a simple "inclusion delay" policy can help managers avoid these situations. Chapter 7 maps out the value of a subtler change to the timing of new bond purchases, in the opposite direction. Rather than waiting to buy a new bond several months after its issuance as in Chapter 6 or to buy it at month-end as the index does, many investors buy bonds immediately upon issuance in the primary market. While purchasing a few days or weeks before index inclusion may create some tracking error, this practice has one major advantage: Pricing in the primary market often includes concessions designed to encourage participation in the new issue. We show that for investors able to regularly take advantage of concessions on new bond purchases, this can be a reliable source of steady outperformance.

Chapters 8 and 9 take aim at the performance cost of investment constraints, specifically those relating to forced selling of downgraded bonds. As described, a portfolio constraint that requires immediate selling of downgraded bonds exactly when they leave the IG index can be very costly due to the selling pressure associated with these events. One approach we have suggested is to extend the time limit for liquidation to allow the selling pressure to subside. In Chapter 8, we investigate an alternative approach, in which the ratings threshold at which a bond must be sold may be different from the limit for index inclusion. For example, a mandate for an insurance company portfolio might specify that only IG bonds should be purchased but that, if they are downgraded, they may continue to be held in the portfolio unless their rating is cut to below BB−. The key observation here is that the long-term risk/return performance of a given asset class is determined in part by the sell discipline that is in place for the portfolio. Plan sponsors need to explicitly recognize the effect of the sell discipline as an intrinsic part of the asset allocation process. Chapter 9 takes a closer look at the performance effect of any quality constraint that forces bonds to be sold once their rating falls beneath a given threshold. The focus of our studies of FA bonds was on the selling pressure that occurs when bonds leave the IG index. However, there is another aspect of forced sales—or any other stop-loss measure—that hurts long-term performance even when this element is absent. For example, some portfolios impose a ratings threshold of A– or better, leading to forced sales of any bond downgraded to BBB. As only a small number of investors operate under this constraint, there is no selling pressure associated with such an event, and the expected loss would be in line with the typical spread differential between the bond's old and new ratings. Nonetheless, the requirement to sell upon a loss essentially locks in that loss and gives up the chance to recover it as the bond matures, leading to a loss of value over time. Chapter 9 quantifies the impact that such ratings stop-loss rules would have had on credit portfolio returns over several decades.

After we published our work on downgrade tolerant benchmarks and fallen angel strategies in 2010, we wondered if enough market participants would change their behavior to make the observed phenomena disappear. Yet, as we show in Chapter 4, FA strategies continue to perform well past this date. In discussions, managers of passive index funds made it clear that they consider it their mission to passively track index returns, not to outperform them. Thus, even when they are fully aware that certain index conventions lead to inefficiency, they will continue to follow index rules faithfully in managing their portfolios. With the continued flow of assets into passive funds linked to bond indices, these effects promise to be a force for some time to come. For investors looking for systematic strategies to generate outperformance, it is therefore a very worthwhile effort to carefully study index dynamics in search of inefficiencies that can create pockets of value on the other side of the trade. The following chapters offer a start in that direction.

REFERENCE

Ng, K. Y., and B. Phelps. 2011. "Capturing Credit Spread Premium." *Financial Analysts Journal* 67(3): 63–75.

Fallen Angels: Index Liquidation

CHAPTER 2

Fallen Angels
Characteristics, Performance, and Implications for Investors

INTRODUCTION

The Bloomberg Barclays US Corporate Index is widely used by investors as the benchmark against which they manage their US investment-grade credit allocation. Because of the index dominance, changes in its constituents have the potential to affect not only the composition of investors' portfolios but also the pricing of its underlying securities.

Changes in credit ratings are one of the key reasons the index population varies over time. In particular, corporate bonds that are part of the index and are downgraded below investment-grade (IG) status (commonly termed "fallen angels") are excluded from the index at its next monthly rebalancing. Investors who are benchmarked to the index and own fallen angels have strong incentives to sell them at the time of downgrade, for two main reasons. First, many investors have explicit constraints on their ability to continue to hold fallen angels. Pension fund mandates, for example, typically require selling such bonds within a predefined period following the downgrade. Similarly, insurance companies are subject to regulation that imposes large capital charges on speculative-grade bonds. In addition, holding out-of-benchmark securities, particularly those that are likely to be more volatile than the average high-grade bond, can lead to an increase in the tracking errors of portfolios.

Fallen angels as a group represent a significant proportion of the overall high-yield (HY) market, as much as 15 to 25% in some years. As a result, if a large number of investors are forced to sell their holdings in these bonds within a short period around the downgrade date, it can depress prices beyond any negative effects from the information contained in the rating change announcement. In such scenarios, the prices of fallen angels may temporarily drop below their fundamental values, but the prices would return to equilibrium levels over time as the selling imbalance abates. The limited supply of prospective buyers is another factor that can facilitate a temporary price distortion. Investors in HY bonds usually are active only in this market, which has different characteristics than the high-grade market. Consequently, the two markets are highly segmented, as documented by Ambastha, Ben Dor, Dynkin, Hyman, and Konstaninovsky (2010).

Determining whether fallen angels are subject to price pressures induced by forced selling has important implications for investors. Is there an optimal time for traditional credit investors who use the Bloomberg Barclays Corporate Index as their benchmark to sell their holdings of fallen angels after a downgrade? Should these investors adopt more flexible investment mandates that do not necessitate the disposition of fallen angels?

Can the price dynamics of fallen angels offer attractive profit opportunities for absolute return investors such as hedge funds?

The evidence on the price behavior of fallen angels around their downgrades is mixed. Ellul, Jotikasthira, and Lundblad (2011) examined this issue using transaction data from insurance companies, which hold more than one-third of all outstanding IG corporate bonds. They found that companies that were more constrained by regulation were, on average, more likely to sell downgraded bonds. In addition, downgraded bonds that were widely held by constrained insurance companies experienced significantly elevated selling pressures and larger price reversals. However, Ambrose, Cai, and Helwege (2011) reached the opposite conclusion and documented negligible, if not nonexistent, price pressure effects using the same database.[1] Ng and Phelps (2011) found that not excluding fallen angels from the Bloomberg Barclays Corporate Index after their downgrade led to a significant performance pickup without a corresponding increase in risk. Furthermore, combining the index instead with the same proportion of bonds from the Bloomberg Barclays High Yield Index did not generate nearly as much improvement, consistent with the existence of price pressures.

Our first goal is therefore to provide a conclusive answer to the question of whether fallen angels are subject to price pressures due to forced selling. Using a large sample of more than 1,400 bonds that migrated from IG to non-IG status between 1990 and 2009, we analyze the characteristics and price dynamics of fallen angels during the three-year period around their downgrade date. Consistent with the implications of price pressures, we find that after their downgrade, fallen angels initially underperform HY bonds with similar characteristics, with a subsequent reversal lasting up to two years after the rating change. Moreover, the magnitude of price recovery by individual issuers tends to increase with the size of their initial underperformance. In contrast, price reversal is not evident for bonds that were upgraded from high-yield to high-grade status and were not subject to selling (or buying) induced by investment constraints.

An alternative explanation for these patterns is based on investor over-reaction. In this case, selling is voluntary and motivated by behavioral biases rather than investment constraints. Under this scenario, investors *overreact* to the negative informational content of the downgrade event, which depresses bond prices below their fundamental value. Over time, these mis-valuations are gradually corrected and fallen angels outperform HY bonds as their prices mean revert. We do not find any evidence supporting this theory.

To establish an explicit link between the magnitude of forced selling and the performance of fallen angels, we analyze two possible measures of price pressures. First, we examine the interplay between trading volumes and the liquidity of fallen angels. Under typical market conditions, an increase in trading volumes is associated with a decrease in trading costs and improved liquidity. However, if higher volumes are a result of forced selling, liquidity should decline rather than rise. This reflects the execution immediacy demanded by investors and the fact that trading activity mostly represents down-volume. Indeed, we find that trading volumes in the six-month window around the downgrade event increase by a factor of four, but the bid–ask spreads for fallen angels increase simultaneously, well beyond those for peer HY bonds.

Second, we look at the behavior of the cash–CDS spread basis. Credit default swaps are not subject to the same investment constraints that moti-vate the selling of fallen angels' bonds. As a result, the spread basis between the bonds and CDS of fallen angels should also exhibit mean reversion, widening initially and then gradually converging to their long-term equilib-rium levels. We find that while swap spreads widen as expected, they do so to a lesser degree than the spreads of cash bonds. Consequently, the cash–CDS basis widens, on average, to about 225bp in the first three months after the downgrade and then declines steadily to the long-term mean of about 40bp. Overall, the two measures are able to explain about 40% of the cross-sectional variation in the performance of fallen angels. Bonds that experience a deterioration in liquidity despite higher turnover and a widen-ing of their cash-CDS basis between the downgrade month and the end of the following quarter perform worse than other downgraded bonds but exhibit greater outperformance in the subsequent 12 months.

Can investors exploit the price pressures following the downgrade of fallen angels? In the second part of this chapter, we analyze the performance of a dynamic strategy that invests solely in these bonds. The risk–return profile of such a strategy reflects not only the typical price behavior of fallen angels after their downgrade but also their supply dynamics. Therefore, while the findings based on the event-study approach used in the first part of the study are indicative, one needs to examine the results from a portfolio perspective.

We analyze the characteristics and performance of several rule-based portfolios with different investment guidelines over time. We find that portfolios of fallen angels consistently outperform their peers by about 8.5% per year on average, with information ratios in excess of one, using a relatively simple set of rules based on time relative to the downgrade event and a "rich"/"cheap" indicator. While the magnitude of the outperformance is not constant, primarily because of the variation in the supply of fallen angels, it is not confined to a specific period and is evident throughout the sample. Even incorporating the higher costs of trading fallen angels compared with other HY bonds did not significantly diminish their attractiveness. We conclude with a short discussion of the implications of our findings for investors.

DATA AND METHODOLOGY

Sample Construction

The sample used in our analysis consisted of all bonds that were part of the Bloomberg Barclays Corporate Index and experienced a rating event between January 1990 and December 2009. A "rating event" is defined as an exclusion from the index due to a downgrade from any IG rating to HY status or, conversely, an inclusion in the index following an upgrade to IG status from any HY rating. Bonds that qualified under the second category serve as a control group. Since these bonds were not subject to selling (or buying) induced by investment constraints or regulation, their performances were unlikely to be affected by price pressures. The final sample contains a total of 761 unique issuers representing 2,251 bonds, of which 1,485 were downgraded and 766 were upgraded. The large difference between the number of unique issuers and individual bonds reflects the fact that some of the issuers experienced several rating events or had multiple bonds outstanding at the time of the rating event.

The period in which prices may be affected by investors' selling their holdings in fallen angels is likely to be short-lived and concentrated around the rating-event month during which the rating event took place. It is not clear, however, how fast the ensuing price recovery process may be, and we therefore employed a relatively long analysis window during which we tracked all bonds in the sample. The analysis window started a year before the rating-event month and ended 24 months after it, with the exception of defaulted bonds.[2] Since investing in defaulted bonds requires specialized knowledge, we postulate that once a bond defaults, most investors do not continue to hold it. Bonds that defaulted therefore exit the sample at the month-end following the default month, and their prices at that time constitute their final value.[3]

Each of the statistics for fallen angels that we analyze in this study (such as performance) is adjusted by the contemporaneous value of a peer group with similar characteristics. Peer groups are defined based on industry (financials, industrials, and utilities) and credit quality (A and higher, Baa, Ba, B, and Caa and lower). In addition, with the exception of the lowest credit-quality category, separate buckets were constructed for short-/intermediate- and long-maturity bonds (up to 10 years and above 10 years, respectively), resulting in a total of 27 peer groups. Our goal in defining such partitions is to capture the primary risk factors of corporate bonds while keeping the peer groups sufficiently populated to minimize idiosyncratic effects.

To prevent possible contamination, peer groups were populated monthly using the universe of bonds that composed the Corporate or High Yield indices and had not experienced a rating event in the previous 24 months. To compute flow statistics, such as relative returns and turnover, bonds were matched to their appropriate peer group at the beginning of each month (based on industry, credit quality, and remaining maturity at that time). In contrast, for point-in-time measures such as spreads and trading costs, a bond's peer group was determined once, based on its characteristics immediately following the rating event, and held constant throughout the analysis window. A "static" peer group (as opposed to matching every month) was used to avoid the discontinuity in the rating-event month resulting from the change in credit quality.[4]

Monthly relative statistics for each bond were computed whenever the peer group was populated by at least 20 bonds. Otherwise, they were recorded as missing. Relative statistics were then aggregated by issuer using the market values of the underlying bonds throughout the study, except for the last section, which employs individual bonds to examine the performance of a strategy of investing in fallen angels.

To examine the joint behavior of trading volumes and the liquidity of fallen angels, we use monthly data since January 2007 from two separate sources.[5] Transactions data were retrieved from TRACE (Trade Reporting and Compliance Engine) files, which contain individual trades at the cusip level.[6] Analyzing liquidity has always been a more difficult task because of both the shortage of data and lack of a uniformly accepted measure. We employ a measure of bond liquidity known as LCS (liquidity cost score), which was described in detail in Konstantinovsky, Ng, and Phelps (2016). It represents the cost of an institutional-size round-trip transaction in a bond as a percentage of its market price based on traders' quotes. We also employ data from Markit Partners to compare the behavior of fallen angels' bonds with CDSs on the same underlying entity. The cash–CDS basis was constructed as the difference between each issuer's Libor–OAS and a weighted combination of 5y and 10y swaps with the same RPV01 as the issuer's spread duration. CDS returns were computed in a similar fashion.

Descriptive Statistics

Table 2.1 reports the number of issuers and the market value of their outstanding bonds (as of the beginning of the rating event month) in dollar terms and as a proportion of the index to which they migrated, as the average OAS of the Corporate Index by year.

Two key observations emerge from the table. First, the number of downgrades generally varied with the business cycle (proxied by the average OAS of the Corporate Index), while the number of upgrades was distributed more uniformly over time. The largest spikes in downgrades occurred during the 2001–2002 recession and the 2008–2009 financial crisis. The fluctuations in market values were even more pronounced, with the exception of 2005 because of the downgrade of Ford and GM. Second, the market value of downgraded bonds as a percentage of the High Yield Index was much larger than the share of upgraded bonds in the Corporate Index. Downgrades made up more than a quarter of the High Yield Index in some years, while upgrades represented at most 3% of the Corporate Index. The significant proportion of fallen angels in the high-yield universe explains why they may be susceptible to price pressures after their downgrades.

Table 2.2 displays the distribution of beginning and ending credit qualities in the rating event month separately for upgraded and downgraded bonds. Panel A shows that of the 1,485 fallen angels, 1,055 (71%) were rated Baa3 just before the rating event, and 626 of those were downgraded only one notch, to the highest non-IG credit quality (Ba1). Almost the same proportion of upgraded bonds migrated from a Ba1 rating (71.3%), of which 441 switched to the lowest IG quality rating (Baa3). These statistics suggest that both downgrades and upgrades should not have come as a surprise to the market. Given that public information on bond issuers is updated regularly, the rating events would have been anticipated by many investors; thus, their information content would have been small.

TABLE 2.1 Issuer Population and Market Value by Year and Rating Event Type

Year	Downgrades			Corporate Index Average OAS (bps)	Upgrades		
	# Issuers	Market Value ($mn)	Market Value as % of HY Index		# Issuers	Market Value ($mn)	Market Value as % of Corporate Index
1990	15	4,095	7.8%	106	5	2,463	0.5%
1991	15	8,459	14.2%	107	14	8,888	1.5%
1992	9	4,913	6.9%	92	9	2,519	0.4%
1993	15	7,676	5.9%	78	21	7,651	1.1%
1994	9	6,725	4.8%	73	10	2,877	0.4%
1995	7	4,840	3.2%	66	16	10,459	1.4%
1996	12	10,194	5.4%	59	19	6,774	0.9%
1997	8	2,148	0.9%	58	34	9,452	1.0%
1998	27	18,823	5.8%	95	39	31,933	3.0%
1999	20	12,937	3.7%	113	27	16,230	1.4%
2000	16	14,345	4.7%	161	22	13,092	1.1%
2001	37	41,771	13.7%	172	21	21,632	1.5%
2002	64	100,611	28.8%	197	9	5,428	0.3%
2003	51	37,733	7.9%	127	9	12,327	0.7%
2004	20	33,207	5.8%	92	15	12,184	0.7%
2005	17	93,211	15.4%	90	22	18,133	1.1%
2006	16	18,329	3.0%	90	16	22,387	1.4%
2007	20	30,767	4.7%	124	22	34,253	1.9%

(Continued)

TABLE 2.1 *(Continued)*

	Downgrades				Upgrades		
Year	# Issuers	Market Value ($mn)	Market Value as % of HY Index	Corporate Index Average OAS (bps)	# Issuers	Market Value ($mn)	Market Value as % of Corporate Index
2008	25	36,257	6.6%	356	15	19,343	1.0%
2009	39	46,797	8.1%	326	9	7,718	0.3%

Note: Market value is measured as of the beginning of the rating-event month. The market value and OAS of the indices are based on averaging monthly values in each year.
Source: Bloomberg, Barclays Research

TABLE 2.2 Distribution of Beginning and Ending Credit Qualities in Rating Event Month

Panel A. Rating Transitions for Downgraded Bonds

Rating at Start of Event Month	Rating at End of Event Month					Total	% of total
	Ba1	Ba2	Ba3	B	Caa / C		
Aaa/Aa	0	0	0	1	0	1	0.1%
A	7	19	1	14	4	45	3.0%
Baa1	38	18	7	2	4	69	4.6%
Baa2	209	66	10	27	3	315	21.2%
Baa3	626	268	110	46	5	1055	71.0%
Total	880	371	128	90	16	1485	
% of total	59.3%	25.0%	8.6%	6.1%	1.1%		

Panel B. Rating Transitions for Upgraded Bonds

Rating at Start of Event Month	Rating at End of Event Month					Total	% of total
	Aaa/Aa	A	Baa1	Baa2	Baa3		
Ba1	2	14	27	54	441	538	71.3%
Ba2	1	1	5	4	53	64	8.5%
Ba3	5	4	4	9	28	50	6.6%
B	4	9	18	19	48	98	13.0%
Caa/C	0	3	2	0	0	5	0.7%
Total	12	31	56	86	570	755	
% of total	1.6%	4.1%	7.4%	11.4%	75.5%		

Note: The results are based on all bonds in the sample except for 11 bonds that were upgraded to IG status and were not rated before the rating event.
Source: Bloomberg, Barclays Research.

Before analyzing performance, we examine how the population of bonds in the sample evolved between the rating-event month and the end of the analysis window. In particular, did fallen angels maintain their HY rating, or were they likely to revert to IG status? What proportion of fallen angels ended up in default?

Table 2.3 summarizes the status of bonds at the end of the 24-month period following the rating-event month.[7] If a bond was still trading at the end of the analysis window, it was defined as "active" and its status was recorded as either investment grade or high yield. Inactive bonds were assigned to one of three categories: matured, defaulted, or called. The table reports the total number of bonds and the proportion each classification represented in the overall population of rating events in each year.

The results indicate that the vast majority of fallen angels were still trading two years after their downgrade. Most (70–80%) maintained their high-yield status, although a non-negligible percentage regained IG rating. In fact, the actual percentage of fallen angels that returned to IG status was higher, because bonds that were called mostly had an IG rating at that time. Upgraded bonds exhibited a similar pattern and generally preserved their new credit status. An exception was in 2001, when almost a third of the upgraded bonds eventually returned to a high-yield rating.[8]

The relative number of maturing bonds was fairly stable, reflecting the minimum of one year remaining to maturity required of all bonds in the Corporate Index. In contrast, the short-term default rate among fallen angels exhibited considerable variation. Default rates surged in 2000 to 2004 (mostly because of 2001, which had a 25% default rate; 20% in terms of market value), but were generally much lower, reaching a nadir of 0.5% in 1995 to 1999. Altman and Bana (2004) found similar results and reported

TABLE 2.3   Status of Bonds 24 Months after the Rating Event

Rating Event Year	Total # Bonds	Active		Inactive		
		HY	Inv. Grade	Matured	Defaulted	Called
Downgraded Bonds						
1990–1994	173	69.9%	9.8%	7.5%	2.9%	9.8%
1995–1999	211	71.6%	15.2%	8.5%	0.5%	2.8%
2000–2004	678	66.2%	9.3%	5.9%	15.5%	2.1%
2004–2009	404	80.4%	5.0%	6.7%	6.4%	1.5%
Upgraded Bonds						
1990–1994	112	2.7%	64.3%	7.1%	0.0%	23.2%
1995–1999	273	4.8%	72.2%	6.2%	0.0%	12.5%
2000–2004	168	15.5%	54.8%	6.0%	6.0%	17.9%
2004–2009	202	4.5%	73.3%	3.0%	1.5%	15.3%

Note: The table reports the status of bonds in the sample at the end of the analysis window, 24 month after the rating-event month. A bond that was still trading at that time was defined as active, and its credit rating (investment grade or high yield) was recorded. Inactive bonds were classified as matured, defaulted, or called. We were unable to determine the exact classification for 30 inactive bonds.
Source: Bloomberg, Barclays Research

that the annual default rate among bonds rated below investment grade at issuance was almost uniformly higher between 1985 and 2004. Interestingly, the number of defaults did not surge during the 2008–2009 financial crisis, consistent with the findings by Dastidar and Phelps (2011).[9]

PERFORMANCE DYNAMICS AROUND RATING EVENTS

Table 2.4 reports the performance of downgraded and upgraded issuers during the analysis window by quarter relative to the event month.[10] For each quarter, the table displays the number of observations, average monthly relative returns, and associated t-statistics, as well as the cumulative relative returns as of the end of the quarter.[11] For downgraded issuers, these statistics were calculated using both equal and value weighting (based on the total market value of bonds outstanding for each issuer).

The value-weighted monthly relative returns earned by downgraded issuers were all negative and highly significant during the three quarters prior to the rating-event month and in the downgrade month itself, resulting in a cumulative underperformance of 15.09%. The fact that performance turned negative well before the actual downgrade is not surprising. Hite and Warga (1997); Steiner and Heinke (2001); Hull, Predescu, and White (2004); and Norden and Weber (2004), among others, found evidence suggesting that prices anticipate bond and CDSs downgrades. In addition, many of the issuers in the sample had already been downgraded within investment grade in the year before the eventual downgrade to high-yield status.

The trend continued in the first three months after the downgrade but weakened substantially (with monthly relative returns marginally negative and no longer significant). Price dynamics then reversed course, and downgraded issuers consistently outperformed their peers until the end of the analysis window by a total of 6.63%. Interestingly, about two-thirds of the overall outperformance was concentrated in just six months (Quarters 4 and 5). These results are very similar in spirit to the findings by Hradsky and Long (1989), who analyzed the performance of defaulted bonds over 1977 to 1988. Cumulative excess returns over the four-year period centered on the default date also declined sharply, as investors uncovered the signs of financial distress long before the default announcement, followed by a strong price reversal afterward. Furthermore, Hradsky and Long (1989) reported that a large part of the price correction of bankrupt securities was concentrated between the fifth and tenth months after the default.

While the evidence of a price reversal is consistent with the existence of forced selling, it also supports an alternative explanation based on investor overreaction. Under this scenario, investors process the negative information that served as the basis for the rating event but overreact to it. As a result, bonds' prices decline below their fundamental value even before the actual change in credit rating. Following the rating event, the misevaluations are gradually corrected, and fallen angels outperform HY bonds as their prices mean revert. Therefore, the overreaction theory implies that the performance patterns reflect investors' behavioral biases, which lead to *voluntary* selling, while we posit that selling is *involuntary* and driven by regulatory and investment constraints.

To disentangle the theories, we first contrast the value-weighted and equal-weighted returns of downgraded issuers. If the strong price reversal after the downgrade was a correction to investors' earlier overreaction, we would have expected the effect to be more pronounced for smaller issuers. Larger issuers are generally more closely followed by market participants, as they typically play a bigger role in investors' portfolios. As a result, their prices, on average, are more likely to reflect their "true" intrinsic values than are those of smaller issuers. In contrast, if selling activity is mostly involuntary, the magnitude of initial underperformance and subsequent recovery should increase with issuers' size, which is what we observed in practice. The effect of a downgrade on larger issuers was much more severe; using value weighting leads to a cumulative underperformance (relative to peers) of 9.67% over the entire period, while equally weighting all issuers results in a total underperformance of only 2.82%. Furthermore, the strong performance reversal in Quarters 4 and 5 is not evident when returns were equally weighted.

Another way to distinguish between the two explanations is to compare the performance of upgraded and downgraded issuers. In the case of forced selling, upgraded issuers should not exhibit a reversal, since they are not subject to induced buying (or selling) by investors. The overreaction theory, however, implies that the performance of upgraded issuers is likely to be the reverse image of what we observed for downgraded issuers. This is based on the notion that if investors have a tendency to overreact, it is reasonable to expect that they would do so for both negative and positive information. For example, Easterwood and Nutt (1999) found that equity analysts underreact to negative information but overreact to positive information.

The results in Table 2.4 suggest that upgraded issuers outperformed their peers in the rating event month and throughout the year before, but the magnitude (in absolute terms) was only about a third of the underperformance observed for downgraded issuers (5.66% vs. −15.09%). In addition, despite the evidence in Table 2.2 that the distribution of rating transitions between downgraded and upgraded issuers was fairly symmetric, fallen angels underperformed their peers by 277bp in the rating-event

TABLE 2.4 Quarterly Average and Cumulative Relative Returns around Rating Events

Quarter Relative to Rating Event	Downgraded Issuers							Upgraded Issuers			
	Market Value-Weighted				Equal Weighted			Market Value-Weighted			
	# Obs.	Avg. Rel. Monthly Ret. (bp)	t-stat.	Relative Cumulative Return	Avg. Relative Monthly Ret. (bp)	t-stat.	Relative Cumulative Return	# Obs.	Avg. Rel. Monthly Ret. (bp)	t-stat.	Relative Cumulative Return
−4	1114	−23.6	−1.82	−0.69%	−4.1	−0.22	−0.12%	842	35.4	2.46*	1.05%
−3	1150	−71.3	−4.10**	−2.79%	−32.6	−1.79	−1.09%	887	26.8	1.61	1.89%
−2	1194	−103.6	−4.31**	−5.78%	−112.7	−3.72**	−4.40%	944	44.3	2.48*	3.25%
−1	1231	−247.6	−6.91**	−12.66%	−145.6	−3.69**	−8.51%	965	47.3	4.18**	4.72%
0	415	−277.6	−5.86**	−15.09%	−345.7	−5.71**	−11.67%	319	89.3	8.68**	5.66%
1	1201	−8.8	−0.18	−15.29%	71.2	1.48	−9.76%	1090	−16.7	−1.81	5.10%
2	1143	12.1	0.46	−15.01%	64.9	1.87	−7.99%	1017	−3.1	−0.20	5.01%
3	1141	15.7	0.70	−14.61%	38.2	1.17	−6.94%	966	−13.9	−0.98	4.57%
4	1149	69.0	3.26**	−12.82%	27.8	0.97	−6.15%	937	−16.5	−0.88	4.05%
5	1134	65.5	3.53**	−11.12%	53.6	2.20*	−4.65%	903	−0.8	−0.04	4.03%
6	1056	35.2	1.81	−10.18%	13.5	0.48	−4.26%	873	11.3	0.76	4.39%
7	1013	11.5	0.63	−9.87%	48.8	1.30	−2.86%	846	6.4	0.36	4.58%
8	980	7.5	0.50	−9.67%	1.5	0.05	−2.82%	808	−10.2	−0.65	4.26%

Note: The table reports the performance of issuers during the analysis window by quarter relative to the rating event month (defined as quarter 0). Average monthly relative returns were computed by pooling relative returns across all issuers and months in each quarter using either value or equal weighting. *t*-statistics were adjusted for serial and cross-sectional correlation. *, ** denote significant at the 5% and 1% levels, respectively. Cumulative relative returns were calculated by first averaging issuers' relative returns by month and then cumulating them since the beginning of the analysis window. Cumulative relative returns are reported as of the end of each quarter.

Source: Bloomberg, Barclays Research

month, whereas bonds in the control group outperformed only modestly (89bp), consistent with the effects of forced selling. Most important, while the prices of fallen angels following the rating event exhibited a clear reversal, such a pattern is not evident for upgraded issuers, and their performance was in line with that of their peers.

In another attempt to corroborate our findings and distinguish between the two competing explanations, we identify a subset of downgraded issuers for which the information component contained in the rating event was likely to be limited. Specifically, we focus on issuers that were rated Baa3 throughout the year before the rating event and were then downgraded only one notch, to Ba1. These issuers then maintained their new ratings until the end of the analysis window. While it is certainly possible that the downgrade did come as a surprise in some cases, it is likely that the magnitude of new information contained in the downgrade event was more limited for such issuers relative to other issuers in the sample. If overreaction were an important driver of the reversal pattern, we would expect its magnitude to be smaller for this subset of issuers.

Figure 2.1 plots the median beginning-of-month relative spreads for the entire group of downgraded issuers, upgraded issuers, and the subset of issuers that experienced a rating change from Baa3 to Ba1 during the analysis window.[12] Not surprisingly, spreads of upgraded issuers were initially much wider than their (future) IG peers, but the gap declined consistently

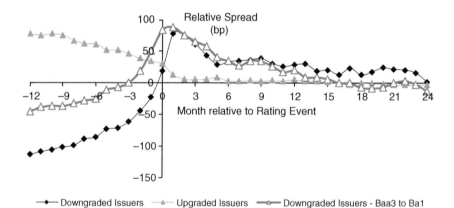

FIGURE 2.1　　Relative Spreads of Upgraded and Downgraded Issuers
Note: The graph plots the median issuer beginning-of-month relative spread during the analysis window.
Source: Bloomberg, Barclays Research

from 78bp at the start of the analysis window to 13bp at the end of the rating-event month (which corresponds to Month 1 in the plot). Following the upgrade, relative spreads continued to compress until they became essentially zero or even slightly negative in the last year.

In contrast, the spreads of all downgraded issuers, as well as the subset that migrated only from Baa3 to Ba1, exhibited very different behavior. Their spreads widened rapidly by about 130bp from at the beginning of the analysis window until just before the rating event (–112bp to 19.5bp and –45bp to 83bp for all issuers and the subset, respectively), as the market apparently anticipated (on average) the eventual downgrade. The rating change brought further widening, as relative spreads increased to 78bp (for the full set of downgraded issuers) immediately following the downgrade month. Spreads then reversed course and declined fairly consistently until they reached parity with spreads of other HY bonds. Hence, there does not seem to be any meaningful difference in the spread dynamics between the subset of issuers downgraded from Baa3 to Ba1 and the overall sample, suggesting that it is unlikely that the price (and spread) reversal reflected investor overreaction.

Cross-Sectional Variation in the Performance of Fallen Angels

The performance results in Table 2.4 point to a strong recovery, on average, of fallen angels in the two years following the rating event, but do not capture the degree of variability among issuers. While many of the downgraded issuers outperformed their peers and even regained IG status, others were downgraded further, and some ended in default, as shown in Table 2.3. To better understand the cross-sectional differences among downgraded issuers, Figure 2.2 displays the mean cumulative returns of downgraded issuers over peers since the beginning of the rating event month alongside the 25th, 50th, and 75th percentiles of the distribution.

The distribution of relative cumulative returns was generated by first compounding the total returns of each issuer over different horizons starting at the rating event month and then subtracting the contemporaneous cumulative return of its peer group.[13] If an issuer left the sample before the end of the analysis window because all of its outstanding bonds matured, were called, or defaulted, we assumed that it continued to earn the same return as its peer group for all remaining months in order to prevent any survivorship bias that would alter the shape of the distribution.

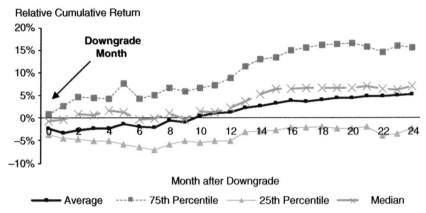

Relative Cumulative Return

FIGURE 2.2 Distribution of Relative Cumulative Performance since the Downgrade
Note: The distribution of relative cumulative returns was generated by first compounding the total returns of each issuer starting at the rating event month and then subtracting the contemporaneous cumulative return of its peer group. If an issuer left the sample before the end of the analysis window because all its outstanding bonds matured, were called, or defaulted, we assumed that it continued to earn the same return as its peer group for all remaining months.
Source: Bloomberg, Barclays Research

The chart clearly illustrates that fallen angels were not all created alike. The top quartile of issuers outperformed their peers throughout the entire period, including the downgrade month, by a total of 15.5%. This suggests that some issuers may not have been subject to large-scale forced selling or that most of the selling activity took place before the rating event. In contrast, the performance of the bottom quartile of issuers deteriorated over time, reaching a minimum of −7.1% seven months after the downgrade. Even the worst-performing issuers exhibited a modest reversal, however, as the 25th percentile of the return distribution at the end of the analysis window was −2.3%, higher than the corresponding −3.7% figure in the rating-event month. Similar to Ellul et al. (2011), Figure 2.2 also suggests that the minimum (average) return was reached only one month following the downgrade, at which point the price reversal process began.

Another important cross-sectional dynamic that was not addressed in Table 2.4 is the relation between the magnitude of initial underperformance and the subsequent price reversal. Did issuers that experienced worse performance (relative to their peers) shortly after their downgrades, perhaps reflecting price pressures, also experience a larger bounce-back afterward? To answer this question, we first need to determine over what periods the initial underperformance and ensuing reversal should be measured.

Figure 2.3 presents the distribution of the time (by quarter) in which the minimum relative cumulative return (measured since the beginning of the rating event month) for each downgraded issuer occurred. The histogram indicates that for almost half of the issuers (46.1%), the minimum relative (cumulative) performance was realized in the downgrade month or during the three months immediately following it. In contrast, the relative performance of only 10.6% of the issuers continued to deteriorate up to eight quarters after the rating event.

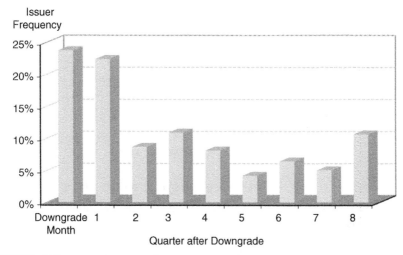

FIGURE 2.3 Distribution of Minimum Relative Cumulative Return Month by Quarter
Note: The histogram displays the percentage of downgraded issuers that realized their minimum relative cumulative return (measured since the beginning of the rating event month) in each quarter as a fraction of the total number of downgraded issuers in the sample. Relative cumulative returns are calculated as in Figure 2.2.
Source: Bloomberg, Barclays Research

The highly skewed distribution in Figure 2.3 has two implications. First, for those considering an investment in fallen angels, it indicates a potential optimal buying time (on average) about three months after the downgrade. We explore this issue further in the second part of the study, which compares various strategies for investing in fallen angels. Second, it suggests that the period of initial underperformance can be represented by the time between the downgrade month and the end of the quarter following it.

To study the relation between the magnitude of initial underperformance and the subsequent price reversal, issuers were first sorted based on their average relative returns during a formation period of four months, starting at the rating event month. They were then assigned to one of 20 performance buckets, with the worst-performing 5% of all issuers populating the first bucket and so on. Figure 2.4 displays the median average relative returns of issuers in each of the buckets during the formation period and three separate six-month periods following it.

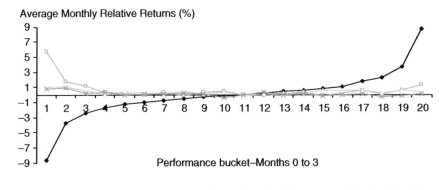

FIGURE 2.4   Median of Issuers' Average Monthly Returns Conditional on Formation Period Performance
Note: Downgraded issuers were first sorted based on their average relative returns during a formation period of four months starting at the rating-event month. They were then assigned to one of 20 performance buckets, with the first bucket containing the worst performing 5% of all issuers and so on. Each observation represents the median average relative returns of issuers in each of the buckets during the formation period or three separate six-month periods following it.
Source: Bloomberg, Barclays Research

The chart suggests an asymmetric relation between the performance during the formation period and subsequent periods. Issuers that were assigned to one of the bottom four buckets experienced a strong rebound in relative performance, whereas high-performing issuers during the formation period earned substantially lower returns but still managed to outperform their peers slightly.[14] Furthermore, the reversal pattern in the six months immediately after the formation period was much stronger than in the other two periods. For example, the worst-performing issuers outperformed peers by 5.75%, 1.04%, and 0.86% in the first, second, and third 6-month periods, respectively, compared with an average monthly relative return of −8.66% in the formation period.

Both results are consistent with the implications of price pressures. Ellul et al. (2011) found that issuers that were more widely held by constrained insurance companies experienced significantly elevated selling pressure and larger price reversals. Hence, forced selling should not uniformly affect all issuers. Poor performers during the formation period were more likely to be subject to forced selling and, therefore, to experience a subsequent reversal, unlike top performers. Similarly, the magnitude of the reversal should be larger soon after the selling pressures abate, as we see in practice.

Relationship between Performance and Forced Selling

While the results in the previous sections were fully consistent with the implications of forced selling, the evidence was indirect. To establish an explicit link between the magnitude of forced selling and the performance of fallen angels, we investigated two possible measures of price pressure based on the interplay between trading volumes and liquidity of fallen angels and the dynamics of the cash–CDS basis. We first established the relation at the aggregate level and then employed a set of regressions to show that it also holds for the cross-section of issuers.

Volume, Liquidity, and Cash-Derivative Basis as Proxies for Price Pressure

Under typical market conditions, an increase in trading volumes is associated with a decrease in trading costs and improved liquidity. However, if higher volumes are a result of forced selling, liquidity should decline rather than rise. This reflects the execution immediacy demanded by investors and the fact that trading activity mostly represents down-volume.

Figure 2.5 plots the median relative LCS alongside the median absolute and relative turnover around the rating event month for a group of 84 issuers that were downgraded between January 2007 and December 2009.[15] The patterns that emerge from the graph are striking. Absolute turnover increased by factor of almost four, from 5.1% to just over 18%, in the rating-event month but then declined rapidly within four months, to almost the same level as in the beginning of the analysis window. This pattern is similar to what was reported by Ellul et al. (2011), who found that the net dollar volume of fallen angels turned negative from about 20 weeks before the downgrade and then spiked up in the event week. Starting the week following the downgrade, the selling pressure dropped sharply, by 60% in just five weeks.[16] Furthermore, Ellul et al. reported that the net selling volume of fallen angels in the event week was almost three times larger than that of the control group, composed of IG bonds that were downgraded to just a notch above high-yield status (Baa3). The dynamics of the relative turnover in Figure 2.5 indicate similar behavior.

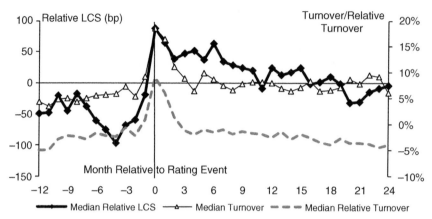

FIGURE 2.5   Relative Turnover and Liquidity of Downgraded Issuers
Note: Turnover is the ratio of monthly aggregate volume to the amount outstanding of all bonds by the same issuer. Relative turnover is an issuer turnover less its respective peer group turnover. LCS represents the cost of an institutional-size round-trip transaction in a bond as a percentage of its market price based on traders' quotes. All values represent median values based on 84 issuers that were downgraded between January 2007 and December 2009.
Source: Bloomberg, Barclays Research, TRACE

The timeline of the selling imbalance in Ellul et al. (2011) also ties in well with the changes in relative LCS. At the beginning of the sample window, the trading costs of downgraded issuers were 50bp lower than their soon-to-be high yield peers and declined even further on a relative basis, to 96bp, only four months before the rating event. The relative LCS then shot up by almost 200bp, rising to 88bp in the downgrade month, and started to decline consistently until it converged to about the same level as other HY bonds two years after the rating event.

A second measure we use to proxy for the magnitude of price pressures while controlling for the possible effect of information contained in the rating event is the basis between the spread of cash securities and CDS. CDS contracts should not be subject to the same level of fire sales as bonds (if any). These dynamics reflect the fact that investors who are subject to the investment constraints that motivate the sale of fallen angels do not generally obtain credit exposure through the use of CDSs. Consequently, while default swap spreads are expected to rise around the rating event, they should do so to a lesser extent than the spreads of bonds from the same issuers, causing the basis to widen initially and then slowly converge to its long-term equilibrium level.[17]

Figure 2.6 illustrates the changes in the spread basis during the analysis window, using the median value across the 65 downgraded issuers for which data were available since January 2004.[18] The results point to the same dynamics as in Figure 2.1. The basis widened consistently from about 40bp to more than 100bp in the rating-event month and rose even further, to almost 225bp, three months after the downgrade. The additional widening of the cash–CDS basis is consistent with the significant selling activity of fallen angels shortly after the rating event, which exacerbated any existing price declines due to negative information. As before, once the selling pressures abated, we observe a strong reversal pattern, and the basis declined again to roughly the same level as 18 to 24 months before the downgrade. Notice also that these results are again inconsistent with the overreaction theory. If our findings were driven by investors' overreaction to negative information, then the cash–CDS basis should have remained fairly stable around the rating event, as both spreads would have moved in tandem.

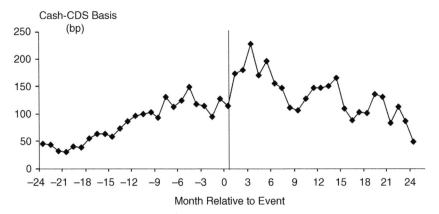

FIGURE 2.6 Median Cash-CDS Basis Relative to Rating Event Month
Note: The cash-CDS basis was constructed as the difference between each issuer's Libor-OAS and a weighted combination of 5y and 10y swaps on the same underlying entity with RPV01 equal to the issuer's spread duration. Median value is based on a sample of 65 issuers that we were able to match since January 2004.
Source: Bloomberg, Barclays Research, Markit Partners

Predictability in the Cross-Section of Fallen Angels' Returns

If the performance of fallen angels is affected by forced selling, then any measure that is correlated with the magnitude of price pressures should explain the cross-sectional variation in the performance of fallen angels. For example, based on the evidence in Figures 2.5 and 2.6, issuers that experienced a larger widening of their cash–CDS basis or a higher increase in turnover accompanied by a simultaneous rise in their trading costs relative to other downgraded issuers would be expected to perform worse initially but earn higher returns subsequently.

To test these predictions, we used two separate regression models. The first investigates the relation between the performance of downgraded issuers during the "underperformance period" in which they are subject to selling pressures and their *contemporaneous* liquidity, turnover, and cash–CDS basis. We define the "underperformance period" to be the same as the "formation period" in Figure 2.4 —the four months between the start of the rating-event month and the end of the next quarter. In contrast, the second regression is predictive in nature. It examines whether the realizations of these variables in the underperformance period can explain the future returns of downgraded issuers during the 12-month "reversal period" immediately following.

Panel A of Table 2.5 presents the estimation results for the first regression model, in which the dependent variable is the relative return (of an issuer) in any of the four months composing the underperformance period. The first specification examines whether the performance of downgraded issuers relative to peers can be explained by information contained in the rating event.[19] The performance during the rating-event month and shortly after, however, should be affected only by new information that the market did not anticipate previously. We therefore include three proxies for the magnitude of possible "surprise" embedded in the rating event.

The first variable, "HY at Downgrade" is a dummy variable that equals one if an issuer carried an investment-grade rating from all three major rating agencies at the time of the "rating event" and 0 (zero) otherwise. We find this to be the case for only 74% of issuers, since the credit ratings used throughout the study are based on the index rating method, which combines the ratings of the three agencies.[20] A second dummy variable, "Rating Change Size," controls for the magnitude of the rating revision. As shown in Panel A of Table 2.2, about 76% of fallen angels were downgraded by only one or two notches. Therefore, a rating change of more than two notches may not be expected by the market on average. The "Rating Change Size" is set to one if the downgrade was more than two notches and to 0 (zero) otherwise. The lagged one-month relative return of each issuer is also included to control for the possibility that informational effects may be incorporated over several months. The estimation results, however, indicate that none of the variables has any significant explanatory power, and the adjusted R^2 is only 0.013.

TABLE 2.5 Cross-Sectional Regressions of Fallen Angels Performance

Panel A: Contemporaneous Regressions

	Model I			Model II			Model III		
	Coef.	t-stat.	P value	Coef.	t-stat.	P value	Coef.	t-stat.	P value
Intercept	−1.23	−1.32	0.19	−1.52	−1.30	0.19	2.95	0.57	0.57
Measures of New Information									
HY at Downgrade	−0.39	−0.43	0.67	0.43	0.41	0.68			
Rating Change Size	−1.00	−0.82	0.41	−0.99	−0.55	0.58			
Lagged 1-mth Relative Return	0.07	1.31	0.19	0.06	0.93	0.35			
Measures of Price Pressure									
Change in Cash–CDS Basis				−1.63	−5.80	<.0001	−1.68	−6.33	<.0001
Lag change in Cash–CDS Basis				−0.31	−1.29	0.20			
Change in Rel. LCS*Rel. Turnover							−0.13	−6.08	<.0001
Size							−0.38	−0.52	0.61
Observation	411			246			173		
Adjusted R²	0.013			0.144			0.298		

(Continued)

TABLE 2.5 (*Continued*)

Panel B: Predictive Regressions

	Model I			Model II			Model III		
	Coef.	t-stat.	P-value	Coef.	t-stat.	P-value	Coef.	t-stat.	P-value
Intercept	0.74	3.96	<.0001	0.21	1.66	0.10	0.18	0.11	0.91
Avg. Relative Ret. Month 0–3	−0.09	−2.61	0.01	−0.01	−0.56	0.58	−0.10	−2.76	0.01
Measures of Price Pressure									
End of Month 3 Cash–CDS Basis				0.15	2.69	0.01			
ΣRelative LCS*Turnover							0.004	2.05	0.05
Size							0.11	0.47	0.64
Observation	64			58			55		
Adjusted R²	0.085			0.089			0.152		

Note: The dependent variable in Panel A is the relative return for each issuer in the rating-event month or in one of the following three months (underperformance period). The dependent variable in Panel B is the average relative return of each issuer over the 12-month period following the underperformance period. HY at Downgrade is a dummy variable that equals 1 if an issuer carried an investment-grade rating from all three major rating agencies (Moody's, S&P, and Fitch) at the time of the rating event and 0 (zero) otherwise. Rating Change Size is a dummy variable that equals 1 for issuers that were downgraded by more than two notches during the month of downgrade and 0 (zero) otherwise. The change in the cash–CDS basis and relative LCS are the differences between the cash–CDS basis and relative LCS at the end of the current and previous months. Relative Turnover is the ratio of the monthly aggregate volume to the amount outstanding for each issuer in excess of the peer group. Size is the natural logarithm of each issuer's market value as of the end of its downgrade month. ΣRelative LCS*Turnover is the sum of the product of relative LCS and turnover between the downgrade month and the end of the following quarter.

Source: Bloomberg, Barclays Research

The second specification includes the first measure of price pressure, the change in the cash–CDS basis, in addition to the proxies for information. The lagged change in the cash–CDS basis is included as well to control for the possibility that the CDS market will react before the cash market does. We find that the coefficient of the change in the cash–CDS basis is highly significant (*t*-statistic of –5.80) and implies that a 1% widening of the basis leads to an additional underperformance of 1.63% per month in the cash market relative to peers during the underperformance period. In contrast, the coefficients of the lagged change in cash–CDS basis, as well as the variables controlling for information, are all insignificant.

The findings in Figure 2.5 suggest that an increase in trading volumes that is coupled with a simultaneous rise in illiquidity (as measured by an increases in bid–ask spreads) may signal the existence of price pressures. To capture the joint dynamic of volume and liquidity, the third specification includes the product of the change in relative LCS and relative turnover. The product term reflects the notion that if a larger trading volume for an issuer (relative to peers) is due to forced selling, its LCS should rise as well, reflecting the one-sided nature of the market and the increased risk premium demanded by dealers for holding the security in their inventory. The value of the product term in this case would be positive, and a negative coefficient would be consistent with the effect of price pressure. Notice that for the more common cases in which LCS rises because of lack of sufficient trading volume (i.e., negative relative turnover) or declines as a result of abnormally high trading activity, the product term would be negative. In addition to the change in the cash–CDS basis, we include the logarithm of issuer's size based on the results in Table 2.4, which suggest a size effect.[21]

The results of the third specification support the view that the combination of high volume and bid–ask spreads is a likely sign of price pressure. The coefficient of the product term is negative, as expected, and significant at the 1% level (*t*-stat. of –6.08). Moreover, the coefficient of the change in the cash–CDS basis remained highly significant and essentially unchanged (–1.68 instead of –1.63). This implies that the two measures capture different aspects of price pressure and combined are able to explain 30% of the cross-sectional variation in the performance of fallen angels.

Two additional results are worth mentioning. First, despite the evidence in Table 2.4, larger issuers did not earn significantly lower returns, although the coefficient of size does have a negative sign. This is likely due to the difference in compositions and the small subset used in the estimation, which reduces the power of the regression considerably.[22] Second, the intercept changed sign, from negative in the first specification to positive (albeit insignificant in both). This implies that the relative return of downgraded issuers during the underperformance period is no longer negative, on average, once the effects of price pressure on performance are removed.

To test the second prediction, Panel B examines the relation between our two proxies for price pressure and future returns. In particular, in the second regression, issuers' average relative returns during the 12-month "reversal period" (the dependent variable) are regressed against the cash–CDS spread basis and a combination of volume and the bid–ask spread level at the end of the "underperformance period" (i.e., the end of month 3 after the downgrade). Issuers that experienced a greater degree of price pressure during the underperformance period based on these measures would be expected to exhibit a larger performance reversal.

To set the stage, the first specification includes only each issuer's average relative return in the underperformance period as an explanatory variable. Hence, it almost exactly corresponds to the analysis in Figure 2.4, which showed the relation between performance in the formation period and returns in three subsequent six-month periods. Indeed, the performance reversal observed in Figure 2.4 is now manifested by the negative and significant coefficient (at the 1% confidence level) of the "Avg. Rel. Return Month 0–3." This implies that issuers with worse initial underperformance experienced a stronger rebound.

However, once the proxies for price pressure are added to the regression model, the coefficient of past performance is no longer significant. In the second specification, the coefficient of the level of the cash–CDS basis is positive and significant, suggesting that a 1% widening of the basis during the underperformance period leads to an average of 15bp per month in the next 12 months. In the third specification, the cash–CDS basis is replaced by ΣRelative LCS*Turnover, which is the sum of the monthly product of relative LCS and turnover during the underperformance period and the issuer's size. As in the second specification, past performance has no explanatory power, whereas issuers that experienced higher volume coupled with a decrease in liquidity relative to other issuers enjoyed greater outperformance than their peers.[23] Overall, the results in Panel B confirm that the observed relation between the degree of initial underperformance and subsequent outperformance is a reflection of the magnitude of price pressure.

INVESTING IN FALLEN ANGELS AS A STRATEGY

The evidence in the first part of this study suggests that fallen angels as a group exhibit a strong reversal pattern starting shortly after their downgrade. The primary driver of this phenomenon does not seem to be overreaction to information but rather the structural inefficiency stemming from the segmentation between the investment and non-investment-grade markets. The collective need by many investors to divest former IG issues in a short period of time temporarily brings the price of fallen angels below their equilibrium level.

What would be the performance of a strategy that seeks to exploit this structural inefficiency? The second part of the study investigates the properties and performance of a dynamic rule-based strategy that would have invested in fallen angels over the sample period. While results in the previous sections are indicative, they reflect an event study approach in which all events (downgrades) were time-aggregated. As Table 2.1 demonstrates, the supply of fallen angels varies considerably over time, which can greatly affect the risk–return profile of such a strategy. Its performance would reflect not only the typical price behavior of fallen angels after they are downgraded but also their frequency over time.

A strategy that focuses solely on fallen angels can be viewed as an addition to an existing portfolio of HY bonds or as a separate strategy for absolute return investors who find its risk–return profile appealing. Our goal in constructing this strategy was to emulate the experience of a typical portfolio manager who consistently buys fallen angels. While the strategy does not engage in individual name selection as an actual portfolio manager would, we incorporated several features into the construction process to reflect our findings and the way that bond portfolios are managed in practice. Although several important features of any realistic strategy, such as trading costs, were not incorporated, we believe the results provide a good illustration of the potential benefits and risks of investing in fallen angels relative to other HY bonds.

Construction Method

We constructed three dynamic portfolios of fallen angels that differed in their bond inclusion and exclusion criteria. (Table 2.6 provides a summary of the criteria.) The portfolios were fully seeded with cash at inception (January 1991), with no leverage allowed. All portfolios were rebalanced thereafter at the end of each month employing the same approach for sizing the positions of individual bonds.

The first portfolio, "Buy All," was meant to represent the performance of the broad universe of fallen angels after downgrade. Hence, every fallen angel bond was acquired at the end of its rating-event month. For issuers with multiple bonds, only the bond with the highest market value was purchased to limit issuer concentration.[24] In addition, a position size limit was imposed to reduce the exposure to any single issuer. In general, the tighter the cap, the more it would reduce the effect of a default or sharp price decline, but in periods in which the population of fallen angels was limited, it would likely result in the portfolios not being fully invested. We therefore set the maximum position size at 10% and assumed that any uninvested cash portion earned a return equivalent to the one-month Libor rate.

TABLE 2.6   Bond Inclusion/Exclusion Criteria by Portfolio

Portfolio		**Buy All**	**3-Month Reversal**	**Flexible Reversal**
Buy Conditions (if all satisfied)	Timing	Downgrade Month	Month 3	Month 1–6
	Min. Relative Spread	N/A	≥ 40 bps	≥ 40 bps
	Min. Price	N/A	N/A	≥ 40
	Chg. in Relative Spread	N/A	N/A	Tighten
Sell Triggers (if any one satisfied)	Technical	Yes	Yes	Yes
	Timing	Month 24	Month 24	Month 24
	Relative Spread	N/A	Negative	Negative

Note: The technical trigger for selling a bond refers to bonds that matured, defaulted, or were called. The relative spread change condition requires a bond relative spread to tighten compared with the previous month.
Source: Barclays Research

At each rebalancing date, bonds that satisfied any of the following conditions were sold:

1. The bond has defaulted, been called, or matured during the month;
2. Two years have passed since the rating-event month.

The first trigger can be seen as technical in nature, since the bonds had stopped trading. Otherwise, bonds would be sold at the end of the analysis window (24 months after the downgrade). In both cases, the end-of-month sale price represented the bond's final value for performance calculation purposes.

Once the list of bonds to be added and sold was finalized, we assumed that the new set of bonds that constituted the portfolio for the following month was equally weighted. For example, suppose that after the portfolio was rebalanced at the end of June 2009, it included eight bonds with a 10% weight each and a 20% allocation to cash. Assume further that at the end of the next month, two of the bonds were sold and five new bonds were added. The total number of bonds in the portfolio would have increased to 11, with each having an equal weight of 9.09% of the total portfolio value.

While this weighting scheme is not likely to be used in practice, it is better suited for our purpose, which is to capture the performance of fallen angels as a group, for two reasons. First, using differential weights would make the strategy more sensitive to the performance of certain issuers. Second, our approach guarantees that all fallen angels that satisfied the inclusion criteria will be represented in the portfolio even if it was fully invested. Under alternative weighting schemes, some fallen angels may not be purchased simply because they were downgraded in a period in which the portfolio was fully invested. This, in turn, would introduce a subjective component to the analysis. The clear disadvantage of using equal weighting in practice, in contrast, is the relatively high turnover it introduces.

In the second portfolio, termed "3-Month Reversal," fallen angels were purchased at the end of the third month following their downgrade. This was motivated by the evidence in Figure 2.3, which indicated that for more than 45% of fallen angels, the price reversal process started in the first three months after the downgrade. Another aspect in which this portfolio differed from the "Buy All" portfolio was the incorporation of pricing data. Only bonds trading at relative spreads of at least 40bp were eligible for purchase, in order to screen out bonds that were not cheap on a relative basis and were, therefore, less likely to outperform their peers. When the relative spread of bonds already in the portfolio became negative, they were sold, as their potential upside was limited.

The last portfolio, "Flexible Reversal," aimed to exploit the general pattern of price reversion as well but also to acknowledge that not all fallen angels exhibit the same behavior. Some fallen angels never experience any reversion and continue straight to default. In addition, even when fallen angels do experience a price reversal, the timing may vary.

A bond qualified for purchase by the "Flexible Reversal" portfolio if it satisfied *all* the following:

1. Its relative spread was higher than 40bp and had tightened compared with the previous month.
2. No more than six months have passed since the downgrade month (e.g., months one through six after the rating event).
3. The end-of-month bond price was over $40 (per $100 par amount).
4. It was not part of the portfolio before.[25]

The first condition can be seen as an indicator for the timing of a possible reversal. A tightening of relative spreads may suggest that the selling imbalance caused by the downgrade has mostly diminished. The second requirement was motivated by the notion that since price pressures due to fire sales are temporary, price reversals should occur within a fairly short period of time following the downgrade. The selection of a six-month window was driven by the evidence in Figure 2.5, which suggested that selling activity declined sharply after that timeframe, as well as those in Figure 2.3.

The condition for a minimum purchase price was imposed to avoid buying bonds for which the price decline may have been driven primarily by (negative) information rather than by price pressures. Including such bonds would likely result in higher portfolio volatility and reduce our ability to properly measure the benefit related to exploiting reversals resulting from price pressures.[26] Existing bonds, however (i.e., after they were initially purchased), were not subject to this requirement, and their prices could have dropped below the $40 threshold. The exclusion criteria for the "Flexible Reversal" portfolio were similar to those of the "3-Month Reversal" portfolio.

Portfolio Characteristics

Before we evaluate performance, we examine various statistics reported in Table 2.7 regarding the properties of the three portfolios. Not surprisingly, the "Buy All" portfolio had the largest number of bonds per month on average, 47.1, compared with 11.7 and 13.4 for the "3-Month Reversal" and "Flexible Reversal" portfolios, respectively. The larger population of the "Buy All" portfolio reflects, in part, its formulation, as all fallen angels were purchased unconditionally. The primary reason, however, had to do with the difference in selling triggers. In the "Buy All" portfolio, bonds were held for the duration of the two-year period after the downgrade, unless they became inactive, whereas in the two other portfolios, they could be sold earlier if their spreads relative to peers were sufficiently tight.

The effect of the additional sale trigger is illustrated in Table 2.8, which reports the percentage of bonds in every portfolio that were sold in order to satisfy each exclusion criterion. Whereas the passage of the two-year period represented 80% of the sales in the "Buy All" portfolio, consistent with the evidence in Table 2.3, it constituted less than 18% in the "3-Month Reversal" and "Flexible Reversal" portfolios. Instead, the main reason in these portfolios was the relative spread trigger, which was responsible for about 75% of the bonds that were sold. As a result, the average holding period for the "Buy All" portfolio was 21.7 months, whereas the average holding periods for the "3-Month Reversal" and "Flexible Reversal" portfolios were only 9.7 and 9.8 months, respectively (Table 2.7). Note also that although the

TABLE 2.7　Portfolio Composition Summary Statistics

	Mean	Median	Min	Max
Buy All				
Number of bonds	47.1	36.0	0.0	148.0
Holding period (months)	21.7	24.0	1.0	24.0
Turnover	15.2%	12.6%	0.0%	51.0%
% in financials relative to HY Index	13.0%	8.9%	−8.3%	48.2%
% in industrials relative to HY Index	−22.8%	−25.0%	−81.4%	18.0%
% in utilities relative to HY Index	9.9%	8.8%	−11.8%	35.7%
% cash in portfolio	1.6%	0.0%	0.0%	100.0%
3-Month Reversal				
Number of bonds	11.7	9.0	0.0	52.0
Holding period (months)	9.7	8.0	1.0	21.0
Turnover	19.0%	16.6%	0.0%	84.2%
% in financials relative to HY Index	17.5%	7.8%	−9.6%	96.5%
% in industrials relative to HY Index	−15.7%	−10.0%	−91.7%	18.5%
% in utilities relative to HY Index	−1.8%	−5.9%	−12.5%	41.7%
% of cash in portfolio	30.8%	10.0%	0.0%	100.0%
Flexible Reversal				
Number of bonds	13.4	11.0	1.0	60.0
Holding period (months)	9.8	7.5	1.0	23.0
Turnover	19.4%	15.8%	0.1%	80.0%
% in financials relative to HY Index	12.4%	5.8%	−9.6%	96.5%
% in industrials relative to HY Index	−12.8%	−7.7%	−89.6%	18.6%
% in utilities relative to HY Index	0.8%	−4.9%	−12.5%	53.7%
Percentage of cash in portfolio	26.0%	0.0%	0.0%	90.0%

Note: Turnover is calculated as the sum of the absolute changes in weights of all bonds based on the portfolio composition before and after the monthly rebalancing.
Source: Bloomberg, Barclays Research

default rate in the "Buy All" portfolio (9.3%) was more than double that of the two other portfolios, its net effect on performance cannot be easily determined, since the larger population of the "Buy All" portfolio resulted in a much smaller weight allocated to each bond. Another implication of the additional sale trigger was more frequent trading. The "3-Month Reversal" and "Flexible Reversal" portfolios had higher turnover rates (19.0% and

19.4% per month, respectively) than the "Buy All" portfolio (15.2%). Although the unusually high turnover rates reflect the unrealistic equal-weighted scheme that we adopted, we examine their effect on performance in the next section.

TABLE 2.8   Distribution of Bonds Sales by Exclusion Triggers

	Buy All		3-Month Reversal		Flexible Reversal	
Passage of 24 months since downgrade	369	79.5%	47	17.6%	53	17.4%
Relative Spread Negative	0	0%	199	74.5%	230	75.7%
Matured	34	7.3%	7	2.6%	8	2.6%
Called	18	3.9%	1	0.4%	0	0.0%
Defaulted	43	9.3%	13	4.9%	13	4.3%
Total Sells	464		267		304	

Source: Bloomberg, Barclays Research

Two additional portfolio characteristics of interest are presented in Table 2.7. First, relative to the High Yield Index, all three portfolios over-weighted the financial sector and underweighted the industrial sector, but with considerable variation over time. During the 2008–2009 financial crisis, for example, all three portfolios had an overweight to financials of about 40%. Second, the 10% position limit caused the "3-Month Reversal" and "Flexible Reversal" portfolios to have a 25 to 30% allocation to cash on average. These averages, however, mask the large change in the number of bonds between the first and second halves of the sample. Figure 2.7 displays the number of bonds in the portfolio over the sample period for each of the three portfolios. Irrespective of the portfolio, the population exhibited large variations over time, consistent with the evidence in Table 2.1, peaking in 2001–2003 period and during the financial crisis as the deterioration in market conditions increased the supply of fallen angels. As a result, between 2001 and 2010, the average cash holdings for the "3-Month Reversal" and "Flexible Reversal" portfolios were only 3.1% and 1.6%, respectively.

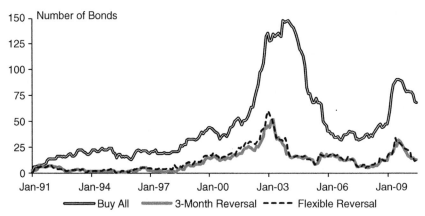

FIGURE 2.7   Monthly Portfolio Bond Population
Source: Bloomberg, Barclays Research

Performance and Analysis

Panel A of Table 2.9 reports various statistics for the three portfolios regarding their absolute and relative returns between January 1991 and June 2010.[27] Several key results are evident from the table.

Despite the simple construction rules underlying the "Buy All" portfolio, it outperformed its peers by about 3.6% a year on average during the analysis period, leading to an information ratio of 0.64. The higher volatility of the portfolio compared with the peer group (2.77% vs. 2.14%) is at least partly a reflection of the larger number of bonds in the peer group. To have a more proper comparison, the column titled "Modified Peer Group" presents the performance of an alternative peer benchmark with the same number of bonds as the portfolio.[28] The volatility of the Modified Peer Group was indeed somewhat higher than that of the broad peer group we used so far, but so was its performance (0.80% vs. 0.73%), and this pattern held irrespective of the portfolio and time period. As a result, information ratios were lower when the Modified Peer Group served as the benchmark, but fallen angels still handsomely outperformed these HY bonds. The tail statistics of the "Buy All" portfolio were similar to those of the peer group and better than the Modified Peer Group. The worst one-month and three-month returns were −12.36% and −24.89%, respectively, compared

TABLE 2.9 Performance of Fallen Angels Portfolios

Panel A: Full Sample					
	Portfolio	Peer Group	Ret. over Peer Group	Modified Peer Group	Ret. over Modified Peer Group
Buy All					
Average (Monthly)	1.04%	0.73%	0.31%	0.80%	0.24%
Volatility (Monthly)	2.77%	2.14%	1.68%	2.50%	1.77%
Sharpe/Inf. Ratio (Ann.)	0.87	0.64	0.64	0.64	0.48
Worst Month	−12.36%	−14.24%	−5.81%	−13.53%	−5.37%
Worst 3-Month	−24.89%	−23.51%	−5.19%	−26.49%	−7.56%
5%-tile of Return Distribution	−2.33%	−2.57%	−1.90%	−3.12%	−2.52%
3-Month Reversal					
Average (Monthly)	1.46%	0.67%	0.78%	0.74%	0.72%
Volatility (Monthly)	3.83%	2.11%	2.62%	2.63%	2.69%
Sharpe/Inf. Ratio (Ann.)	1.01	0.56	1.03	0.53	0.93
Worst Month	−10.76%	−14.46%	−8.45%	−12.72%	−10.94%
Worst 3-Month	−26.01%	−22.74%	−9.29%	−27.48%	−8.90%
5%tile of Return Distribution	−3.81%	−1.93%	−2.64%	−2.00%	−2.90%
Flexible Reversal					
Average (Monthly)	1.21%	0.68%	0.53%	0.76%	0.45%
Volatility (Monthly)	3.54%	2.09%	2.27%	2.68%	2.37%

	Panel A: Full Sample			
	Portfolio	Peer Group	Ret. over Peer Group	Modified Peer Group	Ret. over Modified Peer Group
Sharpe/Inf. Ratio (Ann.)	0.85	0.57	0.81	0.54	0.66
Worst Month	−13.34%	−13.75%	−7.01%	−12.08%	−6.78%
Worst 3-Month	−29.66%	−22.92%	−14.60%	−27.68%	−11.05%
5%tile of Return Distribution	−3.95%	−2.14%	−2.59%	−2.75%	−2.88%

	Panel B: 3-Month Reversal Portfolio by Period			
	Portfolio	Peer Group	Ret. over Peer Group	Modified Peer Group	Ret. over Modified Peer Group
January 1991–December 2000					
Average (Monthly)	0.92%	0.52%	0.40%	0.54%	0.38%
Volatility (Monthly)	1.90%	0.81%	1.71%	0.92%	1.86%
Sharpe/Inf. Ratio (Ann.)	0.89	0.40	0.80	0.42	0.71
Worst Month	−5.70%	−3.05%	−6.25%	−2.15%	−6.11%
Worst 3-Month	−5.76%	−6.24%	−8.98%	−3.62%	−8.90%
5%tile of Return Distribution	−1.03%	−0.78%	−1.83%	−1.25%	−2.30%
January 2001–June 2010					
Average (Monthly)	2.02%	0.83%	1.19%	0.94%	1.08%
Volatility (Monthly)	5.09%	2.90%	3.28%	3.64%	3.32%

(Continued)

TABLE 2.9   (*Continued*)

	Panel B: 3-Month Reversal Portfolio by Period				
	Portfolio	Peer Group	Ret. over Peer Group	Modified Peer Group	Ret. over Modified Peer Group
Sharpe/Inf. Ratio (Ann.)	1.21	0.72	1.25	0.68	1.13
Worst Month	−10.76%	−14.46%	−8.45%	−12.72%	−10.94%
Worst 3-Month	−26.01%	−22.74%	−9.29%	−27.48%	−8.38%
5%tile of Return Distribution	−5.51%	−2.91%	−2.97%	−4.31%	−3.69%

Note: The returns for the portfolios' peer and modified peer groups were computed as the equally weighted performances of the individual bonds' peer groups (as explained in the Methodology section) and single matched peer bonds. Sharpe ratio was calculated using 1m Libor. Information ratio is the ratio of average and standard deviation of relative returns.
Source: Bloomberg, Barclays Research

with −13.53% and −26.49% for the modified peer group; similarly, the fifth percentile of the portfolio monthly return distribution was −2.33%, compared with −3.12% for the modified peer group.

Comparing the results across portfolios suggests that the "3-Month Reversal" and "Flexible Reversal" portfolios had substantially higher performance than the "Buy All" portfolio, with information ratios for the "3-Month Reversal" portfolio (based on both peer benchmarks) almost doubling, from 0.64 and 0.48 to 1.03 and 0.93. Despite the attempt to improve performance by using a bond-specific signal for the beginning of the reversal process, the "Flexible Reversal" portfolio actually generated lower returns than the "3-Month Reversal" portfolio. An important reason for this was that by trying to identify the inflection point for each issuer, the portfolio gave up, by construction, some spread tightening. Hence, timing an investment in fallen angels individually (as opposed to using a uniform rule) may be difficult to achieve.

The two portfolios experienced higher volatility and slightly worse tail properties than the "Buy All" portfolio. For example, the fifth percentile of the distribution of relative returns and the worst 3-month period using the Modified Peer Group benchmark declined from −2.52% and −7.56%, respectively for the "Buy All" portfolio to –2.90% and –8.90% for the "3-Month Reversal." This increased risk was mostly related to the difference in the number of bonds between the two portfolios and the "Buy All" portfolio. As Figure 2.8 indicates, the distribution of relative returns for the "3-Month Reversal" portfolio was symmetric and exhibited fat tails (skewness and kurtosis were 0.72 and 4.38 using the modified peer benchmark, respectively), with positive relative performance in 63% of months.

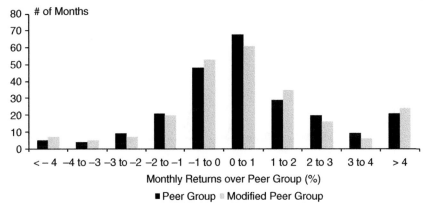

FIGURE 2.8   Distribution of Monthly Relative Returns for the 3-Month Reversal Portfolio
Source: Bloomberg, Barclays Research

Robustness Tests

Is there a relation between the performance of fallen angels and their supply dynamics? As Figure 2.7 illustrates, the population of bonds in the portfolios was characterized by two distinct states that correspond quite closely to the first and second halves of the sample period. The number of bonds was fairly stable until 1999 but rose sharply thereafter following the two credit episodes of 2001–2002 and 2008–2009.

To address this question, Panel B of Table 2.9 displays the same statistics for the "3-Month Reversal" portfolio as in Panel A, separately for the first and second halves of the sample. The results show a clear difference in portfolio risk and performance between the two periods. Volatility almost doubled despite the larger portfolio population, but the monthly average relative return was higher by a factor of three (1.19% vs. 0.40%). Consequently, the information ratio increased from 0.8 to 1.25 in the first and second halves, respectively. These changes in performance were driven in part by the difference in cash holdings between the two periods. During most of the first decade, the portfolio was not fully invested and had an average cash position of 54%, which contributed to the lower returns and volatility.[29]

The portfolio's relative performance was also sensitive to the macroeconomic environment and overall conditions in the HY market. This is illustrated in Figure 2.9, which displays the rolling 6-month average relative returns of the "3-Month Reversal" portfolio against the average absolute returns of the Bloomberg Barclays High Yield Index over the same time frame. The chart shows that the portfolio relative returns tend to covary with the absolute performance of the HY market, with a monthly correlation of 0.22.

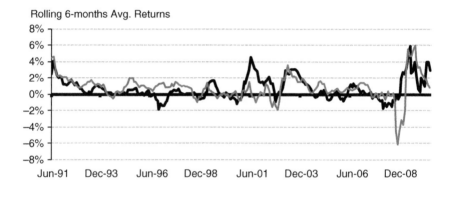

FIGURE 2.9 Rolling 6-Month Average Relative Returns of the 3-Month Reversal Portfolio and High Yield Index
Source: Bloomberg, Barclays Research

One possibility for this phenomenon is that the peer group (and modified peer group) formulation that we used did not properly capture all relevant risk factors. As a result, the relative returns of the "3-Month Reversal" portfolio still reflected exposures to systematic risks that were also present in the broader market. We tested several alternative peer group specifications, but all produced similar results.

A more likely explanation, which is also supported by evidence in Ellul et al. (2011), is that the performance of the High Yield Index serves as a proxy for the level of demand for high-yield securities. Past research has shown that investors' inflows tend to follow strong positive performance, and vice versa. This is especially the case for individual investors, who constitute a large part of the high-yield investor base through mutual funds holdings. Ellul et al. found that the degree of initial price declines and subsequent reversals was related to the potential demand for fallen angels, which they measured using the assets under management of high-yield mutual funds and distressed focused hedge funds. Their results indicate that the price drops and reversals are indeed larger when the capital of potential buyers was relatively scarce.[30]

Another important question is the degree to which our results are sensitive to the exact parameter values used. Table 2.10 reports the relative performance statistics over the entire period for the "3-Month Reversal" portfolio using various alternative parameter specifications. Comparing the importance of the timing confirms again that the optimal buying time of fallen angels is three months after their downgrade (represented by the original portfolio formulation). The table also suggests that the properties of the "3-Month Reversal" portfolio were fairly robust to changes in other key parameters. In fact, using a 5% position limit would have generated higher performance and lower risk compared with the original results based on a 10% position limit.

Performance Net of Transactions Costs

Overall, the findings in this section suggest that inefficiency in the pricing of fallen angels could be exploited using a simple set of rules based on time relative to the downgrade event and pricing relative to peers. While the benefit from the mispricing of fallen angels certainly varies over time as a function of supply dynamics and market conditions, the outperformance of portfolios was not confined to a single episode but was evident throughout the sample. However, given the high turnover rates we found, would the results of the "3-Month Reversal" portfolio still be attractive to investors after we factor in trading costs?

Although it is not feasible to provide an exact answer, an estimate of the net performance of the portfolio can be computed as follows (all values are based on averages):

$$\text{Net Performance} = \text{Portolio Monthly Return} - \tfrac{1}{2} \times \text{LCS} \times \text{Turnover}$$

Notice that since LCS represents the round-trip trading cost of a bond and our turnover calculation does not distinguish between "buys" and "sells," the product of the two should be divided by two to get a correct estimate of the portfolio rebalancing costs.

Figure 2.5 indicates that the average round-trip trading cost for a fallen angel shortly after the downgrade was about 50–60bp higher than a similar HY bond, or about 4 to 5% in absolute terms. Combining the LCS data with the average "3-Month Reversal" portfolio turnover (19%) and relative

TABLE 2.10 Performance of "3-Month Reversal" Portfolio over Peer Group with Alternative Specifications

	Original Formulation	Buy Bonds instead in				Position Limit	Min. Relative Spread	Min. Abs. Price
		Month 1	Month 2	Month 4	Month 5	5%	20 bps	$40
Average (Monthly)	0.78%	0.64%	0.67%	0.75%	0.66%	0.64%	0.70%	0.61%
Volatility (Monthly)	2.62%	2.52%	2.72%	3.02%	3.11%	2.10%	2.59%	2.05%
Inf. Ratio (Ann.)	1.03	0.87	0.85	0.86	0.73	1.07	0.93	1.03
Worst Month	−8.45%	−7.41%	−9.13%	−8.52%	−9.97%	−8.45%	−7.77%	−6.25%
Worst 3-Month	−9.29%	−14.00%	−11.12%	−11.67%	−11.53%	−7.67%	−10.55%	−9.29%
5%tile of Return Distribution	−2.64%	−2.51%	−2.54%	−3.08%	−3.47%	−1.65%	−2.75%	−2.33%

Source: Bloomberg, Barclays Research

performance translates into a net average monthly relative performance of 72.7bp. The average monthly total return, which is of greater interest to absolute return investors, can be computed similarly and is equal to 103.25bp per month (146bp – 0.5 × 450bp × 19%), or about 12.39% a year since 1991. This translates into an annualized information ratio of 0.94 after trading costs.[31]

Two additional observations are worth mentioning. First, the LCS data underlying Figure 2.5 coincided with a severe liquidity crisis. Hence, the long-term trading costs of fallen angels may be lower in general. Second, our simple strategy can be enhanced using an overlay of CDSs. This will reduce both risk and the correlation of the strategy with the overall corporate market.

SUMMARY

Typical mandates for investment-grade corporate bond portfolios and the current regulatory environment either explicitly or implicitly require portfolio managers to sell bonds that are downgraded to non-IG status. The collective need to divest downgraded bonds in a short period of time can create pressures that temporarily bring fallen angel prices below equilibrium.

The findings of this chapter support the existence of such price pressures. We document strong price reversal patterns at both the aggregate and cross-sectional levels. Our results suggest that investors begin to sell their soon-to-become fallen angels before the rating change event in anticipation of the downgrade and continue to sell for up to about three months after it. As the selling intensity dissipates, price declines are reversed, and fallen angels outperform peer HY bonds by a total of 6.63% in the two-year period after the downgrade. In addition, the price recovery of individual issuers is negatively correlated with the magnitude of their initial underperformance. Furthermore, we find no support for an alternative behavioral explanation to these results based on investors' overreaction to the negative information of the downgrade event.

We also provide direct evidence linking price pressures to the performance of fallen angels in the two-year period after their downgrade. Cross-sectional regressions indicate that the extent of initial underperformance in the three months following the downgrade (as well as the downgrade month) is related to the magnitude of the contemporaneous cash–CDS spread basis widening as well as to changes in relative liquidity and turnover. These factors were also shown to have predictive power for issuers' relative performance in the subsequent 12 months. In particular, a wider cash–CDS basis and higher liquidity costs at the end of the first quarter after the downgrade were positively and significantly related to future relative performance across issuers.

In the second part of the chapter, we analyzed the characteristics and performance of several dynamic portfolios with different guidelines for investing in fallen angels over time. We found that portfolios of fallen angels consistently outperform their peers by about 8.5% per year on average, with information ratios in excess of one, using a relatively simple set of rules based on time relative to the downgrade event and a "rich/cheap" indicator. While the magnitude of the outperformance is not constant, it is not confined to a specific period and is evident throughout the sample. Even incorporating the higher costs of trading fallen angels compared with other HY bonds does not significantly diminish their attractiveness.

Our findings have several important implications for investors. First, traditional credit investors who use the Bloomberg Barclays Corporate Index as their benchmark and own fallen angels at the time of their downgrade may be better off not liquidating their holdings at once but unwinding them gradually instead, starting about three months after the rating change. Second, investors such as plan sponsors should consider the merits of adopting more flexible investment mandates that do not necessitate the disposition of fallen angels. Ng and Phelps (2011) show that an alternative index that is similar to the Bloomberg Barclays Corporate Index but does not exclude fallen angels can lead to a significant performance improvement without a corresponding increase in risk. Even investors who are not willing to implement such dramatic changes should, at a minimum, allow for a longer period of time (perhaps two years) during which fallen angels can be sold. Our findings suggest that the vast majority of fallen angels do not default during that time frame and that their spreads decline consistently relative to those of their high-yield peers, reaching parity only at the end of that period. Third, for absolute return investors such as hedge funds, the pricing inefficiency and return predictability of fallen angels can provide attractive profit opportunities. This may be especially the case if the simple portfolio construction rules we tested are enhanced and an overlay of CDS is used to eliminate default risk.

REFERENCES

Altman, E., and G. Bana. 2004. "Defaults and Returns on High-Yield Bonds," *Journal of Portfolio Management* 30(2): 58–73.

Ambastha, M., A. Ben Dor, L. Dynkin, J. Hyman, and V. Konstantinovsky. 2010. "Empirical Duration of Corporate Bonds and Credit Market Segmentation." *Journal of Fixed Income* 20(1): 5–27.

Ambrose, B., K. Cai, and J. Helwege. 2011. "Fallen Angels and Price Pressure." *Journal of Fixed Income* 21(3): 74–86.

Dastidar, S. G., and B. D. Phelps. 2011. "Credit Spread Decomposition: Decomposing Bond-Level Credit OAS into Default and Liquidity Components." *Journal of Portfolio Management* 37(3): 70–84.

Easterwood, J. C., and S. Nutt. 1999. "Inefficiency in Analysts' Earnings Forecasts: Systematic Misreaction or Systematic Optimism?" *Journal of Finance* 54(5): 1777–1797.

Ellul, A., C. Jotikasthira, and C. Lundblad. 2011. "Regulatory Pressure and Fire Sales in the Corporate Bond Market." *Journal of Financial Economics* 101(3): 596–620.

Hite, G., and A. Warga. 1997. "The Effect of Bond-Rating Changes on Bond Price Performance." *Financial Analysts Journal* 53(3): 35–51.

Hradsky, G. T., and R. D. Long. 1989. "High-Yield Default Losses and the Return Performance of Bankrupt Debt." *Financial Analysts Journal* 45(4): 38–4.

Hull, J., M. Predescu, and A. White. 2004. "The Relationship between Credit Default Swap Spreads, Bond Yields, and Credit Rating Announcements." *Journal of Banking and Finance* 28: 2789–2811.

Konstantinovsky, V., K. Y. Ng, and B. D. Phelps. 2016. "Measuring Bond-Level Liquidity." *Journal of Portfolio Management* 42(4): 116–128.

Ng, K. Y., and B. Phelps. 2011. "Capturing Credit Spread Premium." *Financial Analysts Journal* 67(3): 63–75.

Norden, L., and M. Weber. 2004. "Informational Efficiency of Credit Default Swap and Stock Markets: The Impact of Credit Rating Announcements." *Journal of Banking and Finance* 28: 2813–2843.

Steiner, M., and V. G. Heinke. 2001. "Event Study Concerning International Bond Price Effects of Credit Rating Actions," *International Journal of Finance and Economics* 6, 139–157.

NOTES

1. To control for any new information revealed in the downgrade event, Ambrose, Cai, and Helwege (2011) restrict their sample to include only bonds for which the issuers' stock had no significant reaction to the rating change. They argue that the trading activity by insurance companies in their dataset is therefore more likely to be driven by regulatory pressure than by information-motivated trading.

2. Rating events that occurred less than 36 months after an earlier rating event were excluded to avoid spill over effects. For example, fallen angels that were upgraded to IG status less than three years before the later downgrade may have been subject to less selling pressure if they were being held by different clientele than fallen angels that had originally been issued as IG bonds.

3. Another reason for excluding bonds from the sample shortly after they defaulted is that the quality of pricing data tends to deteriorate as time passes after the default date.

4. To illustrate this point, consider a case in which we examine the relative spreads of fallen angels when peer groups are determined monthly. The relative spreads would likely be positive for some time before the rating event (i.e., wider than their peers) as investors anticipate the pending downgrade but may become negative immediately after the downgrade, as the spreads of the new peer groups containing HY bonds are much higher.
5. LCS estimates are available monthly for all bonds in the Bloomberg Barclays US Corporate and High Yield indices only since January 2007. TRACE market coverage before that date is also incomplete.
6. TRACE truncates the sizes of large transactions at $1mn and $5mn for HY and IG bonds, respectively, which may cause our estimates of turnover to be downward biased. Alternative transaction caps can be imputed based on equating the sum of individual trades with the aggregate volume figures reported by TRACE. This procedure yields higher transaction limits of $4MM and $12.5MM for HY and IG bonds, respectively. In addition, in order to focus on trading activity by institutions, transactions of less than $100,000 were excluded.
7. If the rating event occurred less than 24 months before the last sample month (June 2010), we recorded the bond status as of the last available date.
8. The large proportion of upgraded bonds that were called reflects the prevalence of the call feature among bonds that were rated high yield at issuance. As the financial health of their issuers improved, they were called and replaced by other funding alternatives at a lower cost.
9. Dastidar and Phelps (2011) present a framework for decomposing credit spreads into liquidity cost, expected default, and risk premium. They found that most of the widening in credit spreads during the 2008–2009 financial crisis reflected an increase in illiquidity rather than expectations of future defaults.
10. The rating event month was defined as quarter zero. The three months following it correspond to Quarter 1 and so on.
11. Formally, the relative cumulative return of downgraded (D) or upgraded (U) issuers from the start of the analysis window until month T is given by $R_j^T = \prod_{t=-12}^{T}\left(1+\sum_i w_{i,t}\left(R_{i,t}-R_{i,t}^p\right)\right)-1$ $j \in D,U$, where $w_{i,t}$, $R_{i,t}$ are the relative weight and total return of issuer i in month t, respectively. $R_{i,t}^p$ is the contemporaneous weighted return of all the peer groups corresponding to issuer i's outstanding bonds.
12. Recall that the peer group was determined once, based on each bond's characteristics at the rating-event month. Issuers that were downgraded or upgraded again following the rating-event month may have traded at very large positive or negative spreads relative to their peers. The use of the median rather than the average spread was meant to neutralize such effects.
13. Formally, the cumulative return of issuer i relative to its peers over T months since the rating event month is given by $R_i^T = \prod_{0\le t\le T}\left(1+R_{i,t}\right)-\prod_{0\le t\le T}\left(1+R_{i,t}^p\right)$ where,

as before, $R_{i,t}$ is the total return of issuer i in month t. $R_{i,t}^p$ is the contemporaneous (weighted) return of all the peer groups corresponding to issuer i's outstanding bonds.

14. Of the 17 issuers in the best-performing bucket, 11 were downgraded in 2009 and eight belonged to the financial sector. For example, Lincoln National Corp. and Hartford Financial had monthly average relative returns of 39% and 24%, respectively, during Months 0 to 3.

15. As before, issuer-level LCS and turnover were calculated by weighting the LCS of outstanding bonds by their respective market values and aggregating all trading volume and amount outstanding linked to the underlying cusips, respectively.

16. Ellul et al. (2011) report that the average total volume per bond-week for this sample is almost $2.5mn in the event week, declining to less than $1mn just five weeks later.

17. Hence, this argument is unrelated to the long-term level of the cash–CDS basis, which is beyond the scope of this chapter.

18. To reduce the likelihood of stale quotes, months with ten or more daily consecutive unchanged observations were excluded.

19. Because of the limited amount of data available for LCS, turnover, and CDS, the number of issuers used in each specification varies and is only a subset of the overall sample.

20. The index method for determining a bond's credit rating has changed several times during the sample period. Prior to October 2003, it was based on Moody's, or S&P if Moody's was unavailable. From October 2003 to July 2005, it was the lower of Moody's and S&P. Since July 2005, it has been the middle rating of Moody's, S&P, and Fitch.

21. Given the limited number of observations in the third specification, the variables that were found to be insignificant before were excluded in order to maximize statistical power.

22. In other words, the small number of observations increases the likelihood that the estimated size coefficient is insignificant even if there is a relation between issuer performance and size.

23. The third specification does not include the cash – CDS basis because it would have decreased the sample size even further.

24. Specifically, the largest bond in the short/intermediate maturity bucket was selected (i.e., remaining maturity of ten years or less). If none of the qualifying bonds were in this bucket, then the largest bond in the longer maturity bucket (ten years or more) was selected. The reason for this procedure was to reduce the frequency of missing peer group returns, as the population of the long-maturity bucket was typically smaller than the short/intermediate bucket.

25. This was meant to prevent a situation in which, for example, a bond that was purchased a month after the downgrade and sold two months later, when its relative spread became negative, would have returned to the portfolio because it widened again to 45bp within three months.

26. Portfolio volatility is likely to rise since, over time, these bonds would proceed to default or recover, resulting in large positive returns.
27. Peer groups returns were calculated by equal weighting the performance of the peer groups matched to every fallen angel in the portfolio, as explained in the Methodology section. When a fallen angel's peer group was populated by fewer than 20 bonds, the High Yield Index return was used instead. The relative return of any unused cash allocation was set to zero.
28. The Modified Peer Group was constructed by matching each fallen angel with the largest bond (in terms of market value) that had the same quality, industry, and maturity characteristics and had not yet been matched to another fallen angel in the portfolio. The Modified Peer Group returns were computed as the equally weighted returns of all bonds that were matched to fallen angels.
29. Similar patterns were also observed for the "Buy All" and "Flexible Reversal" portfolios but were not reported for the sake of brevity.
30. Ellul et al. (2011) found that the median cumulative abnormal return in the downgrade week during periods of low demand was –17.3%, compared with –3.4% for high-demand periods.
31. The results were unchanged when we repeated the calculation of the net performance and volatility using the individual monthly turnover.

CHAPTER 3

Fallen Angels: Capacity, Transaction Costs, and the Bond-CDS Basis

INTRODUCTION

In Chapter 2, we presented a detailed analysis of the characteristics and price dynamics of fallen angels during the three-year period around their downgrade. In this chapter, we address a number of practical implementation issues regarding investing in fallen angels. The first part of this chapter examines the performance stability of fallen angels over time and across markets, and possible explanations for the profitability of the three-month reversal strategy. Specifically, how much time variation is observed in the outperformance of fallen angels over peers? Is the price pressure experienced by fallen angels limited to the US corporate market, or is it also evident in the European market? To what extent does the performance of the three-month reversal strategy reflect a general pattern of mean reversion in the high-yield (HY) market, and is its superior return a result of higher default rates (relative to other HY bonds)?

The second part focuses on implementation issues resulting from the unique characteristics of fallen angels. The supply of fallen angels varies considerably. Thus, the capacity of a strategy investing only in fallen angels may be limited. Moreover, the impact of transaction costs on the performance of such a strategy is likely to be larger than usual. Forced selling, which drives the price reversal patterns, also makes fallen angels less liquid relative to other HY bonds (which does not necessarily mean lower volumes but rather higher bid–offer spreads). Furthermore, periods in which overall supply of fallen angels is high and resulting initial underperformance is large often coincide with a decrease in overall market liquidity.

127

We investigate both issues in turn. First, we examine what is a realistic size for a portfolio of fallen angels. Specifically, we study how the performance of our rule-based strategies varies with portfolio size when positions in individual issuers are constrained to a set fraction of their amount outstanding. Second, we incorporate bond level bid–ask spreads based on Konstantinovsky, Ng and Phelps's (2016) Liquidity Cost Scores (LCS) into the calculation of strategy returns. This gives us a more accurate read on the actual returns that can be expected when investing in fallen angels, especially given the relative illiquidity in the subperiod for which LCS data are available (since 2007) relative to the overall sample since 1991.

The fallen angels strategies discussed in Chapter 2 significantly outperformed peer HY bonds during the sample period but required investors to purchase fallen angels' bonds outright. This may be appropriate for HY managers, who can substitute exposure to one universe of HY bonds (e.g., originally issued) with another (fallen angels). However, many investors may want to benefit from the temporary dislocation in the pricing of fallen angels without taking on the systematic and idiosyncratic credit risks associated with holding a limited number of HY bonds.

An alternative strategy would be to trade the bond–credit default swap (CDS) basis of fallen angels. CDS are not subject to the same investment constraints that spur managers to sell fallen angels once they are excluded from their benchmark index. Thus, CDS spreads should widen by less than bonds after downgrade, and the basis should also exhibit mean reversion, widening initially and then gradually converging to its long-term equilibrium level. The last part of the chapter investigates a rule-based strategy designed to benefit from mean reversion in the bond-CDS basis of fallen angels. We track the characteristics and performance of such a strategy from 2004, using more than 100 individual issuers. Consistent with past results, we find that over 85% of pairs earn positive returns, with average gross and net (after transaction costs) Sharpe ratios in excess of 1.7 and three, respectively.

Chapter 2 introduced three rule-based dynamic portfolios of fallen angels with different construction methodologies. The "Buy All" portfolio was meant to capture the collective performance of fallen angels and therefore acquired all bonds at the end of the downgrade month and held them for up to 24 months. A second portfolio, "three-Month Reversal," purchased only the subset of bonds that were trading at spreads of at least 40bp over high-yield peers three months after downgrade (once forced selling had on average subsided). In addition, bonds were sold from this portfolio prior to the end of the holding period if their relative spread to peers declined to zero. In the last portfolio, "Flexible Reversal," bonds were purchased any time in the first six months after downgrade, once their relative spreads were higher than 40bp, as before, but had also tightened, compared with the previous month. The last condition was meant to be an indicator that the selling imbalance caused by the downgrade had mostly dissipated.[1] Throughout the chapter, we focus on the Buy All and three-Month Reversal strategies because the former reflects the performance of the entire universe of fallen angels, whereas the latter consistently generated the best returns of the three strategies.

The rest of the chapter is organized as follows. The first section examines the performance stability of fallen angels over time and across markets, and possible explanations for the profitability of the three-Month Reversal strategy. The second section focuses on implementation issues resulting from the unique characteristics of fallen angels. The third section evaluates an alternative strategy of trading the bond-CDS basis of fallen angels. We conclude with a short discussion of the implications of our findings for investors.

REVISITING THE PERFORMANCE OF FALLEN ANGELS

In this section, we consider stability, geographical scope, mean reversion, and default rates of fallen angels.

Stability

To examine the general stability over time (or lack thereof) of fallen angels recovery after the downgrade, Table 3.1 presents the one- and two-year post-downgrade cumulative returns of fallen angels (over peers) as well as the two-year information ratio for four roughly equal time periods since 1990.

The results in Table 3.1 reflect a large degree of consistency across periods, with fallen angels outperforming peers by about 5.5 to 9.5% during the two years after downgrade. Furthermore, the similarity in information ratios implies that not only the cumulative performance but also the month-to-month variation in returns during the 24 months was fairly stable over time. Even the one-year cumulative return between 1995 and 1999, which was a clear exception, was essentially on par with that of other HY bonds.

The results in Table 3.1 indicate that the strong performance reversal pattern we documented for fallen angels after their downgrade was not driven by a single period but was evident throughout the entire sample. This of course does not imply a lack of change over time, as the results in the table would exhibit more variation had they been presented annually. In addition, as we illustrate in the next section, the degree of initial underperformance and subsequent reversal are affected by the aggregate supply of fallen angels, which is in turn correlated with overall market conditions.

TABLE 3.1 Post-Downgrade Relative Performance of Fallen Angels by Period

Downgrade Year	# Bonds	Cum. Returns over Peers afterDowngrade		Information Ratio over
		1 Year	2 Year	2-Year Period
1990–1994	173	3.03	7.88	0.36
1995–1999	211	−0.52	5.46	0.42
2000–2005	771	4.16	8.77	0.50
2006–2011	372	7.06	9.25	0.49

Note: The table reports the cumulative returns in the first 12 and 24 months after the downgrade by period. Cumulative returns were calculated by first averaging the returns of fallen angels' bonds over peers each month after the downgrade and then cumulating the first 12 or 24 months. Information ratio is the ratio of relative returns of fallen angels averaged over the 24-month period after the downgrade divided by the volatility of the monthly time series.
Source: Bloomberg, Barclays Research

Geographical Scope: Fallen Angels in the Euro Corporate Market

Many European investors have inquired as to whether European fallen angels exhibit price dynamics similar to those we have documented in the US market. There are three possible reasons why the results of Chapter 2 may not extend to European fallen angels. First, in the United States, the Bloomberg Barclays Corporate Index is the most widely used benchmark against which investors manage their US investment-grade (IG) credit allocation. Bloomberg Barclays's Euro Corporate Index, however, does not have such a dominant position. Hence, changes in its constituents may result in less forced selling and consequently have smaller pricing implications. Second, differences in regulation and the formulation of investment mandates in the Euro market may weaken the incentive to sell fallen angels at the time of downgrade (or shortly prior to it), which would reduce the magnitude of forced selling. Third, the US HY market is four to five times larger than the corresponding European market. This results not only in a lower absolute supply of European fallen angels but also in a larger variation in their share of the aggregate HY market. For example, Table 3.2 shows that in 2002, 2005 and 2009, fallen angels' share of the European HY market was 77.7%, 30.7% and 32.5%, respectively, while in the United States, the corresponding figures were never higher than 15.5% (with the exception of 2002).

TABLE 3.2   Issuer Population and Market Value of Fallen Angels by Year in the Euro Market

	Euro Fallen Angels			
Downgrade Year	# Issuers	Market Value (€mn)	Market Value as % of Euro HY Index	Market Value of US Fallen Angels as % of US HY Index
2000	3	787	4.2%	4.7%
2001	4	1,926	8.8%	13.7%
2002	16	20,006	77.7%	28.8%
2003	8	8,764	15.9%	7.9%
2004	4	3,027	4.6%	5.8%
2005	15	22,996	30.7%	15.4%
2006	5	5,529	6.7%	3.0%
2007	3	1,838	2.2%	4.7%
2008	11	7,146	13.0%	6.6%
2009	35	25,054	32.5%	8.1%
2010	16	11,462	8.5%	1.9%
2011	21	27,833	17.8%	1.4%

Note: For fallen angels' issuers, market value is measured as of the beginning of the downgrade month. For the indices, market values are based on averaging monthly figures in each year.
Source: Bloomberg, Barclays Research

Table 3.3 repeats the event study analysis in Chapter 2 for the sample of European fallen angels downgraded between 2000 and 2011. The table reports the average monthly relative returns (and associated *t*-statistics) by quarter relative to the downgrade month as well as the cumulative relative returns as of the end of each quarter.[2] These statistics are presented for the entire sample and separately for two states of the market based on the share fallen angels represented out of the aggregate high-yield market. "High Supply Years" correspond to years where that percentage was above 30% (2002, 2005, and 2009); the remaining years are called "Low Supply Years."

Consistent with the results for the United States in Chapter 2, the monthly relative returns in the downgrade month and during the previous three quarters were all negative and highly significant for European issuers, resulting in a cumulative underperformance of 18.54% over the entire sample. Price dynamics then reversed course, and the downgraded issuers consistently outperformed their peers in the following two years. Although the

TABLE 3.3 Quarterly Average and Cumulative Relative Returns of Euro Issuers Downgraded to HY

Quarter Relative to Downgrade Month	Full Sample				Low Supply Years				High Supply Years			
	# Obs.	Avg. Rel. Monthly Ret. (bp)	t-stat.	Rel. Cum. Ret.	# Obs.	Avg. Rel. Monthly Ret. (bp)	t-stat	Rel. Cum. Ret.	# Obs.	Avg. Rel. Monthly Ret. (bp)	t-stat.	Rel. Cum. Ret.
-4	289	-18	-0.52	-0.55%	181	14	0.26	0.43%	108	-68	-1.49	-1.62%
-3	310	-77	-2.07*	-2.81%	193	-37	-1.03	-0.73%	117	-160	-1.7	-5.06%
-2	357	-146	-2.63**	-7.02%	202	-72	-2.09	-2.84%	155	-274	-1.98*	-11.28%
-1	361	-259	-3.88**	-14.12%	207	-191	-2.86**	-8.29%	154	-350	-2.68**	-19.72%
Downgrade Month	123	-516	-4.85**	-18.54%	71	-671	-5.12**	-14.44%	52	-264	-2.10*	-22.61%
1	337	78	0.83	-16.62%	188	-12	-0.1	-14.61%	149	257	1.06	-19.02%
2	305	-10	-0.17	-16.81%	174	-24	-0.26	-14.90%	131	72	-0.01	-19.04%
3	302	43	0.84	-15.73%	159	69	0.66	-13.15%	143	29	0.61	-18.33%
4	301	24	0.57	-15.12%	143	-33	-0.4	-14.02%	158	55	1.09	-17.09%
5	287	22	0.56	-14.56%	134	-19	-0.22	-14.46%	153	23	1.08	-16.11%
6	265	14	0.41	-14.17%	130	20	0.26	-13.91%	135	28	0.39	-15.80%
7	257	5	0.13	-14.03%	120	-24	-0.3	-14.55%	137	-4	0.43	-15.31%
8	231	44	0.62	-12.90%	87	86	1.63	-12.32%	142	33	0.24	-14.68%

Note: The table reports the performance of Euro issuers by quarter relative to their downgrade month for the entire sample (2000–2011) and separately for high supply years (2002, 2005, and 2009) and low supply years (2000, 2001, 2003, 2004, 2006–2008, 2010, 2011). Average monthly relative returns were computed by pooling returns over peers (relative returns) across all issuers and months in each quarter weighted by market value. t-statistics were adjusted for serial and cross sectional correlation. *, ** denote significant at the 5% and 1% levels, respectively. Cumulative relative returns were calculated by first averaging issuers' relative returns each month and then compounding them, starting 12 months before the downgrade. Cumulative relative returns are reported as of the end of each quarter.
Source: Bloomberg, Barclays Research

individual monthly relative returns (over peers) are not statistically significant (given the relatively small sample size), they accumulate to a total outperformance of 6.93%. This figure is remarkably similar to the 6.63%
outperformance documented in Chapter 2 for US issuers, despite the much
longer period used in the sample in that chapter. The results are also consistent with Bolognesi, Ferro, and Zuccheri (2014), who document an abnormal return of –5% during the event month and 0.81% in the following
quarter (compared with –5.16% and 0.78%, respectively, in Table 3.3)
despite the use of a different index, data frequency, and period.[3]

In contrast, comparing the performance dynamics in High Supply and
Low Supply years reveals striking differences both before and after downgrade. Issuers downgraded in High Supply years experienced larger initial
losses (–22.61% vs. –14.44% in Low Supply years) but then posted much
stronger recoveries (cumulative outperformance from the downgrade of
10.24% and 2.48%, respectively). The difference between High Supply and
Low Supply years is fully consistent with the effects of forced selling when
market demand is limited.[4] The lack of prospective buyers facilitate a temporary price distortion, with prices initially dropping below their fundamental values and then returning to equilibrium levels over time as the
selling imbalance abates.

Mean Reversion

After analyzing the stability of fallen angels' price dynamics across time and
markets, we turn to the performance of the 3-Month Reversal strategy. To
what extent did its strong performance (relative to high-yield peers) ema-
nate from the existence of a mean-reversion pattern in the HY market as
opposed to characteristics unique to fallen angels?[5] Pospisil and Zhang
(2010), for example, find evidence of reversal effects in HY bonds during
periods of decreasing credit spreads.[6]

At first, it may seem that one need only compare the performance of the
3-Month Reversal to that of the Buy All strategy, which does not condition
buy/sell decisions on relative pricing information. Over the 20 years of the
sample period in Chapter 2, the 3-month reversal strategy earned an average
relative return of 0.78% per month with an information ratio of 1.03 vs.
0.31% per month and an information ratio of 0.64 for the Buy All strategy
(see Table 2.9). However, the two strategies differ in terms of the inclusion
month, which may affect performance considerably. In fact, the formulation
of the 3-Months Reversal strategy was formulated to capitalize on
Chapter 2's findings that the optimal time to purchase fallen angels was, on
average, three months after their exclusion from the Bloomberg Barclays
Corporate Index. Chapter 2 showed, for example, that if a One-Month

Reversal strategy were implemented by buying fallen angels at the end of the first month after their downgrade, the relative performance and information ratio would fall to 0.64% per month and 0.87, respectively.

To properly quantify the contribution of mean reversion to the performance of the three-Month Reversal strategy, we apply the same strategy to the universe of HY bonds that are not fallen angels.[7] The alternative "Mean Reversion" portfolio is rebalanced monthly and purchases any HY bond trading at relative spreads to peers of at least 40bp. As with fallen angels, these bonds are sold from the portfolio once their relative spreads become negative or if 21 months have passed since the date they were acquired.[8]

Table 3.4 displays various performance statistics for several variants of the Mean Reversion portfolio, as well as for the Bloomberg Barclays High Yield Index and the three-Month Reversal strategy. Comparing the Sharpe ratio of the equally weighted and market value–weighted mean-reversion portfolios to that of the High Yield Index suggests the existence of a mild reversal pattern concentrated among smaller issuers. However, even the equally weighted mean reversion portfolio did not earn a risk-adjusted return that was substantially higher than that of the High Yield Index (0.72 vs. 0.66, respectively, over the entire sample period). Furthermore, once the monthly returns of the equally weighted mean-reversion portfolio are adjusted to reflect the uninvested cash position of the three-Month Reversal strategy (termed "Mean Reversion Port. (EW) with Matching Cash allocation"), the performance difference is striking.[9] Not only is the performance of the three-Month Reversal strategy superior in both subperiods (0.92% vs. 0.44% and 1.86% vs. 1.11% in the first and second halves of the sample, respectively), but its tail risk properties, such as the worst one- and three-month returns, are consistently better than the Mean Reversion Port. (EW) with Matching Cash allocation, even though the latter has a more diversified population of bonds. These results confirm that the performance of the three-Month Reversal strategy does not simply reflect a general mean reversion pattern in HY bonds but rather price dynamics specific to fallen angels.

Default Rates

Some investors expressed concerns that fallen angels are susceptible to higher default rates. Although the performance figures reported for all strategies reflect the effect of bonds that defaulted while in the portfolio, we compare the default rates among fallen angels and other high-yield issuers directly. There are at least two reasons why such an analysis is important. First, since investing in defaulted bonds requires specialized knowledge, we assumed that most investors would liquidate their positions at prices corresponding to the month-end following the default month. In some cases,

TABLE 3.4 Performance of Mean Reversion Portfolios Using High–Yield Bonds vs. Three–Month Reversal Strategy

	High–Yield Index	Mean Reversion Port. (VW)	Mean Reversion Port. (EW)	Mean Reversion Port. (EW) w. Matching Cash Allocation	Three-Month Reversal Portfolio
January 1991–December 2011					
Avg. return (Monthly)	0.82%	0.88%	1.14%	0.80%	1.41%
Std return (Monthly)	2.66%	3.73%	3.93%	3.48%	3.71%
Sharpe ratio (Ann.)	0.66	0.53	0.72	0.48	1.02
Worst month	−15.91%	−16.42%	−19.35%	−19.35%	−10.76%
5%tile of return distribution	−3.23%	−5.14%	−4.60%	−3.77%	−3.47%
Worst 3 months	−29.82%	−34.62%	−34.96%	−34.96%	−26.01%
January 1991–December 2000					
Avg. return (Monthly)	0.90%	0.99%	1.15%	0.44%	0.92%
Std return (Monthly)	1.83%	2.64%	2.78%	1.39%	1.90%
Sharpe ratio (Ann.)	0.90	0.73	0.90	0.03	0.89
Worst month	−5.52%	−8.89%	−8.87%	−6.48%	−5.70%

(Continued)

135

TABLE 3.4 (*Continued*)

	High-Yield Index	Mean Reversion Port. (VW)	Mean Reversion Port. (EW)	Mean Reversion Port. (EW) w. Matching Cash Allocation	Three-Month Reversal Portfolio
5%tile of return distribution	-1.52%	-3.17%	-3.36%	-1.83%	-1.03%
Worst 3 months	-9.41%	-18.20%	-14.86%	-14.69%	-5.76%
January 2001–December 2011					
Avg. return (Monthly)	0.74%	0.77%	1.12%	1.11%	1.86%
Std return (Monthly)	3.25%	4.51%	4.76%	4.61%	4.76%
Sharpe ratio (Ann.)	0.57	0.44	0.67	0.69	1.20
Worst month	-15.91%	-16.42%	-19.35%	-19.35%	-10.76%
5%tile of return distribution	-3.78%	-6.19%	-5.39%	-5.38%	-4.79%
Worst 3 months	-29.82%	-34.62%	-34.96%	-34.96%	-26.01%

Note: The mean reversion portfolio is rebalanced monthly and purchases any high–yield bond trading at relative spreads to peers of at least 40bp. Bonds are sold from the portfolio once their relative spreads become negative or if 21 months have passed since the date they were acquired. The portfolio returns are weighted either equally or by market weights. The Mean Reversion Port. (EW) with Matching Cash allocation includes a monthly cash position equal to that in the Three–Month Reversal portfolio.
Source: Bloomberg, Barclays Research

TABLE 3.5   Annual Default Rates in the Bloomberg Barclays High Yield Index by Issuer Type

Year	# Defaulted Issuers		Amt Outstanding of Defaulted Issuers ($mn)	
	Fallen Angels	Other High Yield	Fallen Angels	Other High Yield
1990	0	18	0	6,767
1991	2	41	1,150	10,963
1992	1	41	100	10,224
1993	0	19	0	3,380
1994	0	4	0	368
1995	0	18	0	3,714
1996	0	19	0	3,652
1997	1	6	279	1,369
1998	0	17	0	2,791
1999	1	61	125	14,937
2000	2	110	1,500	26,692
2001	14	143	10,724	44,589
2002	20	108	37,927	60,231
2003	14	80	13,504	21,603
2004	1	34	200	8,053
2005	6	27	11,487	6,741
2006	1	14	1,740	4,620
2007	0	11	0	2,729
2008	2	43	2,404	17,445
2009	22	90	35,920	53,813
2010	1	19	800	6,464
2011	6	20	1,576	12,525
Total	94	943	119,438	323,668
Issuer population in High Yield Index	616	3,870	980,401	2,053,583
Aggregate Default Rate	15%	24%	12%	16%

Note: "Other High Yield" refers to any issuer that was part of the High Yield Index at some point and was never downgraded from investment-grade status. The calculation of default rates disregards bonds' vintage years.
Source: Bloomberg, Barclays Research

however, these prices may not be transactable or investors may be unwilling to sell at that time. Second, beyond the direct effect on prices, default events may bring additional reputational and legal costs for some investors, which our performance figures do not capture.

Table 3.5 presents the annual number and amount outstanding of defaulted fallen angels as well as other issuers that were part of the Bloomberg Barclays High Yield Index.[10] Over the 22-year period since 1990, 88 issuers classified as fallen angels defaulted out of an overall population of 614 issuers that were fallen angels at some point, with most defaults occurring during 2001 and 2003 and the 2008–2009 financial crisis. These figures translate into a default rate of 15%, compared with almost twice that rate (24%) among other HY issuers. Not surprisingly, in terms of amount outstanding, the difference in default rates between the two populations was much smaller (12% and 16%, respectively), reflecting the larger average size of debt rated IG at issuance (as are fallen angels), compared with non-IG debt. In 2002, the amount outstanding that defaulted peaked at $38bn, reflecting the WorldCom bankruptcy in July 2002.[11] Overall, the table indicates that the default rates of fallen angels are certainly not higher and generally are even lower compared to other HY bonds.

CAPACITY AND COST OF IMPLEMENTING A FALLEN ANGELS STRATEGY

Investors interested in committing capital to exploit the price dynamics of fallen angels face two important considerations. First, what is the capacity of a strategy dedicated to fallen angels? More specifically, what is the relation between the amount of capital allocated to the strategy and its performance? Second, what is the impact of transaction costs? Would the strategy become unattractive once transactions costs were incorporated in performance statistics? In this section, we study these implementation issues in detail.

Investment Capacity

Chapter 2 did not address the scalability of the rules-based strategies. The return figures reported there did not account for possible degradation in performance as a result of possible price impacts once the strategies were employed in practice. The analysis in Chapter 2, thus, implicitly assumed that the capital invested in any of the strategies would be sufficiently small relative to the aggregate supply of fallen angels to not affect their pricing.

A direct analysis of scalability requires a model of price impact, which is beyond the scope of this chapter. Instead, we assume that the maximum position size of any issuer in the portfolio is capped at a certain percentage of its total market value to minimize any price impact. Given this constraint, we vary the size of the portfolio and analyze the effect on performance. Specifically, we assume that the dollar holding in any issuer is no more than 5% of its market value while the sizes of the fallen angels' portfolios vary from $125mn to $2bn.[12] For example, suppose the portfolio size is $500mn and there are 12 eligible issuers. If there are no capacity constraints, each issuer would have a weight of 8.33%, or $41.67mn in dollar terms. With a maximum position size of 5%, the constraint will be binding for any issuer with a market value of less than $833.33mn. In the case of an issuer with a market value of $500mn, the actual position size would be $25mn (equivalent to 5% of its total market capitalization), and the portfolio will have a cash position of 3.33%.

Notice that the weight of any issuer in the portfolio is determined by the ratio of the cap and portfolio size. Hence, a $500mn portfolio with a market value cap of 5% would have the same return profile as a $250mn portfolio with a cap of 2.5%. This is easily seen from the formula for issuer *i*'s weight:

$$W_i = min\left(\frac{1}{N}, 10\%, \frac{Cap \times MV_i}{Port.size}\right), \tag{1}$$

where

$\frac{1}{N}$ represents the base case of equal allocation to each issuer. 10% is the limit on issuer concentration introduced in Chapter 2, and

$\frac{Cap \times MV_i}{Port.size}$ is the constraint on the size of the dollar position in issuer *i*.

For relatively small portfolios, the capacity constraint may not be binding for any issuer, and the portfolios will be identical to the ones in Chapter 2. In contrast, for sufficiently large portfolios, the capacity constraint would apply to all issuers, and the non-cash component of the portfolio will be market value weighed. More generally, there are two deviations from the compositions of our original portfolios as their size increases. First, the non-invested component (i.e., allocation to cash) becomes larger as more issuers reach the capacity limit. Second, the portfolio tilts from being equally weighted toward being market-value weighted.

Figure 3.1 shows the average (over a rolling 12-month window) non-cash percentage in the Buy All and Three-Month Reversal portfolios for different levels of capital investment.[13] As portfolio size increases, the

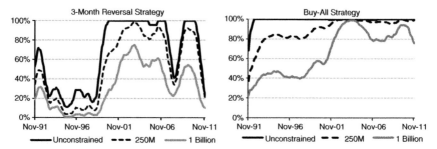

FIGURE 3.1 Proportion Invested in Fallen Angels as a Function of Portfolio Size
Source: Bloomberg, Barclays Research

allocation to fallen angels generally declines as more issuers meet the capacity limit; the magnitude of the effect, however, varies with the supply of fallen angels and across strategies. Not surprisingly, the impact is typically more pronounced for the Three-Month Reversal portfolio since the eligible investable universe is considerably smaller. For example, for a portfolio size of $1bn, only 53% of the Three-Month Reversal strategy would have been invested in fallen angels in August 2004, compared with 98% in the case of the Buy All strategy.

Table 3.6 presents various performance statistics for the Buy All and Three-Month Reversal strategies across a range of portfolio sizes. Cash allocation (as a percentage of the strategy committed capital) increases with size, leading to a decrease in average return as well as in volatility. As expected, the effect is more pronounced for the Three-Month Reversal strategy. For example, the average monthly return of the Three-Month Reversal strategy drops by 74bp as size increases from $125mn to $2bn, while the drop for the Buy All strategy is only about 27bp. In terms of Sharpe ratios, the decline is very modest for the Buy All strategy. Even in the case of the Three-Month Reversal strategy, the Sharpe ratio decreases to 0.95 (from 1.14) for a portfolio size of $2bn, well above that of the High Yield Index (0.65).

Overall, the results in Table 3.6 suggest that although capacity considerations do affect the performance of the fallen angels' portfolios, the degradation is modest; both the Buy All and Three-Month Reversal strategies outperform the High Yield Index over time, irrespective of the amount of capital invested.

Liquidity and Transaction Costs

Evaluating the performance of any strategy requires a consideration of its transactions costs. This is especially important when investing in fallen

TABLE 3.6 Performance of Buy All and Three–Month Reversal Strategies by Portfolio Size

	$125mn	$250mn	$500mn	$1bn	$2bn
Buy All (January 1991–December 2011)					
Avg. return (Monthly)	1.04%	1.01%	0.96%	0.88%	0.77%
Std return (Monthly)	2.71%	2.64%	2.52%	2.22%	1.75%
Sharpe ratio (Ann.)	0.92	0.90	0.88	0.88	0.88
Worst month	–12.54%	–12.38%	–12.15%	–10.96%	–7.99%
5%tile of return distribution	–2.62%	–2.10%	–2.11%	–1.70%	–1.20%
Worst 3 months	–25.20%	–25.06%	–24.95%	–23.02%	–18.28%
Three–Month Reversal (January 1991–December 2011)					
Avg. return (Monthly)	1.37%	1.24%	1.03%	0.81%	0.63%
Std return (Monthly)	3.17%	2.85%	2.27%	1.68%	1.13%
Sharpe ratio (Ann.)	1.14	1.12	1.08	1.02	0.95
Worst month	–7.57%	–7.03%	–5.86%	–4.45%	–2.83%
5%tile of return distribution	–2.63%	–2.47%	–1.89%	–1.35%	–0.79%
Worst 3 months	–17.63%	–16.81%	–14.14%	–10.80%	–7.09%

Source: Bloomberg, Barclays Research

angels since the forced selling that eventually leads to performance reversal also results in lower liquidity (relative to other HY bonds) shortly after the downgrade. Therefore, we explicitly incorporate transaction costs into our performance estimates using a measure of bond liquidity known as LCS (liquidity cost score) described in detail in Konstantinovsky et al. (2016). It represents the cost of an institution-sized round-trip transaction in a bond as a percentage of its market price based on traders' quotes and is available at the cusip level since January 2007.

Figure 3.2 plots the average LCS of our rule-based strategies along with that of the High Yield Index. As expected, the LCS of the fallen angel port-folios closely tracked that of the High Yield Index and all reached record highs during the height of the financial crisis. Although the LCS of the Buy All strategy was very similar to the High Yield Index with an average differ-ence of only 3bp, the transaction costs associated with the Three-Month Reversal strategy were typically higher. This reflects the fact that bonds eli-gible for the Three-Month Reversal strategy generally had higher spreads and, as a result, higher LCS values.[14]

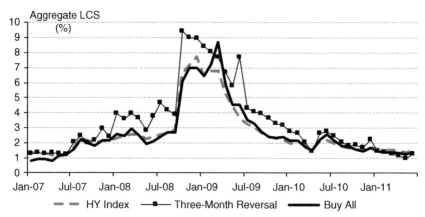

FIGURE 3.2   LCS Values for Fallen Angel Strategies and the High Yield Index
Source: Bloomberg, Barclays Research

The returns calculated in Chapter 2 for the Buy All and Three-Month Reversal strategies were based on prices at the bid. To capture the effect of transaction costs on performance, we mark the price of each bond when it was acquired to reflect the ask level based on its LCS value at that time.[15] Table 3.7 compares the performance of the two strategies before and after transaction costs. Not surprisingly, the impact on the Three-Month Reversal strategy is much larger than on the Buy All strategy (a decline of 59bp/month compared with 37bp/month, respectively). This reflects not only the higher LCS and turnover of the Three-Month Reversal strategy but also the strong positive correlation between turnover and LCS. In other words, the Three-Month Reversal portfolio experiences larger turnover at times when the LCS values are higher.

The results in Table 3.7 suggest that even net of transaction costs, both strategies provide attractive returns, with Sharpe ratios around 0.65 vs. 0.43 for the High Yield Index. It is also important to note that our LCS data most likely overstates the true cost incurred by investors for three reasons.

1. It is based only on quotes from a single broker-dealer and may not represent the inside market.
2. The period for which LCS data is available coincided with a severe liquidity crisis. Hence, the long-term trading costs of fallen angels may be lower in general.
3. The portfolios' construction method, which assumes monthly rebalancing (based on equal weighting all bonds), results in excessive turnover and is unlikely to be used.

TABLE 3.7   Effect of Transaction Costs on Performance of Fallen Angels Strategies

February 2007–December 2011	Buy All		Three-Month Reversal		HY Index	
	Gross	Net	Gross	Net	Gross	Net
Avg. return (Monthly)	1.28%	0.91%	1.80%	1.21%	0.69%	0.66%
Std return (Monthly)	4.53%	4.29%	5.79%	5.49%	4.14%	4.13%
Sharpe ratio (Ann.)	0.86	0.61	0.98	0.66	0.45	0.43
Average Turnover	18.0%		23.6%			
Average LCS	2.67%		3.30%		2.64%	
Correlation btw. Turnover and HY LCS	0.13		0.61			

Note: Net performance figures are based on using LCS values to reflect ask prices for bonds when they are purchased into the portfolio. See also note 15. The estimates of transaction costs for the High Yield Index are based on Dastidar and Phelps (2011).
Source: Bloomberg, Barclays Research

TRADING THE BOND-CDS BASIS OF FALLEN ANGELS

Many investors are interested in exploiting the temporary dislocation in the pricing of fallen angels without taking on both the systematic and idiosyncratic credit risk associated with holding a limited number of HY bonds (e.g., holding the Buy All portfolio and, to a larger extent, the Three-Month Reversal portfolio). One possible approach is trading the bond-CDS basis.

The forced selling of fallen angels' bonds is not accompanied by a similar dynamic in the CDS referencing these issuers. As a result, CDS spreads generally widen after the downgrade but to a lesser extent than those of bonds, and the basis exhibits mean reversion, widening initially and then gradually converging to its long-term equilibrium level. In this section, we investigate in detail a rules-based strategy designed to benefit from the expected mean reversion in the bond-CDS basis of fallen angels.

Sample Construction and Methodology

To analyze the properties of a bond-CDS basis investment strategy, we use a subset of the sample in Chapter 2, which consists only of issuers downgraded to high yield between 2004 and 2010 and referenced by actively traded CDS contracts. Issuers downgraded as a result of a corporate event (i.e., the reference entity was acquired by or merged into a new entity) were excluded because of the change in the corresponding CDS contract.

Following Chapter 2, for each CDS we compile a time series of monthly spread and DV01 data over a Three-year window starting 12 months prior to the downgrade month. Our main data source is Markit, but quotes from Barclays' traders are used as a secondary source whenever data from Markit is unavailable or stale. We clean out spreads once they are unchanged for over three months. CDSs for which we obtain less than one year of data in the analysis window or less than six months during the first year following the downgrade were excluded.

Table 3.8 reports the number of issuers and the aggregate market value of their bonds (as of the beginning of the downgrade month) in our matched bond-CDS sample as well as for the dataset used in Chapter 2. The final sample consists of 101 matched bond-CDS pairs, which represent annually between 64% and 94% of the issuers included in Chapter 2's original study and 66% in terms of market value, on average.[16]

Table 3.9 presents the average and median spreads of bonds and CDS in our sample by year, measured at the end of the downgrade month. Until 2007, median CDS spreads were similar to or slightly higher than those of bonds, but the financial crisis that started that year resulted in a much larger

TABLE 3.8 Annual Population and Market Value of Matched CDS-Bond Sample

	Sample in Chap. 2		Matched Cash–CDS Sample		Ratio of Matched Cash–CDS Sample to Sample in Chap. 2	
Year	# Issuers	Total Market Value ($mn)	# Issuers	Total Market Value ($mn)	# Issuers	Total Market Value
2004	20	33,207	14	25,428	70%	77%
2005	17	93,211	13	59,597	76%	64%
2006	16	18,329	15	15,702	94%	86%
2007	20	30,767	13	17,854	65%	58%
2008	25	36,257	16	28,866	64%	80%
2009	39	46,797	27	23,635	69%	51%
2010	4	2,517	3	1,655	75%	66%
Total	141	261,085	101	172,737	72%	66%

Note: Unsecured bonds trading under the same CDS were aggregated by market value as of the beginning of the downgrade month.
Source: Markit, Bloomberg, Barclays Research

TABLE 3.9　Spreads of Bonds and CDS at Downgrade Month by Year (bp)

	Bond Spreads			CDS Spreads		
Year	Median	Average	Bloomberg Barclays HY Index	Median	Average	CDX HY Index
2004	200	276	329	207	279	380*
2005	249	529	298	246	580	350*
2006	157	204	266	232	229	312
2007	202	270	311	207	250	366
2008	642	1045	899	535	1025	788
2009	1393	1468	991	706	866	950
2010	559	590	603	139	195	555

Note: Spreads are measured as of the end of the downgrade month and capped at the 95th percentile (20%). The CDX High Yield Index is the on-the-run CDX. NA.HY. Spreads of the CDX.NA.HY for 2004–2005 are imputed based on the relation between the bases of the investment-grade and high-yield markets in later years (defined using the spreads of CDX.NA.IG and the Corporate Index and the CDX. NA.HY and High Yield Index, respectively). The correlation between the two bases was 75% in the years 2006 to 2010. Values for the High Yield Index and the CDX HY are averages of month-end Libor–OAS spreads for that year.
Source: Markit, Bloomberg, Barclays Research

widening of cash spreads relative to CDS. Average and median spreads were generally similar, with 2005 and 2008 being notable exceptions. The higher average spread (relative to the median) in 2005 was mostly driven by downgrades in the airline industry, while in 2008 it reflected additional downgrades in that sector as well as the downgrade and eventual default of Ambac Financial Group. More generally, spreads around downgrade events may widen to levels that are not tradable and mostly reflect the illiquidity of the CDS or security. To limit the effect of these "theoretical" quotes, we cap spreads at the 95th percentile (20%). Note also that spreads in our sample were largely below those of the High Yield Index (with the exception of 2009), since most fallen angels were downgraded to the highest speculative-grade rating.[17]

We define the cash–CDS basis as the difference between the spread of a 5y CDS and the market value-weighted OAS (computed relative to the Libor curve) of all unsecured bonds issued by the underlying reference entity.[18] We examined two alternative specifications for the basis, but both generated results that were qualitatively and quantitatively very similar.[19]

Since the purpose of the investment strategy we analyze is to exploit issuer-specific mean reversion, it is important to control for changes in the cash–CDS basis that are driven by systematic factors. For example, Desclée, Ng, Phelps, and Polbennikov (2009) showed that the sharp rise of the basis between the Corporate Index and CDX.NA.IG[20] in 2007 and the subsequent reversal were driven to a large degree by the marked change in market liquidity conditions.[21] To isolate the idiosyncratic part of the cash–CDS basis, we define the market-adjusted basis for issuer i as:[22]

$$(5y\ CDS\ spread - market\text{-}value\ weighted\ OAS\ of\ bonds) -$$

$$(On\text{-}the\text{-}run\ 5y\ CDX.NA.HY\ spread - High\ Yield\ Index\ OAS) \qquad (2)$$

Table 3.10 displays the distribution of the market-adjusted basis of fallen angels, measured at the end of the downgrade month, by year. Overall, the dynamics are similar to those of the broad market (Table 3.9)—tight in the first years of the sample but increasingly negative in the last couple of years of the sample. A notable exception was the positive average basis in 2008, driven by downgrades in the airlines sector (United Airlines and American Airlines), where debt was largely secured and bonds generally traded richer than the corresponding CDSs. In 2009–2010, the basis of fallen angels was significantly larger (in absolute terms) than that of the overall HY market, suggesting that the impact of forced selling was significantly exacerbated during the liquidity crisis.

TABLE 3.10 Distribution of Market-Adjusted Cash–CDS Basis by Year

Year	Mean	P_{10}	P_{25}	Median	P_{75}	P_{90}
2004	−46	−106	−65	−52	−31	18
2005	−27	−98	−83	−60	26	103
2006	−24	−139	−62	−8	31	83
2007	−79	−106	−97	−88	−66	−42
2008	50	−218	−184	−89	328	443
2009	−544	−1,233	−903	−476	−186	24
2010	−353	−606	−606	−387	−66	−66

Note: The market-adjusted basis is measured as of the end of the downgrade month and defined as: (5y CDS spread – Market-value weighted OAS of issuer i bonds) – (On-the-run 5y CDX.NA.HY spread – High Yield Index OAS). Spread data is capped at the 95th percentile (20%).
Source: Markit, Bloomberg, Barclays Research

Analysis of the Cash–CDS Basis

Chapter 2 documented large variability in the performance of fallen angels after downgrade. While most outperformed peers and some even regained high-grade status, others were downgraded further or even defaulted. To identify which fallen angels were more likely to exhibit price reversal, we consider spread relative to peers, among other criteria.

Table 3.10 documents both time and cross-sectional variation in the sign and magnitude of the cash–CDS basis at the end of the downgrade month. In particular, it highlights the fact that for some issuers, the basis was even positive at times. Figure 3.3, therefore, examines the relationship between the magnitude of the market-adjusted basis on downgrade and its subsequent dynamics. The analysis is conducted for the top third of issuers in terms of market-adjusted basis (36 issuers with a basis larger than 120bp in absolute terms) and, separately, for the others.

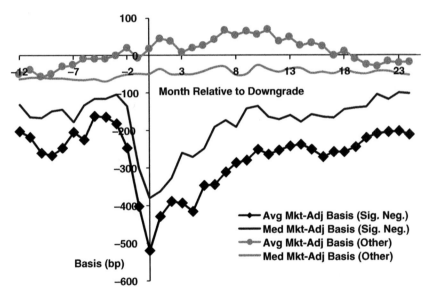

FIGURE 3.3   Dynamics of the Market-Adjusted Cash–CDS Basis by Magnitude on Downgrade
Note: The market-adjusted basis is measured as of the end of the downgrade month and defined as: (5y CDS spread – Market-value weighted OAS of issuer *i* bonds) – (On-the-run 5y CDX.NA.HY spread – High Yield Index OAS). "Significant negative basis" includes 36 issuers with a negative market-adjusted basis larger in absolute value than 120bp. "Other" includes all remaining 65 issuers in the sample.
Source: Markit, Bloomberg, Barclays Research

Those with a significant negative basis indeed experienced strong mean reversion, as reflected in the median and the mean basis. The two rose sharply in absolute value in the six months prior to downgrade, from −130bp and −220bp, respectively, to −380bp and −520bp, respectively. In the following two years, they gradually mean-reverted back to their initial levels.[23] In contrast, the median basis of the second group (comprised of a roughly similar number of issuers with positive and with small negative basis) was relatively constant at low negative values, while its average hovered tightly around zero leading up to the downgrade and for most of the following year. It widened to 50bp approximately 12 months after the downgrade and then quickly declined to zero.

As Table 3.10 suggests, the downgrades in the two subgroups of issuers were not distributed uniformly over the sample years. Issuers with a significant negative basis were largely downgraded in 2009, while issuers with a small negative basis or even a positive basis were mostly downgraded earlier, between 2004 and 2007 (Figure 3.4). The results again suggest that the liquidity crisis exacerbated the effect of forced selling on bond prices, driving cash spreads of fallen angels to extremely wide levels relative to other years in our sample.

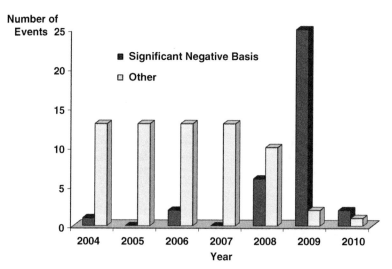

FIGURE 3.4   Sample Distribution by Basis on Downgrade and Year
Note: "Significant negative basis" includes 36 issuers with a negative market-adjusted basis larger in absolute value than 120 bp. "Other" includes all remaining 65 issuers in the sample.
Source: Markit, Bloomberg, Barclays Research

The concentration of downgrades with a significant negative basis in 2009 also meant that their industry representation was highly skewed toward financials (17 out of 36 issuers). Issuers included in the second group were distributed much more uniformly across Auto, Airlines, & Rail; Media and Telecommunications; Retail; and Technology industries (Table 3.11). In particular, all issuers but one in the Airlines and Railroad industry had positive bases, reflecting the fact that debt in these industries is largely secured and bonds typically trade rich relative to CDS. The Media and Telecommunications industry and the Technology industry were heavily targeted by private equity firms between 2004 and 2007; the leveraged buyout targets were often downgraded to speculative grade shortly after the corporate events.

Exploiting the Dynamics of Fallen Angels' Cash–CDS Basis

To exploit the behavior of fallen angels' cash–CDS basis, we examine the performance of a strategy that acquires fallen angel bonds and buys

TABLE 3.11   Industry Distribution by Basis on Downgrade

	Significant Negative Basis	Other	Total
Total	36	65	101
Auto, Airlines, & Rail	1	10	11
Financials & REITs	17	6	23
Gaming & Lodging	2	7	9
Healthcare	1	3	4
Industrials	0	2	2
Manufacturing	4	1	5
Media & Telecom	2	12	14
Metals & Mining	1	0	1
Oil & Gas	0	4	4
Paper	3	3	6
Retail	2	8	10
Technology	1	8	9
Utilities	2	1	3

Note: Industry classification is based on Bloomberg Barclays Index conventions. "Significant negative basis" includes 36 issuers with a negative market-adjusted basis larger in absolute value than 120bps. "Other" includes all remaining 65 issuers in the sample.
Source: Markit, Bloomberg, Barclays Research

protection on their issuers in the CDS market. Unlike Chapter 2, we do not form portfolios that are dynamically rebalanced but rather aggregate all individual (issuer) trades over time. Hence, we do not address the issues relating to cash management and the variability of supply discussed earlier. We first analyze the performance of several strategies with incremental holding criteria and then examine in greater detail the risks associated with their implementation.

Strategy Formulation   The base case formulation is akin to the Buy All cash strategy and initiates a trade on the basis of all the issuers in our sample at the end of the downgrade month. Our long cash position consists of a market value-weighted aggregate of each issuer's outstanding bonds (to ensure results are not driven by bond selection), accompanied by a short position in the corresponding CDS. The position is maintained for 24 months, unless the issuer defaults or all of its outstanding bonds are called or mature before the end of the two-year period.

The second formulation, termed "Sell Tight," incorporates pricing data into the exclusion criteria. Specifically, instead of a uniform holding period of 24 months, a trade is unwound once the basis tightens to the market basis level so that additional tightening is less likely (i.e., the market-adjusted basis is zero). The next formulation ("Sell Tight-Buy Wide") focuses on the subset of issuers with a market-adjusted negative basis of at least 120bp (in absolute terms) that seem to offer the best prospect of mean reversion (Figure 3.3). Once the position has been established, this criterion is no longer enforced.

In the final formulation, which is comparable to the Three-Month Reversal portfolio, positions are initiated only three months after the downgrade month (in addition to the aforementioned inclusion and exclusion criteria). The timing is motivated by evidence in Chapter 2 showing that the price reversal process starts three months after the downgrade, on average. We term this strategy "Sell Tight-Buy Wide in Month 3." Table 3.12 summarizes inclusion and exclusion criteria by strategy.

Performance Analysis   Table 3.13 displays portfolio characteristics of the four strategies (Panel A) as well as performance statistics for the overall strategies over time (Panel B) and for individual pairs (Panel C). It also reports net Sharpe ratios based on estimates of average transaction costs per trade. The calculation of transaction costs assumes paying the ask and receiving the bid prices upon initiating and terminating the trade, respectively.[24] Figure 3.5 plots the strategies' cumulative gross returns.

TABLE 3.12 Cash–CDS Basis Investment Strategy Formulation

Strategy	Indicator	Buy All	Sell Tight	Sell Tight, Buy Wide	Sell Tight, Buy Wide Month 3
Inclusion Criteria (if all apply)	Timing	Downgrade Month	Downgrade Month	Downgrade Month	Month 3
	Market-Adjusted Basis	N/A	N/A	<–120bp	<–120bp
Exclusion Criteria (if one applies)	Technical	Yes	Yes	Yes	Yes
	Market-Adjusted Basis	N/A	>0	>0	>0
	Timing	Month 24	Month 24	Month 24	Month 24

Note: Technical criteria are triggered if an issuer defaults or if all of its outstanding bonds are called or mature.
Source: Barclays Research

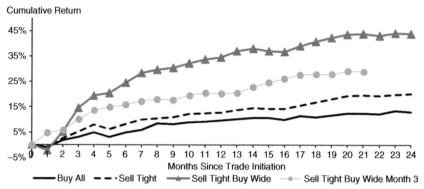

FIGURE 3.5   Cumulative Gross Returns from Trade Initiation
Note: The graph displays the cumulative gross returns of the four cash–CDS basis strategies as a function of the time since trades were initiated.
Source: Markit, Bloomberg, Barclays Research

The base case strategy ("Buy All") earned an average return of 0.5% a month with a volatility of 1.0%, resulting in a Sharpe Ratio of 1.05 and a net Sharpe Ratio of 0.26 (based on an average bid-ask estimate of 4.9%). The strategy generated fairly consistent returns, with a drawdown of only 1.8%, and 85% of the pairs earning positive total returns. Consistent with prior evidence, over 60% of the strategy's two-year cumulative performance was realized in the first eight months (Figure 3.5). Comparing the results in Panels B and C reveals that, as expected, average performance is similar, but volatility is much higher for individual pairs (8.1%). This volatility is largely driven by extreme positive realization (as suggested by the positive skewness) but there are also months of large negative performance, with the worst 5% of returns below –6.9%. A more detailed analysis reveals that most of the large negative returns were incurred by issuers with a positive basis (immediately following the event) or by issuers downgraded in 2009.

In the second formulation ("Sell Tight"), 50 trades were unwound before the end of the 24-month period. Most were liquidated shortly after their inception, weeding out the tight-basis pairs, with an overall holding period of 14 months on average. In terms of performance, the inclusion of the relative basis condition led to higher average returns (0.8% vs. 0.5% in the base case) with the same volatility and better drawdown (1.6%). The shorter holding period compared with the "Buy All" strategy (14 vs. 24 months, respectively) resulted in an almost quadrupling of the net Sharpe ratio to 0.97, although transaction costs were unchanged. Most of the performance pickup vs. the Buy All strategy was achieved in the second year, having sold off pairs that were unlikely to tighten further.

TABLE 3.13 Portfolio Composition and Performance Statistics for Bond-CDS Basis Strategies

	Buy All	Sell Tight	Sell Tight, Buy Wide	Sell Tight, Buy Wide Month 3
Panel A. Portfolio Composition				
Initial # Pairs	91	91	33	32
# of Early Sells (before 2 yr)	0	50	11	8
Avg. Holding Period (months)	24	14	18	17
Panel B. Performance Statistics over Time				
Average Return (monthly)	0.5%	0.8%	1.8%	1.4%
Return Volatility (monthly)	1.0%	1.1%	2.6%	1.4%
Avg./Vol. (ann.)	1.79	2.54	2.43	3.39
Sharpe Ratio (ann.)	1.05	2.04	2.38	3.30
Skewness	0.05	−0.06	1.38	1.01
Maximum Drawdown	1.8%	1.6%	2.3%	0.5%
Net Sharpe Ratio (ann.)	0.26	0.97	1.30	1.74
Transaction Costs	4.9%	4.9%	10.1%	5.7%
Panel C. Performance Statistics Across Pairs				
% Pairs with Positive Return	85%	85%	93%	93%
Average Return (monthly)	0.8%	1.5%	2.5%	1.6%
Return Volatility (monthly)	8.1%	7.7%	10.3%	7.7%
Median Return	0.4%	0.6%	1.0%	0.9%
Skewness	1.21	5.96	4.54	6.01
5%tile of Return Distrib.	−6.9%	−4.1%	−5.0%	−5.1%
Panel D. Performance Statistics with a Maximum Loss Constraint of 5% Per Trade				
Trades Closed due to Stop-Loss Trigger	30	16	7	6
Avg. Holding Period (months)	18	11	14	14

(Continued)

TABLE 3.13 (*Continued*)

	Buy All	Sell Tight	Sell Tight, Buy Wide	Sell Tight, Buy Wide Month 3
Sharpe Ratio (ann.)	0.74	1.45	2.31	2.68
Net Sharpe Ratio (ann.)	0.05	0.63	1.23	1.53

Note: The table displays population and performance statistics for all four strategies presented. Initial number of pairs stands at 91, as returns could not be computed for 10 pairs due to missing DV01 values. Panel B presents statistics for the overall value-weighted portfolio of pairs, held from the downgrade month or three months following it (varying by strategy) till the end of the analysis window (month 24). Panel C displays statistics across all pairs and months. The time series statistics in Panel B are based on time-aggregating returns of all pairs by market value (relative to the trade initiation date), while Panel C statistics reflect disaggregated data.
Source: Markit, Bloomberg, Barclays Research

Limiting our universe to issuers with a wide negative basis at downgrade ("Sell Tight, Buy Wide") resulted in a much smaller sample (33 issuers), with average performance more than doubling to 1.8% a month. Furthermore, more than half of the total cumulative return was realized in the first six months with 93% of the trades earning positive cumulative returns. However, as volatility rose sharply as well (from 1.1% to 2.6%), the Sharpe ratio increased only marginally to 2.38 from 2.04 for the "Sell Tight" strategy. In addition, part of the improvement reflects the lower financing rates in 2009, during which time most of the trades were initiated. Yet this strategy still delivered a better net Sharpe ratio (1.3) despite transaction costs doubling compared with the Buy All and Sell Tight strategies.

The last column in Table 3.13 displays the statistics for the "Sell Tight, Buy Wide Month 3" strategy. The results indicate that initiating the trade three months after the downgrade led to a lower monthly return (1.4% vs. 1.8%), which was more than offset by a commensurate drop in volatility (1.4% vs. 2.6%). In addition, the cross-sectional tail risk properties improved as the strategy avoided continued widening of the basis in some pairs in the first three months. Overall, the strategy delivered the highest Sharpe ratio (3.30), with the lowest drawdown (0.5%). As the liquidity of fallen angels generally improved in the first quarter after downgrade, transaction costs fell to 5.7%, resulting in a net Sharpe ratio of 1.74.

Effects of Basis and Default Risk on Performance   The key risk associated with cash–CDS convergence strategies is widening of the basis due to idiosyncratic or systematic factors. The performance statistics in Panels B and C of Table 3.13 capture the realizations of this risk only partially, as the formulation of our strategies assumes investors can maintain all holdings regardless of possible drawdowns in individual pairs. In practice, a stop-loss trigger is often applied. Hence, profit from trades where the basis ultimately tightened, but only after initially widening further, is reflected in Panels B and C, although it may not have been realized in practice. For example, the spreads on the bonds of LEN, PHM and MWV continued to widen following the downgrade and only later started to tighten, resulting in a positive cumulative return for the trades overall.

To address this issue, we incorporate into each of the strategies what we consider to be a fairly conservative stop-loss trigger, such that once the cumulative loss on a trade is larger than 5%, the position is liquidated immediately (irrespective of any other criteria listed in Table 3.12). Panel D of Table 3.13 reports the number of trades liquidated prematurely as a result of the trigger, the average holding period, and the updated gross and net Sharpe ratios.

A comparison of the new results to those in Panels A and B indicates that sensitivity to basis risk is not uniform across the strategies. In the case of the Buy All strategy, a third of the trades (30 out of 91) were liquidated and the net Sharpe ratio dropped from 0.26 to 0.05. In contrast, for the Sell Tight, Buy Wide and Sell Tight, Buy Wide Month 3 strategies, only about 20% of the trades were affected, and the net Sharpe ratios decreased very moderately (from 1.30 and 1.74 to 1.23 and 1.53, respectively). Therefore, it seems that if trades are initiated only when the basis is sufficiently large, the risk from further significant widening is limited, despite the fact that almost half of the trades in the two strategies realized negative returns at some point over the holding period.

While trading bond-CDS pairs of fallen angels assumes basis risk (although the results in Panel D of Table 3.13 suggest that, historically, the risk was small and did not materially affect performance), investors are protected in the event of a default. Moreover, in cases where bonds were already trading at a deep discount when downgraded, being made whole upon default would have resulted in significant capital gains.

Our sample includes three firms that defaulted within the 24-month period after downgrade. To illustrate the difference in returns between buying the bond outright and using a CDS overlay, Table 3.14 reports price and spread information for the bonds and CDS of Delphi, one of the three defaulted issuers. The table also displays the returns for an investor trading the basis compared with just bonds by two trade initiation dates.

TABLE 3.14   Trade Statistics for Bond and Basis Investors in Delphi
Automotive LLP

	Downgrade(Dec-04)	3 Months after Downgrade(Mar-05)	Default (Oct-05)
Bond / CDS Price Statistics			
Bond Price	99.9	87.9	76.8
Bond Spread	1.9%	4.5%	
CDS Premium	1.8%	5.0%	
Market-Adjusted Basis (bp)	–50	10	
Returns to Bond Trade Initiated in Respective Month			
Bond Price Return	–23.1%	–12.5%	
Total Return	–17.5%	–8.7%	
Returns to Basis Trade Initiated in Respective Month			
Bond Price Return	0.1%	13.8%	
Total Return	4.2%	14.8%	

Note: The table presents month-end price and basis statistics for Delphi Automotive LLP bonds and CDS for various dates as well as returns to bond-only and
basis investors by month of trade initiation. The bond statistics are based on market value weighting four Delphi bonds (cusips 247126AB, 247126AC, 247126AD,
247126AE). For a definition of market-adjusted basis, see Equation 2. Bond price
returns assume the buyer of protection in the basis trade receives par upon default.
Total return is computed as Bond price return + (Bond carry – CDS premium) *
Proportion of the year position was held.
Source: Markit, Bloomberg, Barclays Research

Following the downgrade, an investor would have paid only slightly
below par for the bond, resulting in a loss of 23.1% for a bond investor,
given the default price of 76.8. Factoring in the CDS premia and interest
payments based on a (weighted) coupon of 6.7% would have generated a
total loss of 17.5% for an investor in Delphi bonds but a gain of 4.2% for
a basis trader (the annual cost of protection on Delphi, 1.8%, was more
than covered by the interest payments on the bond). Initiating the trade
three months after the downgrade, when the bond was already trading
lower, at 87.9, would have resulted in a smaller loss for a bond investor
(8.7%) and a larger gain for a basis investor (14.8%). It should be noted,
however, that since the market-adjusted basis was not sufficiently negative

in either month (i.e., larger than 120bp in absolute terms), a basis trade would not have been initiated by either the Sell Tight, Buy Wide or the Sell Tight, Buy Wide Month 3 strategies.

SUMMARY

The results in this chapter broadly reinforce the recommendations put forward in Chapter 2. We provide evidence on the similarity of fallen angels' price dynamics in US and European markets and on the relative stability over time of mean-reversion post-downgrade. Thus, a policy of quickly liquidating fallen angels in the three months after the rating change, implemented by many investors who are benchmarked to the Bloomberg Barclays Corporate Indices, would be suboptimal. Instead, investors should consider the merits of adopting more flexible investment mandates that do not necessitate the disposition of fallen angels or at least allow for a sufficiently long selling period (perhaps up to two years) in order to benefit from the gradual price recovery.

We previously also argued that the pricing inefficiency and return predictability of fallen angels offer attractive profit opportunities for absolute return investors such as hedge funds, as (simple) rules-based portfolios of fallen angels consistently outperformed peers by about 8.5% per year on average, with information ratios in excess of one. Despite the strong return figures, investors had two key concerns: (1) practical implementation and (2) the large systematic and idiosyncratic credit risk associated with these strategies.

In this chapter, we show that despite their supply dynamics, a portfolio invested in fallen angels would be scalable up to a size of $2bn with only minimal degradation in performance. Moreover, while forced selling renders fallen angels less liquid than other HY bonds, fallen angels continue to outperform even after their relatively high transaction costs are taken into account. With respect to mitigating credit risk, we investigate in detail the idea raised in Chapter 2 of using a credit default swap overlay. A rules-based strategy trading the cash–CDS basis of fallen angels achieves a Sharpe ratio of three, with over 90% of pairs earning a positive return.

As we demonstrate in this chapter, not only does the mean reversion of fallen angels not extend to other HY bonds, but it is also not evident in equity of fallen angel issuers. A complementary analysis focused on the price reaction of stocks of issuers downgraded to high yield found no evidence of a "correction" in the equity market, while the corresponding bonds exhibited clear mean reversion. (See Figure 3.6.)

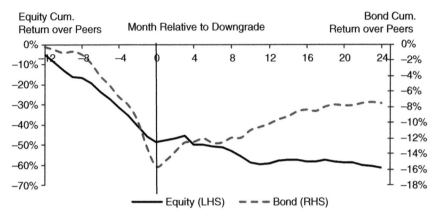

FIGURE 3.6   Cumulative Returns of Fallen Angels' Bonds and Equities Around the Downgrade
Note: The figure presents the cumulative performance of bonds and equities of fallen angels over peers around the downgrade month. The sample is comprised of all issuers that were downgraded from investment-grade to high-yield status as in Chapter 2 and have both public debt and equity. Equity and bond peer groups are based on one-digit SIC's and a combination of industry, rating class, and maturity, respectively.
Source: Compustat, Bloomberg, Barclays Research

These results provide additional evidence that the selling pressure associated with fallen angels is limited to the bond market. The performance stability of the fallen angels' strategy over time and its high capacity suggest investors need not engage in market timing based on supply of fallen angels or market liquidity. Increased default risk, likewise, does not seem to be a substantial concern. High-yield managers might choose to benefit from these selling pressures via an outright investment in fallen angel bonds. Investors with a mandate allowing the use of derivatives might opt to hedge systematic and idiosyncratic default risk by simultaneously buying protection in the CDS market, possibly also hedging the resulting exposure to market basis risk.

REFERENCES

Blanco, R., S. Brennan, and I. W. Marsh. 2005. "An Empirical Analysis of the Dynamic Relationship between Investment-Grade Bonds and Credit Default Swaps." *Journal of Finance* 60(5): 2255–2281.

Bolognesi, E., M. Ferro, and A. Zuccheri. 2014. "The Impact of Fallen Angels on Investment Grade Corporate Bonds Portfolios: Evidence from the European Market." *International Journal of Finance & Economics* 19(4): 267–278.

Dastidar, S., and B. Phelps. 2011, September. "Manager Performance Drag from Uncompensated Transaction Costs." Barclays Capital.

Desclée, A., M. Ng, B. Phelps, and S. Polbennikov. 2009, October 7. "Replicating Bond Index Baskets (RBI®s1): Performance, Risks, and Alternative RBI Baskets." Barclays Capital.

Konstantinovsky, V., K. Y. Ng, and B. D. Phelps. 2016. "Measuring Bond-Level Liquidity." *Journal of Portfolio Management* 42(4): 116–128.

McAdie, R., and D. O'Kane. 2001, May. "Explaining the Basis: Cash vs. Default Swaps," Lehman Brothers Structured Credit Research.

Pospisil, L., and J. Zhang. 2010. "Momentum and Reversal Effects in Corporate Bond Prices and Credit Cycles." *Journal of Fixed Income* 20(2): 101–115.

Zhu, H. 2006. "An Empirical Comparison of Credit Spreads between the Bond Market and the Credit Default Swap Market." *Journal of Financial Services Research* 29(3): 211–235.

NOTES

1. For complete details on the construction methodologies, see Chapter 2.
2. Formally, the relative cumulative return of downgraded issuers (D) from the start of the analysis window until month T is defined as $R_j^T = \prod_{t=-12}^{T} \left(1 + \sum_i w_{i,t}\left(R_{i,t} - R_{i,t}^p\right)\right) - 1 \; j \in D$, where $w_{i,t}$, $R_{i,t}$ are the relative weight and total return of issuer i in month t, respectively, and $R_{i,t}^p$ is the contemporaneous weighted return of all the peer groups corresponding to issuer i's outstanding bonds.
3. Bolognesi et al. (2014) use daily data from the Merrill Lynch Investment grade EMU Non Financial Corporate Index from January 2000 to December 2009.
4. Notice that the proportion fallen angels constitute of the Euro high-yield market is affected by their aggregate supply as well as by the absolute size of the market. For example, despite the similar market value of fallen angels in 2002 and 2005, their share was 77.7% and 30.7%, respectively.
5. Recall that the Three-Month Reversal portfolio purchased only bonds that were trading at spreads higher than their high-yield peers by at least 40bp. Those bonds were then sold once their relative spreads declined to zero.
6. Pospisil and Zhang (2010) find that a strategy which buys past HY winners provides higher cumulative returns than a strategy of buying past losers over 1998 to 2009 and is related to the behavior of credit spreads during a credit cycle. Specifically, the momentum effect is strongest during periods of widening credit spreads and dominates the reversal effect that can be observed during periods of decreasing credit spreads.

7. Specifically, the universe is comprised of all bonds that were included in the Bloomberg Barclays High Yield Index and did not have an investment-grade rating in the previous 24 months. (See the construction of peer groups in the "Data and Methodology" section in Chapter 2 for more details.)

8. The 21 months correspond to the period between the timing of fallen angels purchase in the Three-Month Reversal strategy and the end of the analysis window (24 months after the downgrade).

9. Recall that to mitigate issuer concentration risk, analysis in Chapter 2 imposes a 10% position limit per issuer. Thus, the Three-Month Reversal would have an allocation to cash any time the number of issuers in the portfolio is less than 10.

10. "Other High Yield" refers to any issuer that was part of the high yield index at some point and was never downgraded from investment-grade status.

11. Notice that issuers that proceeded to default directly from IG status, such as Lehman Brothers in 2008, are not included in the analysis in Table 3.5.

12. In Chapter 2, the strategies were implemented using individual bonds, and the portfolios consisted of only one bond per issuer. Since this will underestimate capacity, we use issuer-level data when all underlying bonds were aggregated by market value.

13. Portfolio size is assumed to remain constant over time in order to neutralize the impact of monthly performance and to focus on the issue of capacity.

14. Wider spreads are typically associated with higher LCS. Recall that only bonds trading at spreads higher than their HY peers by at least 40bp are eligible for the Three-Month Reversal portfolio, while the Buy All portfolio purchases all fallen angel bonds.

15. Specifically, the net portfolio return is defined as $\sum_i \left(w_{i,t} \times R_{i,t} \right) - LCS_{i,t-1} \times \max \left(w_{i,t} - w_{i,t-1}, 0 \right)$ where $w_{i,t}$, $R_{i,t}$ are the relative weight and total return of issuer i in month t, respectively. $LCS_{i,t-1}$ is the bid–ask spread of bond i as of the end of the previous month $(t-1)$.

16. All bonds referenced by the same CDS contract were aggregated monthly by market value.

17. The fact that spreads of fallen angels in our sample are lower than that of the High Yield Index is not inconsistent with the evidence in Chapter 2, since Chapter 2 reports spreads relative to peers matched by credit quality (as well as by industry and maturity).

18. We use contracts with the no restructuring clause (XR) as per the current US market standard. We do, however, use the modified restructuring (MR) contract for names where it was significantly more prevalent.

19. The first alternative specification used only the two bonds straddling the five-year point such that their weighted maturity was equal to that of the CDS. (When two such bonds were not available for an issuer on a specific month, the bond with maturity closest to five years was used instead.) In the second specification, the bond trading at the widest spread each month was used instead of the market-weighted bond aggregate to better represent the effect of the cheapest-to-deliver option.

20. Markit's North American Investment Grade CDX Index, or the CDX.NA.IG Index (the IG Index), is composed of 125 of the most liquid North American entities with investment-grade credit ratings that trade in the CDS market.
21. For additional discussion on the determinants of the cash–CDS basis, see Blanco, Brennan, and Marsh (2005); McAdie, and O'Kane (2001); and Zhu (2006).
22. To avoid discontinuity, we do not change the definition of the systematic component of the basis in the downgrade month following the migration from investment-grade to high-yield rating.
23. Comparing the dynamics of the absolute and market-adjusted basis confirms that controlling for the behavior of the broad market basis mostly represents a level shift and does not generate the reversal pattern we observe.
24. Bid–ask spreads are based on LCS values. LCS for CDS are assumed to be 25% of LCS on the reference issuer underlying bonds. Missing individual LCS values were back-filled using the contemporaneous sample median value. Prior to 2007, when LCS data was not available, values were imputed based on the sample median LCS in 2007 adjusted by the ratio of spreads for the respective years.

CHAPTER 4

Introducing the Fallen Angel Reversal Scorecard

INTRODUCTION

In Chapter 2 we introduced a simple systematic rules-based strategy, three-month reversal, aiming to capitalize on the general dynamics of fallen angels' reversal dynamics. The three-month reversal strategy treats all fallen angels equally based on the average reversal dynamics of all fallen angels and does not fully incorporate the reversal characteristics of each individual fallen angel. In this chapter, we present fallen angel reversal (FAR) scores, which are bond-level rankings on each fallen angel's attractiveness. FAR scores further enhance the rules-based strategies by taking into consideration of each fallen angel's reversal dynamics, such as their price trajectories and trading dynamics.

Given the consistent outperformance of the three-month reversal strategy documented in Chapters 2 and 3, what are the additive benefits from the FAR scores? The additive benefits come from two aspects: how FAR scores are constructed and how FAR scores can be used by investors. Construction-wise, because the FAR scores look at individual fallen angel's reversal dynamics, they are able to capture some return opportunities that would have been missed by the three-month reversal strategy. Regarding how the two can be used by investors, the three-month reversal strategy is fairly inflexible: Each fallen angel bond is either in or out of the portfolio, determined at a fixed point (three months after downgrade) with a fixed spread cut-off (40bp). As a comparison, FAR scores rank all fallen angels on their attractiveness on a monthly basis starting right after downgrades. Therefore, FAR scores can help investors better exploit the variation in profitability across fallen angels by offering more flexibility in portfolio construction. The flexibility comes in two dimensions: time of inclusion (investors can choose when to include each fallen angel in their portfolio) and attractiveness (investors can be more or less selective or vary the weights on fallen angels based on their FAR scores).

Regarding the timing of inclusion, the three-month reversal strategy purchases all fallen angels at the end of the three months after initial downgrades because results in Chapter 2 indicate that by the end of the three-month period, most fallen angels have started mean reversion. In reality, each fallen angel may start mean reversion sooner or later than the three-month mark. When constructing FAR scores, we assess the likelihood of each individual fallen angel entering into the reversal cycle by employing several sources of information, such as the past spread change trajectory and a bond's trading dynamics relative to its peers. The fixed timing rule of the three-month reversal may lead the portfolio to include some bonds that are not very good choices and at the same time miss some bonds that might have been good buys; the FAR scores are more comprehensive in capturing the good investment opportunities. For example, if price and trading patterns indicate that a fallen angel may start the reversal before the average three-month mark, the bond could be included into the portfolio immediately after the downgrade, not at the fixed three-month point as in the three-month reversal strategy. This way we would catch the golden opportunity in the initial months when price reverses its course at a very fast pace. As another example, if a fallen angel was not cheap enough compared to peers at the three-month point, it will never be included in the three-month reversal strategy. If the bond later becomes cheap enough relative to peers (thus a good buy), its FAR score would recognize the investment opportunity and give the bond a favorable ranking to suggest inclusion in the portfolio.

The second dimension of flexibility is that the FAR scores rank each individual fallen angel on its attractiveness (i.e., expected mean reversion in relative spread in the subsequent month). In the three-month reversal strategy, all bonds passing the fixed relative spread cut-off (40bp) at the three-month point are included and receive equal weights in the portfolio. Investors may also want to be more or less selective of the fallen angels than suggested by the three-month reversal strategy due to their different capacity. With FAR scores, an investor can either be very selective and focus only on bonds with top rankings or be more inclusive and invest in all fallen angels. An investor may also want to vary the weights based on the attractiveness of the investment opportunity presented by each bond, and the individual rankings through FAR scores make it possible.

Despite their differences, the FAR scores and the three-month reversal strategy are conceptually consistent. For example, the three-month reversal strategy uses relative spreads as its buy and sell triggers. The FAR scores also use relative spreads as one of the inputs to gauge the expected reversal magnitude. Fallen angels with higher relative spreads are more likely to be ranked higher among all fallen angels and thus are more likely to be included in the portfolio, similarly as in the three-month reversal. Given the overall consistency, the FAR scores provide more granular information on distinguishing investment opportunities among fallen angels by incorporating details in individual fallen angel's reversal dynamics.

We find the FAR scores to be very informative of subsequent performance. Fallen angel bonds with higher FAR scores outperformed their peers more than fallen angel bonds with lower FAR scores, in terms of both returns and information ratio. The outperformance was persistent over subperiods. Moreover, the FAR scores worked more effectively than alternative scores based on relative OAS alone. In a more practical setting, we construct a high-yield portfolio with a fallen angel tilt by using FAR scores in selecting fallen angels and in determining their overweight. We find that the FA-tilted portfolio using FAR scores outperformed the HY Index and another FA-tilted portfolio in which all fallen angels are equally weighted.

The rest of the chapter is organized as follows. The first section describes the sample coverage and the construction of FAR scores in detail. The second section examines the effectiveness of FAR scores in predicting subsequent performance over peers. The last section concludes.

CONSTRUCTING FAR SCORES

Universe

The analysis in this chapter covers fallen angels with positive relative spreads immediately following the downgrades and keeps track of the bonds for as long as their relative spreads remain positive within the 24-month window following downgrades. We focus only on fallen angels with positive relative spreads because these are the fallen angels identified in Chapter 2 as being cheaper than peers and having profit potentials. We exclude any fallen angels after 24 months following downgrades because results in Chapter 2 indicate that the prices of fallen angels generally will have reverted to their fundamental levels at the end of the 24-month period. The sample period is from January 2007 to December 2019. The sample period starts later than that in Chapters 2 and 3 because high-quality Trade Reporting and Compliance Engine (TRACE) data that we use to measure bond trading volume starts in January 2007.

Construction

There are three steps in constructing the FAR scores. The first step is to identify which stage a fallen angel is at within its mean-reversal cycle post-downgrade: Is the spread still widening, or has it started mean reversal yet? To identify the stage, we examine the spread change trajectory up to each point in time and the bond-level trading dynamics. The second step is to predict the mean-reversal magnitude conditional on each stage. We rely on two predictors, the relative spread to peers and the remaining number of months until the end of the reversal cycle. The former measures how far away a fallen angel is from its long-term fundamental price level, and the latter measures how many remaining months the bond has to adjust to that fundamental price level. Putting the two predictors together gives us the average adjustment speed as a baseline. However, the next month's expected spread change is also dependent on the stage. Therefore, we use a regression approach to estimate stage-dependent sensitivities of subsequent month's spread change to current month's relative spread separately for each stage of the mean-reversal cycle. The last step is to put together both the stage information and the sensitivities to come up with one unified score.

Step I: Identify Expected State of Fallen Angels Within Their Reversal Cycles

We first discuss ex post, with the knowledge of the whole mean-reversal cycle, how we can classify the cycle into different stages. The purpose of this part is to have a good understanding of a typical mean-reversal cycle covering the two-year span following the downgrades so that we know when the best time is to enter and exit. The next part discusses the real time prediction approach: In real time with a price trajectory only up to a particular month, how we can identify which stage a fallen angel is in without the whole price trajectory in view? Note that the goal of the prediction is to identify the stage during the post-downgrades reversal cycle to take advantage of the FAR dynamics. It does not attempt to predict the downgrades, which is a separate topic and out of the scope of this chapter.

Ex Post Classification of Stages Ex post, a fallen angel's typical mean-reversal cycle can be broken down into three stages: widening, inflection point, and tightening, as illustrated in Figure 4.1 Panel A. After downgrades, the relative spread[1] of a fallen angel may keep widening as there is consistent selling pressure from institutional investors who are forced to liquidate their fallen angel holdings within a short amount of time. After a while, the selling pressure slows down and the widening reaches its peak, the inflection point, where a fallen angel bond transitions from widening to tightening. Based on the whole price trajectory, the inflection point is defined as the month when a fallen angel's relative spread is the highest within the 24-month window following its downgrade. We classify the periods before and after the inflection month as the widening stage and the tightening stage, respectively (both excluding the inflection month and within the 24-month window following the downgrade). Note that the widening period is not defined as months with constant spread widening. Although the widening period is generally characterized by spread widening, relative spreads could also temporarily decline from the general ascend.

Figure 4.1 Panel B presents the actual historical pattern of spread changes surrounding inflection months by showing the median monthly change in relative OAS by the number of months from the inflection point. In the months leading up to the inflection point, there is consistent spread widening. The one month right after the inflection point has the biggest spread reversal, with a median of 122bp. Following that, the fallen angel mean-reversal cycle enters into a stage with more uniform-size reversals lasting until the end of the cycle.

Real-Time Prediction of Stages   In real time, it is relatively easier to tell whether a month is in the widening/inflection stages vs. the tightening stage and is harder to distinguish between the widening and inflection months. The reason is that in real time, the price trajectory leading up to a widening month and an inflection month look very similar: consistent spread widening, as shown in Figure 4.1 Panel B. It is only with ex post knowledge of the whole trajectory in view that we can classify a month as inflection with confidence. Then the question is whether it is worth the trouble trying to tell the widening and inflection months apart. The answer is yes. The median change in relative spread in the subsequent months following a widening month is a further widening of 13bp, so it is a good idea to avoid holding fallen angels in the widening months. However, if we do not distinguish the widening vs. inflection months and avoid holding fallen angels in those months all together, we would be missing out on some golden investment opportunities: The median tightening speed following an inflection month is very high at 122bp, seven times of the median reversal following a typical tightening month (17bp). The big subsequent spread reversals make the inflection months the most profitable point to enter and hold fallen angels. Another possibility is to hold a fallen angel as soon as its downgrade to ensure that the big reversal following the inflection month is captured. This is not optimal either because one could be stuck with several months of spread widening that would dilute the overall profits.

The real-time prediction takes two phases : The first phase is to distinguish whether a fallen angel is in a widening/inflection month vs. in a

Panel A. Illustration of a Typical Fallen Angel Spread Mean Reversal Cycle

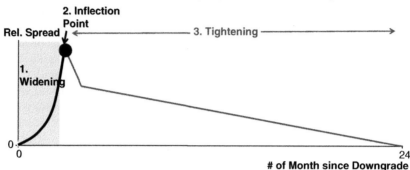

Panel B. Median Monthly Change in Rel. OAS by the Number of Months relative to Inflection Month

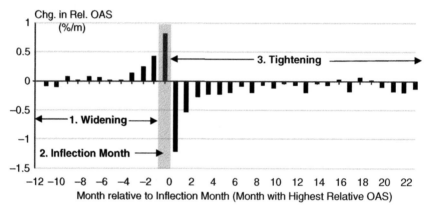

FIGURE 4.1   Relative Spreads of Fallen Angels around Inflection Months
Source: Barclays Research
Note: All statistics are based on data from January 1991 to December 2019. Inflection month is defined as the month when the relative OAS of a fallen angel is the highest in the [0m,24m] window following downgrades.
Source: Bloomberg, Barclays Research

tightening month. If a bond lands in the widening or inflection bucket, the second phase is to estimate the probability of a month being an inflection month. For the first phase, we propose to rely on a fallen angel's price trajectory from downgrades up to the month in evaluation. For the second phase, we use a bond's trading dynamics: its trading volume relative to peers.

1. Real-Time Indicator *Pre-Reversal* Based on Price Trajectory

To predict whether a month is in the widening/inflection bucket or the tightening bucket, we define a 0/1 indicator variable, denoted as *Pre-Reversal*, which equals 1 in month t if relative OAS in month t is the highest in the window from downgrade to month t and 0 otherwise.[2] The *Pre-Reversal* = 1 periods are supposed to pick up the widening and inflection months, and the *Pre-Reversal* = 0 periods are supposed to pick up the tightening months.

How effective is this predictor indicator in real time? In the tightening stage, the variable *Pre-Reversal* would always have a value of 0 (correct classification), because by definition of the tightening stage, the fallen angels have already passed their maximum spread point. In the inflection months, the *Pre-Reversal* would always have a value of 1 (also correct), because the relative spread achieves maximum in these months. In the widening months, we have mixed results. In some widening months, *Pre-Reversal* would be 1 (correct), but in some other widening months, it could also be 0 (wrong classification) when the spread declines temporarily on the path to the inflection point.[3] Table 4.1 illustrates the effectiveness of the indicator variable *Pre-Reversal* by showing the translation between the predicted value of *Pre-Reversal* and its mapped ex post stages. The fraction of the monthly fallen angel observations falling in each stage over the whole sample is included in the parentheses, and the median subsequent month relative OAS change is included in the line below.

Empirically, the indicator variable *Pre-Reversal* does a decent job in identifying the tightening period. Of all months with *Pre-Reversal* = 0, 70% (51% / (22%+51%)) of them are indeed in the tightening period. The remaining 30% (22% / (22%+51%)) of months with *Pre-Reversal* = 0 are the months still in the widening period but where spread temporarily tightened on the course to the inflection point.

However, the *Pre-Reversal* indicator by itself does not do a good job at predicting subsequent relative spread changes, as suggested by the median spread change in subsequent months in Table 4.1. The median change in subsequent month relative OAS is a tightening of 14bp when *Pre-Reversal* = 1 and a tightening of 6bp when *Pre-Reversal* = 0. The majority of the *Pre-Reversal* = 1 months are characterized by widening, so it is counterintuitive that following a *Pre-Reversal* = 1 month the median spread change is a tightening. This is because the *Pre-Reversal* indicator cannot distinguish the inflection months from other widening months. When the inflection point happens, the magnitude of the spread tightening is so large such that those changes dominate the spread widening in the noninflection months. Next, we use a fallen angel's trading dynamics to predict the probability of inflection to disentangle the inflection months from other widening months.

TABLE 4.1 Real-Time Predictor Variable *Pre-Reversal* vs. Ex Post Stages

Real-Time Predictor	Ex Post Stage Classification		Effectiveness of Real-Time Predictor
↑	Inflection (8%)		Right
Pre-Reversal=1 (27%)	Median(Sub. Rel. OAS chg.) = −122bp		
Median(Sub. Rel. OAS chg.) = −14bp	Widening (41%)	Increasing Spread (20%)	Right
↓		Median(Sub. Rel. OAS chg.) = 9bp	
↑	Median(Sub. Rel. OAS chg.) = 13bp	Temporarily spread declining (22%)	Wrong
Pre-Reversal=0 (73%)		Median(Sub. Rel. OAS chg.) = 16bp	
Median(Sub. Rel. OAS chg.) = −6bp	Tightening (51%)		Right
↓	Median(Sub. Rel. OAS chg.) = −17bp		

Note: The frequency of monthly observations in each state is in parentheses. All statistics are based on data from January 1991 to December 2019. The indicator variable *Pre-Reversal*=1 if rel. OAS of month t is the maximum of all relative OAS from month 0 (downgrade month) to month t. Inflection month is defined as the month when the relative OAS of a fallen angel is the highest in the [0m,24m] window following downgrades.

Source: Bloomberg, Barclays Research

2. Using Change in Relative Turnover to Estimate Probability of Inflection

We rely on trading dynamics because the initial price drops and subsequent reversals are driven by supply and demand imbalance instead of firm fundamentals. Therefore, looking at prices alone is insufficient to pinpoint the inflection point in the price pattern since it is not a pure price phenomenon. To predict when the selling pressure has dissipated and when the price trajectory will change course, we have to look at the other key piece in the supply and demand dynamics: quantity. Chapter 2 finds that the turnover of fallen angels relative to their peers[4] captures their price pressure from forced selling around downgrade. In particular, we find that fallen angels' median relative turnover spiked at downgrade months, which are usually peaks of forced selling. Following downgrades, the median relative turnover decreased slowly as the selling pressure dissipated.

Can turnover also be used to identify the inflection months? Figure 4.2 plots the median and average of changes in monthly relative turnover from the previous month (denoted as *Chg. in Rel. Turnover*) before and after inflection months for the period January 2007 to December 2019. During inflection months, the relative turnover had the largest increase over the previous months, with an average of 6%. This relation is also confirmed in Table 4.2, which shows the results of regressing individual bond's monthly *Chg. in Rel. Turnover* on the *Inflection Dummy*, which equals 1 if the fallen angel is in inflection month in the current month and 0 otherwise. In both the whole sample and the subsample with *Pre-Reversal* = 1, the *Chg. in Rel. Turnover* is significantly higher during inflection months than during non-inflection months. Note that the difference in *Chg. in Rel. Turnover* between inflection and noninflection months is much smaller for the *Pre-Reversal* = 1 subsample. This is because this subsample contains widening and inflection months, which are both in general characterized by forced selling and increases in relative turnover, and thus are very difficult to tell

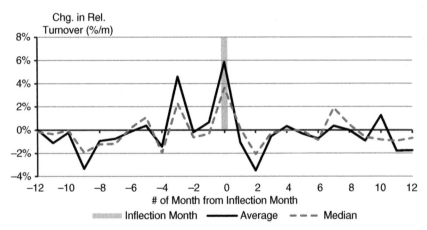

FIGURE 4.2 Monthly Change in Relative Turnover Around Inflection Months
Note: Inflection month is defined as the month when the relative OAS of a fallen angel is the highest in the [0m,24m] window following downgrades. The indicator variable *Pre-Reversal* = 1 if relative OAS of month *t* is the maximum of all relative OAS from month 0 (downgrade month) to month *t*. The sample periods are from January 2007 to December 2019 because our TRACE data start in 2007.
Source: TRACE, Bloomberg, Barclays Research

TABLE 4.2   Change in Relative Turnover in Inflection Months vs. Noninflection Months

Dependent Variable: *Chg. in Rel. Turnover*

Coefficient	Whole Sample	Subsample with *Pre-Reversal* = 1
Intercept	–0.33%	3.44%***
Inflection Dummy (=1 if month *t* is an inflection month, 0 otherwise)	6.20%***	2.43%**

Note: Inflection month is defined as the month when the relative OAS of a fallen angel is the highest in the [0m,24m] window following downgrades. The indicator variable *Pre-Reversal* = 1 if rel. OAS of month *t* is the maximum of all rel. OAS from month 0 (downgrade month) to month *t*. The sample periods is from January 2007 to December 2019 because our TRACE data start in 2007.
Source: TRACE, Bloomberg, Barclays Research

apart. The tightening periods associated with *Pre-Reversal* = 0 have *Chg. in Rel. Turnover* much closer to 0. Therefore, in the whole sample with all three stages, we observe a bigger difference between inflection and noninflection months, as the average change in turnover of the noninflection month is lower due to the inclusion of *Pre-Reversal* = 0 months with small values in *Chg. in Rel. Turnover*.

Based on the turnover dynamics, we use a parsimonious nonparametric method to estimate the inflection probability in the sample with *Pre-Reversal* = 1. We focus on the subsample with *Pre-Reversal* = 1 because by construction of the variable, a month with *Pre-Reversal* = 0 cannot be an inflection month since its relative spread is not even the highest since downgrades while the inflection month is defined as the month with the maximum in relative spread in the 24m window post downgrade.

To examine the effectiveness of this method, we first divide fallen angel monthly observations into two groups based on their *Chg. in Rel. Turnover*, with a cut-off of 5%. The 5% cut-off was chosen based on the median (4%) and mean (6%) of the *Chg. in Rel. Turnover* values during the inflection months. Results are robust to using alternative cut-off values in the 4 to 6% range, or using median/mean values estimated from trailing windows. Over the whole sample period, the two groups indeed had very different probabilities of inflection. As shown in Table 4.3, the probability of inflection of the small turnover change group is much lower than that of the large turnover change group among all fallen angels in our sample (5% vs. 12% respectively) and also among fallen angels in months with *Pre-Reversal*=1 (24% vs. 32% respectively).

TABLE 4.3 Probability of Inflection by Groups of Change in Relative Turnover

	Whole Sample		Subsample with Pre-Reversal = 1	
	# Monthly Obs.	Prob. of Inflection	# Monthly Obs.	Prob. of Inflection
Small Change Group (*Chg. in Rel. Turnover* <5%)	3,457	5%	744	24%
Large Change Group (*Chg. in Rel. Turnover* >= 5%)	1,349	12%	523	32%

Note: The indicator variable *Pre-Reversal* = 1 if relative OAS of month t is the maximum of all relative OAS from month 0 (downgrade month) to month t. Inflection month is defined as the month when the relative OAS of a fallen angel is the highest in the [0m,24m] window following downgrades. Relative turnover is calculated as a bond's turnover (total monthly trading volume over its total amount outstanding) over the value-weighted turnover of its peer group (matched by rating and industry). *Chg. in Rel. Turnover* is calculated as the difference from a bond's current month's relative turnover over its last month's relative turnover. The sample period is from January 2007 to December 2019.
Source: Trace, Bloomberg, Barclays Research

In real time, we use the empirical distribution of inflection months in the trailing five-year window (subsample with *Pre-Reversal* = 1) to estimate the probabilities of inflection at any point in time. Each month we calculate the fraction of inflection months in each group based on the available data in the trailing five-year window and use the empirical fraction of inflection months in each group as an estimate of the inflection probability for that group in the coming month. Figure 4.3 shows the historical monthly estimates of inflection probability using trailing five-year data. There is some time-series variation in the probability of inflection, but the inflection probabilities in the large change group (*Chg. in Rel. Turnover>=5%*) are always higher than that in small change group (*Chg. in Rel. Turnover <5%*) at any point in time.

Step II: Sensitivity of Subsequent Relative Spread Change in Each State

The variable we are interested in predicting is the magnitude of a fallen angel's relative spread change in the subsequent month. This variable is

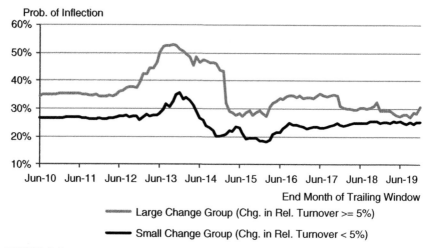

FIGURE 4.3 Rolling Estimation of Probability of Inflection by Change in Relative Turnover Groups (trailing five-year window)
Note: The universe for the rolling estimation of probability of inflection is the subsample with *Pre-Reversal* = 1. The indicator variable *Pre-Reversal* = 1 if relative OAS of month *t* is the maximum of all relative OAS from month 0 (downgrade month) to month *t*. Inflection month is defined as the month when the relative OAS of a fallen angel is the highest in the [0m,24m] window following downgrades. Relative turnover is calculated as a bond's turnover (total monthly trading volume over its total amount outstanding) over the value-weighted turnover of its peer group (matched by rating and industry). *Chg. in Rel. Turnover* is calculated as the difference from a bond's current month's relative turnover over its last month's relative turnover. The sample periods are from January 2007 to December 2019.
Source: Trace, Bloomberg, Barclays Research

calculated in two parts. The first part is to estimate a baseline for monthly spread reversal, incorporating both the current relative spread and how many months the fallen angel still has to adjust its spread back to its long-term level. The second part is to estimate how sensitive the next month's spread changes are to this baseline separately for each stage through regressions.

Baseline Monthly Spread Change: Normalize Relative Spreads by the Number of Remaining Months Until the End of the Reversal Cycle To establish a baseline for next month's spread change, we normalize the current month's relative spread level by the number of remaining months until the end of the reversal cycle (24m period following downgrade based on findings in Chapter 2). The idea is that the current relative spread of a bond captures the deviation of its spread from its long-term fundamental level (proxied by peer spread). Chapter 2 finds that a fallen angel's spread in general fully adjusts back to its long-term level (i.e., 0 spread relative to peers) at the end of the 24m period. If we assume such reversal happens at a uniform speed during the remaining months, the expected adjustment speed per month can be calculated as the current relative spread divided by the number of remaining months. We denote this quantity as *rel. OAS/m*, and it is calculated as:

$$Rel.OAS / m = \frac{Spread\ Relative\ to\ Peers}{24 - \#\ of\ Months\ since\ Downgrade + 1}$$

Estimate Conditional Sensitivities　We classify three stages in the regression using the stage variable *Pre-Reversal* and *Inflection Dummy*:

1. The tightening stage proxied by *Pre-Reversal* = 0.
2. Inflection month captured by the *Inflection Dummy*, which equals 1 when the month is an inflection month.
3. The noninflection widening month during the subsample with *Pre-Reversal* = 1 (captured by *Pre-Reversal* * (1 − *Inflection Dummy*)).

We try to characterize stages with the variable *Pre-Reversal* instead of the ex post characterization of tightening and widening stages because the *Pre-Reversal* variable is observable in real time. In the regressions, we had to use the *Inflection Dummy*, which cannot be calculated in real time for the current month but is known ex post for other months for the purpose of calibration. In calculating the FAR scores, we use the estimated probability of inflection and not the *Inflection Dummy* so that the scores can be calculated in real time.

To estimate the sensitivity in each stage, we regress subsequent month's relative OAS change on the interaction terms of the three state dummies and *rel. OAS/m* (baseline model). The whole sample results are reported in Table 4.4. The sign and relative magnitude of the coefficients are as expected. The sensitivity is −0.82 in the tightening periods, which means that in tightening months, fallen angels on average have a spread tightening with the size of 82% of the baseline adjustment (current month's *rel. OAS/m*). The sensitivity in inflection month is −4.26, which means that in inflection months, the average price reversal is much larger at 4.26 times of the baseline adjustment, which is to be expected, as we discussed earlier that the inflection months are followed by the largest reversals. The sensitivity in noninflection widening months is 1.86, which means that in these months, relative spreads would continue widening in the subsequent month with the change being 1.86 times of the baseline adjustment.

In model 2, we include an additional variable *Pre-Reversal* to test whether there is a difference in the level of subsequent spread changes when *Pre-Reversal* = 1 vs. when *Pre-Reversal* = 0 besides the differences in their sensitivities. The coefficient on *Pre-Reversal* is insignificant, and there is minimal difference in the adjusted R^2 between the baseline model (23.42%) and model 2 (23.45%). The sensitivity coefficients are also similar. The results confirm that the subsequent month's spread changes do not differ in level between *Pre-Reversal* = 1 vs. *Pre-Reversal* = 0 months, and the three sensitivities are enough to capture the differences. The coefficients reported in Table 4.4 are based on the full sample in order to give a comprehensive depiction of the general fallen angel dynamics. In calculating the FAR scores, the sensitivity coefficients are computed from a trailing 5-year window using only that data available up to the evaluation months to avoid any look-ahead bias.

Step III: Putting the Stages and Sensitivities Together

The last step is to integrate the results from the first two steps, reversal stages and sensitivities, together into a single score that captures the expected spread reversal magnitude in the subsequent month for each individual fallen angel at each month. The raw scores are constructed as follows (outlined in Table 4.5): The scores are conditional on the state variable *Pre-Reversal*. If *Pre-Reversal* = 0, the score is equal to (– Sensitivity_Tightening * *rel. OAS/m*). If *Pre-Reversal* = 1, the score is equal to the expected relative spread change across the two states (inflection month and noninflection months), which is calculated as the sum across states of the product of probability of each state and the predicted subsequent spread change in each respective state (which is – sensitivity coefficient * *rel. OAS/m*). The sensitivity coefficients are betas of the subsequent relative spread change to current month's *rel. OAS/m* in each state estimated from regressions discussed in the previous section. When we construct the raw scores, we multiply *rel. OAS/m* by the negative of the sensitivity coefficients because the sensitivity predicts future spread changes, and fallen angels with more negative spread changes (tightening) observe more positive returns and thus should receive a higher score as they are more attractive. For easy interpretation, the final FAR scores are normalized to be between 0 and 100 as the percentile ranking on a bond's raw score among all fallen angel bonds within the FAR universe in a particular month. A higher FAR score indicates a more positive expected return reversal in the coming month.

TABLE 4.4 Sensitivities of Subsequent Relative Spread Change to Relative OAS/m

		Dependent Variable: Subsequent Month Relative OAS Change		
Coefficient	Denoted as		Baseline Model	Model 2
Intercept			-0.05	-0.01
Rel. OAS/m *(1 − Pre-Reversal)	Sensitivity_Tightening		-0.82**	-0.85**
Rel. OAS/m * Pre-Reversal * Inflection Dummy	Sensitivity_Inflection		-4.26***	-4.23***
Rel. OAS/m * Pre-Reversal * (1 − Inflection Dummy)	Sensitivity_Widening		1.86***	1.91***
Pre-Reversal				-0.17
Adj. R^2			23.42%	23.45%

Note: The indicator variable *Pre-Reversal* = 1 if relative OAS of month t is the maximum of all relative OAS from month 0 (downgrade month) to month t. The *Inflection Dummy* = 1 for month t if it is an inflection month and 0 otherwise. These regressions are based on fallen angel observations from July 2005 to December 2019. The starting month corresponds with the starting month of the trailing window used for sensitivity estimation (July 2005).
Source: Bloomberg, Barclays Research

TABLE 4.5   Construction of Fallen Angel Reversal Score

FAR Score	
Meaning	
A higher score indicates a larger reversal magnitude in spread (higher return) relative to peers in the subsequent month.	
Scenario	**Raw Score**
If *Pre-Reversal* = 0 (Rel. OAS < max since DG)	$-$ Sensitivity_Tightening $*$ *Rel. OAS/m*
If *Pre-Reversal* = 1 (Rel. OAS = max since DG)	P_inflection$*(-$ Sensitivity_Inflection)$*$*Rel. OAS/m* $+$ $(1 -$ P_inflection)$*(-$ Sensitivity_Widening$*$*Rel. OAS/m*)
Normalization	
The final scores are normalized to be between 0 and 100 as the percentile ranking of all fallen angel bonds in the FAR universe within a month on the raw score.	
Universe	
The universe includes all fallen angels with positive relative spreads immediately following the downgrades and keeps track of the fallen angel bonds for as long as their relative spreads remain positive within the 24-month window following downgrades.	

Note: Rel. OAS/m is calculated as relative OAS divided by (24 $-$ # months since downgrade + 1). Sensitivity_Tightening, Sensitivity_Inflection, and Sensitivity_Widening are estimated from trailing five-year regression of subsequent month's relative OAS on the interaction terms of *Rel. OAS/m* and three state dummies. P_inflection is determined by the empirical fraction of inflection months in the two groups of *Chg. in Rel. Turnover* (<5% and >=5%) in the trailing five-year window with subsample having *Pre-Reversal* = 1.
Source: Barclays Research

To avoid any look-ahead bias, we only use the data available up to each point in time to calculate FAR scores each month. We estimate both the probabilities of inflection and subsequent spread sensitivities using a trailing five-year window.[5] We choose to use a fixed-length window and not an expanding window because FAR dynamics could change over time. As an example, Ben Dor and Xu (2015) show that the supply–demand dynamics of fallen angels have changed over time, and such change had a material impact on average fallen angel performance. Ben Dor and Guan (2018) also show that from 2015 to 2018, the reversal of fallen angels happened at a faster pace than in the sample period examined in Chapter 2 (1990–2010). If there are any changes to FAR dynamics, a fixed-length trailing windows would capture the changes in a timelier manner than an expanding window, in which the more recent changes may be diluted by the early months before such changes.

We start the estimation of FAR scores in June 2010. We choose this date for two reasons. First, our TRACE data for calculating turnover starts in January 2007 and we need a long-enough period for the initial real-time estimation. Second, we want the sample period to best correspond to our fallen angel strategy subperiod analysis in earlier publications for comparison (such as in Ben Dor and Xu 2015). June 2010 is the choice after balancing the two criteria. For the period from June 2010 to November 2011, we have less than five years of data each month in estimating empirical probabilities of inflection. We do have full five-year data for estimating spread change sensitivity coefficients since spread data starts well before 2007.

EFFICACY OF FAR SCORE

We perform two types of analysis to assess the efficacy of FAR scores. In the first analysis, we sort all eligible fallen angels into two groups each month based on their FAR scores and compare their performance. In a more practical setting, we construct a high-yield portfolio with a fallen angel tilt by using FAR scores in selecting fallen angels and in determining their overweight.

Top and Bottom Portfolios Sorted on FAR Scores

To evaluate the efficacy of FAR scores, we form a monthly rebalanced long-short portfolio that buys the top half of fallen angels with highest FAR scores and shorts the bottom half of fallen angels with lowest FAR scores. All bonds are equally weighted subject to a 10% cap to reduce the impact of any single bond. If there are less than 10 bonds in either portfolio, the excess capital will be allocated to 1m Libor.

We evaluate the performance of the top, bottom, and top-over-bottom portfolios with the performance measured by total returns relative to peers.[6] If the score has predictive power of subsequent spread reversals, we will expect the top portfolio to outperform the bottom portfolios more and the top-over-bottom portfolio to have a positive information (inf.) ratio. Besides the FAR scores, we also consider two other predictors, relative OAS and *rel.*

OAS/m, as benchmarks to evaluate the additive performance from using FAR scores.

The performance statistics of each portfolio's returns over peers are reported in Table 4.6. The first three columns show the relative returns of the top and bottom portfolios sorted on a naive ratio: each fallen angel's relative OAS alone. From July 2010 to December 2019, the top-over-bottom relative OAS portfolio had average relative return of 3.88% per year with an information ratio of 0.40. This means that the top portfolio outperformed peers more than the bottom portfolio by 3.88% per year. When we adjust for the remaining time in the reversal cycle and use *rel. OAS/m* to sort fallen angels into top and bottom half portfolios (Columns 4–6), the information ratio of the top–bottom portfolio increased to 0.51 with an average return of 4.69% per year. Finally, as we further augmented *rel. OAS/m* with the trajectory of spread changes, trading dynamics as well as different sensitivities in the three stages of reversal cycle to construct the FAR scores, the top-over-bottom portfolio sorted on FAR scores had the highest information ratio of 0.65 and also the highest average return of 5.67% per year. In the two subperiods July 2010–December 2014 and January 2015–December 2019, the top-over-bottom portfolio sorted on FAR scores also generated higher information ratio than those sorted on relative OAS or *rel. OAS/m*. Besides having higher information ratio in all subperiods, the FAR score top-over-bottom portfolio also had better risk properties (lower volatility and better tail risk measures) than the other two in both subperiods. The maximum drawdown of FAR score top-over-bottom portfolio was less than half of that of the other two (–9.42% vs. –26.12% and –23.90%). The persistent performance of FAR top-over-bottom portfolio as well as its better risk properties indicate that the FAR scores are more effective at predicting subsequent price reversals than either relative OAS or *rel. OAS/m*.

Furthermore, if we look at the top and bottom portfolios separately, the top FAR score portfolio had higher information ratio and better maximum drawdown than the bottom FAR score portfolio in all subperiods, indicating that FAR scores are not simply loading on spread risk and are indeed effective in identifying fallen angels with higher subsequent price reversals. In contrast to the FAR score portfolio, the top *rel. OAS/m* portfolio had lower information ratio (0.75) than the bottom portfolio (0.88) in the January 2015–December 2019 period and worse tail risk statistics than the bottom portfolio in all subperiods. The same is true for the relative OAS portfolios as well. The fact that the top portfolios sorted on relative OAS and *rel. OAS/m* had higher returns, higher volatility, but similar information ratios and worse tail risk properties is consistent with these two measures picking up risky bonds, not necessarily bonds with likely subsequent reversals.

TABLE 4.6 Return over Peers of Top over Bottom Sorted on Relative Scores

Scores			Relative OAS			Relative OAS/m*			FAR Score†		
			Top over Bottom	Top Half	Bottom Half	Top over Bottom	Top Half	Bottom Half	Top over Bottom	Top Half	Bottom Half
Full Sample	Jul. 2010–Dec. 2019	Average (%/yr)	3.88	8.05	4.17	4.69	8.46	3.77	5.67	8.95	3.28
		Volatility (%/yr)	9.68	11.77	5.57	9.25	11.31	6.16	8.75	10.56	7.08
		Inf. Ratio (Ann.)	0.40	0.68	0.75	0.51	0.75	0.61	0.65	0.85	0.46
		Worst Monthly Ret.(%)	-9.29	-8.75	-4.92	-9.03	-8.62	-4.47	-6.54	-5.42	-8.52
		Max. DD (%)	-26.12	-23.41	-4.92	-23.90	-20.17	-8.02	-9.42	-12.72	-15.03
Subperiods	Jul. 2010–Dec. 2014 (1st half)	Average (%/yr)	2.67	4.46	1.79	5.07	5.67	0.59	4.38	5.33	0.95
		Volatility (%/yr)	5.42	6.16	3.01	5.73	5.72	4.01	4.55	4.96	4.25
		Inf. Ratio (Ann.)	0.49	0.72	0.59	0.89	0.99	0.15	0.96	1.08	0.22
		Worst Monthly Ret.(%)	-5.36	-5.40	-2.02	-5.73	-5.58	-3.87	-2.38	-3.91	-3.78
		Max. DD (%)	-8.69	-11.16	-3.62	-7.84	-9.21	-6.69	-4.45	-7.39	-7.81
	Jan. 2015–Dec. 2019 (2nd half)	Average (%/yr)	4.97	11.27	6.30	4.34	10.97	6.63	6.83	12.20	5.37
		Volatility (%/yr)	12.37	15.15	7.11	11.59	14.64	7.53	11.30	13.77	8.88
		Inf. Ratio (Ann.)	0.40	0.74	0.89	0.37	0.75	0.88	0.60	0.89	0.61
		Worst Monthly Ret.(%)	-9.29	-8.75	-4.92	-9.03	-8.62	-4.47	-6.54	-5.42	-8.52
		Max. DD (%)	-24.96	-20.91	-4.92	-23.90	-20.05	-4.47	-9.42	-11.70	-13.72

Note: All performances reported are fallen angel total returns over peer group returns. A fallen angel's peer bond group contains all index bonds in the same level-3 industry and with the same rating as the fallen angel. The peer return for a fallen angel is calculated as the market value–weighted average return of all bonds in its peer group.

*Adjusted for remaining time in reversal cycle

†*Augmented with trend of spread changes, trading dynamics, and different spread change sensitivities throughout reversal cycleSource:*
Source: TRACE, Bloomberg, Barclays Research

Another observation is that the bottom portfolio based on FAR scores had positive returns relative to peers in all subperiods. This is consistent with the general finding that fallen angels represent good investment opportunities (Chapter 2). Even not-so-attractive fallen angels ranked low by the FAR scores still delivered outperformance over peers, just not as much as the highly ranked ones.

Figure 4.4 plots the time-series of cumulative returns over peers of the top-over-bottom portfolios based on FAR scores and alternative scores. The top FAR score portfolio persistently outperformed the bottom FAR score portfolio throughout the time. As a comparison, the performance of the top-over-bottom portfolio based on relative OAS and *rel. OAS/m* were not as persistent over time and suffered substantial drawdowns around the second half of 2015.

Using FAR Scores in a Fallen Angel-Tilted High-Yield Portfolio

The evidence in Table 4.6 and Figure 4.4 suggests that FAR scores are effective at selecting fallen angels that outperform other fallen angels. As discussed in the beginning of the chapter, FAR scores offer more flexibility in portfolio construction compared to the three-month reversal strategy,

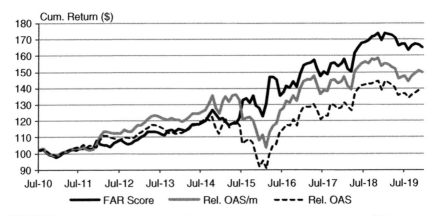

FIGURE 4.4   Time Series of Cumulative Returns (Returns over Peers) of Top-over-Bottom Portfolios
Note: All performances reported are fallen angel total returns over peer group returns. A fallen angel's peer bond group contains all index bonds in the same level-3 industry and with the same rating as the fallen angel. The peer return for a fallen angel is calculated as the market value-weighted average return of all bonds in its peer group.
Source: TRACE, Bloomberg, Barclays Research

both in terms of weighting and security selection. In this part, we illustrate through an example of how FAR scores can be used to enhance the performance of a high-yield portfolio by overweighting fallen angel bonds with high FAR scores. In this example, to best utilize the information in FAR, the FAR scores will be used both as a selection metric to choose the bond with the highest expected reversal magnitude for each fallen angel issuer and also to determine the overweight allocated to each fallen angel issuer, proportional to their signal strength.

In particular, the HY portfolio with a fallen angel tilt (denoted as the FA-tilted portfolio) is constructed as follows on a monthly basis:

- For each fallen angel issuer, we select the bond with the highest FAR score.
- Among all fallen angel issuers, the issuer with the highest FAR score receives a 3% overweight. The rest of the fallen angel issuers receive less overweight proportional to their FAR scores (3% * FAR_Score/Max_FAR_Score).
- The rest of the weights will be allocated to the Bloomberg Barclays US High Yield Index.

The weights assigned to fallen angels in the second step can be viewed as overweight to these fallen angel bonds because these bonds are already part of the HY Index. The fallen angel overweight varies from month to month depending on the total number of fallen angel issuers in our universe. Table 4.7 lists the distribution of the fallen angel overweight. On average, the portfolio overweights fallen angels by 23%, with the maximum reaching 50%. Figure 4.5 presents the total overweight and the number of fallen angel issuers in the FAR universe by month. One thing worth noting is that the fallen angel overweight in this portfolio can be substantial. In reality, an investor can tune up or down the magnitude of the fallen angel tilt by changing the weight allocated to the fallen angel issuer with the highest FAR score (currently 3%). The performance of FA-tilted portfolio will change, but the sign and the magnitude of the information ratio of the outperformance over the HY Index will stay the same.

TABLE 4.7 Distribution of Monthly Allocation to Fallen Angels Overweight

Average	Minimum	Q1	Median	Q3	Maximum
23%	5%	18%	22%	29%	50%

Source: TRACE, Bloomberg, Barclays Research

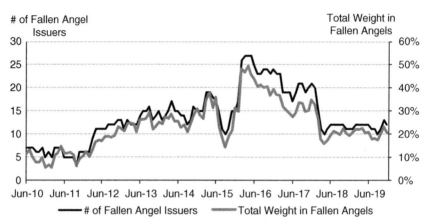

FIGURE 4.5 Number of Fallen Angel Issuers in FAR Universe and Overweight Assigned to Fallen Angels
Source: TRACE, Bloomberg, Barclays Research

Table 4.8 shows the performance of the FA-tilted portfolio compared to the HY Index, reported separately for the two subperiods, July 2010 to December 2014 and January 2015 to December 2019. In both periods, the FA-tilted portfolio delivered higher average total returns and higher Sharpe ratios than the HY Index. The FA-tilted portfolio outperformed the HY Index by 1.07% per year and 5.32% per year in the two subperiods with information ratios around one (1.31 and 0.98).

One possible explanation for the outperformance of the FA-tilted portfolio is that it has higher risk than the index, and the higher returns are a compensation for the risk. To control for the risk difference, we constructed a similar portfolio as the FA-tilted portfolio, but instead of overweighting the selected fallen angels, we assign the same overweight in the industry-and-rating-matched peer bonds for each selected fallen angel. This portfolio is denoted as the peer-tilted portfolio. The peer-tilted portfolio had lower returns and Sharpe ratios than the FA-tilted portfolios and did not generate as much outperformance. Moreover, the FA-tilted portfolio had higher Sharpe ratios than the index in both subperiods, indicating that the outperformance of the FA-tilted portfolios is not entirely driven by higher risk. Figure 4.6 plots the time-series cumulative returns of the FA-tilted and peer-tilted portfolios vs. the index. The FA-tilted portfolios demonstrated steady outperformance over the HY Index while the peer-tilted portfolio had similar performance as the index.

TABLE 4.8 Performance of Fallen Angel-Tilted High-Yield Portfolios

		Weight by FAR Score					EW	FAR-Weighted over EW
		FA-tilted portfolio	Peer-tilted portfolio	HY Index	FA-tilted-portfolio over Index	Peer-tilted-portfolio over Index	FA-EW-tilted portfolio	FA-tilted over FA-EW-tilted portfolio
		(1)	(2)	(3)	(1) – (3)	(2) – (3)	(4)	(1) – (4)
Subperiod 1 (Jul. 2010– Dec. 2014)	Avg. Ret (%/Yr.)	9.91	8.96	8.84	1.07	0.12	9.64	0.27
	Vol. (%/Yr.)	6.38	6.09	6.15	0.82	0.29	6.36	0.41
	Sharpe (inf.) Ratio (ann.)	1.52	1.44	1.40	1.31	0.41	1.48	0.67
Subperiod 2 (Jan. 2015– Dec. 2019)	Avg. Ret (%/Yr.)	11.43	6.60	6.11	5.32	0.50	9.61	1.81
	Vol. (%/Yr.)	9.47	5.54	5.29	5.45	0.72	8.38	1.92
	Sharpe (inf.) Ratio (ann.)	1.08	0.98	0.93	0.98	0.68	1.00	0.94

Source: TRACE, Bloomberg, Barclays Research

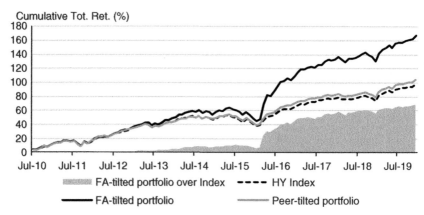

FIGURE 4.6   Cumulative Total Returns of FA-Tilted Portfolio and the HY Index
Source: TRACE, Bloomberg, Barclays Research

To evaluate the efficacy of FAR scores in selecting fallen angels that outperform other fallen angels, we construct the FA-tilted portfolio in an alternative approach without using the FAR scores. In this approach, we invest in all fallen angel bonds of each issuer in the same universe (value-weight among bonds of an issuer) and then equally weight all fallen angel issuers. The total overweight allocated to all fallen angel bonds is set to be the same as in the original approach on a monthly basis. We denote this portfolio as the FA-EW-tilted portfolio and show its performance in the second-to-last column of Table 4.8. The FA-EW-tilted portfolio had lower average returns and Sharpe ratios than the original FAR-score-weighted FA-tilted portfolio in both subperiods. The differences were small, partially because fallen angels only accounted for a small fraction of the overall portfolio on average. A better way to assess the efficacy of using FAR scores for weighting is to look at the difference in monthly returns of the two portfolios and evaluate its persistence. The last column of Table 4.8 reports the performance statistics on the monthly return difference of the FAR-score-weighted FA-tilted portfolio over the equally weighted FA-EW-tilted portfolio. The FAR-score weighted portfolio had information ratio of 0.67 and 0.94 over the EW portfolio in the two subperiods. The sizable information ratio suggests that using FAR scores as a selection and weighting metric indeed improved performance over indiscriminately investing in all fallen angels equally.

CONCLUSION

This chapter introduces FAR scores that rank fallen angels on their attractiveness (the magnitude of their expected spread reversal relative to their peers in the subsequent month). The FAR scores incorporate multiple dimensions of a fallen angel's reversal dynamics, such as past trajectories of spread changes and trading dynamics. Fallen angels with higher FAR scores had higher subsequent average returns relative to peers, higher information ratios over peers, and better tail risk properties than fallen angels with lower FAR scores, with similar patterns persistent in subperiods. We also illustrate in an example of how to use FAR scores as selection and weighting metrics in constructing a HY portfolio with a fallen angel tilt. Such a FA-tilted portfolio delivered outperformance over the HY Index as well as over a tilted portfolio that equally weights all fallen angels. Overall, FAR scores provide an effective and versatile metric for investment in fallen angels.

REFERENCES

Ben Dor, A., and J. Guan. 2018, June 13. "Fallen Angel Strategy Performance—An Update." Barclays Research.
Ben Dor, A., and J. Xu. 2015, June 1. "Revisiting the Performance Dynamics of Fallen Angels." Barclays Research.

NOTES

1. The relative spread of a fallen angel is calculated as its spread over the average spread of its peer group. A fallen angel's peer group contains all index bonds with the same credit rating and industry as the fallen angel bond. The spread of all bonds in a peer group are value weighted.
2. An alternative is to monitor past months' spread change and declare a month to be in the *Pre-Reversal* bucket if the fallen angel's spread has been increasing. There are a couple of caveats to this type of definition. First, if one requires a sequence of spread widening to classify a month as widening, one would misclassify months when the previous months had temporarily deviated from the general spread widening trajectory but had come back to course as tightening. If one just uses the previous month's spread change to do the classification, a second caveat is that during the tightening stage, a fallen angel's relative spread could temporarily deviate from the general reversal pattern but later go back to the original trajectory. These months would be misclassified as widening if one just monitors the past month's spread change. Monitoring the maximum level of relative spreads avoids these caveats.

3. These periods include two types of months in this temporary tightening during the widening stages: months in which the spreads have (1) temporarily tightened and (2) subsequently widened (right after the temporary tightening) but have not yet reached the pre-tightening spread level.

4. A bond's turnover is calculated as the ratio of its monthly trading volume scaled by its amount outstanding to normalize its size. Next, to control for any market-wide systematic trading dynamics, the turnover of a bond's peer group is subtracted from the bond's own turnover to get the bond's relative turnover over peers. Peer group turnover is calculated as the market value-weighted average of all peer bonds' turnover in each month.

5. One issue to be handled with care in constructing the trailing windows is that to identify the inflection month, the full 24-month history of each fallen angel since downgrade is needed. Such history is not available for all fallen angels at the time of estimation. One option is to delete all fallen angels that do not have the full 24-month history at the month of estimation, but by doing so, a big chunk of the sample would be lost. Instead one could revise the definition of inflection month in constructing the real-time sample to balance using only data available to investors at each point in time and not losing too much data. At each month, fallen angels that have less than 6 months of post-downgrade data at that month were dropped and the inflection point was redefined as the months with the highest relative spread from downgrade to the earlier of either 24 months following downgrade or the end of the estimation window.

6. Any excess capital allocated to Libor would receive 0 (zero) return relative to peers.

New Issuance: Index Inclusion

CHAPTER 5

Issuance Dynamics and Performance of Corporate Bonds

INTRODUCTION

Corporate bond investors often benchmark their portfolios to market-weighted indices. Such indices have several characteristics that make them attractive to market participants–they represent the asset class, have relatively low turnover, and are easy to replicate. Even though some investors adopted alternative weighting schemes, market-weighted indices remain dominant.

Market-weighted corporate bond indices automatically include newly issued securities that satisfy index inclusion rules. As a result, index composition often becomes a function of issuance dynamics. However, corporate issuers might have goals that differ from investors' objectives. While portfolio managers try to achieve high returns, corporate treasurers try to minimize cost of capital.

Are these conflicting objectives likely to be reconciled in the corporate bond market? On one hand, prices of newly issued securities should represent supply–demand equilibrium. Assuming market efficiency, abnormal future returns should be precluded. On the other hand, portfolio managers, whose performance is measured relative to an index, can have neutral views on securities added to the benchmark. From their perspective, buying newly issued bonds entails little risk because their benchmark buys them as well. At the same time, scrutinizing newly issued bonds with an objective to underweight unwanted names is typically a strategy with low alpha, especially in a tight spread environment.[1] Also, newly issued bonds are often priced at a concession relative to the secondary market.[2] This can provide an additional incentive to add these securities to the portfolio. The lack of a strong motivation for a portfolio manager to scrutinize newly issued bonds included in the credit benchmark might lead to bond prices underreacting to issuance announcements.

In this chapter, we analyze long-term effects of issuance on the subsequent performance of corporate bonds in the US credit market. We divide the study into four parts.

First, we document a negative relationship at the macro level between issuance rate and subsequent performance of corporate bonds as corporate treasurers exploit credit cycles to minimize their long-term cost of funding.

Second, we demonstrate a negative relationship between issuance and subsequent excess returns at the sector level. We show that this results in a performance drag for corporate bond indices, with dynamic sector weights working as a propagation mechanism. We explain and measure the negative contribution of sector weight dynamics to index performance.

In the third part, we show that historical excess returns of issuers borrowing at a high pace ("aggressive" issuers) have been consistently lower than those of their peers issuing at a lower rate ("moderate" issuers). We check the robustness of our conclusions by using alternative criteria to identify "aggressive" issuers and by controlling for spread exposure.

Finally, we discuss possible alternative weighting of credit indices that alleviate some of the problems associated with issuance dynamics.

DEBT ISSUANCE AND CREDIT PERFORMANCE

We begin by analyzing the relationship between debt issuance and subsequent performance of corporate bonds at the macro level. The data used in our study covers the entire range of USD-denominated corporate bonds, from investment grade (IG) to high yield (HY).[3] We combine Bloomberg Barclays US Corporate, US 144A, and US High Yield indices into a composite US Corporate All Ratings index. Table 5.1 shows the market structure of this composite index split into eight customized sectors as of 31 July 2014.[4] IG bonds represent 78.1% of the index market value. Banks and brokerages have the largest weight (19%) among IG sectors. Other large industry sectors include communication and technology, consumer noncyclical, transportation and energy, and basic and capital goods with respective weights of 11.5%, 10.1%, 10.0%, and 8.5%.

The snapshot of the USD corporate bond universe presented in Table 5.1 is a function of cumulative issuance over the preceding years. The issuance rate has varied significantly over time as a function of global and sector-specific cycles, as shown in Figure 5.1.[5] Indeed, corporations aim to minimize their cost

TABLE 5.1 Market Structure of the US Corporate All Ratings, 31 July 2014

Sector	# Issuers	# Bonds	Amt Outstanding, $bn	Market Value %	Yield to Worst, %	OAD, yr	OAS, bp
Total	2,091	8,207	5,599	100	3.61	6.3	167
Investment Grade	**1,032**	**6,030**	**4,335**	**78.1**	**3.02**	**6.9**	**105**
Basic and Capital Goods	171	757	475	8.5	3.27	7.3	120
Cyclical	70	395	275	4.9	2.70	6.5	84
Noncyclical	139	799	569	10.1	2.92	7.3	89
Communication and Technology	106	682	633	11.5	3.20	7.6	108
Transportation and Energy	130	867	548	10.0	3.34	7.7	117
Utilities	90	772	314	5.8	3.40	9.2	104
Banks and Brokerage	155	988	1,075	19.0	2.58	5.0	100
Financial Others	171	770	447	8.2	3.18	6.9	116
High Yield	**1,059**	**2,177**	**1,264**	**21.9**	**5.70**	**4.3**	**388**
Basic and Capital Goods	266	464	239	4.1	5.87	3.9	419
Cyclical	188	381	184	3.1	6.37	4.2	456
Noncyclical	133	240	152	2.6	5.58	4.1	381
Communication and Technology	159	419	303	5.3	5.62	4.5	373
Transportation and Energy	200	403	218	3.8	5.76	4.4	383
Utilities	22	66	42	0.7	5.23	4.9	333
Banks and Brokerage	24	58	42	0.8	4.42	5.3	253
Financial Others	67	146	86	1.5	5.07	4.0	332

Note: option-adjusted spread (OAS); option-adjusted duration (OAD)
Source: Bloomberg, Barclays Research

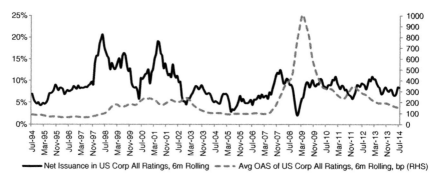

FIGURE 5.1   Rolling Six-Month Net Issuance as % of Amount Outstanding vs. Rolling Six-Month Average OAS of the US Corporate All Ratings Index
Source: Barclays Research

of capital by increasing debt issuance when rates and spreads are relatively low. In contrast, issuance typically declines when credit spreads are high.

We analyze the relationship between aggregate *net issuance rate* and subsequent excess returns of the US Corporate All Ratings index. We calculate net issuance in the index over six-month rolling periods. *Issuance rate* is calculated as the ratio of six-month net issuance to the amount of debt outstanding at the end of the period.[6] We then report cumulative index excess returns over duration-matched treasuries in the subsequent six months.

We split all observations in our sample into issuance rate quartiles. Observations with net issuance rates in the bottom 25% of the sample are assigned to Quartile 1 (Q1), while observations in the top 25% are assigned to Quartile 4 (Q4). Panel A of Figure 5.2 shows average excess returns calculated for each quartile. Average issuance rate for each quartile is reported next to the quartile label of the x-axis.

Corporate excess returns seem to be negatively related to past issuance rates. Periods of low issuance are followed by higher excess returns. In contrast, high issuance typically is followed by a relatively poor performance. A qualitatively similar pattern is observed for total returns, as shown in panel B of Figure 5.2.

The negative relationship between issuance and performance also holds for individual industry sectors. For each sector, we calculate historical issuance rates and subsequent excess returns over rolling six-month periods. Monthly observations are partitioned into issuance rate quartiles. Table 5.2 shows the difference in average excess returns between the first and the fourth quartiles. Positive differences indicate that sector returns are higher

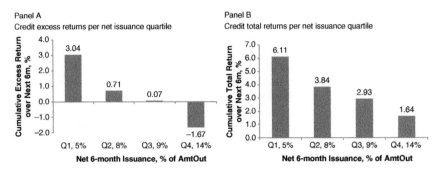

FIGURE 5.2 Credit Performance per Volume of Net Issuance, August 1994–July 2014
Source: Barclays Research

TABLE 5.2 Differences in Average Excess Returns Between Bottom and Top Issuance Quartiles by Sector, % over Six Months

	Low (Q1)–High (Q4)		
	Aug 1994–Jul 2014	Jul 1994–Dec 2005	Jan 2006–Jul 2014
Basic and Capital Goods	0.56	2.11	–1.96
Cyclical	3.19	2.62	4.47
Noncyclical	0.40	1.00	0.61
Communication and Technology	4.45	6.10	–0.33
Transportation and Energy	2.66	3.14	2.58
Utilities	1.76	2.14	0.02
Banks and Brokerage	4.65	0.64	9.50
Financial Others	5.09	1.67	14.66
Total	4.72	2.61	7.26

Source: Barclays Research

after low issuance (Q1) than after high issuance (Q4). We repeat this exercise for two subperiods: from August 1994 to December 2005 and from January 2006 to July 2014. Even though the differences in average returns between bottom and top quartiles seem to vary, the results point to the same conclusion: Periods of high issuance tend to be followed by lower returns.[7] Differences in excess returns seem to be larger for sectors significantly affected by credit cycles (cyclical, communication and technology, and financials). In the first subperiod, the negative relationship between issuance and performance holds for all sectors but is especially strong for communication and technology due to the dot-com crisis of 2001. The second subperiod is relatively short, so the results are strongest for sectors affected by the 2008 crisis: financials and cyclical. In contrast, the issuance cycle for basic and capital goods and for communication and technology in the second subperiod is relatively mild. As a result, the relationship between issuance and performance for these two sectors breaks down.

Does issuer size affect the negative relationship between issuance and performance? Intuitively, larger borrowers should be in a better position to exploit discretionary issuance with a view to manage their cost of capital. A stronger negative relationship between issuance and performance should therefore be expected for larger firms. To verify this, we sort issuers into quartiles of debt outstanding in the index. Small borrowers fall into the bottom quartile (Q1) and large ones into the top quartile (Q4). We calculate historical issuance rates over 6-month rolling periods together with subsequent 6-month excess returns for each quartile and report correlation between issuance rates and subsequent excess returns. Panel A of Figure 5.3 shows that correlations

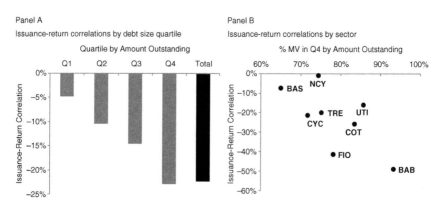

FIGURE 5.3 Correlations Between Issuance Rates and Subsequent Excess Returns (August 1994–July 2014)
Source: Barclays Research

decline when issuer size increases, reaching almost –25% for the largest borrowers represented by the top quartile. Interestingly, 80% of the index market value falls into the top quartile of issuer size.[8] This suggests that the previously obtained results are likely driven by large borrowers.

Correlations between issuance rate and subsequent returns can also be calculated for individual sectors. To infer whether a sector is represented by larger borrowers, we measured the percentage of sector's market value in the top quartile by amount of debt outstanding. Panel B of Figure 5.3 shows that sectors represented by larger companies generally have more negative correlations between issuance rate and subsequent excess returns. The most negative correlation of –49% is observed for banks and brokerage (BAB) as 93% of this sector falls in the top size quartile. In contrast, only 67% of debt issued by the basic goods sector falls in the top quartile, so the issuance-return correlation for this sector is only –7.6%.

SECTOR WEIGHTS DYNAMICS AND INDEX PERFORMANCE

The negative relationship between issuance and performance can be detrimental to the returns of a market-weighted corporate bond index. Dynamic sector weights, which represent cumulative net issuance over time, work as a transmission mechanism for the performance drag. Sector weights tend to be high during periods of poor performance as high issuance is followed by poor returns. In contrast, sector weights tend to be low during recovery periods as low issuance is followed by stronger performance.

We illustrate this with simple examples: Figure 5.4 shows the historical weights of the communication and technology and the financial sectors in the US Corporate All Ratings index. Both sectors experienced episodes of significant underperformance at different times. The communication and technology sector was strongly affected by the 2002 crisis, while financials suffered in 2008. Both sectors entered their respective crises with relatively high weights as firms had been issuing debt aggressively in prior years. Elevated sector weights during market downturns made negative contributions to index performance relatively high. In contrast, the weights of both sectors experienced sharp declines during and after their respective crises as affected corporations lost their ability, or willingness, to issue new debt. As a result, sector weights were relatively low during post-crisis recoveries. This limited the contribution of any recovery in sector performance to index returns. These two examples illustrate that time-varying sector weights associated with issuance dynamics can have an adverse effect on the performance of a market-weighted corporate index over time.

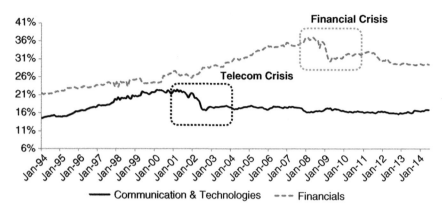

FIGURE 5.4   Historical Market Weights of Selected Corporate Sectors in US Corporate All Ratings
Source: Bloomberg, Barclays Research

To quantify the effect of sector weight dynamics on index performance, we create an alternative corporate bond benchmark with *constant* sector weights. These weights are set to time-average weights of respective sectors in the US Corporate All Ratings index. The contribution of weight dynamics can be measured as the incremental excess return of the standard (market-weighted) index over the one with constant sector weights.

Table 5.3 reports the return statistics for the market-weighted and alternative indices over different periods. The index with constant (time-average) sector weights significantly outperforms the market-weighted one. The right-most column shows the excess return attributed to sector weight dynamics calculated as differences between the excess returns of the two indices. Since sector weights are identical when averaged over time, the return differences represent contributions from weight variations. The performance drag attributed to sector weights dynamics in the US Corporate All Ratings index is 14bp/year from February 1994 to July 2014. This effect is more than doubled in the global financial crisis from 10bp/year before to 23bp/year during and after the crisis. This underperformance of the market-weighted index is persistent over time, with an information ratio of −0.60.

The performance drag of 14bp/year can be decomposed into contributions from individual sectors. The contribution of an individual sector is calculated as a time average of the product of excess returns and sector weights minus the product of time-average excess returns and time-average weights. Figure 5.5 shows the attribution results.

TABLE 5.3 Contribution of Dynamic Sector Weights to Index Performance

US Corporate All Ratings	Historical Market Weights (MW, Dynamic)	Time-Average Weights (Constant)	Weight Contribution (TE)(MW-Const)
Feb 1994–Jul 2014			
Avg. Exc. Ret., %/yr	0.98	1.12	−0.14
Volatility, %/yr	5.38	5.40	0.24
Information Ratio	0.18	0.21	−0.60
Feb 1994–Jun 2007			
Avg. Exc. Ret., %/yr	0.63	0.73	−0.10
Volatility, %/yr	3.10	3.03	0.13
Information Ratio	0.20	0.24	−0.79
Jul 2007–Jul 2014			
Avg. Exc. Ret., %/yr	1.65	1.87	−0.22
Volatility, %/yr	8.12	8.22	0.36
Information Ratio	0.20	0.23	−0.60

Source: Barclays Research

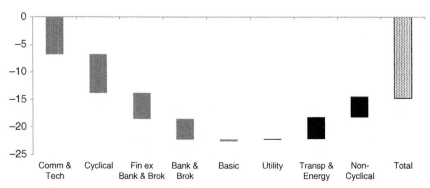

FIGURE 5.5 Contributions of Dynamic Weights to Index Returns by Sector, February 1994–July 2014
Source: Barclays Research

Dynamic weights of sectors affected by credit cycles (cyclical, communication and technology, and financials) contribute negatively to index excess returns. Other, more stable sectors (noncyclical, energy, and utilities) have positive contributions. Different signs of individual sector contributions are not surprising because changes in weights in the index are relative–an increase in weight of one sector results in a weight decrease for others.

DO AGGRESSIVE ISSUERS TEND TO UNDERPERFORM?

Our results suggest that, at the sector level, the negative relationship between debt issuance and credit returns translates into a performance drag for market-weighted corporate indices. Is this negative relationship between issuance and performance also observed at the issuer level? Do issuers that opportunistically rely on debt financing ("aggressive" issuers) tend to underperform their conservative peers ("moderate" issuers) over time?

In this section, we limit our universe to issuers successfully mapped to Compustat GVKEY identifiers. The Compustat database contains historical financial report data of individual firms. Using Compustat identifiers allows us to track debt issued by individual firms historically.[9] This reduced universe covers about 80% of the bonds in the original corporate bond index.

For each issuer in the new universe, we calculate *issuance rate* as the ratio of net issuance over past 12 months divided by the amount of debt outstanding in the index at the end of the period.[10] Because the amount of debt outstanding in the index changes and, in general, increases over time, we consider the rate of issuance of individual firms relative to the index. If a company issuance rate exceeds the one of the index, we classify that issuer as "aggressive"; otherwise, it is called "moderate." Panel A of Figure 5.6 shows the performances of market-weighted portfolios of aggressive and moderate issuers by broad sectors between August 1994 and July 2014. The portfolio of aggressive issuers underperformed the portfolio of moderate issuers in all three sectors. At the aggregate level, the average excess return of moderate issuers is almost double that of aggressive issuers. At the same time, excess return volatilities of both portfolios are similar. Panel B of Figure 5.6 compares cumulative excess returns of aggressive and moderate issuers. The underperformance of aggressive issuers seems to be persistent over time.

A possible explanation of the outperformance of moderate issuers is that this group might include many bonds downgraded into high yield (fallen angels). Indeed, companies downgraded below investment grade may be constrained in their capacity to issue new debt and therefore become moderate issuers. At the same time, fallen angels are known to outperform their peers after they have been downgraded below investment grade.[11] They should

Panel A: Performance Statistics (August 1994–July 2014)

Sector	Statistics	Mod.	Agg.	Mod.–Agg.
Industrial	Avg. Exc. Ret., bp/m	12.0	8.7	3.3
	Volatility, bp/m	163	154	49
	Information Ratio	0.26	0.20	0.24
Utility	Avg. Exc. Ret., bp/m	12.8	5.9	6.9
	Volatility, bp/m	171	165	61
	Information Ratio	0.26	0.12	0.39
Financial	Avg. Exc. Ret., bp/m	10.3	6.8	3.6
	Volatility, bp/m	151	167	82
	Information Ratio	0.24	0.14	0.15
Total	*Avg. Exc. Ret., bp/m*	*11.9*	*6.1*	*5.9*
	Volatility, bp/m	*154*	*150*	*60*
	Information Ratio	*0.27*	*0.14*	*0.34*

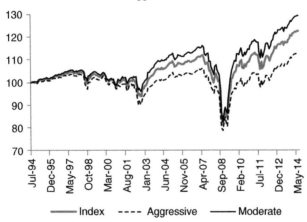

Panel B
Cumulative excess returns: aggressive vs moderate issuers

——— Index   - - - - Aggressive   ——— Moderate

FIGURE 5.6   Performance Statistics of Aggressive (Agg.) and Moderate (Mod.) Issuers by Broad Industry Sectors, August 1994–July 2014
Source: Bloomberg, Barclays Research

therefore contribute positively to the performance of the group of moderate issuers, assuming their capacity or willingness to issue new debt is limited.

Table 5.4 reports the performance of aggressive and moderate portfolios in each rating category. Aggressive issuers underperform moderate ones

TABLE 5.4 Performance Statistics of Moderate (Mod.) and Aggressive (Aggres.) Issuers by Rating Category, August 1994–July 2014

Rating	Avg. Excess Returns, [bp/m]			Volatility, [bp/m]			Information Ratio		
	Mod.	Aggres.	Diff.	Mod.	Aggres.	Diff.	Mod.	Aggres.	Diff.
Aaa–Aa	4.9	1.5	3.4	96	95	52.6	0.18	0.05	0.23
A	7.6	-3.7	11.3	130	147	82.0	0.20	-0.09	0.48
Baa	7.3	10.3	-3.0	156	163	52.8	0.16	0.22	-0.20
Ba–B	31.8	14.0	17.8	255	279	88.9	0.43	0.17	0.69
Caa– C	54.2	23.1	31.1	489	565	387.9	0.38	0.14	0.28
Total	11.9	6.1	5.8	154	150	60.1	0.27	0.14	0.34

Note: Diff. stands for difference.
Source: Barclays Research

across all ratings except Baa. The average excess returns of moderate issuers are over double those of aggressive ones, while volatilities are broadly comparable. This result is strongest for the Ba–B bucket, where the information ratio of return differential (moderate over aggressive) reaches 0.69. However, moderate issuers slightly underperform aggressive ones in the Baa quality bucket.

Results for Baa and Ba–B buckets can be influenced by downgraded bonds (fallen angels). Fallen angels are likely to be classified as moderate issuers because their capacity to issue new debt is likely to be constrained. Companies might partially lose their market access before a downgrade or could reduce borrowing to avoid higher cost of capital. Prior to a downgrade to high yield, most fallen angels fall into the Baa category and tend to underperform their peers. After the downgrade, fallen angels most often end up in the Ba–B rating category and generally experience a strong recovery. Therefore, excess returns of moderate issuers over aggressive ones are low in the Baa bucket and relatively high in the Ba–B bucket.

The fact that aggressive issuers tend to underperform moderate ones across most rating categories (except Baa) shows that the phenomenon cannot be explained by the presence of fallen angels only. Indeed, most fallen angels transit from Baa into Ba–B and so cannot explain performances in other rating categories.

Another possible cause of the poor relative performance of aggressive issuers might be related to differences in credit exposure. If moderate issuers have systematically higher spreads or longer durations than aggressive issuers, one could expect a portfolio of moderate issuers to outperform over the long term.[12] We therefore try to measure the relative performance of the two portfolios while controlling for issuer spread exposure, as measured by duration times spread (DTS).[13]

Each month we run a cross-sectional regression of individual issuers' excess returns on their DTS, distinguishing between aggressive and moderate issuers in broad sector categories using dummy variables.[14]

$$\text{Exc. Ret.} = \text{Exc. Ret. per DTS} \times \text{DTS} \times 1\{\text{issuance}\} \times 1\{\text{sector}\} + \text{Residual}$$

Estimated coefficients correspond to monthly average excess returns of aggressive and moderate issuers *per unit of credit exposure* (DTS) in three broad sectors. Table 5.5 shows that moderate issuers continue to outperform aggressive ones after controlling for DTS exposure. The outperformance is 0.38bp/month and 0.42bp/month for Industrial and Utility sectors, respectively. Information ratios are also significant with the exception of Financials, for which exposure-adjusted outperformance of moderate issuers over aggressive is relatively weak. These performance numbers

TABLE 5.5 Returns per Unit of DTS for Different Issuer Categories, August 1994–July 2014

| | Avg. Excess Return, [bp/m] | | | Volatility, [bp/m] | | | Information Ratio | | |
	Mod.	Aggres.	Mod.–Aggres.	Mod.	Aggres.	Mod.–Aggres.	Mod.	Aggres.	Mod.–Agg
Industrial	1.23	0.85	0.38	8.25	9.60	2.80	0.52	0.31	0.47
Utilities	1.14	0.72	0.42	9.05	10.10	4.31	0.44	0.25	0.34
Financial	1.22	1.13	0.09	7.87	8.99	3.52	0.54	0.44	0.09

Note: Mod. and Aggress. stand for Moderate and Aggressive, respectively.
Source: Barclays Research

are reported per unit of DTS (e.g., 1 unit of DTS would correspond to a duration of 2.5 years and a spread of 40bp). For an actual corporate bond portfolio, DTS is typically higher. Assuming a portfolio DTS of 10 (close to the current DTS of the US Corporate All Ratings index), these numbers become 3.8bp/month and 4.2bp/month, which is broadly consistent with the results reported in Panel A of Figure 5.6.

Are our results robust with respect to the definition of "aggressive" and "moderate" issuers? After all, there are other ways to measure issuer aggressiveness that do not rely on amounts outstanding in a bond index. In fact, our definition of an aggressive issuer is subject to two caveats. First, we define "issuance rate" as the ratio of net issuance to existing amount outstanding in the corporate bond index. As a result, large companies with relatively little outstanding debt could be classified as aggressive when issuing new bonds, although their leverage remains modest. Second, bond indices might not represent all liabilities of a firm, as they do not include private debt, bank loans, or credit lines from consumers and suppliers. Therefore, our results could be less relevant for companies that obtain financing outside of the corporate bond market.

We repeat our analysis using an alternative definition of "aggressive" and "moderate" issuers based on accounting data from issuers' financial statements rather than bond index data. Instead of looking at 12-month net debt issuance in the index, we consider the net increase in firm's liabilities divided by the total assets of the firm at the end of the 12-month period.[15] As a result, we obtain a rolling 12-month net increase in liabilities as a percentage of total assets for each company in our sample. Firms that grow liabilities at a higher pace than the index average are classified as aggressive, while firms that issue at a slower than average pace are called moderate. Figure 5.7 reports performances of market-weighted portfolios of aggressive and moderate issuers using this new partitioning by growth in liabilities as a percentage of total assets.

Similar to our findings in Figure 5.6, issuers that grow liabilities at a faster pace (aggressive) significantly underperform issuers that grow liabilities at a lower rate (moderate). The difference between average excess returns of moderate and aggressive issuers becomes even larger than in the previous case based on net debt issuance in the bond index. Information ratios of excess returns of moderate over aggressive issuers increase as well.[16] Results for financial sector are weaker, which is probably not surprising, given inherent difficulties in objectively measuring assets and liabilities of financial firms.

Panel A: Performance statistics (August 1994–July 2014)

Sector	Statistics	Mod.	Aggres.	Mod.–Aggres.
Industrial	Avg. Exc. Ret., bp/m	14.2	6.0	8.2
	Volatility, bp/m	161	152	43
	Information Ratio	0.31	0.14	0.66
Utility	Avg. Exc. Ret., bp/m	12.3	6.2	6.1
	Volatility, bp/m	162	190	90
	Information Ratio	0.26	0.11	0.23
Financial	Avg. Exc. Ret., bp/m	10.0	9.8	0.2
	Volatility, bp/m	179	136	67
	Information Ratio	0.19	0.25	0.01
Total	*Avg. Exc. Ret., [bp/m]*	*13.5*	*5.6*	*7.9*
	Volatility, [bp/m]	*158*	*134*	*39*
	Information Ratio	*0.30*	*0.14*	*0.70*

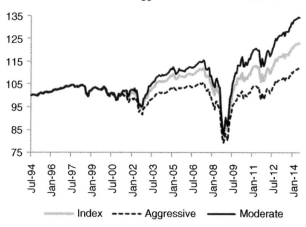

Panel B
Cumulative excess returns: aggressive vs moderate issuers

⸺ Index   - - - - Aggressive   ⸻ Moderate

FIGURE 5.7   Performance Statistics of Aggressive and Moderate Issuers by Sector Using Accounting Data (August 1994–July 2014)
Note: Mod. and Aggress. stand for Moderate and Aggressive, respectively.
Source: Bloomberg, Barclays Research

POSSIBLE DEPARTURES FROM MARKET WEIGHTS IN THE INDEX

We have shown in the previous sections that issuance dynamics is generally detrimental to the performance of market-weighted corporate indices. At the index level, dynamic sector weights contribute negatively to index performance. At the issuer level, aggressive issuers tend to underperform moderate ones.

We now discuss two possible departures from market weights in corporate bond indices that alleviate problems related to issuance dynamics. The first weighting scheme, implemented at the sector level, is designed to address the negative contribution to index performance from the dynamics of sector weights. This is achieved by weighting all sectors in the index equally.[17] The second departure from market weights is implemented at the level of individual issuers and under- (over-)weight aggressive (moderate) issuers relative to market capitalization-based weights.

Starting with sector-based customization, Table 5.6 reports performances of market-weighted, equally weighted, and equal-notional corporate bond indices. The equal notional sector allocation is very similar to equal sector weights. It should, however, have a lower turnover because changes in relative prices of corporate bonds would not lead to rebalancing. Results in Table 5.6 show that alternatively weighted indices outperformed the market-weighted one by 1.4 to 1.5bp/month (or about 17bp/year), with information ratios close to 0.4.

TABLE 5.6 Alternative Sector Weighting-Comparative Statistics, February 1994–July 2014

	Market Value (MW)	Equal Weights (EW)	EW– MW	Equal Notional (EN)	EN– MW
Avg. Exc. Ret., bp/m	8.2	9.7	1.5	9.5	1.4
Volatility, bp/m	155	155	13	154	14
Information Ratio	0.18	0.22	0.40	0.21	0.33
Worst Month, bp	–907	–1002	–95	–1007	–99
Best Month, bp	671	697	100	678	109

Source: Barclays Research

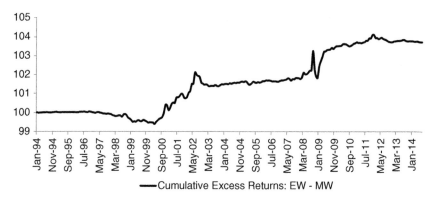

—Cumulative Excess Returns: EW - MW

FIGURE 5.8 Cumulative Excess Returns of the Index with Equally Weighted Sectors over the Market-Weighted Index, January 1994–July 2014 (January 1994 = 100)
Source: Barclays Research

Figure 5.8 shows cumulative excess returns of the equal sector weight index over the market-value weighted one. The former outperformed the latter by 3.5% from January 1994 to July 2014, predominantly during crisis periods and in subsequent recoveries. This is not surprising, given the sector weight dynamics discussed previously. More generally, investors could consider indices with constant sector weights as alternative benchmarks that reduce the performance drag associated with issuance cycles (dynamic sector weights) in standard market-weighted corporate bond indices.

Next, we discuss an alternative corporate index designed to underweight aggressive issuers and overweight moderate ones relative to market capitalization-based weights. We call this new issuer weighting scheme *contrarian*. At inception date, all issuers in the new index are market-value weighted, as in the standard index. Issuer weights in the contrarian index are then adjusted each month. The weights of aggressive issuers are reduced by the net percentage increase of their debt over the percentage growth of debt in the overall universe of eligible bonds. In contrast, the weights of moderate issuers are increased by the net absolute percentage changes in their outstanding debt over the percentage growth of amount outstanding in the bond universe. Monthly weight changes are limited to +10% or –10% of beginning-of-month issuer weights to avoid extreme changes in the index composition. New issuers are included into the index at their full market weights.

Table 5.7 shows numerical examples of contrarian issuer weighting for aggressive and moderate issuers. Panel A shows changes in market weights of an aggressive issuer. The original market weight of the issuer in the index

TABLE 5.7 Numerical Examples of Contrarian Issuer Weighting

Panel A: Aggressive Issuer

	Mth 0	Mth 1	Mth 2	Mth 3
Index Rate		2.0%	2.50%	3.0%
Issuer Rate		5.0%	8.0%	11.0%
Target Weight Change		−2.9%	−5.1%	−7.2%
Issuer Weight	5.00%	4.86%	4.61%	4.28%

Panel B: Moderate Issuer

	Mth 0	Mth 1	Mth 2	Mth 3
Index Rate		2.0%	2.50%	3.0%
Issuer Rate		0.0%	0.5%	−8.0%
Target Weight Change		2.0%	2.0%	10.0%
Issuer Weight	5.00%	5.10%	5.20%	5.72%

Source: Barclays Research

is 5%. The first row of the table reports the rates of issuance for the entire index. The total amount of debt outstanding in the index increased by 2% in month 1 while amount outstanding of our aggressive issuer increased by 5%. According to the contrarian methodology, the issuer weight is then reduced by 2.9%,[18] which is the excess issuance rate of our example issuer over that of the index. Panel B shows a similar example for a moderate issuer. The issuance rate for this issuer in the first month is 0%, while the index rate is 2%. As a result, the issuer weight increases by 2%.

Table 5.8 reports the performances of the US Corporate All Ratings index and its contrarian counterpart by sector. The contrarian index outperforms the market-weighted one in terms of absolute and risk-adjusted returns across most sectors. Contrarian issuer weighting almost doubles average excess return and information ratio at the overall index level. It also reduces excess return volatility slightly, even though volatilities of some individual sectors are higher than in the market-weighted index.

A practical problem with the contrarian issuer weighting scheme is high turnover and, hence, high transaction costs. This problem is likely to be exacerbated by the relatively low liquidity of the contrarian index compared with the market-weighted index. Newly issued bonds with large amounts outstanding tend to be more liquid than the average liquidity in the index. Underweighting such bonds is likely to reduce the average liquidity of the portfolio.

TABLE 5.8 Contrarian vs. Market Issuer Weighting in US Corp All Ratings, February 1994–July 2014

Sector	Market Issuer Weights			Contrarian Issuer Weights		
	Avg. Exc. Ret., bp/m	Volatility, bp/m	Inf. Ratio	Avg. Exc. Ret., %/m	Volatility, bp/m	Inf. Ratio
Basic and Capital Goods	11.9	136	0.30	19.1	163	0.41
Cyclical	13.3	203	0.23	17.7	284	0.22
Noncyclical	10.0	116	0.30	13.0	115	0.39
Communication and Technology	8.7	201	0.15	15.3	188	0.28
Transportation and Energy	11.9	152	0.27	12.3	107	0.40
Utilities	9.0	162	0.19	10.8	151	0.25
Banks and Brokerage	8.6	156	0.19	13.3	140	0.33
Financial Others	11.2	177	0.22	19.3	194	0.34
Total	9.4	148	0.22	14.7	146	0.35

Source: Barclays Research

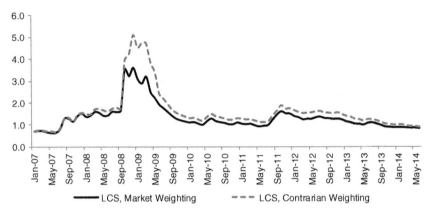

FIGURE 5.9 Liquidity Cost Score of Corporate Indices with Contrarian and Market Issuer Weighting, February 1994–July 2014
Source: Barclays Research

We can use liquidity cost scores (LCS) of the market-weighted and contrarian indices to verify this conjecture. Barclays has been publishing LCS of individual securities in the US corporate bond market since 2007. Liquidity cost scores are defined as estimates of a round-trip transaction cost, so less liquid bonds have higher LCS than more liquid ones.[19] Figure 5.9 shows that the average LCS of the contrarian index has been systematically higher than that of the market-weighted index, especially during the 2008 crisis.

The transaction costs associated with maintaining a contrarian index could be controlled in various ways. Portfolio rebalancing styles could include avoiding new issues of aggressive issuers, but then the average portfolio LCS would increase over time, or attempting to maintain liquidity and capture new issue concessions by replacing older bonds with newly issued ones.

CONCLUSION

We find that debt issuance tends to be negatively related to the subsequent returns of corporate bonds at three levels. At the macro level, high debt supply occurs in periods of low risk aversion, typically signaling weaker future returns. Debt issuance often slows in periods of market distress, which are eventually followed by recovery.

Likewise, issuance cycles cause sector weights in corporate bond indices to change over time. We provide empirical evidence that sector weight dynamics contribute negatively to index performance.

At the issuer level, we find strong evidence that aggressive issuers tend to underperform conservative borrowers. The difference in performance is significant and persistent over time. This result holds across broad industry sectors and quality buckets. Controlling for the credit exposure of individual issuers or using an alternative definition of issuance aggressiveness based on balance sheet data does not change our conclusions.

Possible departures from market-capitalization weighting in benchmark indices include imposing constant sector weights and overweighting moderate issuers over aggressive ones. Investors might also consider similar approaches as part of active strategies.

REFERENCES

Ben Dor, A., L. Dynkin, J. Hyman, P. Houweling, E. Van Leeuwen, and O. Penninga. 2007. "DTS^{SM} (Duration Times Spread)." *Journal of Portfolio Management* 33(2): 77–100.

Ben Dor, A., and J. Xu. 2011. "Fallen Angels: Characteristics, Performance, and Implications for Investors." *Journal of Fixed Income* 20(4): 33–58.

Ben Dor, A., and J. Xu. 2015a, January 23. "Concessions in Corporate Bond Issuance: Magnitude, Determinants, and Post-Issuance Dynamics." Barclays Research.

Ben Dor, A., and J. Xu. 2015c. "Should Equity Investors Care about Corporate Bond Prices? Using Bond Prices to Construct Equity Momentum Strategies." *Journal of Portfolio Management* 41 (4): 35–49.

Ben Dor, A., and J. Xu. 2015b, January 23. "Concessions in Corporate Bond Issuance: Magnitude, Determinants, and Post-Issuance Dynamics." Barclays Research.

Dynkin, L., J. Hyman, and V. Konstantinovsky. 2002. "Sufficient Diversification in Credit Portfolios." *Journal of Portfolio Management* 29(1): 89–114.

Konstantinovsky, V., K. Y. Ng, and B. D. Phelps. 2016. "Measuring Bond-Level Liquidity." *Journal of Portfolio Management* 42(4): 116–128.

Ng, K. Y., and B. Phelps. 2015. "The Hunt for a Low-Risk Anomaly in the USD Corporate Bond Market." *Journal of Portfolio Management* 42(1): 63–84.

ENDNOTES

1. Active returns that can be generated by underweighting unwanted names are typically low because of benchmark composition constraints. The maximum underweight in a security cannot exceed its weight in the benchmark unless net short positions are possible. As a result, the strategy of underweighting issuers typically

generates lower alpha than overweighting favorite names. This is especially true in low-spread environments. See Dynkin, Hyman, and Konstantinovsky (2002).

2. Our analysis of issuance concessions showed that new corporate issues in the primary market typically are priced at a concession relative to their peers in the secondary market. The study further analyzes various factors that affect the size of the concession. The strategy that replaced old bonds in the portfolio with newly issued bonds of the same issuer has historically generated a positive alpha with relatively low market risk. See Ben Dor and Xu (2015a).

3. Combining IG and HY indices precludes situations in which issuers disappear from the universe due to a rating downgrade. This allows tracking individual issuers over long time horizons.

4. Customized sectors are defined to minimize issuer-specific effects. They are constructed by grouping together Class 3 industry categories of Barclays bond indices to ensure that all sectors remain sufficiently populated in our sample period.

5. We calculate net issuance in the index as the following: New Gross Issuance – Redemption – Maturing Bonds. The latter is measured by the amount of bonds excluded from the index with a 12-month lag as the index invests in bonds with at least one year remaining until maturity.

6. We use *end-of-the-period* amount outstanding (as opposed to *beginning-of-the-period*) to calculate the issuance rate. In the following sections, we calculate issuance rates for individual issuers, so using end-of-the-period debt will allow us to handle new issuers in the index. We use a similar approach at the macro level for consistency reasons. Using *beginning-of-the period* amount outstanding leads to the same conclusions.

7. Note that return differentials for the two subperiods in Table 5.2 cannot simply be recombined into the results for the overall sample because issuance ranking is implemented independently for each period in isolation.

8. This result is not shown in the figure.

9. In contrast, corporate bond tickers were not always suitable to track individual issuers historically. The mapping between our bond and Compustat universes is described in Ben Dor and Xu (2015b).

10. We measure issuance rate with respect to the amount outstanding *at the end* of the period to process issuers appearing in the index for the first time. The amount outstanding of those issuers at the beginning of the period is zero, which would not make possible to define issuance rate based on beginning-of-the period debt outstanding. This problem can be avoided by excluding new issuers from the sample. This alternative approach does not change results qualitatively.

11. See Ben Dor and Xu (2011).

12. Higher credit risk typically is compensated for by higher risk premium; see Ng and Phelps (2015).

13. Previously published research shows advantages of using DTS to measure portfolio credit risk. See Ben Dor et al. (2007).

14. We remove observations with extreme return realizations. Observations in the top and bottom 1% of the sample sorted by excess returns are eliminated.

15. Historical measures of firms' assets and liabilities are taken from Compustat, which stores financial statement data published by individual companies. We

take total assets at the end of the period to be consistent with our previous methodology of calculating issuance rate.

16. We also repeated the analysis of excess returns per unit of DTS for the alternative definition of aggressive issuers. Results are qualitatively similar to those reported in Table 5.5.

17. Essentially, the key is to impose constant sector weights, thus removing the influence of issuance patterns. Equal weights are selected here for simplicity, but other constant weighting schemes could be considered as well.

18. The reduction in issuer weight is obtained as the growth in outstanding issuer debt relative to the growth of debt in the index: $(1+2\%) / (1+5\%) - 1 = -2.9\%$.

19. See Konstantinovsky, Ng, and Phelps (2016).

CHAPTER 6

The Value of Waiting to Buy: Inclusion-Delay Investment-Grade Corporate Indices

INTRODUCTION

The Bloomberg Barclays Investment Grade (IG) Corporate index is a market value-weighted index representing all outstanding institution-sized, publicly traded issues that meet index inclusion criteria. As new eligible issues come to market, the index adds them automatically. Portfolio managers tend to like such issues, which typically have decent two-way trading flow and strong underwriter participation. Consequently, new issues may enter the index with a liquidity premium that dissipates as the bonds season. Must the benchmark of a long-term passive investor rush to buy new issues? Why not wait for new issues to season and cheapen?

Investors appreciate that standard index rules may involve inefficiencies that an alternative benchmark might be able to avoid. There is an emerging trend to move away from standard market capitalization-weighted indices toward a weighting scheme that allocates more weight to bonds with some desirable characteristics that have an expectation of better long-term relative value. For example, in Chapter 5 we explored the possibility of modifying index weighting schemes to seek constant sector weights and avoid aggressive issuers. Similarly, investors are increasingly adopting such alternative benchmarks as "downgrade-tolerant," "issuer-capped," "value-weighted," and "liquidity-enhanced" indices.[1] At the same time, such alternative indices maintain high long-term correlation with standard indices and so do not change the portfolio asset allocation scheme.

215

Along these lines, there is interest in an alternative index that waits some time before adding new issues—an "inclusion-delay" index. The underlying idea is to wait for any new-issue liquidity premium to melt away before adding the bonds to the benchmark. In this chapter, we investigate whether investors can indeed obtain an enhanced credit beta by adopting such an index. If so, how long should the delay be to generate enhanced returns? What exactly is the source of any enhanced returns? Is it avoidance of a liquidity premium, or something else? Also, does an inclusion-delay index have strong correlation with standard indices? If yes, such indices could attract investors looking for enhanced credit beta that maintains the asset allocation properties of the standard indices.

To investigate, we construct alternative IG corporate bond indices that wait X months before adding an eligible new issue to the index.[2] For example, if X = 3, the delay index will not include a new bond until the third month after it entered the standard IG Corporate index (a zero-month delay index). We then compare the returns of this three-month inclusion-delay index with those of the IG Corporate index. Importantly, a bond must remain index eligible before it can be added to a delay index. For example, suppose Bond A is announced in Month 0 and enters the Returns Universe at the end of Month zero. The three-month delay index will add Bond A to its index at the end of Month 3, provided that Bond A is still index eligible. If, for example, Bond A is downgraded to high yield in Month 2, then the bond was in the zero-month delay index for two months, then removed, but would not be added to the three-month delay index. Also, to be clear, we are measuring delay in months from the time that the bond would join the Returns Universe of the IG Corporate index. Consequently, we are ignoring any new-issue concession in the days around a bond's issuance.[3]

There are some complications when comparing inclusion-delay indices with standard indices. First, as we discuss in the first section, an X-month inclusion-delay index uses the bid price (beginning of the month)-to-bid price (end of the month) convention ("bid-to-bid") to compute price returns for all bonds, including new bonds entering the delay index.[4] This convention will tend to increase the performance of a delay index relative to the IG Corporate index, which uses an offer price (beginning of the month)-to-bid price (end-of-month) convention ("offer-to-bid") for calculating returns for new issues. So, we need to compare a delay index with a bid-price adjusted corporate index to remove any difference in returns arising from the difference in pricing conventions. For clarity, because the IG Corporate index has zero delay, we will label a bid-price adjusted IG Corporate index as the "0-month delay index." Consequently, all inclusion-delay indices discussed in this chapter use bid-to-bid pricing for new issues. The standard IG Corporate index (offer-to-bid) is labeled simply "IG Corporate Index."

A second complication is the inevitable contemporaneous difference in index composition between the zero-month delay index and any other delay index. For example, suppose immediately prior to Month zero there is a rash of financial sector issuance. The zero-month delay index will likely see a boost to its financial sector market value weight from these new issues in Month zero. However, this boost will not appear in the X-month inclusion-delay index for X months as the "natural" weight of its financial sector will be based on its then-current holdings of financial bonds. In other words, it will take X months for the boost in financials to appear in the delay index. However, if the financial sector outperforms/underperforms the other sectors during this X-month window, then it becomes difficult to compare the relative performance of a delay index and a standard index.[5]

To deal with this complication, in addition to delay indices with "natural weights," we construct delay indices with adjusted market value weights to reflect the same contemporaneous sector/quality weights as the IG Corporate index. We label these delay indices as having "adjusted weights." Adjusted weights match the market value weights of the IG Corporate index for 12 index buckets: three sectors (FIN, IND, and UTL) and four quality levels (AAA, AA, A, and BAA). So, for example, if the IG Corporate index has a 10% market value weight in A-rated financials in a particular month, then we use this same sector/quality weight for the X-month delay index for that same month. However, we note that the issuer/issue composition of the financial sector will likely differ between the two indices.

BID-PRICE ADJUSTMENT OF IG CORPORATE INDEX

The Bloomberg Barclays IG Corporate index computes returns using bid-side prices. However, there is an exception to this rule. New issues entering the index do so at the bond's offer price at the beginning of the first month of the bond's index inclusion. Thereafter, they are valued using bid-side prices. In other words, for their first-month return calculation, new issues follow an "offer-to-bid" pricing convention, referring to the offer price at month-beginning and bid price at month-end. After that, they revert to the "bid-to-bid" pricing convention used for all other index bonds.[6]

The offer-to-bid convention produces lower returns compared with those based on the bid-to-bid convention. Our goal is to adjust index returns assuming the bid-to-bid pricing convention in the first month. To make this adjustment, we use Barclays Liquidity Cost Scores (LCS).[7]

Let Month zero represent the month in which an index-eligible bond is announced. The bond will enter the index at the end of Month zero and will be part of the index's returns in Month one. At the end of Month zero, we estimate the bond's bid price using the bond's published offer price (i.e., index price) and the bond's LCS.

We estimate the bid price as follows: Let $LCS_t = (OP_t - BP_t)/BP_t$ where OP_t and BP_t represent a bond's offer and bid price, respectively, at time t. Let $t = 0$ represent the beginning of the month (i.e., end of Month zero) that the bond enters the index (Returns Universe). Given OP_0, the bond's bid price equals $BP_0 = OP_0/(1 + LCS_0)$. For LCS_0, we use the trader's bid-offer quotes, if available in the LCS database at Time zero. If not available, then we use the bond's published LCS value for Month zero (i.e., the month in which the bond is announced). If this is not available, then we estimate the bond's LCS_0 using the LCS extended coverage model, which estimates LCS based on a bond's attributes (including time since issuance).[8] The period for this part of our study is from January 2007 to August 2016, the period for which we have simultaneous trader bid-offer quotes and LCS values.

As an example of our bid price calculation, suppose a newly issued bond's $OP_0 = 100.2$ and its $LCS_0 = 0.200\%$. Then we estimate the bond's bid price, BP_0, to be $100.2/1.002 = 100.0$.

Once we have a bid price for a new issue entering the index, we can calculate its bid-price adjusted price return. Let $t = 1$ be the end of Month one. We calculate the newly issued bond's bid-to-bid adjusted monthly price return as follows:

$$AdjPriceRet_{month\_1} = [BP_1 - BP_0]/[BP_0 + AI_0]$$

where AI_0 is accrued interest at Time zero

$$= [BP_1 - OP_0/(1 + LCS_0)]/[OP_0/(1 + LCS_0) + AI_0]$$

$$= [BP_1 \times (1 + LCS_0) - OP_0]/[OP_0 + AI_0 + AI_0 \times LCS_0]$$

$$= [(BP_1 - OP_0) + BP_1 \times LCS_0]/[OP_0 + AI_0], \text{assuming } AI_0 \times LCS_0 \text{ is small}$$

$$= ReportedPriceRet_{month\_1} + BP_1 \times LCS_0/[OP_0 + AI_0]$$

For new issues, the bid-to-bid convention significantly increases their first month's returns compared with the offer-to-bid convention. From February 2007 through August 2016, the new issues' average first-month market value weighted index excess return was –11bp following the offer-to-bid convention but +42bp following the bid-to-bid convention, an average increase of 53bp.

To compute the adjusted index level return, we recalculate the beginning-of-the-month index market value weights for all index constituents to reflect the lower value of new issues entering the index at the bid price.[9]

Table 6.1 shows the results for the IG Corporate index. Applying the bid-to-bid convention to new issues over the sample period has increased index monthly total and excess returns by about 0.9bp/m, or 11bp per year, an approximately 14% increase.

Figure 6.1 shows the time series of monthly return differences between the bid-to-bid IG Corporate index and the standard, offer-to-bid index. The monthly difference is usually in the 0.5 to 1.0bp/m range, although it spiked to about 2bp/m during the global financial crisis, when LCS levels were elevated.

TABLE 6.1 USD IG Corporate Index Returns, Offer-to-Bid and Bid-to-Bid Pricing Conventions, February 2007–August 2016

	Offer to Bid (IG Corp Index) (bp/m)		Bid to Bid (Bid-adj. IG Corp Index) (bp/m)		Difference (bp/m)	
	Tot. Ret.	Exc. Ret.	Tot. Ret.	Exc. Ret.	Tot. Ret.	Exc. Ret.
Mean	50.7	6.3	51.5	7.2	0.9	0.9
Stdev	175.8	176.3	175.9	176.4	0.1	0.1
Annual. IR	1.00	0.12	1.01	0.14	0.02	0.02

Source: Barclays Research

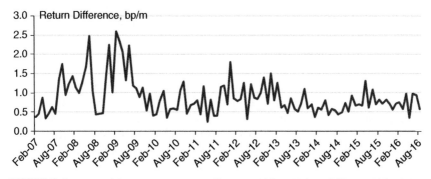

FIGURE 6.1 Monthly Excess Return Difference: Bid-to-Bid vs. Offer-to-Bid Pricing Conventions, USD IG Corporate Index, bp/m, February 2007–August 2016
Source: Barclays Research

TABLE 6.2 USD IG Long Corporate Index Returns, Offer-to-Bid and Bid-to-Bid Pricing Conventions, bp/m, February 2007–August 2016

	Offer to Bid (IG Long Corp Index) (bp/m)		Bid to Bid ("Bid-adj. IG Long Corp Index") (bp/m)		Difference (bp/m)	
	Tot. Ret.	Exc. Ret.	Tot. Ret.	Exc. Ret.	Tot. Ret.	Exc. Ret.
Mean	68.6	1.9	70.0	3.3	1.4	1.4
Stdev	307.6	283.3	307.7	283.3	0.1	0.1
Annual. IR	0.77	0.02	0.79	0.04	0.02	0.02

Source: Bloomberg Barclays Indices, Barclays Research

Table 6.2 shows the offer-to-bid and bid-to-bid total and excess returns for the IG Long Corporate index. The average monthly return increase from bid-to-bid pricing is higher at 1.4bp/m, reflecting the higher transactions costs of longer-duration corporate bonds. In terms of excess return, the bid-to-bid convention return increase is about 16bp a year, or approximately 72%, over the study period.[10]

INCLUSION-DELAY IG CORPORATE INDICES

The IG Corporate index typically adds eligible new issues in the month following their announcement date.[11] As mentioned earlier, to construct an X-month inclusion-delay index, we wait X months following the month in which an index-eligible new issue would normally enter the IG Corporate index before adding it to the delay index.[12] A bond must still be index eligible at the time it is added to a delay index. In addition, all delay indices use the bid-to-bid pricing convention for return calculations for all index constituents.

An inclusion-delay index with weights adjusted to match the sector/quality allocation of the IG Corporate index would require monthly rebalancing. For now, we assume that investors considering a delay index will likely choose natural weights to avoid these rebalancing costs. Later, when we examine the sources of delay index performance relative to the IG

Corporate index, we will look at delay indices with adjusted sector/quality weights.[13]

We calculate index returns for a variety of inclusion-delay indices: one month, three month, six month, 12 month, 18 month, and 24 month. We then compare the performance of these indices with the 0-month delay index, which, again, is the IG Corporate index with the same bid-to-bid pricing convention.

Table 6.3 shows the results.[14] In terms of total returns, we observe little or no advantage for delays less than a year. In fact, the zero-month delay index outperforms the three-month delay index by 0.6bp/m (51.5bp/m vs. 50.9bp/m) and underperforms the 12-month delay index by only 0.2bp/m. Apparently, waiting a few months does not enhance relative performance.

In terms of excess returns, the zero-month delay index also outperforms the one- and three-month delay indices. A bit surprising, perhaps, is that the one-month delay index underperforms the zero-month delay index by 0.7bp/m. If new issues trade rich, they seem to get even richer in the month following index inclusion. Not until six months have passed do the delay indices start to match or exceed the performance of the zero-month delay index. The 12-month and longer delay indices outperform the zero-month delay index, and with modestly lower volatility, as well. The 24-month delay index outperforms the zero-month delay index by a meaningful 3.2bp/m. Over the 115 months covered, this produced a cumulative return advantage of approximately 372bp. In addition, there is a slight reduction in the volatility of the delay index returns as the delay extends, producing a small increase in the annualized IR. The correlation of all inclusion-delay indices' total and excess returns with the IG Corporate index is 1.00, suggesting that an inclusion-delay index is a reliable source of market capitalization credit beta that investors expect for their asset allocation purposes.

We see similar results for the IG Long Corporate index (Table 6.4). In terms of excess returns, for delays of 12 months or less the delay indices match or underperform the zero-month delay index, while the 18-month and 24-month delay indices outperform, by 0.9bp/m and 1.1bp/m, respectively. The correlation of all inclusion-delay indices' total and excess returns with the IG Corporate index is also 1.00.

Apparently, delay indices do not start outperforming zero-month delay indices until well after new issues are reasonably assumed to have lost most, if not all, of their liquidity premium. So, what accounts for the significant outperformance of delay indices with delays of 12 months or longer?

TABLE 6.3 USD IG Corporate Index Total and Excess Returns, Various Delay Indices, bp/m, Natural Weights, February 2007–August 2016

Total Returns (bp/m)

	IG Corp Index (Offer to Bid)	0-Mth Delay (Bid to Bid)	1-Mth Delay	3-Mth Delay	6-Mth Delay	12-Mth Delay	18-Mth Delay	24-Mth Delay
Mean	50.7	51.5	50.8	50.9	51.2	51.7	52.4	53.1
Stdev	175.8	175.9	175.5	175.6	174.9	170.2	166.7	162.9
Annual. IR	1.0	1.0	1.0	1.0	1.0	1.1	1.1	1.1
Corr. w. index		1.0	1.0	1.0	1.0	1.0	1.0	1.0

Excess Returns (bp/m)

	IG Corp Index (Offer to Bid)	0-Mth Delay (Bid to Bid)	1-Mth Delay	3-Mth Delay	6-Mth Delay	12-Mth Delay	18-Mth Delay	24-Mth Delay
Mean	6.3	7.2	6.5	6.7	7.3	8.3	9.5	10.4
Stdev	176.3	176.4	176.3	176.6	176.5	173.7	171.5	167.5
Annual. IR	0.1	0.1	0.1	0.1	0.1	0.2	0.2	0.2
Corr. w. index		1.0	1.0	1.0	1.0	1.0	1.0	1.0

Source: Bloomberg Barclays Indices, Barclays Research

TABLE 6.4 USD IG Long Corporate Index Excess Returns, Various Delay Indices, Natural Weights, bp/m, February 2007–August 2016

Total Returns (bp/m)

	Long Corp Index (Offer to Bid)	0-Mth Delay (Bid to Bid)	1-Mth Delay	3-Mth Delay	6-Mth Delay	12-Mth Delay	18-Mth Delay	24-Mth Delay
Mean	68.6	70.0	68.8	68.8	69.3	69.5	70.0	70.0
Stdev	307.6	307.7	308.1	308.4	306.3	301.3	296.8	293.6
Annual. IR	0.77	0.79	0.77	0.77	0.78	0.80	0.82	0.83
Corr. w. index		1.00	1.00	1.00	1.00	1.00	1.00	1.00

Excess Returns (bp/m)

	Long Corp Index (Offer to Bid)	0-Mth Delay (Bid to Bid)	1-Mth Delay	3-Mth Delay	6-Mth Delay	12-Mth Delay	18-Mth Delay	24-Mthonth Delay
Mean	1.9	3.3	2.1	2.1	2.8	3.3	4.2	4.4
Stdev	283.3	283.3	284.0	284.5	282.8	280.4	277.4	275.0
Annual. IR	0.02	0.04	0.03	0.03	0.03	0.04	0.05	0.05
Corr. w. index		1.00	1.00	1.00	1.00	1.00	1.00	1.00

Source: Bloomberg Barclays Indices, Barclays Research

DRIVER OF DELAY INDEX PERFORMANCE: ISSUANCE DYNAMICS

Recall that we can construct an X-month delay index so that its sector/ quality market value weights are determined solely by its current constituents (natural weights). Consequently, its excess return in a given month may differ from that of the zero-month delay index because of structural mismatches, be they differences in sector/quality weights or in issuer/issue composition.

To illustrate, we examine the performance of the financial sector (see Figure 6.2). As we saw in Chapter 5, the financial sector's amount outstanding rose sharply while its excess returns were falling in the two-year period leading up to the financial crisis. Once the crisis hit, the amount outstanding in financials fell substantially due to defaults and downgrades to high yield. In addition, the market value declined faster than the amount outstanding reflecting the large drop in price levels. The financial sector weight for the 24-month delay index will lag that of the zero-delay index by 24 months. Consequently, the 24-month delay index did not see its financial sector MV% increase until the beginning of 2009, by which time the sector was starting to recover.

Figure 6.3 shows the cumulative monthly financial sector excess return difference between the 24-month delay index (natural weights) and the zero-month delay index, using December 2006 as the starting month. As the financial sector began to deteriorate in 2007, the 24-month delay index started to outperform for two reasons. First, the 24-month delay index was relatively underweight financials for the entire period of poor financial performance up to January 2009. By the time the 24-month delay index became relatively overweight financials, they were already on the verge of a strong recovery.

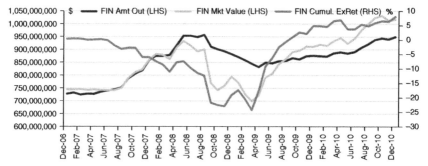

FIGURE 6.2 USD IG Corporate Index, Financial Sector, Cumulative Excess Returns and Amount Outstanding, December 2006–December 2010
Source: Bloomberg Barclays Indices, Barclays Research

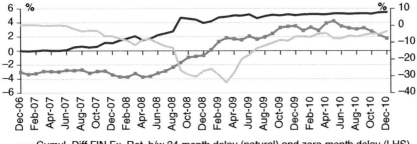

— Cumul. Diff FIN Ex. Ret. b/w 24-month delay (natural) and zero-month delay (LHS)
—— Diff in FIN MV% b/w 24-month delay (natural) and IG Corp index (LHS)
...... IG Corp FIN Cumul. Ex. Ret. since 12/06 (RHS)

FIGURE 6.3 USD IG Corporate 24-Month Inclusion-Delay Index Cumulative Excess Return Difference with zero-Month Delay Index, Natural Weights, Financial Sector Only, December 2006–December 2010
Source: Bloomberg Barclays Indices, Barclays Research

The second reason for the 24-month index's strong relative performance was the better quality of its issuer composition within the financial sector compared with the 0-delay index. Financial firms—in particular, soon-to-be distressed financial firms (e.g., LEH)—issued bonds before the crisis that the delay indices, to varying degrees, did not include until after the crisis or avoided altogether. For example, suppose LEH announced a new issue during July 2008. This issue would enter the zero-month delay index in August 2008, and the index would suffer the return consequences in September 2008 when LEH defaulted. However, the 24-month delay index would never include this LEH issue as it would be ineligible for inclusion in August 2010.

Both the 24-month and the zero-month delay indices benefited from the financial sector recovery in early 2009. Consequently, the excess return difference leveled out, but the 24-month index continued to do better because it was overweight financials during this sector's period of strong performance.

Figure 6.4 shows the overall performance of various IG Corporate delay indices versus the zero-month delay index. We would expect the one-month and the three-month indices to show much less divergence because their sector/quality market value weights are much closer to those of the zero-month delay index, and the issuer/issue composition of their sector/quality buckets is also very similar.

We have shown that the difference in sector/quality weights between an X-month delay index and the zero-month delay index affects their relative performance. What if we construct delay indices using adjusted weights? As mentioned earlier, an adjusted weighting scheme maintains the same

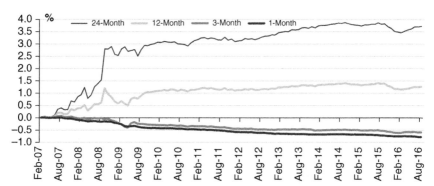

FIGURE 6.4 USD IG Corporate Index Cumulative Excess Return Difference, Various Delay Indices Less Zero-Month Delay Index, Natural Weights (February 2007–August 2016)
Source: Barclays Research

sector/quality weights as the IG Corporate index. Continuing to use the financial sector for illustration, Figure 6.5 shows the relative performance of the 24-month delay index using adjusted weights versus the zero-month delay index. Hence, the horizontal line for the difference in financial sector weights. However, while the sector/quality weights are always the same, the issuer/issue composition can still be different.

Note also that the financial excess return difference line in Figure 6.5 differs slightly from that in Figure 6.3. This is because of differences in quality allocation within the financial sector when using natural weights or adjusted weights.

Comparing Figure 6.5 with Figure 6.3 highlights the effect of the weighting scheme used in delay indices. Figure 6.5 shows that the cumulative financial sector excess returns for the 24-month delay index (adjusted weights) began to exceed that of the zero-month delay index in mid-2007. This is identical to the natural weights pattern we observe in Figure 6.3. However, unlike the delay index with natural weights, the delay index with adjusted weights did not benefit from being underweight financials when it performed poorly, nor did it benefit from being overweight financials when the sector performed well. Consequently, the delay index (adjusted weights) did not outperform the zero-month delay index by as much as the delay index (natural weights), as shown in Figure 6.6.

A comparison of Figures 6.4 and 6.6 suggests that the longer delay indices outperform the zero-delay index by so much because of larger differences in issuer/issue composition. A long delay index avoids adding new

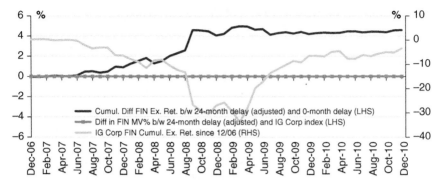

FIGURE 6.5   USD IG Corporate 24-Month Inclusion-Delay Index Cumulative Excess Return Difference with Zero-Month Delay Index (Bid to Bid), Adjusted Weights, Financial Sector Only, December 2006–December 2010
Source: Bloomberg Barclays Indices, Barclays Research

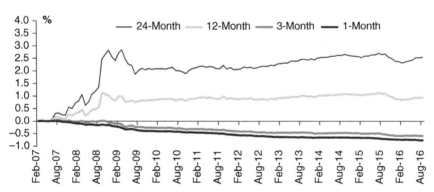

FIGURE 6.6   USD IG Corporate Index Cumulative Excess Return Difference, Various Delay Indices less 0-Month Delay Index, Adjusted Weights, February 2007–August 2016
Source: Barclays Research

issues from soon-to-be-troubled issuers. A zero-month delay index, or a short-delay index, has no choice but to include them. As avoiding large negative returns is often the key to success in fixed income investing, perhaps a long-delay index is a way to control the downside risk of new issues from troubled issuers that is a part of standard indices?

In the next section we analyze in more detail the strong outperformance of the 24-month delay index.

COMPONENTS OF DELAY-INDEX OUTPERFORMANCE

Figure 6.6 shows that a 24-month delay index (adjusted weights) strongly outperforms the zero-month delay index. Since February 2007, the outperformance has averaged 2.2bp/m in excess returns (9.4bp/m vs. 7.2bp/m). As discussed, much of this outperformance is likely due to the ability of the 24-month delay index to avoid including new issues that are downgraded or default (so-called problem bonds) in the 24-month window after standard index inclusion. However, is there any liquidity/seasoning component to this outperformance as well? While both components are legitimate parts of the value of waiting to buy, can we determine the magnitude of each component?

To do so, we create a "Clean" zero-month delay index (again, bid to bid) using adjusted weights. This index is based on the usual IG Corporate index eligibility criteria except that each month we peek ahead and exclude any problem bond from inclusion (i.e., any bond that is downgraded to high yield or defaults within 24 months after it becomes index-eligible). With problem bonds excluded from both the Clean zero-month and the 24-month delay indices, any return difference between the two can only be caused by factors other than avoiding problem bonds.

The 24-month delay index is a subset of the Clean zero-month delay index. The remainder of the Clean index is a "Young & Clean" index that contains all nonproblem bonds issued within the past 24 months.[15] Figure 6.7 summarizes the relationship among the three indices.

To measure the value of seasoning we could choose to compare either the Clean index or the Young & Clean index to the 24-month index. However, as the Clean and 24-month index both include a large fraction of seasoned bonds, their returns will tend to be more similar, except for the impact of the delay period from a relatively small set of bonds.

To measure the value of seasoning more precisely we may be tempted to compare the returns of the Young & Clean zero-month delay index with those of the 24-month delay index. Both the Young & Clean and the Clean indices are affected by the returns of newly issued (nonproblem) bonds before they enter the 24-month delay index. For example, if there is a flurry of new issuance as spreads are widening, the Young & Clean and Clean indices will tend to show poor returns relative to the 24-month delay index during this period. More important, however, if the issues recover (as we know they will as they are not problem bonds) after they have joined the 24-month delay index, then the Young & Clean index will continue to underperform the 24-month delay index as the Young & Clean index will no longer be holding these bonds while the 24-month index will enjoy their recovery. By contrast, the Clean index will still be holding these bonds and

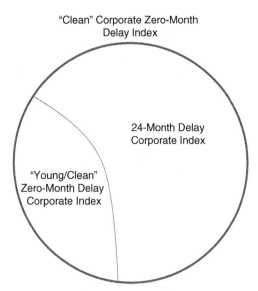

FIGURE 6.7   Clean Zero-Month Delay, 24-Month Delay, and Young & Clean Zero-Month Delay Corporate Indices, Schematic
Source: Barclays Research

will benefit from their recovery. Compared to the Clean index, the Young & Clean index performance will be more sensitive to the timing of when bonds recover any spread widening (tightening) shortly after issuance. Consequently, we would expect the Young & Clean index to be a more volatile index relative to the Clean zero-month delay index.

Since the Clean zero-month delay index is not as sensitive as the Young & Clean index to the timing of spread movements between issuance and inclusion into the 24-month delay index, the return advantage of waiting to buy is better measured by comparing the Clean zero-month delay index with the 24-month delay index over an extended period of time.

Ideally, we would wish to generate returns for all three indices (adjusted weights) as far back as possible to dilute the influence of periods of rapid spread widening/narrowing (e.g., the global financial crisis) on the comparisons. Yet, as we need bid-to-bid pricing for new issues, we are limited by the availability of LCSs, which go back only to 2007. To extend the results further back, we use the actual average return impact on a new issue when switching from an offer-to-bid to a bid-to-bid pricing convention in their first index month and apply this to all new issues prior to 2007. We separate bonds into intermediate and long maturity categories and use two different return impacts: +42.5bp for intermediate issues and +79.3bp for long issues

(we also adjust the bond-level index market value weights accordingly).
Using these estimates, we extend our analysis back to 1990. Table 6.5 presents the results.

First, as expected, we see that the Clean zero-month delay index outperformed the zero-month delay index, by 1.2bp/m (60.4bp/m − 59.2bp/m) in total return and by the same amount (6.8bp/m − 5.6bp/m) in excess return. This is the value of having avoided problem bonds over a period of 26 years.

What about the value of the seasoning component of inclusion delay? Perhaps unexpectedly, the Clean zero-month delay index also outperforms the 24-month delay index, by 0.3bp/m (6.8bp/m − 6.5bp/m) in excess returns. So, there was a −0.3bp/m disadvantage to waiting for bonds to

TABLE 6.5   Clean Zero-Month Delay, Young & Clean, and 24-Month Delay US IG Corporate Indices, Total & Excess Returns, Adjusted Weights, January 1990–August 2016

		Total Returns (bp/m)			
	IG Corp Index (offer to bid)	Zero-Month Delay (bid-to-bid)	Clean Zero-Mth Delay (bid-to-bid)	24-Mth Delay (bid-to-bid)	Young & Clean Zero-Mth Delay (bid-to-bid)
Mean	58.3	59.2	60.4	58.5	64.0
Stdev	151.9	151.9	150.0	140.2	167.8
Annual. IR	1.33	1.35	1.39	1.45	1.32
Corr. w. index		1.00	1.00	1.00	1.00

		Excess Returns (bp/m)			
	IG Corp Index (offer-to-bid)	Zero-Mth Delay (bid-to-bid)	Clean Zero-Mth Delay (bid-to-bid)	24-Mth Delay (bid-to-bid)	Young & Clean Zero-Mth Delay (bid-to-bid)
Mean	4.7	5.6	6.8	6.5	7.7
Stdev	115.2	115.2	112.3	108.1	120.2
Annual. IR	0.14	0.17	0.21	0.21	0.22
Corr. w. index		1.00	1.00	1.00	0.99

Source: Bloomberg Barclays Indices, Barclays Research

season 24 months before adding them to the index.[16] Over this 26-year period, it was not beneficial to wait for new issues to season before adding them to the index.

Figure 6.8 shows the cumulative return difference between the Clean zero-month delay index and the 24-month delay index. It also contains the option-adjusted spread (OAS) time series for the IG Corporate index (since May 1993). The difference in excess returns between the Clean zero-month delay and 24-month delay indices is sensitive to changes in the OAS level. In fact, the correlation of the difference in excess returns to changes in the monthly IG Corporate index OAS level for the entire period is –0.53. We observe that when OAS spikes higher, the Clean index tends to underperform the 24-month delay index. This may be due to rapid issuance from companies in some degree of trouble (but not problem bonds) whose spreads widen rapidly after issuance. If the bonds recover before the 24-month window closes, the Clean index's relative performance snaps back. If the bonds take longer than 24 months to recover, both indices benefit, and any divergence in relative performance is limited. This is why it is necessary to examine relative performance over long periods, to better measure the relative advantage of a delay-inclusion index by minimizing the influence of OAS spikes.

In terms of the seasoning component, the delay index underperforms long term yet has outperformed since 2009. Table 6.6 provides the details, separating the study period into two subperiods and excluding the February 2007–July 2009 financial crisis (and recovery) period. Although the 24-month delay index underperformed the Clean zero-month delay index by 1.0bp/m from January 1990 to January 2007, the 24-month delay index

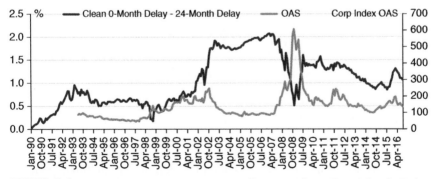

FIGURE 6.8 Cumulative Excess Return Difference, Clean Zero-Month Delay Index Less 24-Month Delay Index, Adjusted Weights, January 1990–August 2016
Source: Bloomberg Barclays Indices, Barclays Research

TABLE 6.6 Excess Returns (bp/m) of Clean Zero-Month Delay, Young & Clean, and 24-Month Delay US IG Corporate Indices, Adjusted Weights, During Two Subperiods: January 1990–January 2007 and July 2009–August 2016

	January 1990–January 2007				
	IG Corp Index (Offer to Bid)	Zero-Mth Delay (Bid to Bid)	Clean Zero-Mth Delay (Bid to Bid)	24-Mth Delay (Bid to Bid)	Young & Clean Zero-Mth Delay (Bid to Bid)
Mean	3.8	4.7	5.9	4.9	8.0
Stdev	58.0	58.0	56.4	54.8	60.1
Annual. IR	0.23	0.28	0.36	0.31	0.46
Corr. w. index		1.00	1.00	0.99	0.98

	July 2009–August 2016				
	IG Corp Index (Offer to Bid)	Zero-Mth Delay (Bid to Bid)	Clean Zero-Mth Delay (Bid to Bid)	24-Mth Delay (Bid to Bid)	Young & Clean Zero-Mth Delay (Bid to Bid)
Mean	6.8	7.7	9.1	9.9	7.7
Stdev	180.2	180.3	175.8	168.9	188.2
Annual. IR	0.13	0.15	0.18	0.20	0.14
Corr. w. index		1.00	1.00	1.00	1.00

Source: Bloomberg Barclays Indices, Barclays Research

has outperformed by 0.8bp/m since July 2009. This reversal in the 24-month index's relative performance due to the seasoning component likely reflects the change in the liquidity environment since the financial crisis. To the extent that trading activity has become more concentrated in new issues since the financial crisis, new issues may be relatively expensive compared with seasoned bonds, reflecting their liquidity premium.

Since July 2009, the 24-month delay index has outperformed the IG Corporate index by 3.1bp/m (9.9bp/m − 6.8bp/m). We can use Tables 6.5 and 6.6 to identify the components of this outperformance, summarized in Table 6.7. The change due to the switch from offer-to-bid to bid-to-bid pricing has the same average impact of 0.9bp/m for all three periods.

TABLE 6.7   Average Monthly Excess Return Difference and Return Components, 24-Month Delay Index Less IG Corporate Index, Adjusted Weights, bp/m, January 1990–August 2016 and Two Subperiods

Sources of Excess Return Relative Performance (bp/m)

	Jan 1990–Aug 2016	Jan 1990–Jan 2007	Jul 2009–Aug 2016
Bid-to-bid adj. pricing	0.9	0.9	0.9
Avoidance of problem bonds	1.2	1.1	1.4
Seasoning	−0.3	−1.0	0.8
Total	1.8	1.1	3.2

Source: Barclays Research

This similarity is due, in part, to the use of LCS values from the post-2007 period to compute the pricing adjustment for all prior months.

Interestingly, the benefit of avoiding problem bonds is also roughly the same for all three periods, a healthy 1.2bp/m on average. This is a reasonable estimate of the value of an active manager's judgment in avoiding such new issues relative to the index that has no choice but to buy them.

The most noticeable change in Table 6.7 is in the seasoning component. Prior to 2007, it was −1.0bp/m, suggesting that new issues did not have a liquidity premium and outperformed seasoned bonds. Since 2009, however, the seasoning component has been +0.8bp/m, indicating that new issues have underperformed seasoned bonds.

INCLUSION-DELAY INDICES AS AN ALTERNATIVE TO THE IG CORPORATE INDEX

What do these results mean for an investor searching for a better-performing credit benchmark (or an investment strategy) as an alternative to the Bloomberg Barclays IG Corporate index? For this question we assume that the investor will want to use an index with natural weights to avoid additional rebalancing to match the IG Corporate index's weights. The investor will allow the delay index sector/quality weights to evolve independently.

Figure 6.9 shows the performance since January 2007 of the various inclusion-delay indices (natural weights) against the standard Bloomberg

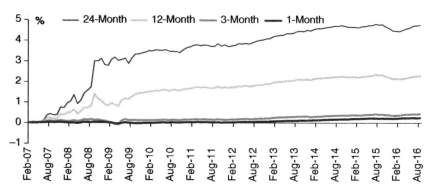

FIGURE 6.9 USD IG Corporate Index Cumulative Excess Return Difference, Various Delay Indices (Natural Weights) Less IG Corporate Index, February 2007–August 2016
Source: Barclays Research

Barclays IG Corporate index (offer-to-bid for new issues). This figure shows the actual return improvement if an investor were to switch from the standard IG Corporate index to an inclusion-delay index.

Short-delay indices offer little advantage. The small improvement in their performance is an artifact of using bid-to-bid pricing for new issues compared to the IG Corporate index's offer-to-bid convention. However, long-delay indices have done much, much better, even allowing for the difference in pricing convention.

Figure 6.10 shows the components of the 24-month delay index over the IG Corporate index since January 1990. The top line shows the cumulative excess return outperformance of the 24-month delay index. Over the past 26 years, this has amounted to 716bp, while the correlation of monthly excess returns to the IG Corporate index has been 1.00. The figure also shows the components of outperformance. The difference in pricing convention for new issues (i.e., bid to bid vs. offer to bid) accounts for 296bp of the cumulative outperformance, which probably cannot be harvested by investors unless their manager is very skilled at trading and can buy bonds at the bid price. The ability of the 24-month delay index to avoid problem bonds accounts for 432bp of cumulative outperformance, clearly making a delay index attractive for long-term investors. As expected, this component of outperformance tends to increase in periods of credit stress and remains fairly flat during quiet credit quality periods.

Finally, the cumulative performance of the seasoning component for the delay index is a very small, and negative, –12bp. From a seasoning perspective (bottom line), there has been no advantage to avoiding new issues in

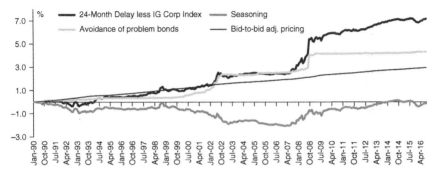

FIGURE 6.10　Average Monthly Excess Return Difference and Return Components, 24-Month Delay Index Less IG Corporate Index, bp/m, Adjusted Weights, January 1990–August 2016
Source: Barclays Research

their first 24 months since issuance. However, most striking in Figure 6.10 is the change in trend for the seasoning component beginning in mid-2007. While the trend had been clearly negative leading up to the financial crisis, it has become and stayed positive since the crisis, likely reflecting the high liquidity premium of new issues. Given the ongoing structural changes in the cash corporate bond market, this trend may continue.

Are long inclusion-delay indices realistic benchmarks that can replace the traditional market-capitalization IG Corporate index? As we saw in Table 6.4, the correlations of monthly total returns and excess returns with the IG Corporate index are approximately 1.00. In addition, a delay index using natural weights involves no rebalancing and the associated additional transactions costs.[17] The benefits of a delay index are avoiding adding issues from sectors or issuers who boost issuance just before getting into serious trouble and, as of late, avoiding overpriced new issues with an embedded liquidity premium.

One potentially problematic issue for delay indices as benchmarks is replicability. For example, can a portfolio manager replicate a 24-month delay index? The key question is whether the manager can buy at a reasonable cost bonds issued two years ago. Figure 6.10 assumes that "newly included" issues of a delay index are bought at the bid side. However, a bond's LCS is positively related to its age (correlation = 0.27) and only modestly related to its trading volume (correlation = –0.06). A 24-month-old bond may have an LCS 50% higher than the LCS it had as a new issue, which would add to the manager's cost if the bonds are added at the offer price, a cost not borne by the index. However, this additional cost for seasoned issues is modest compared with the magnitude of the delay index's outperformance. Also, some long-term investors may function as market liquidity providers and strive to buy seasoned bonds on the bid side rather than on the offer side.

Overall, the liquidity premium in new issues and the ability to avoid some problem bonds makes a 24-month delay index an attractive benchmark for credit investors.

REFERENCES

Dastidar, S., and B. Phelps. 2009, October 6. "Introducing LCS: Liquidity Cost Scores for US Credit Bonds." Barclays Research.

Dynkin, L., A. Gould, J. Hyman, V. Konstantinovsky, and B. Phelps. 2007. *Quantitative Management of Bond Portfolios.* Princeton, NJ: Princeton University Press.

Konstantinovsky, V., K. Y. Ng, and B. D. Phelps. 2016. "Measuring Bond-Level Liquidity." *Journal of Portfolio Management* 42(4): 116–128.

Ng, K. Y., and B. Phelps. 2011. "Capturing Credit Spread Premium." *Financial Analysts Journal* 67(3): 63–75.

Ng, K. Y., and B. Phelps. 2016, October 27. "The Value of Waiting to Buy: Inclusion-Delay IG Corporate Indices." Barclays Research.

NOTES

1. For downgrade-tolerant indices, see Ng and Phelps (2011). For issuer-capped indices, see Dynkin, Gould, Hyman, Konstantinovsky, and Phelps (2007), Chapter 13. For liquidity-constrained indices, see Dastidar and Phelps (2009).
2. We continue to allow upgraded high-yield (HY) bonds to enter the IG Corporate Index in the month following their upgrade to IG.
3. Concessions on new corporate bond issues are the topic of Chapter 7.
4. As will be discussed, an inclusion-delay index is not required to use bid-to-bid pricing for newly included issues. However, constructing delay indices using index prices, which are all bid-side prices except for new issues added shortly after issuance, produces delay indices that use bid-to-bid prices for return calculations.
5. In addition, there are modest contemporaneous differences in duration and OAS between the IG Corporate index and an inclusion-delay index. Not unexpectedly, these differences grow with the length of the delay, and are greatest for the maximum delay we investigated, 24 months. Over the period, the duration of the 24-month index was 0.27 shorter than the IG Corporate index and its OAS was 8bp higher.
6. In contrast, upgraded HY bonds entering the IG Corporate index do so at their bid prices. Note, also, that the Bloomberg Barclays High Yield index follows a different convention than the IG Corporate index wherein new HY issues enter the index at their bid prices.

7. See Konstantinovsky, Ng, and Phelps (2015).

8. From January 2007 to August 2016, there were 7,431 new issues. Of these, 3,659 issues had a trader bid-offer quote in the LCS database at t = 0 (i.e., the day the bond entered the index (Returns Universe) – end of Month zero). Of the remaining 3,772 issues, 1,037 had published LCS values for Month zero that were based solely on trader quotes. Of the remaining 2,735 issues (= 7,431 – 3,659 – 1,037), 2,724 had published LCS for Month zero that were estimated using the LCS model. This left only 11 issues whose Month zero LCS was computed using the "extended coverage model."

9. This results in a very small adjustment.

10. For the IG Long Corporate index, from February 2007 through August 2016, the market value–weighted average excess return for new issues averaged –18bp following the offer-to-bid convention, but it was +62bp following the bid-to-bid convention, a difference of 79bp.

11. For this study we used the "time from dated date" field in the index database to determine when a bond is added to a delay index.

12. We continue to allow upgraded HY bonds to enter the IG Corporate index in the month following their upgrade to investment grade, as per index rules.

13. Performance results for delay indices can be calculated for many different parameters and variations: with natural or adjusted weights, different delays, and different quality subsets. For brevity, we have chosen to report results for selected combinations. A set of appendixes including adjusted-weight results for the complete IG index as well as natural-weight results for quality-constrained subsets (A/Baa-only and Baa-only Corporate indices) may be found in Ng and Phelps (2016).

14. We commence construction of all delay indices well before January 2007 so that all delay indices fully reflect the impact of the delay beginning with the first month of returns (i.e., February 2007).

15. Clearly, neither the Clean index nor the Young & Clean index is a realistic performance benchmark, as both require looking ahead 24 months. These indices are purely theoretical constructs to help isolate the roles of different effects on the performance of inclusion delay indices.

16. We can see this same finding more sharply by comparing the Young & Clean index with the 24-month delay index. In terms of excess returns, the Young & Clean index outperforms the delay index by 1.2bp/m.

17. The delay indices (adjusted weights) require relatively modest rebalancing each month compared to the IG Corporate index, ranging from a monthly average of approximately 1.2%/m for the shorter-delay indices to 1.45%/m for the longer-delay indices.

CHAPTER 7

Concessions in Corporate Bond Issuance: Magnitude, Determinants, and Post-Issuance Dynamics

INTRODUCTION

The volume of corporate bond issuance since the end of the global financial crisis reached record levels as firms took advantage of the attractive interest rate environment and low spreads in the market. In 2013 alone, for example, corporations issued more than $1 trillion of investment-grade bonds. The issuance was met with high demand from investors, partly due to the relatively low liquidity in the secondary market.[1]

A key feature of the issuance process is the price (i.e., spread) at which the new bonds are offered to investors. To entice investors' demand, the bonds are typically offered at a spread that is wider than that of similar bonds from the same issuer. The "concession," or the difference in spreads between the newly issued bond and otherwise similar outstanding bonds, is a key factor in determining the level of investors' participation in any individual offering, and its dynamics at the aggregate level affects both the primary and secondary markets.

Using a unique database of bond concessions from the Barclays US Syndicate desk, we study the determinants of concessions accounting for both demand and supply side factors. We find that the magnitude of concessions is fairly predictable with only a few factors accounting for over 60% of the variation across issues. Next, we investigate the dynamics of concessions post-issuance and show that the typical discount relative to the secondary market is eliminated within a week on average. We conclude with an analysis that highlights the importance of concessions as a source of alpha for investors. Specifically, the newly issued bonds become part of the

Bloomberg Barclays US Corporate Index (and hence investors' benchmark) only on the last day of the month in which they were issued. As a result, concessions offer investors a source of alpha that is not reflected in the pricing of the index constituents. We find that concessions represent a very important source of outperformance and constitute about half the alpha a typical credit investor can hope to generate by employing various active strategies.

DATA AND METHODOLOGY

Concessions: Overview and Definition

The issuance process for a corporate bond starts typically with an announcement of the planned deal prior to market opening on that day and includes initial price thoughts, a spread range within which the deal is likely to be priced. The spread range is based on market conditions at the time and is set relative to a Treasury bond within the same maturity bucket. The difference between the spreads at which the new bond is offered and that of its benchmark bond (a corresponding bond with similar characteristics typically issued by the same issuer) is known as the concession. In most cases, the concession is positive (i.e., the issued bond's spread is wider than the benchmark bond's spread) in order to entice demand from investors.

Throughout the day, the syndicate tries to narrow the spread range as it gains a better understanding of the potential demand from investors. At the same time, prospective investors may revise their demand based on the updated range. At some point, a final indicative price range is communicated to investors, and investors' demand becomes firm. The deal is priced near market close, with the final spread typically falling in the communicated indicative spread range, although it can be materially different. Investors therefore bear pricing uncertainty as well as uncertainty regarding the fulfillment of their requested allocation.

To analyze the dynamics of concessions, we employ two separate data sources. Our primary source is the Barclays US Investment Grade Syndicate desk, which maintains a comprehensive dataset of bond issuance data, irrespective of whether Barclays is part of the underwriting syndicate. For each new bond, the dataset includes information on the issue date, issuing entity, size, use of proceeds, and magnitude of the concession as well as a detailed list of bond-specific attributes (e.g., maturity, coupon, rating, seniority, callability features). The concession is calculated as the difference between the (ask) spread of the newly issued bond on the offer day and the prior day (bid) spread of its benchmark bond. The benchmark bond is selected out of the issuer's outstanding bonds based on various considerations, such as maturity, seniority, size, and liquidity.[2]

Concession data in the syndicate database is not available prior to 2008, which limits our ability to study its behavior over time in different market regimes. In addition, the identity of the benchmark bond is not specified and cannot be inferred since the selection process is not fully rules-based.[3] As a result, we cannot observe the dynamics of the concession in the days immediately following the offer date or examine whether the spread gap between the newly issued bond and the benchmark bond is eliminated and over what period.

To address these issues, we construct a second concession dataset by combining (ask) spreads of new issues available from Bloomberg with (bid) spread data for the benchmark bond from POINT (henceforth the B/P database).[4] This allows us to extend our historical coverage of new issuance further back to the year 2000 and to increase the overall sample population from 1,218 bonds to 3,334 bonds (representing 876 and 2,643 issuance events, respectively). In addition, unlike in the syndicate dataset, in the B/P dataset, the benchmark bond selection process is completely rules-based.[5] This allows us to study the behavior of concession following the issue date.

Table 7.1 reviews the concession calculation process used in both datasets and reveals at least three additional differences. First, the concession in the syndicate database is adjusted for the maturity difference between the newly issued bond and the benchmark bond, whereas in the B/P database, the concession is simply the difference between the two.[6] Since the maturity of the benchmark bond is typically somewhat shorter, adjusting for it should typically lower the concessions in the B/P database as spread curves are usually upward sloping. Second, the (bid) spread of the benchmark bond in the B/P database is as of the market close on the day of the offer (day t), unlike in the syndicate case, where it is based on the previous day. This difference is not likely, however, to introduce any systematic bias as overall market spread is equally likely to widen or tighten. A third reason the (bid) spread of the benchmark bond may vary is that the B/P data reflects only Barclays' quotes, while the syndicate relied on multiple pricing sources.

In light of these differences, Table 7.2 compares various statistics related to the distribution of individual concessions in both databases. To allow for a proper comparison, the table also reports the figures separately for a subset of bonds in the B/P dataset that are also included in the syndicate dataset (shown in the rightmost column).

The median value in the Syndicate sample (9bp) is 3bp lower compared with the corresponding figure in the matched B/P subset, consistent with the lack of maturity gap adjustment in the B/P dataset.[7] In addition, its standard deviation is almost 50% higher than that of the Syndicate sample. Notice

TABLE 7.1 Comparison of Concession Databases

	Barclays Syndicate	Bloomberg / POINT (B/P)
Sample start	2008	2000
# Issues (bonds)	1,218	3,334
Rules-based benchmark bond selection?	No	Yes
Identity of benchmark bond	Unknown	Known
Adj. for maturity diff. btw. new issue and benchmark bond?	Yes	No
Concession definition	$ask_t - bid_{t-1}$	$ask_t - bid_t$
Benchmark bond pricing source	Multiple	Point

Source: Bloomberg, Barclays Research

TABLE 7.2 Descriptive Statistics for Concession Datasets

		B/P	
	Barclays Syndicate	Full Dataset	Subset Matched to Syndicate Sample
P_{25} (bps)	0	–2	0
Median (bps)	9	9	12
P_{75} (bps)	18	22	26
Avg. (bps)	13.28	9.97	12.86
Std. (bps)	20.98	30.57	30.26
% of Neg. values	12%	27%	24%
Corr. with B/P subset	0.53		

Source: Bloomberg, Barclays Research

also that 24% of the issues in the matched B/P subset were characterized by negative concessions vs. only 12% in the Syndicate sample. However, while the bond-level pairwise correlation of concessions between the datasets is only 53%, the correlation on a monthly basis (of median values) increases to 91% as shown in Figure 7.1.

Overall, these results suggest that the concession calculation in the B/P dataset resulted in a larger degree of noise, or measurement errors, compared with the data collected by Barclays syndicate. However, once the concession data are aggregated, most of the noise gets canceled out, and the

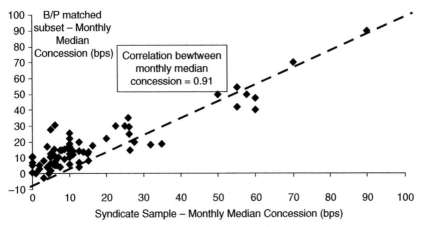

FIGURE 7.1   Monthly Median Concession: Syndicate vs. B/P Matched Subset
Source: Bloomberg, Barclays Research

two datasets are very similar. Hence, we use the Syndicate dataset for studying the bond level variation in issuer concessions and the B/P dataset with its longer history and broader coverage to analyze the concessions post-issuance dynamics.

DETERMINANTS OF CONCESSIONS

The pricing process of new corporate bond issues determines the magnitude of concession as a result of the balance of supply and demand for the new issue. We therefore divide the possible factors affecting concessions into three broad categories: supply-side drivers, aggregate/systematic demand, and issuer-/issue-specific demand. We present the rationale and definition of each factor and then estimate a multivariate regression to assess its statistical and economic importance via several scenarios.

Supply-Side Drivers

Perhaps the most obvious measure of supply is the issuance size. Intuitively, if demand for a good is downward-sloping, larger supply will result in a lower equilibrium price (i.e., larger concession). However, how should an issue size be measured is not immediately clear. Using the absolute dollar value is an obvious choice, but this measure also suffers from several drawbacks. First, the typical issue size has increased over time as issuers' nominal balance sheet increased. Hence, a $1bn issue may have been very large in the past but not in today's market. Second, a few very large deals may have a disproportional effect on the results, and distort the overall pattern. Third, intuitively, a $1bn issue for a company with a $15bn of debt outstanding is not equivalent to a case where a company with only $1bn in debt outstanding would issue that amount. Thus, in addition to the absolute dollar value (in log terms), we measure issue size as the percentage of issuer's outstanding debt ("relative size").[8]

Beyond current supply (represented by both measures of issuance size), the concession may also be affected by past issuance as higher overall supply may necessitate a higher concession. Even the possibility of future issuance may affect concession at present since investors will need a larger incentive (i.e., concession) to buy the current issue rather than wait and participate in the next bond offering from the same issuer. To represent the past supply of an issuer, we use the dollar amount issued by the issuer in the trailing 12-month period. To capture the likelihood of additional supply, we use a dummy variable that equals 1 if the issuer is a "frequent issuer" and zero (0) otherwise, where a frequent issuer is defined as one with four or more issuance events during the trailing 12-month period. Table 7.3 summarizes the supply side drivers of concessions.

TABLE 7.3 Supply-Side Drivers of Concessions

Factor	Reason for Inclusion	Variable Definition	Predicted Effect on Concession
Absolute deal size	Direct measure of supply in dollar terms	Log of total issuance size	+
Relative deal size	Measure of supply relative to issuer's outstanding debts, which proxies for passive demand (i.e., index fund)	Ratio of total issuance size to outstanding debt	+
Past supply	Less supply shortage	Debt issued during trailing 12 months	+
Frequent issuer	Higher likelihood of future supply	Dummy variable that equals 1 if issuer had four or more issuance events during trailing 12 months, zero (0) otherwise	+

Source: Bloomberg, Barclays Research.

Demand-Side Drivers

Figure 7.2 plots the median concession by year since 2000 (based on the B/P dataset) alongside the average spread of the Bloomberg Barclays Corporate Index. The chart reveals a clear association between the magnitude of the typical concession and the level of spreads with a correlation of 0.72.[9] Prior to the 2008 financial crisis, the median concession ranged between 5 and 10bp; it increased to over 20bp during the crisis and has declined consistently since then. This relationship is fully consistent with Ben Dor et al.'s (2007) work on Duration Times Spread (DTS), in which they found that spread risk (represented by spread volatility) is proportional to spread level. Since market uncertainty tends to increase with risk and is likely to result in lower demand for new issues (and lead to larger concessions), we should expect to see the positive association observed in the chart. Hence, we employ the spread of the Corporate Index as a proxy for market uncertainty.

Not only the level but also the direction of spreads is important when trying to capture market uncertainty/sentiment. To measure the sentiment in the overall market, we use the change in spread of the Corporate Index over the month prior to the pricing date, with spread tightening representing improved sentiment. In addition, we also try to reflect sentiment toward the issuer's particular sector by looking at sentiment to his peer issuers in a similar way (the change in spread experienced by peer issuers over the previous month).

Another factor that can affect demand for new issues is liquidity in the secondary market, through a substitution effect. When the secondary market liquidity is poor, investors seeking exposure to a certain "name" may do so more efficiently in the primary market. Hence, lower liquidity should lead to higher demand and consequently lower concessions. As a proxy for market liquidity, we use Liquidity Cost Scores (LCS), a measure of liquidity in fixed income markets based on traders' quoted bid–ask spreads. (See Konstantinovsky, Ng, and Phelps (2016.) Specifically, we use the aggregate LCS of the Corporate Index.

An additional determinant of the demand for new issues is the amount of cash available to investors. Higher levels of cash may lead to higher demand (or alternatively more competition among investors for a given supply) and hence lower concessions. We use data on in/outflows to/from investment grade mutual funds collected by Lipper to measure the level of cash in the hands of investors and separately account for the total amount of debt that matured or was called in the month preceding the issue date.

Beyond market-wide factors, the demand for a new issue may vary as a function of issue/issuer-specific characteristics. First is the intended use of the proceeds from the sale of the new bonds. Using the proceeds for

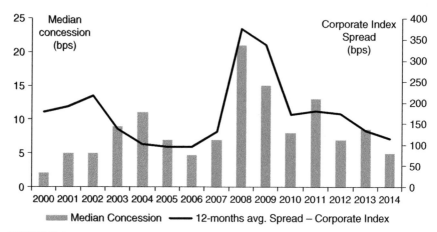

FIGURE 7.2 Median Concession by Year vs. Corporate Index Spread
Source: Bloomberg, Barclays Research

a corporate action (e.g., leveraged buyout) is likely to result in a larger concession compared with financing a business expansion. Second, the issuer's credit rating and industry group may play a role if investors have certain preferences (e.g., avoiding financial issuers after the 2008 financial crisis). Similarly, concessions may also vary as a function of the bond maturity as different parts of the spread curve may have specific investors.

The last driver we consider is the spread of the issuer, which reflects issuer-specific uncertainty. However, unlike aggregate market spreads, which can be considered as largely exogenous, the issuer's spread immediately prior to the pricing date can be endogenous as it may already incorporate expectations of the new issue concession. To avoid the problem associated with the endogeneity in our regression analysis we use the spread of the issuer measured 15 business days prior to the pricing date. Table 7.4 summarizes the demand side drivers of concessions.

Analyzing the Determinants of Concessions

Table 7.5 reports the average and median concession by key issuance characteristics, such as credit rating, industry, use of proceeds, and issuance size. The table suggests that issuance size was positively related to the magnitude of concessions. The median concession in the smallest issuance size quintile (less than \$400mn) was 6bp, less than half the median concession in the largest issuance size quintile (greater than \$2,000mn). The difference between the two groups was both statistically and economically significant. Except for issuance size, the relation between issuance characteristics and

TABLE 7.4 Demand Side Drivers of Concessions

Factor	Reason for Inclusion	Variable Definition	Predicted Effect on Concession
Market Wide			
Market uncertainty	Uncertainty (spread volatility) proportional to spread (DTS paradigm). Higher uncertainty should lead to lower demand	Corporate Index spread 1 day prior to pricing date	+
Market sentiment	Positive market sentiment should lead to higher demand	Corporate Index spread change in month prior to pricing date	+
Sentiment to peers	Positive sentiment to issuer's peers may lead to higher demand	Peer spread change over previous 3 months	+
Secondary market liquidity	New bonds are substitutes to outstanding bonds. Worse secondary market liquidity should increase demand for new issues	LCS in month prior to pricing date	−
Cash available to Investors	Demand may increase with level of cash available to investors	Bond redemption (redeemed or called) and flows to IG funds	−

(Continued)

TABLE 7.4 (*Continued*)

Factor	Reason for Inclusion	Variable Definition	Predicted Effect on Concession
Issue/Issuer Specific			
Use of proceeds	Some issues may require tighter concession to entice investors	Dummy variables for MA, Financing, and Capex (Base case—GCP)	?
Issuer characteristics (rating, industry, maturity)	Investors may prefer/dislike certain characteristics	Dummy variables for rating, industry, and maturity buckets	?
Issuer spread	Issuer-specific uncertainty like market-wide uncertainty may affect demand	Issuer spread 15 business days prior to pricing date	+

Note: Flows to investment-grade funds are based on the average flows (as a percentage of total fund assets) over the four-week period prior to the issue date from Lipper. Data on the planned use of proceeds is available from Dealogic and is classified into four broad categories: Merger and Acquisition, Financing, Capital Expenditure, and GCP (General Corporate Purposes).
Source: Bloomberg, Barclays Research, Dealogic, Lipper

TABLE 7.5 Concession Size by Issuance Characteristic

	# Issues	Average	Median
Credit Rating			
AA and above	470	11.54	10.0
A	1492	10.04	8.0
BAA	1372	9.35	9.0
Industry Group			
Financials	979	8.00	8.0
Industrials	1862	11.28*	10.0
Utilities	493	8.91	7.0
Use of Proceeds			
GCP	1771	9.89	8.0
Financing	810	10.15	8.0
MA	152	12.39	12.0
CapEx	88	2.04*	5.0
Size Quintile			
1 (< 400mm)	696	7.30	6.0
2 (400mm–675mm)	609	8.46	6.5
3 (675mm–1,000mm)	710	8.51	7.0
4 (1,000mm–2,000mm)	740	11.75*	10.0
5 (>2,000mm)	579	14.28*	13.0

Note: GCP: general corporate purpose; Financing: repay debt and refinancing; MA: merger and acquisition; CapEx: capital expenditure.*denotes that the difference from the first group is statistically significant.
Source: Bloomberg, Dealogic, Barclays Research

concessions were less clear, sometimes counterintuitive. For example, the median concession of bonds rated as AA or above was higher than for bonds with lower ratings, although the difference was small (1–2bp) and statistically insignificant. This likely reflects the fact that the typical issue size of highly rated issuers was much larger than that of lower-rated issuers. Hence, this pattern reflects the effect of issuance size, not rating.

To understand the marginal effect of each of the supply and demand factors we identified, we employ a multivariable regression approach in which the size of the concession in each issue is regressed against the complete set of factors we listed earlier. The regression results are reported in Table 7.6, while Table 7.7 illustrates the economic significance of the results using several scenarios.

TABLE 7.6   Estimated Regression Coefficients for Drivers of Issuer Concessions

Jan. 2008–Feb. 2014	Syndicate Concession	
Driver	Coef.	t-stat.
Intercept	−73.46	−8.13***
Supply Factors		
Abs. issue size (log)	5.21	9.05***
Ratio of issue size to debt outstanding	3.19	3.00***
Frequent issuer?	2.37	1.88*
Past issuance size (log)	0.12	1.72*
Demand Factors—Market Specific		
Corporate Index OAS$_{d-1}$	0.16	10.68***
Corporate Index OAS Change$_{t-1,t}$	0.12	5.87***
LCS$_{t-1}$	−0.15	−4.54***
Three-month peer spread diff.	0.01	0.93
Bond redemption (prior month in log)	−2.83	−1.29
Flows to IG funds (4wk avg., % total assets)	−5.65	−1.87*
Demand Factors—Issue/Issuer Specific		
Use of Proceeds Dummies		
MA deal?	−2.95	−1.67*
Financing deal?	−4.38	−4.33***
Capex deal?	−2.52	−0.69
Maturity Dummies		
Less than or equal to 5yr	0.41	0.35
Greater than or equal 15yr	2.07	1.85*
Industry Dummies		
Financials?	2.15	1.88*
Utilities?	1.43	1.09
Rating Dummies		
AA or Above?	−0.92	−0.59
A?	−1.16	−1.09
Issuer Spread (−15d)	0.02	3.41***
# obs.	1218	
Adj. R^2	61%	

Note: The regression is estimated using Barclays syndicate concessions dataset over the period January 2008 to February 2014. *, **, *** represent statistical significance at the 10%, 5%, and 1% levels.
Source: Bloomberg, Dealogic, Lipper, Barclays Research

As can be seen in Table 7.6, the combined set of factors explained more than 60% of the total variation in concessions, with most coefficients having the expected signs, and many of them being highly significant. Of the supply factors we listed, issuance size (both absolute and in relative terms) had the largest effect. The estimated coefficients of the absolute and relative issuance size were 5.21 and 3.19, respectively, with t-statistics of 9.05 and 3.00.[10] To see the economic significance of these results, consider Scenario 1 in Table 7.7, in which an issuer with $1bn of outstanding debt plans to increase new issuance from $1bn to $2bn. This on average would result in concessions increasing by 7bp, of which 4bp are attributed to the increase in absolute issuance size. Past supply and the likelihood of a future issue also affected concessions as frequent issuers (four or more issuance events in the prior 12 months) offered concessions that were 2.4bp higher on average.

With respect to market-wide demand factors, market uncertainty and sentiment had the largest effect on concessions, both economically and statistically, with t-statistics of 10.68 and 5.87, respectively. For example, in a case where the spread of the corporate index widens from 100bp a month ago to 120bp on the day just prior to the pricing date, an issuer would need to offer 5.5bp more in concessions compared with the previous month. However, as spread widening is often associated with deteriorating liquidity in the secondary market, part of the increase in concessions (3bp) would be offset.[11] The two proxies for the cash available to investors had the expected sign as more cash in hand led to lower concessions. However, the estimated coefficients were neither economically nor statistically insignificant. For example, the estimated coefficient for flows into investment-grade funds was statistically significant, but a 10% inflow, which is very large by historical standard, would only reduce concession by 0.6bp.

Compared with the market-wide demand factors, issue/issuer-specific factors explained less of the variation in concessions. Out of the 10 variables used, only four were statistically significant at the 10% level, in contrast to seven out of the 10 market-wide demand factors. Furthermore, the issuer's spread, while significant, had a much smaller effect on concessions than that of the market spread. Its estimated coefficient was only 0.02, one-eighth of the estimated coefficient of market spread. Issues classified as financing deals offered concessions lower by 4.4bp compared with otherwise similar general corporate purpose (GCP) issues (the difference is statistically significant) since most financing deals did not increase or even lower the issuer leverage. However, issues classified as Merger and Acquisitions also offered lower concessions, although they typically result in higher leverage. Notice, however, that these results lack power (insignificant t-stats) due to the limited number of Merger and Acquisitions issues in the sample relative to

TABLE 7.7   Economic Significance of Concession Drivers

Factors	Change in Factors	Estimated Coef.	Predicted Effect on Concession
Scenario 1:	Issuer with $1bn debt outstanding plans to increase issuance size from $1bn to $2bn		
Issuance size (log)	0.69	5.21	3.63
Issuance to secondary ratio	1	3.19	3.17
Total effect (bp)			6.79
Scenario 2:	Corporate Index spread widens from 100bps/month before issue to 120bps day prior		
IG spread level (bp)	20	0.16	3.13
IG spread change (bp)	20	0.12	2.4
Total effect (bp)			5.53
Scenario 3:	Secondary market illiquidity increases (LCS increases 10bp)		
LCS level	+10bp	−0.15	−1.52
Total effect (bp)			−1.52

Source: Bloomberg, Barclays Research

other types of issues. In terms of industry, financial issuers offered 2.2bp more in concessions compared with industrial or utility issuers. This result may be attributed to the relatively short period spanned by our sample and the dominance of the 2008–2009 crisis years.

How useful is our regression model when it comes to explaining (or predicting) the concession in specific issues? Table 7.8 presents two such examples, the GE Capital 1.5% 3y issued on 7/9/2013 (cusip 36962G6Z), and the Verizon 6.55% 30y issued on 09/11/2013 (cusip 92343VBT). The table displays their key characteristics, the model imputed concession value and the realized concession.

In the case of the GE bond (A-rated), the model imputed value was very similar to the concession observed in practice (14.7 vs. 15.0bp, respectively). For the Baa-rated Verizon bond, the difference is much larger (68bp vs. 90bp, respectively). However, the Verizon issue was the largest ever and included multiple bonds. If one were to calculate the size-weighted concession for the entire issue, the concession was 74bp, more in line with our model prediction.[12] The remaining difference can be attributed to the unusual size of the issue that in effect required the model to extrapolate beyond

TABLE 7.8 Predicting Concessions Using the Regression Coefficients

Issue	Total Size ($Bln)	Ratio of Issue Size to Debt Outstanding	Freq. Issuer?	User of Proceeds	Debt Issued over Trailing 12-Months ($ Bln)	Market Spread Prior to Issue Date (bps)	Market Spread Change over Month prior to Issue Date (bps)	Previous Month LCS (bps)	Concession (bps) Predicted	Realized
GE Capital 1.5% 3Y issued 7/9/2013	1.25	0.01	Yes	GCP	17.8	148	+9.7	93	14.7	15
Verizon 6.55% 30Y Issued 09/11/2013	45	1.34	No	M&A	4.5	142	+4.6	90	68	90

Source: Bloomberg, Barclays Research

the range of the data used for estimating the coefficients, although the issue was part of our dataset.

Post-Issuance Dynamics, Secondary Bonds, and Alpha   The findings on the average size of concessions reported in the previous section bring up several questions: What are the dynamics of issuer concession post-issuance? Do they disappear on the day following the issue date, or do they still trade cheap compared with the benchmark bond for some time? Moreover, does primary issuance affect an issuer's outstanding (i.e., secondary) bonds? Finally, do concessions represent an important source of alpha for investors?

Post-Issuance Concession Dynamics   Figure 7.3 plots the dynamics of concessions over the 20 trading days post-issuance using the B/P dataset. The figure indicates that the median concession tightened from 9bp on the pricing date to 3bp at the end of the first trading date and to 2bp after a week but did not decline any further.

To understand why the concession did not converge to zero, recall that the newly issued bonds typically had a slightly longer maturity than their benchmark bonds, and the concession calculation did not adjust for the maturity gap. In addition, the data used to compute the concession (or spread difference) after the issue date came from POINT, which only reports bid quotes. Hence, unlike the concession figures used so far, which were based on (ask) spread of a new bond minus (bid) spread of the benchmark, the post-issuance concession was calculated as bid spread minus bid spread.

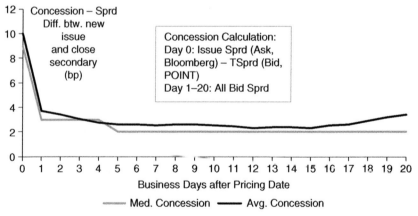

FIGURE 7.3   Post-Issuance Concession Dynamics
Source: Bloomberg, Barclays Research

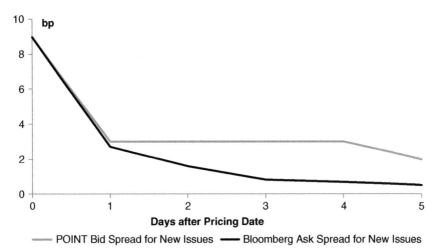

FIGURE 7.4   Effect of Bid/Ask Spread on Convergence of Concessions
Note: The benchmark bond spread is based on bid data from POINT. The new issue spread after the issue date is either ask spread from Bloomberg or bid spread from POINT.
Source: Bloomberg, Barclays Research

To see the effect of the transition from ask spread to bid spread for the new issue, Figure 7.4 plots the same post-issuance concession dynamics for a subset of the new issues for which we can find ask spread data on Bloomberg. The chart presents both the POINT concession (bid minus bid) and a new concession value based on the ask spread obtained from Bloomberg for the new issue. Not surprisingly, the new concession is lower than the concession figure based on the POINT data. Unlike in Figure 7.3, the concession (based on the Bloomberg data) keeps declining after Day 1 to as low as 0.5bp one week after the pricing date. Given the maturity gap is still affecting our calculations, these results suggest that the relative "cheapness" of the new issue almost completely disappeared on the first day of trading.

Spread Behavior of Secondary Bonds   The size of the primary issuance may not only affect the magnitude of concessions demanded by investors but also cause the spread of the issuer's outstanding bonds at the time of the issue (i.e., secondary bonds) to widen via two channels. First, even if the issuer's credit rating is unchanged, the market may view the issue's leverage as increasing (e.g., depending on the intended use of the proceeds), leading to a higher spread. Second, there may also be a transient liquidity effect due to the imbalance between supply and investor demand. In such a case, the spread widening would be reversed within a short time after the issue date.

A good example of the latter dynamic could be observed in the Verizon $45bn issue that took place in September 2013. Figure 7.5 shows the aggregate (market-weighted) absolute spread of Verizon's outstanding bonds at the time of the issue and relative to peer bonds during a 40-day window centered on the issue date.[13] The chart indicates that the spread of Verizon bonds started to widen nine days prior to the issue, reaching 190bp just before the issue day. The close resemblance between the absolute and relative spread series indicates that the widening was not market driven but specific to Verizon. Overall, its bonds widened by about 80bp in just eight days. However, notice that relative spreads started to tighten immediately following the offer, declining by a total of 40bp, roughly half the magnitude of the initial widening. This reversal pattern highlights the large but transient nature of the demand/supply imbalance in this issue.

The results shown in Figure 7.5 are not typical, however. Panel A of Figure 7.6 plots the median relative spread as a function of issue size during a longer window of eight weeks centered on the issue date. The plot suggests that the mean-reversion pattern was limited to the largest 10 issues in our sample (> $9bn). In all other issues, secondary spreads continued to widen after the pricing date, suggesting that the market underreacted prior to the pricing date. In fact, the underreaction was smaller (in percentage of total spread increase) for the larger issues (Figure 7.6 Panel B).

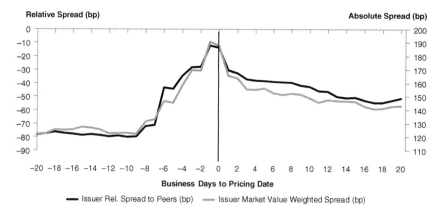

FIGURE 7.5 Spread of Verizon Outstanding Bonds during the September 2013 Issue
Source: Bloomberg, Barclays Research

Panel A

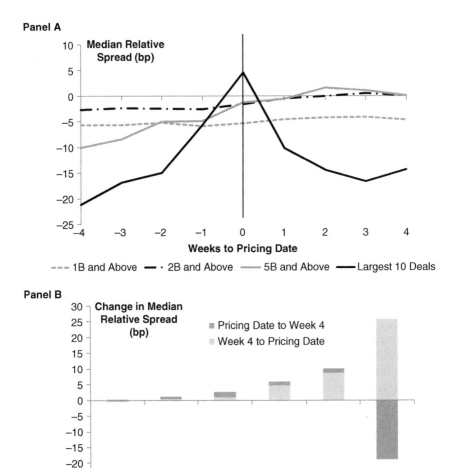

FIGURE 7.6 Dynamic of Issuers' Secondary Bond Spread by Size
Source: Bloomberg, Barclays Research

Concessions as a Source of Alpha The magnitude of concessions (and their post-issuance dynamics) and the fact that the newly issued bonds become part of the Bloomberg Barclays Corporate Index only on the last day of the month in which they were issued implies that concessions may represent a valuable source of alpha for credit portfolio managers. To understand the magnitude of alpha they offer in comparison to typical strategies employed by credit managers, we need to first quantify the magnitude of alpha offered by concessions.

Consider an investor who holds a portfolio mimicking the Bloomberg Barclays Corporate index and replaces secondary bonds with new issues monthly. What would the outperformance, "alpha," be relative to the Corporate index? The alpha offered by a single issue i is equal to:

Alpha of new issue i $\cong$ Concession $\times$ Spread duration$_i$ $\times$ MV$_i$ / MV of Corporate index

Assuming our manager is allocated bonds in proportion to the portfolio (i.e., the market) weights, alpha will equal the cumulative alpha offered by concessions.

Figure 7.7 shows that concession constituted an important alpha source with an average of 14bp/year since 2008. In particular, in 2008 and 2009, the alpha generated by concessions was above 20bp.

Next, we compare these figures to estimates of alpha generated by common credit strategies employed by portfolio managers. Desclée, Dynkin, Hyman, Maitra, and Polbennikov (2014) examined the time dynamics of credit active returns focusing on three specific strategies: market timing, sector rotation, and issuer selection.[14]

Table 7.9, which is taken from their study, reports the average alpha, volatility, and information ratio for these strategies for different time periods, assuming "typical" levels of skill. The table shows that since 2000, the magnitude of alpha generated by concession was comparable to that generated by market timing and sector rotation. Issuer selection generated much higher alpha due to the fact that the "breadth" of the strategy is much larger than the other two. Hence, the results in Table 7.9 suggest that concession

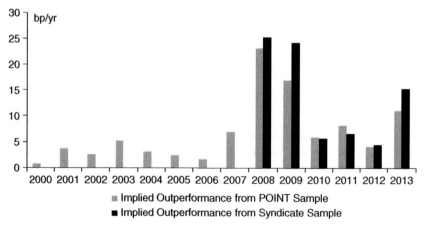

FIGURE 7.7   Estimated "Outperformance" Due to Concessions
Source: Bloomberg, Barclays Research

TABLE 7.9 Simulated Alpha with Skill

		Issuer Selection (5% skill, 20 issuers)	Sector Rotation (10% skill)	Market Timing (10% skill, 10% of Index)
1996–2013	Avg. α (bp/yr)	37.1	12.6	9.6
	Volatility (bp/yr)	96.4	67.8	47.8
	Information ratio	0.38	0.19	0.2
2000–2003	Avg. α (bp/yr) (Avg. Index OAS : 164bp)	48.5	16	8
2004–2007	Avg. α (bp/yr) (Avg. OAS : 94bp)	15.1	3.5	2.7
2007–2010	Avg. α (bp/yr) (Avg. OAS : 296bp)	80	28.9	25
2010–2013	Avg. α (bp/yr) (Avg. OAS : 163bp)	31.4	12.8	11

Note: The table is taken from Desclée et al. (2014, Figure 14).
Source: Bloomberg, Barclays Research

indeed serves as an important source of alpha for portfolio managers, which because of the current index rules does not require "skill" in the sense it is needed for the other strategies. However, being able to take advantage of this source of alpha does require access to the primary market, which may not be equally available to all portfolio managers.

CONCLUSION

The results in this study have important implications for both investors and issuers. Not only can issuers predict to a large extent the cost (i.e., concession) of new issuance, but by changing the timing and some of its characteristics, they may also reduce their expected cost. For investors, concessions offer an important source of alpha that requires mostly access to the allocation process, unlike active strategies, which require investment skill.

REFERENCES

Ben Dor, A., L. Dynkin, J. Hyman, P. Houweling, E. Van Leeuwen, and O. Penninga. 2007. "DTS^SM (Duration Times Spread)." *Journal of Portfolio Management* 33(2): 77–100.

Desclée, A., L. Dynkin, J. Hyman, A. Maitra, and S. Polbennikov. 2014, May 27. "Time Dynamics of Credit Active Returns." Barclays Research.

Konstantinovsky, V., K. Y. Ng, and B. D. Phelps. 2016. "Measuring Bond-Level Liquidity." *Journal of Portfolio Management* 42(4): 116–128.

Konstantinovsky, V., and B. Phelps, 2012, May 10. "Implications of Constrained Broker/Dealer Inventories for Corporate Market Liquidity." Barclays Research.

NOTES

1. Konstantinovsky and Phelps (2012) document the decline in US corporate bond market liquidity as dealer inventories have fallen since 2008 in response to various regulatory changes. They estimate that the inventory decline led to an 18% drop in illiquidity, which translates to approximately 13bp/year in additional transaction cost for a portfolio with 100% yearly turnover.
2. Notice that the calculation of concession in this way represents the profit or loss (after being converted into price space) from a trade that substitutes a secondary bond (short) with the newly issued bond (long).
3. The selection of the benchmark bond takes into account considerations such as liquidity, which are not defined using a rules-based approach.
4. POINT (Portfolio Index Tool) was a Barclays in-house portfolio management analytics software that was subsequently sold to Bloomberg.
5. The benchmark bond is defined as a bond issued by the same issuer, having the same credit notch rating and callability features, that is closest in maturity to the newly issued bond.
6. The issue-specific Bloomberg yield analysis calculator was used to adjust the maturity difference between the new issue and the secondary.
7. The average concession in both datasets is higher than the median, indicating positive skewness (i.e., the existence of outliers).
8. Defining absolute issue size in log terms reduces the positive skew (right tail) caused by the largest issues (this is important since OLS regression assumes that the errors [residuals] are normally distributed). In addition, the estimated coefficient would represent percentage change. Hence, an increase of $1bn in issue size would have a different effect if it is from $2bn to $3bn or from $14bn to $15bn.
9. At a monthly frequency, the correlation between spread level and concession size was even higher (0.89).
10. The value of the t-statistic represents the likelihood (probability) that the estimated coefficient is different from zero. Under the normal distribution, a t-statistic above 3 implies a probability of less than 0.001 that the coefficient is no different from zero.

11. The LCS coefficient (–0.15 with a *t*-statistic of –4.54) indicates that a 20bp increase would lead to a decline in concession on average.
12. Notice that our regression model is estimated at a bond level and not the overall issue level.
13. The relative spread was calculated for each Verizon bond using all Industrial bonds with the same rating (Baa) in its maturity bucket (<5y, 5–10y, >10y) and then aggregated based on market value.
14. Desclée et al. (2014) use the notion of imperfect foresight to represent skill. Foresight means that the manager exhibits skill at anticipating market direction. For example, a 10% skill means that the probability of overweighting credit exposure in a month with positive excess return is 55%, and the probability of incorrect positioning is 45%. An unskilled manager has a 50% probability of correctly anticipating market direction. Market timing is implemented by setting the strategy's active position to a constant 10% of the index market value. This means that Desclée et al. assume that the portfolio's active weight to credit will be either +10% or –10% in market value terms, depending on the directional view of the skilled manager. The sector rotation strategy is formulated as over-/under-weighting to one out of the three main industry sectors (financial, industrial, and utility) vs. the other two. The strategy is DTS neutral to avoid directionality on overall market performance and shifts predefined amounts of DTS contribution across the three sectors. The issuer selection strategy invests in a predetermined number of issuers with skewed probability of picking winners. Imperfect foresight is reflected in the probability of selecting issuers with positive idiosyncratic excess returns. The strategy samples from the largest 200 index issuers and allocates an equal DTS contribution to each selected issuer while matching the overall corporate index DTS. The results for this strategy are based on 1000 simulations every month to obtain cross-sectional distributions of issuer-selection strategy returns.

Performance Cost of Investment Constraints

CHAPTER 8

"Try-and-Hold" Credit Investing

INTRODUCTION

Many long-term credit investors may refer to their mandates as taking a "buy and hold" approach, in which investors buy bonds on a regular basis and hold on to them without exception until they either mature or default. The long-term return on such a strategy can be measured and analyzed in terms of the bonds' yields upon purchase (book yield) and the realized default experience.[1]

In real life, however, the majority of these investors do not actually follow this strategy. They may well buy bonds with the intention of holding them to maturity, but when credit deterioration strikes, they are often forced to sell the bonds at a loss well in advance of any possible default event. In so doing, they may prevent larger losses due to default, but they must record realized losses upon the sale of the bond. Investors in this situation do not necessarily view the risk/return trade-off of different asset classes using the same metrics as mark-to-market total return investors, who carefully measure month-over-month portfolio total returns and compare them with those of a benchmark. However, their performance considerations are also quite different from those described for the pure buy-and-hold case. The primary loss event in this case is not default but forced sales of degraded credits. We refer to this paradigm—in which investors buy bonds for the long term but may be forced to sell them upon some trigger event—as "try and hold" investing. In this chapter, we develop a framework for analyzing risk and return in such portfolios.

Our analysis of risk in long-horizon portfolios relies on long-term estimates of both the likelihood of adverse credit events and the severity of the accompanying losses. Probabilities of defaults and downgrades are estimated based on data collected and published by rating agencies. To estimate the realized losses upon a given downgrade event, we use the differential between the average spreads for bonds of different ratings. For investors forced to sell "fallen angel" bonds as they cross the boundary from investment grade (IG) to high yield (HY), we add an additional performance penalty to reflect the selling pressure typical in such situations, as demonstrated in Chapter 2. We then examine the extent to which both types of estimates should be conditioned on the current spread environment. We find that higher spreads are indicative of higher probabilities of downgrades and defaults over a horizon of about two years. They are also accompanied by greater losses in case of forced sales, due to larger spread differentials between ratings categories. These effects are mitigated by the higher spreads themselves, which generate greater returns for bonds that are held to maturity, and by the tendency of spreads to mean revert toward their long-term averages over a time frame of about two years.

The result of our analysis is a model for the return distribution of a corporate bond over a long horizon (e.g., five years) that depends on the current spread environment and the stated sell discipline for handling distressed securities. In this chapter, we present the basic elements of the model and supporting empirical research and show examples of the model's output for a single bond given different assumptions concerning credit ratings, spread levels, transition matrices, and sell disciplines.[2]

PURE BUY-AND-HOLD APPROACH

To motivate our model, we begin with a simple analysis of the long-term risk/return trade-off among different credit asset classes, using a back-of-the-envelope–type analysis corresponding to a pure buy-and-hold assumption. In this simplest possible view of credit investing, there are only two possible outcomes: either a bond survives to maturity or it defaults. In case of default, the recovery value is assumed to be fixed and known in advance. In Table 8.1, we compare bonds of three different credit ratings based on long-term average spreads, default probabilities, and recovery rates.

We assume a return horizon of five years and use historical five-year cumulative default frequencies from Moody's[3] to approximate the probability of default. A representative average recovery rate of 40% is assumed, such that a loss of 60% is assumed to be incurred with the specified probability. The expected default loss over the five-year horizon is then calculated as the product of the two. The analysis in Table 8.1 shows, for example, that the average 309bp/year spread promised by Ba-rated securities over this time period includes compensation for 122bp/year of expected default losses, leaving 187bp/year of expected return; for Baa-rated debt, the spread of 162bp/year carries an expected default loss of 23bp/year, for an expected

TABLE 8.1 Pure Buy-and-Hold Analysis of Expected Default Loss over a Five-Year Horizon

Rating	Spread	Five-Yr Default Probability	Recovery Rate	Five-Yr Expected Default Loss	Annual. Expected Default Loss	Annual. Expected Excess Ret.
A	1.10%	0.87%	40%	0.52%	0.10%	0.99%
Baa	1.62%	1.88%	40%	1.13%	0.23%	1.40%
Ba	3.09%	10.19%	40%	6.11%	1.22%	1.87%

Note: The fifth column represents expected loss from default over a five-year horizon for A, Baa, and Ba-rated bonds. Default probabilities are based on Moody's long-term average five-year rates from 1970 to 2012, and spreads are averages obtained from Bloomberg Barclays Corporate Bond Index data, adjusted to reflect the same time period.
Source: Moody's, Barclays Research

return of 140bp/year. By this analysis, the expected return differentials among the different rating categories are much smaller than those indicated by the average spread levels.

This analysis is overly simplified in many ways.[4] We have presented it to draw attention to two key issues that must be addressed to create a practical approach to asset allocation. First, this pure buy-and-hold viewpoint is not relevant for investors who are forced to sell distressed credits as a defensive measure to avoid default losses. We will demonstrate that when sell triggers are taken into account, the loss distribution has very different characteristics. Second, the analysis uses historical measures to represent both the return side of the analysis (as a historical average spread) and the associated risk (using rating agency data). To address an investment decision as of a particular date, a manager can easily adjust the spreads to reflect the current market environment. However, it is much less clear how to project forward-looking estimates of default or downgrade frequencies. Is it reasonable to use an unchanged long-term estimate of risk regardless of the market environment, or should estimates of expected credit losses show some dependence on spread levels? In this chapter, we develop an alternative model that focuses on the risk of forced sales due to downgrades as well as default losses. We present several empirical studies of the dependence of credit risk on spread levels and incorporate the results into the model's design. Finally, we use the model to illustrate the effect of the sell discipline on the risk/return trade-off for credits of different ratings and maturities under various spread environments.

TRY-AND-HOLD MODEL

The try-and-hold approach to credit investing seeks a middle ground between pure mark-to-market investing, in which the risk/return trade-off is viewed in terms of expected excess returns vs. the monthly volatility of excess returns, and the binary maturity-or-default analysis presented above. To achieve this, we maintain the notion of spread carry as the main source of return but key off credit transition matrices rather than just default probabilities to flesh out the set of possible loss scenarios that should be considered. We assume there is a ratings threshold that governs the portfolio and that a rating downgrade to below this level will require the bond to be sold. In such a case, the amount of the loss that will need to be written down is approximated using the difference between the book spread at which the bond was purchased and the average spread of bonds carrying the new lower rating.[5]

Table 8.2 illustrates how this approach can be used to evaluate the loss probability over a one-year horizon for a single Baa-rated bond. The top row of the table presents the average spread level for a given rating; the spread levels indicated are long-term average spreads[6] for Bloomberg Barclays indices of bonds with the indicated letter-grade ratings. The second row indicates the implied average spread change that a bond would experience upon a ratings change from Baa to any other rating. For example, it would tighten by an average of 53bp upon a one-notch upgrade to A. This logic would similarly suggest that upon a downgrade to Ba, the spread would widen by 147bp, the difference between the average spreads of Baa and Ba bonds.

This simple difference between the average spreads of bonds with different ratings, while intuitive, does not fully represent the losses investors are likely to realize from forced sales of fallen angel bonds that are downgraded from IG to HY. As shown in Chapter 2, the collective need to divest downgraded bonds in a short period of time can create pressures that temporarily drive fallen angel prices below equilibrium levels. We found forced selling to be associated with an additional penalty of 78bp, on average, incurred by investors selling shortly after the downgrade to HY. These investors cannot benefit from any of the subsequent documented recovery of fallen angels. This additional spread widening, shown in the third row of Table 8.2, is imposed whenever a bond starts the year as IG, gets downgraded to HY, and must be sold immediately. In such cases, the spread widening locked in by selling upon the downgrade will include both the typical difference in spread between the starting and ending rating classes and the additional fallen angel penalty.

The profit or loss upon liquidation, shown in the fourth row of the table, is calculated by multiplying the spread change experienced by a bond (including the fallen angel penalty, where applicable) by an assumed average spread duration of 4.5, corresponding to a bond that started the year with a five-year duration and is sold at an unknown time between the start of the year and the one-year horizon.[7]

The transition probabilities, which specify the likelihood of the bond having a given rating as of the one-year horizon, are obtained from the appropriate line of a Moody's historical one-year credit transition matrix.[8] The expected loss for a given event is obtained by multiplying the event probability by the loss that would be experienced. However, we record the expected loss only for events that would trigger a liquidation according to our sell discipline.

An analysis based on a one-year horizon does not fully express the viewpoint of a long-horizon investor. To extend an analysis of this type to a

TABLE 8.2 Example of the Try-and-Hold Approach: Loss Distribution for a Five-Year, Baa-Rated Bond over a One-Year Horizon, with Forced Sale upon a Downgrade to Ba or Lower

	Aaa	Aa	A	Baa	Ba	B	Caa	Ca-C	Default
Average spread (bp)	68	79	110	162	309	463	839	1863	
Spread change from Baa (bp)	-94	-83	-53	0	147	300	677	1701	
Fallen angel penalty (bp)					78	78	78	78	
P/L upon liquidation	4.24%	3.75%	2.37%	0.00%	-10.13%	-17.03%	-33.96%	-60.00%	-60.00%
Transition probability	0.04%	0.18%	4.36%	89.95%	4.30%	0.80%	0.17%	0.02%	0.18%
Expected loss					-0.44%	-0.14%	-0.06%	-0.01%	-0.11%

Note: Credit transition probabilities are based on Moody's average one-year transition rates from 1970 to 2012; spreads are averages obtained from Bloomberg Barclays Corporate Bond index data, adjusted to reflect the same period. Spread duration of the bond upon downgrade is assumed to be 4.5 years. Forced selling is assumed to occur on a downgrade to Ba or below.
Source: Moody's, Barclays Research

longer horizon, say five years, one approach would be to simply replace the one-year credit transition matrix used in Table 8.2 with a five-year cumulative transition matrix, also available from the rating agencies. However, we instead carry out the analysis in annual steps, using repeated application of a one-year transition matrix, as shown in Figure 8.1.[9]

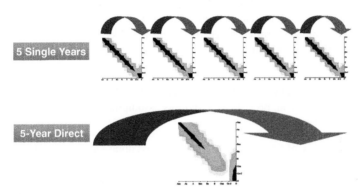

FIGURE 8.1   Analyzing Downgrade Losses Year by Year
Note: The credit transition matrix is depicted in the form of a heat map. Darker areas along the diagonal indicate high probabilities of unchanged ratings or one-notch transitions. More distant transitions are shown to be less likely at a one-year horizon and more likely at a five-year horizon.
Source: Moody's, Barclays Research

We prefer this year-by-year approach over a one-step analysis using a five-year matrix for several reasons. First, in the event that a bond gets downgraded after one year and then defaults after another two, the five-year matrix will record this as a default; in the year-by-year approach, the bond will be sold and written down at a loss upon crossing the ratings threshold, but the default event will be avoided. Second, to properly record the performance effect of a sale upon downgrade, we need to know the spread duration as of the forced sale. A downgrade in year 1 will incur a much greater loss than a similar downgrade in Year 4 due to the natural shortening of the bond's duration over time. Finally, the year-by-year structure allows use of a different matrix for each year; in a later section, we show how this can be used to condition on current spread levels.

We are now in position to repeat the try-and-hold analysis of a single Baa-rated five-year bond, as shown in Table 8.2, on a five-year return horizon. In this case, we have many more loss events to consider. A downgrade to Ba can occur in any year of the analysis; each such event will have a different probability and a different loss upon downgrade. This analysis is shown in Table 8.3. The severity of the loss upon a downgrade to a given rating decreases over time due to the shortening spread duration. The probability of downgrades decreases over time as well, largely due to the effect of upgrades; bonds upgraded to A are much less likely to be subsequently downgraded to Ba or below.

TABLE 8.3   Try-and-Hold Loss Distribution for a Five-Year, Baa-Rated Bond, over a Five-Year Horizon: probabilities and loss assumptions for downgrades, by final rating and event year

	Probability of Downgrade / Default			Loss upon Downgrade / Default		
Year	Ba	B	Default	Ba	B	Default
1	4.30%	0.80%	0.18%	−10.13%	−17.03%	−60.00%
2	4.09%	0.76%	0.18%	−7.88%	−13.24%	−60.00%
3	3.92%	0.73%	0.17%	−5.63%	−9.46%	−60.00%
4	3.76%	0.70%	0.16%	−3.38%	−5.68%	−60.00%
5	3.63%	0.68%	0.16%	−1.13%	−1.89%	−60.00%

Note: Forced selling is assumed to occur upon any downgrade to Ba or below. Downgrades to Caa and Ca–C ratings are calculated as well but omitted from this table due to space limitations.
Source: Barclays Research

This table of possible adverse outcomes, together with the desired outcome in which the bond is held to maturity and earns its promised spread, can be considered an approximate representation of the distribution of excess returns for the bond. We can use this to tabulate various measures of risk and return. Expected losses can be broken down into those due to forced sales and those due to default; total losses are subtracted from the total spread carry to arrive at the expected return. Various risk measures can be calculated from the distribution of five-year cumulative returns: risk can be characterized by the standard deviation or by various measures of tail risk.

One additional assumption that must be considered to complete this analysis is the reinvestment policy to be used for the proceeds of forced sales and defaults. The simplest case would be to assume that after any such loss event, the proceeds are held in cash until the return horizon. This, however, is not a realistic assumption. If a portfolio's mandate specifies that it should be invested into credits of a particular type, the proceeds from sales or defaults typically would be invested into similar credits. In addition, holding these sums in cash would result in the loss of spread carry, creating additional drag on portfolio performance. We therefore assume reinvestment into like credits with similar remaining maturity. For example, when we analyze a five-year Baa-rated bond, we assume that if we are forced to sell it after three years due to a downgrade to B, we would invest the proceeds in a new Baa-rated bond with two years remaining to maturity.

This complicates the calculation of tail risk. Whereas the worst possible outcome shown in Table 8.3 is a loss of 60% in case of default, the reinvestment assumption allows for even worse outcomes: two or more loss events could occur within the five-year horizon. For example, if we recover 40% from a default and reinvest that in a second bond that takes a similar loss, we will be left with just 16 cents on the dollar of our initial investment. The probabilities of such events are quite low, but they should be taken into account. In what follows, we use a simulation approach to calculate the reported tail risk statistics.

The results of this analysis are shown in Table 8.4 for bonds with four different initial credit ratings. Three different versions of the analysis are shown, each of which corresponds to different sell disciplines.

The first set of outputs from our analysis concerns the cumulative probability of experiencing a loss event over the five-year horizon (Columns 3–4). We find that under the pure hold-to-default assumption, the probabilities of experiencing a default range from 0.1% for Aaa debt to 1.9% for Baa. If we assume that a stop-loss mechanism is in place and bonds will be sold after a downgrade beyond some threshold, the probability of default is reduced, but the overall probability of a loss event is much greater. For Baa-rated debt, the probability that a forced sale will occur at some time over the five-year horizon is 23.7% if forced to sell upon any downgrade to Ba or lower, and 7.2% under the less aggressive policy of selling upon a downgrade to B or lower.[10] As a result, when we calculate the expected losses under each policy, we find that the more aggressive the sell discipline, the greater the expected losses (Columns 5–6). The small decrease in the probability of a large loss due to a default is more than offset by the much larger increase in the probability of losses due to forced sales, even though the loss experienced in each such event is much smaller. As a result, the cumulative expected excess return over the five-year horizon decreases as the sell discipline becomes more aggressive. For example, A-rated debt has an expected cumulative return of 509bp under the hold-to-default assumption, but this decreases to 505bp under the sell-at-B policy and to 483bp under the most aggressive sell-at-Ba policy. This effect is present, though much smaller, for higher-rated debt, and is even more pronounced for lower-rated debt.

TABLE 8.4 Try-and-Hold Analysis of Risk and Return over a Five-Year Horizon, for a Single Five-Year Bond, by Credit Rating and Sell Discipline, Using Long-Term Averages for Spreads and Transition Matrix

Rating	Long-Term Spread (bp)	Cum. Prob. of Loss (%)		Cum. Expected Loss (bp)		Cum. Expected Return (bp)		Risk Measures (bp)		
		Forced Sales (Downgrades)	Defaults	Forced Sales (Downgrades)	Defaults	Carry	Total	Volatility (Return)	VAR [98%]	CVaR [98%]
Sell upon downgrade to Ba										
Aaa	68	0.4%	0.1%	-3	-3	340	335	146	341	53
Aa	79	1.4%	0.2%	-9	-13	394	373	297	395	-723
A	110	5.6%	0.3%	-42	-18	544	483	424	-510	-1,724
Baa	162	23.7%	0.8%	-165	-47	782	570	728	-1,083	-3,364
Sell upon downgrade to B										
Aaa	68	0.1%	0.1%	-1	-3	341	336	143	341	116
Aa	79	0.4%	0.2%	-4	-13	395	378	301	395	-482
A	110	1.8%	0.4%	-20	-22	546	505	426	278	-1,610
Baa	162	7.2%	1.1%	-72	-66	800	662	753	-1,083	-3,937
Hold to default										
Aaa	68	0.0%	0.1%	0	-4	341	337	148	341	159
Aa	79	0.0%	0.3%	0	-15	395	380	310	395	-379

(Continued)

TABLE 8.4 (Continued)

Rating	Long-Term Spread (bp)	Cum. Prob. of Loss (%) Forced Sales (Downgrades)	Defaults	Cum. Expected Loss (bp) Forced Sales (Downgrades)	Defaults	Cum. Expected Return (bp) Carry	Total	Volatility (Return)	Risk Measures (bp) VAR [98%]	CVaR [98%]
A	110	0.0%	0.6%	0	-39	548	509	493	548	-1,427
Baa	162	0.0%	1.9%	0	-114	807	693	853	811	-5,117

Note: The table presents the cumulative probability of selling upon downgrade or default (Columns 3–4), expected losses from selling upon downgrade or default (Columns 5–6), expected cumulative carry (Column 7), and total expected return (column 8), all over a horizon of five years. The three rightmost columns present risk measures: the standard deviation of cumulative five-year returns, and their value at risk (VaR) and conditional value at risk (CVaR) at a 98% threshold. Computations assume transition rates according to Moody's long-term average rates from 1970 to 2012 and average spreads of Bloomberg Barclays Corporate Bond indices over the same period (shown in Column 2). We also assume a fallen angel penalty of 78bp when selling upon any direct downgrade from IG to HY. Losses from rating transitions are capped at 60%. Calculations assume proceeds from bonds sold upon a downgrade are reinvested in bonds of the original rating and maturity. Cumulative expected carry return includes an adjustment for lost carry due to expected forced sales and defaults. The first panel reports results when investors are forced to sell at a Ba rating, the second at B, and the third assumes bonds are held until maturity (or default).
Source: Moody's, Barclays Research

The largest expected losses from forced sales can be found in the fourth line of Table 8.4. When investors who are required to sell upon any downgrade to HY purchase Baa-rated bonds, the cumulative expected loss from forced selling over the horizon is 165bp. This is due to a combination of two effects. The proximity of the initial rating of Baa to the sell threshold at Ba means that just a single-letter downgrade will trigger a sale, leading to a very high cumulative loss probability of 23.7%. Second, the losses in case of such forced sales will be increased due to the fallen angel effect described earlier.

As shown in Chapter 2, it is suboptimal to sell immediately upon a downgrade to HY. The fact that many investors follow such policies creates strong selling pressure for bonds downgraded to HY, causing them to temporarily drop below their fundamental values. Selling immediately upon a downgrade locks in these losses. As the selling intensity dissipates, however, these price declines tend to reverse, and fallen angels outperform peer HY bonds.

This behavior provides motivation for investors to adopt more flexible investment mandates, allowing either continued holding of fallen angels or selling only upon further credit deterioration beyond Ba status. A policy to sell only at a B rating, for example, would allow investors to avoid, at least in part, the high penalty of selling at exactly the "wrong" time.[11] Table 8.4 shows that for Baa bonds over a five-year horizon, changing from a sell-at-Ba policy to a sell-at-B policy helps to decrease the expected loss due to forced sales from 165bp to 72bp, thus increasing the expected return from 570bp to 662bp.

Why do so many investors choose to sell upon any downgrade to HY despite this performance penalty?[12] By their nature, bond investors tend to be conservative. A large loss event such as a default can be particularly unpleasant for bond investors or portfolio managers. They would therefore prefer a higher probability of a less extreme loss event such as a forced sale. The risk reduction benefits of an aggressive sell discipline can be seen in the rightmost three columns of Table 8.4. The volatility of returns is always decreased by more aggressive selling. We also show tail risk measures, VaR and CVaR, at the 98% confidence level. VaR and CVaR are defined relative to a particular confidence level. The 98% VaR, shown here, is the level of cumulative five-year return that the bond will exceed with 98% probability. The 98% CVaR is the average return across the 2% of events with returns below this level. The numbers in the rightmost column show that these worst-case returns can entail large losses. For Baa bonds in particular, the tail risk is most extreme in the hold-to-default case, and the use of a sell trigger can limit the losses in these worst-case events.[13]

To illustrate this risk/return trade-off, Figure 8.2 presents the entire distribution of cumulative loss over a five-year horizon for Baa-rated bonds, by selling threshold. Investors who systematically sell upon a credit deterioration are less likely to experience large (default) losses; the higher the threshold, the lower the chance of encountering such losses. They are, however, more likely to incur smaller write-downs due to forced selling; the probability of such events increases with the rating threshold. This effect is most pronounced when holding bonds rated just above the sell cut-off (i.e., for Baa-rated bonds).

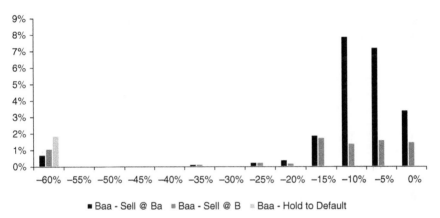

FIGURE 8.2 Loss Distribution for a Five-Year, Baa-Rated Bond, over a Five-Year Horizon, by Sell Discipline
Note: Represents the projected loss distribution for Baa bonds assuming Moody's long-term average transition rates from 1970 to 2012 and average spreads obtained from Bloomberg Barclays Corporate Bond index data, adjusted to reflect the same period. We assume a fallen angel penalty of 78bp whenever selling occurs immediately upon a downgrade to HY. Losses from rating transitions are capped at 60%. Calculations assume proceeds from bonds sold upon a downgrade are reinvested in bonds of the original rating. The figure reports results by sell discipline.
Source: Moody's, Barclays Research

Another comparison worth noting in Table 8.4 is that across rating classes. The risk/return trade-off positions carry against potential losses from forced sales and downgrades. As a result, the increase in total expected excess return (Column 8) obtained by moving down in credit is not as large as that promised by average spread levels (Column 2); this effect is exacerbated by an aggressive sell discipline. For example, the average Baa spread is 162bp, which is 47% higher than the average A spread of 110bp. Due to the increased expected losses in lower-rated debt, the expected return advantage is lower: in the hold-to-default case, Baa debt is expected to earn

36% more than A-rated debt (693bp to 509bp); this advantage decreases to 31% under the sell-at-B policy and just 18% under sell-at-Ba. These results are depicted in Figure 8.3. The length of each bar in the figure represents the full carry return promised by the bond's spread; the part of each bar above the horizontal axis represents the net returns after subtracting expected losses due to forced sales and defaults. All returns are cumulative over a five-year horizon. Long-horizon credit investors who sell upon a credit deterioration will, on average, incur larger losses from downgrades but significantly lower default losses relative to pure buy-and-hold investors. Again, this effect is most pronounced when holding bonds rated just above the sell cut-off.

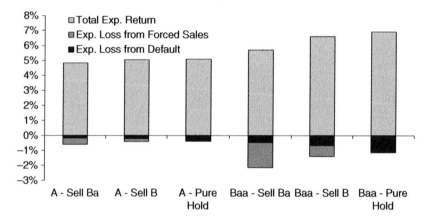

FIGURE 8.3 Expected Cumulative Excess Returns for Five-Year, A- and Baa-Rated Bonds over a Five-Year Horizon, by Sell Discipline
Note: Represents total expected return, expected losses from defaults, and expected losses from downgrade for A and Baa bonds assuming Moody's long-term average transition rates from 1970 to 2012 and average spreads of Bloomberg Barclays Corporate Bond indices over the same period (shown in Column 2 of Table 8.1). We assume a fallen angel penalty of 78bp when selling upon downgrade to Ba. Losses from rating transitions are capped at 60%. Calculations assume proceeds from bonds sold upon a downgrade are reinvested in bonds of the original rating. The figure reports results by sell discipline.
Source: Moody's, Barclays Research

The net effect of the sell discipline on expected return is much more pronounced for Baa-rated debt than for A-rated debt. As a result, the expected return advantage of Baa debt is much more compelling for a pure hold-to-default investor than for one who is forced to sell upon any downgrade to Ba or lower.

In Figure 8.4, we use the data from Table 8.4 to portray the effect of the sell discipline on the risk/return trade-off.[14] We find that, as expected, Baa-rated debt has both greater expected return and greater risk than A-rated debt, regardless of sell discipline. However, the effect of the sell discipline is clear. For bonds in both rating categories, the sell-at-B policy seems to give the best return per unit of risk. Going from there to a hold-to-default policy gives a large increase in risk for a small pick-up in expected return; adopting a sell-at-Ba policy gives a large decrease in expected return and just a small decline in risk. As noted earlier, this effect is much stronger for Baa-rated than A-rated bonds. Therefore, when comparing the two asset classes on a risk/return basis, the sell discipline will have a strong influence. Investors following a pure hold-to-default policy or a sell-at-B policy may find that although Baa debt carries more risk over the long term, it also promises a sufficient improvement in expected return to justify this additional risk. Under the sell-at-Baa policy, the smaller increase in expected return may make it harder to justify taking on the additional risk.

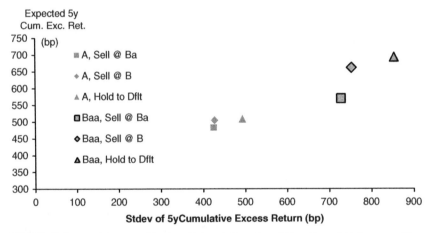

FIGURE 8.4   Risk/Return Trade-off for A-Rated and Baa-Rated Debt on a Five-Year Horizon under Different Sell Disciplines
Source: Barclays Research

Maturity Effects

In Table 8.3, we saw that the forced sale of a bond upon being downgraded to a given credit quality can have very different effects on performance depending on when it occurs. During the first year of the analysis, when the bond has a relatively long remaining spread duration, the loss upon default is expected to be much greater than in later years, as the spread duration continues to shorten. With this in mind, we can explore how our model represents the effect of investing in credits of different maturities. In Figure 8.5, we simply vary the maturity of the bond, leaving all other model parameters unchanged. We show the expected cumulative five-year excess returns for A-rated and Baa-rated bonds, for sell disciplines in which we are forced to sell bonds upon a downgrade to either Ba or B. In all cases, we find that our model shows expected losses increasing with maturity, and thus expected returns decrease for longer bonds.

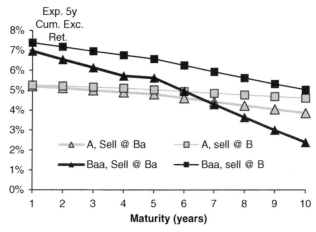

FIGURE 8.5   Effect of Bond Maturity on Five-Year Cumulative Expected Excess Returns, Under a Flat Term Structure Assumption
Source: Barclays Research

We must keep in mind that Figure 8.5 is extremely unrealistic. One of the assumptions that we have relied upon until now was a flat term structure of credit spreads; just a single average spread level is used to represent each quality, regardless of maturity. When we compare one credit quality to another, this simplification is largely immaterial. However, if we are specifically trying to compare bonds of different maturities, it is important to recognize that longer-dated bonds typically have higher spreads. Depending on the slope of the spread curve, this effect could largely offset the decreasing trends shown in this figure.

However, even with these limitations in mind, we can pull some valuable lessons from Figure 8.5. For A-rated bonds, which are far from either sell threshold, the decline in expected performance with increasing maturity (at unchanged spread) is rather mild; the difference between the results for the two sell disciplines is small as well. For Baa-rated bonds, both effects are much stronger: the decrease in performance for longer-maturity bonds is striking, and the choice of the sell discipline has much greater performance implications. In fact, for investors forced to sell any bond downgraded to HY, we see that the expected losses due to forced sales are sufficiently large to entirely offset the spread advantage of Baa bonds over A-rated ones at longer maturities, leaving the A-rated bonds with higher expected cumulative excess returns over the Five-year horizon. This suggests that such investors, to the extent that they buy Baa-rated credits, should prefer shorter maturities.

In Figure 8.6, we repeat this analysis, this time with an adjustment for a typical term structure of spreads. Based on a long-term analysis[15] of spreads of corporate bonds with different ratings in three maturity buckets (one to three years, three to seven years, and seven–10 years), we used average spreads of 81bp, 110bp, and 119bp for A-rated bonds with nominal maturities of two, five and 10 years, respectively. The corresponding spreads for Baa-rated bonds were 131bp, 162bp, and 169bp. We used these numbers to represent the average spreads of the different asset classes; this introduces a return incentive for moving out on the curve, which offsets the increase in expected losses from forced sales shown in Figure 8.5. The net result of these competing forces is shown in Figure 8.6. The effect of extending from

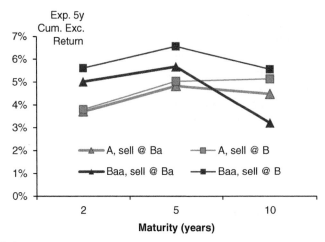

FIGURE 8.6 Effect of Bond Maturity on Five-Year Cumulative Expected Excess Returns, Including Term Structure of Spreads
Source: Barclays Research

two-year to five-year maturities seems to be net positive in all four cases shown; the net effect of a further extension to 10 years is positive for A-rated bonds with a sell-at-B policy but negative for the other three cases shown. The inclusion of the term structure of spreads does not seem to negate the primary conclusion of Figure 8.5: Long-horizon investors with a sell-at-Ba policy in place should avoid buying Baa credits with long maturities.

Moving Beyond Long-Term Averages

The framework presented thus far allows investors to evaluate the long-term performance implications of the sell discipline adopted for dealing with distressed credits and to examine the risk/return trade-off among different credit asset classes under a specific policy. However, a number of the simplifying assumptions we have made are rather limiting and need to be adjusted.

First, all the numbers presented up to this point are based on long-term averages. The credit transition matrices that underlie this approach were 40-year averages obtained from Moody's, and the spreads were long-term averages adjusted to be consistent with the same period of time. This may help to set investment policy over a very long horizon. However, most portfolio investment decisions and analyses are more immediate in nature. Even a manager with a long return horizon, such as five years, will want to examine the projected risk and return of the portfolio over the five years starting today. Our best projection of expected excess returns cannot be based solely on long-term average spreads; it must account for the spreads currently available in the market.

Second, we have essentially assumed that as time progresses, nothing changes but ratings. Not only do the average spreads of each rating category remain unchanged, but transition rates are kept constant at unconditional long-term averages. In practice, spreads as well as transition rates would be anything but constant, affecting carry, downgrade losses, and the like.

Can we improve on this model? Can we use an intuitive observable, such as current spread levels, to better estimate transition rates and spreads in the upcoming and subsequent years? We begin by studying the predictive power of spreads.

PREDICTIVE POWER OF SPREADS

In this section, we examine the historical relationships between the spreads of corporate bonds and the various contributors to corporate bond risk: default probabilities, ratings transition rates, and the cost of a downgrade, as represented by the spread differences between different ratings. We find clear connections among all of these quantities over the short term, which tend to dissipate with the passage of time. These results suggest that the information contained in spreads can be used to estimate conditional values for the various parameters of our model.

Spreads and Default Risk

We first study the relationship between corporate default rates and credit spreads. We utilize two main sources of data: historical spreads from Bloomberg Barclays Corporate and High Yield Bond indices and Moody's reported cumulative issuer-weighted default rates by annual cohort over 1991 to 2012.[16] Figure 8.7 plots the beginning-of-year spreads of the Bloomberg Barclays High Yield Index versus Moody's HY cumulative default rates for the corresponding annual cohorts over one-, two-, three-, four-, and five-year horizons. Figure 8.8 presents the same information for IG issuers.

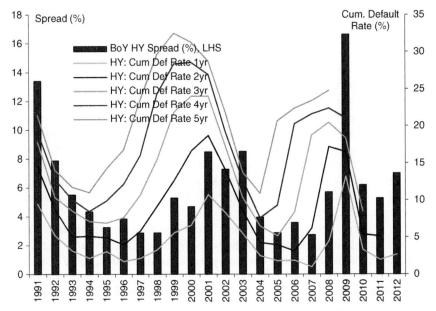

FIGURE 8.7 Moody's Cumulative Default Rates vs. Beginning-of-Year Spreads by Annual Cohort: High Yield
Source: Moody's, Barclays Research

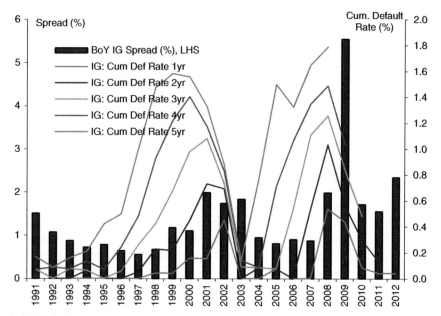

FIGURE 8.8 Moody's Cumulative Default Rates vs. Beginning-of-Year Spreads by Annual Cohort: Investment Grade
Source: Moody's, Barclays Research

For both rating groups, a clear positive relationship emerges for short and medium horizons (one to two years). Purchasing bonds when spreads are high is clearly associated with higher-than-average default rates over a horizon of one or two years. The same waves of elevated defaults during crisis periods can be seen in the data for longer-horizon cumulative defaults, except that they no longer line up well with spreads as of the start of the period. For example, the high cumulative five-year realized defaults ultimately realized by the 1998 cohort make sense because they include results from the dot-com crisis of 2001–2002. However, the low spreads as of the beginning of 1998 gave no indication of the future crisis.

The patterns observed in Figure 8.7 and Figure 8.8 translate into high positive correlations between beginning-of-period spreads and realized defaults over short horizons. For one-year realized defaults, these correlations are 0.84 and 0.63 for HY and IG, respectively, and in Year 2, they are 0.12 and 0.18. By Year 3, the relationship has dissolved, and correlations have gradually become negative.

These results suggest investors can improve on unconditional historical default frequencies for predicting default rates on one- and two-year horizons by utilizing information from current spread levels. Our results also illustrate just how difficult it is to make a five-year prediction based on current spreads. An investor at the start of 1998 or 2006 saw very low spreads, which gave no clue as to the crises that later unfolded. Similarly, investors in high spreads at the start of 2003 and 2009 had no clear indication of future improvement.

Spreads and Downgrade Risk

Given the rarity of defaults from IG status, the risk of a downgrade to speculative grade rating is clearly more prominent for managing a high-grade credit portfolio. We demonstrated that spread levels are closely tied to default frequencies at horizons of one or two years; can investors utilize information incorporated in current spreads to estimate the conditional probabilities of downgrades as well? Do spreads also predict transition rates?

For this study we utilize data on bonds in Bloomberg Barclays Corporate and High Yield indices for 1991 to 2013. We construct issuer-level data by aggregating all outstanding bonds for an issuer each month using market-value weighting. We then compose annual cohorts by rating and compute empirical frequencies of rating transitions over horizons of one to five years.

Figure 8.9 plots the realized one-year downgrade frequency against the beginning-of-year spread level for A-rated issuers from different annual cohorts. Spreads are market value-weighted averages of outstanding bonds. Frequency includes all downgrades to a lower full-letter-grade rating in the corresponding year.[17] We find strong visual evidence of a trend toward higher downgrade frequencies when spreads are higher. Nevertheless, the observed outcomes can be quite far from the trend line. For example, near the center of Figure 8.9 there is a vertical strip of observations representing cohorts with similar beginning-of-year spreads of 140 to 160bp but very different realized downgrade rates, ranging from 2.48%, for the 2010 observation to 20.90% in 2003. Figure 8.10 shows the corresponding data for Baa-rated issuers. We find similar results: higher downgrade rates for higher spreads, but no strong convergence to a specific linear relationship.

Note that in Figure 8.9 and Figure 8.10, we have omitted the data point corresponding to the 2009 cohort, which is a clear outlier. Corporate spreads at the start of 2009 were unusually high: 488bp for A-rated bonds and 698bp for Baa. Realized downgrade rates were not nearly as high as might have been expected based on these spreads: 14.61% for A-rated issuers and 5.29% for Baa. These levels would be far to the right of all of the observations shown in these figures, but not particularly high up; they would thus strongly bias the results.[18] Furthermore, a large part of the elevated spreads at the start of 2009 was due to the lack of liquidity in the market rather than

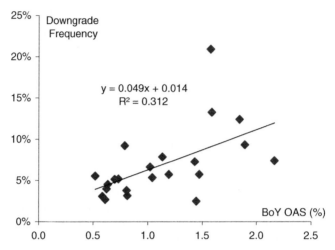

FIGURE 8.9 Dependence of One-Year Downgrade Frequency on Beginning-of-Year Spreads for A-Rated Issuers
Note: Based on annual data from Bloomberg Barclays US Corporate Bond index, 1991–2013, excluding 2009.
Source: Barclays Research

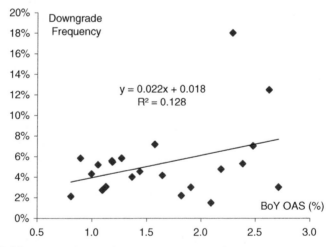

FIGURE 8.10 Dependence of One-Year Downgrade Frequency on Beginning-of-Year Spreads for Baa-Rated Issuers
Note: Based on annual data from Bloomberg Barclays US Corporate Bond index, 1991–2013, excluding 2009.
Source: Barclays Research

to default concerns.[19] For both of these reasons, we have chosen to exclude the 2009 cohort from this analysis.

The results of linear regression analysis of the relationship between spreads and downgrades are shown as trend lines in Figure 8.9 and Figure 8.10. In each case, we can also calculate the correlation coefficients between beginning-of-year spreads and realized downgrade rates in the subsequent period. The resulting coefficients, again excluding 2009, are 56% for A-rated bonds and 36% for Baa-rated bonds.

What if we try to predict downgrades beyond the one-year horizon? To address this question, we continue to track our issuer cohorts over longer periods. For each annual cohort, we track realized downgrade rates in year one as described. We then calculate the realized Baa downgrade rate for year two using only issuers with a Baa rating as of the beginning of both years one and two and a non-missing rating at the end of year three. We continue in this fashion to obtain realized downgrade rates for years three, four, and five after the initial formation of the cohort (and the observation of the beginning-of-period spread). We then calculate the correlation between the downgrade rates experienced by each annual cohort in year n with the spread as of the cohort formation date. The results obtained for A-rated and Baa-rated issuers are shown in Figure 8.11. For both qualities, we show strong positive correlations between beginning spreads and subsequent downgrade rates in both year one and year two. However, as seen

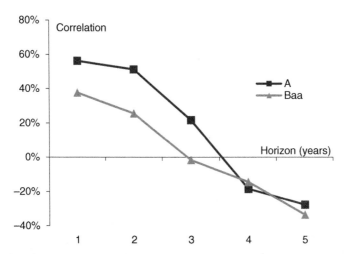

FIGURE 8.11 Correlation of Downgrade Frequencies with Spreads, by Credit Quality and Horizon
Note: Based on annual data from Bloomberg Barclays US Corporate Bond index, 1991–2013, excluding 2009.
Source: Barclays Research

with defaults, there is a strong drop-off in this correlation in year three, and by years four and five the correlation is slightly negative. It seems that two years is a long time in the context of the credit cycle; when we try to look beyond two years forward, there is little confidence that the state of the credit markets will resemble current conditions.

We can extend our cohort study to look at spreads as well. To what extent does the Baa spread today correlate with Baa spreads *n* years in the future? To make sure we are comparing the spreads of the same bonds at two different points of time, and not two different bond populations, we form a cohort of bonds outstanding at time *t* and then revisit the same set of bonds *n* years later. From within this set of bonds, we find an average spread level corresponding to each whole-letter quality rating at both the beginning and end of the period. We carry out this analysis for cohorts starting in January of each calendar year from 1991 through 2013, for horizons of one through five years.[20] We then compute the correlations between beginning spread and horizon spread for each quality and horizon. The results are reported in Figure 8.12. We once again find that today's spreads are highly correlated with spreads one year or two years into the future but that this correlation disappears and turns negative by the end of year 3.

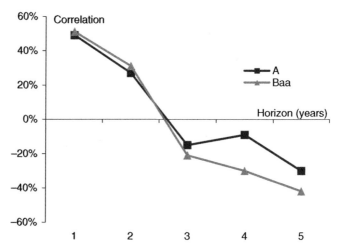

FIGURE 8.12   Correlation of Current Spreads with Future Spreads, by Credit Quality and Horizon
Note: Based on annual data from Bloomberg Barclays US Corporate Bond index, 1991–2013, excluding 2009.
Source: Barclays Research

These results are consistent with direct analysis of the time series of corporate spreads, which demonstrates a strong tendency toward mean reversion, with a time frame consistent with the listed results.[21]

In this section, we have documented a positive relationship between spread levels and downgrade frequencies. Based on empirical studies using aggregated rates of downgrades to any lower rating, we have strong evidence suggesting that transition probabilities are different in different spread environments. However, to support an analysis of downgrade risk, such as the one we developed in the first section of this chapter, investors typically depend on complete transition matrices, such as those published periodically by the rating agencies. How can one construct a complete transition matrix conditional on the current spread environment?

To answer to this question, we sort the years in our sample by their respective overall one-year probability of downgrade and classify the top and bottom quartiles of years as "high" and "low" downgrade states. We classify the years 1993–1994, 1996–1997, 2010, and 2013 as the "low" state, while 1999, 2001–2003, and 2008–2009 comprise the "high" state. We can pool the realized one-year issuer transition data from our index database to form a separate historical transition matrix from each of these subsets of the overall time period. Table 8.5 presents the average one-year empirical transition rates for the "high" and "low" states as well as the average long-term transition matrix reported by Moody's for 1970 to 2012. We note that as we move farther off the diagonal, the number of observations upon which the downgrade rates are calculated declines considerably, reducing the accuracy of our estimates. Furthermore, index issuers are largely concentrated in the A–Baa rating groups, so the numbers shown for these qualities should be the most accurate. As expected, based on the way these matrices were constructed, downgrade frequencies are significantly higher (lower) across the board in the "high" ("low") state than in the long-term average matrix. Conversely, the frequencies of unchanged ratings or upgrades tend to be below (above) average in the "high" ("low") state.

In Table 8.6, we compare the overall A and Baa downgrade frequencies in the three downgrade states to their long-term averages from the Moody's matrix. We also calculate the average spreads in each of these subperiods and compare these with the long-term average spreads from Table 8.1. We then express each of these quantities, for each downgrade state and quality rating, as a ratio relative to the long-term average. We find that in the "high" downgrade state, downgrade frequencies are roughly double the long-term average, and in the "low" state, they are about half. Consistent with our findings in Figure 8.9 and Figure 8.10, spreads are also about double their average levels in the high-downgrade state. The low- and medium-downgrade states do not have significantly different beginning spreads.

TABLE 8.5 One-Year Transition Matrices Calculated Empirically Based on Data from "Low," "Medium," and "High" Downgrade States, Compared with Moody's Long-Term Transition Matrix

Low Downgrade Prob.	Aaa	Aa	A	Baa	Ba	B	Caa	Ca–C
Aaa	98.4%	0.8%	0.8%	0.0%	0.0%	0.0%	0.0%	0.0%
Aa	0.0%	92.6%	7.2%	0.2%	0.0%	0.0%	0.0%	0.0%
A	0.1%	1.4%	94.5%	3.7%	0.3%	0.1%	0.0%	0.0%
Baa	0.1%	0.1%	5.8%	91.4%	2.4%	0.1%	0.1%	0.0%
Medium Downgrade Prob.	Aaa	Aa	A	Baa	Ba	B	Caa	Ca–C
Aaa	90.0%	10.0%	0.0%	0.0%	0.0%	0.0%	0.0%	0.0%
Aa	0.4%	88.3%	11.0%	0.2%	0.0%	0.0%	0.0%	0.0%
A	0.0%	3.3%	90.8%	5.5%	0.3%	0.1%	0.0%	0.0%
Baa	0.0%	0.2%	5.5%	89.6%	3.9%	0.6%	0.1%	0.0%
High Downgrade Prob.	Aaa	Aa	A	Baa	Ba	B	Caa	Ca–C
Aaa	88.0%	12.0%	0.0%	0.0%	0.0%	0.0%	0.0%	0.0%
Aa	0.8%	72.2%	25.6%	1.1%	0.3%	0.0%	0.0%	0.0%
A	0.2%	2.0%	84.7%	11.7%	1.0%	0.2%	0.1%	0.0%
Baa	0.1%	0.0%	2.8%	87.1%	7.8%	1.5%	0.6%	0.0%
Moody's 1970–2012	Aaa	Aa	A	Baa	Ba	B	Caa	Ca–C
Aaa	90.8%	8.5%	0.7%	0.0%	0.0%	0.0%	0.0%	0.0%
Aa	1.0%	89.5%	8.9%	0.5%	0.1%	0.0%	0.0%	0.0%
A	0.1%	2.6%	90.7%	5.8%	0.6%	0.1%	0.1%	0.0%
Baa	0.0%	0.2%	4.4%	90.0%	4.3%	0.8%	0.2%	0.0%

Note: The top three categories are empirical transition matrices computed using index issuer data from selected years of our data sample. "Low" and "high" downgrade probability states are formed from the years with the smallest and highest total downgrade rates, respectively, across our sample years 1991–2013. "High" state years include: 1999, 2001–2003, and 2008–2009. "Low" state years are: 1993–1994, 1996–1997, 2010, and 2013. The bottom table shows Moody's long-term average transition rates over 1970 to 2012.

Source: Moody's, Barclays Research

TABLE 8.6 Ratios of Downgrade Frequencies and Spreads in "High" and "Low" Downgrade States to Corresponding Long-Term Averages

	Low State		Medium State		High State		Moody's Long Term	
	A	Baa	A	Baa	A	Baa	A	Baa
Downgrade Freq.	4.1%	2.6%	5.8%	4.6%	13.0%	9.9%	6.59%	5.47%
Avg. BoY OAS	1.10	1.74	1.20	1.66	2.42	3.26	1.10	1.62
Downgrade Freq. / Long-Term Rate	0.62	0.48	0.89	0.84	1.98	1.82		
BoY OAS / Long-Term Avg.	1.00	1.07	1.09	1.02	2.20	2.01		

Note: The table reports overall empirical downgrade frequencies in the three different downgrade states for A-rated and Baa-rated bonds and compares these with the long-term average frequencies from Moody's long-term transition matrix (1970–2012). Similarly, average beginning-of-year (BoY) spreads over these three states are compared with long-term average spreads. Downgrade frequencies include the sum of all transitions from the specified rating to lower whole-letter grade ratings based on the matrices shown in Table 8.5. Ratios are used to express the downgrade frequencies and spreads in each state relative to the long-term averages.

Source: Moody's, Barclays Research

We have established that high-spread environments are associated with high probabilities of downgrades and, hence, forced sales. However, expected losses from forced sales are determined not only by the probabilities of such events but by the magnitude of the loss realized upon such events; in times of stress, these can be elevated as well. We have modeled the loss upon a downgrade as proportional to the spread differential between the average spreads in the different quality ratings. Typically, periods of heightened credit risk are characterized not only by higher spreads but also by greater average spread differentials between different quality ratings. This is illustrated in the next pair of figures: Figure 8.13 plots the differential between the average spreads of Baa-rated and A-rated credits against the A spread; Figure 8.14 plots the Ba to Baa spread difference against the Baa spread. In both cases, wider spreads are associated with steeper spread differences. This means that a high-spread environment carries a two-pronged increase in the risk of forced sales: Not only is the risk of a downgrade elevated, but the loss realized upon such a downgrade is likely to be larger as well.

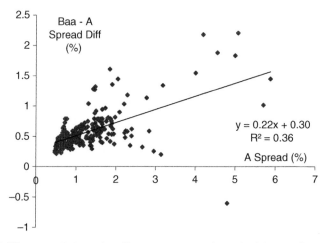

FIGURE 8.13   Baa–A Spread Difference vs. Spread Level of A-Rated Bonds
Source: Barclays Research

ENHANCED TRY-AND-HOLD MODEL

In the first section of this chapter, we presented a framework for evaluating portfolio losses for try-and-hold investors that explicitly considers the risk of downgrades and forced sales in addition to outright defaults. However, we limited ourselves to a through-the-cycle analysis, assuming a static environment based on long-term averages. Transition rates were set to unconditional long-term average levels, regardless of the spread environment, and kept constant throughout the investment horizon. Similarly, spreads were assumed to remain at their initial levels. In the last section, we found empirical evidence that current spreads can help form expectations for transition rates and spread changes over the near term. In this section, we show how our try-and-hold framework can be modified to incorporate the results of our empirical analysis.

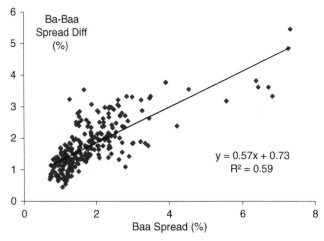

FIGURE 8.14   Ba–Baa Spread Difference vs. Spread Level of Baa-Rated Bonds
Source: Barclays Research

Model Enhancements

Our empirical analysis has shown that current spread levels are highly correlated with future spread levels, and with transition rates, at horizons of one to two years. Higher spreads are associated with higher downgrade frequencies and higher future spreads. Therefore, we now require both current and long-term average spread levels as inputs to our model. The level of the former vs. the latter determines the current market "state" and, consequently, the value of new transition rate adjustment parameters. We impose a simple structure on the transition matrix in which a single constant scales up the probability of all downgrade transitions, and a second scales down the probability of upgrades. Figure 8.15 shows the result of perturbing the one-year transition matrix to reflect modified estimates of transition probabilities corresponding to a high-downgrade state of the

Long–Term Transition Matrix

	Aaa–Aa	A–Baa	Ba–B	Caa–D
Aaa–Aa	95.20%	4.80%	0.05%	0.02%
A–Baa	1.50%	95.40%	2.90%	0.24%
Ba–B	0.10%	3.60%	89.60%	6.80%
Caa–D	0.00%	0.10%	4.60%	95.40%

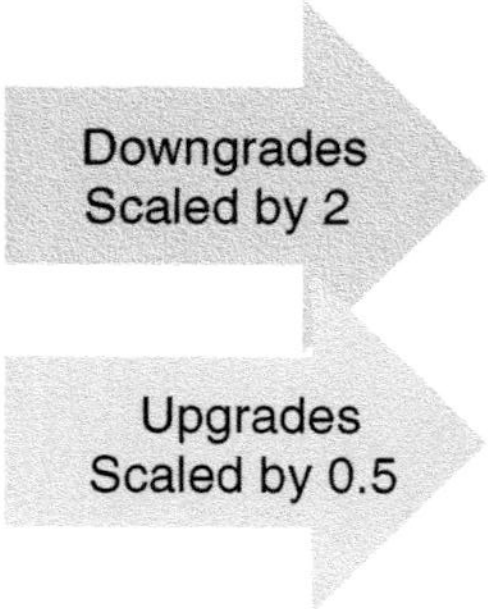

Downgrades Scaled by 2

Upgrades Scaled by 0.5

Perturbed Transition Matrix

	Aaa–Aa	A–Baa	Ba–B	Caa–D
Aaa–Aa	90.26%	9.60%	0.10%	0.04%
A–Baa	0.75%	92.97%	5.80%	0.48%
Ba–B	0.05%	1.80%	84.55%	13.60%
Caa–D	0.00%	0.05%	2.30%	97.65%

FIGURE 8.15 Perturbed Transition Matrix Example: High Spread Environment
Source: Barclays Research

environment. In Table 8.6, we found that in such an environment, downgrades are roughly twice as frequent on average and upgrades are about half as frequent. Therefore, for this example, we set our downgrade scalar to 2 (and upgrade scalar to 0.5) and adjust probabilities of unchanged ratings (along the diagonal) such that each row sums to 100%.

We have further found a strong relationship between spread levels and downgrade rates. To reflect this, we represent the state of the environment by the ratio of current spread levels to their long-term averages. We use this ratio as the downgrade multiplier and its reciprocal to scale the rate of upgrades. However, as shown in Figure 8.11 and Figure 8.12, the correlation between today's spreads and future downgrade rates (or spreads) declines over time and has mostly dissipated by Year 3. This motivates the incorporation of a mean reversion parameter, which controls the evolution of both spreads and transition rates.

In Figure 8.16, we illustrate how the technique of chaining five year-by-year transition matrices introduced in Figure 8.1 can accommodate the results of our empirical studies. If high current spreads are double their long-term rates, indicating that we are in a high-downgrade-frequency environment, we perturb the transition matrix used for the first year of the analysis by a downgrade multiplier of 200% to reflect the higher probabilities of downgrades. This is illustrated by stronger upper off-diagonal elements in the matrix used for Year 1. We then incorporate the mean reversion effect by reducing the downgrade multiplier in subsequent years of the analysis.[22] In the example shown, we have converged to something very close to the long-term average transition matrix by Year 3 of the analysis.

Note that the mean reversion assumption affects our expectation of spreads as well as conditional downgrade frequencies. Spreads will also be assumed to converge to their long-term averages. The spreads assumed to be

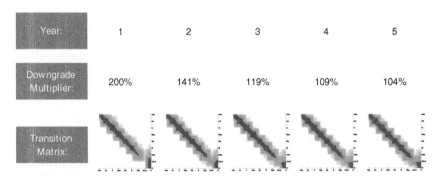

FIGURE 8.16   Example: Applying Different Transition Matrices in Different Years
Source: Barclays Research

in place at different points in time will affect the size of the loss experienced upon any forced sale event and the spread to be earned when reinvesting the proceeds of any loss.

We now show how our model can be used to condition the long-horizon risk/return analysis on a particular spread environment, incorporating the results of our empirical studies. We use the model to reproduce the risk/ return trade-off between an A-rated and a Baa-rated bond under different sell disciplines, which was shown in Figure 8.4 using long-term averages. Now, however, we condition the model on the spread environment at a particular point in time. Figure 8.17 provides an example from a low-spread environment, using spreads as of the end of January 2007; Figure 8.18 gives a high-spread example, using spreads as of the end of November 2011. In each case, the model has been conditioned on spreads as follows. We start with the Moody's long-term transition matrix based on data from 1970 to 2012. We then input to the model two distinct sets of spreads: the long-term average spread per quality, as shown in Table 8.2, and the current average spread per quality as of a particular point in time. We then use the ratio of current to long-term spreads to perturb the transition matrix used for the first year, as illustrated in Figure 8.15.[23] For subsequent years of the analysis, we assume that the spreads and downgrade multipliers for each quality converge towards their long-term averages as shown in Figure 8.16; the transition

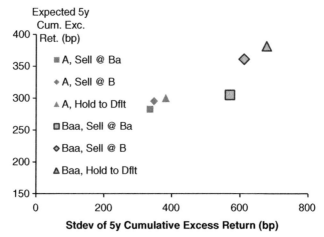

FIGURE 8.17 Modeled Risk/Return Trade-off by Quality and Sell Discipline, for a Five-Year Bond on a Five-Year Return Horizon, Conditioned on a Low-Spread Environment (as of January 31, 2007)
Source: Barclays Research

matrices are recalculated for each subsequent year based on the spreads assumed to pertain. (As a result, the transition matrix should also converge towards the long-term average.)

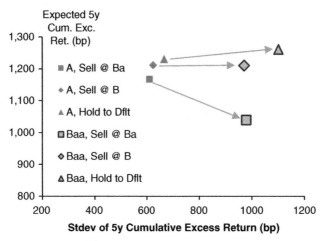

FIGURE 8.18 Modeled Risk/Return Trade-off by Quality and Sell Discipline, for a Five-Year Bond on a Five-Year Return Horizon, Conditioned on a High-Spread Environment (as of November 30, 2011)
Source: Barclays Research

The first difference between the two figures is the scale of the two axes. The high-spread environment shown in Figure 8.18 is characterized by much higher levels of both risk (as measured by standard deviation of cumulative 5y excess return) and expected return than the low-spread environment of Figure 8.17. However, the relationship between the results for different asset classes and sell disciplines does not scale linearly; in the different spread environments, some conclusions remain consistent while others can be very different. When comparing performance using the three sell disciplines considered according to this risk metric, the sell-at-B discipline seems to offer the best risk/return trade-off for both A and Baa bonds in both low-spread and high-spread environments. However, the size of this effect, as well as the relative performance of A and Baa assets, appears very different. In the low-spread environment, extending from A to Baa credits brings both increased risk and increased expected return, regardless of the sell discipline; for investors forced to sell at Ba, the pickup in expected return is smaller, and possibly not worth the risk, but it is positive nonetheless. In the high-spread environment, the expected losses from forced sales have a stronger negative effect on Baa-rated assets. In this case, a Baa bond has just slightly larger expected return than an A-rated bond when using the sell-at-B or hold-to-default disciplines but significantly worse expected returns under the sell-at-Ba discipline. For investors forced to liquidate any bond downgraded below IG, this analysis suggests strongly against purchasing Baa-rated bonds in a high-spread environment.

Comparing the two figures, though, we find a suggestion that the high-spread environment may offer an excellent opportunity to buy A-rated debt. The level of risk shown for A-rated debt in this case, about 600 to 700bp, is similar to that shown for Baa-rated debt in the low-spread environment, but it comes with significantly higher expected returns (about 1200bp over the Five-year horizon, as opposed to 300–400bp for Baa-rated bonds in the low-spread environment).

CONCLUSION

We have developed an approach to modeling risk and expected return in credit portfolios over a relatively long horizon that stakes out a middle ground between monthly mark-to-market risk measurement and pure hold-to-default analysis. This approach is relevant to mandates in which bonds are typically purchased to be held for an extended period of time, but sold early if the credit degrades beyond a certain point. We believe this description applies to a majority of credit portfolios and that this modeling approach should therefore be widely relevant.

The main point we would like to emphasize is that the sell discipline enforced for liquidation of distressed credits can have a profound effect on the long-term performance characteristics of different credit asset classes. Consideration of these effects can be applied at different points in the portfolio decision process. Ideally, they should be considered when establishing the sell discipline for a portfolio. As we have concluded in earlier studies, fallen angel bonds downgraded from IG to HY are subject to selling pressure immediately after the downgrade event; a policy that requires immediate forced selling of such bonds is therefore suboptimal. However, even after such a policy is chosen, it is still important to model its effect. For example, the asset allocation decision among different IG asset classes can and should be influenced by the sell discipline that is imposed.

Our model recognizes the importance of forced sales in determining the loss distribution in credit portfolios. We use credit ratings as the primary representation of credit quality; it is therefore important to use a complete transition matrix to model loss events rather than simply focusing on the risk of default. Furthermore, we have found strong empirical evidence that credit transitions, at least over the short term, are strongly linked to spread levels. We therefore need a mechanism by which to estimate the best available transition matrix conditioned on the current spread environment.

Our empirical results, based on data from the past 20 to 30 years, indicate that high spreads signal greater risk of credit losses in several ways. Not only do high spreads indicate greater frequencies of defaults and downgrades over the next one to two years, but high spreads also tend to be accompanied by high spread differentials between different quality ratings, increasing the severity of loss upon a forced sale as well as the likelihood of such events. These effects are especially harmful when purchasing Baa bonds under a sell discipline that would require selling them immediately upon a one-letter downgrade to Ba; they are exacerbated when investing in long-maturity bonds. However, we have also found a strong tendency for spreads and downgrade rates to mean revert within about two to three years. This means that long-term risk does not increase by as much as spread and that periods of high spreads may indeed be viewed as buying opportunities—but perhaps with a bias toward shorter maturities and/or higher qualities.

Bonds near the threshold for forced selling are most sensitive to increased risk. Our model includes a performance penalty based on empirical evidence of the selling pressure experienced by fallen angel bonds. Results of this model seem to suggest that a more relaxed selling discipline that allows bonds to be held in the portfolio until they are downgraded to B should tend to outperform the more widely used sell-at-Ba discipline. For investors who retain the sell-at-Ba discipline, our model suggests that depending on the level of spreads and the shape of the spread curve, it may be advisable to adopt a bias toward A-rated rather than Baa-rated credits or to bias the Baa holdings to shorter maturities. Furthermore, these biases should be strengthened in elevated risk environments.

This chapter presents just the bare bones of the model and attempts to illustrate some of the fundamental effects that must be considered. However, the model constructed here is not a complete model of long-horizon risk for a credit portfolio because it is subject to some very limiting assumptions. First of all, we have limited ourselves to modeling the loss distribution of a single bond, not a portfolio. Second, the spread scenarios that we considered here concerned only expectations. In the first section of the chapter, we used long-term spreads and assumed them to be static; in the final section, we relaxed this assumption to allow conditioning on current spreads, with mean reversion to the long-term mean. This is reasonable concerning the expected path of spreads, but it does not begin to model all the possible evolutions of spreads over our return horizon, which may include some major spread widenings that would in turn imply a systematic increase in downgrade frequencies.

REFERENCES

Dastidar, S. G., and B. D. Phelps. 2011. "Credit Spread Decomposition: Decomposing Bond-Level Credit OAS into Default and Liquidity Components." *Journal of Portfolio Management* 37(3): 70–84.

Dynkin, L., A. Gould, J. Hyman, V. Konstantinovsky, and B. Phelps. 2007. *Quantitative Management of Bond Portfolios*. Princeton, NJ: Princeton University Press.

Dynkin, L., J. Hyman, and V. Konstantinovsky. 2002. "Sufficient Diversification in Credit Portfolios." *Journal of Portfolio Management* 29(1): 89–114.

Longstaff, F. A., and E. S. Schwartz. 1995. "Valuing Credit Derivatives." *Journal of Fixed Income* 5(1): 6–12.

Ng, K. Y., and B. Phelps. 2011. "Capturing Credit Spread Premium." *Financial Analysts Journal* 67(3): 63–75.

Ou, S., D. Chiu, B. Wen, and A. Metz. 2013, February 28. "Annual Default Study: Corporate Default and Recovery Rates, 1920–2012", Moody's Investors Service.

NOTES

1. For investors of this type who use book value accounting techniques, it can be difficult to evaluate manager performance due to the lack of appropriate benchmarks. A methodology for building customized book value benchmarks was presented in Dynkin, Gould, Hyman, Konstantinovsky, and Phelps (2007), Chapter 9.
2. Additional issues arise when applying this approach to a diversified credit portfolio; we have addressed some of these in further research, but this work is beyond the scope of this chapter.
3. Ou, Chiu, Wen, and Metz (2013).
4. Even for a pure buy-and-hold investor, there are many relevant refinements that should be considered. For example, recovery rates are not fixed: they can vary widely between 0% and 100%, their averages vary by sector, seniority, and bond price, and they are correlated with default rates. These effects have been studied in the past and are beyond the scope of this study; our focus is on the effect of forced sales rather than the intricacies of defaults and recoveries. Our analysis shows that forced sales comprise the bulk of the loss distribution for many investors.
5. A similar model of downgrade risk, combining downgrade probabilities with estimated losses upon downgrade, was explored in Dynkin, Hyman, and Konstantinovsky (2002). However, the emphasis there was on sufficient diversification to control tracking error volatility in mark-to-market portfolios.
6. The long-term average spreads used in this chapter were calculated to give our best representation of "typical" spreads over the period covered by the transition matrix used (1970–2012). For the majority of the period, we use spreads reported for the appropriately rated components of the Bloomberg Barclays US Corporate Bond and US High Yield Indices. To extend those series back to 1970, we use several approximations and adjustments to arrive at the best available representation. An eight-month period from the peak of the global financial crisis (September 2008–April 2009) was omitted from this average.

7. The loss in case of default is estimated as 60%, which is the complement of the earlier assumption of a constant recovery rate of 40%. This loss is also used to cap the loss in case of a downgrade with a very wide spread differential, as shown for a transition from Baa to Ca in Table 8.2.

8. The matrix used was obtained from Ou et al. (2013), Exhibit 26: Average One-Year Letter Rating Migration Rates, 1970–2012. We adjusted the matrix slightly to account for withdrawn ratings by prorating the probabilities on each line so that they sum to 100%.

9. Note that multiplying the historical one-year transition matrix by itself five times does not produce the historical five-year cumulative transition matrix. Further research could investigate ways to adjust the one-year matrix to make it as consistent as possible with the five-year matrix.

10. Assuming the proceeds of forced sales will be reinvested complicates the analysis by making it possible to experience more than one loss event over the horizon. Technically, the "cumulative probability of forced sales" reported here is the expected frequency of occurrence of forced sales; the probability of experiencing one or more forced sales to the horizon is slightly smaller.

11. In Chapter 2, we found that spreads of fallen angel bonds widen excessively in the first zero to three months following a downgrade but then revert to fair value after 12 to 24 months. No similar effect was found for a downgrade within HY, such as from Ba to B. To reflect these findings, we assume that if a bond is downgraded in one year to Ba and then in the subsequent year to B, investors who sell the bond immediately upon the downgrade will suffer the full extent of the selling pressure, modeled as a spread widening of 78bp beyond fair value. However, an investor who sells the bond after the second downgrade from Ba to B is assumed to receive full fair value for a B-rated security.

12. The above answer to this question focuses on risk. Another contributing factor linked to the strong selling pressure on fallen angels is that the rules governing many standard bond market benchmarks, including the Bloomberg Barclays US Aggregate Index, drop bonds at month-end immediately following a fall in index rating to below investment grade. Continuing to hold such bonds after they have exited the index can lead to an increase in tracking error volatility. To help ease this problem for investors who wish to relax their sell discipline, Barclays has introduced a series of downgrade-tolerant benchmarks that allow fallen angel bonds to remain in the portfolio. See Ng and Phelps (2011) for details.

13. These effects are not as clear for A-rated bonds. This highlights one drawback of tail risk measures: They do not provide a single number, but a set of risk numbers, for different confidence levels. For A-rated bonds, with default probabilities under 1%, even the 98% and 99% CVaR numbers represent averages over default events and less severe losses.

14. We use the standard deviation of cumulative five-year excess return as the measure of risk in Figure 8.4. The risk/return trade-off may indeed look different (and in this case might favor A-rated bonds even more) were we to choose a tail risk measure at a specific confidence level, such as 98% CVaR, as our primary risk metric. Investors must decide upon the risk metric (and confidence level, if applicable) most relevant to their own situations.

15. The long-term average spreads for the five-year maturity are assumed to be equal to the long-term average spreads reported earlier in Table 8.2 and Table 8.4. To approximate the term structure of spreads, we used US Corporate Index data to produce time series of average spreads for each quality in three maturity buckets from May 1993 through November 2013. We computed the ratio of short-maturity to medium-maturity spreads, and a similar long-to-medium spread ratio each month. We then took the median values of this spread ratio over this relatively short time period and multiplied them by the longer-term average levels for the five-year cell to obtain the representative spread levels shown above.

16. Default rates for annual cohorts are obtained from Ou et al. (2013), Exhibit 41, using summary data for IG and HY debt. We have chosen to base our study on default rates rather than the annual number of defaults. The results of a study based on default counts might be misleading, since the number of issuers varies over time.

17. One distortion inherent in this type of analysis is that a one-notch downgrade from A3 to Baa1 counts as a downgrade, while a two-notch downgrade from A1 to A3 does not. Nevertheless, as the ratings boundaries used for setting investment policy usually occur at full-letter-grade transitions, we believe this to be the relevant approach.

18. The much higher downgrade rates for A-rated bonds over Baa-rated bonds in 2009 is due to a preponderance of A ratings among the many financial issuers that experienced downgrades in that year. Including 2009 would reduce the calculated slope of the dependence for both A and Baa bonds, but this effect would be much stronger for Baa because that downgrade rate was essentially on par with long-term averages despite record high spreads.

19. This is corroborated by the large negative basis at that time between the spreads of cash bonds and CDS. The strong role of the liquidity component in the high spreads of 2008–2009 was demonstrated in Dastidar and Phelps (2011).

20. We eliminate spread observations as of the beginning of January 2009 from this analysis. To do so, we drop both the cohort beginning on this date as well as the observations from prior-year cohorts whose spread change horizon occurs on that date.

21. For example, see Longstaff and Schwartz (1995). The authors demonstrate consistent mean reversion toward a long-term average by regressing monthly changes in log spreads against beginning-of-month log spreads. They report a half-life of convergence toward the mean ranging from 0.7 to 1.0 years for industrial bonds and from 1.5 to 4 years for utility bonds. Our own similar study of corporate spreads gives a half-life between one and two years.

22. The mean reversion assumption shown here reflects exponential convergence in log spreads, with a half-life of one year, consistent with the model of Longstaff and Schwartz (1995).

23. The ratio of current spreads to long-term spreads varies by quality. In this analysis, unlike the simpler uniform rule depicted in Figure 8.15, we rescale each row of the transition matrix using a different downgrade multiplier, set equal to the appropriate spread ratio for each quality.

CHAPTER 9

Effect of Rating-Based Stop-Loss Rules on Performance

INTRODUCTION

Investment guidelines of institutional credit mandates often include rating-based liquidation rules that require selling issues downgraded to or below a certain quality level. Stop-loss rules are generally meant to limit mark-to-market as well as default losses and therefore reduce market risk. A potential reduction in portfolio volatility and tail risk can be a strong motivation for excluding downgraded bonds from credit portfolios.

For example, credit investors often buy investment-grade (IG) bonds and sell those downgraded into high yield (HY) to limit exposure to riskier quality sectors. Ng and Phelps (2011) document that by selling downgraded bonds falling into HY, IG Corporate indices miss out on a significant portion of the credit spread premium. In fact, only a relatively small proportion of downgraded bonds proceeds to default, while the majority mature at par and generally perform well post-downgrade.[1]

While the Ba rating threshold associated with downgrades to HY is probably the most common rating stop-loss, it is not the only one. Conservative investors, such as central banks, insurance companies, or commercial banks, often have sell thresholds at higher ratings.[2] At the same time, less conservative investors set liquidation thresholds at lower ratings, such as B or Caa, to capture part of the premium associated with the post-downgrade performance of fallen angels while limiting exposure to default.

In this chapter, we document the effects of rating-based stop-loss rules on the risk and return of diversified corporate bond portfolios.

Intuitively, selling bonds following a downgrade to or beyond a certain rating threshold should reduce both risk and return because riskier issues with higher spread carry get excluded from the portfolio. An overview of the average spreads of bond indices and rating transition frequencies is shown in Table 9.1. To illustrate the effect of a rating stop loss, consider a portfolio invested into Aa-rated bonds. This portfolio has an average spread of 92bp between 1994 and 2015 (see the first column of the table). In comparison, the average spread of the A-rated subindex over the same period is 126bp. If a rating stop loss is introduced at A, the average effect of this decision on portfolio performance is likely to be negative. Indeed, the Aa-rated index buys bonds at the average spread of 92bp and sells them at 126bp. Assuming the average duration of sold downgraded securities is 5.5 years, the return associated with a downgrade to A would be a negative 187bp (~5.5yr × [126bp − 92bp]).[3]

Only a small fraction of Aa bonds gets downgraded every year, though. The annual downgrade rate of the Aa-rated firms is only 9.6% (see the last column of the table), as indicated by Moody's transition probabilities.[4] The effect on the performance of the Aa portfolio is therefore −18bp/year (= −187 × 9.6%).

In the following sections, we seek an empirical validation of the intuition just presented and measure the effects of various rating-based stop-loss rules on the risk and return of diversified portfolios. We use Bloomberg Barclays Corporate bond index data and contrast the performance of subindices that sell downgraded bonds at different rating thresholds. In the first section that follows, we analyze rating stop-losses in portfolios of USD corporate bonds investing in different rating categories. The following section provides an explanation of the negative effect of rating stop-losses. Next, we compare downgraded bonds with their peers in the rating category to which they are downgraded. Finally, we study the effect of rating stop-loss rules in the euro and sterling markets. Appendix 9.1 explains the role of duration in the effects of stop-loss rules.

EFFECTS OF RATING STOP-LOSS RULES IN USD CREDIT

To evaluate the effects of rating-based stop-loss rules on the performance of USD corporate portfolios, we create a set of customized indices with different rating-specific buy and sell rules. Bonds are selected from the combined universes of Bloomberg Barclays US Corporate and US HY indices. These customized indices effectively represent diversified portfolios assembled according to predetermined investment and liquidation rules. They are market capitalization-weighted and are rebalanced every month-end. Each portfolio buys issues within a given rating range and sells bonds rated at or below a prespecified sell (stop loss) rating. Portfolios without a liquidation

TABLE 9.1 Average Spread of US Corporate Bonds by Rating and Moody's One-Year Transition Frequencies

Rating Bucket	Avg. OAS (bp) Jan 1994–Jan 2015	Moody's One-Year Transition Frequencies, 1970–2014								Total Downgrade Prob.
		Aaa	Aa	A	Baa	Ba	B	Caa	Default	
Aaa	71		8.48%	0.65%	0.00%	0.03%	0.00%	0.00%	0.00%	9.2%
Aa	92	0.94%		8.94%	0.52%	0.07%	0.02%	0.01%	0.02%	9.6%
A	126	0.05%	2.54%		5.84%	0.57%	0.11%	0.03%	0.06%	6.6%
Baa	183	0.04%	0.17%	4.19%		4.06%	0.75%	0.16%	0.17%	5.1%
Ba	350	0.01%	0.05%	0.36%	6.16%		8.08%	0.64%	1.11%	9.8%
B	515	0.01%	0.03%	0.12%	0.33%	5.00%		6.86%	3.90%	10.8%
Caa	913	0.00%	0.02%	0.02%	0.11%	0.42%	9.55%		13.46%	13.5%

Source: Moody's, Barclays Research

rule are called buy and hold (BH). BH portfolios also buy bonds in prespecified rating categories every month-end but hold them to default or maturity. We use these BH portfolios as benchmarks to measure the effect of rating-based stop-loss rules in relative terms.[5]

Table 9.2 shows the effects of rating stop-loss rules on risk and return characteristics of USD corporate portfolios investing across different rating categories. All returns are measured in excess of duration-matched Treasuries to segregate credit performance from exposure to interest rates.

The top two panels of the table show return statistics. The top-left panel includes returns of portfolios invested in individual rating categories. Each row corresponds to a specific buy rating at which bonds are included into a portfolio while each column represents a different liquidation threshold. The first column shows average excess returns of BH portfolios. Returns of portfolios with rating-based stop losses appear in the next five columns as incremental returns over corresponding BH portfolios. These columns represent return contributions of the various stop-loss rules considered.

Table 9.2 indicates that rating-based stop-loss rules have generally been detrimental to portfolio return between 1993 and 2015. The negative effect becomes larger as the "distance" between the original buy rating of a portfolio (at which bonds are purchased) and its sell-rating threshold declines. This is consistent with the relatively high transition probabilities for nearby rating categories reported in Moody's rating transition matrix in Table 9.1, immediately to the right of its main diagonal.

For example, the second row of the top-left panel of Table 9.2 shows average excess returns of portfolios invested into A-rated bonds.[6] The average return of the BH portfolio is 66bp/year. The A-rated portfolio with Caa rating threshold[7] underperforms its BH peer by 4bp/year (second column). This underperformance becomes larger as the stop loss is set at higher ratings, closer to the original rating category of the portfolio. Thresholds at B, Ba, and Baa lead to underperformance relative to the BH portfolio of 7bp, 13bp, and 22bp/year, respectively.[8] Similar patterns are observed across other buy-rating categories.

One surprising outcome is that the BH portfolio invested in A-rated bonds underperforms the one invested into Aaa–Aa bonds despite its higher average spread. Indeed, the average return of the Aaa–Aa portfolio is 74bp/year while that of the A portfolio is only 66bp/year. The reason for this anomaly is that the BH portfolio invested in A-rated bonds contained financial issuers that defaulted in 2008–2009: for example, Lehman Brothers (LEH) and Washington Mutual (WM). When these issuers are excluded, the anomaly disappears. Rating-based stop-loss rules do not protect against jump to default.

TABLE 9.2 Return and Risk of Corporate Bond Portfolios Incepted in December 1992, January 1993–January 2015

| | | Incremental over BH | | | | | | | Incremental over BH | | | | |
Rating Cat.	BH	Sell @ Caa	Sell @ B	Sell @ Ba	Sell @ Baa	Sell @ A	Cum. Rating Range	BH	Sell @ Caa	Sell @ B	Sell @ Ba	Sell @ Baa	Sell @ A
						Average Excess Return (bp/y)							
Aaa–Aa	74	−1	−3	−6	−11	−41	Aaa–Aa	74	−1	−3	−6	−11	−41
A	66	−4	−7	−13	−22		Aaa–A	63	−4	−7	−11	−19	
Baa	116	−13	−22	−39			Aaa–Baa (IG)	75	−8	−12	−20		
Ba	288	−35	−69				Aaa–Ba	89	−9	−16			
B	242	−41					Aaa–B	91	−8				
Caa	275						Aaa–Caa	94					
						Volatility (bp/y)							
Aaa–Aa	366	0	−1	−3	−8	−59	Aaa–Aa	366	0	−1	−3	−8	−59
A	448	−5	−10	−15	−27		Aaa–A	418	−4	−8	−13	−27	
Baa	538	−16	−27	−48			Aaa–Baa (IG)	450	−8	−15	−25		
Ba	805	−49	−99				Aaa–Ba	470	−11	−21			
B	992	−83					Aaa–B	506	−18				
Caa	1,352						Aaa–Caa	520					
						Max Drawdown (bp)							
Aaa–Aa	1,825	0	−5	0	−11	−126	Aaa–Aa	1,825	0	−5	0	−11	−126
A	2,542	−46	−85	−105	−71		Aaa–A	2,356	−36	−69	−87	−91	
Baa	2,943	−111	−227	−314			Aaa–Baa (IG)	2,590	−55	−113	−169		
Ba	3,896	−204	−523				Aaa–Ba	2,676	−57	−134			
B	4,424	−304					Aaa–B	2,828	−88				
Caa	5,595						Aaa–Caa	2,907					

Source: Barclays Research

Investment guidelines of credit portfolios often define only the minimum rating, allowing managers to buy higher-quality bonds. In other words, rating categories are often defined as cumulative ranges. Accordingly, the right panel of Table 9.2 illustrates the effect of rating stop-loss rules on the performance of portfolios invested across cumulative rating categories.

For example, the third row of the top-right panel shows average excess returns (over BH peers) of portfolios that buy bonds rated Baa and higher (Aaa–Baa) and sell at prespecified rating thresholds: Caa, B, and Ba. The portfolio that sells bonds downgraded to or below Ba coincides in composition with the standard US Corporate IG index, which also sells securities following a downgrade to HY. This portfolio underperforms its BH equivalent by 20bp/year as a result of the rating stop loss. The size and the magnitude of the effect align with the results of Ng and Phelps (2011). The reductions in return to the Aaa–A and Aaa–Ba portfolios caused by respective Baa and B sell thresholds are comparable with the one associated with selling fallen angels from the investment-grade portfolio. An even stronger negative effect is observed for the Aaa–Aa portfolio with A stop-loss. This can be attributed largely to the systemic downgrades of financial firms in 2008.

The four bottom panels of Table 9.2 show risk statistics for the same portfolios. The middle panels display the effect of rating stop-loss rules on portfolio volatility while the bottom panels include maximum drawdown. Similar to the average excess returns, the effects of stop-loss rules are reported in increments over the risk of BH portfolios shown in the first column of each panel.

As expected, imposing rating stop-loss rules generally reduces portfolio risk. For example, the volatility of the Aaa–Aa portfolio with a stop loss at A is 59bp/year lower (first row, sixth column of the mid-left panel) than that of its BH peer (366bp/year). The corresponding reduction in maximum drawdown, shown in the bottom-left panel, is 126bp (from 1,825bp to 1,699bp). In comparison, the average return of this portfolio declines by 41bp/year (first row, sixth column of the top-left panel). In percentage terms, the return reduction significantly exceeds the reduction in risk (56% vs. 7 or 16%, depending on the risk measure).

Results are similar across cumulative rating categories reported in the right panels of the table. For example, the Aaa–Baa portfolio selling at Ba (US Corporate IG index) is 25bp/year less volatile than its BH counterpart (425bp/year vs. 450bp/year). Its maximum drawdown is 169bp less than that of its BH peer (2,590bp vs. 2,421bp). These reductions in risk are only 5 to 7% when expressed in relative terms while return drops 27%, from 75bp/year to 55bp/year. Similar results are found for other buy and sell rating categories. We find that rating stop-loss rules have a much stronger effect on portfolio return than on risk.

In Appendix 9.1, we present a simple model that explains why stop-loss rules have a larger effect on return than on risk. It turns out that the percentage decline in return is proportional to the duration of downgraded bonds while the percentage reduction in volatility is not.[9] We contrast the effect of stop-loss rules on portfolios of different maturities and find that empirical evidence corroborates the model.[10]

Our empirical results contradict somewhat the commonly accepted view that rating sell thresholds (a) limit losses in the portfolio and thus enhance return and (b) reduce market risk. We observe, instead, that the first goal is failed outright: Rating stop-loss rules lead to significant declines in return. This outcome is consistent with Kaminski and Lo (2014), who demonstrate that in the absence of return momentum, a stop-loss rule which replaces a higher-yielding asset with a lower-yielding one (as is the case with selling downgraded bonds) leads to losses in expected performance. This negative effect is stronger when asset returns exhibit mean reversion, which is likely to be the case for corporate bonds as they end up reaching maturity and repaying principal in the absence of default. Our findings are also consistent with the evidence that credit markets anticipate rating downgrades.[11] Indeed, if market prices incorporate negative news prior to the downgrade, an actual rating change does not per se signal a further spread widening, so that the scope for stopping further market losses by selling downgraded bonds might be limited.

The relatively small effect of stop-loss rules on portfolio risk is surprising. For example, the difference in volatilities of the A portfolio selling at Baa and its BH counterpart is only –27bp/year (421bp/year vs. 448bp/year). At the same time, a large portion of the BH portfolio invested in A-rated issues migrates to lower ratings as a result of downgrades. Figure 9.1 reports the historical rating composition of portfolios that buy A-rated bonds. Over time, some bonds are upgraded or downgraded. Issues upgraded to Aaa–Aa remain in the portfolios. However, bonds downgraded to Baa or below are sold subject to the stop-loss rule (Panel A) but remain in the BH portfolio (Panel B). As a result, a significant proportion of the BH portfolio may transition to lower ratings over time. Panel B shows that, on average, over 10% of the portfolio market value is invested in bonds rated Baa or below. This significant difference in composition leads to a relatively modest difference in risk.

To some extent, the small reduction in risk can be explained by the high level of diversification of the underlying portfolio. Indeed, while rating stop-losses are designed to limit issuer-specific risk of individual downgraded issuers, they are perhaps less suited to handle the risk of a systematic wave

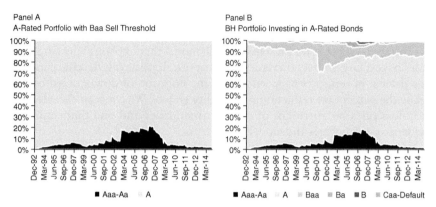

FIGURE 9.1   Rating Allocation of Buy and Hold (BH) Portfolios over Time
Source: Barclays Research

of downgrades, as seen in 2001 or 2008. It is doubtful that selling a significant portion of a portfolio at depressed prices, following systemic downgrades through a crisis, helps improve performance, especially if most bonds
were purchased at tight spreads. Furthermore, the added value of a
security-level stop-loss rule can be limited in diversified portfolios. Indeed,
idiosyncratic risk declines quickly as the number of issuers increases, even
without any stop-loss rules.

Rating-based liquidation rules can be more effective in reducing the
risk of concentrated portfolios, especially when default risk is considered
as well. Indeed, while the probability of observing a default in a concentrated portfolio is relatively small, its occurrence can result in a very large
loss. Rating stop-loss rules can reduce default-related tail risk if, by following a stop-loss rule, investors are able to sell downgraded bonds prior
to default.

We next look at how rating stop-loss rules have affected performance of
corporate bond portfolios in financial and nonfinancial sectors. There are
three reasons to consider financial and nonfinancial sectors separately. First,
rating agencies use different methodologies for financial and nonfinancial
firms. Second, the financial sector might be more sensitive to ratings given
its balance sheet–intensive business model. Finally, credit cycles are likely to
affect financial and nonfinancial sectors differently. For example, a larger
proportion of financial firms were downgraded following the 2008 crisis
than industrial companies.

Table 9.3 shows the effect of rating stop-loss rules on return and volatility of financial (left panel) and nonfinancial (right panel) portfolios.
Rating-based liquidation rules set immediately below the original buy

TABLE 9.3 Average Return and Risk of Financial and Nonfinancial Corporate Bond Portfolios Incepted in December 1992, January 1993–January 2015

Financials

Rating Cat.	BH	Incremental over BH				
		Sell @ Caa	Sell @ B	Sell @ Ba	Sell @ Baa	Sell @ A
Average Excess Return (bp/y)						
Aaa–Aa	108	−1	−1	−5	−9	−46
A	87	−2	−4	−11	−29	
Baa	178	−10	−16	−31		
Ba	457	−143	−125			
B	610	−277				
Caa	665					
Volatility (bp/y)						
Aaa–Aa	414	−1	−1	−4	−8	−77
A	580	−1	−4	−10	−22	
Baa	637	−9	−23	−54		
Ba	1,501	−255	−397			
B	2,146	−674				
Caa	2,806					

Nonfinancials

Rating Cat.	BH	Incremental over BH				
		Sell @ Caa	Sell @ B	Sell @ Ba	Sell @ Baa	Sell @ A
Average Excess Return (bp/y)						
Aaa–Aa	50	−3	−5	−6	−12	−16
A	54	−3	−8	−9	−9	
Baa	101	−10	−21	−41		
Ba	268	−21	−58			
B	219	−23				
Caa	217					
Volatility (bp/y)						
Aaa–Aa	296	0	−5	−6	−24	−39
A	394	−8	−12	−19	−37	
Baa	536	−15	−26	−47		
Ba	774	−40	−87			
B	974	−72				
Caa	1,329					

Source: Barclays Research

ratings are especially detrimental to the performance of financial portfolios invested in Aaa–Aa and A bonds. Indeed, the Aaa–Aa financial portfolio with a sell threshold at A underperforms its BH counterpart by 46bp/year while the underperformance of the similar nonfinancial portfolio is only 16bp/year. Similarly, financial and nonfinancial portfolios invested in A-rated bonds and selling at Baa underperform their BH peers by 29bp/year and 9bp/year, respectively.

The bottom panels of Table 9.3 show the effects of rating stop losses on portfolio volatility. As expected, volatility is reduced across all rating categories. This reduction is especially significant for financial portfolios in lower rating categories (Ba and B). These portfolios were very concentrated prior to 2008 as few financials were then rated below investment grade. For example, in December 2005, the number of financial bonds in our universe was only 33 Ba, and 18 B-rated, but 250 Baa, 625 A, and 299 Aaa–Aa-rated. As a result, volatility reductions of the Ba and B portfolios from sell thresholds set at B and Caa, respectively, are 26% (from 1,501bp/year to 1,104bp/year) and 31% (from 2,146bp/year to 1,472bp/year) in relative terms. For financial portfolios that invest in higher rating categories, the reductions in volatility relative to BH peers are much smaller than the percentage reductions in return.

The composition of credit portfolios subject to stop-loss rules is often path-dependent. Generally, portfolios that follow separate buy and sell rating rules depend on rating history and, hence, inception date. For example, an A-rated portfolio that sells bonds downgraded to Ba buys all bonds rated A1, A2, or A3 in a given month and keeps them until they get downgraded to or below Ba. This means that a bond downgraded by one notch to Baa remains in the portfolio. In contrast, a portfolio created after the downgrade would not include this bond because its new Baa rating does not meet the A-rating investment criterion.

Similarly, the composition of all BH portfolios except Aaa–Caa also depends on their inception dates. The only portfolios that are not path-dependent are those that invest in a cumulative rating range and have a liquidation threshold set immediately next to the lower boundary of that investment range: Aaa–Aa selling at A, Aaa–A selling at Baa, Aaa–Baa selling at Ba, Aaa–Ba selling at B, Aaa–B selling at Caa, and the BH portfolio that includes all rating ranges (Aaa–Caa).

Would the results of our analysis change qualitatively as a function of the inception date and sample period? Table 9.4 shows the effects of stop-loss rules in two separate subperiods.

The two left panels of Table 9.4 relate to portfolios incepted in December 1992 while the two right panels correspond to portfolios incepted in December 2004.

TABLE 9.4 Average Return and Risk of Corporate Portfolios with Inception Dates in December 1992 or December 2004

Rating Cat.	January 1993–December 2004							January 2005–January 2015						
	BH	Incremental over BH						BH	Incremental over BH					
		Sell @ Caa	Sell @ B	Sell @ Ba	Sell @ Baa	Sell @ A			Sell @ Caa	Sell @ B	Sell @ Ba	Sell @ Baa	Sell @ A	
Average Excess Return (bp/y)														
Aaa–Aa	51	-1	-2	-2	-5	-4		98	-1	-2	-9	-16	-82	
A	62	-3	-6	-7	-4			62	-2	-5	-12	-41		
Baa	92	-13	-25	-38				135	-9	-12	-34			
Ba	226	-32	-87					376	-42	-52				
B	152	-18						355	-72					
Caa	91							501						
Volatility (bp/y)														
Aaa–Aa	155	0	-1	-2	-7	-17		520	-1	-1	-5	-8	-90	
A	209	-1	-4	-11	-32			619	-1	-3	-7	-19		
Baa	336	-7	-16	-42				706	-16	-28	-48			
Ba	598	-25	-70					1,034	-68	-125				
B	836	-51						1,165	-111					
Caa	1,189							1,574						

Source: Barclays Research

For high-quality portfolios (Aaa–Aa and A), the reduction in return is much larger in the second period than in the first one. For example, the Aaa–Aa portfolio selling at A underperforms its BH peer by 4bp/year from 1993 to 2004 and by 82bp/year from 2005 to 2015. This can be explained by the large proportion of highly rated financials downgraded following the 2008 crisis. The underperformance of Baa portfolios selling fallen angels is comparable in both periods (38bp/year and 34bp/year, respectively).

The financial crisis of 2008 amplified the negative return impact of stop-loss rules in higher rating categories. The wave of systemic downgrades accompanied by elevated credit spreads caused substantial losses due to selling downgraded bonds.

EXPLAINING THE PERFORMANCE DROP

Historical data of diversified US corporate bond indices show that a rating-based stop-loss rule reduces portfolio risk but, at the same time, leads to a disproportional decline in return. In this section, we try to better understand the mechanism through which this performance drop arises. We take the portfolio that buys Aaa–Aa bonds and sells bonds downgraded to A as a working example.

In the introduction, we used Moody's annual transition probabilities and differences in average spreads between rating categories to explain the return effect of a rating stop loss. That logic still applies but needs to be expanded.

On average, a portfolio that buys Aaa–Aa bonds invests at a spread lower than the one of A-rated bonds. The spread of a bond downgraded to A generally widens relative to its value when that bond joined the portfolio. When downgraded bonds are sold, the losses associated with the spread widening are realized and cannot be recovered if spreads subsequently tighten. Bonds in higher rating categories rarely proceed to default so that their spreads tend to tighten as bond prices are pulled to par closer to maturity. This causes the Aaa–Aa portfolio with the A sell threshold to underperform its BH peer. In practice, this effect is magnified because downgrade probabilities and credit spreads are positively correlated.

In Figure 9.2, we plot the difference, averaged over 12 months, between the average spread of A bonds that have been downgraded from Aaa–Aa and that of Aaa–Aa bonds. The figure also plots the rolling 12-month downgrade frequencies in the Aaa–Aa portfolio.

We can make two important observations. First, the spread difference between bonds downgraded to A and the Aaa–Aa portfolio can be substantial, especially in times of market turmoil. The loss from selling a downgraded

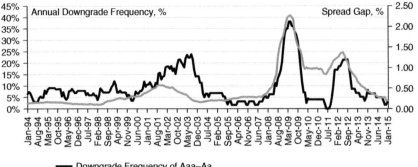

FIGURE 9.2 Downgrade Frequency of Aaa–Aa Bonds and Spread Gap Between Bonds Downgraded to A and Aaa–Aa Bonds Averaged over 12 Months
Source: Barclays Research

bond can be approximated by the product of this spread difference and bond duration. Assuming a 5.5-year duration, the loss given downgrade could reach 12.5% (227bp × 5.5year) in the peak of the financial crisis 2008. Second, downgrade rates and spread differentials (and hence losses given downgrade) are positively correlated. Their correlation is 66% in our sample. This positive correlation amplifies the negative effect from selling downgraded bonds. Indeed, if the correlation between downgrade frequencies and losses was zero, the performance drop from selling downgraded bonds could be estimated as the product of the sample-average downgrade loss (average spread gap times duration) and the average downgrade probability.[12] Since the correlation between downgrade rates and losses is positive, the covariance between these two terms must be added to the expression.

The expected loss due to downgrades can then be calculated as the expectation of the product of the downgrade frequency and the loss given downgrade. We can therefore estimate the effect of selling downgraded bonds as the sum of two terms.[13] The first term is related to average losses and downgrades and the second one reflects the positive correlation between downgrade frequencies and losses:

$$\text{Exp. Loss} = E[\text{DG Freq} \times \text{DG Loss}] = E[\text{DG Freq}] \times E[\text{DG Loss}]$$
$$+ \text{Cov}[\text{DG Freq}, \text{DG Loss}]$$

The average spread difference between downgraded A-rated bonds and Aaa–Aa bonds plotted on Figure 9.2 is 50bp, while the average downgrade frequency is 9.5%/year. This can be used to calculate the first term of the expression, 26bp/year (= 5.5year × 50bp × 9.5%). The correlation-related effect can be expressed as the product of the correlation between downgrade frequencies and losses, the volatility of downgrade frequencies, and the volatility of downgrade losses. The volatility of downgrade losses in our sample can be estimated as the volatility of the spread difference between A and Aaa–Aa rated bonds (48bp/year) multiplied by duration (5.5 years). The estimated magnitude of the correlation effect is 13bp/year (= 66% × 7.6%/ year × 48bp/yr × 5.5year), where the correlation between downgrade frequency and the spread differential is 66%, and the volatility of downgrade frequency is 7.6%/year. The overall estimated effect of the stop loss at A for the Aaa–Aa portfolio is 39bp/year (=26bp/year + 13bp/year). This number is close to the actual loss of 41bp/year observed in our sample and shown in the top-left panel of Table 9.2.

CHARACTERISTICS OF DOWNGRADED BONDS

As discussed in the previous section, the negative effect from a rating-based stop-loss rule on portfolio return does not require downgraded bonds to have special characteristics. A performance drag from selling downgraded bonds should manifest itself as long as downgraded bonds perform in line with peers in the rating category to which they are downgraded. However, the effect is stronger when downgraded bonds outperform their new peers. Indeed, since downgraded bonds are retained in the BH portfolio but sold from the original portfolio, their subsequent performance determines the cost of the stop-loss rule.

For example, bonds downgraded from investment grade to high yield (fallen angels) tend to outperform their new peers after the downgrade due to price pressures around the downgrade event.[14] Also, Ng and Phelps (2011) design an experiment in which downgraded bonds in a downgrade tolerant index are replaced by broad HY or Ba indices and show that the resulting composite portfolio underperforms the BH portfolio that retains downgraded bonds.

We perform a similar analysis for portfolios investing across cumulative rating ranges and subject to predefined liquidation thresholds. For each portfolio, we design a peer that matches its rating allocation with rating-specific subindices. Downgraded bonds are replaced by subindices of the corresponding rating and the weights of individual rating buckets are adjusted monthly to match the rating allocation of the rule-based portfolio that retains downgraded bonds.

Quality-matched portfolios should underperform original portfolios that hold downgraded securities if downgraded bonds perform better than their new peers. This is what we see in Table 9.5, which compares the original rule-based portfolios with corresponding quality-matched portfolios.

TABLE 9.5 Risk and Return of Rule-Based Portfolios Incepted in December 1992 vs. Those of Rating-Matched Peers, January 1993–January 2015

Portfolios with Buy and Sell Rating Rules (B&S)

Average Excess Return (bp/y)

	BH	Sell @ Caa	Sell @ B	Sell @ Ba	Sell @ Baa	Sell @ A
Aaa–Aa	74	73	71	68	63	33
Aaa–A	63	59	56	51	44	
Aaa–Baa (IG)	75	67	63	55		
Aaa–Ba	89	80	73			
Aaa–B	91	83				
Aaa–Caa	94					

Volatility (bp/y)

	BH	Sell @ Caa	Sell @ B	Sell @ Ba	Sell @ Baa	Sell @ A
Aaa–Aa	366	366	365	363	358	307
Aaa–A	418	413	409	405	391	
Aaa–Baa (IG)	450	442	435	425		
Aaa–Ba	470	459	449			
Aaa–B	506	488				
Aaa–Caa	520					

Maximum Drawdown (bp)

	BH	Sell @ Caa	Sell @ B	Sell @ Ba	Sell @ Baa	Sell @ A
Aaa–Aa	1,825	1825	1820	1825	1814	1699
Aaa–A	2,356	2320	2287	2270	2265	
Aaa–Baa (IG)	2,590	2535	2477	2421		
Aaa–Ba	2,676	2618	2541			
Aaa–B	2,828	2740				
Aaa–Caa	2,907					

Peer Portfolios with Matching Rating Allocation

Average Excess Return over B&S (bp/y)

	BH	Sell @ Caa	Sell @ B	Sell @ Ba	Sell @ Baa	Sell @ A
Aaa–Aa	-24	-22	-22	-20	-15	0
Aaa–A	-12	-10	-8	-5	0	
Aaa–Baa (IG)	-9	-6	-3	0		
Aaa–Ba	-8	-5	0			
Aaa–B	0	0				
Aaa–Caa	0					

Volatility over B&S (bp/y)

	BH	Sell @ Caa	Sell @ B	Sell @ Ba	Sell @ Baa	Sell @ A
Aaa–Aa	-20	-20	-20	-18	-17	0
Aaa–A	-11	-10	-8	-6	0	
Aaa–Baa (IG)	-6	-5	-3	0		
Aaa–Ba	-4	-3	0			
Aaa–B	0	0				
Aaa–Caa	0					

Maximum Drawdown over B&S (bp)

	BH	Sell @ Caa	Sell @ B	Sell @ Ba	Sell @ Baa	Sell @ A
Aaa–Aa	93	91	92	85	73	0
Aaa–A	3	8	18	27	0	
Aaa–Baa (IG)	-39	-38	-19	0		
Aaa–Ba	-22	-21	0			
Aaa–B	-4	0				
Aaa–Caa	0					

Source: Barclays Research

The quality-matched portfolios are shown in the right panels of the table in terms of incremental performance over respective original portfolios with buy and sell rating rules.

The left panels of Table 9.5 repeat information provided in Table 9.2, while the right panels show that quality-matched portfolios tend to underperform their rule-based peers. The underperformance is larger for portfolios that match the quality allocation of BH portfolios. For example, the Aaa–Aa BH portfolio outperforms its composite rating-matched peer by 24bp/year, while the portfolio that sells at Baa outperforms by only 15bp/year. The quality-matched portfolios also have slightly lower volatilities, while maximum drawdown statistics are similar.

While a detailed event study of downgraded bonds is outside the scope of this chapter, our results indicate that downgraded bonds tend to outperform their composite rating peers. In other words, retaining a downgraded bond tends to be a better strategy than replacing it with a similar nondowngraded bond of the same destination rating.

Another way to look into this is to compare the performance of downgraded bonds with that of their BH peers invested in the rating category to which they get downgraded. Table 9.6 compares the performance of BH portfolios with downgraded bonds (DG) for various rating buckets. DG portfolios outperform their BH peers in all rating categories except Caa, both in terms of return and information ratio. For example, the second row of the table contrasts bonds downgraded from Aaa–Aa to A with the BH portfolio originally invested into A-rated bonds. The DG portfolio has an average excess return of 103bp/year, which is substantially larger than the 66bp/year of the comparable BH portfolio.

TABLE 9.6 Performance of BH Portfolios vs. Performance of Downgraded (DG) Bonds by Rating Category, March 1993–January 2015

	BH Portfolios			DG Portfolios		
	Avg. Exc. Return (bp/y)	Volatility (bp/y)	Information Ratio	Avg. Exc. Return (bp/y)	Volatility (bp/y)	Information Ratio
Aaa–Aa	74	366	0.20			
A	66	448	0.15	103	478	0.22
Baa	116	538	0.22	180	604	0.30
Ba	288	805	0.36	434	973	0.45
B	242	992	0.24	492	1,213	0.41
Caa	275	1,352	0.20	257	1,453	0.18

Source: Barclays Research

EFFECTS OF RATING STOP-LOSS RULES
IN NON-USD CREDIT MARKETS

Having found that rating-based liquidation rules often reduce the performance of credit portfolios in the US dollar market, we now turn to the euro and sterling credit markets. These two markets have less historical data than the US market, as corporate bond indices are available only from 1999. Table 9.7 reports the effects of rating stop losses on return and risk of diversified portfolios of euro-denominated corporate bonds for various rating categories and rating sell thresholds.

Table 9.7 is broadly consistent with our findings for the USD market: Stop-loss rules reduce portfolio return. The drop can be significant, especially when a rating sell threshold is set immediately below the original buy rating range of the portfolio. For example, the portfolio that buys Baa-rated bonds and sells them at Ba (third row, fourth column of the top-left panel) underperforms its BH peer (column 1) by 57bp/year. The average excess return of the BH portfolio invested into Baa bonds is 155bp/year. This means that the average excess return of the Baa portfolio selling at Ba is 98bp/year, 37% lower than the return of the corresponding BH portfolio.

The top-right panel of the table illustrates portfolios with cumulative buy-rating ranges. For example, the portfolio invested into Aaa–Baa bonds and selling at Ba underperforms its BH peer by 24bp/year. As in the case of the USD market, this portfolio matches the composition of the standard Euro Investment-Grade Corporate index, which invests into IG bonds and sells upon downgrade to HY. The average excess return of this portfolio is 55bp/year (=79 – 24bp/year), 31% lower than the average excess return of the corresponding BH portfolio invested into Aaa–Baa securities (79bp/year).

The two bottom panels of the table show changes in portfolio volatility corresponding to different stop-loss rules. As in the US market, introducing a stop loss reduces portfolio volatility. When measured in relative terms, reductions in volatilities are much smaller than the corresponding declines in average return. For example, the volatility of the Aaa–Baa BH portfolio is reduced by 16bp/year (from 335bp/year to 319bp/year) when a Ba sell threshold is imposed. This 4.5% risk reduction is accompanied by a 31% reduction in return, from 79bp/year to 55bp/year.

Stop-loss rules have similar effects in sterling corporate portfolios. Table 9.8 presents results in the same format as Table 9.7 and provides the same insight. Generally, the reductions in return due to rating stop losses are larger for the sterling market than for USD or euro ones. This can be related to the higher average duration of sterling corporate bonds: 7.6 years as opposed to 6 years for the US corporate index, which makes downgrade losses of sterling portfolios larger in magnitude. For example, the A portfolio with a Baa sell threshold underperforms its BH equivalent by 91bp/year.

TABLE 9.7 Average Excess Return and Volatility of Euro Corporate Portfolios Incepted in December 1998, January 1999–January 2015

		Incremental over BH							Incremental over BH				
Rating Cat	BH	Sell @ Caa	Sell @ B	Sell @ Ba	Sell @ Baa	Sell @ A	Cum. Rating Range	BH	Sell @ Caa	Sell @ B	Sell @ Ba	Sell @ Baa	Sell @ A
Average Excess Return (bp/y)													
Aaa–Aa	66	0	–2	–11	–29	–47	Aaa–Aa	66	0	–2	–11	–29	–47
A	72	–3	–9	–25	–49		Aaa–A	67	–2	–6	–18	–39	
Baa	155	–7	–18	–57			Aaa–Baa (IG)	79	–3	–8	–24		
Ba	581	–31	–46				Aaa–Ba	85	–4	–10			
B	315	–73					Aaa–B	85	–5				
Caa	360						Aaa–Caa	84					
Volatility (bp/y)													
Aaa–Aa	285	–1	–2	–5	–19	–79	Aaa–Aa	285	–1	–2	–5	–19	–79
A	382	–3	–6	–14	–35		Aaa–A	321	–2	–5	–11	–30	
Baa	457	–7	–15	–39			Aaa–Baa (IG)	335	–3	–6	–16		
Ba	1,058	–41	–45				Aaa–Ba	346	–4	–8			
B	1,384	–106					Aaa–B	361	–7				
Caa	2,117						Aaa–Caa	363					

Source: Barclays Research

TABLE 9.8 Average Excess Return and Volatility of Sterling Corporate Portfolios Incepted in August 1999, September 1999–January 2015

Rating Cat.	BH	Incremental over BH					Cum. Rating Range	BH	Incremental over BH				
		Sell @ Caa	Sell @ B	Sell @ Ba	Sell @ Baa	Sell @ A			Sell @ Caa	Sell @ B	Sell @ Ba	Sell @ Baa	Sell @ A
Average Excess Return (bp/y)													
Aaa–Aa	86	-2	-5	-20	-47	-65	Aaa–Aa	86	-2	-5	-20	-47	-65
A	62	-7	-20	-39	-91		Aaa–A	73	-6	-15	-31	-70	
Baa	197	-13	-33	-70			Aaa–Baa (IG)	84	-6	-17	-35		
Ba	749	-74	-158				Aaa–Ba	90	-7	-19			
B	730	-100					Aaa–B	88	-8				
Caa	1,139						Aaa–Caa	88					
Volatility (bp/y)													
Aaa–Aa	512	-1	-2	-6	-24	-109	Aaa–Aa	512	-1	-2	-6	-24	-109
A	628	-4	-11	-21	-35		Aaa–A	551	-3	-8	-17	-36	
Baa	628	-6	-16	-41			Aaa–Baa (IG)	546	-3	-8	-16		
Ba	1,181	-28	-72				Aaa–Ba	549	-3	-9			
B	1,403	-49					Aaa–B	552	-4				
Caa	1,771						Aaa–Caa	552					

Source: Barclays Research

Similarly, the Aaa–Baa portfolio selling at Ba underperforms its BH version by 35bp/year. This portfolio matches the composition of the Sterling Corporate IG index, so that a portfolio referencing this index could boost returns by 70% (from 49 to 84 bp/year) if holding bonds to maturity or default instead of selling upon downgrade to HY.

The bottom panel of Table 9.8 reports changes in portfolio volatility relative to respective BH portfolios due to stop-loss rules. Again, volatility numbers decline only moderately compared with the large declines in respective average excess returns when measured in percentage terms.

CONCLUSION

Investment guidelines of institutional credit mandates often require selling bonds downgraded to or below a certain quality level. This requirement can be seen as a stop-loss rule and typically is introduced to limit credit losses and control portfolio risk.

Our analysis illustrates the effects of different stop-loss rules on the historical performances of various corporate bond subindices. We find that rating-based stop-loss rules lead to lower portfolio returns. This result is observed for diversified portfolios of different rating qualities and for all liquidation rating thresholds considered.

While rating stop-loss rules do reduce portfolio risk, the reduction in volatility and drawdown risk is, in the diversified portfolios considered in our analysis, much less than proportional to the decline in return. The percentage drop in return is proportional to duration, but the percentage drop in volatility is not. This makes stop-loss rules particularly detrimental to risk-adjusted returns of long-duration credit portfolios.

The magnitude of the performance drag associated with rating stop losses can be significant, even for portfolios of high-quality bonds. This is especially true when liquidation thresholds are set immediately below the target quality of a credit portfolio, so that the probability of forced liquidation is high.

We find that downgraded bonds tend to perform better than their rating peers. This phenomenon contributes to the performance drag of selling downgraded securities.

As the risk-adjusted performance of diversified credit portfolios does not seem to benefit from rating-based stop-loss rules, it may be preferable to incorporate rating only in terms of investment rule, but not liquidation rule. For example, rating guidelines could require that bonds be rated A or higher to join a portfolio but would allow downgraded bonds to be retained. If rating-based liquidation rules cannot be avoided, setting them relatively far from the original investment rating of the portfolio helps limit their negative impact on performance. For example, a portfolio manager investing in A-rated bonds can set a stop-loss threshold at B instead of Baa to limit the performance drop associated with forced selling upon a downgrade.

APPENDIX 9.1

Relative Effects of Rating Stop-Loss Rules on Portfolio Return and Volatility

Our empirical results indicate that the decline in portfolio return associated with a rating stop-loss rule is typically much larger than the corresponding decline in volatility when expressed in percentage terms, relative to the corresponding BH portfolio. Here is an analytical explanation of why the percentage drop in return is larger than that in volatility.

Consider two portfolio strategies that invest in a single Aa-rated bond with spread S_L and duration D.[15] The first strategy, which we call *sell at downgrade* (SG), implements a rating stop loss at A and therefore sells the bond upon downgrade. The bond spread when rated A is $S_H > S_L$. The strategy replaces the downgraded bond with a new Aa-rated bond with the same characteristics as the original one. The second strategy, called *buy-and-hold* (BH), retains the original bond regardless of downgrade. To simplify, we assume no default and that the abovementioned downgrade is the only possible event affecting the strategy.[16] What is the effect of the sell threshold on strategy return and volatility?

The return of the BH strategy, which retains the original bond indefinitely, is:

$$R_{BH} = S_L$$

The return of the SG strategy, which sells and replaces the downgraded bond, is:

$$R_{SG} = S_L - pD(S_H - S_L),$$

where p is the annual downgrade probabilityThis formula expresses the return of the SG strategy as the originally promised spread minus the expected loss due to downgrades.

From these two equations, the effect of the rating stop loss on strategy returns measured in percentage terms is:

$$\frac{R_{SG} - R_{BH}}{R_{BH}} = \frac{-pD(S_H - S_L)}{S_L} = -pD\left(\frac{S_H}{S_L} - 1\right) \tag{1}$$

TABLE 9.8 Percentage Change in Return and Volatility Due to Rating Stop–Loss Rules, January 1993–January 2015

Rating	Avg. Excess Return (bp/y) BH	% Change in Avg. Excess Return over BH					Rating	Volatility (bp/y) BH	% Change in Volatility over BH				
		Sell @ Caa	Sell @ B	Sell @ Ba	Sell @ Baa	Sell @ A			Sell @ Caa	Sell @ B	Sell @ Ba	Sell @ Baa	Sell @ A
All Maturities													
Aaa–Aa	74	−2%	−4%	−8%	−15%	−56%	Aaa–Aa	366	0%	0%	−1%	−2%	−16%
Aaa–A	63	−6%	−11%	−18%	−30%		Aaa–A	418	−1%	−2%	−3%	−6%	
Aaa–Baa (IG)	75	−10%	−17%	−27%			Aaa–Baa (IG)	450	−2%	−3%	−6%		
Aaa–Ba	89	−10%	−18%				Aaa–Ba	470	−2%	−5%			
Aaa–B	91	−8%					Aaa–B	506	−3%				
Aaa–Caa	94						Aaa–Caa	520					
Maturities from 1 to 5 years													
Aaa–Aa	87	0%	0%	−1%	−3%	−33%	Aaa–Aa	228	0%	0%	0%	−1%	−18%
Aaa–A	84	−1%	−3%	−4%	−12%		Aaa–A	262	0%	0%	−1%	−5%	
Aaa–Baa (IG)	96	−4%	−8%	−12%			Aaa–Baa (IG)	272	−1%	−3%	−5%		
Aaa–Ba	113	−7%	−12%				Aaa–Ba	295	−3%	−6%			
Aaa–B	125	−7%					Aaa–B	317	−4%				
Aaa–Caa	136						Aaa–Caa	332					

Source: Barclays Research

Next we calculate the effect on strategy volatility. We express the volatility of strategy excess return using Duration Times Spread (DTS) as risk exposure. The variance of the SG strategy is:

$$V_{SG} = V\left\{ D \times S_L \times \frac{dS}{S} \right\} = \left[D \times S_L \times \sigma \right]^2,$$

where σ is the volatility of relative spread changes

Note that since the strategy replaces downgraded bond with a new Aa-rated bond with original characteristics, its DTS exposure to credit spread risk does not change.

The variance of the BH strategy is less straightforward to formulate as its DTS exposure changes when the bond is downgraded.

$$V_{BH} = V\left\{ \left(\Pi_{DG} DS_H + \Pi_{\overline{DG}} DS_L \right) \times \frac{dS}{S} \right\},$$

where $\Pi_{DG} = 1 - \Pi_{\overline{DG}}$ is the downgrade indicator

Assuming that downgrades and relative spread changes are independent, we can rewrite the formula as:

$$V_{BH} = \left[DS_L \sigma \right]^2 \times E\left\{ \left(\Pi_{DG} \frac{S_H}{S_L} + \Pi_{\overline{DG}} \right)^2 \right\} = \left[DS_L \sigma \right]^2 \times \left[\frac{S_H^2}{S_L^2} E\{\Pi_{DG}\} + E\{\Pi_{\overline{DG}}\} \right]$$

Finally,

$$V_{BH} = \left[DS_L \sigma \right]^2 \times \left\{ 1 + \left(\frac{S_H^2}{S_L^2} - 1 \right) p \right\}.$$

Therefore, the effect of the stop loss on portfolio volatility expressed in percentage terms is:

$$\frac{V_{SG}^{1/2} - V_{BH}^{1/2}}{V_{BH}^{1/2}} = \frac{1 - \sqrt{\left\{ 1 + \left(\frac{S_H^2}{S_L^2} - 1 \right) p \right\}}}{\sqrt{\left\{ 1 + \left(\frac{S_H^2}{S_L^2} - 1 \right) p \right\}}} \tag{2}$$

Comparing equations (1) and (2), we see that the return reduction is proportional to duration while the volatility reduction is not. This explains why the percentage changes in return are larger than percentage changes in volatilities. In Table 9.9, we compare declines in portfolio return and volatility from imposing rating stop-loss rules in short-duration (1–5 year) and long-duration (all maturities) portfolios. The declines are reported in percentage terms over corresponding BH peers.

Table 9.9 confirms the predictions of our model. First, the return impact of rating stop-loss rules is indeed larger in longer duration portfolios. The percentage declines in return of shorter-maturity portfolios (bottom-left panel) are smaller than those of longer-maturity portfolios (top-left panel). This is consistent with equation (1). Second, percentage declines in volatility do not seem to be affected by the duration of downgraded bonds: Declines in volatilities in the top-right and bottom-right panels are comparable. This is consistent with equation (2). The model introduced in this appendix ignores some important aspects, so its output should not be used as a precise forecast. Nevertheless, its insight is validated by our empirical results.

REFERENCES

Ben Dor, A., L. Dynkin, J. Hyman, P. Houweling, E. Van Leeuwen, and O. Penninga. 2007. "DTS^{SM} (Duration Times Spread)." *Journal of Portfolio Management* 33(2): 77–100.

Dynkin, L., J. Hyman, and V. Konstantinovsky. 2002. "Sufficient Diversification in Credit Portfolios." *Journal of Portfolio Management* 29(1): 89–114.

Kaminski, K. M., and A. Lo. 2014. "When Do Stop-Loss Rules Stop Losses?" *Journal of Financial Markets* 18: 234–254.

Morahan, A., and C. Mulder. 2013, May. "Survey of Reserve Managers: Lessons from the Crisis." IMF Working Paper.

Ng, K. Y., and B. Phelps. 2011. "Capturing Credit Spread Premium." *Financial Analysts Journal* 67(3): 63–75.

NOTES

1. The performance of fallen angels around the downgrade event is documented in Chapter 2.
2. For example, many central bank reserve portfolios are subject to a Baa-rating liquidation rule. See Morahan and Mulder (2013).
3. We ignore spread carry in our back-of-an-envelope calculations, assuming that the cash proceeds from selling downgraded bonds would be reinvested at the original Aa spread.
4. Note that Moody's transition probabilities in Table 9.1 are calculated for a one-year horizon. As a general rule, we conservatively assume that Aa securities reach the sell A threshold before proceeding to lower ratings. This is why we use the average spread of the A-rated portfolio across all lower rating categories in the loss calculations.

5. In practice, bonds are also excluded due to index rules unrelated to rating. For example, securities with maturities below one year would be excluded. Effects from these auxiliary rules are documented by Ng and Phelps (2011). Explicitly accounting for these rules would not significantly change our results as the rules would be applied equally to portfolios with rating stop-losses and to their BH benchmarks.
6. These include A1-, A2-, and A3-rated issues.
7. For the Caa stop-loss, bonds are sold from the portfolio at Caa1 or below.
8. Note that upgraded bonds are retained in the portfolios, while bonds down-graded to or below sell thresholds are sold.
9. Portfolio risk is proportional to duration times spread (DTS), so when changes in risk are analyzed in relative terms, durations in the numerator and the denominator cancel out. For an introduction to DTS, see Ben Dor et al. (2007).
10. Table 9.9 in appendix 9.1 shows that percentage reductions in return are smaller for shorter-maturity portfolios than for longer ones, while percentage declines in volatility are similar.
11. See, for example, Dynkin, Hyman, and Konstantinovsky (2002).
12. In the introduction, we did exactly this using average spreads of Aa and A bonds and Moody's one-year transition probabilities.
13. Here we use the fact that $E[XY] = E[X]E[Y] + Cov(X,Y)$.
14. See Chapter 2.
15. We assume a constant duration as a realistic portfolio continues buying newly issued bonds, so that its average duration remains broadly stable over time.
16. Adding default or other ratings would complicate the model without changing results qualitatively.

Three

Performance Implications of Portfolio Characteristics

Part II explained how understanding index inefficiencies can help investors generate alpha and outperform their benchmarks. In this part, we discuss whether bond and portfolio characteristics—coupon, maturity, and environmental, social, and governance (ESG) rating—can be systematically associated with performance. These characteristics are not related to portfolio dynamics or to bond pricing. They can be seen as systematic sources of return and can be considered for implementation in the absence of any discretionary views on individual securities.

Chapter 10 explores the effects of coupon level on the pricing and performance of corporate bonds. We find that bonds with low coupons (discount bonds) tend to have lower spreads than bonds with high coupons (premium bonds), reflecting the fact that bonds trading at a discount are better shielded from default risk by recovery values. This phenomenon has an asymmetric effect on empirical duration. Corporate bonds trading at a discount have a reduced sensitivity to rising interest rates and an increased sensitivity to falling rates; bond trading at a premium exhibit the opposite effect. To investigate whether this convexity-like advantage can help enhance portfolio returns, we design a portfolio strategy that goes long discount bonds vs. premium bonds while controlling for issuer exposures. We find that this strategy has delivered a persistently positive performance, especially in times when default risk is perceived to be highest.

Credit investors have long known that short-dated corporate bonds tend to deliver higher return per unit of risk than long-dated ones. The intuition is simple: While spread generally increases with maturity, risk increases faster, as it is essentially a linear function of duration. Several factors explain the poor risk-adjusted reward for duration extension in credit. Portfolio managers with long-dated liabilities consistently place excess demand on the long end of the curve. In addition, aversion to leverage — which has been suggested as the explanation for the low-risk anomaly in other asset classes — makes extending bond maturity the preferred way for many investors to add rates exposure to portfolios. In Chapter 11, we find that, despite their higher average spreads, long-dated corporate bonds have delivered not only lower information ratios but also lower average excess returns than short-maturity ones over a long (25-year) period of history of the US investment-grade corporate bond market. We attribute realized excess returns to various factors, including carry, roll-down on the term structure of spreads, sample-specific change in spread, and downgrade-related costs. We find strong maturity dependence for all these factors. Roll-down of the spread curve and costs associated with rating migration are factors that persistently favor short- over long-dated bonds. Surprisingly, a significant part of the difference in excess returns between long- and short-dated bonds can be associated with sample-specific changes in spread, despite the length of the period considered in our study.

Another set of characteristics that investors consider increasingly often are those relating to ESG issues. Whereas coupon and maturity are specific to fixed income markets, an ESG rating, or score, is assigned to a corporation and is generally associated with all its securities, across the capital structure. While coupon and maturity characteristics of a corporate bond are easily observable, this is not the case with ESG. The ESG characteristics of an issuer are less objectively measured, with significant divergence among ESG ratings from different providers. The key question we address in Chapter 12 is whether a link exists between ESG characteristics and the performance of corporate bond portfolios. We pay particular attention to unintended biases that can affect portfolio risk exposures when an ESG tilt is introduced. We use an original portfolio simulation approach to measure the effect of an ESG tilt while controlling exposure to major credit risk dimensions. We find that an ESG tilt has had the effect of enhancing return in the period of our study. Of the three pillars of ESG, governance has the strongest effect on performance in the US market, while environment is more important in Europe. We also measure the effect of ESG characteristics on valuation and discuss the possibility—which we find unlikely—that the historical outperformance of an ESG-tilted portfolio could have been the result of a systematic richening of high-ESG issuers due to excess demand.

These studies share two common themes. First, the many different characteristics of fixed income securities can make it very difficult to isolate the effect of a particular one. Any purchase of a corporate bond has an effect on every single portfolio characteristic, including duration, issuer exposure, sector exposure, quality, subordination, liquidity, age, coupon, and ESG rating, to name a few. This complicates both the analysis required to identify the performance effect of a particular trait and the practical implementation of a strategy to harvest such an effect. Second, when a certain characteristic is found to carry a price premium, it typically means that a significant group of market participants finds that characteristic attractive. It is important to understand why this is so and whether this attractiveness is due to economic considerations that affect all investors equally or to constraints on some investors that can result in opportunities for others. For example, we shall see that investor preferences for bonds with low coupons and high ESG ratings seem to be justified in economic terms while a systematic preference for longer maturities is not.

CHAPTER 10

Coupon Effects in Corporate Bonds:
Pricing, Empirical Duration, and Spread Convexity

INTRODUCTION

Bond portfolio managers rely on various types of duration measures to manage risk, such as option-adjusted durations (OAD) or key rate durations (KRD) to measure exposures to changes in rates, or option-adjusted spread durations (OASD) to measure spread exposures. Typically, these measures are based on individual bond calculations in which the projected cash flows promised by a bond are discounted by a combination of rates and spreads, with no distinction between principal and interest cash flows and no explicit modeling of default and recovery. In this framework, at first glance, there is no reason to expect discount bonds to behave any differently than premiums; bonds with higher coupons will naturally trade at accordingly higher prices, but once all the cash flows have been properly discounted along the curve, the standard duration measures should be equally accurate and applicable regardless of coupon or price.

An alternative viewpoint can be reached if we explicitly consider the role of default and recovery in the pricing model. In survival-based pricing, rather than discounting all the cash flows of a credit-risky security at a spread over the risk-free curve, we discount all cash flows using the risk-free curve but adjust each for the probability of its occurrence. In each time period from now to maturity, there is a certain probability that the bond will default; should this occur, the bondholders will immediately receive some recovery value but will forfeit all future cash flows. This type of model captures the effect of a corporate bond market reality that is ignored in the spread-based models: In case of default, recovery values are expressed as a percentage of par. Should corporation XYZ default on its debt, all holders of its bonds at a given seniority level will receive the same amount per dollar of face value, regardless of the fact that the investors holding their 8% coupon bond paid considerably more than those holding the 4% coupon.

Consideration of this survival-based pricing approach leads to the conclusion that, all else equal, a lower-priced (lower-coupon) bond is less exposed to default risk than a higher-priced bond from the same issuer, since the recovery value of the firm protects more of the bond's value.[1]

In some market environments, such coupon effects are immaterial. Most bonds are priced at par upon issuance, and if yields and spreads remain stable, each issuer might be characterized by a particular range of coupons. However, when a large shift in Treasury yields causes new issues to come to market at very different yield levels than previously existing debt, we can find wide dispersion among the coupons of outstanding bonds within a single issuer.

In the years following the global financial crisis, with Treasury stimulus actions keeping interest rates pinned to zero for several years, seasoned bonds issued before the onset of the crisis tended to carry much higher coupons than newer issues. Yet investors were well aware that should rates move higher again, those low-coupon issues then trading near par would become discounts under a higher interest rate regime. For this reason, they expressed interest in gaining a better understanding of how coupon levels should affect corporate bond pricing and performance. In this chapter, we present historical evidence of the effect that coupon level has had on relative pricing and performance.

We carry out empirical studies of three distinct effects. First, can we detect a clear relationship between the price of a bond and its spread relative to other bonds of the same issuer? Second, can we find that coupon level has an effect on the empirical duration of a bond—that is, its sensitivity to changes in Treasury yields? Finally, do these effects present an opportunity for portfolio outperformance?

We begin our study with a comparison of simple spread-based and survival-based pricing models applied to several bonds from a single corporate issuer, to illustrate some of the effects just described. We then address each of the listed questions in turn, using appropriate data samples from within the Bloomberg Barclays US Corporate Bond Index database. At each stage, we will face the challenge of isolating the coupon effect from all of the other fine distinctions among different securities.[2]

WHY SHOULD PRICE LEVEL MATTER?

At first glance, it may seem that there should be no reason to expect coupon levels to influence spreads. We all are familiar with pricing formulas that express the price of a bond as the present value of future cash flows, discounted by a spread over Treasuries. For example, we could write:

$$P = \sum_t \frac{CF_t}{\left(1 + \frac{r_t + s}{2}\right)^{2t}}$$

(10.1)

where CF_t denotes the cash flow occurring at time t,
r_t is the Treasury rate for maturity t, and
s is a constant spread over the Treasury curve that will make the formula tie out with the bond's price.

Consider two bonds from the same issuer, with the same seniority level and maturity date but with two different coupons. If we use equation 1 to price the two bonds at the same spread s over the Treasury curve, we will get different prices, with the higher coupon bond commanding a higher dollar price.[3] Shouldn't this price differential fully account for the difference in coupon?

The answer is that the model shown in equation 1 does not fully account for what may happen in case of default. All promised cash flows are considered fixed.[4] The model adjusts for the possibility that these cash flows may not arrive due to default simply by discounting them at a spread over the Treasury curve. This spread may be considered roughly equivalent to a hazard rate (annual probability of default) if we assume that when a bond defaults, investors forfeit all future cash flows and receive no further compensation (e.g., the recovery rate is assumed to be zero).

An alternative approach to modeling credit-risky securities is to use a modelling framework like the one used to value a credit default swap (CDS). In this approach, we use hazard curves to estimate the probability that an issuer will default at a particular point in time and then value the cash flow obtained at time t under three distinct possibilities. If the security is not in default at time t, the investor receives the cash flow scheduled to occur at that time. If the security goes into default at time t, the investor is assumed to be able to liquidate the position immediately for some recovery value equal to a fixed percentage of face value. If the security has defaulted in the past, no further cash flows are received. The expected cash flow is obtained by weighting these three possibilities by the estimated probabilities of each event (based on the hazard curve), and the stream of these expected cash flows is then discounted along the Libor curve. In this type of model, the adjustment for credit risk is reflected explicitly in the probability of obtaining a cash flow, so no further spread is needed in the discounting process.

Such a model is presented in Pederson (2006). It starts by taking data from the CDS market to fit an issuer-specific hazard curve that correctly prices CDS of different maturities for a specific issuer and seniority level. This model can then be used, as described, to obtain a fair price for a bond based on its scheduled cash flows and an assumed recovery rate. To adjust for the fact that a bond's actual price is different from this fair price, the model introduces a constant shift to the hazard curve, pushing all default probabilities either higher or lower, until the model price matches the actual price of the bond. This shifted hazard curve is then used to find the CDS spread corresponding to the maturity of the bond.[5] This spread is called the bond-implied CDS (BCDS) spread. To illustrate the dependence of spread on coupon as viewed by the BCDS model, we examine the spreads of four Verizon bonds with very similar maturities of 24 to 25 years but carrying very different coupons. Table 10.1 shows a snapshot of these four bonds as of April 28, 2014. All four of these bonds are struck with coupons significantly higher than their current yield levels of 5.0% to 5.2% and thus all trade at premium to par. This effect is quite extreme due to the long maturity of the bonds, and the highest coupon bond trades at over 150% of face value. The table shows both the zero-volatility (ZV) spreads of the bonds (similar to equation 1 and to the option-adjusted spread (OAS) model typically used for corporate bonds) and their BCDS spreads.[6] These spread levels are also plotted in Figure 10.1.

TABLE 10.1 Spreads of Four Verizon bonds as of April 28, 2014

Coupon	Maturity	Price	Yield	ZV Spread	BCDS Spread	ZVS @ 163BCDS
6.4	2/15/2038	118.97	5.024	174.3	162.0	175.3
6.9	4/15/2038	125.15	5.074	180.4	164.4	179.1
7.35	4/1/2039	130.27	5.174	190.5	170.4	182.8
8.95	3/1/2039	154.18	5.084	183.9	155.1	192.9

Source: Bloomberg Barclays Indices; Barclays Research

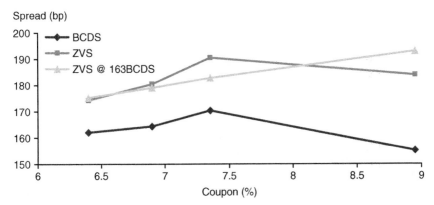

FIGURE 10.1 Spreads of Verizon Bonds as a Function of Coupon, April 28, 2014
Source: Barclays Research

For the first three bonds in this list, we see a clear trend of spreads increasing with coupon level. The fourth bond, with the 8.95% coupon, seems to violate this rule. Any number of technical factors could be creating demand for this specific bond, which seems to be trading rich to its peers. To eliminate any such pricing noise and highlight the difference between the BCDS and ZV models, we took the average BCDS of these four bonds, 163bp, repriced all four bonds at exactly this level, and recorded the resulting ZV spreads. As shown in Figure 10.1, these spreads follow a straight-line relationship, continuing to increase with coupon level. That is, if one believes that the BCDS approach is the correct one and recovery rates are nonzero, there is a theoretical basis for the assumption that higher-coupon bonds should trade at higher spreads. In the remainder of this chapter, using historical OAS of index bonds, we test the extent to which the market has priced in this effect historically.

DO PREMIUM CORPORATES HAVE HIGHER SPREADS?

We now turn to the first empirical question we have outlined: Do spreads depend on the extent to which a bond is premium or discount? To address this question, we gathered a dataset of bonds from frequent issuers, such that each issuer would have a well-defined issuer spread curve. Specifically, using corporate bond data from January 1992 through April 2014, we selected the set of issuers with seven or more bonds outstanding each month.[7] We regress bond spreads against coupon levels, after adjusting for the slope of the issuer spread curve. Specifically, we run a separate cross-sectional regression each month as follows:

$$OAS_{i,j} - \overline{OAS_j} = \alpha_j \cdot \left(sprdDur_{i,j} - \overline{sprdDur_j} \right) + \beta \cdot \left(Coupon_{i,j} - \overline{Coupon_j} \right)$$

where each of the dummy variables α_j represents the slope of the issuer spread curve for issuer j in the selected month. Variable β represents an additional dependence of spread on coupon across all issuers, above and beyond the term structure of spreads for each issuer.

This regression can be viewed as equivalent to a two-step process, in which we first fit a slope α_j to each issuer spread curve to explain as much as possible of the variation in spreads across each issuer. We then take the extent to which each bond's spread is rich/cheap relative to its issuer curve, pool together all the bonds in a single month, and regress these against coupons to see if we can identify a market-wide coupon effect. A positive value for β implies that higher coupons have higher spreads. Figure 10.2 charts the results of this regression over time, including both the value of the coefficient β and the t-statistic measuring the strength of the relationship. We find that since 2008, this coefficient has been high, with a value of about 0.1 and strong statistical significance. The value of 0.1 for β means that if there are two otherwise identical bonds from the same issuer with coupons 1% apart, we would expect the higher coupon bond to trade 10bp higher in spread.

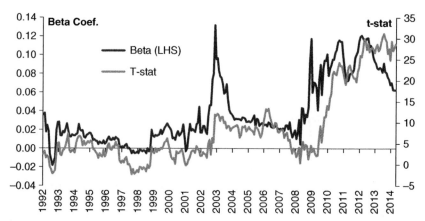

FIGURE 10.2   Time Series of Regression Results for Dependence of Spread on Coupon
Source: Barclays Research

We note that the high values for β from 2008 to 2012 were achieved in one earlier episode as well. Toward the end of 2002, β spiked to a level above 0.1 and then steadily decayed back down to more moderate levels over the course of 2003. As in 2008, this corresponds to a period at the end of the dot-com crisis, when portfolio managers had reason to be especially wary of default risk. We investigate this in more depth later in the chapter.

HOW DOES COUPON LEVEL AFFECT EMPIRICAL DURATION?

Once we have established that investors indeed consider premium bonds to carry more credit risk and hence higher spreads, we can start to think about how this affects spread dynamics. Specifically, how will credit spreads of discount and premium bonds change in reaction to changes in Treasury rates, and what effect will this have on empirical durations?

To test this, we set up a regression of corporate bond returns against changes in Treasury yields. We begin by assembling a dataset of monthly returns and explanatory variables for all noncallable bonds in the Bloomberg Barclays US Investment-Grade Corporate Index[8] from January 1992 through April 2014. As a control, we first set up a simple regression of returns against yield changes, allowing for dependence of empirical duration on spread but not yet including any coupon effect, as follows:

$$R_{i,t}^{adj} = -\beta_{treas}D_{i,t}\Delta y - \beta_{spread}D_{i,t}S_{i,t}\Delta y + \varepsilon_{i,t}$$

We refer to this base case as Model 1. In this regression, our dependent variable $R_{i,t}^{adj}$ represents the carry-adjusted return of bond i at time t, calculated as the bond's total return minus one-twelfth of the beginning-of-month yield.[9] Note that this is a pooled regression, using all index bonds across all observed months to solve for just two constants, β_{treas} and β_{spread}. The interpretation of the results is that to obtain the best estimate for the empirical duration of a bond, or the sensitivity of its return to changes in Treasury yield,[10] we should adjust it by an empirical hedge ratio that is a linear function of spread:

$$\frac{D_i^{emp}}{D_i} = \beta_{treas} + \beta_{spread} \cdot S_i$$

If, as is often assumed, the duration of a bond gives the best estimate of its sensitivity to changes in Treasury yield, the results would be that $\beta_{treas} = 1$

and $\beta_{spread} = 0$. We do not find this to be the case; we instead find strong evidence that β_{spread} is negative, and hence that empirical duration decreases as spreads rise.

Both the setup and the results of this first regression are consistent with earlier work we have done on empirical durations of credit securities.[11] Using a pooled regression of daily data, with a formulation similar to this one, we found that empirical durations of credit securities tend to be less than their analytical durations and that this effect becomes stronger as spreads widen. We found this effect to be connected to the negative correlation that usually prevails between changes in rates and spreads. When rates fall, bond prices increase. Due to this negative correlation, however, spreads tend to widen, and thus the bond prices do not increase by as much as would have been expected based on analytical duration alone. We traced the spread dependence of this effect to other empirical work of ours on Duration Times Spread (DTS).[12] Here we found that spread changes tend to follow a proportional pattern, in which bonds trading at wider spreads react more strongly to systematic spread changes in the market. Due to this effect, the price impact of the negative correlation of rates and spreads is greater for bonds with higher spreads.

To explore the coupon effect, we now modify this regression, inserting an additional term reflecting a dependence of empirical duration on bond price. We now look for a relationship of the form:

$$\frac{D_i^{emp}}{D_i} = \beta_{treas} + \beta_{spread} \cdot S_i + \gamma \cdot PriceDistPar_i$$

where $PriceDistPar_i$ denotes the absolute distance of the price of bond i from par.

Bonds trading further from par in either direction—either deep discounts or premiums—are assumed to require an additional adjustment to their empirical durations, and γ represents the extent to which this adjustment should depend on the distance of a bond's price from par. However, we suspect that the required adjustment might be different for premium and discount bonds and that each of these groups is likely to react differently to upward and downward yield changes.[13] Therefore, our modified regression, which we refer to as Model 2, includes not just a single γ coefficient but four distinct ones corresponding to premium and discount bonds in months with upward and downward Treasury yield changes.

In this model, we label as "discounts" all bonds with prices of 90 or less and as "premiums" all bonds with prices of 110 or more. For bonds trading near par (e.g., with prices from 90–110), price changes are modeled as in

Model 1, based only on β_{treas} and β_{spread}. For every observation of a discount bond, we include an adjustment using one of our additional coefficients, either γ_{disc}^{up} for observations in which Treasury yields rise or γ_{disc}^{dn} for observations in which they fall. Similarly, premium bonds will have an adjustment controlled by either γ_{prem}^{up} or γ_{prem}^{dn}. In each case, the magnitude of the correction effect is assumed to be proportional to the distance of the bond's price from par. The results of these regressions are summarized in Table 10.2. We indeed find that the results are broadly consistent with our earlier work: In both Model 1 and Model 2, we find that empirical duration is slightly lower than analytical duration for low spreads and continues to decrease as spreads rise. Furthermore, the adjustment terms that measure the sensitivities to rising and falling yields confirm our hypothesis: For premium bonds, rate sensitivity is higher when yields rise and lower when they fall; for discount bonds,

TABLE 10.2 Results of Regression Models for Yield Sensitivity, With and Without Coupon Adjustment

Pooled Data, All Noncallable Bonds in the Bloomberg Barclays US IG Corporate Index, January 1992–April 2014

		Model 1		Model 2	
Coefficient	Interpretation	Coeff.	*t*-stat.	Coeff.	*t*-stat.
β_{treas}	Base case hedge ratio (low spread limit)	0.97	405.0	0.98	355.3
β_{spread}	Hedge ratio sensitivity to spread	–0.13	–144.1	–0.15	–140.6
γ_{prem}^{up}	Sensitivity of premium bonds to rising yields			0.27	14.6
γ_{prem}^{dn}	Sensitivity of premium bonds to falling yields			–0.25	–11.8
γ_{disc}^{up}	Sensitivity of discount bonds to rising yields			–1.09	–41.0
γ_{disc}^{dn}	Sensitivity of discount bonds to falling yields			1.67	76.1
Adjusted R^2		24%		25%	

Note: The *t*-statistics shown in this table are somewhat distorted due to the fact that under the pooled regression, the residuals may be correlated. As a result, the test for statistical significance needs to be adjusted. However, we tested these results by including a monthly dummy factor to capture this dependence and found the resulting coefficients to be little changed.
Source: Barclays Research

the direction is reversed. In both cases, the effect is proportional to the distance of the bond price from par.

These results imply that discount bonds should follow a highly desirable behavior in which they react more strongly to favorable yield changes and less strongly to unfavorable ones—a positive convexity effect. Premium bonds, by contrast, should display the opposite behavior, similar to negative convexity. Table 10.3 illustrates the magnitude of this effect for two hypothetical bonds trading at the same spread of 100bp, but with prices of 110 and 90, respectively. Model 1, based purely on spread, estimates the same empirical hedge ratio of 0.83 for the two bonds. Model 2 includes an additional term based on the distance of the price from par, estimated separately for premium and discount securities. As a result of this effect, we find that our discount bond should have a significantly higher empirical sensitivity to falling yields than our premium bond and a significantly lower sensitivity to rising yields, and should therefore be expected to outperform in both of these environments.

TABLE 10.3   Illustration of Coupon Effect on Empirical Hedge Ratios for Premium and Discount Bonds

	Bond A (Premium)	Bond B (Discount)
Price	110	90
Distance of price from par (absolute value)	10%	10%
OAS (bp)	100	100
Estimated empirical hedge ratio (Model 1)	0.83	0.83
Estimated empirical hedge ratio (Model 2, for falling yields)	0.80	1.00
Estimated empirical hedge ratio (Model 2, for rising yields)	0.86	0.72

Source: Barclays Research

DO DISCOUNT CORPORATES OUTPERFORM?

We have thus shown two clear types of differentiation between the market behavior of premium and discount bonds. In terms of valuation, it seems that there is an investor preference for discount bonds, which translates into higher spreads for premiums. In terms of rates sensitivity, discount bonds enjoy some sort of positive convexity that should help improve performance when rates change. On a long-term performance basis, these two effects should offset each other—but to what extent? If we could compare two portfolios that are otherwise equivalent, except that one is biased toward high-coupon bonds while the other is biased toward low-coupon bonds, which one would achieve better performance over the long term?

We seek to construct two portfolios whose characteristics are as similar to each other as possible, except for a bias toward higher or lower coupons. We then analyze the performance differences between the two portfolios. We considered two distinct approaches to constructing such an experiment. One, using a top-down portfolio construction technique, would use all the bonds in the index and achieve the desired coupon bias by partitioning the index universe and reweighting the cells. A second approach would use a bottom-up construction, using only bonds from frequent issuers. The top-down approach would have the advantage of using much more diversified portfolios. However, we found it very difficult to introduce the desired coupon bias while controlling for all other important portfolio attributes. With this method, it was not clear exactly what additional exposures might have crept into our portfolios—to specific industries or issuers, perhaps—in addition to the premium or discount characteristics that we sought to emphasize. We therefore found it preferable to work with the more limited dataset of frequent issuers and use a bottom-up approach that explicitly matches issuer exposures in the discount and premium portfolios.

Our bottom-up portfolio experiment was carried out as follows. For each month of the study, we first identified the universe of available corporate bonds from frequent issuers, defined as those issuers with seven or more bonds outstanding, as in our earlier analysis of the dependence of spread on coupon. From this set of bonds, we then constructed two portfolios with the same sector and issuer contributions, as follows.

Within each issuer each month, we use the difference between a bond's coupon and its yield[14] to divide the available bonds into two equally populated groups.[15] We then subdivide each of these two groups by duration. Ideally, we can then find a target duration that is between the durations of the long and short cells in both groups and reweight the two halves of each group to match this. When possible, we choose the overall average duration of the issuer as the target duration for both the premium and discount groups; if this would lead to a short position in one of the portfolios, we adjust the target duration accordingly. The only case in which it is not possible to match the durations is when both duration cells of one group (premium or discount) have longer durations than both duration cells of the other group. In such a case, we just omit this issuer from our portfolio. Once we do this at the level of each issuer, we just combine these groups using issuer market weights to form a premium portfolio and a discount portfolio.[16] Without the need for any further adjustments, these two portfolios should be almost perfectly matched in their allocations to issuers, sectors, and qualities, by both market value and contributions to spread duration. While we do not explicitly control for spreads, there is no possibility of large issuer-specific positions.

We carried out the portfolio construction according to this algorithm. Of 28,198 unique issuer/month observations, we needed to discard almost 33% because the durations of the two groups of bonds could not be matched by the simple rebalancing just described. The results of this experiment are shown in Table 10.4. In addition to the discount and premium portfolios, we report results for an active portfolio that goes long the discounts and short the premiums, by taking the difference between the two portfolio returns.

TABLE 10.4   Performance of Discount vs. Premium Portfolios, Bottom-up (Issuer-Matched) Construction, January 1992–April 2014

		Discount Portfolio	Premium Portfolio	Active Portfolio
	Average (bp/mo)	57.1	53.7	3.5
Total	Volatility (bp/mo)	151.1	149.5	12.0
Returns	Inf. Ratio (Annualized)			1.01
	Average (bp/mo)	8.0	4.9	3.1
Excess	Volatility (bp/mo)	119.74	118.31	11.8
Returns	Inf. Ratio (Annualized)			0.91
	OAS (bp)	129.9	133.4	
Portfolio	OAD	5.25	5.25	
Averages	Price	100.59	107.91	
	# Bonds	382.9	424.7	

Source: Barclays Research

We find that the discount and premium portfolios seem to be quite well matched. The average durations are the same, at 5.25. The premium portfolio carries a slightly higher spread on average, as we would have expected based on our earlier result that premium bonds trade at higher spreads. The volatility of the active portfolio is quite small, at just 12bp/month out of an overall return volatility of about 150bp/month for either the discount or the premium portfolio. Given this close tracking between the two portfolios, and despite the spread carry advantage of the premium portfolio, the active portfolio (long the discounts and short the premiums) achieves an impressive average outperformance of 3.5bp/mo, for an information ratio of 1.01. The statistics are roughly the same in terms of excess returns; this is consistent with our hypothesis that the advantage of the discount portfolio over time has to do with subtle differences in the way spread changes in the two types of portfolios are influenced by changing rates.

We then sought to double-check our hypothesis that the outperformance of the discount portfolio was due to a convexity effect in which outperformance is achieved when rates move quickly in either direction. To do this, we partitioned the months of the study into quartiles by the amount of the monthly change of the 10-year fitted Treasury yield. Table 10.5 shows the performance results by quartile for our discount, premium, and active portfolios. We do not find evidence that our strategy is directional in rates; the active portfolio shows positive returns in all four quartiles. It seems to perform best when yields rally. In quartiles 1 and 2, the performance of the active strategy is truly large relative to its risk, earning information ratios of 1.84 and 1.65, respectively.

We similarly want to check whether returns of our strategy are directional with credit spreads. If we instead partition our sample by overall excess returns,[17] we find that the largest outperformance comes in the extreme top and bottom deciles, when there are large positive or negative excess returns across the market. This is shown in Table 10.6. The return of the active strategy is in the range of 6 to 10bp/month in both the top two and the bottom two deciles; in the middle six deciles, the strategy returns are near zero on average. The truly surprising results are those in deciles 9 and 10. Generally, as mentioned, we have found that spread changes tend to be proportional to spreads. We would therefore expect that, if two asset portfolios have the same durations but one has a higher spread than the other, the higher-spread portfolio would show excess returns of greater magnitude in both up and down months. The results in deciles 1 and 2 are consistent with this idea; the premium portfolio, with a spread 2bp higher than the discount portfolio, has returns that are more negative in months of widening spreads. However, deciles 9 and 10 represent large spread rallies, in which all credit assets show positive excess returns. Here, where the spread advantage of the premium portfolio is even greater, we would have expected the premiums to outperform. Yet the discount portfolio outperforms by even more in these deciles.

TABLE 10.5 Performance of Discount vs. Premium Portfolios Partitioned by Treasury Yield Change, January 1992–April 2014

Treasury Yield Change		Total Returns (bp/mo)				Excess Returns (bp/mo)			
Quartile	Yield Change (bp)	Discount Portf.	Premium Portf.	Active Portf.	Inf. Ratio (Ann.)	Discount Portf.	Premium Portf.	Active Portf.	Inf. Ratio (Ann.)
1	< −19	175.5	169.8	5.8	1.84	−36.9	−41.2	4.3	1.50
2	−19 to −2	101.8	96.9	4.9	1.65	13.7	9.3	4.5	1.71
3	−2 to 14	20.6	19.8	0.8	0.29	9.7	8.4	1.3	0.39
4	> 14	−69.4	−71.9	2.5	0.56	45.6	43.2	2.4	0.52

Source: Barclays Research

TABLE 10.6 Performance of Discount vs. Premium Portfolios Partitioned by Excess Return Deciles, January 1992–April 2014

Excess Return Decile	Average Spreads (bp)			Total Returns (bp/mo)				Excess Returns (bp/mo)			
	Discount Portf.	Premium Portf.	Active Portf.	Discount Portf.	Premium Portf.	Active Portf.	Inf. Ratio (Ann.)	Discount Portf.	Premium Portf.	Active Portf.	Inf. Ratio (Ann.)
1	217.4	219.4	−2.0	−60.7	−71.3	10.5	2.42	−213.1	−220.4	7.3	1.40
2	129.9	132.5	−2.6	35.0	28.5	6.5	2.29	−53.2	−59.3	6.1	2.21
3	101.0	105.3	−4.3	6.0	7.2	−1.3	−0.71	−20.1	−18.8	−1.3	−0.98
4	77.4	80.7	−3.4	46.5	47.1	−0.6	−0.54	−3.1	−1.9	−1.2	−0.97
5	85.4	87.6	−2.2	79.0	77.7	1.3	0.67	7.4	6.2	1.2	0.87
6	93.3	95.3	−2.0	38.3	38.5	−0.2	−0.14	16.4	16.3	0.0	0.03
7	90.4	94.0	−3.5	75.6	74.4	1.1	0.77	23.7	22.2	1.5	1.10
8	119.9	123.9	−4.0	62.6	61.4	1.2	0.50	34.4	33.2	1.1	0.47
9	138.6	143.0	−4.4	94.1	86.0	8.0	1.92	60.4	52.9	7.5	1.89
10	253.5	260.0	−6.4	196.0	187.2	8.8	1.29	227.4	218.3	9.1	1.37

Source: Barclays Research

Recalling that our key motivation for investigating the coupon effect was based on a consideration of defaults and recoveries, it stands to reason that these effects should be stronger when credit markets are in a stressed environment and investors are thinking carefully about default risk. Does our discount vs. premium strategy show better performance when expected default rates are high? To address this, we chose to partition our sample by the yield spread between Baa and Aaa bonds.[18] However, we noticed that there was a clear difference in duration between our Baa Credit and Aaa Credit indices. To adjust for this, we reweighted the Intermediate and Long Aaa Credit indices to match the duration of the Baa Credit index and took the difference between their yields. The time series for this metric is shown in Figure 10.3.

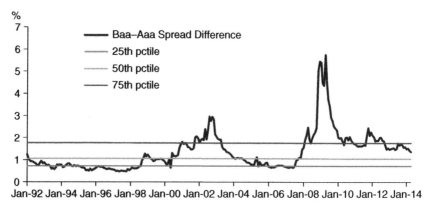

FIGURE 10.3   Credit Spread Premium, Represented by Baa–Aaa Yield Difference, Using Duration-Adjusted Yields of Bloomberg Barclays US Credit Indices, January 1992–April 2014
Note: The credit spread premium shown here is derived based on the Aaa and Baa components of the Bloomberg Barclays US IG Credit Index. A blend of the Long (maturities above 10 years) and Intermediate (maturities below 10 years) Aaa Credit indices is found each month to match the OAD of the Baa Credit Index. We define the credit spread premium as the yield difference between the Baa Credit Index and this duration-matched Aaa Credit Index. *Source:* Barclays Research

We then use this metric to divide our data sample into four quartiles, ranging from those in which the market seems to be the least concerned about credit risk (quartile 1) to the most (quartile 4). The horizontal lines shown in Figure 10.3 mark the breakpoints between these quartiles; the figure thus identifies which time periods are included in each quartile. The performance of our discount and premium portfolios in each of these quartiles is shown in Table 10.7. This analysis indeed shows a very clear differentiation of the performance of the strategy in different credit environments. Quartiles 1 and 2 show near-zero returns for the strategy, with very low risk as well: Active strategy volatility is just 3.2bp/month in quartile 1 and 6.1bp/month in quartile 2. In higher-spread environments, the strategy does quite well: Discounts outperform premiums by 12.2bp/month in quartile 4. Furthermore, this outperformance is accomplished with very little volatility. As a result, the issuer-matched active strategy shows an information ratio of 0.59 in quartile 3 and 2.28 in quartile 4.

TABLE 10.7 Performance of Discount vs. Premium Portfolios Partitioned by Quartiles of Credit Spread Premium, January 1992–April 2014

	Credit Spread Premium	Average Total Returns (bp/mo)			Total Return Volatility (bp/mo)			
Quartile	Baa–Aaa Spread Diff.	Discount Portf.	Premium Portf.	Active Portf.	Discount Portf.	Premium Portf.	Active Portf.	Inf. Ratio (Ann.)
1	< 71 bp	64.7	64.6	0.1	119.1	119.7	3.2	0.14
2	71–106 bp	28.6	28.5	0.1	115.6	114.0	6.1	0.03
3	106–176 bp	57.9	56.3	1.6	132.3	129.1	9.2	0.59
4	> 176 bp	77.4	65.2	12.2	214.5	213.5	18.5	2.28

Source: Barclays Research

We had one final concern regarding the validity of extrapolating forward from these historical results. The average prices of the securities in our "Premium" and "Discount" portfolios over the full period of our study were 107.9 and 100.6, respectively. That is, over the time period studied, the bond market as a whole was more premium than discount, consistent with the steady decrease in yields. If one sees our historical results as primarily a story of newly issued par bonds outperforming more seasoned premium bonds, one could question the extent to which these results would be applicable in a very different environment of rising rates. On that basis, it might be a stretch to predict outperformance of seasoned discount bonds over newly issued par bonds.

To confirm that this is not the case, we profile the performance of our bottom-up discount vs. premium strategy in one more dimension—this time based on the average price of bonds in the Discount portfolio. The results, shown in Table 10.8, demonstrate that despite the bias in our sample toward prices above par, the outperformance was not strongest when the premium portfolio traded at the highest price above par but rather when the discount portfolio traded at the lowest price below par. We therefore see no reason to believe that the market dynamics should change in a rising rates environment.

TABLE 10.8   Performance of Discount vs. Premium Portfolios, Partitioned by Quartiles of Average Price of Discount Portfolio, January 1992–April 2014

	Average Bond Price		Total Returns of Active Portfolio		
Quartile	Discount Portfolio	Premium Portfolio	Average (bp/mo)	Volatility (bp/mo)	Inf. Ratio (Ann.)
1	98.0	105.4	6.5	14.7	1.53
2	101.3	112.7	3.4	8.5	1.39
3	103.4	114.0	3.0	12.8	0.82
4	108.4	120.5	1.0	10.6	0.34

Source: Barclays Research

CONCLUSION

We have suggested one possible motivation for premium and discount bonds to follow different pricing dynamics. Because recoveries in case of default are based on face values rather than market value, premium bonds are at risk to lose more of their value in such events than discount bonds from the same issuers. This effect is not considered by standard models for OAS and duration. Although the probability of default is low, it seems that the market does tend to incorporate this knowledge in several ways.

We have demonstrated that within corporate bonds, all else equal, bonds with higher prices tend to trade at wider spreads.[19] While this means that discount bonds are more expensive, they also exhibit some spread convexity, tending to widen less when rates rally and tighten more when rates rise. Over the long term, and especially in high-credit-risk environments, this results in better performance for discount bonds, despite the initial pay-up to buy them.

It is not clear that this performance effect is large enough to justify a stand-alone active strategy after consideration of transaction costs. However, long-only portfolio managers may wish to maintain a bias toward lower-coupon bonds whenever possible.

If and when the market sees a significant secular rise in yields, existing corporate bonds may offer attractive performance relative to higher-coupon new issues.

REFERENCES

Ambastha, M., A. Ben Dor, L. Dynkin, J. Hyman, and V. Konstantinovsky. 2010. "Empirical Duration of Corporate Bonds and Credit Market Segmentation." *Journal of Fixed Income* 20(1): 5–27.
Ben Dor, A., L. Dynkin, J. Hyman, P. Houweling, E. Van Leeuwen, and O. Penninga. 2007. "DTS^SM (Duration Times Spread)." *Journal of Portfolio Management* 33(2): 77–100.
Pedersen, C. 2006. "Explaining the Bond-Implied CDS Spread and the Basis of a Corporate Bond." *Quantitative Credit Research Quarterly*, Quarter 2: 29–42.

NOTES

1. Note that this argument is based on the assumption that we are comparing two bonds from the same issuer at the same seniority level. For two bonds from different issuers, or at different seniority levels, one possible explanation for differences in pricing would be that the bond with the lower price has a lower expected recovery value. Similarly, if the price of a single bond declines over time, it might be due to a decline in expected recovery.
2. As we proceed through the different sections of this chapter, we alternate among three slightly different metrics for measuring the extent to which one bond is considered more or less premium than another: dollar price, coupon level, and the differential between coupon and yield. Generally speaking, these measures should agree when applied to bonds of similar maturities from the same issuer. For example, whether a bond's coupon is above or below its yield should determine whether it trades above or below par. We choose the metric most appropriate for each specific study.
3. Due to having a higher proportion of present value due to the near-term coupon flows rather than the principal payment at maturity, this model will also show that the higher-coupon bond has a shorter duration.
4. For the purposes of this discussion, we limit ourselves to the case of bullet bonds without embedded options. In this case, cash flows are fixed as long as no default occurs, and we can use equation 1 as is or modify it to reflect default/recovery assumptions. For callable bonds, cash flows cannot be assumed to be fixed, since they depend on the issuer's decision on option exercise. Equation 1 would be replaced by a more complex OAS model, and the treatment of default and recovery assumptions would need to be implemented as a modification to the OAS model.

5. The details of the BCDS model used in this example can be found in Pedersen (2006).
6. All of the BCDS spreads shown here use a base case assumption of a 40% recovery rate.
7. We arrived at this definition of "frequent issuers" as a compromise between two opposing motivating factors. A larger number of bonds per issuer should ensure that each spread curve is well defined; a less stringent requirement would allow more observations overall, and hence allow greater statistical significance in our results. With the requirement of seven bonds per issuer, our dataset includes, on average, 11.7% of index issuers but 40.5% of the eligible bonds. In April 2014, for example, only 158 of 1040 issuers were designated as "frequent," yet these account for 1,757 of the 3,752 eligible bonds in the index. Over the course of the 268 months included in the study, our regressions included bonds from an average of 105 issuers per month.
8. In this section, we do not limit ourselves to bonds from frequent issuers, as we did in the previous section. Before, when we were trying to explain pricing effects, we needed to ensure that we were only detecting differences among bonds from the same issuers. Here we are measuring sensitivity to Treasury yield changes. We already have durations for each bond, but we are seeking to pool as many observations as possible to identify any systematic adjustments to the analytical duration that can help improve our estimate of empirical duration. By including all eligible bonds, our pooled regression includes a total of 737,506 observations over 268 months, of which 171,762 are classified as "premium" and 34,616 as "discount," as will be described.
9. In our prior work on empirical duration, Ambastha, Ben Dor, Dynkin, Hyman, and Konstantinovsky (2010), we used price return as the dependent variable. This removes an estimated carry based on the bond's coupon. This was not a material difference in any case because that study was based on daily returns. In this study, using monthly returns, the difference is more pronounced. Furthermore, the difference between a carry adjustment based on yield and one based on coupon is most pronounced when coupon is far from yield—that is, when bonds are strongly premium or discount: the very cases we want to investigate. For this reason, it was important to us to use a carry adjustment that does not introduce a bias based on coupon level.
10. The Treasury yield change used for each observation is the monthly change in the fitted yield of an appropriate constant-maturity Treasury: For bonds with less than seven years to maturity, we use the 5y Treasury yield; for those with above seven but less than 15 years, we use the 10y; for those with 15 years or more to maturity, we use the 30y.
11. See Ambastha et al. (2010).
12. See Ben Dor et al. (2007).
13. It may even be the case that different root causes drive the behavior of premium and discount bonds, with the price of deep discounts supported by recovery values and the price of premiums suppressed by investor aversion due to

accounting considerations. Perhaps a simple way to view this is that the market tends to resist extreme valuations in either direction.

14. When a bond's coupon is above its yield, it will trade at a price above par; if coupon is less than yield, price will be below par. The extent of this price difference will be greater for longer-duration bonds. In this exercise, we are trying to favor premium bonds while not introducing a bias toward longer or shorter durations. For this reason, we chose to use coupon minus yield as our key metric.

15. We arbitrarily decided that when there are an odd number of bonds from an issuer, the middle bond is assigned to the premium portfolio. Thus, for an issuer with seven bonds outstanding, four would be assigned to the premium portfolio and three to the discount one. For this reason, the premium portfolio contains a greater number of bonds on average.

16. We divide the total market weight of all included bonds for each issuer by the total market weight of all included bonds each month. These overall issuer weights are used to weight both discount and premium portfolios.

17. We arbitrarily chose to use the excess returns of the discount portfolio to carry out this partition. Ranking the months by the excess returns of the premium portfolio or the index as a whole should produce similar results.

18. We did not want to use absolute spread levels because these contain some common components that are not necessarily linked to default expectations. One notable example is liquidity. During the global financial crisis, spreads of cash bonds were hundreds of basis points higher than those of corresponding CDS due to the lack of liquidity in the market. CDS spreads themselves might be a good metric for measuring overall default risk, but historical data is not available for the full extent of our sample period. We therefore chose to work with the Baa–Aaa differential, which is a fairly standard metric in the credit risk literature.

19. The tendency of high-priced bonds to trade at higher spreads may not be due entirely to the default/recovery argument described in this chapter. Other technical factors may contribute to this effect as well. For example, some investors prefer not to invest in premium bonds due to accounting considerations.

CHAPTER **11**

Maturity Dependence of Corporate Bond Excess Returns

INTRODUCTION

Maturity dependence of credit performance is an important consideration for many investors, beyond mutual funds and absolute return investors. For example, insurance and pension fund managers use long-maturity debt to match long-dated liabilities. The decision to invest along the maturity spectrum must therefore be based on a precise understanding of what makes performance vary depending on maturity.

Market practitioners have known for many years that risk-adjusted excess returns of corporate bonds tend to decrease as maturity is extended: The information ratio of credit excess returns is generally lower for long-dated bonds than for short-dated ones. This phenomenon has been extensively discussed and has sometimes been associated with a possible "low volatility anomaly" in the credit market.[1] Such an anomaly would allow investors who systematically overweight short-dated bonds relative to long-dated ones to benefit from positive returns without experiencing higher risk.

We analyze the performance of corporate bonds in the Bloomberg Barclays US Investment Grade (IG) Corporate Bond Index across different maturities over a 25-year period. We find that both average excess returns and information ratios of corporate bonds declined as maturity increased, even though the term structure of spreads retained a positive slope.

What are the factors causing such a phenomenon? We perform a return attribution analysis and highlight contributions of four effects: spread accretion, spread curve roll-down, a sample-specific bear steepening in the spread

tion, spread curve roll-down, a sample-specific bear steepening in the spread

CHAPTER **11**

Maturity Dependence of Corporate Bond Excess Returns

INTRODUCTION

Maturity dependence of credit performance is an important consideration for many investors, beyond mutual funds and absolute return investors. For example, insurance and pension fund managers use long-maturity debt to match long-dated liabilities. The decision to invest along the maturity spectrum must therefore be based on a precise understanding of what makes performance vary depending on maturity.

Market practitioners have known for many years that risk-adjusted excess returns of corporate bonds tend to decrease as maturity is extended: The information ratio of credit excess returns is generally lower for long-dated bonds than for short-dated ones. This phenomenon has been extensively discussed and has sometimes been associated with a possible "low volatility anomaly" in the credit market.[1] Such an anomaly would allow investors who systematically overweight short-dated bonds relative to long-dated ones to benefit from positive returns without experiencing higher risk.

We analyze the performance of corporate bonds in the Bloomberg Barclays US Investment Grade (IG) Corporate Bond Index across different maturities over a 25-year period. We find that both average excess returns and information ratios of corporate bonds declined as maturity increased, even though the term structure of spreads retained a positive slope.

What are the factors causing such a phenomenon? We perform a return attribution analysis and highlight contributions of four effects: spread accretion, spread curve roll-down, a sample-specific bear steepening in the spread curve, and a persistent drift of IG bonds toward lower rating qualities. All four factors exhibit strong maturity dependency, sometimes of opposite sign.

The relative importance of different investor types in short- and long-maturity buckets could lead to market segmentation and also contribute to our results. In particular, the underperformance of long-dated bonds on a risk-adjusted basis may also be a result from the existence of investors who measure risk relative to long-dated liabilities. These economic considerations are not the subject of this study as we instead try to understand the mechanism by which short and long corporate bonds have persistently delivered different performances.

PERFORMANCE BY MATURITY BUCKET

We study IG bonds,[2] which we partition in seven maturity buckets: 1–3-, 3–5-, 5–7-, 7–9-, 9–11-, 11–20-, and 20–35-year buckets, based on average life. The first three buckets rely on breakpoints widely used by index publishers. The 7–9- and 9–11-year buckets keep using a two-year interval up to and including the 10-year sector in which much new issuance is observed. The two longest-maturity buckets cover larger maturity ranges, given the need for diversification within each bucket. Our study period covers 25 years, from the end of January 1994 to January 2019. All returns included in our analysis are excess returns, as reported by the index provider, calculated as the difference between corporate bond total return and the total return of a duration-matched hypothetical Treasury portfolio. Excess returns allow us to isolate the return component associated with credit spreads from the effects of changes in Treasury yields.

The maturity buckets considered in our study can include different sets of issuers or sectors because we would like to represent the market structure as available to investors across all maturities. Indeed, some sectors, such as utilities, account for a large share of long-maturity buckets while others, such as bank and brokerage, have more short-dated debt. However, our attribution analysis is performed using individual issuer curves, as we explain later.

Figure 11.1 shows a clear pattern of decreasing information ratios as maturity is extended: Average excess return per unit of risk, measured as standard deviation of monthly returns, decreases almost monotonically. This phenomenon results from longer-dated bonds having higher duration exposure and hence higher excess return volatility than shorter-maturity ones. Figure 11.2 is more striking as it shows that average returns—even before adjusting for risk—have been lower for long than for short-maturity debt, in an uneven pattern.

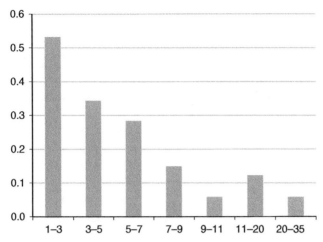

FIGURE 11.1   Information Ratio of Maturity Buckets, 1994 to 2019
Source: Bloomberg, Barclays Research

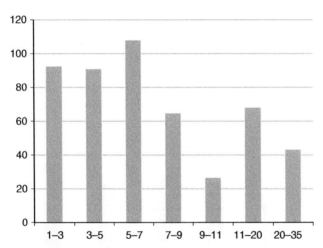

FIGURE 11.2   Average Excess Return of Maturity Buckets, 1994 to 2019 (bp/y)
Source: Bloomberg, Barclays Research

Repeating our calculation of average returns and information ratios for five nonoverlapping five-year windows (shown in Table 11.1), we find that this pattern of decreasing performance with maturity has been persistent, although not monotonic. Extending spread duration was associated with higher returns only in the strong spread rally that followed the 2008 crisis (period 4 in Table 11.1). But even then, information ratios declined with maturity.

TABLE 11.1 Performance of US Investment-Grade Maturity Buckets in Five-Year Subperiods

	1–3	3–5	5–7	7–9	9–11	11–20	20–35
Realized Excess Return (bp/y)							
1. 1994–1999	45	35	11	–4	–30	–4	–28
2. 1999–2004	102	82	94	34	18	45	55
3. 2004–2009	–65	–204	–299	–407	–356	–486	–496
4. 2009–2014	307	439	591	571	406	664	643
5. 2014–2019	73	103	143	130	95	120	41
Information Ratio							
1. 1994–1999	0.92	0.35	0.08	–0.02	–0.15	–0.01	–0.08
2. 1999–2004	0.86	0.45	0.33	0.09	0.05	0.09	0.09
3. 2004–2009	–0.22	–0.49	–0.53	–0.67	–0.60	–0.75	–0.56
4. 2009–2014	1.59	1.34	1.22	1.04	0.65	0.92	0.64
5. 2014–2019	1.20	0.80	0.70	0.49	0.33	0.25	0.07

Source: Bloomberg, Barclays Research

The low returns of long-maturity buckets are somewhat surprising given that average spreads have been higher for longer maturities, as shown in Figure 11.3. The ability of OAS to anticipate excess returns varies significantly across maturities: Short-maturity bonds exhibit average returns close

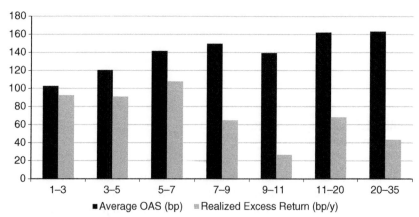

FIGURE 11.3 Average OAS and Average Excess Returns of Subsets of the US IG Corporate Bond Index, 1994 to 2019
Source: Bloomberg, Barclays Research

to their average OAS while returns of long-maturity bonds are much lower than their average OAS.

ATTRIBUTING PERFORMANCE

To understand why average excess returns of corporate bonds tend to decline with maturity, we perform a return attribution exercise. We use four factors to explain performance—spread carry, roll-down return, spread trend, and downgrade costs.

- **Spread carry** represents the spread accretion from holding a bond that trades at a positive spread over the Treasury curve. We observe it at the beginning of each month.
- **Roll-down return** is the price return from valuing a bond at a spread corresponding to a one-month shorter maturity while keeping the spread curve unchanged. If the curve has a positive slope, price returns are positive. Roll-down return is estimated from spread curves of individual issuers calibrated at the beginning of each month.[3]
- **Spread trend** reflects the sample-specific cumulative change in spread that arises because market conditions at the beginning and at the end of our 25-year period could differ substantially. One could be tempted to assume that 25 years is a long enough period for spread variations to cancel out, so as to play only a negligible role on average returns, but, as we will see later, this is not the case.
- **Downgrade cost** represents the price return from relatively rare defaults and more frequent rating downgrades. Although downgrade cost is estimated as the residual term from the three preceding factors, later we explain how it can be further attributed to those costs that are crystallized when bonds leave an index upon monthly rebalancing following a rating downgrade and those that are associated with the spread drift of continuing bonds.

Table 11.2 provides characteristics of the seven maturity buckets together with an estimated return attribution to these four factors for the 25-year period considered. Although the table relates to the entire IG markets, we have found that results are broadly similar for the nonfinancial subset of that market.

Although the spread curve has been positively sloped on average over the period considered, the slope has been more pronounced in short and intermediate maturities, meaning that roll-down returns have been small in long maturities and especially in the 10-year sector, where they are negative.

TABLE 11.2 Characteristics and Performance Attribution of US IG Corporate Maturity Buckets, 1994 to 2019

	1–3	3–5	5–7	7–9	9–11	11–20	20–35
Characteristics							
Average OAS (bp)	103	120	141	149	139	162	163
Average OASD	2.0	3.6	5.1	6.4	7.4	9.6	12.1
Average Spread Slope (bp/y)	8.9	7.4	7.1	0.1	-3.7	2.2	0.1
Trend Change in OAS (bp/y)	1.7	2.5	3.5	3.7	4.0	5.6	4.9
Average Returns							
Spread Carry (bp)	103	120	141	149	139	162	163
Roll-down (bp/y)	16	25	36	0	-27	20	-2
Spread Trend (bp/y)	-3	-9	-18	-24	-30	-53	-60
Residual, including Estimated Downgrade Cost (bp/y)	-23	-45	-52	-61	-56	-60	-58
Realized Excess Return (bp/y)	**93**	**91**	**108**	**65**	**27**	**68**	**43**
Excess Return excluding Spread Trend (bp/y)	96	100	126	88	56	121	103
Volatility and IR							
StDev ER (bp/y)	174	265	380	433	449	551	728
Realized Information Ratio	**0.53**	**0.34**	**0.28**	**0.15**	**0.06**	**0.12**	**0.06**

Source: Bloomberg, Barclays Research

The slope and roll-down data in Table 11.2 are consistent with a dip in average return for the 9–11-year sector, as seen in Figure 11.3. A possible explanation for this effect can be that bonds in this bucket are generally more liquid than those in neighboring buckets and that such liquidity advantage translates into lower spreads. Indeed, the 9–11-year bucket includes the portion of the curve with the largest volume of new issuance. As shown in the rightmost column of Table 11.3, 40% of bonds included in the index at the end of January 2019 were issued with a maturity between 9 and 11 years. That maturity bucket also includes by far the largest proportion of recently issued bonds: 86% issued in the two years to the end of January 2019, as opposed to 44% for the 7–9-year and 35% for the 3–5-year buckets. This large allocation to recent issues can have the effect of making that bucket relatively more liquid, with a low average bond age compared with other buckets.

Another possible explanation relates to the fact that our study is based on index data, with new bonds joining the index at calendar month-end following issuance. Therefore, our analysis does not capture the new issue concession available to investors who participate in the primary market. Capturing issuance concessions has been shown to be a significant source of portfolio performance relative to the index.[4] As new issue volume are most heavily weighted in the 10y bucket, ignoring new-issue concessions, as the index does, may underestimate the performance of investors who participate in the primary market and are able to obtain sufficient allocation of new issuance.

TABLE 11.3　Characteristics of Maturity Subsets of the US IG Corporate Index on 31 January 2019

Maturity Bucket	% Bonds w. Age less than 2yr	Average Age (Year) of Bonds in Maturity Bucket	% New Issuance by Maturity Bucket
1–3	24%	4.5	1%
3–5	35%	4.0	5%
5–7	21%	3.7	13%
7–9	44%	2.8	6%
9–11	86%	2.5	40%
11–20	12%	10.6	2%
20–35	28%	4.3	31%

Source: Bloomberg, Barclays Research

A more direct way of observing a possible liquidity advantage is shown in Figure 11.4 where we plot the average Liquidity Cost Scores (LCS) per unit of Duration Times Spread (DTS) spread exposure of the 7–9-, 9–11-, and 11–20-year buckets. This is reported for the more recent part of our data sample as LCS are available only from January 2007.[5] A low value indicates low transaction cost per unit of risk and hence higher secondary market liquidity. Figure 11.4 shows clearly that bonds included in the 9–11-year bucket have enjoyed persistently higher liquidity than those in adjacent buckets. This liquidity advantage can explain the lower spread of that sector.

Long maturities are characterized by higher average spreads but flatter spread curves. The spread curve has even been persistently inverted in the 9–11-year bucket. In that sector, a vast majority of bonds are recent issues with high liquidity and lower spreads than older bonds. As these bonds age, their liquidity advantage tends to disappear and their spread normalizes relative to peers.[6] This normalization process leads to an inverted or flat spread curve for maturities just below 10 years, which results in lower roll-down returns. In contrast, shorter maturity buckets, up to seven years, are characterized by steeper spread curves and exhibit higher roll-down returns than longer maturity buckets.

The level and shape of the spread curve has changed substantially in the 25-year period considered, as shown in Figure 11.5. These changes account for the third factor in our analysis: spread trend. The average increase in spread is less than 2bp/y for the 1–3-year sector but over 5bp/y for long maturities (see the fourth row of Table 11.2). This secular bear steepening

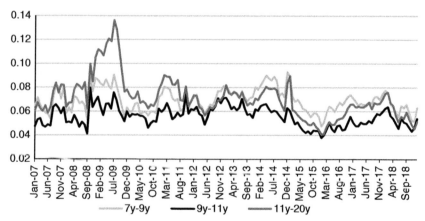

FIGURE 11.4   Liquidity Cost Score per Unit of DTS for Maturity Subsets of the US IG Market
Source: Bloomberg, Barclays Research

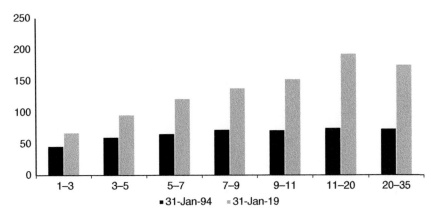

FIGURE 11.5   Average OAS (bp) of IG Maturity Buckets at Beginning and End of 25-Year Time Period
Source: Bloomberg, Barclays Research

leads to negative returns (labeled "Spread Trend" in the middle of Table 11.2) that are much larger for longer maturities than for shorter ones. For example, the return of the longest maturity sector (20–35 years) would have been 103bp/y in the absence of any trend in spread, 60bp/y more than actually realized. In contrast, the effect of the spread trend is only 3bp/y for the 1–3-year bucket.

Excess returns become more similar across maturities if we add back the effect of sample-specific trend in spreads to realized returns, as shown in the bottom row of the middle section of Table 11.2. But even in that case, there is no return advantage of extending maturity beyond seven years.

The fourth factor explaining index returns is measured as the residual term after accounting for the previous three factors: carry, roll-down return, and spread trend. We assume that much of it is associated with realized and unrealized (downward spread drift) changes in credit quality and therefore call it "cost of rating downgrades," although it could also capture the effect of some unrelated spread changes.

Figure 11.6 illustrates a systematic drift toward lower rating quality in our IG universe. For each month, we contrast the month-end average rating quality, expressed in numerical value on a linear scale with its beginning-of-month value. A bar with a positive value indicates a net change toward a lower average rating quality as more and/or stronger downgrades than upgrades were observed in that month. The chart also reports the average OAS of our universe: Rating quality tends to deteriorate more when spreads are high. It is also when average index OAS is high that the difference in

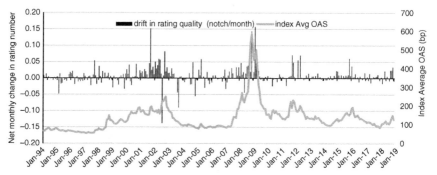

FIGURE 11.6 Net Monthly Change in Rating Quality (in Unit of Fine Rating Notches) Averaged Across All Maturities for the IG Universe
Source: Bloomberg, Barclays Research

spreads between rating buckets becomes the widest and therefore that the return penalty associated with a downgrade is the largest.[7]

Bonds join the IG index as they meet specific quality and other criteria but leave following a default or a downgrade below investment grade. Previous research[8] has shown that most of the underperformance of downgraded bonds relative to peers occurs prior to the downgrade actually happening. Therefore, downgrade-related costs primarily affect the index from which downgraded bonds originate.

It is expected that downgrade cost increases with maturity[9] as such cost can be described as the product of a spread widening times duration. Yet spread widening may not be a parallel shift across all maturities. In particular, a lack of demand for long-dated high-yield bonds can cause long-maturity bonds to underperform on a downgrade. Jump to defaults would typically trigger price to expected recovery values with little relationship to the maturity of the bond. Finally, different industry sector allocations in different maturity buckets may introduce significant noise in the effect of downgrades on performance across maturities.

Figures 11.7 and 11.8 detail performance contributors for the 3–5-year and 9–11-year maturity buckets. Although the average OAS of the 9–11-year bucket has been higher, it has been penalized by a negative contribution from roll-down return, a factor that is strongly positive in the 3–5-year bucket. The systematic steepening of the spread curve observed in our data sample and larger downgrade costs for longer maturities also affect performance. The net effect is that the 3–5-year bucket delivered 91bp/y of excess return while the 9–11-year bucket excess return was only 27bp/y on average over period of the analysis.

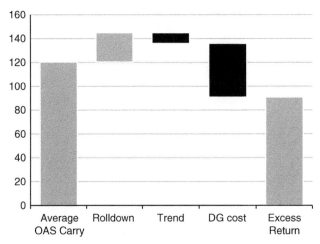

FIGURE 11.7 Attribution of Excess Returns for the 3–5-Year US IG Corporate Index from 1994 to 2019 (bp/y)
Source: Bloomberg, Barclays Research

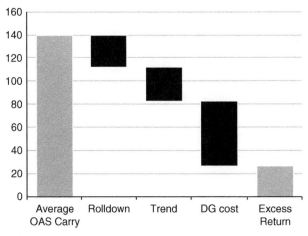

FIGURE 11.8 Attribution of Excess Returns for the 9–11-Year US IG Corporate Index from 1994 to 2019 (bp/y)
Source: Bloomberg, Barclays Research

In the period considered, the spread curve has not been steep enough to compensate for downgrade losses that also tend to increase with maturity. In addition, for the 9–11-year sector, negative roll-down returns weigh heavily on performance.

TABLE 11.4 Characteristics and Performance Attribution of A-Rated and Baa-Rated Maturity Buckets, 1994 to 2019

	A Rated							Baa Rated						
	1–3	3–5	5–7	7–9	9–11	11–20	20–35	1–3	3–5	5–7	7–9	9–11	11–20	20–35
Characteristics														
Average OAS (bp)	84	100	114	119	110	126	132	140	157	175	183	172	199	197
Average OASD	2.0	3.6	5.1	6.5	7.5	9.7	12.4	2.0	3.6	5.1	6.3	7.3	9.4	11.8
Average Spread Slope (bp/y)	8.6	6.9	6.7	-0.8	-5.6	1.1	-0.3	9.5	8.2	7.6	1.5	-1.2	3.2	0.3
Trend Change in OAS (bp/y)	1.1	1.7	2.3	2.5	3.0	4.0	3.3	1.7	2.5	3.9	4.1	3.7	5.9	5.7
Average Returns														
Spread Carry (bp)	84	100	114	119	110	126	132	140	157	175	183	172	199	197
Roll–down (bp/y)	16	23	34	-6	-41	11	-5	16	28	39	9	-9	29	1
Spread Trend (bp/y)	-2	-6	-12	-16	-22	-39	-41	-3	-9	-20	-26	-27	-55	-67
Est. Downgrade Cost (bp/y)	-19	-37	-36	-32	-37	-47	-42	-38	-63	-67	-92	-84	-80	-76
Realized ER (bp/y)	80	79	100	65	10	51	43	115	113	127	74	53	92	56
Excess Return excluding Spread Trend (bp/y)	82	85	112	81	32	90	84	119	122	147	100	79	148	123
Volatility and IR														
StDev ER (bp/y)	163	247	342	384	412	461	648	222	336	454	528	531	667	832
Information Ratio	0.49	0.32	0.29	0.17	0.02	0.11	0.07	0.52	0.34	0.28	0.14	0.10	0.14	0.07

Source: Bloomberg, Barclays Research

Similar performance patterns can be found in quality subsets of the IG market, as shown in Table 11.4. A-rated and Baa-rated corporate bonds have both experienced positive spread curve slopes on average, with a dip for the 10-year sector. Differences in roll-down returns across maturities are more pronounced in A-rated indices, with strongly negative returns for the 9–11-year subset. The effect of spread trends is larger for Baa-rated bonds. In both rating categories, excess returns of the longest and shortest maturity buckets would be nearly identical but inferior to those of the 5–7-year sector, had there been no spread trend in the period considered. (See bottom row of the middle section of Table 11.4.)

The cost of downgrades is smallest for the shortest maturity sector in both universes. It is on average twice as large in the Baa-rated as in the A-rated universe. Indeed, the spread widening observed upon rating downgrade is typically much larger when considering downgrades from Baa to high yield than for rating migration from A to Baa.

In both universes, information ratios decrease monotonically with maturity, with an exception for the 9–11-year sectors, which perform worse than their respective neighbors. Maturity extension beyond seven years has been poorly rewarded in credit markets, for both A- and Baa-rated bonds, in the period of this study.

CONCLUSION

Long-maturity corporate bonds have delivered lower excess returns than short-maturity ones over a 25-year period from 1994 to 2019. Our attribution analysis reveals that this underperformance can, to a large degree, be explained by roll-down and downgrade-related returns, along with sample-specific trend in spreads. The effect of all three factors varies significantly depending on maturity.

Variations in roll-down returns reflect the relative steepness of issuer spread curves across maturity buckets. While spread curves have generally been steeper in short maturities than in longer ones, they have been flat or inverted in the 10-year sector, which has delivered particularly poor roll-down returns. This can be associated with the negative liquidity spread premium of the 10-year sector, in which much new issuance is concentrated. The costs of rating downgrades are also generally larger for longer maturity bonds.

REFERENCES

Ambastha, M., A. Ben Dor, L. Dynkin, and J. Hyman. 2008, March. "Do Short-Dated Corporates Outperform Long-Dated Corporates? A DTS-Based Study." Global Relative Value, Lehman Brothers Fixed Income Research.

Ben Dor, A., L. Dynkin, J. Hyman, P. Houweling, E. Van Leeuwen, and O. Penninga. 2007. "DTS^{SM} (Duration Times Spread)." *Journal of Portfolio Management* 33(2): 77–100.

Hyman, J. 24 January 2017. "Dynamics of Spread Between New and Old Bonds of the Same Issuer." Barclays Research.

Konstantinovsky, V., K. Y. Ng, and B. D. Phelps. 2016. "Measuring Bond-Level Liquidity." *Journal of Portfolio Management* 42(4): 116–128.

Naik, V., M. Devarajan, and E. Wong. 2007. "The Anatomy of Credit Curve Trades Over the Economic Cycle." Lehman Brothers Fixed Income Research, *Quantitative Credit Research Quarterly*, Quarter 2: 16–24.

Ng, K. Y., and B. Phelps. 2011. "Capturing Credit Spread Premium." *Financial Analysts Journal* 67(3): 63–75.

Ng, K. Y., and B. Phelps. 2015. "The Hunt for a Low-Risk Anomaly in the USD Corporate Bond Market." *Journal of Portfolio Management* 42(1): 63–84.

NOTES

1. The low volatility anomaly is a phenomenon related to persistently higher risk-adjusted returns of less risky securities. Useful references include Naik, Devarajan, and Wong (2007); Ambastha, Ben Dor, Dynkin, and Hyman (2008); and Ng and Phelps (2015).
2. We exclude bonds with significant optionality, with average life lower than 1 or higher than 35 at the beginning of any calendar month, or with extremely high OAS.
3. We consider issuers with bonds outstanding in at least three out of seven maturity buckets. For these issuers, we estimate spread curves, which are used to derive bond roll-down returns. The spread curves of eligible issuers are aggregated and used to calculate roll-down return of other similar issuers that have fewer outstanding bonds.
4. See Chapter 7.
5. For an introduction to Barclays Liquidity Cost Scores, see Konstantinovsky and Phelps (2016). For an introduction to Duration Times Spread, see Ben Dor et al. (2007).
6. For more details, see Hyman (2017).
7. The relationship between spread levels and spread differential among rating categories is documented in Chapter 8.
8. See Ng and Phelps (2011) as well as Chapter 2.
9. See Chapter 9.

CHAPTER 12

ESG Investing in Credit

INTRODUCTION

Environmental, social, and governance (ESG) investing started as a small niche style in equity portfolio management and has expanded to bond markets to become more and more mainstream. Investors weighing the merits of incorporating ESG criteria into their portfolios often ask the same critical question: How does this affect performance?

For some of the most committed investors, the knowledge that their funds are being invested to support the values in which they believe is so important that they would accept a lower return on their investments. A much larger group would be happy to support these values, but only once they are convinced that there is limited negative return effect. Finally, if consideration of ESG principles can actually help to improve portfolio performance—as many adherents claim—then it would be hard to justify any resistance to their adoption. The relationship between ESG characteristics of a portfolio and performance is therefore of primary importance.

Many studies have examined this relationship; however, most have focused on equity markets. We use bond data from the Bloomberg Barclays Corporate Bond Indices and ESG ratings from two providers, Sustainalytics* and MSCI ESG Research, to study the effect of ESG investing in US dollar– and euro-denominated investment-grade (IG) bond markets and in US high-yield (HY) markets. In each asset class, we study the effect of ESG in individual industry sectors. We focus on a best-in-class implementation in which all industry sectors, no matter how controversial, remain eligible to invest, with ESG ratings helping distinguish between more and less attractive issuers within each sector. The data used in our analysis covers the period from August 2009 through April 2018.

---

*Sustainalytics' ESG scores used in this chapter are no longer their primary signal.

369

This chapter is organized as follows: First, we provide an overview of the data used in our study and detail the level of index coverage in each target market.

Next, we discuss some key characteristics of the ESG scores obtained from the two providers considered in our analysis. What do they represent? How are they calculated? How stable have they been? How closely correlated are they? Do they exhibit distinct geographical patterns? We then illustrate how a naive ESG tilt can induce unwanted risk exposures in a portfolio.

Then we address the key question of bond market performance. We construct pairs of bond portfolios—one with high ESG scores and one with low ESG scores—designed to be matched as closely as possible with respect to all major risk characteristics. Using this technique, we systematically measure the relative performance achieved when we impose this ESG tilt. We perform this experiment using individual pillar scores as well as with composite ESG scores from either of the two providers. In each market, we focus on individual credit sectors as well as on the overall corporate bond market.

Then we investigate the relationship between ESG rating and bond valuation. Do investors need to pay a premium for bonds with higher ESG scores? If there is an ESG premium, has it changed over time? Does it vary across markets?

In the last section, we investigate these issues in the US HY market, including an analysis of the extent to which a spread premium and/or a performance benefit can be associated with ESG ratings.

Finally, following a short conclusion, Appendix 12.1 provides additional details on the effect of ESG on bond portfolio performance.

ASSEMBLING A DATASET OF ESG RATINGS AND BOND RETURNS

We have assembled a dataset of corporate bonds and their ESG ratings that constitutes the core of this study. We merged data from three distinct sources. Bloomberg Barclays Index data for bond characteristics and returns; to this, we added ESG ratings from two providers: MSCI ESG Research and Sustainalytics.

This process required careful attention because the ESG ratings providers assign ratings to companies, not to specific bonds. Furthermore, as they primarily target equity market investors (and due to data availability), they mostly cover publicly traded companies, and their ratings correspond to equity security identifiers. Thus, to obtain an ESG rating for each bond in our database, one must first map it to an equity security for which an ESG rating is available (for each provider and for each month). We were greatly aided in this process by previous bond-equity mapping exercises, performed when we designed cross-market systematic strategies in equity and in fixed income markets.[1]

The resulting dataset is the set of bonds for which we have ratings from both MSCI ESG and Sustainalytics. In April 2018, this dataset covered close to 90% by market value of the USD and EUR IG Corporate index universes. However, as ESG ratings are relatively new, we find less extensive coverage as we go back in time. Table 12.1 shows how index coverage has evolved for the intersection of the Sustainalytics and MSCI ESG ratings universes. Over the period of our analysis, coverage always exceeded 80% of index market value and 63% of the issuers in the US dollar- and euro-denominated IG markets.[2] The discrepancy between the two metrics implies that the issuers that are not covered tend to be relatively small.

The HY market stands in contrast to the IG market, with a much lower joint coverage by ESG providers. This is, in part, explained by the prevalence of private issuers of HY debt as well as by the usually smaller size of HY issuers relative to IG ones, meaning that covering them could often be a less immediate priority for investors and ESG providers alike than covering larger IG issuers. In addition, the total number of companies covered by either of the two ESG providers can be larger than the number of companies in our intersection dataset.

Coverage considerations lead us to start our data sample at different points in time for our studies of the IG (from August 2009) and HY (from October 2012) markets.

CHARACTERISTICS OF ESG SCORES

Before addressing the effect of ESG scores[3] on bond market performance, we examine some of the characteristics of the scores themselves. First of all, what do these scores measure and how are they calculated? How stable have these scores been? How different are the scores from one provider to another? How do ESG scores tend to relate to other bond characteristics such as credit ratings and spreads?

ESG Scoring Methodologies Are Complex and Vary Across Providers

ESG scoring, by its very nature, is a complex and somewhat subjective enterprise. ESG issues span a wide range of business practices; each of the three main pillar scores are calculated based on a large number of component

TABLE 12.1 Coverage of US IG, Euro IG, and US HY Bond Index Universe by Providers of ESG Scores, at the End of Each Calendar Year

	2009	2010	2011	2012	2013	2014	2015	2016	2017
US IG Index Universe									
Index MV ($bn)	2,555	2,843	3,175	3,651	3,727	4,097	4,401	4,907	5,192
Index bonds	3,387	3,685	4,005	4,467	4,868	5,201	5,680	5,919	5,588
Index issuers	562	606	637	688	725	761	784	783	729
MV coverage	87%	89%	89%	89%	90%	91%	91%	93%	95%
Bond coverage	82%	84%	84%	87%	87%	88%	88%	89%	93%
Issuer coverage	67%	70%	69%	78%	78%	77%	78%	78%	85%
Euro IG Index Universe									
Index MV (€bn)	1,303	1,307	1,209	1,310	1,303	1,442	1,507	1,682	1,865
Index bonds	1,363	1,369	1,297	1,312	1,401	1,532	1,729	1,958	2,229
Index issuers	350	352	348	333	352	396	451	491	538
MV coverage	80%	80%	82%	84%	81%	83%	86%	87%	89%
Bond coverage	75%	76%	80%	83%	79%	81%	85%	85%	87%
Issuer coverage	64%	64%	69%	73%	70%	71%	77%	75%	79%
US HY Index Universe									
Index MV ($bn)	747	930	928	1,145	1,270	1,326	1,199	1,334	1,339
Index bonds	1,642	1,822	1,847	2,009	2,131	2,229	2,174	2,086	2,043
Index issuers	771	879	944	1,013	1,047	1,068	1,011	947	934
MV coverage	30%	24%	32%	43%	43%	47%	54%	56%	59%
Bond coverage	24%	20%	24%	36%	37%	39%	43%	47%	51%
Issuer coverage	12%	9%	12%	24%	25%	26%	27%	30%	34%

Source: Bloomberg, MSCI ESG Research, Sustainalytics

inputs. Within the environmental score, for example, different ESG providers give different focus to criteria such as a company's energy usage, its contribution to air and water pollution, or the extent of its recycling efforts. These criteria are based on nonfinancial information assumed to be material to the long-term sustainability of the company. However, despite standardization efforts by industry bodies, such as the Sustainability Accounting Standards Board[4] and the Global Reporting Initiative,[5] there is no industry-wide consensus on which detailed environmental- and social-related criteria should be used to evaluate a corporation and how the criteria should be weighted.

There are a number of providers of ESG ratings in the market, and each has built a comprehensive system for gathering a large, multidimensional dataset on the ESG records of companies. They collect dozens of indicators within each of the three pillars; the weights given to each of these indicators when forming the E, S, and G scores vary by industry. Once aggregated, top-level scores are then normalized by sector, such that the most relevant comparison is between the scores of two companies in the same industry.

We have chosen to use ESG scores from two providers, MSCI and Sustainalytics. This does not imply that we have deemed these providers to be superior to others; rather, these are the only firms whose scores we have studied.[6]

ESG Scores from Different Providers Do Not Measure Exactly the Same Thing

It is not surprising that scores from different providers do not always agree, given the lack of standardization in methodologies for compiling ESG scores and their qualitative nature. Furthermore, as opposed to credit ratings, which have a well-defined objective of estimating default risk, there is no clear and objective consensus on what ESG ratings should measure. To assess how similar our two ESG datasets are, we ranked the full universe of companies by scores from the two providers and measured the correlation between the two sets of rankings at various points in time. Figure 12.1 shows the time series of these correlations for the overall ESG score and for each pillar score. The ESG scores from the two providers exhibit positive but low correlations as a consequence of the differences in their methodologies.

Figure 12.1 shows that the correlations between the governance scores from MSCI and Sustainalytics have been persistently lower than for other pillars. This highlights a significant methodological difference between the two sets of scores. In the context of the dataset used in this study, the governance score from MSCI ESG research is a measure of the quality of corporate governance, focusing on issues such as the composition of the board

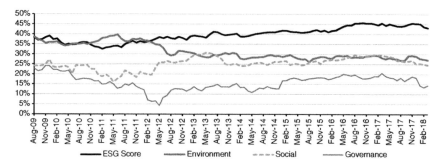

FIGURE 12.1 Correlations Between ESG Scores of MSCI and Sustainalytics
Note: Monthly rank correlations between the E, S, G, and ESG scores of the two providers.
Source: MSCI ESG Research, Sustainalytics, Barclays Research

and executive compensation. While the governance score from Sustainalytics includes some of these issues, it also gives a large weight to the company's governance of environmental and social issues. Sustainalytics also produces a separate set of pure corporate governance scores, but these are not included in our study as they were not the ones that were rolled up into the company's overall ESG scores at the time of our analysis.

ESG Scores Have Been Stable

Understanding the dynamics of ESG ratings is important to bond portfolio managers, as systematically favoring high-ESG bonds might require incremental portfolio turnover and, therefore, entail high transaction costs if these ratings change often. At the same time, one would expect some ESG scores to change as a function of the evolving nature of corresponding risks and of company characteristics, including the effects of management decisions to mitigate ESG risk or to address disclosure of nonfinancial information deemed material to the prospects of the company.

We now return to our combined dataset of all bonds with scores from Sustainalytics and MSCI and examine the stability of these ratings. We first combine the data from all three bond markets considered (US IG, US HY, and Eur IG); since the ratings are assigned at the company level, this division by bond market is not fundamental to the scoring process. We then order all available companies by their ESG score as of a given date and rank them into terciles that we label Low, Medium, and High. We then measure the 12-month transition frequencies among these ESG tiers. Table 12.2 shows the transition matrices obtained for the ESG scores of our two providers. Both sets have been relatively stable. For example, the bottom row of the

TABLE 12.2 Transition Frequencies Across ESG Tiers on a One-Year Horizon, 2009 to 2018

		MSCI				Sustainalytics		
				End of Period				
		Low	Medium	High		Low	Medium	High
Start of	Low	77%	20%	2%	Low	86%	14%	0%
Period	Medium	19%	61%	20%	Medium	11%	75%	14%
	High	2%	19%	79%	High	0%	12%	88%

Source: MSCI ESG Research, Sustainalytics, Barclays Research

table shows that an issuer with a top-tier ESG score at the beginning of a year has a 79% (88%) probability of remaining top tier a year later, according to MSCI ESG rating (Sustainalytics) in our data sample. Table 12.2 has been calculated using overall ESG scores; we have repeated the analysis for each of the three pillars independently and found similar transition patterns, with governance slightly less stable than social and environmental.

An ESG Tilt Can Bias a Portfolio

Although both sets of ESG scores are normalized by sector, a strategy that systematically favors high-ESG bonds over low ones may bring unintended exposures. For example, Table 12.3 shows the characteristics of three equal-size ESG tiers in the US and Euro IG markets, according to our two providers. The top tier is associated with substantially lower spreads than the bottom tier in all four cases considered, with the difference in spread between high- and low-ESG buckets being 15 to 36bp. The spread difference is consistent with the small difference in credit rating shown in the table. Repeating this analysis for individual ESG pillars shows that the environmental score has the strongest association with credit rating and spreads. In other words, a systematic portfolio tilt in favor of issuers that score well on environment is more likely to result in an unintended conservative, low-yield bias.

In the credit markets, a strategy that systematically favors high-ESG bonds without controlling for portfolio risk characteristics can easily underperform just because of its systematic bias towards higher-quality, lower-spread issuers.

Table 12.3 provides a mild indication that corporations with strong credit quality tend to score higher in terms of ESG. To confirm this and to test the linkage with individual pillars, we calculate the correlations between ESG scores and credit ratings. We use the index convention—taking the

TABLE 12.3 Average Differences in Characteristics Between High- and Low-ESG Portfolios, 2009 to 2018

	MSCI				Sustainalytics			
	Low	Medium	High	H-L	Low	Medium	High	H-L
US IG Index Universe								
Average ESG Score	2.5	4.9	7.6	5.0	51	61	70	18
Spread over Treasury Bonds (bp)	162	146	126	-36	162	147	131	-31
Rating Quality	A3	A3	A2		Baa1	A3	A2	
Rating Quality Number	8.3	8.1	7.3	-1.0	8.6	8.0	7.3	-1.2
Euro IG Index Universe								
Average ESG Score	3.8	6.3	8.6	5.0	59	69	77	18
Spread over Treasury Bonds (bp)	166	144	143	-22	162	146	147	-15
Rating Quality	A3	A3	A3		A3	A3	A3	
Rating Quality Number	7.7	7.6	8	0.2	7.8	7.7	7.9	0.1

Note: In the numeric quality scale used here, higher numbers correspond to lower ratings. For example, A2 = 7, A3 = 8, Baa1 = 9.
Source: Bloomberg, MSCI ESG Research, Sustainalytics, Barclays Research

median rating from three agencies (Moody's, S&P, and Fitch) and transforming letter ratings into numbers—and calculate the rank correlations between these index credit ratings and each ESG score each month. The time averages of these correlations over our study period are reported in Figure 12.2. Small positive correlations confirm that ESG ratings are not independent from credit ratings. Correlations are more pronounced for environmental than for governance scores for the two providers. We find this pattern to be similar and stable across major industry sectors.

In addition to quality and spread, we find that ESG ratings can vary according to the country of domicile of the issuer. Table 12.4 presents ESG

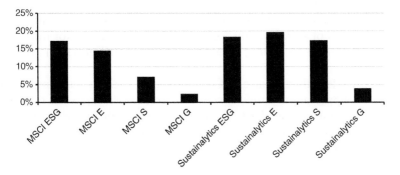

FIGURE 12.2   Average Correlation Between Credit Rating and ESG Score, 2009 to 2018
Source: Bloomberg, MSCI ESG Research, Sustainalytics, Barclays Research

TABLE 12.4   Average ESG Score by Country of Domicile of the Issuer, 2009 to 2018

	USA	Euro Area	Other	All Countries
MSCI ESG	4.9	6.6	5.8	5.4
MSCI Environmental	6.1	6.5	6.2	6.2
MSCI Social	4.7	5.8	5.1	4.9
MSCI Governance	5.2	5.4	5.3	5.3
Sustainalytics ESG	61.0	70.8	66.6	63.7
Sustainalytics Environmental	61.2	70.3	66.0	63.6
Sustainalytics Social	59.4	71.8	65.9	62.7
Sustainalytics Governance	64.8	71.3	69.3	66.7
Average Credit Rating	A3	A3	A2	A3

Source: Bloomberg, MSCI ESG Research, Sustainalytics, Barclays Research

scores for different groups of issuers split by geography. MSCI (on a scale of 10) and Sustainalytics (on a scale of 100) ESG scores are included, together with their individual pillar scores. US-domiciled issuers score, on average, lower on all reported ESG metrics, especially social. Governance scores are relatively more stable across regions.

The pattern found in Table 12.4 might be explained by the joint effect of differences in reporting requirement by region and of the treatment of disclosure by ESG rating agencies. Companies based in European countries must follow stricter disclosure rules on a broad set of non-purely financial metrics. As lack of disclosure can be penalized with a lower ESG rating, the European-based companies can find it easier to obtain a high ESG rating. In addition, local interest in responsible investing and associated demand for high-ESG-rated securities can encourage corporate issuers to conform to high standards of sustainability. Regional differences in investor interest in responsible investing could, therefore, explain differences in average ESG scores.

As it is clear that a naive ESG tilt can come with various unintended biases, it is important to carefully control portfolio risk exposures to ensure that any analysis of the effect of ESG on valuation or on performance is done "everything else equal." Regional variations in ESG scores also point to the need to analyze the effect of ESG investing in the United States and in Europe separately from each other.

EFFECT OF ESG ON PORTFOLIO PERFORMANCE IN IG MARKETS

Does the incorporation of ESG criteria in the investment process improve the financial performance of a portfolio or hurt it? This has been the key question as we evaluate whether and how to incorporate ESG characteristics in portfolios.

One key distinction that can be made is between approaches based on negative screening by industry vs. those based on relative comparisons among the firms in each industry. For example, an investor using a negative screen may choose to exclude coal mining companies from its investment universe. Another investor may use ESG ratings to rank coal mining companies and choose to invest in the ones that have the best overall ranking within the sector. In the first case, in a period in which coal mining companies outperform the market, the investment portfolio may lag a broad market index. In the second approach, the portfolio is neutral with respect to sector exposure but favors those companies with better ESG policies, as these are considered to be less likely to suffer from the risks inherent in the industry.[7]

Bond indices include both types of mechanisms just discussed. For example, socially responsible (SRI) corporate bond indices exist that are based on negative screening and exclude companies involved in controversial industries, such as tobacco, alcohol, or gambling. In contrast, there are sustainability indices which use a best-in-class approach based on ESG ratings to choose the best-performing subset of index bonds within each industry.

In previous research we analyzed the historical returns of both SRI and sustainability indices relative to Bloomberg Barclays' flagship US Corporate IG Index. [8] While both indices had underperformed, some of the underperformance could be traced to systematic biases unrelated to ESG criteria. Once we corrected for these, we found that the return impact due specifically to the ESG tilt in security selection was positive for the sustainability index but negative for the SRI index. We concluded that the wholesale exclusion of entire industries from the investment universe, while it may be desirable based on ethical considerations, is not justified by the evidence based on purely financial criteria.

We therefore focus our attention on attempts to incorporate ESG criteria in portfolio construction by applying an ESG tilt in security selection within each industry. Can such an approach improve portfolio performance over the long term?

To answer this question, we perform a historical simulation of diversified portfolios that match all major index exposures except for a positive or negative ESG tilt. [9] The difference in return between high- and low-ESG portfolios illustrates the performance effect of the ESG characteristic in the period considered. We also study the effect of ESG investing within individual industry sectors with a view to identify which one of E, S, or G has been most influential in each sector.

Constructing Index-Matched Portfolios with an ESG Tilt

To measure the effect of ESG investing on credit portfolio performance in an objective manner, we construct pairs of portfolios that differ substantially in their ESG scores but whose characteristics are otherwise identical across all important dimensions of risk for corporate bonds. By isolating the ESG effect from other sources of risk, we capture the difference in performance between these portfolios that is attributed to the ESG tilt. We then monitor the performance of these portfolios over time.

The core of our portfolio construction technique is a mechanism for building well-diversified portfolios of bonds designed to track a benchmark—in this case, the Bloomberg Barclays US Investment Grade Corporate Bond Index. [10] We constrain portfolios to remain neutral to the benchmark along multiple risk dimensions that are known to affect bond portfolio returns. Specifically, the portfolios are constrained to match the average spread, duration, and Duration Times Spread (DTS) of the index. A quality constraint ensures that the portfolio allocation matches that of the index across three rating buckets. Sector and maturity allocations are matched along a 16-cell partition of eight industry sectors by two maturity buckets for the US IG market. For each industry-maturity cell, the portfolio must match the index market weight, spread duration, and DTS[11] contribution. To reduce idiosyncratic risk, concentration limits ensure that no bond or issuer is significantly overweight in terms of market weight and DTS contribution. These rules make our tracking portfolios highly diversified, with close to 180 bonds, on average.[12]

Several adjustments apply to the Euro market. The benchmark is not the published Bloomberg Barclays Euro IG Corporate Bond Index but its subset that includes bonds covered by MSCI and Sustainalytics. This ensures that portfolio construction is not biased as a consequence of some index bonds being unavailable in the investment universe. We use a 10-cell partition of five industry sectors by two maturity buckets and control for issuer geography.

The specific set of constraints used in each market can be satisfied by many different portfolios. The key to our technique is that the objective function determines which specific bonds should be used to fill each industry-maturity cell. We run the model twice with two different objectives: once to maximize the weighted-average portfolio ESG score subject to these constraints and once to minimize it. The two tracking portfolios are reconstructed every month-end, at the time of monthly index rebalancing, to ensure that they keep pace with any changes in the structure of the corporate bond market and incorporate fresh ESG information. Both are expected to track the index quite well, so that monthly tracking error volatility should be low. The key question is whether substantial differences would arise over time between the average returns of the two portfolios.

The difference between the high- and low-ESG tracking portfolios can be interpreted as an ESG return effect: the return contribution associated with systematically favoring high-ESG corporate bonds over low-ESG ones while keeping everything else equal. This approach does not automatically exclude any issuer or any industry sector, no matter how controversial it might be.

In addition to pairs of portfolios with the minimum and maximum overall ESG rating, we also create portfolio pairs that accentuate the differences in individual E, S, and G scores, to observe which one of these three pillars has the largest effect on performance. All portfolio simulations are carried out using ESG ratings from either MSCI or Sustainalytics.

High-ESG Portfolios Have Outperformed in IG Markets

Figures 12.3 and 12.4 report the cumulative outperformance of high-ESG portfolios over low-ESG ones in the US IG and Euro IG markets. Figure 12.3 shows results based on ESG data provided by MSCI while Figure 12.4 relates to Sustainalytics ESG scores. The performance paths follow a similar pattern:

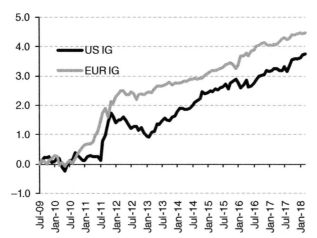

FIGURE 12.3 Cumulative Outperformance (%) of a High-ESG over a Low-ESG Portfolio Using MSCI ESG Data
Source: Bloomberg, MSCI ESG Research, Barclays Research

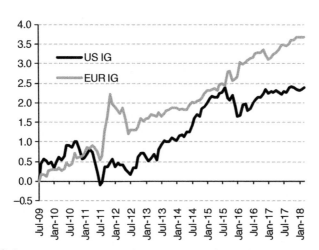

FIGURE 12.4 Cumulative Outperformance (%) of a High-ESG over a Low-ESG Portfolio Using Sustainalytics ESG Data
Source: Bloomberg, Sustainalytics, Barclays Research

In all four cases, the cumulative performance has been positive and trending upward over the period, with some more volatile patches along the way. The period up to 2012 was generally more volatile than more recent years.

Table 12.5 reports performance averaged over time and includes the three individual components of ESG. To put tracking errors results in perspective, the top row includes average returns and volatilities of the respective indices. The returns are expressed in excess of duration-matched local Treasury bond portfolios to keep the focus on credit performance, independently of any fluctuations in the general level of interest rates. Maximizing overall ESG scores from either provider produces a small but steady outperformance, with the best single-pillar results coming from governance, when considering the US market over the entire period. However, we found that an environmental tilt delivered the highest returns in the last two years of the period for the US IG market and in the entire period for the Euro IG market, irrespective of the provider of ESG scores.[13]

The performance numbers for the two markets are strikingly similar, with slightly lower volatility in Europe. As a result, information ratios are higher in Europe. In terms of the role played by different pillar scores, the Euro IG results show less variation among them: All three pillars turn in positive performance, with the largest effect coming from the environmental score. The social score seems to be the least important in both markets for both providers.

Breaking Down ESG Performance by Industry

What is the effect of ESG characteristics in major industry sectors? Has an ESG tilt had a positive return contribution across all sectors? And are E, S, and G contributions similar at sector level to what is shown in Table 12.5 for the entire market?

To address these questions, we repeat our long-short portfolio simulations for eight major sectors of the index in the US market and five sectors in the euro market. The choice of sectors is motivated by the need to have sufficient issuer diversification within each sector for the entire period of the analysis, so that issuer-specific risk remains limited. As in the market-wide portfolios discussed earlier, industry-specific high-ESG and low-ESG portfolios are rebalanced every month to ensure that they have the same risk characteristics while being broadly diversified. Construction rules can vary from one sector to another according to issuer diversity within each sector. In practice, the average number of bonds in each such portfolio varies by industry, ranging from 65 (cyclical) to over 110 (banks and brokerages) in the US market and from 50 (utility) to over 110 (for an enlarged cyclical sector, broader than its US cousin) in the euro market.

Table 12.6 reports the average returns of ESG-tilted sector portfolios in the US IG market. Return contributions of ESG tilts are positive in most

TABLE 12.5 Return Difference Between Portfolios with High ESG Scores over Similar-Risk Portfolios with Low ESG Scores, 2009 to 2018

	US IG Market			Euro IG Market		
	Average (bp/m)	Volatility (bp/m)	Information Ratio	Average (bp/m)	Volatility (bp/m)	Information Ratio
Index ER	17.0	97.5	0.6	16.3	87.0	0.7
		Using MSCI ESG Scores				
ESG	3.6	13.6	0.9	4.3	11.4	1.3
Environmental	2.9	13.3	0.7	2.7	13.5	0.7
Social	–0.8	13.6	–0.2	1.8	10.2	0.6
Governance	5.4	14.4	1.3	2.7	11.0	0.8
		Using Sustainalytics ESG Scores				
ESG	2.3	13.5	0.6	3.5	13.9	0.9
Environmental	1.6	15.8	0.3	3.6	11.1	1.1
Social	0.4	14.5	0.1	2.4	12.1	0.7
Governance	2.1	13.8	0.5	3.4	13.2	0.9

Note: Sustainalytics' governance pillar measures governance of sustainability issues. Sustainalytics has a separate corporate governance rating that is not represented in this study.
Source: Bloomberg, MSCI ESG Research, Sustainalytics, Barclays Research

TABLE 12.6 Return Difference (in bp/Month) Between Portfolios with High ESG Scores over Similar-Risk Portfolios with Low ESG Scores in Various Sectors of the US IG Market, 2009 to 2018

	Basic/Capital Goods	Cyclical	Noncyclical	Comm. & Technology	Transport. & Energy	Utility	Banking & Brokerage	Other Financials
	Using MSCI ESG Scores							
ESG	6.6**	2.0	5.8**	3.4*	6.9**	0.3	6.3**	5.4**
Environmental	7.1**	4.0**	8.2**	1.8	6.5*	1.4	0.4	4.3**
Social	-0.8	-3.2	-0.1	3.3*	-2.7	0.1	3.5*	1.7
Governance	2.6	1.5	4.6**	-0.8	3.9*	0.4	6.5**	2.0
	Using Sustainalytics ESG Scores							
ESG	-1.1	2.4*	10.3**	3.5*	8.3**	2.4*	2.0	3.3**
Environmental	1.8	5.6**	9.3**	3.1*	4.6*	2.1*	0.8	6.0**
Social	-0.5	-3.4	8.8**	0.8	3.8	0.6	0.4	-1.4
Governance	-3.7	0.2	4.3**	-3.5	3.8*	1.7	5.1**	3.0*

Note: * indicates a 5% significance while ** corresponds to a 1% significance for positive results in the sample considered. Sustainalytics' governance pillar measures the governance of sustainability issues. Sustainalytics has a separate corporate governance rating that is not represented in this study.

Source: Bloomberg; MSCI ESG Research; Sustainalytics, Barclays Research

cases. As intuition suggests, governance has the largest effect in banking and brokerages, for both providers of ESG scores. The effect of the environment rating is positive in all sectors and especially significant in noncyclicals or transportation and energy. The effect of social is highly variable, and sometimes negative. The sector with the most significant relationship to ESG (i.e., with the highest information ratio of the high-ESG over low-ESG portfolio) is noncyclical consumer goods, for both ESG providers. While similar results are obtained for the two providers in most sectors, performance diverges from one ESG provider to the other in some sectors (such as basic and capital goods).

Table 12.7 summarizes the results of a similar analysis in the euro market. Given the need for intra-sector diversification, we consider only five sectors. Banking and brokerage and noncyclical consumer goods are the ones in which the link between ESG and performance is most visible; for the less-diversified utility portfolios, high-ESG portfolios have underperformed low-ESG ones. As in the US market, high-low portfolio pairs exhibit similar behavior for the two ESG providers in most sectors but not in the cyclical sector, which is enlarged to include capital goods. We find that ESG tilts have been broadly associated with positive portfolio performance across many sectors, with E and G being the strongest contributors.

TABLE 12.7   Return Difference (in bp/Month) Between Portfolios with High ESG Scores over Similar-Risk Portfolios with Low ESG Scores in Various Sectors of the Euro IG Market, 2009 to 2018

	Cyclical	Noncyclical	Utility	Banking and Brokerage	Other Financials
Using MSCI ESG Scores					
ESG	2.1*	1.3*	−2.5	5.5**	1.5
Environmental	−0.3	1.2	−2.4	1.2	3.1*
Social	1.2	0.5	−3.6	1.2	−0.1
Governance	2.3*	0.3	−0.8	1.4	1.4
Using Sustainalytics ESG Scores					
ESG	−0.4	1.9**	−0.9	3.2*	5.3**
Environmental	−0.7	2.3**	0.9	3.2*	5.7**
Social	0.8	1.4*	−3.1	1.7	2.0
Governance	−0.2	1.0	−0.4	2.5	3.7*

Note: * indicates a 5% significance while ** corresponds to a 1% significance for positive results in the sample considered. Sustainalytics' governance pillar measures governance of sustainability issues. Sustainalytics has a separate corporate governance rating that is not represented in this study.
Source: Bloomberg, MSCI ESG Research, Sustainalytics, Barclays Research

EFFECT OF ESG ON BOND VALUATION

There is a possibility that, as a result of the increased popularity of ESG investing, investor preferences shifted from issuers with poor ESG attributes to those with high ESG scores, resulting in a systematic richening of high-ESG bonds (and cheapening of low-ESG bonds). If that is the case, the returns observed in our analysis should be considered as transient and typical of a specific time period that may not be representative of future market conditions.

If such a systematic ESG-based repricing of bonds happened in the period of our analysis, it should be visible in bond valuations, in particular spreads over Treasuries. However, issuers with high ESG scores could also have tighter spreads for unrelated reasons—they could be tilted toward higher credit ratings, for example. We have seen that ESG characteristics can be associated with differences in spread and other risk attributes and that issuers with strong credit ratings tend to have better ESG scores. Therefore, to determine whether the market is pricing in an ESG premium, we need to control for all other relevant bond risk characteristics.

To isolate the effect of ESG ratings on bond valuation, we run a cross-sectional regression analysis in which we explain the spread of all bonds in our study universe at a particular point in time using the ESG score of their respective issuer while controlling for systematic sources of risk such as credit rating, sector, and duration. In the euro market, we also control for geography, as issuers from peripheral Europe are likely to have been affected by the high volatility of sovereign spreads observed from 2010 to 2012.[14] This analysis provides an attribution of issuer spread, including the component due to ESG characteristics.

Table 12.8 provides a sample result of such a regression in the US IG market using MSCI ESG scores, at the end of March 2018. The regression has a high R^2 (72%), meaning that the full set of bond attributes used (industry, credit rating, option-adjusted spread durations [OASD], and ESG score) explains much of the spread of any given bond at this time. Most of the control variables are highly significant, economically (large coefficient) and statistically (t-statistics well in excess of 2 in most cases). In this case the ESG spread premium, is negative, meaning that high-ESG bonds tend to trade at slightly tighter spreads than low-ESG bonds. The coefficient of –0.6 means that for an increase of 1 standard deviation in the ESG score of an issuer, the spread of its bonds decreases by 0.6bp, making them marginally more expensive than comparable bonds of other issuers. The statistical significance of this coefficient is low (t-stat. of –0.5), as there is substantial uncertainty around that estimate.

TABLE 12.8 Example Spread Attribution to ESG in the US IG Market at the End of March 2018 (Using MSCI ESG Data)

| | ESG | Duration | Credit Rating | | | | | | Industry Sector | | | | | | | |
	Score	OASD	A1	A2	A3	BAA1	BAA2	BAA3	BAS	CYC	NCY	COT	TRE	UTI	BAB	FIO
Coef.	-0.6	8.4	2.3	8.8	18.9	35.7	51.2	77.6	63	65	57	72	77	77	87	76
t-stat.	-0.5	22.7	0.4	1.7	3.8	7.3	10.6	14.6	12	11	12	14	14	13	19	14
R^2	71.8%															

Source: Bloomberg, MSCI ESG Research, Barclays Research

Repeating this analysis every month, we can chart the evolution of the ESG spread premium over time. Any significant changes in the ESG spread premium can point to a change in valuation of bonds resulting from their ESG characteristics. For example, if the spread difference between high- and low-ESG bonds decreases (or becomes more negative), meaning that high-ESG bonds become more expensive relative to low-ESG ones, one could assume that high-ESG bonds benefit from increasing investor appetite. However, such repricing is typically limited in time, as high-ESG bonds cannot continue to become increasingly expensive forever. Therefore, any performance based on such transient phenomenon should not be expected to be sustained but could be exposed to the risk of a reversal.

Figure 12.5 presents the time series of results for the regression in Table 12.8.[15] The solid line in the plot shows the coefficient obtained for the ESG-related spread each month; a negative result means that high-ESG bonds trade at tighter spreads than low-ESG peers. The shaded region around each plot represents the 95% confidence interval. We find that the results of the regression towards the end of the period have been consistent with that shown in the table: there is a slight indication of an ESG spread premium, but it is not often statistically significant.

Figure 12.6 presents the evolution of the ESG spread premium estimates and confidence intervals in the US based on Sustainalytics ESG scores; the following two figures give results for the Euro IG market using scores from

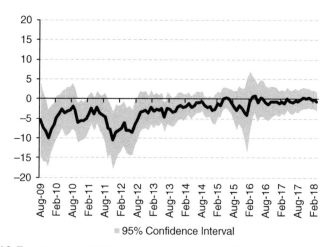

FIGURE 12.5   Historical ESG Spread Premium in the US IG Market (MSCI)
Note: The spread premium is expressed in basis point per standard deviation of ESG score.
Source: Bloomberg, MSCI ESG Research, Barclays Research

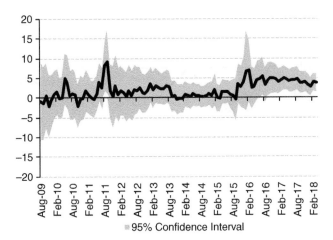

FIGURE 12.6   Historical ESG Spread Premium in the US IG Market (Sustainalytics)
Note: The spread premium is expressed in basis point per standard deviation of ESG score.
Source: Bloomberg, Sustainalytics, Barclays Research

the two providers. Taken together, Figures 12.5 through 12.8 provide several insights.

One might have expected that increased interest in sustainable investing would have driven up the prices (thus reducing spreads) of high-ESG bonds. This hypothesis, which could explain why high-ESG portfolios have outperformed over this period, is not supported by our valuation analysis. We do not observe a downward trend in ESG-related spreads in IG markets; if anything, they seem to have increased.

We find some differences in the level of the ESG premium depending on the provider in the US dollar market but less so in the euro market. In the US market, we were unable to detect a statistically significant premium in most months. When estimating spread premia in the US market, we find that bonds considered high ESG by MSCI have traded at slightly tighter spreads, on average, than their low-ESG peers (but significantly so only for a few months in the early part of the data sample). This is not the case when using Sustainalytics data.

In contrast to the US market, we find that in Europe, high-ESG bonds trade at lower spreads than their low-ESG peers irrespective of the provider. The effect is small: approximately −5bp per standard deviation of ESG score. This could indicate different attitudes to ESG investing in the two markets: European investors might be more prepared to give up performance in favor of desirable ESG characteristics. It also might be a reflection of investor guidelines mandating a focus on high-ESG issuers.

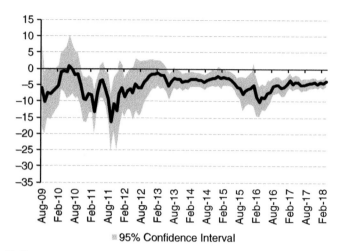

FIGURE 12.7   Historical ESG Spread Premium in the Euro IG Market (MSCI)
Note: The spread premium is expressed in basis point per standard deviation of ESG score.
Source: Bloomberg, MSCI ESG Research, Barclays Research

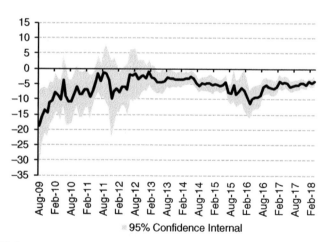

FIGURE 12.8   Historical ESG Spread Premium in the Euro IG Market (Sustainalytics)
Note: The spread premium is expressed in basis point per standard deviation of ESG score.
Source: Bloomberg, Sustainalytics, Barclays Research

Can this tell us which pillar score has been most valued by investors? To address this, we repeat our analysis with two changes: We substitute either the E, S, or G score alone for the overall ESG score in the above analysis; and we pool together the results for all months of the study. Table 12.9 summarizes the results of this pooled analysis for the two providers.

For both providers, all three pillars of ESG are found to have a significant effect[16] on bond valuations in Euro IG credit: A higher ESG rating corresponds to tighter spreads and a cheaper cost of debt. When using MSCI data, we find that governance has the largest and most significant effect. When using Sustainalytics data, we find a slightly different pattern of relationship between ESG attributes and bond spreads: Environmental score has the greatest influence on spreads, followed by social and governance (but remember that for the Sustainalytics data used in this study, governance relates mainly to the sustainability commitment of the corporation while for MSCI it is corporate governance). The same analysis performed in the US IG market is less conclusive: The coefficients are generally smaller in magnitude, and their signs vary depending on the provider and on the pillar considered.

Spread premium analysis reveals differences in appetite for ESG attributes between the US and euro markets. These differences are not very large and did not follow a very clear trend or pattern during the time of our analysis, but they have been significant during the latter part of the period considered. From the perspective of issuers of euro-denominated bonds, high ESG scores have been rewarded with lower credit spreads and hence a lower cost of funding.

The existence of a small negative spread premium in the euro market does not seem to have affected the performance of our simulated long-short ESG strategy. From the data shown in Table 12.5, the annualized outperformance of high-ESG over low-ESG portfolios was 42bp or 51bp/yr, depending on

TABLE 12.9 Average Spread Premium (bp) in the US IG and Euro IG Markets, 2009 to 2018

	MSCI		Sustainalytics	
	US IG	Euro IG	US IG	Euro IG
ESG	−3.0	−5.1	2.1	−6.0
Environmental	−2.2	−2.3	1.1	−5.9
Social	0.0	−2.9	2.6	−4.6
Governance	−4.2	−5.0	1.8	−3.8

Note: The spread premium is expressed in basis point per standard deviation of ESG score.
Source: Bloomberg, MSCI ESG Research, Sustainalytics, Barclays Research

which ESG data source is used. This is much larger than and of opposite sign to the spread premium (about –5bp) discussed in the previous section. This spread premium did not mean revert over the period of the study.

Effect of ESG on Downgrade Rates

If there was no systematic richening of bonds with high ESG rankings, what caused them to outperform? One interpretation could be that poor ESG rankings relate to risks of various types of adverse events and that, even over the relatively short time period of this study, high-ESG portfolios experienced fewer such events than the low-ESG portfolios. Unfortunately, we do not have sufficient data to document such an effect with regard to ESG-specific events. However, we know that in bond markets, negative changes to a company's outlook are often associated with a downgrade in credit ratings as well as negative returns. Do we find that high ESG scores are associated with a lower rate of subsequent credit rating downgrades?

To test this, we partitioned our bond universe into two groups—above and below the median ESG scores—and observed the number and magnitude of credit rating downgrades in each set. This allowed us to report an annual downgrade notch rate capturing both the frequency and intensity of downgrades. (For example, if 10% of the issuers in a given group experience one-notch downgrades and another 3% have two-notch downgrades, the downgrade notch rate for the year would be 16%.) We compared these downgrade rates for bonds scoring high and low in different ESG categories. The most striking difference between the two groups was observed using governance scores. As shown in Figure 12.9, bonds with low governance

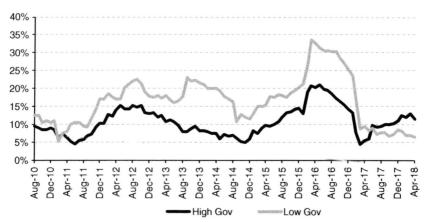

FIGURE 12.9   Rolling Average Number of Downgrade Notches per Issuer and per Year, US IG Market
Source: Bloomberg, MSCI ESG Research, Barclays Research

scores experienced a consistently higher rate of subsequent downgrades than those with high scores throughout our study period with the exception of the last year of the period when downgrade risk was generally milder than in prior years.[17]

FOCUSING ON THE US HIGH-YIELD MARKET

ESG investing poses different challenges in the HY market than in the IG market. Many HY issuers are private issuers, and ESG rating coverage is sparser in HY than in IG. As a consequence, building diversified portfolios of bonds is more difficult in HY than in IG markets, where a larger proportion of the market is ESG rated. However, portfolio diversification is even more important in HY than in IG markets, given the high issuer-specific risk of HY bonds. Extending our analysis of the IG market to HY may therefore yield less precise insights.

Figure 12.10 shows the share of the US HY index that is covered by both ESG providers over time and echoes information reported in Table 12.1. At the end of the period, ESG coverage is just over a third of HY index issuers but close to 60% of the index market value. Coverage jumped in the last quarter of 2012, when the share of HY issuers that were assigned ESG ratings by both providers increased from 16% to 23%. For this reason, we start our study of the HY market in October 2012, as opposed August 2009 for IG markets.

As in IG markets, a naive allocation to high-ESG issuers may entail unintentional exposures. Table 12.10 shows the differences in characteristics between the top and bottom tiers of ESG bonds. It reports average ESG

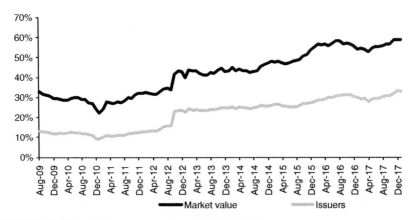

FIGURE 12.10 ESG Coverage of the US HY Market
Source: Bloomberg, MSCI ESG Research, Sustainalytics, Barclays Research

TABLE 12.10 Average Differences in Characteristics Between High- and Low-ESG Portfolios in the US HY Market, 2012 to 2018

	MSCI				Sustainalytics			
	Low	Medium	High	H–L	Low	Medium	High	H–L
Average ESG Score	2.0	3.8	6.1	4.1	47	55	68	21
OAS (bp)	407	385	377	–30	359	363	379	20
OASD	4.4	4.3	4.5	0.0	4.1	4.6	5.1	1.0
Liquidity Cost Score	1.1	1.0	1.1	0.0	1.0	1.0	1.1	0.1
Rating Quality	B1	B1	Ba3		Ba3	Ba3	Ba3	
Rating Quality No.	14.7	14.6	14.5	–0.2	14.5	14.3	13.9	–0.5

Source: Bloomberg, MSCI ESG Research, Sustainalytics, Barclays Research

scores (on a scale of 10 for MSCI and of 100 for Sustainalytics) in each bucket as well as the differences between high- and low-ESG buckets. The second row of the table reports average spreads. Unlike what we found in IG markets, spreads do not necessarily decrease as ESG ratings improve. When using Sustainalytics data, the opposite is true: High-ESG-rated bonds have, on average, provided higher spreads than lower-rated ones. This is related to the one-year longer duration that these higher-rated bonds also happen to exhibit over that of lower-rated ones. As before, any analysis of the effect of ESG must carefully control for differences in systematic risk.

To assess the sign and magnitude of the ESG spread premium, we perform a regression analysis every month, controlling for duration, quality, and sector allocation. Estimated spread premia and corresponding 95% confidence intervals (shaded areas) are shown in Figures 12.11 and 12.12 and display some interesting similarities as well as differences from one provider to the other. In both cases, we find that the spread premium has tended to decrease in the time window considered, although this reduction is small: Starting and ending premia are not significantly different from each other. However, spread premia follow different paths over time, in particular during the energy crisis of 2015–2016, depending on which provider is used. Confidence intervals are very wide throughout, especially during the energy crisis.

To measure the effect of ESG investing in HY bond markets, we assemble diversified portfolios that either minimize or maximize ESG scores while having otherwise matching exposures, such as duration, spread, rating, and sector allocations. High- and low-ESG portfolios included close to 160 bonds, on average. Portfolios are rebalanced monthly, and the cumulative

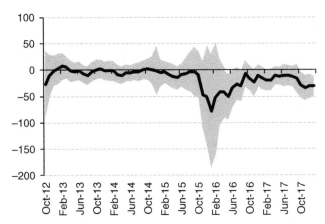

FIGURE 12.11 ESG Spread Premium in the US HY Market (MSCI) (bp)
Source: Bloomberg, MSCI ESG Research, Barclays Research

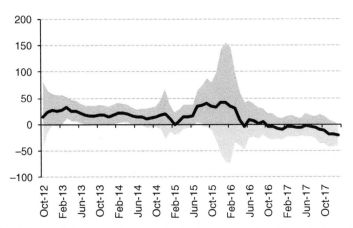

FIGURE 12.12 ESG Spread Premium in the US HY Market (Sustainalytics) (bp)
Source: Bloomberg, Sustainalytics, Barclays Research

excess return of high- over low-ESG portfolios is shown in Figures 12.13 and 12.14 for the two ESG providers. Although cumulative performances end up being positive in both cases, the patterns are different and mirror the patterns of spread premia shown above. In one case, the drop in spread premium seen at the end of 2015 corresponds to high returns of the ESG tilt. This is followed by a spread reversal that corresponds to low returns. In the other case, the spread widening of high-ESG bonds in 2015 corresponds to underperformance, as shown in Figure 12.14, also followed by reversal in

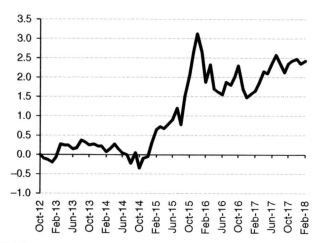

FIGURE 12.13 Cumulative Performance (%) of a High-ESG over a Low-ESG Portfolio in the US HY Market (Using MSCI ESG Data)
Source: Bloomberg, MSCI ESG Research, Barclays Research

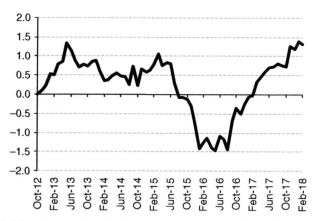

FIGURE 12.14 Cumulative Performance (%) of a High-ESG over a Low-ESG Portfolio in the US HY Market (Using Sustainalytics ESG Data)
Source: Bloomberg, Sustainalytics, Barclays Research

the subsequent years. These contrasting spread and performance patterns illustrate the effect of different methodologies in ESG rating.

A summary of the ESG performance effect is shown in Table 12.11 which includes a split among E, S, and G. The top row reports the excess return of the high-yield index over duration-matched Treasuries. The sections below relate to the two providers. Most, but not all, performances are

TABLE 12.11   Return Difference between Portfolios with High ESG Scores over Similar-Risk Portfolios with Low ESG Scores, 2012 to 2018

	Average (bp/m)	Volatility (bp/m)	Information Ratio
HY Index ER	41.5	152	0.9
Using MSCI ESG Scores			
ESG	3.8	28	0.5
Environmental	–2.4	39	–0.2
Social	2.3	31	0.3
Governance	10.3	32	1.1
Using Sustainalytics ESG Scores			
ESG	2.1	27	0.3
Environmental	2.9	30	0.3
Social	–0.3	30	0.0
Governance	3.5	31	0.4

Note: Sustainalytics' governance pillar measures governance of sustainability issues. Sustainalytics has a separate corporate governance rating that is not represented in this study.
Source: Bloomberg, MSCI ESG Research, Sustainalytics, Barclays Research

positive. Long-short portfolio strategies tilted according to the MSCI environmental score or the Sustainalytics social score had negative returns in the period considered. The highest return, and the only one that exhibits statistical significance, relates to portfolios tilted according to corporate governance (supplied by MSCI).

CONCLUSION

Many investors rely on independent providers of ESG scores and ratings in their investment decisions. We consider two major ESG providers, MSCI and Sustainalytics, and investigate the relationships between their ESG scores and other bond characteristics. We find that ESG scores have been higher, on average, for European than for US issuers and that bonds with higher ESG ratings tend to have higher credit ratings and lower spreads as well. This makes it difficult to adjust the ESG characteristics of a portfolio without introducing a bias in some other direction or to cleanly measure the performance effect of an ESG tilt in isolation.

To limit such biases, we compared the performance of exposure-matched portfolios with high-ESG and low-ESG tilts. We built these portfolios subject to an array of constraints designed to avoid any other systematic bias in our historical back-test. We found that high-ESG portfolios consistently outperformed low-ESG ones, in many cases significantly. For example, using overall ESG scores from either provider, outperformance in the euro market was over 3bp/month, with an information ratio close to 1, over the nearly nine years of our study. We found that governance was the characteristic most closely associated with performance in the US market. An environmental tilt delivered highest returns in the euro market for the entire period, and also in the US dollar market for the most recent two years of our study.

We then carried out an additional set of tests using industry-specific tracking portfolios and obtained less even results. Most, but not all, results were positive, quite a few significantly so. For example, a tilt to high ESG scores, and particularly governance, was significantly positive in the banking and brokerage sector; environmental scores were more significant in the noncyclical sector.

We investigated the relationship between ESG attributes and valuation through statistical analysis. We performed regressions to test for an ESG premium by which high-ESG bonds are systematically priced at tighter spreads than their low-ESG peers of similar industry and quality. Over most of the data sample, we were unable to identify a statistically significant ESG premium in the US IG markets but did find a fairly stable premium of about 5bp (per 1 standard deviation in ESG scores) in euro IG markets in the second part of the period. This implies that European bond markets have placed greater emphasis on ESG criteria than their US counterparts. We did not find any evidence of a systematic richening of high-ESG bonds and therefore refrain from explaining the positive return of an ESG tilt as the result of a change in investor preferences whose effect on return is, by definition, temporary. Rather, we find that high-governance bonds are less subject to downgrade risk. This finding supports the hypothesis that companies that are better prepared to face the broad range of nonfinancial risks covered by ESG scores might be less likely to deliver negative surprises to their investors. More generally, the ESG return benefit may take the form of issuer-specific returns. The benefits of a systematic tilt toward higher ESG issuers might thus be hard to identify as a market-wide ESG factor but still accrue slowly and steadily toward better long-term performance.

In the US HY market, our efforts were hampered by relatively poor coverage; because many HY issuers are private firms, we were unable to map them to ESG scores. We repeated much of the analysis performed for IG bonds but found few significant results. In valuation, we did not detect a significant ESG premium vs. peers. In performance tests of tracking portfolios with ESG tilts, there was a tendency for high ESG to outperform, but with low information ratios.

Appendix 12.1 includes a regression-based analysis of returns. It shows a small positive ESG performance effect, largely corroborating the findings of our portfolio simulation study. For the US HY market, the regression analysis indicates a stronger relationship between ESG attributes and returns than shown in our portfolio simulations.

APPENDIX 12.1

Estimating ESG-Related Returns Through Regression Analysis

As an alternative to the construction of tracking portfolios, we have tested the effect of ESG scores on performance using a statistical analysis very similar to the one we used to assess the ESG spread premium. We carried out monthly cross-sectional regressions of bond excess returns using various control variables such as OAS, OASD and DTS loadings to several industry sectors. One additional variable is added to see whether there is a systematic outperformance or underperformance of high-ESG bonds: the normalized ESG score. The resulting coefficient on the ESG score can be interpreted as the excess return advantage realized in a given month by high-ESG over low-ESG bonds (in basis points per one standard deviation of ESG score). Table 12.12 presents an example result of this analysis, using MSCI overall ESG scores, for the US IG market in February 2018.

We carried out similar analysis for each market covered, using overall ESG scores from each provider, as well as using each pillar score independently. We also included all three pillar scores together. The R^2 values obtained from these monthly regressions varied between 5% and 76%.

Monthly results are aggregated over the entire time window of our analysis and summarized in Table 12.13. Overall, the regression analysis shows weak positive results. Almost all ESG characteristics, for both providers, have positive coefficients, indicating that high-ESG names outperform low-ESG names by about 0.5bp/month to 1bp/month for a one standard deviation tilt in ESG score.

Regression analysis on returns should not be expected to deliver the same results as the tracking portfolio simulations. The regression analysis implicitly gives the same weight to all observations, while portfolio simulations are anchored to the structure of the market capitalization-weighted index, which is unevenly distributed across issuers. Also, the results of such statistical analysis can be heavily influenced by model specifications, such as, for example, the nature of the relationship (linear or not), the weighting

TABLE 12.12 Example Regression Analysis of Monthly Returns Controlling for Spread, Duration, and Sector Exposures, February 2018

	ESG Score	OAS	OASD	BAS	CYC	NCY	COT	TRE	UTI	BAB	FIO
Coef.	0.04	0.69	−0.04	−0.11	−0.10	−0.08	−0.09	−0.08	−0.09	−0.11	−0.09
t-stat.	1.6	8.3	−3.6	−15.6	−7.7	−10.9	−14.3	−11.3	−10.2	−8.8	−12.8
R²	43.7%										

Note: Using normalized MSCI ESG Scores, US IG Market
Source: Bloomberg, MSCI ESG Research, Barclays Research

TABLE 12.13   Average (2009–2018) Regression Coefficients of IG Bond Returns on ESG Scores

		US IG Market			
MSCI	**ESG**	**Environmental**	**Social**	**Governance**	**Combined**
ESG	1.1				
Environmental		0.8			0.6
Social			0.5		0.1
Governance				0.6	0.9
Avg. R^2	29.9%	29.8%	29.7%	29.8%	30.3%
Sustainalytics	**ESG**	**Environmental**	**Social**	**Governance**	**Combined**
ESG	0.9				
Environmental		0.8			0.6
Social			0.8		0.8
Governance				0.1	−0.5
Avg. R^2	29.9%	30.0%	29.9%	29.8%	30.5%
		Euro IG Market			
MSCI	**ESG**	**Environmental**	**Social**	**Governance**	**Combined**
ESG	0.6				
Environmental		0.2			0.4
Social			−0.5		−0.6
Governance				0.5	0.9
Avg. R^2	38.7%	38.9%	38.7%	38.8%	39.5%
Sustainalytics	**ESG**	**Environmental**	**Social**	**Governance**	**Combined**
ESG	0.5				
Environmental		0.4			0.2
Social			0.3		0.2
Governance				0.3	0.1
Avg. R^2	39.0%	39.0%	38.9%	38.8%	39.6%

Note: Control variables are not shown. Coefficients are expressed in bp/Month per Stdev of ESG score.
Source: Barclays Research

of individual observations, or the choice of control variables. We find the portfolio simulations presented in the main body of this chapter to be more intuitive to market practitioners, and we see the regression analysis as a validation of the results obtained in portfolio simulations. In this sense, it is comforting that the results shown here corroborate the overall positive effect of ESG on performance. Furthermore, when measuring the correlations between the monthly regression coefficients for the ESG score and the monthly excess returns of high-ESG over low-ESG simulated portfolios, we found them to be significantly positive—approximately 0.5—for the overall ESG scores of MSCI and Sustainalytics in the US IG and euro IG markets.

The results of portfolio simulations and regression analysis are consistent with each other. When assessing the effect of ESG scores on performance, we find weak but persistent positive relationships in the two IG markets.

In the US HY market also, we performed a regression analysis of issuer monthly returns on ESG scores while controlling for risk characteristics (spread, spread duration, and DTS partitioned to eight industry sectors). Results are shown in Table 12.14.

We find that for all pillars taken individually, coefficients are positive and relatively large. The overall ESG return effect is significant for both providers, as is the governance pillar. The effect of the environmental rating appears to be weak in the HY market. In the combined regression, the governance pillar also has the most significant effect. We must, however, stress two caveats to this analysis: Issuer coverage is low, and the time window is relatively short.

TABLE 12.14   Average (2012–2018) Regression Coefficients of US HY Bond Returns on ESG Scores

MSCI	ESG	Environmental	Social	Governance	Combined
ESG	6.4				
Environmental		1.5			0.7
Social			4.6		5.4
Governance				5.7	5.9
Avg. R^2	33.7%	33.6%	33.9%	33.7%	35.0%
Sustainalytics	ESG	Environmental	Social	Governance	Combined
ESG	5.3				
Environmental		3.0			–1.9
Social			4.6		2.4
Governance				7.4	7.5
Avg. R^2	33.9%	33.7%	33.9%	33.7%	35.0%

Note: Control variables are not shown. Coefficients are expressed in bp/Month per Stdev of ESG score.
Source: Barclays Research

REFERENCES

Ben Dor, A., L. Dynkin, J. Hyman, P. Houweling, E. Van Leeuwen, and O. Penninga. 2007. "DTS^{SM} (Duration Times Spread)." *Journal of Portfolio Management* 33(2): 77–100.
Ben Dor, A., and J. Xu. 2015. "Should Equity Investors Care about Corporate Bond Prices? Using Bond Prices to Construct Equity Momentum Strategies." *Journal of Portfolio Management* 41 (4): 35–49.
Dynkin, L., A. Desclée, M. Dubois, J. Hyman, and S. Polbennikov. 2018, October 22. "ESG Investing in Credit: A Broader and Deeper Look." Barclays Research.
Dynkin L., A. Desclée, J. Hyman, and S. Polbennikov. 2016, November 17. "ESG Investing in Credit Markets." Barclays Research.
Hyman J., A. Baldaque da Silva, Y. Eidenthal-Berkovitz, A. El Khanja, A. Maitra, and S. Polbennikov. 2014. "Sovereign Risk Spillover into Euro Corporate Spreads." *Journal of Fixed Income* 24(1): 51–74.
Polbennikov, S., A. Desclée, L. Dynkin, and A. Maitra. 2016. "ESG Rating and Performance of Corporate Bonds." *Journal of Fixed Income* 26(1): 21–41.

NOTES

1. See Ben Dor and Xu (2015).
2. Our coverage ratios measure the percentage of issuers of each index that is covered by our dataset. This study includes only a small fraction on the many thousands of companies covered by MSCI and Sustainalytics. Our sample is therefore not representative of their work, (it is biased in favor of the larger companies that are represented in bond indices) and our study should not be viewed as a test of the quality of their ratings.
3. We use the terms "ESG scores" and "ESG ratings" interchangeably. Scores are numerical representations of ratings.
4. The Sustainability Accounting Standards Board is an organization that develops and maintains sustainability accounting standards. See www.sasb.org.
5. The Global Reporting Initiative is an organization that promotes sustainability reporting standards. See www.globalreporting.org.
6. The ratings methodology of each of these two firms is discussed in more detail in Dynkin et al. (2016).
7. It may seem at first glance that negative screens provide a much more powerful impetus for social change. However, in the context of our example, which investor is more likely to influence the behavior of a coal mining company executive? The first will not buy his stock in any case, while the second will be reviewing his ESG policies as the basis for the investment decision. Thus, the "best-in-class" approach can be supported even from an idealistic viewpoint as well as from a purely capitalistic one.
8. See Polbennikov et al. (2016).

9. An alternative approach to answering this question uses a statistical analysis. Results are presented in Appendix 12.1 of this chapter and broadly agree with those presented here.

10. To ensure consistency, the universe of bonds considered for portfolio construction is not the entire index, but limited to those for which ESG ratings were available from both MSCI and Sustainalytics.

11. See Ben Dor et al. (2007).

12. The performance of more diversified portfolios, with over 400 bonds in the case of the US IG market, was also studied and commented in Dynkin et al. (2018).

13. See Dynkin et al. (2018).

14. The relationship between sovereign and corporate spreads is discussed in Hyman et al. (2014).

15. For conciseness, neither the charts in Figures 12.5 to 12.8 nor Table 12.9 include results for the control variables related to duration, credit rating, and sectors. They are all key drivers of spread, but our interest is on the incremental effect of ESG rating on spread after controlling for these.

16. We base this conclusion on the prevalence of significant monthly results. T-statistics are not shown for the time-averaged coefficients in Table 12.9.

17. Figure 12.9 illustrates a link between governance scores and subsequent *changes* in credit ratings. Note that this does not contradict Figure 12.2, which shows low correlation between governance scores and contemporaneous *levels* of credit rating.

Four

Factor Investing in Credit

Factor investing has become increasingly popular in recent years. Large pools of assets are currently managed by equity funds utilizing the systematic factor approach, aiming to achieve higher risk-adjusted returns than market indices.

Style factor investing represents strategies that select securities based on characteristics associated with an expectation of higher returns. The justification for the use of style factor investing rests on the expectation that markets offer a risk premium for taking a particular factor exposure. While a plethora of style factors have been proposed since the seminal work of Fama and French in 1992, value, momentum, and size still remain the most recognizable ones in equity markets. Value investing involves buying stocks that appear underpriced relative to their intrinsic value. This philosophy, pioneered by Benjamin Graham and David Dodd in the late 1930s, identifies value opportunities across publicly traded companies using price-to-book and price-to-earnings ratios. Momentum investing takes advantage of the continuation of a market trend by choosing securities that have recently outperformed their peers.[1] Finally, the size factor is a strategy that invests in equities of smaller companies, which, according to empirical evidence, tend to outperform their large peers over the long-term, other things being equal.[2] In many cases, a style factor emerged from the investigation of a market anomaly: a systematic strategy that consistently generates abnormal returns relative to those predicted by the efficient markets hypothesis. Although few

405

style factors have been uniformly adopted and used in academic studies, market practitioners are constantly searching for new strategies to incorporate into their portfolios. If a strategy offers consistent risk-adjusted returns, with low correlations to existing style factors, it will be a welcome addition to many portfolios.

Adoption of factor investing in corporate bonds has been relatively slow in comparison to stocks because implementing quantitative strategies in credit portfolios entails unique challenges. First, structuring portfolios based on systematic factors is more complex for corporate bonds than for stocks. Indeed, while market exposure can capture a significant portion of returns for stock portfolios, corporate bond returns even within the same market vary according to credit quality and duration. As a result, a single market factor is unlikely to explain the returns of different bond portfolios equally well. Next, transaction costs of corporate bonds are relatively high, so excessive turnover can create a significant drag on portfolio performance. Implementing realistic factor portfolios is likely to require turnover controls as well as a reliable way to measure transaction costs. At the same time, the liquidity of corporate bonds varies over time and across individual securities. Some corporate bonds may not trade at all or trade rarely in the secondary market, limiting the breadth of systematic strategies. A practical implementation of style factors in credit should therefore correctly identify and avoid highly illiquid securities. However, the expansion of electronic trading has been welcomed by quantitative investors as it facilitates the synchronized rebalancing of diversified portfolios. Finally, corporate bonds are traded over the counter, so that bond-level historical data required to obtain and validate returns of factor portfolios is not always publicly available. This makes managing data collection and integrity a challenge in its own right.

In this part of the book, we consider credit style factors analogous to the well-known factors in equities. In particular, we investigate systematic factors based on relative value, equity momentum, and issuer size. In order to analyze the properties of these style factors in credit, we need to define style using bond or issuer characteristics. While the methodologies of deriving these factors are significantly different from the ones utilized in equities, the broad logic remains fairly similar. For example, price-to-earnings and price-to-book ratios available from financial statements are frequently used by equity investors as valuation metrics. Analogous measures for corporate bonds need to be defined.

In Chapter 13, we introduce a relative value factor called excess spread to peers (ESP) based on spreads unexplained by issuer fundamentals or bond characteristics. The strategy utilizes option-adjusted spreads as the valuation measure and is designed to identify securities undervalued or overvalued relative to their peers (bonds with similar risk characteristics) over the short- to medium-term. Chapter 14 introduces an alternative specification of a relative value strategy in credit designed to remain effective at long time horizons. The strategy uses spread per unit of debt-to earnings ratio (SPiDER) as the valuation measure to identify over- or under-valued issuers. Unlike ESP, which is a cross-sectional measure, SPiDER measures compensation (spread) per unit of risk (debt to long-term EBITDA), which allows using it over time and across sectors. We show that both ESP and SPiDER relative value strategies have delivered sizable and persistent risk premia over time.

The next chapter introduces a strategy based on equity momentum in credit (EMC), which uses past equity returns to identify debt issuers likely to outperform or underperform their peers. The strategy is based on a strong positive relationship between past stock returns of an issuer and subsequent excess returns of its corporate bonds. In contrast to the momentum strategy in equities, EMC is based on information spillover from the equity to corporate bonds of a given issuer. We document strategy characteristics and analyze its long-term performance. In Chapter 16, we demonstrate that the equity momentum signal aggregated at the sector level can be used by investors to identify outperforming or underperforming sectors in credit and, therefore, to time sector allocation. We show that an allocation strategy that systematically buys sectors with strong equity momentum persistently outperformed benchmark indices in the investment-grade (IG) and high-yield (HY) markets.

Chapter 17 analyzes the effect of issuer size on spread and performance of corporate bonds in the US IG and HY markets. Contrary to the evidence from the equity markets and common beliefs of some credit investors, our results do not support the existence of a size factor that could be systematically exploited in credit. While portfolios of small issuers seem to outperform their peers of large issuers, we find that this outperformance results from unintended differences in rating, duration, sector allocation, and liquidity characteristics. When controlling for these differences, portfolios of small issuers tend to *underperform* portfolios of large issuers with similar systematic risk characteristics, while the average spread premium attributed to size tends to be significantly reduced.

In Chapter 18, we discuss integrating style factors into a realistic credit portfolio. This can be a challenging task because of high transaction costs, large variations of liquidity across individual bonds, and the requirement to follow a benchmark index. We design realistic simulations that illustrate the performance and characteristics of quantitatively managed portfolios of liquid corporate bonds with attractive value and momentum characteristics. We propose two alternative mechanisms for controlling turnover in strategy implementation and illustrate each one with a case study. The first utilizes a turnover buffer to avoid trading bonds with intermediate signal levels. Once a strong buy signal is obtained and a security enters the portfolio, it is held there until a strong sell signal arrives. In the second approach, a turnover budget is used to explicitly control rebalancing volumes. The buffer approach aims to trade only when a transaction is expected to have a sufficiently large impact on performance. However, it can lead to spikes in portfolio turnover, in particular when markets are volatile. The turnover budget approach keeps monthly turnover steady, but can make the strategy less nimble. We find that realistic strategy portfolios based on either of these approaches outperform the benchmark index after transaction costs with high information ratios. The results of our study support the case for systematic investing in credit.

Finally, in Chapter 19 we introduce a quantitative framework, OneScore, that combines value and equity momentum characteristics of credit issuers within industry sectors. The chapter presents the OneScore methodology and provides a summary of its long-term performance within individual sectors and for the overall IG universe. To motivate combining value and momentum signals, we show that the performance of the relative value (ESP) strategy has been pro-cyclical (positively correlated to the market) in volatile periods while that of the equity momentum (EMC) strategy has been contra-cyclical with respect to the market. For both strategies, market directionality can be significantly reduced by ensuring that overweight and underweight positions are matched in terms of risk exposure. In addition to combining quantitative signals, OneScore is aligned with the research process of fundamental analysts. It can therefore help illustrate how quantitative analysis and fundamental research can complement each other in forming issuer views. While quantitative models allow for systematic coverage of broad investment universes, fundamental analysis provides deeper insights to help mitigate selection risk.

We anticipate that investor interest in factor strategies for credit markets will continue to grow alongside more traditional investment approaches. The models described in this part clearly demonstrate the potential of such strategies for adding value in credit portfolios. We continue quantitative research to identify and develop new strategies for systematic investing in credit.

REFERENCES

Asness, C., A. Frazzini, R. Israel, T. J. Moskowitz, and L. H. Pedersen. 2018. "Size Matter, If You Control Your Junk." *Journal of Financial Economics* 129(3): 479–509.

Fama, F. E., and K. R. French. 1992. "The Cross-Section of Expected Stock Returns." *Journal of Finance* 47(2): 427–465.

Jegadeesh, N., and S. Titman. 1993. "Returns to Buying Winners and Selling losers: Implications for Stock Market Efficiency." *Journal of Finance* 48(1): 65–91.

NOTES

1. See Jegadeesh and Titman (1993).
2. See, for example, Fama and French (1992) and Asness et al. (2018).

Value Investing

CHAPTER 13

Relative Value Investing in Credit Using Excess Spread to Peers

INTRODUCTION

Value investing has for long been popular with equity portfolio managers. Pioneered by prominent investors Benjamin Graham and David Dodd, the strategy involves overweighting undervalued securities using, for example, the price-to-book ratio.[1]

Value investing can be used on a systematic basis and is often seen as part of a suite of investment styles that aim to capture thematic risk premia, such as momentum, carry, and size. However, limited liquidity in credit markets makes high-turnover strategies less practical and necessitates long investment horizons consistent with fundamentally driven styles such as value.

In credit, valuation measures typically include spread in addition to fundamentals often used in equity markets. In that sense, value and carry strategies are related to each other. Favoring high-spread bonds has long been popular with fixed income managers, as a higher spread carry bias has indeed proved profitable over long periods. But this can entail significant market risk, given that higher spread typically comes with lower credit quality and higher excess return volatility. Indeed, systematically overweighting high-spread bonds would lead to portfolio biases in quality, sector, and maturity allocations.

Figure 13.1 shows average excess returns[2] of corporate bond portfolios vs. average spreads. Bonds are grouped every month either by credit rating in Panel A or by spread deciles in Panel B. In both cases, average return increases with portfolio average spread. However, this increase in return is accompanied by higher market risk, as shown in Figure 13.2. Overweighting high-spread bonds relative to low-spread ones is highly directional on market returns.

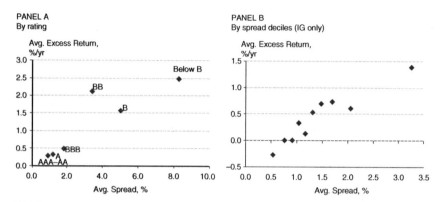

FIGURE 13.1   Average Spread vs. Average Excess Return: US Corporate Investment Grade and High Yield Bonds, January 1993 to January 2016
Source: Barclays Research

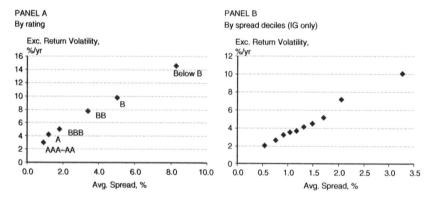

FIGURE 13.2   Average Spread vs. Volatility of Excess Returns: US Corporate Investment Grade and High Yield Bonds, January 1993 to January 2016
Source: Barclays Research

To remove this directionality, one must control for the systematic risk embedded in credit spreads. Several recent studies use such approach when introducing value investment styles in credit that resemble the factor method used by equity investors.[3] Our approach is similar in spirit. We introduce a relative value credit strategy that controls for industry, quality, duration, and issuer fundamentals, which can all affect the credit risk of an issuer.

We identify relative value as the portion of excess spread over peers unexplained by fundamental factors and call this measure excess spread to peers (ESP). We use ESP scores to build portfolios of "undervalued" bonds and analyze their performance and characteristics.

We show that bond portfolios with high ESP tend to outperform their peers in terms of both absolute and risk-adjusted returns. We discuss properties of ESP scores and of relative value portfolios, including directionality on other risk premia and stability of performances. We also describe portfolio applications.

FORMING RELATIVE VALUE SCORES

Our analysis aims to differentiate between bonds and issuers at a given point in time on a relative basis. The methodology used to compare bonds with each other is the key to our approach. Several control mechanisms are considered to limit systematic risk exposures that typically arise when favoring high-spread bonds.

Our objective is to identify securities whose spreads are not fully explained by fundamental credit risk. This can be done by attributing credit spread to a number of risk factors, including the macro-environment and fundamental issuer characteristics. This attribution can be done in different ways. For example, Correia, Richardson, and Tuna (2012) derive theoretical spreads of individual issuers using structural and reduced form credit default models. Excess spread over its derived theoretical value is then used as a valuation measure. Alternatively, one can use a statistical analysis to identify relevant risk factors affecting spreads.

We adopt a practical approach by assuming that, on average, the corporate market is correctly priced, while individual securities can temporally deviate from their fundamental value and can therefore be either under- or overvalued. The fundamental "theoretical" spread is represented by the peer group in our case. Consequently, we compare individual bonds with relevant peer groups, controlling for three major risk dimensions: credit quality, industry, and duration. Exposures to these risk dimensions can be measured at the level of individual securities (e.g., duration, rating) or at issuer level (e.g., industrial sector, fundamental issuer data).

Credit rating is arguably one of the most important characteristics to control for when assessing valuation, as doing so helps avoid systematic biases in credit risk. Indeed, rating agencies put significant resources into assessing credit risk, which they then express through ratings. They extensively use accounting data as well as industry-specific information as inputs for their models. Rating quality is, in our view, informative of long-term credit risk and can form a baseline for cross-sectional comparison of credit issuers.

Although controlling for ratings can be a practical way to account for credit risk, it can also be combined with a direct analysis of fundamental characteristics of an issuer.[4] In our analysis, we include financial leverage,[5] which is one of the important drivers of default risk.[6] We show that controlling for financial leverage moderately improves our results relative to the rating-based approach in isolation.

Controlling for industry helps make issuers broadly homogenous in terms of business dynamics and economic fundamentals. While this comparability is far from perfect, some broad characteristics, such as exposure to economic shocks or business cycles, are often more similar within than across industries.

Finally, controlling for bond duration recognizes that the term structure of spread is not flat, as spreads generally increase with maturity. When assessing whether a high-spread bond is undervalued, comparison should be made with bonds of similar maturities in order to avoid systematic biases in duration exposure.

For each bond from a broad index universe, we produce an ESP score by measuring its excess spread over its rating-industry-duration peers while also controlling for financial leverage. Figure 13.3 provides a crude illustration of the methodology. Excess spread is contrasted with excess leverage for Baa-rated bonds with maturities between three and seven years in the

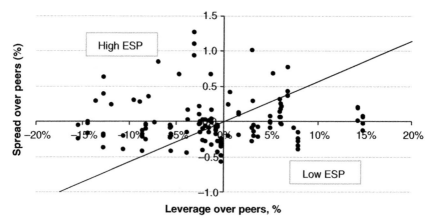

FIGURE 13.3   Excess Spread vs. Excess Leverage over Peers for Consumer Noncyclical 3–7y Baa-Rated Bonds, December 2015
Source: Barclays Research

consumer noncyclical sector. Excess spread and excess leverage are calculated over peer averages in the same rating-industry-maturity category. Bonds in the upper-left part of the figure have higher spreads relative to peers after controlling for financial leverage and are deemed good value while bonds in the lower-right region are seen as relatively expensive.

We estimate ESP scores of individual bonds on a monthly basis and construct 10 portfolios that correspond to deciles of ESP. Our analysis is based on Bloomberg Barclays US Corporate Bond Index filtered to retain noncallable, senior bonds that were successfully mapped to Compustat fundamental data.[7] This universe is large, with more than 2000 bonds per month on average and over 4000 in recent months.

Figure 13.4 plots average excess returns, volatilities, and information ratios of the sorted portfolios. The relationship between ESP and return or information ratio is nearly monotonic: Undervalued portfolios with higher ESP tend to deliver higher risk-adjusted performance over time. This result holds for different subperiods.

To illustrate the incremental contribution of including corporate fundamentals in ESP, Table 13.1 reports the performances of ESP deciles calculated with and without financial leverage. Controlling for leverage moderately helps discriminate across deciles.[8]

Volatility and dynamics of ESP scores can affect the turnover and rebalancing costs of relative value portfolios. Indeed, volatile ESP scores could make a value strategy based on it expensive to maintain and therefore impractical. Table 13.2 shows transition frequencies across ESP deciles on

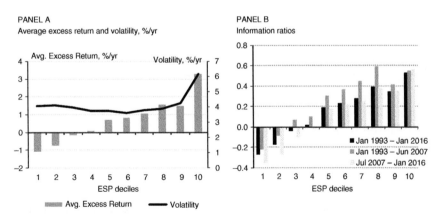

FIGURE 13.4 Performance of Bond Portfolios by ESP Deciles, 1993 to 2016
Source: Barclays Research

TABLE 13.1 Performance of ESP Decile Portfolios With and Without Controlling for Financial Leverage, 1993 to 2016

	Excluding Financial Leverage			With Financial Leverage		
ESP Deciles	Avg. Excess Return, %/yr	Volatility, %/yr	Information Ratio	Avg. Excess Return, %/yr	Volatility, %/yr	Information Ratio
1	−1.19	4.86	−0.24	−1.10	4.08	−0.27
2	−0.48	4.43	−0.11	−0.73	4.12	−0.18
3	−0.13	4.02	−0.03	−0.15	3.95	−0.04
4	0.13	3.67	0.04	0.08	3.73	0.02
5	0.66	3.41	0.19	0.70	3.73	0.19
6	0.66	3.23	0.21	0.83	3.62	0.23
7	0.97	3.46	0.28	1.07	3.81	0.28
8	1.21	3.61	0.34	1.55	3.90	0.40
9	1.60	4.45	0.36	1.47	4.25	0.35
10	2.63	6.28	0.42	3.29	6.16	0.53

Source: Barclays Research

3- and 12-month horizons. It indicates that ESP scores tend to be relatively stable, especially for deciles with the lowest and highest scores. This suggests that portfolio turnover arising from changes in ESP is likely to be moderate. In addition, the transition matrices reveal mean reversion in ESP as high and low scores seem to be pulled to the middle. This is consistent with mean reversion of relative spreads, which itself is the key driver of the strategy performance.

PERFORMANCE OF RELATIVE VALUE INVESTING

The performance of portfolios sorted on ESP (Figure 13.4 and Table 13.1) suggests that it is possible to build a high-ESP portfolio that historically outperforms traditional corporate bond indices.

As a simple approach, we build high- (low-)ESP portfolios each month by selecting bonds with above- (below-)median ESP scores from our investment-grade index universe.

Figure 13.5 shows cumulative returns of high- and low-ESP portfolios[9] as well as of the long-short (high- minus low-ESP) strategy. The outperformance of the high-ESP portfolio over its low-ESP counterpart has been very persistent.

TABLE 13.2   Transition Frequencies of Bond ESP Scores Across ESP Deciles over Three- and 12-Month Horizons, 1993 to 2016

ESP End of Period

	ESP Decile	1	2	3	4	5	6	7	8	9	10
						three-month horizon					
ESP Start of Period	1	70%	20%	5%	2%	1%	1%	1%	0%	0%	0%
	2	19%	42%	23%	9%	4%	2%	1%	1%	0%	0%
	3	5%	21%	33%	22%	10%	4%	2%	1%	1%	0%
	4	2%	8%	21%	29%	22%	10%	4%	2%	1%	0%
	5	1%	4%	9%	20%	28%	22%	10%	4%	1%	1%
	6	1%	2%	4%	9%	19%	29%	22%	9%	3%	1%
	7	1%	1%	2%	4%	9%	20%	32%	23%	7%	1%
	8	0%	1%	1%	2%	4%	8%	21%	38%	23%	3%
	9	0%	0%	1%	1%	1%	3%	6%	20%	50%	17%
	10	0%	0%	0%	0%	0%	1%	1%	3%	16%	77%
						12-month horizon					
ESP Start of Period	1	44%	21%	12%	7%	5%	4%	3%	2%	2%	2%
	2	18%	23%	18%	13%	9%	7%	5%	3%	2%	2%
	3	10%	16%	18%	16%	13%	10%	7%	5%	3%	2%
	4	6%	11%	15%	17%	16%	13%	10%	7%	4%	2%
	5	4%	8%	11%	15%	17%	15%	13%	9%	5%	3%
	6	3%	5%	8%	11%	14%	16%	16%	13%	8%	4%
	7	2%	4%	6%	7%	11%	15%	19%	18%	13%	5%
	8	2%	3%	4%	5%	8%	11%	16%	22%	20%	9%
	9	2%	2%	2%	3%	5%	7%	11%	18%	29%	22%
	10	2%	2%	1%	2%	2%	3%	4%	8%	20%	56%

Source: Barclays Research

Table 13.3 compares the performance of high- and low-ESP portfolios with that of Bloomberg Barclays US IG Corporate Bond Index in different periods. The high-ESP portfolio outperforms both the low-ESP portfolio and the corporate index by 1.78 and 1.18% per year, respectively, with information ratios above 1.2 in all periods. Return differentials of the high-ESP portfolio over the low-ESP portfolio and over the index show a relatively modest risk of underperformance in terms of volatility and maximum drawdown. They also show little or moderate directionality on credit market returns, as indicated by low correlations with the index.

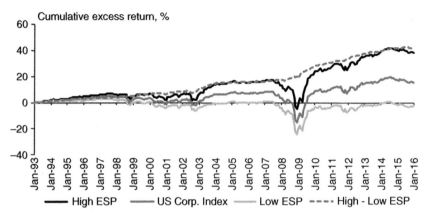

FIGURE 13.5   Cumulative Excess Returns of Relative Value ESP Portfolios
Source: Bloomberg, Barclays Research

TABLE 13.3   Performance of Relative Value ESP Portfolios

	High ESP	Low ESP	US Corp. Index	High– Low ESP	High ESP Index
	Jan. 1993–Jan. 2016			Jan. 1993–Jan. 2016	
Avg. Excess Return, %/yr	1.56	–0.23	0.38	1.78	1.18
Volatility, %/yr	4.12	3.83	4.20	1.18	0.89
Information Ratio	0.38	–0.06	0.09	1.52	1.32
Max. Drawdown, %	–20.1	–24.8	–24.2	–2.0	–1.2
Correlation with Index	98%	99%	100%	20%	–20%
	Jan. 1993–Jun. 2007			Jan. 1993–Jun. 2007	
Avg. Excess Return, %/yr	1.18	0.03	0.43	1.15	0.75
Volatility, %/yr	2.34	1.92	2.08	0.95	0.59
Information Ratio	0.50	0.01	0.21	1.22	1.26
Max. Drawdown, %	–5.7	–8.9	–8.3	–2.0	–1.2
Correlation with Index	97%	97%	100%	43%	33%
	Jul. 2007–Jan. 2016			Jul. 2007–Jan. 2016	
Avg. Excess Return, %/yr	2.19	–0.66	0.28	2.85	1.91
Volatility, %/yr	6.04	5.78	6.36	1.44	1.22
Information Ratio	0.36	–0.12	0.04	1.98	1.56
Max. Drawdown, %	–19.9	–22.6	–24.0	–1.7	–1.0
Correlation with Index	98%	99%	100%	14%	–35%

Source: Bloomberg, Barclays Research

Table 13.4 shows average exposure characteristics of relative value portfolios and of the index over different periods. While the high-ESP portfolio has a lower duration, higher spread, and higher Duration Times Spread (DTS) exposure than the index, the differences are small and not sufficient to explain the performance gain. Indeed, the average spread of the high-ESP portfolio is only 17bp higher than that of the index while the difference in realized return is 118bp per year (see first row of Table 13.3). The outperformance of the high-ESP portfolio cannot be explained by the carry advantage alone but also requires significant mean reversion in relative spreads. We provide a formal statistical analysis of the relationship between performance of corporate bonds and their characteristics, including ESP score, credit spread, duration, and DTS exposure, in the last section of this chapter.

The outperformance of high- vs. low-ESP portfolios holds across credit ratings and broad industry sectors. Table 13.5 provides a split by rating and

TABLE 13.4   Characteristics of Relative Value ESP Portfolios

	High ESP	Low ESP	US Corp. Index	High– Low ESP	High ESP Index
	Jan. 1993–Jan. 2016			Jan. 1993–Jan. 2016	
Spread, bp	155	118	139	37	17
Duration, yr	5.6	6.6	6.1	–0.9	–0.5
DTS, yr × %	9.5	8.4	9.0	1.0	0.4
Average MV, $MM	463	551	512	–89	–49
Numeric credit rating	7.9 (A3)	7.4 (A2)	7.6 (A3)	0.5	0.3
	Jan. 1993–Jun. 2007			Jan. 1993–Jun. 2007	
Spread, bp	120	90	104	29	15
Duration, yr	5.3	6.3	5.8	–1.0	–0.5
DTS, yr × %	7.0	6.2	6.5	0.7	0.5
Average MV, $MM	340	401	369	–61	–29
Numeric credit rating	7.7 (A3)	7.3 (A2)	7.5 (A3)	0.4	0.2
	Jul. 2007–Jan. 2016			Jul. 2007–Jan. 2016	
Spread, bp	216	165	196	50.8	19.5
Duration, yr	6.3	7.0	6.7	–0.7	–0.4
DTS, yr × %	13.7	12.1	13.3	1.5	0.4
Average MV, $MM	670	805	753	–135	–83
Numeric credit rating	8.1 (A3)	7.8 (A3)	7.8 (A3)	0.3	0.3

Source: Bloomberg, Barclays Research

TABLE 13.5 Performance of High- over Low-ESP Portfolios by Quality and Sector

	AAA–AA	A	BBB	HY (BB/B)	Financials	Nonfinancials
	Jan. 1993–Jan. 2016				Jan. 1993–Jan. 2016	
Avg. Excess Return, %/yr	1.01	1.97	1.94	3.80	2.40	1.54
Volatility, %/yr	1.17	1.28	1.85	2.61	1.98	1.08
Information Ratio	0.86	1.54	1.05	1.45	1.21	1.43
Max. Drawdown, %	−4.26	−1.33	−5.35	−5.36	−2.60	−2.65
	Jan. 1993–Jun. 2007				Jan. 1993–Jun. 2007	
Avg. Excess Return, %/yr	0.66	0.95	1.46	3.86	1.06	1.26
Volatility, %/yr	0.62	0.68	1.92	2.73	0.98	1.05
Information Ratio	1.07	1.39	0.76	1.41	1.09	1.20
Max. Drawdown, %	−0.80	−0.78	−5.35	−5.10	−1.25	−2.65
	Jul. 2007–Jan. 2016				Jul. 2007–Jan. 2016	
Avg. Excess Return, %/yr	1.60	3.69	2.75	3.70	4.65	2.02
Volatility, %/yr	1.73	1.80	1.71	2.40	2.89	1.11
Information Ratio	0.92	2.05	1.61	1.54	1.61	1.82
Max. Drawdown, %	−4.26	−1.33	−3.53	−5.36	−2.60	−1.94

Source: Barclays Research

broad financial/nonfinancial industry sectors of the index. High average returns and information ratios of high- over low-ESP portfolios across all subsets of the market indicate that performance is not confined to a particular sector or credit quality.

The performance of the relative value strategy tends to be stronger when cross-sectional variation (dispersion) in ESP is high. Figure 13.6 plots differences in ESP between high- and low-ESP portfolios and subsequent 12 months returns of the relative value strategy. In addition, Figure 13.7 shows the average return per quintile of strategy ESP differential. It is apparent that strategy returns are higher when relative spreads are higher, although the observations in the top quintile are associated with the 2008 crisis episodes when dispersion in ESP became very large.

Figure 13.6 also shows that the strategy delivered negative 12-month returns in 2002 as well as in 2015. These episodes correspond to negative momentum in spreads, when bonds that have become high spread relative to peers keep underperforming. Again, we must emphasize that relative value investing in credit rests on mean reversion in relative spreads.

The average outperformance of high- over low-ESP portfolios also holds across liquidity partition of the US corporate bond universe. We use Trade Efficiency Scores (TES)[10] of corporate bonds to investigate how relative value performance varies across liquidity buckets. TES combines trading costs and volumes with low TES indicating high liquidity. Table 13.6 reports the performance of high- over low-ESP portfolios for various TES quintiles starting

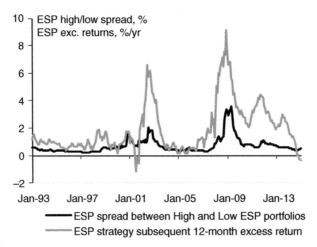

FIGURE 13.6   ESP Spread Between High- and Low-ESP Portfolios and Subsequent 12-Month Excess Returns of the ESP Strategy
Source: Barclays Research

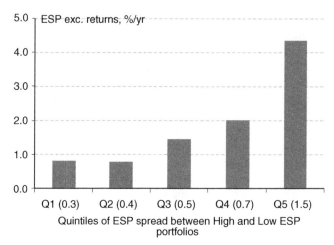

FIGURE 13.7 ESP Strategy Average 12-Month Excess Return per Quintile of High-/Low-ESP Spread
Source: Barclays Research

TABLE 13.6 Performance of High- over Low-ESP Portfolios by Trade Efficiency Score Bucket, 2007 to 2016

	Overall	TES Q1	TES Q2	TES Q3	TES Q4	TES Q5
Avg. Excess Return, %/yr	2.77	2.74	2.93	2.24	2.41	2.99
Volatility, %/yr	1.41	1.74	1.69	1.48	0.99	1.43
Information Ratio	1.96	1.57	1.73	1.51	2.43	2.09
Max. Drawdown, %	−1.69	−1.87	−2.29	−2.71	−0.58	−1.53
Index Beta	6%	5%	8%	9%	−1%	9%

Source: Barclays Research

in 2007, when TES become available. While outperformance of high-ESP portfolios is strong across all liquidity buckets, information ratios are highest for buckets with lower liquidity (higher TES). This implies that high-ESP portfolios could potentially pick up some illiquidity premium.

The relationship between liquidity and ESP is illustrated in Figure 13.8, which plots monthly average trading volumes across ESP deciles. Volume declines as ESP increases, but then jumps for the top ESP decile. At one extreme, bonds with low ESP are likely to be recently issued on-the-run securities with high trading volumes while, at the other extreme, bonds in the top ESP bucket may experience high trading volumes due to issuer specific events.

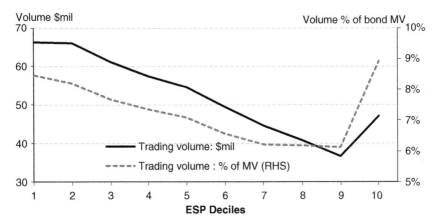

FIGURE 13.8 Monthly Trading Volume by ESP Deciles, 2007 to 2016
Source: Barclays Research

IMPLEMENTING A RELATIVE VALUE STRATEGY

The high-ESP portfolio outperforms the corporate index and its low-ESP peer, but practical considerations, such as transaction costs, can reduce strategy returns in actual bond portfolios. We therefore measure turnover of the high-ESP portfolio and discuss practical ways to reduce it.[11]

Column 1 of Table 13.7 shows that the excess turnover of the value strategy that buys high-ESP (above median) and sells low-ESP (below median) bonds is 11% per month, which is quite high. However, the ESP transition matrices in Table 13.2 indicate that ESP scores are relatively stable over time, especially in the top and bottom ESP categories. Indeed, more than 75% of bonds in the top ESP decile remain in the top two deciles one year after. Similarly, more than 65% of bonds in the bottom ESP decile

TABLE 13.7 Performance of the Relative Value ESP Strategy with Turnover Controls, 1993 to 2016

	No Buffer	10% Buffer	15% Buffer
Avg. Excess Return, %/yr	1.78	1.98	1.86
Volatility, %/yr	1.18	1.52	1.56
Information Ratio	1.52	1.31	1.20
Max. Drawdown, %	−2.00	−3.58	−3.68
Turnover in High-ESP portfolio (%/m)	11.2%	5.7%	4.3%

Source: Barclays Research

remain in the bottom two deciles after one year. In fact, a large part of the high-ESP portfolio turnover is generated by bonds that have ESP scores close to the median. At the same time, bonds with ESP close to the median are likely to add little to the outperformance of the relative value strategy, which suggests that we could reduce turnover and enhance return of the strategy by excluding bonds with ESP scores close to the median.

We therefore propose a modification to the original strategy (long above-median and short below-median ESP bonds). The modified strategy buys bonds with ESP scores in the top 40% and sells when their ESP drops below the median. Otherwise, bonds remain in the portfolio. A similar logic applies to the short leg of the strategy, which includes bonds when they fall in the bottom 40% of ESP and holds them until their ESP exceeds the median. This is shown in Table 13.7, where the original strategy discussed so far is labeled "no buffer" while the new one is called "10% buffer." In a slightly more restrictive specification (called "15% buffer" in the table), the high-ESP portfolio retains bonds until they fall into the bottom 45% while the short leg of the strategy holds bonds until their ESP rank reaches the top 45%. These new strategies focus on issues with stronger relative valuation signals and tend to hold them until this signal has diminished. Note that these new strategies differ from the original one only with regard to the rebalancing logic; the ESP formulation remains unchanged.

Columns 2 and 3 of Table 13.7 indicate that the modified strategies reduce turnover from 11.2 to 5.7 and 4.3% per month, respectively. At the same time, strategy returns increase while information ratios slightly decline due to higher volatility.

Figure 13.9 plots historical 12-month rolling turnover for the original and modified relative value strategies just described. The persistent reduction in strategy turnover is evident, although turnover varies over time and generally tends to be higher when spreads are higher.

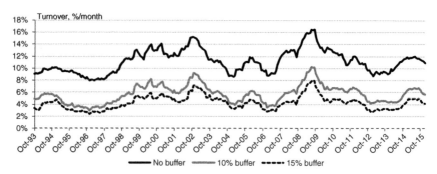

FIGURE 13.9   Rolling 12-Month Turnover of High-ESP Portfolios
Source: Barclays Research

TRACKING PORTFOLIOS BASED ON RELATIVE VALUE

The relative value strategy presented so far is based on Bloomberg Barclays US Corporate Bond Index and covers a large universe of bonds, buying all above-median and selling all below-median ESP bonds. The long-short ESP portfolio is therefore highly diversified and carries little idiosyncratic risk. In most practical cases, however, implementing a relative value investment style involves a concentrated selection of over- and under-weights relative to a benchmark index. For a more detailed description of selection risk, please see Appendix 13.1.

As an example, we build tracking portfolios designed to replicate the Bloomberg Barclays Corporate index while implementing an ESP tilt. Portfolios are constructed every month to maximize ESP score while closely matching the index exposures: DTS, duration and market value contributions across eight sectors.[12] In addition, the portfolios also match the overall DTS and duration of the index. We construct tracking portfolios with 4%, 2%, and 1% issue concentration limits. Ticker concentrations are fixed at double the issue concentration. The portfolios therefore range from highly concentrated (34 bonds) to diversified (more than 100 bonds). Table 13.8 reports the performance of the replicating portfolios. Average returns are substantially higher than the index returns despite very similar durations, DTS, and only slightly different spreads. High-ESP tracking portfolios outperform the index by more than 1.2% per year with information ratios in excess of 1. The concentrated 34-bond portfolio (Portfolio 1) has a slightly higher tracking error volatility than the diversified 109-bond tracker (Portfolio 3). The risk-adjusted outperformance is robust over different horizons.

STATISTICAL ANALYSIS OF THE VALUE PREMIUM

The ESP strategy is constructed with controls for rating and sector. However, systematic exposures might remain. Table 13.4 indicates that the long-short strategy has a positive spread and a negative duration bias, although the net DTS exposure is small. We now measure the value premium controlling for spread, duration, and sector biases. Every month, we run cross-sectional regressions[13] of individual bond excess returns against spread, duration, and ESP scores in addition to sector DTS.[14] This procedure allows us to calculate the return attributable to spread, duration, and value exposures in isolation. The cross-sectional regressions are run each month to obtain a time series of the factor realizations. Table 13.9 reports the average factor returns and associated *t*-statistics.

TABLE 18.8 Performance of Index-Tracking Portfolios Based on ESP

	US Corp. Index	Portf. 1 (max. 4%/bond)	Portf. 2 (max. 2%/bond)	Portf. 3 (max. 1%/bond)	Portf. 1–Index	Portf. 2–Index	Portf. 3–Index
Jan. 1993–Jan. 2016							
Avg. Excess Return, %/yr	0.38	1.75	1.73	1.59	1.37	1.36	1.22
Volatility, %/yr	4.20	3.73	3.67	3.74	1.22	1.12	1.02
Information Ratio	0.09	0.47	0.47	0.43	1.13	1.21	1.19
Max. Drawdown, %	−24.2	−19.4	−19.0	−20.4			
Average Spread, %	*1.39*	*1.55*	*1.55*	*1.54*	*0.17*	*0.16*	*0.15*
Average No. Bonds		34	59	109			
Jan. 1993–Jun. 2007							
Avg. Excess Return, %/yr	0.43	1.27	1.27	1.15	0.84	0.84	0.72
Volatility, %/yr	2.08	2.08	2.00	2.04	0.79	0.66	0.62
Information Ratio	0.21	0.61	0.63	0.56	1.06	1.27	1.16
Max. Drawdown, %	−8.3	−4.6	−3.9	−4.9			
Average Spread, %	*1.04*	*1.15*	*1.15*	*1.16*	*0.10*	*0.11*	*0.11*
Average No. Bonds		34	59	109			
Jul. 2007–Jan. 2016							
Avg. Excess Return, %/yr	0.28	2.55	2.52	2.35	2.27	2.23	2.06
Volatility, %/yr	6.36	5.51	5.44	5.53	1.69	1.60	1.45
Information Ratio	0.04	0.46	0.46	0.42	1.34	1.40	1.43
Max. Drawdown, %	−24.0	−19.2	−18.9	−20.3			
Average Spread, %	*1.96*	*2.24*	*2.22*	*2.18*	*0.28*	*0.26*	*0.21*
Average No. Bonds		34	59	109			

Source: Bloomberg, Barclays Research

The spread factor described in isolation in the first section of Table 13.9 is similar to a pure carry bias. The spread factor has a large and statistically significant premium (t-stat. of 2.7). The average factor realization of 5.2bp per month (roughly 62 bp/y) can be interpreted as the average monthly return of the portfolio that goes long above median spread bonds and short below median spread bonds when controlling for risk allocation across sector.

The duration premium is negative, indicating that extending duration, while keeping DTS constant, has a significant negative premium.[15] When combining spread and duration (fourth section of Table 13.9), we find that both effects are stronger and more statistically significant. Increasing spread or increasing duration, while similar from a risk perspective, have very different effects on return. Indeed, increasing spread produces higher risk and higher returns while extending duration increases risk but reduces returns

TABLE 13.9   Average Risk Premia of Credit Exposures, January 1993 to January 2016

	Spread		Duration		Value		Spread & Duration		All Factors	
	Beta	*t*-stat.	Beta	*t*-stat.	Beta	*t*-stat.	Beta	*t*-stat.	Beta	*t*-stat.
Market Factors (bp/m/unit exposure)										
Spread	5.2	2.7					7.2	3.3	2.2	1.1
Duration			−12.2	−5.4			−14.2	−5.7	−10.9	−4.5
ESP					15.2	8.7			12.4	8.1
Sector DTS Factors (bp/m/unit DTS)										
Basic	0.0	0.0	0.5	1.1	0.1	0.2	0.4	0.8	0.3	0.6
Cyclical	0.0	0.0	0.5	0.8	0.0	0.0	0.3	0.6	0.2	0.4
Noncyclical	0.2	0.4	0.7	1.4	0.2	0.5	0.6	1.4	0.6	1.2
Energy	0.1	0.3	0.6	1.3	0.2	0.4	0.5	0.9	0.4	0.8
Telecom	0.1	0.1	0.5	1.0	0.1	0.2	0.4	0.8	0.3	0.6
Utility	−0.1	−0.2	0.3	0.6	0.1	0.1	0.2	0.3	0.2	0.4
Banks and Brokers	0.8	1.3	1.1	1.7	1.0	1.7	0.9	1.5	1.0	1.6
Other Financial	0.7	1.3	1.1	2.0	0.8	1.6	0.9	1.6	0.9	1.7

Source: Barclays Research

TABLE 13.10 Correlations of Relative Value (ESP), Credit, and Equity Risk Factors, January 1993 to January 2016

		Credit				Equity (F-F factors)		
		Credit Market	Spread	Duration	Equity Market	Size	Value	Momentum
Credit	ESP	–24%	–7%	–22%	–27%	2%	–19%	–6%
	Market		16%	–49%	59%	29%	–4%	–27%
	Spread			–45%	12%	8%	1%	–7%
	Duration				–28%	–15%	6%	15%
Equity (F-F factors)	Market					24%	–23%	–26%
	Size						–35%	8%
	Value							–15%

Source: Kenneth French Data Library, Barclays Research

controlling for DTS. The ESP factor in isolation has an average premium of 15.2bp/month (~ 1.8%/yr), which is highly statistically significant (*t*-stat. of 8.6). This is consistent with the average returns of the long-short value strategy. When we combine all three factors in our regression, the spread factor premium declines substantially and is now statistically insignificant. The ESP factor remains large and highly significant (*t*-stat. of 8.0). This suggests that the cross section of bond returns is much better explained by differences in ESP than just differences in spreads. ESP therefore seems a better candidate to help define a relative-value-based risk premium than traditional bond characteristics such as spread or sector.

Having extracted a clean ESP factor from our regressions, we analyze its correlation with other sources of risk premia, such as the spread, duration, and DTS factors in credit and the Fama–French (F-F) factors in equity markets. Table 13.10 shows that the ESP factor appears to be decorrelated with other credit and equity factors and could therefore be a good diversifier in a factor portfolio.

CONCLUSION

We design a systematic relative value strategy in credit based on excess spreads relative to peer groups that control for fundamental and macro risk characteristics: excess spread to peers.

The strategy has attractive risk and performance characteristics. We find that an ESP strategy that goes long high-ESP bonds and short low-ESP ones performs well, with information ratio of more than 1.5 and a low correlation with the credit market returns.

The strategy performance is robust across liquidity, rating, and sector partitions in different time periods. The outperformance of the ESP strategy is larger when there is a high dispersion in ESP. This is consistent with mean reversion of relative spreads being the main driver of strategy returns.

ESP can be used to form a relative value factor, which we show to be highly significant in explaining average corporate bond excess returns, and distinct from spread, duration, and sector premia.

ESP could have several applications in portfolio management. Implementing a systematic relative value strategy based on ESP can help capture a thematic risk premium that is uncorrelated with the common credit beta. For asset managers seeking to outperform traditional indices, we show that index-tracking portfolios with ESP tilt can deliver a large outperformance (over 1.2% per year) with information ratio of more than 1. We also show that the strategy is robust to turnover constraints as the mean reversion in ESP scores happens relatively slowly.

APPENDIX 13.1

Security Selection Risk

Selection risk can be captured by the volatility of the idiosyncratic (or security-specific) returns, which can be calculated by removing the effects of systematic exposures to factors such as spread, duration, ESP, and sector-related DTS.[16] Figure 13.10 reports the average monthly security-specific volatility[17] across ESP deciles. A risk of 5% per year indicates that the return of a single bond can deviate from its peer group average with a volatility of 5%. Clearly, high ESP bonds have much higher selection risk than bonds closer to the median.

Figure 13.11 incorporates selection risk in a historical simulation of a concentrated long-short overlay. The simulation randomly selects n long positions from the above-median ESP portfolio and n short positions from the below-median portfolio for a total of $2n$ positions each month. When n equals the number of above-median ESP bonds (approximately 2000 bonds in December 2015) in the universe, the long-short overlay is identical to the ESP strategy, and there is no selection risk. As the strategy controls for spread, duration, and

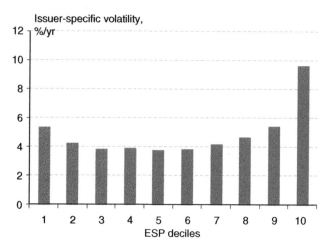

FIGURE 13.10   Security-Specific Volatility by ESP Deciles
Source: Barclays Research

sector DTS, the excess return of such an overlay is the average excess return of the value factor for a given month. When n is small compared with the size of the universe, there can be significant issue-specific risk. Figure 13.11 plots modeled volatility and information ratio as a function of the number of portfolio positions. With roughly 50 positions, the selection risk is reduced substantially, and the overlay achieves an information ratio close to one.

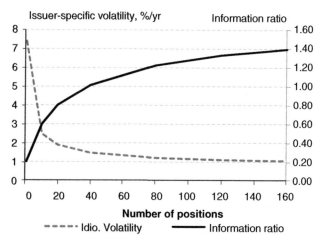

FIGURE 13.11   Security-Specific Volatility and Information Ratio as a Function of Portfolio Concentration
Source: Barclays Research

REFERENCES

Asness, C., A. Frazzini, and L. H. Pedersen. 2019. "Quality Minus Junk." *Review of Accounting Studies* 42: 34–112.

Asness, C., T. Moskowitz, and L. H. Pedersen. 2013. "Value and Momentum Everywhere." *Journal of Finance* 68(3): 929–985.

Correia, M. M., S. A. Richardson, and A. I. Tuna. 2012. "Value Investing in Credit Markets." *Review of Accounting Studies* 17(3): 572–609.

Fama, E., and D. MacBeth. 1973. "Risk, Return, and Equilibrium: Empirical Tests." *Journal of Political Economy* 81(3): 607–636.

Houweling, P., and J. Zundert. 2017. "Factor Investing in the Corporate Bond Market." *Financial Analysts Journal* 73(2): 1–16.

Israel, R., D. Palhares, and S. Richardson. 2018. "Common Factors in Corporate Bond Returns." *Journal of Investment Management* 16(2): 17–46.

Koijen, R., T. Moskowitz, L. H. Pedersen, and E. Vrugt. 2018. "Carry." *Journal of Financial Economics* 127(2): 197–225.

Konstantinovsky, V., K. Y. Ng, and B. D. Phelps. 2016. "Measuring Bond-Level Liquidity." *Journal of Portfolio Management* 42(4): 116–128.

Loffler, G. 2005. "Avoiding the Rating Bounce: Why Rating Agencies Are Slow to React to New Information." *Journal of Economic Behaviour and Organization* 56(3): 365–381.

Merton, R. C. 1974 "On the Pricing of Corporate Debt: The Risk Structure of Interest Rates." *Journal of Finance* 29(2): 449–470.

Ng, K. Y., and B. Phelps. 2015. "The Hunt for a Low-Risk Anomaly in the USD Corporate Bond Market." *Journal of Portfolio Management* 42(1): 63–84.

NOTES

1. Recent publications on value investing in equities and other asset classes include Asness, Frazzini, and Pedersen (2019); Koijen, Moskowitz, Pedersen, and Vrugt (2018); and Asness, Moskowitz, and Pedersen (2013).
2. All corporate bond returns discussed in this chapter are in excess over duration-matched Treasury portfolios, as per Bloomberg Barclays Index conventions.
3. See Houweling and van Zundert (2017) and Israel, Palhares, and Richardson (2018).
4. Rating agencies could be slow in incorporating new data into credit rating because they take a rating action only when it is unlikely to be reversed shortly afterward. See Loffler (2005).
5. Financial leverage is calculated as the book value of debt divided by the sum of the market value of equity and the book value of debt. We conservatively apply a lag of three months when calculating leverage.
6. See Merton (1974). Other metrics could be used, including quick ratio (Current assets/Current liabilities), coverage ratio (EBIT/Interest) and Net Debt/EBITDA for solvency, as well as estimates of asset volatility.

7. We consider all senior noncallable bonds from Bloomberg Barclays US IG Corporate Bond Index that can be mapped to Compustat financial accounting data. We also exclude securities with spreads in the top 0.5% of the sample to avoid extreme outliers.

8. Including accounting fundamentals can raise some practical challenges when comparing firms. Indeed, company management often has a degree of discretion while calculating certain entries in financial reports. This can make comparison difficult without appropriate adjustments.

9. All portfolios are market weighted. We have also tested equally weighted portfolios with one bond per issuer. The performance results were even stronger under such specification.

10. Trade Efficiency Scores (TES) are relative bond-level measures representing an intra-market liquidity rank ranging from one (best) to 10 (worst). TES blends Liquidity Cost Scores and trading volume into a single rank. See Konstantinovsky, Ng, and Phelps (2015).

11. We define turnover as the market value proportion of bonds bought by the high-ESP portfolio.

12. We divide the corporate universe into basic industry, consumer cyclical, consumer noncyclical, energy, TMT, utility, banks & brokerages and other financials.

13. We use Fama-MacBeth regressions. See Fama and MacBeth (1973).

14. In these regressions, factor exposures are calculated from the percentile rank in ESP, duration, and spread and vary between −1 and one for these three factors. For example, a financial bond that has a 60 percentile ESP score and with a median spread and duration would have a loading of 0.2 on the ESP factor and zero on the spread and duration factors respectively. In addition, the bond DTS is multiplied by the relevant sector dummy and captures the market factor.

15. Ng and Phelps (2015) show that increasing spreads has a positive alpha (positive incremental returns over a matched DTS portfolio) while increasing durations has a negative alpha.

16. We use the residuals of the regressions shown in Table 13.9 to control for DTS, spread, and duration exposures.

17. Security-specific variance is calculated as the time-average cross-sectional variance of regression residuals, as specified in Table 13.9 grouped by ESP scores.

CHAPTER 14

Long-Horizon Value Investing in Credit Using Spread per Unit of Debt-to-Earnings Ratio

INTRODUCTION

Value investing is widely practiced by equity investors, and its origin can be traced back at least to Graham and Dodd (1934). The approach discriminates stocks between being over- and under-priced using ratios in the form of a fundamental-based valuation relative to its market valuation. Empirical evidence shows that undervalued stocks indeed outperform the overvalued ones in the United States based on different value measures, such as book-to-market, earnings-to-price, dividend-to-price and cash-flow-to-price ratios (see Chan and Lakonishok, 2004, and references therein). Additional studies also confirm that the phenomenon is present in international equity markets and at the sector level (see, e.g., Fama and French, 1998, for international evidence, and Bunn and Shiller, 2014, for value in sectors).

Motivated by the value premium's strong presence in equity markets, many studies have attempted to extend it to other asset classes and have found positive results. For example, Asness, Moskowitz, and Pedersen (2013) document value in currencies, government bonds, and commodities. They famously dub the premium's universal presence "Value Everywhere." In Chapter 13, we show that the value premium also exists in corporate bonds.[1] Using the excess spread relative to peers, we find that the undervalued corporate bonds generate higher subsequent returns than the overvalued ones.

In this chapter, we propose a new value measure in credit markets. The measure, termed SPiDER (*s*pread *p*er un*i*t of *d*ebt-to-*e*arnings *r*atio), is simple, intuitive, and model-free. It is the ratio between the market price and the fundamental measure of an issuer's default risk. The market price of default risk is captured by credit spreads, which represent the compensation demanded by investors for bearing the possible default loss. The fundamental measure of risk is reflected by the issuer's inability to repay its debt, more specifically, the issuer's debt level over its long-term earnings. Intuitively, a higher debt-to-earnings ratio means that the issuer's earnings power is relatively low compared to its debt level, increasing the likelihood of defaults. High-SPiDER issuers, in which investors demand higher compensation after controlling for issuers' payment ability, are therefore undervalued. In contrast, low-SPiDER issuers are overvalued because of the relatively low compensation commanded by investors.

Unlike other value measures in credit, SPiDER is model-free and does not involve any parametric estimations. Existing measures developed by Houweling and van Zundert (2017) and by Israel, Palhares, and Richardson (2018) use reduced regressions to estimate the "fair" spread based on a variety of bond and firm characteristics. The fair spread is then compared against the market spread to determine whether a bond is overvalued or undervalued. While a regression is able to control for multiple risk characteristics at the same time, it is vulnerable to statistical problems, such as overfitting and instability in coefficients. Other studies use structural models to calculate the fair spread. For example, Correia, Richardson, and Tuna (2012) transform the physical default probability estimated from Merton's model to the risk-neutral default probability and then convert the latter to credit spreads. Although they have a theoretical underpinning, structural models require many input parameters and add opaqueness as they are distribution- and model-dependent.[2] In addition, unlike the relative value measure discussed in Chapter 13, which identifies a bond's relative cheapness by comparing it against its peers, SPiDER is an absolute value measure that models a bond's fundamental value independently from other bonds in the market. This allows the SPiDER measure to be aggregated over multiple bonds—for example, to the sector or the market level—for comparability across sectors and over time. In fact, Ben Dor and Guan (2017) and Ben Dor, Guan, and Polbennikov (2020) find that sector-level SPiDER signals are useful at predicting future sector-level bond returns. All these unique features make SPiDER a complementary addition to the value toolbox in the credit space.

We find strong predictability of SPiDER in bond returns. Using bonds from the Bloomberg Barclays credit indices, we show that nonfinancial issuers with high SPiDER values have consistently outperformed those with low

SPiDER values between March 1993 and February 2020. The outperformance is present in both investment grade and high yield. In particular, we find that the performance is consistent with mispricing and cannot be explained by risk compensations or carry differences. It is evident across all credit ratings and industries and is robust to alternative SPiDER formulations. In order to evaluate the practical relevance of the predictability, we incorporate a variety of constraints that investors are commonly subject to. We find that the performance is still apparent under alternative portfolio exit rules, weighting schemes, rebalancing frequencies, and after transaction costs. Furthermore, we form index tracking portfolios with a tilt toward issuers with high SPiDER values. The tilted portfolio beats the index in both investment grade and high yield, showing that investors can benefit from SPiDER in practice.

The remainder of this chapter is organized as follows. We begin with a discussion of sample construction and the SPiDER measure. The next section examines the performance of a strategy formulated by buying high-SPiDER issuers and short-selling low-SPiDER issuers. Then we investigate what drivers can explain the strategy performance. In the subsequent section, we take account of many practical considerations for implementing the SPiDER strategy in reality and illustrate how investors can use the measure in practice by building index tracking portfolios with a SPiDER tilt.

DATA AND SAMPLE CONSTRUCTION

The starting universe for our sample consists of all bonds included in the Bloomberg Barclays US Corporate and High Yield indices between January 1993 and February 2020. All bonds issued by companies for which we do not have domestic financial statement data in Compustat are removed because fundamental values of firms are needed for the construction of the SPiDER measure and international financial statements may follow different, incomparable accounting standards.[3]

In addition, we impose several filters to make sure that the SPiDER measure is a meaningful value ratio. First, we exclude issuers from the financial sector. Financial companies have a distinct business model that relies heavily on leverage to generate revenue. As a result, the relationship between leverage ratios, such as the debt-to-earnings ratio and fundamental risk, is much more complicated for these firms. Second, we only keep high-yield (HY) bonds that are rated at B or above and have a price not below $50. The rating and price requirements ensure that spreads are a meaningful measure of the default risk perceived by the market and that bonds are not traded to recovery. Third, we also remove firms with less than six years of financial statements as we need a relatively long history to reliably calculate sustainable earnings. Studies, such as Campbell and Shiller (1988), have argued that long-term earnings are more suitable for capturing a firm's earnings power than transient earnings, as the latter is very "noisy." Finally, we require the fiscal quarter or the fiscal year of the statements to end in October, November, and December. This filter ensures that the information from the financial statements is relatively up-to-date and aligned in the cross-section at the time of annual portfolio formation, the details of which are discussed later.

Table 14.1 lists the year-end bond index market values that have been successfully mapped to Compustat and how the sample size is affected by each filter. Panel A shows that in terms of market value, the mapped percentage increases from 85% at the end of 1994 to 98% at the end of 2019 in the investment grade (IG). For HY, the percentage increases from 68% to 83%

TABLE 14.1   Sample Creation

Panel A: Bloomberg Barclays US IG and HY Index Market Value and Percentage Mapped with Compustat, by Year

		1994	1999	2004	2009	2014	2019
IG	Index ($bn)	560	913	1,697	2,555	4,097	5,809
	Mapped	85%	85%	94%	98%	97%	98%
HY	Index ($bn)	144	351	610	747	1,326	1,278
	Mapped	68%	64%	83%	82%	82%	83%

Panel B: Number of Tickers in the Sample After Filters, as of February 2019

	IG	HY
Initial sample: index bonds mapped with Compustat	688	641
Excluding financials	480	586
Excluding ratings below B or price below $50		525
Keeping companies with minimum 6-year history of US financial statements in past 10 years	470	495
Recent fiscal year ends or fiscal quarter-ends between October and December	463	491
Final sample	463	491

Note: Numbers reported in Panel A are year-end statistics. The price filter in Panel B is based on the month-end bond price of February.
Source: Bloomberg Barclays Indices, Compustat, Barclays Research

TABLE 14.2 Characteristics of Issuers in the Final Sample and the Respective Index Benchmark, March 1993 to February 2020

		Characteristics (Monthly Average)					Return Statistics					
	Avg. # Issuers/ Mon	Qual.	OAS (bps)	Dur. (yr)	DTS	MV (MM$)	Avg. Ex. Ret.,%/ Yr	Vol., %/ Yr	Inf. Ratio	Min. Mon Ret. (%)	Max. DD (%)	Corr. w. Benchmark
IG Sample	481	3.28	133	6.86	9.90	2500	0.61	4.03	0.15	−8.20	−22.89	0.99
Bench-mark	637	3.39	136	6.96	10.18	2202	0.63	4.08	0.16	−9.04	−23.23	
HY Sample	333	5.02	329	5.03	15.66	1016	1.86	6.80	0.27	−14.14	−35.20	0.99
Bench-mark	656	5.54	426	4.47	18.70	741	2.21	8.34	0.27	−15.26	−39.43	

Note: The benchmarks for the IG and HY universes are the corresponding Bloomberg Barclays Corporate Index excluding financials. In the high-yield universe, the benchmark further excludes bonds rated below B. The numeric values of quality rating are converted by the following scale: Aaa = 1, Aa = 2, A = 3, Baa = 4, Ba = 5, B = 6. Quality (Qual.), option-adjusted spread (OAS), spread duration (Dur.), and Duration Times Spread (DTS) are all first aggregated across issuers with issuer market value weights on a monthly basis. The reported value is the average of the monthly time series. Max. DD is short for maximum drawdown.
Source: Bloomberg Barclays Indices, Compustat, Barclays Research

over the same period. The mapped percentage is lower for HY because there are more private issuers in HY. Panel B shows that the IG universe is mostly affected by excluding financial companies whereas the rating and price requirement has some additional impact in the HY universe.

Although financials are excluded from the index benchmark, the final sample still does not cover the benchmark completely, owing to the other filters. Despite of the partial coverage, Table 14.2 shows that the final sample is in fact very similar to the respective index benchmark in terms of characteristics and performance. In both IG and HY, the final sample has similar ratings, spreads, and duration and almost identical information ratio as the benchmark. The strong similarity between the sample and the benchmark implies that any dynamics we observe later in the strategy are unlikely to be driven by the sample differences.

UNDERSTANDING THE SPiDER MEASURE

Following equity value signals, we construct SPiDER by taking the ratio between a market valuation and a fundamental valuation of issuer's default risk. Specifically, SPiDER is computed annually at the issuer level for issuer i as:

$$SPiDER_{i,t} = \frac{OAS_{i,t}}{\dfrac{Debt_{i,t}}{Sustainable\ EBITDA_{i,t}}},$$

where,

OAS is the market-value-weighted option adjusted spread of all bonds from the issuer,
$Debt$ is the sum of a firm's long-term and short-term debts, and
$Sustainable\ EBITDA$ is the historical average of the last 10 annual earnings before interest, taxes, depreciation, and amortization (EBITDA) figures with a minimum of six years' data.

While OAS measures the market price of default risks, the ratio between debt and sustainable EBITDA measures the firm's inability to repay its debt and forms our fundamental valuation of default risks. We use sustainable rather than current EBITDA because the former is more capable of capturing the issuer's true earnings power over the long term and is less noisy (see Campbell and Shiller, 1988). In addition, it is much more difficult for a company to manipulate its earnings numbers over several years without being detected.

The SPiDER measure is computed at the end of February each year. While the OAS value is as of the end of February at year t, the financial data is from the fiscal year or quarter ending on the previous year-end (i.e., between October and December of year t–1). If the annual statement is available, then the debt-to-sustainable earnings ratio is computed using numbers from the annual statements. Otherwise, aggregated figures based on the most recent four quarterly statements are used.[4] It is worth noting that although the debt-to-earnings ratio is from the fiscal year ends on year t–1, we still use time script t to represent the fundamental data used at the portfolio formation year t. A lag of two months between the fiscal-year-end date for Debt-to-Sustainable EBITDA ratio (D/E ratio) and the signal formation date is employed to make sure that the financial statement information has been already made publicly available at the formation.

Using SPiDER as a Value Ratio

For SPiDER to be a proper value measure, the D/E ratio, which is used as a valuation benchmark for the market price of default risk, should reflect an issuer's fundamental default risk. In addition, the market should price this fundamental risk correctly most of the time given that the market is largely efficient and mispricing is rare. This means that the market price of risk (OAS) and the fundamental risk (D/E ratio) should move in line with each other most of the time. We verify empirically whether these two conditions are met with the D/E ratio.

D/E Ratio Captures Risk Beyond Ratings To verify that the D/E ratio indeed measures fundamental risks, we investigate whether it can predict future changes in credit ratings beyond the current ratings. At the end of each February from 1993 to 2017, we assign issuers into quintiles within each rating bucket using the D/E ratios from the previous year end.[5] Each rating is assigned a numerical value, and the worse the rating, the higher the value. Each rating notch deterioration is equivalent to an increment of one in the numeric value (e.g., Aaa = 1, Aa1 = 2, Aa2 = 3, . . ., C = 21, D = 22). We then track the rating changes of these issuers over the subsequent one-, two-, and three-year horizons. Table 14.3 shows that after controlling for issuers' initial ratings, issuers in quintile 5 (Q5, high D/E ratio) have realized larger or more downgrades than issuers in quintile 1 (Q1, low D/E ratios) in subsequent years. Compared to Q1, issuers in Q5 on average experience more than one tenth to one fifth of a notch in downgrades. The pattern exists in all rating buckets and is generally more pronounced in the subsequent 24- and 36-month period with the only exception of Ba-rated issuers. This indicates that the D/E ratios are able to predict future downgrades beyond the current rating and therefore are associated with fundamental risk.

TABLE 14.3 Rating Notch Changes by Debt-to-Sustainable EBITDA Quintiles, Rating, and Horizon, February 1993 to February 2017

	Aaa/Aa						A					
Horizon	Q1	Q2	Q3	Q4	Q5	Q5-Q1	Q1	Q2	Q3	Q4	Q5	Q5-Q1
12m	0.083	0.353	0.190	0.265	0.255	0.172	0.162	0.092	0.254	0.160	0.234	0.072
24m	0.199	0.538	0.460	1.116	0.588	0.388	0.334	0.208	0.476	0.414	0.413	0.079
36m	0.359	0.677	0.614	1.403	0.960	0.601	0.536	0.355	0.626	0.641	0.612	0.076

	Baa						Ba					
Horizon	Q1	Q2	Q3	Q4	Q5	Q5-Q1	Q1	Q2	Q3	Q4	Q5	Q5-Q1
12m	0.082	0.082	0.095	0.117	0.164	0.082	-0.004	-0.026	0.079	0.129	0.082	0.086
24m	0.135	0.173	0.193	0.281	0.394	0.259	0.082	0.032	0.091	0.220	0.192	0.110
36m	0.183	0.287	0.288	0.392	0.633	0.450	0.202	0.055	0.087	0.385	0.203	0.001

	B					
Horizon	Q1	Q2	Q3	Q4	Q5	Q5-Q1
12m	-0.024	-0.022	0.093	0.045	0.050	0.074
24m	-0.040	0.052	0.193	0.128	0.167	0.207
36m	-0.184	0.092	0.245	0.231	0.202	0.386

Note: Each rating notch is assigned a numerical value, and the better the rating. the lower the value (Aaa=1, Aa1=2, . . ., C=21, D=22). 1 represents one notch down. Each February we sort issuers into quintiles based on their Debt-to-Sustainable EBITDA ratio from the end of the previous year. The ranking is done within each of the five rating buckets (Aaa/Aa, A, Baa, Ba, and B). For each issuer, we then track its rating changes in the subsequent 12, 24, and 36 months. The rating change is calculated as the difference between the end rating (last available rating at the earlier of the issuer exiting the index or the end of the evaluation window) and the rating at the beginning of the evaluation window. Individual bonds' ratings of an issuer are value-weighted to obtain the issuer's average rating. All issuers' rating changes are equally weighted within each quintile bucket.

Source: Bloomberg Barclays Indices, Compustat, Barclays Research

D/E Ratio and OAS Move in Line with Each Other If the D/E ratio is capable of capturing an issuer's fundamental default risk, we should expect it to be positively correlated with OAS, the market price of the same risk. We find that the D/E ratios and OAS are indeed very much aligned at the cross-sectional level and the aggregate level.

First, there is a positive relation between D/E and OAS at the cross-sectional level. To show that, we run the following cross-sectional regression for each year t,

$$OAS_{i,t} = \sum_j \alpha_{jt} I(\text{industry} = j) + \beta_t * (\text{Debt - to - EBITDA ratio})_{i,t} + \text{error}_{i,t},$$

where $OAS_{i,t}$ is the OAS of issuer i at the end of February of year t (in percentages) and $I(\text{industry} = j)$ are the industry dummies.[6]

As mentioned earlier, despite the time script t, the D/E ratio is computed from financial statements as of the end of the previous year. Panels A and B in Figure 14.1 plot the estimated slopes β_t and their respective t-statistics for each year, using investment-grade and high-yield bonds separately. The slopes are always positive across all the years in both indices, except for 2015 and 2016 in high yield. Moreover, the t-statistics are above two most of the time, suggesting that there is a consistently significant positive association between the D/E ratio and OAS over time. Table 14.4 further reports the average slope coefficients across all the years and their corresponding Fama-MacBeth t-statistics. The average slope coefficient is significantly positive in both IG and HY. On average, a one-standard deviation increment in the D/E ratio increases OAS by 10.7bps in IG and 28.3bps in HY. Perhaps what is more important is that, on average, in the presence of industry dummies, the variations in D/E ratios are able to explain more than 85% of the cross-sectional variation in spreads in both IG and HY, exhibiting strong explanatory power.

Second, the time-series dynamics between the D/E ratio and OAS are also very similar. Figure 14.2 plots the aggregated OAS and D/E ratios over time. In general, the two move in line with each other except in the financial crisis of 2008–2009, during which the spike in OAS did not come with a rise in debt-to-EBITDA ratio. The breakdown of the comovement is a result of an increase in illiquidity instead of default concerns (see Dastidar and Phelps 2011). Overall, the correlation between the changes in aggregate OAS and D/E ratios is 0.30 for IG and 0.39 for HY.

Taken together, Tables 14.3 and 14.4 and Figures 14.1 and 14.2 show that OAS and the D/E ratio closely reflect the default risk from the market and fundamental perspective. Therefore, the SPiDER ratio, which captures the mismatch of the two, can flag possible valuation errors.

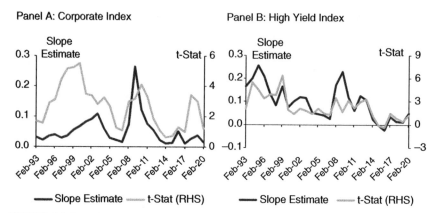

FIGURE 14.1   Slope Estimates from Yearly Cross-Sectional Regressions, February 1993 to February 2020
Source: Bloomberg, Compustat, Barclays Research

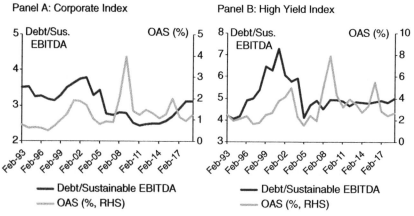

FIGURE 14.2   Time-Series Average OAS and D/E Ratios Across All Issuers, 1993 to 2020
Note: OAS is calculated as the market-value-weighted spread across all issuers. Aggregate debt and sustainable EBITDA are computed separately as the sum of all issuers' debt and sustainable EBITDA respectively. The date in the x-axis is when the portfolio is formed. At portfolio formation, OAS data used are as the end of each February, and the fundamental data used are from the financial statements in the previous year.
Source: Bloomberg Barclays Indices, Compustat, Barclays Research

TABLE 14.4   Time-Series Average and Standard Deviation of the Slope Estimates from Yearly Cross-Sectional Regressions, February 1993 to February 2020

	IG				HY		
Avg. Slope	Std (Slope)	*t*-stat. (Avg./ Std*sqrt(T))	Avg. adj. R²	Avg. Slope	Std (Slope)	*t*-stat. (Avg./ Std*sqrt(T))	Avg. adj. R²
0.05	0.05	5.48	85%	0.10	0.07	6.77	86%

Source: Bloomberg Barclays Indices, Compustat, Barclays Research

Characteristics of the SPiDER Quintiles

Table 14.5 reports the average SPiDER, OAS, and D/E ratio values of issuers in SPiDER quintiles. The quintiles are formed by ranking issuers on the SPiDER value within each industry. On average, there is a decent amount of variation in SPiDER across the quintiles. In both the IG and HY universes, the average SPiDER increases by almost seven-fold from Q1 (low SPiDER) to Q5 (high SPiDER). The rise in SPiDER ratios from Q1 to Q5 is driven more by the decline in the D/E ratio rather than the increases in OAS. In addition, although the average OAS and D/E ratios are greatly different between IG and HY issuers within each quintile, the levels of SPiDER in fact have small differences between the two indices. This finding partly shows that SPiDER has few systematic biases in ratings, confirming that the metric is relatively comparable in the cross-section.

TABLE 14.5   Average SPiDER, OAS, Debt/EBITDA Ratios at the End of Each February Between 1993 and 2019, by SPiDER Quintiles

	SPiDER		OAS (%)		D/E Ratio	
SPiDER Quintile	IG	HY	IG	HY	IG	HY
Q1 (Low)	0.20	0.33	1.12	3.18	5.50	9.67
Q2	0.39	0.55	1.27	3.44	3.23	6.25
Q3	0.55	0.81	1.36	3.75	2.49	4.65
Q4	0.79	1.16	1.55	4.34	1.97	3.76
Q5 (High)	1.40	2.11	1.88	5.62	1.34	2.67
Q5/Q1	6.89	6.41	1.68	1.77	0.24	0.28

Note: Quintile OAS is the equally weighted average of issuer OAS in the quintile. Quintile D/E ratio is calculated as the sum of debt from all issuers over the sum of sustainable EBITDA of all issuers in the quintile. Quintile SPiDER is calculated as quintile OAS over quintile D/E ratio. All the numbers are computed as the end of each February between 1993 and 2019 and are then averaged across all the years.
Source: Bloomberg Barclays Indices, Compustat, Barclays Research

TABLE 14.6 Characteristics of Issuers in SPiDER Quintiles, Monthly Average,
March 1993 to February 2020

SPiDER Quintile	OAS (bps)	Duration	DTS	Rating	Issuer Bond MV ($bn)	Issuer Equity MV ($bn)	EBITDA Vol./ Debt
Panel A: Investment Grade							
1 (Low)	124	6.31	8.46	3.39	3.64	49.08	10%
2	133	6.55	9.24	3.43	2.93	47.40	12%
3	140	6.52	9.62	3.45	2.40	35.84	15%
4	157	6.62	10.68	3.52	1.85	29.89	18%
5 (High)	183	6.51	11.98	3.59	1.33	34.96	33%
Q5–Q1	59	0.21	3.52	0.19	–2.32	–14.12	23%
Panel B: High Yield (Ba & B with Prc>=$50)							
1 (Low)	358	4.48	15.77	5.41	1.44	5.65	10%
2	358	4.29	15.39	5.44	1.11	4.28	9%
3	392	4.24	16.47	5.49	0.96	3.89	11%
4	446	4.11	18.02	5.53	0.86	3.31	13%
5 (High)	542	4.03	21.19	5.59	0.62	3.51	22%
Q5–Q1	184	–0.45	5.43	0.18	–0.82	–2.13	12%

Note: The numeric values of quality rating are converted by the following scale:
Aaa = 1, Aa = 2, A = 3, Baa = 4, Ba = 5, B = 6. OAS, OASD, DTS, and rating are
aggregated by issuer bond market value weight across issuers. The market value
weighted statistics are later averaged across all years. Bond MV, Equity MV, EBITDA
volatility, and EBITDA growth are averaged across issuers in each quintile and are
later averaged across all years. EBITDA volatility is calculated as the volatility of
annualized EBITDA from a trailing 10-year window.
Source: Bloomberg Barclays Indices, Compustat, Barclays Research

Table 14.6 shows other characteristics of the SPiDER quintile portfolios
together with OAS. Results in the table generally confirm that high-SPiDER
issuers are riskier than low-SPiDER issuers. First, credit spreads increase
from Q1 to Q5, which implies that the performance difference between Q5
and Q1 may have a carry component. In the subsequent performance analysis, we control for OAS to remove this component. Second, although duration risk is similar between Q5 and Q1, issuers in Q5 have higher Duration
Times Spread (DTS) than those in Q1 because of the differences in OAS,
indicating that the long-short strategy between Q5 and Q1 might be subject
to market directionality (see Ben Dor et al. 2007 for DTS details). Third, the

credit ratings are a little bit worse in Q5 but are overall similar across all the quintiles. This matches what we find in Table 14.5: SPiDER seems to have little systematic bias in ratings. Fourth, the average bond market value decreases with SPiDER ratios, which implies a decline in firm debts from Q1 to Q5. The same pattern exists in terms of equity market values, but the magnitude of the decrease from Q1 to Q5 is smaller. Last, as further evidence of Q5's higher riskiness, issuers in this quintile have more volatile historical EBITDAs than those in Q1.

UNDERSTANDING THE SPIDER PERFORMANCE

If SPiDER is able to capture mispricing in bonds, then the undervalued cheap issuers, as indicated through their high SPiDER values, would gradually catch up in prices as market value converges to the fundamental value. Similarly, prices of issuers with low SPiDER values would drop as the market corrects for the overpricing. As a result, the SPiDER ratio should be able to predict subsequent bond returns. In this section, we first examine the existence of such predictability and then investigate whether it is indeed driven by mispricing.

To formally test the predictability, we form quintile portfolios by ranking issuers based on their SPiDER within industry at the end of each February. All issuers are equally weighted at the portfolio formation and are held until the next February irrespective of rating changes during the period. A SPiDER "value" strategy is then formulated by buying issuers in the top quintile Q5 (issuers with the highest SPiDER ratios) and shorting those in the bottom quintile Q1 (issuers with the lowest SPiDER ratios). If the predictability exists, we would expect to see that the strategy earns significantly positive returns.

Overall Performance

Table 14.7 and Figure 14.3 present the performance statistics and time-series dynamics of the SPiDER strategy and the long-only SPiDER portfolio from March 1993 to February 2020. As explained earlier, the SPiDER strategy buys issuers in the top SPiDER quintile (Q5) and shorts issuers in the bottom SPiDER quintile (Q1). The long-only SPiDER portfolio consists of issuers only from Q5. Excess returns over duration-matched Treasury portfolios are reported in order to focus on the credit component of performance.

TABLE 14.7 Performance Statistics of the SPiDER Strategy, March 1993 to February 2020

	Investment Grade				High Yield				Equity Value Factors	
	SPiDER Strategy	SPiDER Long (Q5)	Benchmark	Q5 over Benchmark	SPiDER Strategy	SPiDER Long (Q5)	Benchmark	Q5 over Benchmark	Book-to-Market	Earnings-to-Price
Avg. Excess Ret. (%/Yr)	1.61	1.83	0.63	1.20	2.62	3.64	2.21	1.42	7.54	2.84
Vol. (%/Yr)	1.38	3.91	4.08	1.54	3.60	7.68	8.34	4.10	12.48	8.78
Inf. Ratio (ann.)	1.17	0.47	0.16	0.78	0.73	0.47	0.27	0.35	0.60	0.32
Worst Monthly Ex. Ret. (%)	-1.76	-8.71	-9.04	-2.59	-4.37	-15.08	-15.26	-6.25	-15.44	-9.22
Max. Drawdown (%)	-4.68	-23.03	-23.23	-5.74	-9.50	-33.54	-39.43	-14.27	-33.99	-28.08
Corr. w. Benchmark	0.10	0.93			-0.08	0.87				

Note: The benchmarks for the IG and HY universes are the corresponding Bloomberg Barclays credit index excluding financials. In the high-yield universe, the benchmark further excludes bonds rated below B. The equity value factor portfolios are formulated by ranking all NYSE, AMEX, and NASDAQ stocks into quintiles based on book-to-market ratio or earnings-to-price ratio. The factor portfolio buys stocks in the top quintile and shorts stocks in the bottom quintile, both with equal weights. The factor performance is from Ken French's data library and based on returns from March 1993 to January 2020.

Source: Bloomberg Barclays Indices, Compustat, Ken French Data Library, Barclays Research

Table 14.7 shows that the SPiDER strategy delivers an information ratio of 1.17 in IG and of 0.73 in HY from March 1993 to February 2020. As a comparison, equity value strategies generate an information ratio between 0.32 and 0.60 over a similar period. In addition, the long-only portfolio outperforms the respective benchmark both in terms of absolute returns and risk-adjusted performance. In the IG universe, the long-only SPiDER portfolio earns an average annualized excess return of 1.83% and an information ratio of 0.47, almost three times of those for the benchmark (0.63% and 0.16 respectively). In the HY universe, the long-only SPiDER portfolio also generates a higher average excess return and information ratio than the benchmark (3.64% vs. 2.21%, 0.47 vs. 0.27, respectively). In addition, the information ratio of the long portfolio relative to the index benchmark is 0.78 in IG and 0.35 in HY. Last, Figure 14.3 plots the cumulative excess returns of the long and short leg of the SPiDER strategy separately in lines and their cumulative difference in shaded areas. Both panels show that Q5 consistently outperforms Q1 over time since the shaded area has an upward trend for the majority of the sample period.

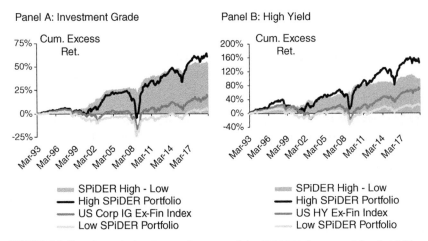

FIGURE 14.3   Cumulative Excess Returns of the SPiDER Strategy, March 1993 to February 2020
Note: The benchmarks for the IG and HY universes are the corresponding Bloomberg Barclays credit index excluding financials. In the high-yield universe, the benchmark further excludes bonds rated below B.
Source: Bloomberg Barclays Indices, Compustat, Barclays Research

Although the SPiDER strategy invests only in the top and bottom quintiles, it is worthwhile to examine the other quintiles to understand the efficacy of the signal. For example, based on the value investing philosophy, the most undervalued bonds (Q5) would be expected to generate a higher subsequent performance than the other less undervalued or even overvalued bonds from Q2, Q3, and Q4. Panel A (IG) and Panel B (HY) of Figure 14.4 show that the average excess returns increase monotonically from Q1 (overvalued) to Q5 (undervalued), confirming that the behavior of all quintiles matches the pattern of a typical value signal. The realized volatilities are very stable across all the quintiles. As a result, the information ratios plotted in Panels C and D also exhibit a monotonic relationship from Q1 to Q5. In addition, the fact that all quintiles have similar realized volatilities suggests that they may have somewhat similar fundamental risk profiles and therefore the outperformance of Q5 over Q1 is unlikely due to risk compensation. We discuss this in more detail in the next section.

What Drives the SPiDER Performance?

What are the drivers behind the outperformance of high-SPiDER issuers? A value story would argue that SPiDER captures issuer-level mispricing. However, there are other possible explanations: risk compensation, being driven by a particular subset of bonds or by the specific form of SPiDER, and so on. We find that none of the alternatives fully explains the performance. Instead, the performance dynamics are more consistent with mispricing.

Risk Compensation or Mispricing? A key risk measure is return volatility. In the credit space, one of the best predictors of a bond's realized volatility in excess returns is DTS (see Ben Dor et al. 2007). Specifically, the volatility of a bond's excess return $\sigma_{\text{Excess Ret.}}$ can be written as:

$$\sigma_{\text{Excess Ret.}} \approx D * S * \sigma_{spread}^{rel},$$

where D is the spread duration,
S is the spread priced by the market (OAS), and
σ_{spread}^{rel} is the volatility in relative spread changes.

Since the volatility of relative spread changes is roughly homogeneous across bonds, the volatility in a bond's excess return is approximately proportional

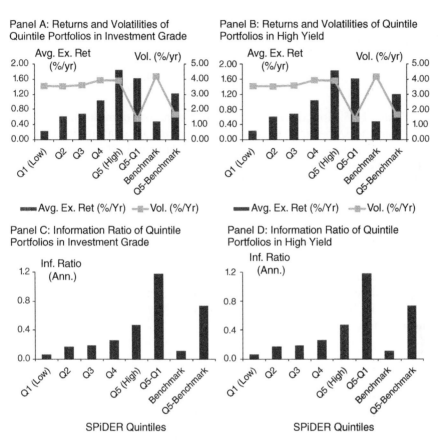

FIGURE 14.4 Average Excess Returns, Volatilities, and Information Ratios by SPi-DER Quintiles, March 1993 to February 2020

Note: The benchmarks for the investment-grade and high-yield universes are the corresponding Bloomberg Barclays US credit index without financials. The benchmark for the high-yield universe further excludes bonds that are rated below B.

Source: Bloomberg Barclays Indices, Compustat, Barclays Research

to its DTS. Then the ratio of the volatilities from two bond portfolios (e.g., σ_{Q5}/σ_{Q1}) should be equal to the ratio of their respective DTS (DTS_{Q5}/DTS_{Q1}). Therefore, we can infer the volatility of a portfolio (say, Q5) based on the volatility of a benchmark portfolio (say, Q1) and the ratio of its DTS to that of the benchmark. In particular, the DTS-implied excess return volatilities of the other quintiles, given the volatility of Q1, are:

$$\sigma_{Q_i}^{\text{DTS-implied}} = \frac{DTS_{Q_i}}{DTS_{Q_1}} \sigma_{Q_1}, i = 2, 3, 4, 5$$

Figure 14.5 plots the realized volatilities across quintiles in the dark color bar and DTS-implied volatilities based on Q1 volatility in the light color bar. The realized volatility reflects fundamental ("fair") risks while the DTS-implied volatility captures the market-perceived risks since DTS is based on market prices (i.e., OAS). The divergence between the two types of volatilities indicates the presence of disagreement in market price spreads and fundamental spreads. Figure 14.5 shows that the DTS-implied volatilities are much higher than the realized volatilities and the difference increases in SPiDER. The inflated DTS-implied volatility over the realized volatility of issuers in quintiles 2 to 5 implies that their spreads are overly high compared to Q1 (therefore, high DTS), and their prices are overly suppressed relative to Q1. Moreover, the level of suppression in prices increases in SPiDER. Such pattern in volatility matches a mispricing phenomenon.

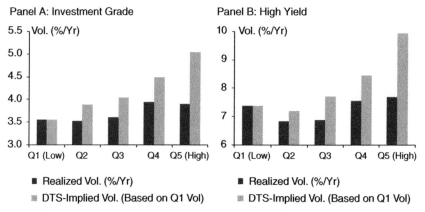

FIGURE 14.5   Realized Volatility vs. DTS-Implied Volatility by Quintiles, March 1993 to February 2020
Source: Bloomberg Barclays Indices, Compustat, Barclays Research

Another way to examine whether the strategy performance is due to risk compensation is to match the risks of all quintile portfolios ex ante and then check if the performance still exists with the risk-adjusted returns. Following Ben Dor et al. (2007), we use DTS as a measure of a portfolio's exposure to market-wide systematic risks (similar to beta in equity markets). Specifically, we scale down the monthly excess returns of Q2 to Q5 so that their ex ante risk is matched to that of Q1 by the DTS ratio,

$$\text{Risk-adjusted excess return}_t^{Q_i} = \frac{DTS_{Q_1}}{DTS_{Q_i}} \text{Excess return}_t^{Q_i}, i = 2,3,4,5$$

where *DTS* is as of the beginning of month t.[7]

Figure 14.6 compares the information ratio of the SPiDER quintile portfolios using DTS-adjusted excess returns (light color bar) vs. using unadjusted excess returns (dark color bar). Performances in Q2 to Q5 are lower when DTS are adjusted, suggesting that part of the performance difference is due to the different level of portfolio risks. However, Q5 still outperforms Q1 by a wide margin, confirming that risk compensation cannot fully explain the outperformance.

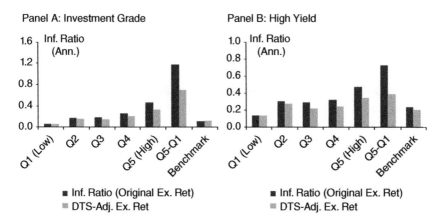

FIGURE 14.6 Information Ratios by Quintiles with DTS Matched Equally Across Quintiles Ex Ante, March 1993 to February 2020
Note: The benchmarks for the investment-grade and high-yield universes are the corresponding Bloomberg Barclays US credit index without financials. The benchmark for the high-yield universe further excludes bonds that are rated below B.
Source: Bloomberg Barclays Indices, Compustat, Barclays Research

Is SPiDER Just Carry?   The second possible explanation for the performance is carry. As shown in Table 14.6, top SPiDER issuers have high OAS, indicating a possible carry component in the strategy returns. However, our analysis shows that carry cannot fully explain the performance.

As a comparison, we formulate a pure carry strategy that buys issuers in the top OAS quintile and short-sells those in the bottom OAS quintile. Table 14.8 shows that this strategy has an average carry of 1.53% in IG and 4.52% in HY, almost three times those of SPiDER. If carry can fully explain the performance of SPiDER, we would expect to see that SPiDER underperforms this strategy because SPiDER has smaller carry. However, Table 14.8 shows the contrary. The information ratio of SPiDER is three to four times larger than the pure carry strategy in both IG and HY. As further evidence of SPiDER's low exposure on carry, Table 14.8 reports very low correlations between SPiDER and the respective market benchmark in both IG and HY, exhibiting a sharp contrast with the correlations between the pure carry strategy and the market.

Another approach to examine performance contributed from carry is to neutralize the effects from OAS by ranking issuers based on SPiDER within each intersected bucket of industry and OAS.[8] This ensures that the top and bottom SPiDER issuers have similar spreads. Indeed, Table 14.8 shows that the OAS-neutral SPiDER strategy has a carry close to zero. More important, after removing the effects from OAS, the top SPiDER issuers still outperform the bottom SPiDER issuers.[9] Collectively, these results demonstrate that the performance of the SPiDER strategy is more than carry.

Is the Performance Driven by a Particular Rating or Industry?   Another possible explanation of the performance is that results possibly are driven by a particular set of issuers. After all, all the previous results are based on aggregated performance from all issuers. In this section, we look at two of the most important dimensions of corporate bond characteristics, credit quality and industry, and examine whether results are unique to just a limited group of issuers.

Table 14.9 reports the strategy performance for each rating group separately. Issuers are ranked on SPiDER into top and bottom halves within buckets formulated by intersecting rating and industry. In each rating group, issuers with high SPiDER values are able to outperform those with low SPiDER values. The average return differences between high- and low-SPiDER issuers increases in ratings.

TABLE 14.8 Performances of SPiDER, Maximum Carry, and OAS-Neutral SPiDER Strategies, March 1993 to February 2020

	Investment Grade				High Yield			
	SPiDER (Original)	Carry (Q5–Q1)	OAS-Neutral SPiDER	Benchmark	SPiDER (Original)	Carry (Q5–Q1)	OAS-Neutral SPiDER	Benchmark
Carry (BOM Avg. OAS (%))	0.59	1.53	0.05	1.36	1.84	4.52	0.23	4.22
Avg. Ex. Ret. (%/yr)	1.61	1.29	0.34	0.63	2.62	1.06	0.97	2.21
Vol. (%/yr)	1.38	3.41	0.66	4.08	3.60	6.44	1.70	8.34
Inf. Ratio	1.17	0.38	0.52	0.16	0.73	0.16	0.57	0.27
Min. Monthly Ret. (%)	-1.76	-6.84	-0.90	-9.04	-4.37	-10.53	-1.99	-15.26
Max. Drawdown (%)	-4.68	-21.06	-1.80	-23.23	-9.50	-34.29	-3.44	-39.43
Corr. w. Benchmark	0.10	0.75	-0.42	0.10	-0.08	0.65	-0.36	-0.08
Corr. w. Original SPiDER		0.48	0.57			0.49	0.70	

Note: The benchmark for each universe is the corresponding Bloomberg Barclays US credit index without financials. In the high-yield universe, the benchmark further excludes bonds that are rated below B. OAS-neutral strategy ranks issuers based on SPiDER values into top and bottom halves within buckets formulated by intersecting industry and OAS (4-quartile OAS buckets). The strategy is long the top 50% of issuers and short the remaining bottom half issuers in each intersected bucket.
Source: Bloomberg Barclays Indices, Compustat, Barclays Research

TABLE 14.9 SPiDER Performance by Credit Ratings, March 1993 to February 2020

	A/A+	Baa	Benchmark	Ba	B	Benchmark
Carry (BOM Avg. OAS (%))	0.12	0.35	1.36	0.60	1.31	4.22
Avg. Ex Ret. (%/yr)	0.40	0.75	0.63	0.71	1.70	2.21
Vol. (%/yr)	0.63	1.00	4.08	2.36	2.69	8.34
Inf. Ratio	0.64	0.75	0.16	0.30	0.63	0.27
Min. Monthly Ret. (%)	−0.68	−1.58	−9.04	−3.80	−2.99	−15.26
Max. Drawdown (%)	−1.81	−3.81	−23.23	−9.96	−5.88	−39.43
Corr. w. Index	0.25	0.02		−0.09	0.05	

Note: The benchmark for each universe is the corresponding Bloomberg Barclays US credit index excluding financials. In the high-yield universe, the benchmark further excludes bonds that are rated below B. Within each rating-industry bucket, issuers are ranked into top and bottom halves based on SPiDER values. The performance statistics reported are of strategies that long the top half (high) SPiDER issuers and short the bottom half (low) SPiDER issuers.
Source: Bloomberg Barclays Indices, Compustat, Barclays Research

Similarly, Figure 14.7 shows that within each industry, high-SPiDER issuers (Q5) deliver higher subsequent returns than low-SPiDER issuers (Q1). The average excess return difference between top and bottom SPiDER issuers is at least 128 bps/yr in IG and 134 bps/yr in HY. In IG, the information ratio ranges from 0.31 to 0.89; in HY, it is between 0.24 and 0.68. There is no clear pattern of the performance across industries. The presence of outperformance from top SPiDER issuers across industries shows that results are not limited to one particular industry.

Is the Performance Driven by the Specific Form of SPiDER?

The last explanation we examine is whether the performance is an in-sample result that relies completely on the specific way we compute SPiDER. The essence of a value ratio is that it reflects the mismatch between one of a firm's market valuations and one of its fundamental valuations. Therefore, although the signal strength could vary, the existence of performance predictability should be robust to mild deviations in the specific construction of the measure.

We find that results are not restricted to the specific way we compute SPiDER. In particular, results are very robust when we consider the following alternative earnings power estimates. First, we use different window lengths

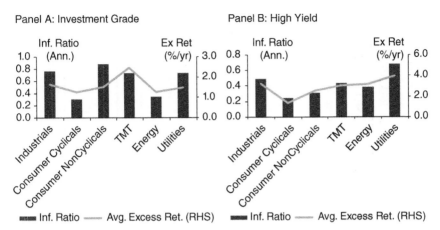

FIGURE 14.7 Performance of SPiDER Strategy (Q5–Q1) by Industry, March 1993 to February 2020
Note: The average excess returns and information ratios reported are for the SPiDER portfolios within each industry group. These portfolios are formulated by buying the top SPiDER issuers (Q5) and short-selling the bottom SPiDER issuers (Q1) within each industry.
Source: Bloomberg Barclays Indices, Compustat, Barclays Research

to calculate the sustainable earnings. Second, to take account for the possible positive or negative growth in earnings, we use the EBITDA extrapolated from a time-trend model to approximate the earnings power instead of using arithmetic averages. Third, we use a forward-looking metric (analyst forecast) as the estimate. In addition, instead of using D/E ratios, we use two alternative ratios to measure the fundamental risk: the inverse of interest coverage ratio and the debt-to-cash ratio.

Table 14.10 reports the performances when different SPiDER definitions are adopted. Two observations are worth noting. First, results are quite robust across all the definitions. Especially in the IG universe, the information ratios barely change. Second, using the debt-to-cash ratio generates the lowest correlation with the original SPiDER strategy both in terms of signal ranking and in return time series. This holds regardless of the index universe. The signal ranking correlation between the original SPiDER and the modified strategy is 0.44 in IG and 0.30 in HY, which implies that debt-to-cash ratios may offer improvements when used in combination with the original SPiDER signal.

TABLE 14.10 Performance with Alternative SPiDER Definitions, March 1993 to February 2020

	SPiDER	Alternative Window Length for Sustainable EBITDA				SPiDER Based on Trend-Adjusted EBITDA				Alternative Fundamental Risk Measure		
		1yr	3yr	5yr	7yr	1%-sig. cutoff	5%-sig. cutoff	10%-sig. cutoff	All	OAS/(1 over Interest Coverage Ratio)	OAS/ Debt-to-Cash Ratio	Bench-mark
IG Avg. Excess Ret. (%/yr)	1.61	1.24	1.38	1.54	1.58	1.40	1.36	1.31	1.39	1.23	0.73	0.63
Vol. (%/yr)	1.38	1.22	1.28	1.26	1.34	1.25	1.26	1.29	1.27	1.17	0.96	4.08
Inf. Ratio (ann.)	1.17	1.02	1.08	1.22	1.18	1.12	1.08	1.01	1.09	1.05	0.76	0.16
Min. Monthly Ret. (%)	-1.76	-1.41	-1.58	-1.64	-1.85	-1.93	-1.67	-1.75	-1.86	-1.20	-1.27	-9.04
Max. Drawdown (%)	-4.68	-3.33	-4.22	-4.56	-5.05	-4.37	-4.32	-4.76	-4.77	-3.52	-3.05	-23.23
Corr. w. Benchmark	0.10	0.11	0.15	0.16	0.08	0.28	0.29	0.30	0.17	0.04	0.00	
Correlation with Original SPiDER Portfolio												
Based on Returns		0.75	0.88	0.93	0.96	0.85	0.84	0.85	0.86	0.84	0.65	
Based on Issuer Rankings		0.82	0.90	0.95	0.98	0.83	0.83	0.83	0.82	0.82	0.44	
HY Avg. Excess Ret. (%/yr)	2.62	1.68	2.48	2.13	2.18	2.44	2.75	2.61	2.41	1.93	2.47	2.21
Vol. (%/yr)	3.60	3.04	3.24	3.50	3.46	3.05	3.32	3.37	3.27	3.49	2.60	8.34

(Continued)

TABLE 14.10 (Continued)

	SPiDER	Alternative Window Length for Sustainable EBITDA				SPiDER Based on Trend-Adjusted EBITDA				Alternative Fundamental Risk Measure		
		1yr	3yr	5yr	7yr	1%-sig. cutoff	5%-sig. cutoff	10%-sig. cutoff	All	OAS/(1 over Interest Coverage Ratio)	OAS/Debt-to-Cash Ratio	Bench-mark
Inf. Ratio (ann.)	0.73	0.55	0.77	0.61	0.63	0.80	0.83	0.77	0.74	0.55	0.95	0.27
Min. Monthly Ret. (%)	-4.37	-3.52	-2.51	-3.17	-3.87	-3.74	-3.69	-3.93	-3.42	-3.54	-2.70	-15.26
Max. Drawdown (%)	-9.50	-6.64	-10.79	-13.06	-10.32	-5.80	-7.98	-8.92	-11.48	-9.79	-9.16	-39.43
Corr. w. Benchmark	-0.08	-0.05	-0.11	0.00	-0.01	-0.05	-0.02	-0.02	0.04	-0.10	0.04	
Correlation with Original SPiDER Portfolio												
Based on Returns		0.65	0.82	0.82	0.91	0.84	0.79	0.79	0.79	0.91	0.32	
Based on Issuer Rankings		0.65	0.80	0.89	0.96	0.77	0.74	0.73	0.69	0.86	0.30	

Note: The benchmarks for the investment-grade and high-yield universes are the corresponding Bloomberg Barclays US credit index without financials. The benchmark for the high-yield universe further excludes bonds that are rated below B. All the alternative strategies are formed with the same population of issuers in the original SPiDER sample that have at least six years of fundamental data. All of them are long top-quintile issuers and short bottom-quintile issuers within each industry. Trended EBITDA is a firm's predicted EBITDA using the coefficients estimated from the following trend model: $\log(EBITDA) = \alpha + \beta * \log(\text{Issuer age})$. The model is estimated annually using the past 10 years' data (minimum six years of history). *Trend-adjusted EBITDA* $= \exp(\hat{\alpha} + \hat{\beta} * (\text{Issuer age} + 1))$. In the 1%-, 5%-, and 10%-significant cutoff, the trend-adjusted EBITDA estimate is used if the slope p-value is below the respective threshold, and sustainable EBITDA is used otherwise. In the specification of "all," the trend-adjusted EBITDA estimate is used regardless of the p-value. Interest coverage ratio is defined as sustainable EBITDA/interest expense. Debt-to-cash ratio is the ratio of a firm's short- and long-term debt over its cash holdings.

Source: Bloomberg Barclays Indices, Compustat, Barclays Research

TABLE 14.11 Strategy Performance When SPiDER Is Based on Analyst EBITDA Consensus Forecasts, March 2003 to February 2020

	IG				HY			
	SPiDER	Analyst forecast	Benchmark		SPiDER	Analyst forecast	Benchmark
Avg. Excess Ret. (%/yr)	1.62	1.41	1.19		2.39	1.71	3.98
Vol. (%/yr)	1.52	1.45	4.67		3.62	2.78	8.62
Inf. Ratio (ann.)	1.06	0.97	0.25		0.66	0.61	0.46
Min. Monthly Ret. (%)	−1.76	−1.89	−9.04		−4.37	−2.34	−15.26
Max. Drawdown (%)	−4.68	−4.38	−22.27		−9.50	−8.71	−39.04
Corr. w. Benchmark	0.20	0.23			−0.12	0.09	
Corr. w. SPiDER		0.85				0.75	

Note: The benchmarks for the investment-grade and high-yield universes are the corresponding Bloomberg Barclays US credit index without financials. The benchmark for the high-yield universe further excludes bonds that are rated below B. The sample starts from 2003 because I/B/E/S starts to have a decent coverage for the EBITDA item only in 2003.
Source: Bloomberg Barclays Indices, Compustat, I/B/E/S, Barclays Research

Table 14.11 reports the performance when forward earnings forecasts rather than the historical EBITDAs are used for SPiDER calculations. Results are reported separately from Table 14.10 because the I/B/E/S analyst forecasts we use only start to have a decent coverage in 2003. The table shows that in both IG and HY universes results are very similar when analyst forecasts are used to compute the SPiDER ratio instead of the historical EBITDA.

IMPLEMENTING SPiDER IN PRACTICE

The SPiDER portfolio presented so far assumes that issuers are held equally weighted until the next rebalancing date in 12 months' time and that trading is cost-free. In this section, we discuss several practical aspects of implementation that deviate from these assumptions.

Selling Issuers Once They Exit the Index

The strategy holds issuers until the next rebalancing date even if they leave the index before that. Investors who have mandates to invest only in index bonds would have to offload these issuers from the portfolio. How would that affect the performance?

Table 14.12 shows that performances in investment-grade bonds are almost unchanged if issuers are sold immediately when they leave the respective index as opposed to until the next rebalancing date. Results are similar for high-yield bonds. One reason for the minimal change in performance is that there are only a few bonds in the top and bottom SPiDER quintiles exiting the index. Table 14.12 shows that the number of issuers in the portfolios under the two rules are almost the same in IG and are only slightly different in HY.

Weighting Schemes

The strategy puts equal weights on each issuer in the portfolio, which can be challenging to scale up. Table 14.13 reports the performance when issuers are value-weighted or value-weighted with a cap of 4% per issuer. The long-only portfolios generate very similar performance when different weighting schemes are used. The information ratios change very little across weighting schemes in both IG and HY. While the performance of long-short (L-S) portfolios is adversely affected by value-weighting, the long leg still outperforms the short leg. The information ratio of the L-S portfolios is 0.58 in IG and 0.57 in HY. Imposing a cap on the weights can improve the performance a little, but not by much.

TABLE 14.12 Effects of the Constituent Exit Rule on Portfolio Performance, March 1993 to February 2020

	Investment Grade			High Yield		
	Original (Issuers Exit Only at Rebalancing)	Issuers Sold Once They Exit Index	Benchmark	Original (Issuers Exit Only at Rebalancing)	Issuers Sold Once They Exit Index	Benchmark
Avg. Ex. Ret. (%/yr)	1.61	1.41	0.63	2.62	2.36	2.21
Vol. (%/yr)	1.38	1.28	4.08	3.60	3.71	8.34
Inf. Ratio	1.17	1.10	0.16	0.73	0.64	0.27
Min. Monthly Ret. (%)	-1.76	-1.84	-9.04	-4.37	-4.89	-15.26
Max. DD (%)	-4.68	-4.98	-23.23	-9.50	-9.88	-39.43
Corr. w. Index	0.10	0.05		-0.08	-0.12	
Avg. # Issuers per month in both long and short	190	189	637	129	117	656

Note: The benchmarks for the investment-grade and high-yield universes are the corresponding Bloomberg Barclays US credit index without financials. The benchmark for the high-yield universe further excludes bonds that are rated below B. The weights from the sold issuers are redistributed evenly to existing issuers.
Source: Bloomberg Barclays Indices, Compustat, Barclays Research

TABLE 14.13 Portfolio Performance Under Different Weighting Schemes, March 1993 to February 2020

		Original Formulation (Equally Weighted)			Value-Weighted			Value-Weighted with 4% cap			
		L-S	L	S	L-S	L	S	L-S	L	S	Benchmark
IG	Avg. Excess Ret. (%/yr)	1.61	1.83	0.22	1.46	1.93	0.47	1.48	1.81	0.33	0.63
	Vol. (%/yr)	1.38	3.91	3.56	2.54	5.26	3.66	1.80	4.49	3.68	4.08
	Inf. Ratio	1.17	0.47	0.06	0.58	0.37	0.13	0.82	0.40	0.09	0.16
	Min. Monthly Ret. (%)	-1.76	-8.71	-8.96	-5.15	-8.87	-6.52	-2.35	-9.12	-8.37	-9.04
	Max. DD (%)	-4.68	-23.03	-25.89	-10.30	-23.04	-19.86	-7.91	-23.24	-22.42	-23.23
	Corr. w. Benchmark	0.10	0.93	0.98	0.50	0.92	0.97	0.33	0.94	0.99	
HY	Avg. Excess Ret. (%/yr)	2.62	3.64	1.02	2.35	3.44	1.09	2.20	3.32	1.11	2.21
	Vol. (%/yr)	3.60	7.68	7.38	4.11	8.36	6.58	3.75	8.29	6.89	8.34
	Inf. Ratio	0.73	0.47	0.14	0.57	0.41	0.17	0.59	0.40	0.16	0.27
	Min. Monthly Ret. (%)	-4.37	-15.08	-15.91	-6.25	-14.95	-13.81	-3.83	-16.83	-13.85	-15.26
	Max. DD (%)	-9.50	-33.54	-40.08	-12.07	-38.89	-36.71	-11.38	-38.07	-35.82	-39.43
	Corr. w. Benchmark	-0.08	0.87	0.95	0.26	0.88	0.95	0.22	0.89	0.96	

Note: The benchmarks for the investment-grade and high-yield universes are the corresponding Bloomberg Barclays US credit index without financials. The benchmark for the high-yield universe further excludes bonds that are rated below B.
Source: Bloomberg Barclays Indices, Compustat, Barclays Research

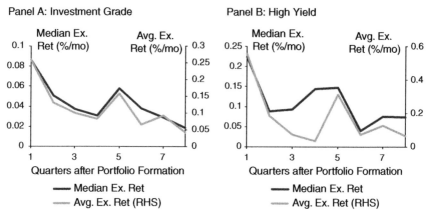

FIGURE 14.8 Strategy Post-Formation Median and Average Performances (L-S) by Quarter, March 1993 to February 2020
Note: Portfolio excess returns are calculated by equally weighting excess returns of all issuers in the portfolio. They are formulated at the end of each February from 1993 to 2018.
Source: Bloomberg Barclays Indices, Compustat Barclays Research

Rebalancing Frequencies

Investors have different preferences of holding horizons for various reasons. In this section, we examine how strategy performance is affected when a quarterly or biannual rebalancing is used instead of the annual rebalancing assumed in the original strategy. Before addressing that, we first evaluate how the signal decays over time.

Figure 14.8 reports the quarterly median and average returns of the L/S portfolio over the first eight quarters subsequent to the portfolio formation. The return difference between issuers from the top and bottom SPiDER-ranked quintiles stays positive for all the quarters. But it declines gradually over time and eventually becomes close to zero at the eighth quarter, exhibiting a signal life of roughly two years. In the figure, the quarterly performance has a small peak over the fifth quarter in both IG and HY. As we show later, this is due to the persistence of the signal (i.e., the empirical evidence that shows that more than half of the issuers in the portfolio tend to remain in their respective position the following year). This means that when the annual report of the following year is released, new information is likely to reinforce the current positions for the majority of the issuers, leading to an increase in performance during the fifth quarter.

Since SPiDER has the highest performance in the first quarter, we first consider rebalancing the portfolio at a quarterly horizon. Although credit investors generally hold bonds for a longer period of time, some sophisticated investors are able to update their portfolios more frequently. One main advantage of having more frequent rebalancing is the ability to use timelier information. To understand how updated information in spreads and financial statements affect portfolio performance, we consider two quarterly rebalanced portfolios. One uses the most recent OAS at the rebalancing but still calculates D/E ratios with financial statements from the end of previous year. The other uses the most recent OAS as well as the most updated quarterly financial statements to compute SPiDER.[10]

Table 14.14 reports the performance of the two quarterly portfolios. Using a timelier OAS improves performance. It increases portfolio returns and information ratios in both IG and HY universes. However, the benefits of calculating D/E ratios with more recent financial statements seem to be inconclusive. While updating both OAS and D/E ratios leads to further improvements in IG, it is not more helpful than simply updating OAS in HY. One possible explanation is that it takes a relatively long time for the market to fully act on the information from financial statements. Therefore, rebalancing too early, before the market corrects the mispricing, would miss out on these return opportunities.

Given that the SPiDER signal does not disappear until the eighth quarter, we consider slowing the rebalancing frequency to 24 months. For the biannually rebalanced portfolio, we follow the standard approach used in Jegadeesh and Titman (1993). Under this formulation, 50% of the issuers in the SPiDER portfolio are rebalanced in any given year and the rest are carried over from the previous year. Specifically, in any given year *t*, the SPiDER portfolio would be comprised of two subportfolios that correspond to the SPiDER portfolios formed in odd and even years. The two subportfolios are assigned with equal weights initially. At the end of each February, we close out the subportfolio formed two years ago and initiate positions of the current subportfolio based on the latest SPiDER rankings, with the subportfolio formed one year ago remaining unchanged. Hence, this formulation enables us to examine the effect of a slower rebalancing frequency independent of the starting year.

Table 14.15 reports strategy performances when the holding period is extended. In IG, information ratios are almost unchanged for both the long-only and the long-short portfolios. Results are similar for the HY universe, with even a slight improvement in information ratio. In general, a less frequent rebalancing reduces portfolio returns slightly but also decreases volatilities and therefore has little impact on the risk-adjusted performance.

TABLE 14.14 Performance with Quarterly Rebalancing, March 1993 to February 2020

	Original SPiDER			SPiDER w. Quarterly OAS Update			SPiDER w. Quarterly Financial Statement and OAS Update		
	Avg. Ex. Ret. (%/Yr)	Vol. (%/Yr)	Inf. Ratio (Ann.)	Avg. Ex. Ret. (%/Yr)	Vol. (%/Yr)	Inf. Ratio (Ann.)	Avg. Ex. Ret. (%/Yr)	Vol. (%/Yr)	Inf. Ratio (Ann.)
IG Q1	0.22	3.56	0.06	0.15	3.37	0.04	0.11	3.33	0.03
Q2	0.60	3.38	0.17	0.44	3.50	0.13	0.40	3.48	0.12
Q3	0.68	3.31	0.19	0.61	3.64	0.17	0.62	3.58	0.17
Q4	1.03	3.29	0.26	0.96	3.92	0.25	0.98	3.90	0.25
Q5	1.83	3.07	0.47	1.95	4.01	0.49	2.01	3.94	0.51
Q5–Q1	1.61	1.14	1.17	1.80	1.46	1.24	1.89	1.43	1.33
Benchmark	0.63	4.08	0.16						
HY Q1	1.02	7.38	0.14	1.13	6.95	0.16	0.97	7.22	0.13
Q2	2.10	7.08	0.31	2.36	6.99	0.34	2.24	6.95	0.32
Q3	1.97	6.85	0.29	2.14	6.85	0.31	2.43	7.00	0.35
Q4	2.42	6.94	0.32	2.41	7.58	0.32	2.83	7.47	0.38
Q5	3.64	6.44	0.47	4.11	8.08	0.51	3.86	8.12	0.48
Q5–Q1	2.62	3.02	0.73	2.99	3.67	0.81	2.90	3.79	0.76
Benchmark	2.21	8.34	0.27						

Note: The benchmarks for the investment-grade and high-yield universes are the corresponding Bloomberg Barclays US credit index without financials. The benchmark for the high-yield universe further excludes bonds that are rated below B.
Source: Bloomberg Barclays Indices, Compustat, Barclays Research

Portfolio Turnover and Transaction Cost

Compared to other anomalies in the equity market, the value phenomenon is usually associated with low turnovers. For example, Frazzini, Israel, and Moskowitz (2012) find that value has a turnover similar to the size anomaly but much lower than that of momentum and short-term reversals.[11] In this section, we examine the turnover of the SPiDER strategy in credit markets. Given the higher transaction costs of corporate bonds, the turnover analysis is especially relevant for the profitability of actual bond portfolios. We first examine turnover from the perspective of signal persistence and the impact of rebalancing frequencies. We then report the net performance after transaction cost.

Table 14.16 reports the percentage of issuers that are ranked as one of the five quintiles or out of the universe in next rebalancing dates by their current quintile rankings. Given that the signal life is roughly eight quarters, we consider two rebalancing horizons, one and two years. The SPiDER rankings exhibit strong persistence, especially for issuers in Q1 and Q5. In the IG universe, more than half of the issuers in Q1 and Q5 maintain their rankings one year later. The percentage decreases two years later but is still above 40%. Results are similar in high yield. One thing worth noting is that although issuers' departures from the universe matter to turnover, most of these departures have nothing to do with the use of the SPiDER strategy. For example, issuers that exit the index because of changes in ratings and maturities would exit the universe anyway, regardless of the underlying strategy.

Figure 14.9 reports the annual portfolio turnovers under the two rebalancing frequencies by year. As discussed before, the biannually rebalanced portfolio is comprised of two equal subportfolios that correspond to the SPiDER portfolios formed in the current year and one year ago. Therefore, roughly half of the portfolio is rebalanced each February. The annual turnover in the biannually rebalanced portfolio is about one third less than that of the annually rebalanced portfolio in both IG and HY. On average, the annual turnover with a 12-month rebalancing is about 43% in IG, compared to 28% with a 24-month rebalancing. In HY, the numbers are 55% vs. 35%, respectively. The biannual rebalanced portfolio also has a lower time-series standard deviation in annual turnovers in both IG and HY, exhibiting less variation in turnover over time.

To examine the effect of turnover and transaction costs, we assume that the average cost of trading the long-only SPiDER portfolio is approximately the average annual turnover multiplied by the average Liquidity Cost Score (LCS) of the issuers in Q5. LCS is a bond-level metric that measures the cost of an immediate, institutional-size, round-trip transaction and is expressed

TABLE 14.15 Performance with Biannual Rebalancing, March 1993 to February 2020

| | Investment Grade | | | | | | | High Yield (Ba & B and Price>=50) | | | | | | |
| | 12m (Original) | | | 24m Rebalancing | | | | 12m (Original) | | | 24m Rebalancing | | | |
	L-S	L	S	L-S	L	S	Bench-mark	L-S	L	S	L-S	L	S	Bench-mark
Avg. Excess Ret. (%/yr)	1.61	1.83	0.22	1.29	1.69	0.40	0.63	2.62	3.64	1.02	2.38	3.97	1.59	2.21
Volatility (%/yr)	1.38	3.91	3.56	1.17	3.91	3.63	4.08	3.60	7.68	7.38	3.13	7.59	7.38	8.34
Inf. Ratio	1.17	0.47	0.06	1.10	0.43	0.11	0.16	0.73	0.47	0.14	0.76	0.52	0.22	0.27
Min. Monthly Ret. (%)	-1.76	-8.71	-8.96	-1.35	-9.28	-8.75	-9.04	-4.37	-15.08	-15.91	-3.23	-14.86	-15.94	-15.26
Max. DD (%)	-4.68	-23.03	-25.89	-4.08	-23.21	-24.40	-23.23	-9.50	-33.54	-40.08	-6.70	-34.06	-38.01	-39.43
Corr. w. Benchmark	0.10	0.93	0.98	0.09	0.94	0.98		-0.08	0.87	0.95	-0.10	0.89	0.95	

Note: The benchmarks for the investment-grade and high-yield universes are the corresponding Bloomberg Barclays US credit index without financials. The benchmark for the high-yield universe further excludes bonds that are rated below B. Results for the 24-month rebalancing are based on returns of two portfolios rebalanced either in even or odd years (i.e., every 24 months).
Source: Bloomberg Barclays Indices, Compustat, Barclays Research

TABLE 14.16 Transition Matrix of SPiDER Quintile Rankings Between Year t and Year t+i, February 1993 to February 2018

%		Year t+1 Ranking						Year t+2 Ranking					
Year t Ranking		Q1	Q2	Q3	Q4	Q5	Exit Universe	Q1	Q2	Q3	Q4	Q5	Exit Universe
IG	Q1	63	23	5	2	0	8	49	24	9	3	1	13
	Q2	15	43	27	7	2	7	17	32	23	11	4	13
	Q3	5	20	35	26	6	8	8	19	27	22	9	15
	Q4	3	7	19	38	22	12	4	9	17	29	22	19
	Q5	2	2	5	18	56	17	2	4	8	17	42	27
HY	Q1	53	20	5	2	0	20	37	19	8	3	1	32
	Q2	15	36	22	7	1	18	14	24	17	8	2	35
	Q3	5	18	31	22	6	19	6	15	20	19	7	33
	Q4	2	6	18	34	20	21	3	7	14	23	18	35
	Q5	1	3	6	17	48	25	1	4	7	15	34	40

Note: The number in row Q-k (row number is under "Year t Ranking") and column Q-j (column number is under "Year t+i Ranking", i=1 or 2) represents the percentage of issuers that were in SPiDER quintile k (row) at year t being ranked in SPiDER quintile j (column) in year t+i or leaving the universe.

Source: Bloomberg Barclays Indices, Compustat, Barclays Research

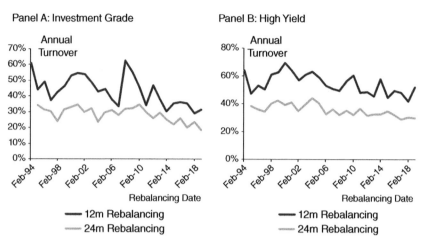

FIGURE 14.9   Annual Portfolio Turnover of the Long-Only Portfolio (Q5) with Annual and Biannual Rebalancing
Source: Bloomberg Barclays Indices, Compustat, Barclays Research

as a percentage of the corporate bond's price. (For more details, see Konstantinovsky, Ng, and Phelps 2016.) Note that a cost estimate based on LCS is conservative because these scores are quotes from Barclays traders, and investors can get a price at least as good as that when they can shop around.

Table 14.17 presents the costs of trading the SPiDER portfolios. The original, 12-month rebalancing, long-only portfolio still outperforms the benchmark in the IG universe after transaction costs. The portfolio's net of cost information ratio relative to its benchmark is 0.33. In addition, when a 24-month rebalancing is used, the net-of-cost performance further improves. The long-only portfolio has an information ratio of 0.37 relative to the benchmark after transaction costs. Note that outperformances are underestimated, as we assume investing in the benchmark is costless.

In the HY universe, the long-only SPiDER portfolio with 12-month rebalancing no longer outperforms the benchmark if transaction costs are considered. However, as discussed before, it is not really a fair comparison because the benchmark is assumed to be costless to invest. Nevertheless, when a 24-month rebalancing is used, the long-only SPiDER portfolio is able to outperform the benchmark net of the cost.

TABLE 14.17 Performances, Transaction Costs, and Tracking Errors of Top-Quintile Portfolios, March 2007–February 2020

	Investment Grade					High Yield				
	12m Reb. Q5 (Original)	24m Reb. Q5	Benchmark	12m Q5 over Benchmark	24m Q5 over Benchmark	12m Reb. Q5 (Original)	24m Reb. Q5	Benchmark	12m Q5 over Benchmark	24m Q5 over Benchmark
Gross Ex. Ret. (%/yr)	2.11	1.96	1.05	1.06	0.91	3.46	3.88	2.82	0.64	1.06
Volatility (%/yr)	5.18	5.22	5.29	1.77	1.63	9.02	8.92	9.47	3.99	3.61
Inf. Ratio	0.41	0.38	0.20	0.60	0.56	0.38	0.44	0.30	0.16	0.29
Average LCS (%)	1.21	1.20	0.86			1.84	1.82	1.37		
Turnover (%/yr)	40%	26%				50%	32%			
Transaction Cost (%)	0.48	0.31				0.93	0.59			
Net Ex. Ret. (%/yr)	1.63	1.65		0.58	0.59	2.53	3.29		-0.29	0.48
Net Inf. Ratio	0.31	0.32		0.33	0.37	0.28	0.37		-0.07	0.13

Note: The sample starts from 2007 because LCS becomes available only after 2007. The benchmarks for the investment-grade and high-yield universes are the corresponding Bloomberg Barclays US credit index without financials. The benchmark for the high-yield universe further excludes bonds that are rated below B. When rebalancing every 24 months, there are two portfolio returns: one rebalanced in odd years and one rebalanced in even years. The overall portfolio initially assigns 50% to each track and each year rebalances the corresponding odd- or even-year track while keeping the other track untouched. Transaction cost is estimated as the average annual turnover times the average LCS of the top-quintile portfolio (Q5).

Source: Bloomberg, Compustat, Barclays Research

Overall, we find that after transaction costs, the 24-month rebalancing window earns higher returns and better risk-adjusted performance than the 12-month rebalancing window. The 24-month rebalancing window outperforms the benchmark even under very conservative assumptions of transaction costs in both IG and HY.

Tracking Index Portfolios Based on SPiDER

The results discussed so far assume that the long portfolios hold all index bonds from issuers in the top quintile with equal weighting. However, in reality, a lot of investors are benchmarked to the index, and holding only the top-quintile portfolio could produce a very large tracking error from the index, due either to constituent difference or to weights and characteristics mismatch. In this section, we consider a realistic portfolio with a SPiDER tilt that is constructed to have small tracking errors from the indices. Specifically, we show how SPiDER improves the performance of a tracking portfolio that replicates index benchmarks with only a small set of liquid bonds. The benchmarks are Bloomberg Barclays US Corporate and High Yield indices excluding financials. For the high yield, the benchmark further excludes bonds that are rated below B.

Next we provide details on how we build the tracking portfolio. The portfolio is constructed on an annual basis with two steps. In the first step, we form a universe of liquid bonds as candidates for index tracking. The tracking universe starts with bonds that satisfy the following set of eligibility criteria:

- Senior bonds;
- Time to maturity is more than three years;
- Notional is greater than the 25th-percentile of the notional amounts of all bonds in the corresponding Bloomberg Barclays US index.

After that, if an issuer has multiple eligible bonds, we select one bond to represent the issuer and remove the others based on the following rule: If an issuer has any eligible bonds with ages less than two years, we remove the bonds with ages more than two years. If there are still multiple eligible bonds for the issuer, we select the one with duration closest to the industry average. As a result, the final tracking universe consists at most of one bond per issuer in the index representing only liquid names.

In the second step, we build bond portfolios to track the benchmarks, using bonds from the tracking universe. We constrain the tracking portfolio to match the risk profiles of the benchmark while tilting the portfolio toward issuers with higher SPiDER values by maximizing a portfolio's weighted average of SPiDER. In particular, we implement the following constraints on the tracking portfolios. First, we cap the weight on each bond in the portfolio at 1% (or 2% if there are not enough bonds from the tracking universe) to ensure that the tracking portfolios are not too concentrated and that idiosyncratic risks are minimized. Second, to match the risk profile of the benchmark and eliminate unintended risk exposures, we require the tracking portfolio to have the same characteristics as the benchmark across the following dimensions of risks: sector weights and index-DTS exposures. Such matching is implemented on an annual basis.

Table 14.18 shows the characteristics of the tracking portfolio, tracking universe, and benchmark. First, as reported in the table, the number of bonds in the tracking portfolio is about 100. The number of bonds in HY is smaller than 100 because there are months when the cap weight is relaxed to 2% to account for the limited names in the universe. Second, the performance of the tracking universe is similar to that of the index, assuring that any performance difference between the tracking portfolio and the index is unlikely to be driven by the universe difference. Third, the monthly average OAS and DTS of the tracking portfolio are very similar to those of the index, but they are not exactly the same. This is due to the risk matching being done annually rather than monthly.

Table 14.19 reports the performance of the tracking portfolios. Apart from the portfolio construction specifications we discussed earlier, we also consider several other portfolio construction specifications. One is to impose an additional restriction to further match index OAS. The other is to relax the cap on the weight of each bond from 1% to 2%. First, as shown in Table 14.19, tracking portfolios with a SPiDER tilt are able to outperform the benchmark regardless of the specification. Second, when a portfolio's OAS is matched to the benchmark in addition to the other risk characteristics, the tracking error is reduced, as the tracking portfolio becomes more similar to the benchmark. The return performance is also reduced in investment grade, whereas it does not change much in high yield. Third, having a more concentrated portfolio (2% cap) increases the tracking error, but returns also generally go up. As a result, the direction of change in the information ratio of the tracking portfolio over the benchmark is less clear. The information ratio increases for all the specifications except in the high-yield universe when both DTS and OAS are matched.

TABLE 14.18 Characteristics of Bonds in the Benchmark, Tracking Universe, and Tracking Portfolio, March 1993 to February 2020

| | | | | | | | Avg. Bond | | Excess Returns | | |
	Avg. # Bonds/m	Quality	OAS (bps)	Duration (yr)	DTS	LCS	MV ($MM)	Turnover	Avg. Ret. (%/Yr)	Vol. (%/Yr)	Inf. Ratio
IG Benchmark	2527	8.19	136	6.96	10.18	0.87	535		0.63	4.08	0.16
Tracking Universe	487	8.34	142	6.98	10.06	0.87	581		0.67	4.10	0.16
Tracking Portfolio	104	7.80	137	7.08	9.89	1.00	565	40%			
HY Benchmark	1152	14.63	422	4.47	18.70	1.38	410		2.21	8.34	0.27
Tracking Universe	470	14.93	435	4.48	19.43	1.43	431		2.02	8.54	0.24
Tracking Portfolio	92	14.36	426	4.15	17.71	1.55	411	49%			

Note: The benchmarks for the investment-grade and high-yield universes are the corresponding Bloomberg Barclays US credit index excluding financials, respectively. The high-yield universe benchmark further excludes bonds that are rated below B. The tracking portfolio has a tilt on SPiDER while matching index DTS, OAS, and industry weights and subject to bond weights no more than 1% (or 2% if there are not enough bonds). The numeric values of quality ratings are converted by the following scale: AAA=1, AA=2, A=3, BAA=4, BA=5, B=6, CAA=7, C/CA=8, and D=9. The reported LCS numbers use only the sample starting from 2007 because that is when LCS becomes available. Quality, OAS, Spread Duration, DTS, and LCS are all first aggregated by the market value weight across issuers on a monthly basis. The reported value is the average of the monthly time series.

Source: Bloomberg, Compustat, Barclays Research

TABLE 14.19 Performance Summary Statistics of the Index-Tracking Portfolios with SPiDER Tilt, March 1993 to February 2020

Constraints	Matched Benchmark DTS + Sector Weight		Matched Benchmark DTS + OAS + Sector Weight	
Issuer Cap	Tracking Portfolio (Max-SPiDER)	Max-SPiDER over Benchmark	Tracking Portfolio (Max-SPiDER)	Max-SPiDER over Benchmark
Panel A: Corporate Index				
1% Avg. Ex. Ret. (%/Yr)	1.25	0.62	0.83	0.20
Vol. (%/Yr)	3.77	1.21	3.66	1.02
Inf. Ratios (ann.)	0.33	0.51	0.23	0.19
Worst Return (%/mo.)	-9.54	-1.78	-9.02	-1.29
Corr. w. Index	0.96	-0.39	0.97	-0.51
2% Avg. Ex. Ret. (%/Yr)	1.52	0.89	0.99	0.35
Vol. (%/Yr)	3.82	1.44	3.76	1.12
Inf. Ratios (ann.)	0.40	0.62	0.26	0.32
Worst Return (%/mo.)	-9.17	-2.78	-9.34	-1.66
Corr. w. Index	0.94	-0.35	0.96	-0.41

(Continued)

TABLE 14.19 (Continued)

Constraints	Matched Benchmark DTS + Sector Weight		Matched Benchmark DTS + OAS + Sector Weight	
Issuer Cap	Tracking Portfolio (Max-SPiDER)	Max-SPiDER over Benchmark	Tracking Portfolio (Max-SPiDER)	Max-SPiDER over Benchmark
Panel B: High-Yield Index				
1% Avg. Ex. Ret. (%/Yr)	2.41	0.20	2.51	0.30
Vol. (%/Yr)	7.69	2.40	7.62	2.38
Inf. Ratios (ann.)	0.31	0.08	0.33	0.13
Worst Return (%/mo.)	−17.84	−5.66	−17.69	−5.77
Corr. w. Index	0.96	−0.40	0.96	−0.43
2% Avg. Ex. Ret. (%/Yr)	2.59	0.38	2.39	0.18
Vol. (%/Yr)	7.59	2.80	7.62	2.71
Inf. Ratios (ann.)	0.34	0.14	0.31	0.07
Worst Return (%/mo.)	−17.35	−5.41	−17.53	−5.45
Corr. w. Index	0.94	−0.42	0.95	−0.42

Note: The rebalancing of the tracking portfolios is done at the end of each February from 1993 to 2019.
Source: Bloomberg Barclays Indices, Compustat, Barclays Research

The outperformance of the tracking portfolio also confirms what we observed earlier, for example, in Table 14.8 and Figure 14.7. It shows that the strategy performance of SPiDER cannot be fully explained by DTS exposures or carry given the tracking portfolio matches the benchmark on the two dimensions.

CONCLUSION

We use a new value measure, termed SPiDER (spread *per* un*i*t of *d*ebt-to-*e*arnings *r*atio) to distinguish over- and under-valued corporate bonds. SPiDER measures the compensation demanded by the market per unit of fundamental risk, which is measured by the firm's debt level relative to its long-term earnings. It is simple, intuitive, and model-free. We find that non-financial issuers with high SPiDER values (wide spread per unit of debt to earnings) have consistently outperformed similar issuers with low values in both IG and HY. The strategy performance is consistent with mispricing rather than risk compensation or carry. It holds across industries and rating buckets and is robust to different SPiDER formulations.

More important, we find that investors are able to benefit from the measure in practice. The strategy performance still exists after incorporating various practical constraints and transaction costs. As an example of application, we show that index-tracking portfolios with tilts toward high SPiDER issuers are able to outperform the respective benchmark in both IG and HY.

REFERENCES

Asness, C., T. Moskowitz, and L. H. Pedersen. 2013. "Value and Momentum Everywhere." *Journal of Finance* 68(3): 929–985.

Ben Dor, A., L. Dynkin, J. Hyman, P. Houweling, E. Van Leeuwen, and O. Penninga. 2007. "DTS[SM] (Duration Times Spread)." *Journal of Portfolio Management* 33(2): 77–100.

Ben Dor, A., and J. Guan. 2017, January 25. "Value Investing in Credit using SPiDER (Spread per unit of Debt to Earnings Ratio)—An Update." Barclays Research.

Ben Dor, A., J. Guan, and S. Polbennikov. 2020, January 23. "Sector Timing in Credit Using Value and Momentum Signals." Barclays Research.

Bunn, O. D., and R. J. Shiller. 2014. "Changing Times, Changing Values: A Historical Analysis of Sectors within the US Stock Market 1872–2013." NBER Working paper.

Campbell, J. Y., and R. J. Shiller. 1988. "Stock Prices, Earnings, and Expected Dividends." *Journal of Finance* 43(3): 661–676.

Chan, L. K. C., and J. Lakonishok. 2004. "Value and Growth Investing: Review and Update." *Financial Analysts Journal* 60(1): 71–86.

Correia, M. M., S. A. Richardson, and A. I. Tuna. 2012. "Value Investing in Credit Markets." *Review of Accounting Studies* 17(3): 572–609.

Dastidar, S. G., and B. D. Phelps. 2011. "Credit Spread Decomposition: Decomposing Bond-Level Credit OAS into Default and Liquidity Components." *Journal of Portfolio Management* 37(3): 70–84.

Fama, E. F., and K. French. 1998. "Value versus Growth: The International Evidence." *Journal of Finance* 53(6): 1975–1999.

Frazzini, A., R. Israel, and T. J. Moskowitz. 2012. "Trading Costs of Asset Pricing Anomalies." SSRN Working paper.

Graham, B., and D. Dodd. 1934. *Security Analysis*. New York: McGraw-Hill.

Houweling, P., and J. Zundert. 2017. "Factor Investing in the Corporate Bond Market." *Financial Analysts Journal* 73(2): 1–16.

Israel, R., D. Palhares, and S. Richardson. 2018. "Common Factors in Corporate Bond Returns." *Journal of Investment Management* 16(2): 17–46.

Jegadeesh, N., and S. Titman. 1993. "Returns to Buying Winners and Selling Losers: Implications for Stock Market Efficiency." *Journal of Finance* 48(1): 65–91.

Konstantinovsky, V., K. Y. Ng, and B. D. Phelps. 2016. "Measuring Bond-Level Liquidity." *Journal of Portfolio Management* 42(4): 116–128.

NOTES

1. Other studies that have looked at the value phenomenon in credit markets include Correia, Richardson, and Tuna (2012), Houweling and van Zundert (2017), and Israel, Palhares, and Richardson (2018).
2. For example, common input parameters include recovery rates, market risk premium, and market risk sensitivity.
3. We follow Compustat's convention on whether the source of fundamental data is domestic or international. "Domestic" financial statements are statements from US or Canadian companies or companies with American depositary receipts.
4. The annual earnings is the sum of the four quarterly earnings and the debt is from the most recent quarterly statement.
5. The sample stops at 2017 because one of the evaluation windows we use is 36 months.
6. $I(\text{industry} = j)$ equals 1 if issuer is from industry j and 0 otherwise. The industries are level 3 fixed income sectors.
7. As a comparison, in equity markets, this adjustment would be equivalent to scaling down the equity returns of a portfolio by its beta relative to the beta of a benchmark to adjust for the market systematic risks.
8. Each year issuers were sorted into four buckets within industry based on their OAS. Then we ranked issuers within each industry-OAS bucket into top and bottom buckets based on their SPiDER. The OAS-neutral SPiDER strategy then longs the top SPiDER bucket and shorts the bottom SPiDER bucket in each industry-OAS bucket.

9. The information ratio of the OAS-neutral SPiDER is lower than that of the original SPiDER strategy. However, the difference in the performance is not entirely due to the removal of the carry component. Note that the OAS-neutral SPiDER strategy buys the top half and shorts the bottom half of issuers in the universe. As a result, the signal efficacy is much more diluted compared to the original SPiDER strategy, which longs the top quintile and shorts the bottom quintile. We divide issuers into top and bottom halves in the OAS-neutral SPiDER strategy because there are fewer issuers in each bucket when the ranking is done within each OAS and industry bucket, and we would like to keep the portfolios diversified.

10. Regardless of the rebalancing frequency, we leave at least a two-month lag between the financial statement fiscal year-/quarter-end and the portfolio formation to make sure that the financial statement data would have been available in real time at the portfolio formation date.

11. Though the turnover of value is similar to that of size, its capacity is much higher, making value one of the most scalable anomalies in the equity market.

Momentum Investing

CHAPTER 15

Equity Momentum in Credit

INTRODUCTION

Cross-asset momentum, particularly between equity and credit markets, has received special attention given the fact that bonds and stocks constitute the building blocks of a firm's capital structure and form the core of most investor portfolios.

Stock price returns and subsequent excess returns of corporate bonds tend to be positively related. To illustrate this, we sort constituents of the Bloomberg Barclays US Corporate Bond Index by equity price momentum[1] over three months and report subsequent bond performance of top and bottom quintiles (20%). Figure 15.1 shows a strong and persistent outperformance of the top quintile portfolio over the index and the bottom quintile portfolio.

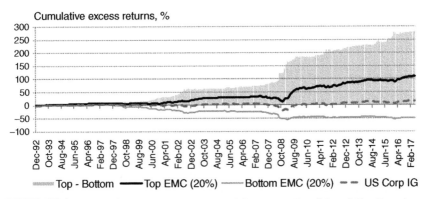

FIGURE 15.1 Cumulative Excess Returns of Corporate Bond Portfolios Based on Issuer's Three-Month Equity Price Momentum, December 1992 to May 2017 (%)
Source: Bloomberg, Barclays Research

Equity momentum in credit (EMC) is closely related to the momentum strategy in stocks where stocks with high past returns tend to continue to outperform, an empirical fact well known to investors. Indeed, numerous studies show that the momentum strategy of buying past winners and selling past losers has proved effective in the US stock market,[2] stock markets in other developed countries, and also in emerging markets. More recently, Asness, Moskowitz, and Pedersen (2013) established that the momentum strategy (along with value) has also worked well in many other asset classes, including currencies, government bonds, and commodities.

In stock markets, the main reasons that momentum exists are believed to be behavioral in nature, such as herding, over- and under-reaction, and confirmation biases; the most prominent interpretation is that stocks tend to underreact to new information.

EMC, however, might have different reasons to exist. For example, Lin, Wang, and Wu (2013) attribute a large part of the phenomenon to liquidity risk.

In contrast, according to a poll of large institutional bond managers conducted by Barclays QPS Research in the summer 2017,[3] EMC is seen as predominantly associated with the segregation of equity and bond markets as well as with the fact that stocks tend to be more sensitive to new information flows than bonds. Figure 15.2 summarizes the poll results.

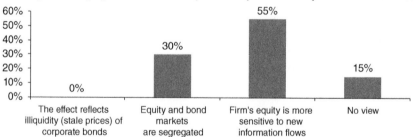

FIGURE 15.2   Results of the Survey Among US Institutional Bond Managers, QPS American Advisory Council, 25 June 2017
Source: Barclays Research

In this chapter, we document the relationship between stock price momentum and subsequent excess returns of corporate bonds of the same issuer. We consider the EMC strategy that buys corporate bonds of issuers with strong momentum and sells bonds with weak or negative momentum. We study the performance of the EMC strategy in different parts of the US corporate bond universe (by sector, quality, and liquidity) and analyze its characteristics in different macro regimes. We also discuss robustness, selection risk, signal decay over time, and portfolio turnover.

A number of studies have also looked at the relationship between equity momentum and subsequent returns of corporate bonds. Naik, Trinh, and Rennison (2002) showed that equity returns tend to predict subsequent returns of corporate bonds, especially in lower-quality sectors.[4] More recently, Haesen, Houweling, and Van Zundert (2017) suggested using firm-specific stock returns to improve risk properties of momentum-based bond portfolios.

EQUITY MOMENTUM IN CREDIT

We analyze the phenomenon of EMC using Bloomberg Barclays US corporate bond data. Our universe consists of all bonds included in Bloomberg Barclays US Corporate Investment Grade (IG) and High Yield (HY) indices in the period between December 1992 and May 2017. The sample contains monthly bond excess returns over duration-matched treasuries[5] as well as bond analytics, such as spreads and durations.

In order to measure equity price momentum of individual issuers, we assemble a historical mapping between corporate bonds and respective stocks.[6] Issuers with missing equity data are excluded from the sample.[7]

We measure equity momentum as equity price return in a formation period. Let us consider a signal formation period of three months as an illustration. At the beginning of each month, corporate bonds are sorted into decile portfolios based on three-month equity momentum. We then report subsequent returns of the resulting portfolios. Figure 15.3 shows average returns and volatilities of all decile portfolios and provides evidence

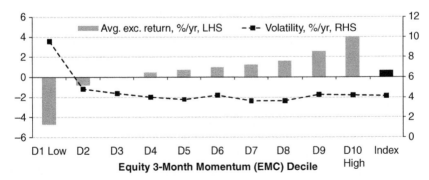

FIGURE 15.3 Average Excess Returns and Volatilities of Corporate Bonds by Equity Momentum Deciles, January 1993 to May 2017
Source: Bloomberg, Barclays Research

of a strong positive relationship between equity momentum and subsequent returns of corporate bonds: Average portfolio returns increase monotonically as equity momentum strengthens.[8]

The bottom decile portfolio (D1) contains bonds with the weakest or most negative equity momentum. It delivered negative average excess return of –4.7% per year between 1993 and 2017. In contrast, the average excess return of the top decile portfolio (D10), with the strongest equity momentum, was +4.01% per year. These numbers are highly economically significant, as the average excess return of the Bloomberg Barclays US Corporate IG index was only 0.67% per year in the same period. Interestingly, return volatilities, also reported on Figure 15.3, seem to be relatively stable across decile portfolios, excluding the bottom one (D1). The volatility of the bottom portfolio is almost twice as high as that of the other portfolios, which indicates higher risk for issuers with strong negative equity momentum.

The three-month signal formation period used to measure equity momentum in Figure 15.3 was chosen arbitrarily. In Appendix 15.1, we try different horizons (one, three, and six months) for signal formation and show that equity momentum appears to retain the predictive power for bond returns irrespective of the chosen horizon. Therefore, in the subsequent analysis, we use a momentum signal constructed as an equally weighted combination of stock returns over most recent one, three, and six months, rescaled for different lengths of the respective formation periods.[9] The benefits of this approach are twofold. First, equity momentum signals measured at different horizons might not be perfectly correlated, so that a diversified signal might be cleaner and have a stronger predictive power for bond returns. Second, combining momentum signals at different horizons helps to validate (confirm) trends in stock prices. Indeed, a stock with continuing upward price trend over the previous six months has a stronger combined signal than a stock with positive price return over the past month only. Using multiple horizons in signal formation helps distinguish between issuers with trending and fluctuating stock prices. Table 15.12 in Appendix 15.1 compares the performance of corporate bond portfolios sorted on equity momentum measured over one, three, and six months as well as on the combined momentum signal.

The predictive relationship between equity returns and excess returns of corporate bonds may be formally evaluated by looking at the performance of a long-short portfolio that buys bonds with strong equity momentum and sells bonds with negative equity momentum. For the purpose of this exercise, we build diversified quintile portfolios sorted by equity momentum and define the equity momentum strategy in credit (EMC strategy) as running a long position in the top-quintile portfolio (Q5) against a short position in the bottom-quintile portfolios (Q1). Table 15.1 reports the performance of the EMC strategy in different periods and compares the top-quintile portfolio (Q5) with the bottom-quintile portfolio (Q1) and the Bloomberg Barclays US Corporate Index. The EMC strategy performed well in both subperiods (1993–2007 and 2007–2017), delivering average return of 6.34% per year with an information ratio of 1.56 in the overall sample. These statistics validate a persistently positive relationship between equity momentum and subsequent bond returns.[10]

TABLE 15.1 EMC Strategy Performance in Different Periods

	US Corp IG Index	Q1 (Bottom)	Q5 (Top)	EMC Strategy: Q5–Q1	Q5–Index
	January 1993–May 2017			January 1993–May 2017	
Avg. Exc. Return, %/yr	0.67	−2.83	3.5	6.34	2.84
Volatility, %/yr	4.15	6.54	4.54	4.07	1.74
Information Ratio	0.16	−0.43	0.77	1.56	1.63
	January 1993–June 2007			January 1993–June 2007	
Avg. Exc. Return, %/yr	0.41	−1.5	2.53	4.03	2.11
Volatility, %/yr	2.09	3.28	2.25	2.34	1.2
Information Ratio	0.2	−0.46	1.12	1.72	1.77
	July 2007–May 2017			July 2007–May 2017	
Avg. Exc. Return, %/yr	1.04	−4.78	4.93	9.71	3.89
Volatility, %/yr	6.01	9.47	6.58	5.59	2.28
Information Ratio	0.17	−0.51	0.75	1.74	1.71

Source: Bloomberg, Barclays Research

Next, we analyze the performance of the EMC strategy by credit quality. We split the US investment-grade bond universe into bonds rated A3 or higher (Aaa–A) and bonds rated Baa. We also report the EMC strategy performance in the high-yield market.

Table 15.2 shows that, irrespective of credit quality, bond excess returns tend to increase with equity momentum. The effect seems to be stronger, however, for lower-quality names. Indeed, the average return of the EMC strategy for bonds rated A3 and higher is 3.9% per year with an information ratio of 0.83. In comparison, average returns of the EMC strategy among Baa-rated and HY bonds in the same period were 8.8% per year and 19.9% per year with information ratios of 1.87 and 1.74, respectively. The corresponding average returns of top-quintile portfolios (Q5) by equity momentum across the three quality buckets were 2.02% per year, 4.74% per year, and 10.38% per year, respectively. Equity momentum appears to be a highly informative signal for lower quality names.

TABLE 15.2   EMC Strategy Performance by Credit Quality, January 1993 to May 2017

Rating Buckets	Q1 (Bottom)	Q2	Q3	Q4	Q5 (Top)	EMC Strat.
Annualized Avg. Excess Return, %/yr						
Aaa–A	–1.88	0.08	0.86	1.25	2.02	3.9
Baa	–4.11	0.09	1.42	2.36	4.74	8.8
HY	–5.5	2.57	3.66	5.52	10.38	15.9
Annualized Volatility, %/yr				'		
Aaa–A	7.26	3.86	3.25	3.56	4.57	4.72
Baa	6.94	5.1	4.92	4.93	5.35	4.72
HY	12.95	8.31	7.83	7.8	9.47	9.11
Information Ratio						
Aaa–A	–0.26	0.02	0.26	0.35	0.44	0.83
Baa	–0.59	0.02	0.29	0.48	0.89	1.87
HY	–0.42	0.31	0.47	0.71	1.1	1.74

Source: Barclays Research

CHARACTERISTICS OF THE EMC STRATEGY

Equity momentum signals tend to vary significantly over time and deteriorate quickly, so investors face the practical choice of holding bonds with weakened equity momentum and poorer performance prospects or incurring transaction costs that could significantly reduce returns. Investment horizons along with turnover and transaction costs all need to be considered to assess the practical value of the EMC strategy to portfolio managers.

Table 15.3 reports average transition probabilities of issuer equity momentum ranks over three-month horizons between 1993 and 2017.

TABLE 15.3 Average Three-Month Equity Momentum Rank Transition Frequencies, December 1992 to May 2017

	Equity Momentum Deciles—End of Period									
	D1 Low	D2	D3	D4	D5	D6	D7	D8	D9	D10 High
D1 Low	16%	15%	13%	10%	11%	9%	8%	7%	6%	6%
D2	9%	15%	13%	13%	12%	11%	10%	7%	6%	4%
D3	7%	12%	13%	13%	13%	13%	11%	8%	7%	3%
D4	6%	12%	13%	13%	13%	12%	12%	9%	7%	3%
D5	4%	10%	12%	13%	13%	13%	12%	11%	8%	4%
D6	4%	10%	12%	12%	13%	13%	12%	11%	9%	4%
D7	4%	8%	11%	12%	12%	13%	13%	11%	11%	5%
D8	4%	8%	10%	11%	11%	13%	13%	12%	11%	6%
D9	3%	6%	9%	9%	11%	12%	12%	14%	13%	9%
D10 High	4%	5%	7%	8%	8%	9%	11%	14%	16%	17%

Equity Momentum Deciles—Beginning of Period

Source: Barclays Research

These transition probabilities are high. For example, an issuer with equity momentum in the top 10% (D10) has only a 17% probability of remaining top ranked after three months and an 83% probability of transiting into a lower decile.

Panel A of Figure 15.4 shows the average number of above-median momentum issuers as a function of holding period. The number of issuers that remain above median drops by 31% in the first month after momentum signal formation. After six months, 52% of issuers drop out. Both Table 15.3 and Figure 15.4 indicate that equity momentum-based corporate bond portfolios could experience relatively high turnover.

PANEL A
Number of issuers with above-median
equity momentum, July 2007 – May 2017

PANEL B
Average outperformance of High
(above median) vs. Low (below median)
EMC portfolios after inception,
July 2007 – May 2017

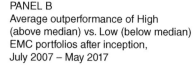

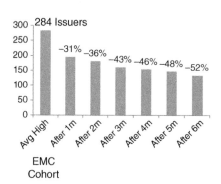

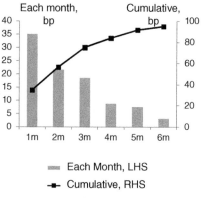

FIGURE 15.4   Turnover and Returns of EMC Portfolios as a Function of Time Since Inception
Source: Barclays Research

While equity momentum seems to be a relatively volatile signal, Panel B of Figure 15.4 shows that the high-EMC portfolio (bonds of issuers with above-median equity momentum) continued to outperform the low-EMC one (below-median equity momentum) in the six months that follow signal formation. A fixed cohort of bonds with high equity momentum outperformed a similar cohort of bonds with low equity momentum by 35bp, 22bp, and 19bp in months 1, 2, and 3 respectively. The cumulative outperformance after six months was 95bp, with the first three months accounting for nearly 80% of the outperformance.

While a quarterly rebalancing period offers a suitable trade-off between turnover and performance, there appears to be little penalty for keeping the portfolio unchanged for longer as the high-EMC portfolio continued to outperform.[11]

However, even a volatile signal could potentially be useful when a portfolio manager must deploy new cash or sell bonds. Indeed, high-EMC bonds could be selected when adding new bonds to the portfolio, while low-EMC bonds could be chosen when liquidating positions. EMC could potentially be used as a filter for issuer selection and may also be combined with other signals with a view to providing robust outperformance. In Appendix 15.2 we discuss a potential impact of turnover and transaction costs on strategy performance in more detail.

The EMC strategy performance just presented is based on very broad portfolios of several thousand bonds. Realistic portfolios are often much more concentrated and subject to selection risk. Therefore, a concentrated portfolio of bonds with strong equity momentum could potentially underperform a portfolio with negative momentum.

To assess selection risk, we plot return distributions of concentrated bond portfolios with high and low EMC. The distributions, shown in Figure 15.5, are obtained by randomly selecting 100 bonds with equity momentum rank in top 30% or bottom 30% while ensuring that portfolio

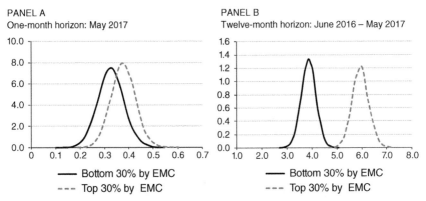

PANEL A
One-month horizon: May 2017

PANEL B
Twelve-month horizon: June 2016 – May 2017

— Bottom 30% by EMC
--- Top 30% by EMC

— Bottom 30% by EMC
--- Top 30% by EMC

FIGURE 15.5   Return Probability Distributions of 100-Bond EMC Portfolios with Randomly Selected Bonds
Source: Barclays Research

allocations remain broadly in line with that of the IG index. In particular, we match the index allocation by sector (financials, nonfinancials), rating (A3–Aaa, Baa3–Baa1), and maturity (1–5y, 5+y). The return distributions presented in Figure 15.5 use 5000 randomly resampled portfolios of 100 bonds.

Panel A of Figure 15.5 shows a very large overlap between May 2017 return distributions of high- and low-equity momentum portfolios, meaning that, in that month, there was a relatively high probability for a randomly chosen portfolio of 100 bonds with top 30% equity momentum to underperform a similarly constructed portfolio with equity momentum in the bottom 30%. Panel B of Figure 15.5 shows that over longer time horizons (one year, from June 2016 to May 2017 in this example), the probability that a high-EMC portfolio underperforms a low-EMC portfolio was very low.[12]

The EMC (Q5–Q1) strategy has delivered strong and robust performance over time. Did varying strategy credit exposure played a role? Panels A and B of Figure 15.6 plot time series of the net option-adjusted spread (OAS) of the EMC strategy together with the S&P 500 index and the average spread of the US corporate index. As Panel A of Figure 15.6 illustrates, the strategy net spread tends to decline and become negative during equity down-cycles. Panel B shows a similar pattern for credit down-cycles.

Panels A and B of Figure 15.6 suggest that credit exposure of the EMC strategy is directional on the performance of the overall equity market: The EMC strategy is long spread and therefore has a positive credit exposure in benign environments and negative exposure in market down-cycles.[13] In

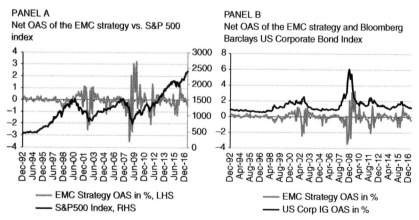

FIGURE 15.6 Historical Net OAS of the EMC Strategy (Q5–Q1), December 1992 to May 2017
Source: Bloomberg, Barclays Research

equity down markets, the "risk-off" would lead to selling of risky stocks, which creates a negative momentum for EMC. As a result, risky high-OAS bonds are likely to fall in the negative momentum quintile (Q1). In market rallies, the opposite is likely to occur with risky high-OAS bonds falling into the top equity momentum quintile (Q5).

Table 15.4 splits our sample by monthly return of S&P500 into bottom 30%, mid-40%, and top 30%, and reports characteristics of the EMC strategy: net option-adjusted spread (OAS), net option-adjusted duration (OAD), and net Duration Times Spread (DTS). The table confirms the pattern seen in Figure 15.6: The EMC strategy tends to have a negative credit exposure during a bearish market and a positive credit exposure during a bullish market. These results point to potential diversification properties of the EMC strategy with respect to equity or credit market returns.

EMC STRATEGY RETURNS IN DIFFERENT MARKET ENVIRONMENTS

We saw in the previous section that the net spread of the strategy tends to be positive when equity markets perform well and when spreads rally. Does this mean that returns of the EMC strategy are correlated with credit, treasury, and equity returns?

Table 15.5 reports correlations of the EMC strategy returns with fixed income and equity market factors. These are excess returns of the Bloomberg Barclays US Corporate IG index (US Corp), total returns of the Bloomberg Barclays US Treasury index (US Tsy), and a selection of equity risk factors that comprises Fama–French Market (EQ MKT), Size (EQ SMB), Value (EQ HML), and Momentum (EQ MOM) factors as well as a Quality Minus Junk (EQ QMJ) equity factor.[14]

EMC is negatively correlated with corporate excess returns (−43%) and with returns of the equity market (−38%). These negative correlations reflect the contra-cyclical dynamics of credit exposure highlighted in Figure 15.6 and Table 15.4. As a result, the strategy should have attractive diversification properties for credit or equity investors. Correlations of the EMC strategy with Treasury returns and equity size, value and momentum factors are also low or negative. Finally, the strategy is positively correlated with the quality minus junk (QMJ) equity factor, which also has defensive properties with respect to credit and equity allocations. EMC correlation with the equity momentum factor (EQ MOM) is positive but low and statistically insignificant, which illustrates the different nature of the two strategies. This may be because momentum is defined differently for EQ MOM and EMC[15] or because the subsequent performance of bonds is different from that of equities.

TABLE 15.4 Exposures of the EMC Strategy by Equity Market Regimes (S&P500), January 1993 to May 2017

	Bottom 30% = −4.2%			Mid 40% = 1.0%			Top 30% = 5.1%		
	Btm EMC (Q1)	Top EMC (Q5)	EMC Strategy (Q5–Q1)	Btm EMC (Q1)	Top EMC (Q5)	EMC Strategy (Q5–Q1)	Btm EMC (Q1)	Top EMC (Q5)	EMC Strategy (Q5–Q1)
OAS, %	1.95	1.64	−0.31	1.43	1.37	−0.06	1.45	1.59	0.14
OAD, yr	6.03	6.46	0.43	6.34	6.28	−0.06	6.35	6.15	−0.2
DTS, %×yr	11.47	10.53	−0.94	9.09	8.71	−0.38	9.16	9.62	0.45

Source: Barclays Research

TABLE 15.5 Correlation of EMC Returns with Equity and Fixed Income Market Factors, January 1993 to May 2017

	EMC	US Corp	EQ MKT	EQ SMB	EQ HML	EQ MOM	EQ QMJ
US Corp	−43%						
EQ MKT	−38%	55%					
EQ SMB	−8%	20%	22%				
EQ HML	−9%	−2%	−15%	−30%			
EQ MOM	9%	−33%	−27%	9%	−18%		
EQ QMJ	31%	−52%	−65%	−50%	15%	29%	
US Tsy	11%	−33%	−21%	−19%	4%	19%	20%

Source: Bloomberg, Data Library of Kenneth French, AQR Data Library, Barclays Research

The negative correlation of EMC with credit market returns implies that the strategy may do well during credit down-cycles. We verify this using the available history of corporate bond excess returns.

Figure 15.7 plots cumulative excess returns of the Bloomberg Barclays US Corporate IG index and highlights periods of significant drawdowns. Based on this chart, we identify six bearish episodes in the credit market: August 1997–October 1998 (LTCM, Asian, Russian crisis), January 2000–December 2000 (dot-com crisis), April 2002–October 2002 (telecom crisis), March 2007–November 2008 (financial crisis), May 2011–November 2011 (European sovereign crisis), August 2014–February 2016 (energy sector crisis). For each of these episodes, we report the performance of EMC alongside that of other equity market factors.

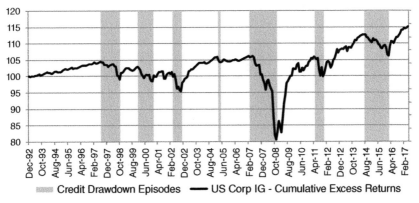

FIGURE 15.7 US Credit Drawdown Episodes, December 1992 to May 2017
Source: Bloomberg, Barclays Research

Table 15.6 shows the performance of the EMC strategy and equity factors in credit drawdown episodes. The first column defines the down-cycle periods. Cumulative excess returns of the corporate index are reported in the second column and are all significantly negative. The third column includes cumulative returns of EMC, while the rest of the table shows equity factor portfolios: market, size, value, momentum, and quality. Consistent with the correlations shown in Table 15.5, the performance of EMC during credit down-cycles is positive, highlighting its contra-cyclical nature. During the telecom, financial, and energy crises, EMC returns before transaction costs exceeded 10%.

While Table 15.6 reports only drawdown episodes, Table 15.7 includes the entire period of our analysis split into two subsets—credit down-cycles and recoveries—and shows annualized returns of EMC alongside various market indices or factors. While the corporate index has average returns of

TABLE 15.6 Returns of the EMC Strategy and Equity Factor Portfolios During Credit Down-Cycles in %, December 1992 to May 2017

Credit Down-Cycle Episodes	US Corp IG	EMC: Q5–Q1	Equity MKT	Equity SMB	Equity HML	Equity MOM	Equity QMJ
Aug 1997–Oct 1998	–5.2	6.8	6.7	–19.4	6.4	13.5	14.6
Jan 2000–Dec 2000	–4.4	6.5	–16.7	–5	38.2	16.7	23.7
Apr 2002–Oct 2002	–5.7	12.4	–22.6	–1.7	0.3	28.2	22.9
Mar 2007–Nov 2008	–24.2	35.4	–37.9	–6.3	–11.6	54.6	52.3
May 2011–Nov 2011	–5.8	7	–8.6	–5.6	–7.7	0.7	19.7
Aug 2014–Feb 2016	–5.8	16	1.2	–5.1	–12.1	21.7	36.1

Source: Bloomberg, Data Library of Kenneth French, AQR Data Library, Barclays Research

TABLE 15.7 Annualized Returns of the EMC Strategy in Credit Down-Cycles and Recoveries in %/yr, January 1993 to April 2017

	Drawdown			Recovery			Overall		
	Avg. Ret., %/yr	Volatility, %/yr	Inf. Ratio	Avg. Ret., %/yr	Volatility, %/yr	Inf. Ratio	Avg. Ret., %/yr	Volatility, %/yr	Inf. Ratio
US Corp IG	-8.07	5.15	-1.57	4.12	3.18	1.29	0.65	4.15	0.16
EMC (Q5–Q1)	11.53	5.43	2.13	4.3	3.22	1.34	6.35	4.06	1.56
EQ MKT	-12.34	18.12	-0.68	15.73	12.56	1.25	7.75	14.76	0.53
EQ SMB	-6.24	15.55	-0.4	5.14	9.11	0.56	1.9	11.37	0.17
EQ HML	1.74	12.53	0.14	3.58	9.93	0.36	3.06	10.7	0.29
EQ MOM	18.36	17.08	1.07	0.26	17.23	0.02	5.4	17.29	0.31
EQ QMJ	22.58	11.77	1.92	-1.54	8.66	-0.18	5.32	10.11	0.53

Source: Bloomberg, Data Library of Kenneth French, AQR Data Library, Barclays Research

−8.07%/yr in drawdown episodes and 4.12%/yr in recovery times, the EMC strategy performed well in both regimes: 11.53%/yr in credit drawdowns and 4.30%/yr in recoveries. No other factors had comparable performance characteristics in the two regimes.

Next we analyze the performance of the EMC strategy during Federal Reserve (Fed) monetary cycles. Monthly observations are associated with monetary tightening or monetary easing regimes. Monetary easing includes months when the federal funds target rate declined,[16] while tightening includes months when the federal fund target rate increased. Figure 15.8 highlights monetary easing and tightening episodes in our sample. In addition, we separately split each tightening or easing period into two halves: early and late tightening/easing (not shown).

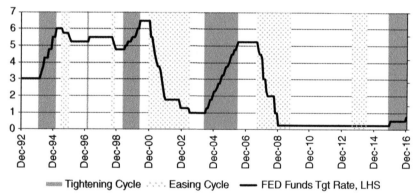

FIGURE 15.8   Federal Reserve Easing and Tightening Episodes
Source: Barclays Research

The chart in Figure 15.9 and Table 15.8 report average excess returns and information ratios of EMC in the different Fed cycles. The strategy performed best during early and late monetary easing with average excess returns over 8%/yr. In all other monetary regimes, average returns were below 5%/yr. Nevertheless, the EMC strategy also demonstrated very high risk-adjusted performance during pre-easing (information ratio of 3.7) and early tightening (information ratio of 2.4) periods, which probably reflects low dispersion and volatility of corporate excess returns in these two periods.

Table 15.8 summarizes the performance of the EMC strategy during Fed monetary cycles and contrasts it with that of the corporate index. Strategy performance is much stronger during monetary easing and weaker during monetary tightening. These results are not surprising in light of the

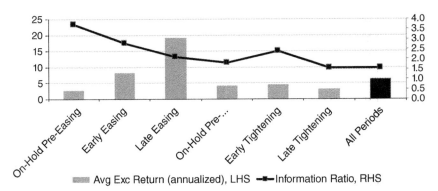

Avg Exc Return (annualized), LHS ■ Information Ratio, RHS

FIGURE 15.9 Annualized Returns of the EMC Strategy in FED Cycles, January 1993 to May 2017
Source: Barclays Research

contra-cyclicality of EMC returns documented earlier. Indeed, Fed monetary cycles are likely to coincide with economic downturns (Fed easing) and recoveries (Fed tightening).

IS EMC A LIQUIDITY PHENOMENON?

One possible explanation for the performance of EMC is that it is an artifact of the illiquidity of corporate bonds, as discussed by Lin et al. (2013). Indeed, bonds may react more slowly than stocks to news affecting a corporation. This can be due to various factors, including market structure and differences in transaction costs and liquidity. In this case, the relationship between equity momentum and subsequent returns of corporate bonds can be an illusion: Investors, trying to implement the strategy, would in reality be offered "updated" prices of corporate bonds that would adjust for recent equity returns.

This logic implies that, on paper, the EMC strategy should perform better for less liquid corporate bonds than for liquid ones. We test the liquidity explanation of EMC by first sorting corporate bonds by a liquidity measure and then by equity momentum within each liquidity category. If illiquidity plays a significant role, EMC should perform better when applied to illiquid bonds.

In this exercise we use bond-level Trade Efficiency Scores (TES) published by Barclays QPS Research, a relative measure of liquidity that combines information on Liquidity Cost Scores (bid–offer spreads) and monthly trading volumes of individual securities to rank all constituents

TABLE 15.8 Annualized Returns of the EMC Strategy in Fed Cycles, January 1993 to May 2017

		EMC Strategy			US Corporate IG Index		
	# Obs	Avg. Exc. Ret. %/yr	Volatility %/yr	Inf. Ratio	Avg. Exc. Ret. %/yr	Volatility %/yr	Inf. Ratio
On-Hold Pre-Easing	42	2.61	0.7	3.73	-0.87	1.5	-0.58
Early Easing	40	8.2	2.94	2.79	-1.52	3.95	-0.39
Late Easing	38	19.06	8.96	2.13	1.97	8.93	0.22
On-Hold Pre-Tightening	103	4.02	2.21	1.82	1.59	3.03	0.52
Early Tightening	46	4.51	1.88	2.41	1.58	2.28	0.69
Late Tightening	24	3.06	1.97	1.55	-0.77	1.29	-0.6
All Periods	293	6.34	4.06	1.56	0.67	4.14	0.16

Source: Bloomberg, Barclays Research

of the corporate index on a monthly basis. TES increases as corporate bond liquidity declines, so bonds with lower TES are more liquid and actively traded.

We split bonds into three TES buckets: liquid, actively traded bonds with TES between one and three; moderately liquid bonds with TES between four and seven; and illiquid infrequently traded bonds with TES between eight and 10. We further sort bonds in each TES bucket into five equity momentum quintile portfolios and calculate return of the EMC strategy as the return differential between top- (Q5) and bottom- (Q1) quintile portfolios.

Table 15.9 reports the performance of the EMC strategy and of the five momentum quintile portfolios in each TES bucket in the period from 2007 to 2017.[17] We observe that the average returns of the EMC strategy are broadly similar across TES buckets while volatility declines for less liquid bonds, so that the information ratio increases from 1.48 to 1.99 as liquidity worsens. Nevertheless, strategy performance remains very strong for the most liquid and actively traded securities. So we cannot state that the illiquidity of corporate bonds is the main factor explaining the EMC phenomenon.

TABLE 15.9 Performance of the EMC Strategy by Bond Trade Efficiency Scores (TES), February 2007 to May 2017

TES Range	Q1 (Bottom)	Q2	Q3	Q4	Q5 (Top)	EMC Strategy: Q5–Q1
	Annualized Avg. Excess Return, %/yr					
TES 1–3 (liquid)	−4.78	−0.26	2.25	2.23	4.67	9.45
TES 4–7	−4.03	0.17	1.72	2.8	5.38	9.41
TES 8–10 (illiquid)	−4.04	0.16	1.91	3.03	4.77	8.81
	Annualized Volatility, %/yr					
TES 1–3 (liquid)	10.41	6.45	5.56	5.94	7.11	6.39
TES 4–7	8.76	5.71	5.34	5.78	6.64	5.38
TES 8–10 (illiquid)	7.34	5.93	5.27	5.72	5.7	4.43
	Information Ratio					
TES 1–3 (liquid)	−0.46	−0.04	0.41	0.38	0.66	1.48
TES 4–7	−0.46	0.03	0.32	0.49	0.81	1.75
TES 8–10 (illiquid)	−0.55	0.03	0.36	0.53	0.84	1.99

Source: Barclays Research

Autocorrelation of corporate bond excess returns can also be used as a measure of liquidity. Indeed, if corporate bond prices are only updated infrequently and are subject to "stale" pricing, their returns are likely to be positively correlated as new information slowly gets priced in. Using this logic, we look at the performance of the EMC strategy within buckets sorted by the autocorrelation of monthly bond excess returns.

We sort bonds by autocorrelation calculated in the previous 12 months and form three buckets: low (bottom 30%), medium (mid 40%), and high (top 30%). Then, within each autocorrelation bucket, we sort bonds by equity momentum to form quintile portfolios and measure the performance of the EMC strategy (Q5–Q1).

As shown in Table 15.10, the EMC strategy works equally well in all autocorrelation buckets. The strategy performance does not seem to be attributed to illiquidity of corporate bonds.

In contrast, average returns of individual quintile portfolios show an interesting pattern: As autocorrelation of bond returns increases, so do returns across all quintile portfolios. This could be seen as potential evidence of momentum in corporate bond excess returns.

TABLE 15.10   Performance of the EMC Strategy by Autocorrelation of Bond Excess Returns, January 1993 to May 2017

Autocorrelation of Corp. Excess Returns	Q1 (Bottom)	Q2	Q3	Q4	Q5 (Top)	EMC Strategy: Q5–Q1
	Annualized Avg. Excess Return, %/yr					
Low (–33%)	–3.74	0.24	0.96	1.57	2.82	6.55
Med (–4%)	–2.24	0.08	1.11	1.65	3.61	5.85
High (25%)	–1.92	0.52	1.59	2.14	4.26	6.18
	Annualized Volatility, %/yr					
Low (–33%)	8.4	4.02	3.82	4.05	4.77	5.7
Med (–4%)	5.33	4.13	3.76	3.9	4.62	3.69
High (25%)	6.32	4.52	3.81	3.99	4.33	4.9
	Information Ratio					
Low (–33%)	–0.44	0.06	0.25	0.39	0.59	1.15
Med (–4%)	–0.42	0.02	0.29	0.42	0.78	1.58
High (25%)	–0.3	0.12	0.42	0.54	0.98	1.26

Source: Barclays Research

COMBINING EQUITY MOMENTUM WITH RELATIVE VALUE

EMC can be combined with other systematic strategies with the aim of achieving better performance. This can be done by combining the EMC signal with other model-driven signals. If individual signals are predictive of future performance and imperfectly correlated with each other, a significant increase in portfolio performance could be achieved.

Let us consider EMC in combination with a credit relative value signal (ESP) discussed in Chapter 13, which is designed to identify relative value opportunities in credit. ESP ranks individual bonds based on their excess spread over peers adjusted for issuer fundamentals. Excess spreads over peers unexplained by fundamentals are scored from one to 10. High scores (6–10) indicate potentially undervalued securities while low scores (1–5) indicate potentially overvalued securities with tight spreads over peers given issuer fundamentals.

Figure 15.10 shows the performance of corporate bond portfolios sorted by ESP scores in the period between 1993 and 2017. The performance of credit portfolios increases monotonically with ESP scores, with higher-ESP portfolios generating superior returns on average.

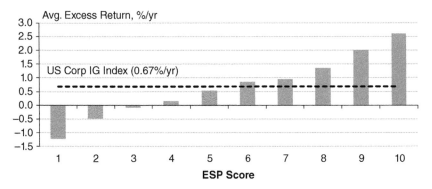

FIGURE 15.10 Average Excess Returns of US Corporate IG Portfolios by ESP Score, January 1993–May 2017
Source: Bloomberg, Barclays Research

There are many different ways to construct a credit portfolio that combines value and momentum signals. We choose a simple and intuitive approach to illustrate the properties of the combination. In order to combine momentum (EMC) and relative value (ESP) signals, we double-sort bonds to form four buckets: high ESP and high EMC (HH), high ESP and low EMC (HL), low ESP and high EMC (LH), and low ESP and low EMC

(LL). Panel A of Figure 15.11 illustrates the approach. The High (Low) ESP bucket includes bonds with ESP scores between six and 10 (one and five). Similarly, the High EMC bucket includes issuers with above-median equity momentum while the low EMC bucket includes issuers with below-median equity momentum.

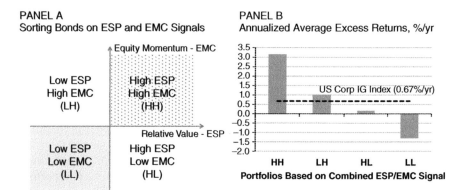

FIGURE 15.11 Combining Relative Value (ESP) and Equity Momentum (EMC) Signals, January 1993 to May 2017
Source: Barclays Research

Panel B of Figure 15.11 shows average returns of these four credit portfolios based on the combination of relative value (ESP) and equity momentum (EMC) signals. The portfolio with high ESP and EMC signals (HH portfolio) significantly outperforms the other three combinations as well as the index.

Table 15.11 reports the performance of the High ESP (top 50% by ESP) and High EMC (top 50% by EMC) portfolios as well as the portfolio based on the combination of ESP and EMC signals (HH) and compares their performance statistics with those of the Bloomberg Barclays US Corp. IG Index. Combining the two signals increases portfolio performance very significantly.

In the overall sample, High ESP and High EMC portfolios outperformed the index by 0.85%/yr and 1.43%/yr, respectively, with information ratios of 1.54 and 1.44. The combined portfolio (HH), in contrast, outperformed the index by 2.49%/yr with an information ratio of 2.14. As the two signals complement each other, the portfolio based on the signal combination outperformed the index by more than the sum of the two strategies taken in isolation.

TABLE 15.11 Performance of Relative Value (ESP) and Equity Momentum (EMC) Style Portfolios Relative to the Index

	Absolute Performance				Performance over Index		
	Index	High ESP	High EMC	Combined (HH)	ESP-Index	EMC-Index	Comb-Index
January 1993–May 2017							
Avg. Exc. Return, %/yr	0.67	1.52	2.09	3.15	0.85	1.43	2.49
Volatility, %/yr	4.15	4.43	3.97	4.17	0.56	0.99	1.16
Information Ratio	0.16	0.34	0.53	0.76	1.54	1.44	2.14
Corr. w. Index	100%	99%	97%	96%	46%	-30%	-12%
January 1993–June 2007							
Avg. Exc. Return, %/yr	0.41	0.97	1.24	2	0.56	0.83	1.59
Volatility, %/yr	2.09	2.42	1.89	2.13	0.48	0.57	0.7
Information Ratio	0.2	0.4	0.66	0.94	1.18	1.46	2.28
Corr. w. Index	100%	99%	96%	95%	63%	-47%	-10%
July 2007–May 2017							
Avg. Exc. Return, %/yr	1.04	2.32	3.34	4.83	1.28	2.3	3.79
Volatility, %/yr	6.01	6.31	5.79	6	0.63	1.35	1.54
Information Ratio	0.17	0.37	0.58	0.81	2.02	1.7	2.46
Corr. w. Index	100%	100%	97%	97%	43%	-27%	-14%

Source: Bloomberg, Barclays Research

CONCLUSION

We analyze the effect of equity price momentum on excess returns of corporate bonds issued by the same firm and find a strong positive relationship. Stronger equity momentum leads to higher corporate bond returns. Equity momentum could therefore be used systematically as a signal for issuer selection.

We design a strategy (EMC) that buys corporate bonds of issuers with strong equity momentum and sells bonds with negative momentum. The strategy has demonstrated strong and persistent performance in the period from 1993 to 2017 with average excess returns of 6.34%/yr (US IG) and 15.9%/yr (US HY) and information ratios above 1.5 before transaction costs.

The results are robust with respect to the exact specification of equity momentum and hold for liquid and illiquid corporate bonds. We do not find that EMC strategy performance can be explained by bond illiquidity.

The EMC strategy has been negatively correlated with equity and credit markets but positively correlated with a quality factor. Returns of the EMC strategy have been particularly strong during credit down-cycles.

High turnover and transaction costs can significantly reduce the performance of the EMC strategy. Nevertheless, equity momentum signal can still be used to inform any portfolio rebalancing or as a building block in a combined signal.

Credit investors could consider combining EMC and relative value signals by buying undervalued bonds with strong issuer equity momentum. This strategy has delivered robust absolute and risk-adjusted returns since January 1993.

APPENDIX 15.1

Robustness of the EMC Strategy

Does EMC strategy performance depend on the signal formation period? Table 15.12 reports the performance of credit portfolios sorted by equity price momentum observed in the previous one, three, and six months. Performance is consistent across all formation periods: Portfolio returns and information ratios increase as equity momentum strengthens. The combined strategy that equally combines signals measured over different horizons (after adjusting for differences in length of the formation periods) delivers

TABLE 15.12 Performance of the EMC Strategy by Signal Formation Period, January 1993 to May 2017

EMC Formation Period	Q1 (Bottom)	Q2	Q3	Q4	Q5 (Top)	EMC Strategy: Q5–Q1
Annualized Avg. Excess Return, %/yr						
6 months	−1.78	0.3	0.73	1.58	2.58	4.36
3 months	−2.46	0.23	0.78	1.43	3.13	5.59
1 month	−2.15	0.25	0.96	1.52	2.71	4.85
Combined	−2.83	0.09	1.08	1.64	3.5	6.34
Annualized Volatility, %/yr						
6 months	7.18	4.12	3.91	3.63	3.57	5.15
3 months	6.79	4.11	3.99	3.58	3.96	4.75
1 month	5.8	3.97	3.88	4.14	4.55	3.78
Combined	6.54	4.24	3.75	3.98	4.54	4.07
Information Ratio						
6 months	−0.25	0.07	0.19	0.44	0.72	0.85
3 months	−0.36	0.06	0.2	0.4	0.79	1.18
1 month	−0.37	0.06	0.25	0.37	0.59	1.28
Combined	−0.43	0.02	0.29	0.41	0.77	1.56

Source: Barclays Research

the highest absolute and risk-adjusted returns. Results do not change qualitatively according to the length of the signal formation period.

Another important issue could be that the momentum signals are measured over periods ending at a point when the EMC portfolios are constructed (usually the last business day of a month). One could argue that, from a practical perspective, end-of-period stock prices should be taken with a lag to give enough time to build a corporate bond portfolio. Table 15.13 shows the performance of quintile portfolios sorted on the combined equity momentum signal but with end-of-period stock prices lagged by one, two, or three business days.[18] The lag in stock prices does not change results much, and the equity momentum signal is found to work well across all specifications.

TABLE 15.13 Performance of the EMC Strategy with Lagged Stock Prices, January 1993 to May 2017

EMC Signal Lag	Q1 (Bottom)	Q2	Q3	Q4	Q5 (Top)	EMC Strategy: Q5–Q1
Annualized Avg. Excess Return, %/yr						
0 days	-3	-0.01	1	1.56	3.43	6.43
1 days	-2.57	-0.04	0.72	1.77	3.26	5.83
2 days	-2.47	0.1	0.69	1.52	3.41	5.89
3 days	-2.68	0.14	0.82	1.45	3.4	6.08
Annualized Volatility, %/yr						
0 days	6.63	4.29	3.8	4.03	4.6	4.12
1 days	6.35	4.41	3.86	3.95	4.54	3.88
2 days	6.42	3.99	4.1	4.07	4.28	4.29
3 days	6.4	3.98	4.04	4.18	4.14	4.25
Information Ratio						
0 days	-0.45	0	0.26	0.39	0.75	1.56
1 days	-0.4	-0.01	0.19	0.45	0.72	1.5
2 days	-0.39	0.02	0.17	0.37	0.8	1.37
3 days	-0.42	0.04	0.2	0.35	0.82	1.43

Source: Barclays Research

The EMC strategy that goes long the top-quintile and shorts the bottom-quintile portfolios sorted by equity momentum shows time-varying credit exposure (see Figure 15.6 and Table 15.4). In credit down-cycles, the strategy typically has a negative net spread, while during recoveries, the strategy has a positive net spread. Haesen et al. (2017) argued that this varying exposure can make the strategy vulnerable in periods of market turning points, for example when a market downturn is followed by a recovery. The authors suggested that risk and performance characteristics of the EMC strategy can be improved if equity momentum is measured from issuer-specific stock returns, having taken out the market (or, more generally, systematic) return component.

Table 15.14 shows the performance of top- and bottom-quintile credit portfolios sorted on residual equity momentum after a beta-adjusted market

TABLE 15.14 Performance of the EMC Strategy Based on Issuer-Specific Equity Momentum, January 1993 to May 2017

	US Corp. IG Index	Q1 (Bottom)	Q5 (Top)	EMC Strategy: Q5–Q1	Q5–Index
	January 1993–May 2017			January 1993–May 2017	
Avg. Exc. Return, %/yr	0.67	−2.52	3.52	6.04	2.85
Volatility, %/yr	4.15	6.3	4.53	4.32	1.9
Information Ratio	0.16	−0.4	0.78	1.4	1.5
	January 1993–June 2007			January 1993–June 2007	
Avg. Exc. Return, %/yr	0.41	−1.67	2.23	3.9	1.82
Volatility, %/yr	2.09	3.58	2.34	2.49	1.1
Information Ratio	0.2	−0.47	0.95	1.57	1.66
	July 2007–May 2017			July 2007–May 2017	
Avg. Exc. Return, %/yr	1.04	−3.76	5.41	9.17	4.37
Volatility, %/yr	6.01	8.9	6.51	5.99	2.61
Information Ratio	0.17	−0.42	0.83	1.53	1.67

Source: Bloomberg, Barclays Research

returns[19] were taken out. The results are slightly worse than those reported in Table 15.1, where total price returns were used to measure equity momentum. So, issuer-specific equity momentum signal does not lead to an improvement in strategy performance in our case.[20]

APPENDIX 15.2

Controlling Turnover and Transaction Costs

The EMC strategy presented in our analysis can raise some portfolio construction challenges. First, selling short the bottom momentum portfolio is likely to be infeasible due to the limitations of the financing market for corporate bonds. Second, portfolio turnover is likely to be high as momentum signal tends to be volatile.

So, we briefly discuss a practical approach to long-only portfolio construction that recognizes the need to limit turnover and accounts for estimated transaction costs.

Figure 15.12 outlines how turnover can be limited. In the top panel, the buy/sell signal can flip sign as soon as a security crosses a particular threshold, such as, for example, the population median. In that case, frequent migration around the threshold can generate high and undesirable turnover. In contrast, the bottom panel illustrates a rebalancing logic that buys bonds only when the signal is sufficiently strong and sells when the signal is sufficiently weak, with a large no-trade buffer zone in between. It requires choosing distinct thresholds for triggering either purchase or liquidation of a bond. The farther apart these thresholds are from each other, the lower the portfolio turnover. However, aggressively restricting turnover can also have a negative impact on performance.

Table 15.15 illustrates long-only EMC portfolios based on different buy and sell rules. The second column of the table summarizes index performance while the next three columns show different EMC portfolios and the last three present portfolio performances relative to the index. All portfolios rebalance at calendar month-end according to EMC signals.

The first portfolio holds only bonds in the top decile of equity momentum, meaning it buys when a bond passes the top 10th percentile and sells when it drops below it. Turnover is very high (73% per month) and performance before transaction costs is also very high (return of 7.31%/yr, or 6.34%/yr in excess of the index, with information ratio of 1.90 over the index) but transaction costs are so large that, once accounted for, both absolute and relative performance becomes negative.

The second portfolio buys when a bond passes the top 10th percentile but sells only when a bond drops below the 90th percentile of EMC. In that case, the existence of a large buffer between buy and sell triggers allows for

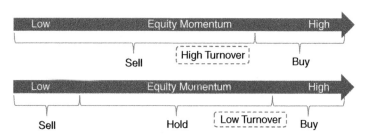

FIGURE 15.12 Reducing Turnover Using a Hold Buffer Between "Buy" and "Sell" Triggers
Source: Barclays Research

TABLE 15.15 Performance of EMC Portfolios Controlling for Turnover and After Transaction Costs, February 2007 to May 2017

	US Corp. IG	Buy Top 10% Sell Otherwise	Top 10%, Sell if Bottom 10%	Liq. Top 10%, Sell if Bottom 10%	Buy Top 10%, Sell Otherwise	Top 10%, Sell if Bottom 10%	Liq. Top 10%, Sell if Bottom 10%
	Index	EMC1	EMC2	EMC3	EMC1—Index	EMC2—Index	EMC3—Index
Avg. Turnover, %/m	-	73.3	8.9	8.9	73.3	8.9	8.9
Avg. Trans. Costs, bp/m	-	76.8	8.4	7.4	76.8	8.4	7.4
Before Transaction Costs							
Avg. Return, %/yr	0.97	7.31	2.76	2.77	6.34	1.79	1.79
Volatility, %/yr	5.89	6.4	5.1	5.26	3.34	1.35	1.35
Information Ratio	0.17	1.14	0.54	0.53	1.9	1.32	1.32
After Transaction Costs							
Avg. Return, %/yr	0.97	-1.9	1.76	1.88	-2.87	0.78	0.91
Volatility, %/yr	5.89	5.49	5.04	5.21	2.74	1.33	1.31
Information Ratio	0.17	-0.35	0.35	0.36	-1.05	0.59	0.7

Source: Bloomberg, Barclays Research

a considerable reduction in portfolio turnover, to 8.9%/m. Before cost, performance is much lower than that of Portfolio 1, but it remains positive and substantially higher than that of the index after transaction costs (estimated using Barclays Liquidity Cost Scores). Portfolio 2 outperforms the index by 0.78%/yr with an information ratio of 0.59 after transaction costs.

The third portfolio is similar to Portfolio 2 but only buys liquid bonds. In this context, a bond is deemed liquid if its TES is between one and three. This constraint makes portfolio simulation realistic. It has virtually no effect on before cost performance, but after transaction costs, both excess return over the index (0.91%/yr) and information ratio vs. the index (0.70) improve relative to Portfolio 2.

One should note that these long-only portfolios are not assembled to closely match the risk profile of the index and so some scope remains to improve tracking error volatility and enhance risk-adjusted performance relative to the index. However, their absolute performances (shown on the left-hand side of Table 15.15) compare well with the index not only in terms of return but also in terms of volatility. For example, the volatility of Portfolio 3 excess returns (after costs) is 5.21%/yr, markedly lower than that of the index (5.89%/yr).

REFERENCES

Asness, C., A. Frazzini, and L. H. Pedersen. 2019. "Quality Minus Junk." *Review of Accounting Studies* 42: 34–112.

Asness, C., T. Moskowitz, and L. H. Pedersen. 2013. "Value and Momentum Everywhere." *Journal of Finance* 68(3): 929–985.

Ben Dor, A., and J. Xu. 2015. "Should Equity Investors Care about Corporate Bond Prices? Using Bond Prices to Construct Equity Momentum Strategies." *Journal of Portfolio Management* 41 (4): 35–49.

Gebhardt, W. R., S. Hvidkjaer, and B. Swaminathan. 2005. "Stock and Bonds Market Interaction: Does Momentum Spill Over?" *Journal of Financial Economics* 75(3): 651–690.

Haesen, D., P. Houweling, and J. Van Zundert. 2017. "Momentum Spillover from Stocks to Corporate Bonds." *Journal of Banking and Finance* 79: 28–41.

Jegadeesh, N., and S. Titman. 1993. "Returns to Buying Winners and Selling Losers: Implications for Stock Market Efficiency." *Journal of Finance* 48(1): 65–91.

Jegadeesh, N., and S. Titman. 2001. "Profitability of Momentum Strategies: An Evaluation of Alternative Explanations." *Journal of Finance* 56(2): 699–720.

Lin, H., J. Wang, and C. Wu. 2013. "Liquidity Risk and Momentum Spillover from Stocks to Bonds." *Journal of Fixed Income* 23(1): 5–42.

Naik, V., M. Trinh, and G. Rennison. 2002. "Introducing Lehman Brothers ESPRI: A Credit Selection Model Using Equity Returns as Spread Indicators." Lehman Brothers, *Quantitative Credit Research Quarterly*, Quarter 1: 26–39.

NOTES

1. Corporate bonds issued by private companies were excluded.
2. See, for example, Jegadeesh and Titman (1993).
3. Polling results from the 17th QPS Americas Analytics Advisory Council, an interactive forum where Barclays QPS Research discusses a variety of research topics with large institutional asset managers.
4. See also Gebhardt, Hvidkjaer, and Swaminathan (2005).
5. All bond returns reported in this analysis are in excess of duration-matched Treasury portfolios, as provided by Bloomberg Barclays bonds indices.
6. Please see Ben Dor and Xu (2015) for the detailed description of the bond-equity mapping.
7. For example, private companies are excluded.
8. Please note that these results do not account for transactions costs.
9. Equity returns measured at one-, three-, and six-month horizons would have different magnitudes, with six-month returns likely to be larger in absolute terms. In order to put different period returns on equal footing, we normalize them by the square root of period lengths over which they are measured, which corresponds to the increase in return volatility with time.
10. All returns ignore transaction costs as, at this stage, we aim to illustrate broad performance patterns and properties of the strategy. Transaction costs and turnover are discussed in Chapter 18.
11. Additional turnover reduction techniques may be implemented in actual portfolios. Investors could introduce a hold buffer, an "acceptable" range of the equity momentum signal where new bonds would not be added to the portfolio and previously bought old bonds would be kept unchanged. (See Appendix 15.2.) Alternatively, investors could implement implicit turnover budget, so that bonds with the most negative momentum would be replaced by new bonds with the positive momentum to the extent the turnover budget permits. We discuss both turnover reduction methods in Chapter 18.
12. Portfolios are assumed to be rebalanced monthly based on issuer equity momentum and broad index composition.
13. Similar results were obtained by Haesen et al. (2017), who proposed to measure equity momentum using idiosyncratic stock returns (by first subtracting beta-adjusted market returns from those of individual stocks) to improve the performance of the strategy around market turning points. The respective results, albeit with otherwise different specification of the momentum signal (as per our previous discussion in the text), are reported in Appendix 15.1.
14. Fama–French equity factors are available in the web data library of Kenneth R. French: http://mba.tuck.dartmouth.edu/pages/faculty/ken.french/data_library.html. For an introduction to the Quality Minus Junk (QMJ) factor, see Asness, Frazzini, and Pedersen (2017).
15. Equity momentum in EQ MOM strategy uses 12-month stock returns excluding the last month (due to mean reversion), while the EMC strategy uses an equally weighted combination of equity returns in the previous six, three, and one months.

16. After 2008, as the Fed rate reached its lower bound, we also qualified as monetary easing the periods when Fed assets expanded at a rate faster than 25% p.a. This occurred in 2009 and 2013.
17. Bond efficiency scores (TES) for constituents of the US Corporate IG index are available from January 2007.
18. In our analysis we used monthly stock prices available on the last business day of each month. For this exercise, however, we used daily equity prices. Hence the small differences in the results related to the zero-lag case.
19. We used returns of the S&P 500 index as the market component. Price returns of individual stocks were regressed on returns of S&P500 in a 12-month rolling window to estimate market beta and obtain the residuals. Residual returns over one, three, and six months were rescaled to account for differences in period lengths and equally weighted to measure issuer-specific equity momentum.
20. Our signal formation period is different from the periods used in Haesen et al. (2017).

CHAPTER 16

Corporate Sector Timing Using Equity Momentum

INTRODUCTION

In Chapter 15, we documented a strong relationship between the equity price returns of an issuer and the subsequent performance of its corporate bonds. This motivated the introduction of our Equity Momentum in Credit (EMC) Scorecard, a framework that ranks credit issuers from one to ten according to relative equity momentum.

EMC scores have been useful in helping to predict performance of corporate bonds. Figure 16.1 shows average performance of US investment-grade corporate bonds sorted by EMC scores. Portfolios are formed at the beginning of each month, and excess returns are recorded in the following month.

The relationship between EMC scores and subsequent performance of corporate bonds has been almost monotonic in the 10-year period between 2007 and 2017. The average excess return[1] of the portfolio of bonds with the lowest equity momentum (EMC = 1) was –7.2%/yr, while the portfolio with best momentum (EMC = 10) had an average return of 8.10%/yr. In comparison, the average excess return of the Bloomberg Barclays US Corporate Bond Index was 1.43%/yr in the same period.

Equity returns used to derive EMC scores are not normalized within individual sectors. As a result, sector average EMC scores can vary significantly depending on industry-specific conditions. Could equity momentum provide a useful signal for timing corporate bond sector allocation? In this chapter, we disentangle effects of issuer selection and sector allocation in the performance of the EMC strategy and then study a momentum-based sector allocation strategy using Level 3 industry classification of Bloomberg Barclays Corporate Bond indices.

515

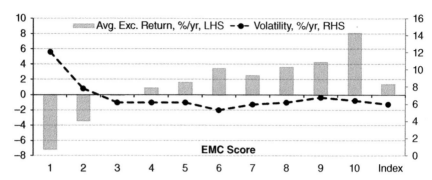

FIGURE 16.1 Average Excess Returns and Volatilities of Corporate Bonds Grouped by EMC Scores, November 2007 to October 2017
Source: Bloomberg, Barclays Research

ATTRIBUTING PERFORMANCE OF THE EMC STRATEGY

Our original EMC framework assigns scores to individual issuers according to equity momentum without controlling for industry sectors. As a result, a portfolio based on EMC is not sector neutral but can overweight sectors with strong equity momentum and underweight sectors with weak or negative momentum, thereby creating an implicit sector allocation overlay. Can we attribute the EMC strategy performance to sector rotation and issuer selection components?

In order to do this, we create a sector-neutral version of the EMC strategy with issuers sorted by equity momentum *within* individual sectors. In each sector the strategy buys bonds of issuers in the top 20% (Q5) and sells bonds in the bottom 20% (Q1) of equity momentum. Table 16.1 shows the performance of this EMC strategy within eight industry sectors derived from Level 3 classification of the Bloomberg Barclays bond indices.[2]

The performance of the issuer selection strategy based on equity momentum has been strong across all sectors and index universes. Information ratios of our hypothetical long-short portfolios are slightly weaker for banks and brokerage in US investment grade (IG), transportation and energy and financials in European IG, and financials in US high yield (HY). Strategy returns have been lower for less cyclical sectors, such as consumer noncyclical and utility across all three universes.

We form top and bottom momentum portfolios within sectors and aggregate them across sectors, using sector weights of the respective benchmark indices to obtain a sector-neutral EMC strategy.[3] The difference in

TABLE 16.1 Performance of the EMC Strategy Within Individual Sectors, November 2007 to October 2017

Sector	US IG: Top (Q5)–Bottom (Q1)			Euro IG: Top (Q5)–Bottom (Q1)			US HY: Top (Q5)–Bottom (Q1)		
	Avg. Return %/yr	Volatility %/yr	IR	Avg. Return %/yr	Volatility %/yr	IR	Avg. Return %/yr	Volatility %/yr	IR
Basic & Cap. Goods	6.97	3.96	1.76	4.32	3.2	1.35	10.96	5.27	2.08
Cons. Cyclical	7.96	5.84	1.36	3.68	3.16	1.17	17.77	13.84	1.28
Cons. Noncyclical	3.56	1.84	1.93	1.91	1.36	1.41	5.94	4.55	1.31
Comm. & Tech	7.05	4.61	1.53	2.9	2.63	1.1	13.54	7.73	1.75
Transport. & Energy	7.83	3.92	2	2.35	2.99	0.79	15.96	8.58	1.86
Utility	3.62	2.22	1.63	0.92	2.4	0.38	6.89	6.38	1.08
Banks & Brokerage	6.83	10.38	0.66	5.48	4.95	1.11	30.22	31.58	0.96
Financial Other	10.19	9.24	1.1	4.95	5.4	0.92	17.09	19.89	0.86

Source: Bloomberg, Barclays Research

TABLE 16.2 Contribution from Sector Allocation to the Performance of the EMC Strategy, November 2007 to October 2017

		Top (Q5) over Bottom (Q1)			Top (Q5) over Index		
		EMC Unconstrained	EMC Sector-Neutral	Contrib. from Timing Sector Allocation	EMC Unconstrained	EMC Sector-Neutral	Contrib. from Timing Sector Allocation
US IG	Avg. Return, %/yr	10.03	6.98	3.05	3.98	3.01	0.97
	Volatility, %/yr	5.3	3.92	2.2	2.26	1.42	1.4
	IR	1.89	1.78	1.39	1.76	2.11	0.69
Euro IG	Avg. Return, %/yr	5.67	4.21	1.46	2.64	1.94	0.7
	Volatility, %/yr	3.45	2.91	1.49	1.38	0.93	0.88
	IR	1.65	1.45	0.98	1.91	2.09	0.79
US HY	Avg. Return, %/yr	18.73	13.2	5.52	9.76	6.38	3.38
	Volatility, %/yr	9.84	5.6	4.93	6.24	3.19	4.4
	IR	1.9	2.36	1.12	1.56	2	0.77

Source: Bloomberg, Barclays Research

returns between the unconstrained EMC strategy and its sector-neutral equivalent can be attributed to sector rotation. We can also calculate volatilities and information ratios of these return differences (contributions) to assess the significance of the effect. Table 16.2 reports the contribution of sector allocation to the performance of the unconstrained EMC strategy in the three corporate bond universes: US IG, US HY, and Euro IG.

Contributions from sector rotation to the performance of the top-quintile EMC portfolios over benchmark indices were all positive: 0.97%/yr for US IG, 0.70%/yr for Euro IG, and 3.38%/yr for US HY in 2007 to 2017. These contributions represent 24 to 35% of the total outperformance over the index.

EQUITY MOMENTUM IN CORPORATE SECTOR TIMING

The exercise of attributing EMC strategy performance to issuer selection and sector rotation, conducted in the previous section, indicates that equity momentum appears to be useful for sector rotation. In this section, we calculate equity momentum signals for a larger set of industry sectors, construct a corresponding sector allocation strategy, and evaluate its performance against benchmark indices.

We start with an illustration that equity momentum can vary significantly across sectors as shown in Figure 16.2. Panel A shows equity momentum[4] across sectors in the US IG and Euro IG universes as of 31 October 2017, while Panel B shows equity momentum by sector of the US HY index. Differences can be substantial. For example, equity momentum signals of the technology sectors in US and Euro IG are +4.3%/m and +3.3%/m respectively, while equity momentum of the financing sectors were –5.9%/m and –9.9%/m respectively at the end of October 2017.[5]

Does equity momentum signal help predict subsequent excess returns of the sector? To address this question, we sort sectors by equity momentum at the beginning of each month and then measure returns in the subsequent month. Figure 16.3 plots the average equity return (horizontal axis) and subsequent bond excess returns (vertical axis) for each sector cell. The rightmost dot in the scatter chart represents the highest equity momentum sector in any given month.

Panels A and B of Figure 16.3 show that average excess returns tend to increase with equity momentum with each 1%/m of additional equity momentum translating into an extra 5 to 8bp of bond excess returns. This relationship has been stronger in US HY (Panel B) and weaker in the Euro IG market (Panel A).

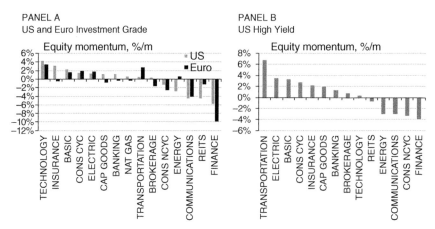

FIGURE 16.2 Equity Momentum of Class 3 Sectors as of 31 October 2017
Source: Bloomberg, Barclays Research

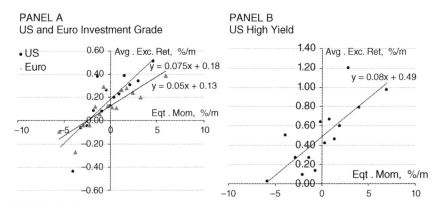

FIGURE 16.3 Average Excess Returns of Corporate Sectors Sorted by Equity Momentum, November 2007 to October 2017
Source: Barclays Research

How would a sector allocation strategy based on equity momentum have performed historically? For this, we form a market-weighted portfolio of the top five sectors (out of 15) in terms of equity momentum at the beginning of each month and measure its subsequent performance.[6] The portfolio is rebalanced every month.

Figure 16.4 plots cumulative excess returns of portfolios invested into the top five sectors along with those of the respective indices. Panel A relates to the US IG and Panel B relates to the US HY market. In both cases, the sector timing strategy outperforms the underlying index consistently over the 10 years of our analysis, with much of the outperformance observed in 2008 and 2009.

Figure 16.5 shows annual outperformance of these sector timing portfolios over their respective indices. Panel A shows annual outperformance in US IG and Euro IG markets. Returns were high during volatile periods, such as the global financial crisis (2008–2009), the European sovereign crisis (2011), and the energy crisis (2015–2016). In contrast, strategy returns were small during benign periods. This is not surprising, because returns of different sectors are likely to diverge during turbulent periods. A similar pattern can be observed in Panel B, which relates to the US HY market.

Table 16.3 compares the performance of market capitalization–weighted portfolios that invest in either the top or the bottom five sectors based on equity momentum. The last two columns report the outperformance of the top portfolios over the bottom ones and over respective indices. In all three markets, this sector allocation strategy has been profitable from 2007 to 2017. Portfolios of the top five sectors outperformed their respective indices by 2.38%/yr (US IG), 1.77%/yr (Euro IG), and 4.04%/yr (US HY) with information ratios above 1. Investors, however, need to exercise some

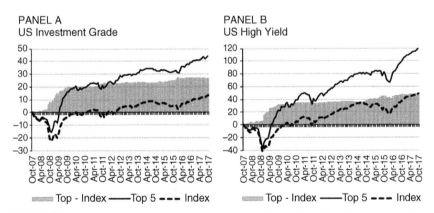

FIGURE 16.4 Cumulative Excess Returns over Index of Top Five Sector Portfolios Based on Equity Momentum
Source: Bloomberg, Barclays Research

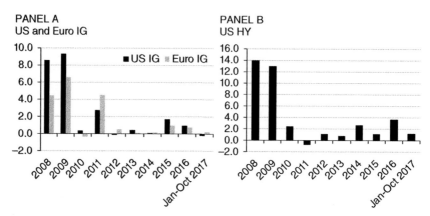

FIGURE 16.5 Annual Excess Returns over Index of Top Five Sector Portfolios Based on Equity Momentum
Source: Bloomberg, Barclays Research

caution when implementing these strategies as the returns could be significantly reduced by transaction costs.

CONCLUSION

Although initially designed as an issuer signal, equity momentum in credit has also been useful for timing corporate bond sector allocation.

A portfolio strategy that systematically invests in sectors with strong equity momentum outperformed the index by 2.38%/yr in US IG, by 4.04%/yr in US HY, and by 1.77%/yr in Euro IG in the 10 years between 2007 and 2017, with information ratios above one before transaction costs.

A 1%/month increase in equity momentum added 5 to 8bp/month to subsequent performance of a credit sector on average.

Our attribution analysis indicates that sector rotation contributed about 30% of the overall performance of the issuer selection strategy based on equity momentum.

TABLE 16.3 Performance of Sector-Based Equity Momentum Portfolios, November 2007 to October 2017

		Index	Top 5	Bottom 5	Top 5–Bottom 5	Top 5–Index
US IG	Avg. Exc. Return, %/yr	1.43	3.81	−0.86	4.67	2.38
	Volatility, %/yr	5.96	5.47	6.74	3.57	1.97
	Max. Drawdown, %	−22.34	−15.74	−28.63	−1.73	−1.04
	IR	0.24	0.7	−0.13	1.31	1.21
Euro IG	Avg. Exc. Return, %/yr	1.04	2.82	−1.03	3.85	1.77
	Volatility, %/yr	4.09	3.72	5.03	2.8	1.63
	Max. Drawdown, %	−16.15	−10.97	−23.5	−3.08	−1.8
	IR	0.26	0.76	−0.2	1.38	1.09
US HY	Avg. Exc. Return, %/yr	4.71	8.75	1.01	7.75	4.04
	Volatility, %/yr	12	13.25	12.51	6.57	3.83
	Max. Drawdown, %	−41.55	−38.28	−46.71	−6.57	−2.81
	IR	0.39	0.66	0.08	1.18	1.05

Source: Bloomberg, Barclays Research

NOTES

1. All returns in this chapter are calculated in excess of duration-matched Treasury bonds, as per Bloomberg Barclays index conventions.
2. The choice of these eight sectors is motivated by the need to have a sufficiently diverse set of issuers in each sector throughout the history of our analysis.
3. Sector-specific top and bottom momentum portfolios in the sector-neutral EMC are aggregated using index sector weights, so that long and short legs of the strategy have identical allocations across sectors. However, they can still have different sector DTS contributions.
4. The equity momentum signal is the average of issuer stock price returns over one-, three-, and six-month horizons normalized by the lengths of the respective periods. This methodology is consistent with that used to calculate issuer equity momentum in Chapter 15.
5. One should expect a higher variation of equity momentum across sectors during turbulent periods.
6. Note that in contrast to the performance attribution exercise, where we used eight customized sectors, here we use 15 Class 3 industry sectors, out of which we select the top five by equity momentum every month. A more granular sector partition was possible here because the allocation exercise was implemented at the macro level, so that we did not need to pick individual issuers within each sector.

Size Effect

CHAPTER 17

Issuer Size Premium in Credit Markets

INTRODUCTION

The effect of company size on stock returns has been well documented by investors and in academic literature: Small firms tend to outperform large firms with similar fundamental characteristics.[1]

Size premium in credit markets is less well researched. Houweling and Van Zundert (2017) find a positive size premium in corporate bonds, when using issuer's index weight as a measure of size. Alquist, Israel, and Moskowitz (2018) use market capitalization of issuer's equity as a measure of size and argue that the size premium in credit is weak or negative. These examples highlight a lack of consensus among investors regarding not only the existence of a size premium but also how size should be defined in credit markets.

Indeed, it is possible to define issuer size in various ways. For example, Table 17.1 reports size according to three different metrics for industry sectors of Bloomberg Barclays US Investment Grade (IG) (left panel) and High Yield (HY) (right panel) indices.[2] The table also reports the total number of issuers and public issuers in each sector. As of 31 May 2018, US Corporate IG and HY indices included 629 and 784 issuers (column 1 of each panel) or 573 and 576 public issuers (column 2 of each panel) domiciled in the United States.

Column 3 of each panel of Table 17.1 reports average issuer size defined as the amount of an issuer's debt outstanding in the index universe.[3] According to this measure, the average size of an issuer was $6.8bn in US IG and $1.6bn in US HY at the end of May 2018.[4]

527

TABLE 17.1 US Corporate Bonds: Measuring Issuer Size by Sector, 31 May 2018

	US Corporate IG, US Domiciled					US HY, US Domiciled				
	# Issuers	# Public Issuers	Index Amt, $bn	Total Debt, $bn	Equity Mkt Cap, $bn	# Issuers	# Public Issuers	Index Amt, $bn	Total Debt, $bn	Equity Mkt Cap, $bn
Basic industry	30	29	3.2	7.1	29.9	75	63	1.0	1.8	3.7
Capital goods	60	60	3.6	7.7	35.8	91	53	1.0	1.9	3.9
Cyclical	51	51	5.8	12.5	68.3	144	106	1.1	3.0	5.7
Noncyclical	108	76	7.1	15.7	61.6	98	67	1.8	4.9	6.6
Transportation	17	17	6.1	14.7	59.4	15	9	1.8	8.9	8.0
Communications	19	19	20.1	34.1	69.5	69	54	3.1	8.9	10.0
Technology	49	48	8.6	11.4	95.5	61	44	1.6	3.6	10.6
Energy	52	51	6.8	13.4	37.6	115	97	1.5	4.4	4.6
Industrial other	16	3	1.0	2.6	14.0	26	18	0.6	1.3	2.5
Utility	50	45	6.4	16.0	27.7	18	12	2.3	15.1	9.4
Banking	35	35	24.8	164.2	72.4	6	6	17.2	106.6	36.1
Brokerage/ exchanges	19	19	2.1	4.5	23.2	10	6	0.7	4.8	11.7
Insurance	57	54	3.7	7.5	32.0	22	15	1.2	3.8	7.4
Finance companies	8	8	9.6	23.8	18.9	15	9	2.0	17.9	3.2
REITs & other	58	58	2.2	4.5	9.6	19	17	1.1	4.3	3.8
Total	629	573	6.8	21.0	46.6	784	576	1.6	5.5	6.3

Source: Barclays Research

Another way to measure size is to look at the total debt reported on an issuer's balance sheet. Average issuer sizes calculated using this approach are reported in column 4 of Table 17.1. Relying on balance sheet information limits us to the universe of *public* companies, which are obliged to publish financial statements.[5] In addition to publicly traded bonds, debt reported on the balance sheet includes bank loans, leases, and repurchase agreements, so that total debt is often significantly higher than the amount outstanding in corporate bond indices. Indeed, the average total debt of issuers in IG and HY is $21bn and $5.5bn, respectively. These numbers are more than three times higher than the amounts included in corporate indices. For an issuer, index debt on average represents only 30% of its overall corporate debt.

Finally, similarly to equity markets, issuer size can be measured as its stock market capitalization. This approach limits our analysis to the universe of companies whose stocks are traded on public exchanges. The average equity capitalization of an issuer in our universe is $46.6bn in IG and $6.3bn in HY. Issuers included in corporate indices tend to be large.

Table 17.1 shows that, irrespective of the way size is measured, substantial variations in issuer size exist across industry sectors. For example, issuer sizes in the banking, finance companies, communication, and technology sectors are much larger than those in basic industry, capital goods, brokerage and exchanges, and insurance. This finding suggests that portfolios sorted on size, without controlling for sector allocation, could potentially be over-/under-represented in some sectors.

In our analysis, we take the amount of an issuer debt outstanding in the index as a size measure. This measure is relevant for corporate bond investors who utilize bond indices as performance benchmarks. Additionally, it is not exclusively restricted to public companies, so we can retain a broader set of issuers in our study. The other two size measures have serious drawbacks: Equity capitalization incorporates pricing information into the definition of size, so that the estimated size premium could be contaminated by valuation; total debt, in contrast, is reported only quarterly with different firms having different reporting cycles.

In this chapter we analyze effects of issuer size on spread and performance of corporate bonds in US IG and HY markets. Is issuer size a priced factor in credit? Is it rewarded with a risk premium that can be captured in a systematic investment style? Would investing into bonds issued by smaller-size issuers be a candidate to join Smart Beta strategies in credit markets?[6]

ISSUER SIZE IN THE US CORPORATE BOND MARKET

Taking the amount of debt outstanding in Bloomberg Barclays US Corporate IG and HY indices as a measure of issuer size, we can report its cross-sectional distribution in the IG index at a point in time.

Figure 17.1 shows distributions of issuer count and percentage of market value by its size in the US Corporate IG index as of 31 May 2018. A large proportion of issuers are of small to moderate size (equal or below $2bn), while only 7.6% of issuers are above $20bn in size. At the same time, these large issuers represent 46.8% of the overall market value. Therefore, it should not be surprising that the corporate bond market's performance, measured by index returns, is more affected by returns of a few large issuers, while the contribution of small issuers is usually relatively low.

While Table 17.1 and Figure 17.1 show snapshots of the corporate indices, the corporate bond market has evolved significantly over time. Figure 17.2 reports historical average sizes of US issuers in IG and HY since 1994. Average issuer sizes have grown dramatically over time: from $1.4bn to $6.8bn in IG, and from $0.6bn to $1.6bn in HY. The growth has been stronger in IG than in HY: 380% vs. 150%. We therefore focus on the relative rather than the absolute size of corporate issuers. In other words, we consider size relative to peers, which means that an issuer with the same amount outstanding could be qualified as "large" in past years and as "small" or "medium" in later years.

Relative issuer size is likely to be a slowly moving variable. Indeed, issuers can be expected to retain their size characteristics for a considerable time, as new bonds get issued and old bonds get retired only gradually. Tables 17.2 and 17.3 confirm this intuition by reporting average transition frequencies across issuer size deciles calculated over 12-month rolling periods in IG and HY markets, respectively. A US IG issuer that falls into the lowest-size decile (D1) in the beginning of the period has a 72% probability to remain in the same category after 12 months and only a 10% probability to move into the next larger-size category (D2). Persistence of relative size

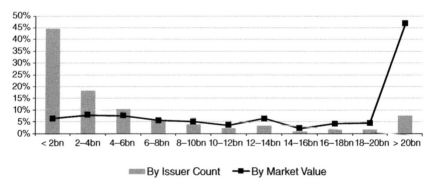

FIGURE 17.1 Distribution of Issuer Count and Market Value by Size in the Bloomberg Barclays US Corporate Index, 31 May 2018 *Source*: Barclays Research

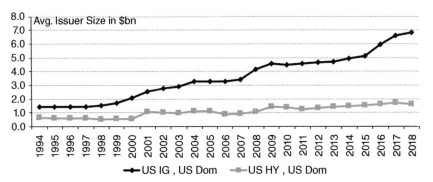

FIGURE 17.2 Evolution of Average Issuer Size in the US Corporate IG and HY Indices *Source:* Barclays Research

was even stronger for large-size issuers. Issuers in the largest-size category (D10) had 90% chance to remain there after 12 months and only 10% probability to transit into the next lower-size decile (D9). Also, small issuers (D1–D2) had a good chance to transit into larger-size deciles (D3, D4, D5, and D6) after 12 months, growing their outstanding debt significantly. In contrast, the largest issuers in D10 almost never experienced a sharp decline in size, so that their probabilities to transit into lower-size deciles (D8, D7, D6, etc.) remained practically zero.

Table 17.3 reports qualitatively similar results for HY issuers, although the contrast in transition probabilities of small- and large-size issuers is weaker.

Tables 17.2 and 17.3 indicate that investment strategies based on issuer size could be feasible for portfolio managers, as they would be unlikely to generate excessively high turnover. However, do portfolios of smaller issuers systematically offer higher spreads and returns?

CORPORATE BOND PORTFOLIOS SORTED ON SIZE

Similar to the approach frequently utilized in academic literature, we start our analysis by sorting issuers on size to form small-, medium-, and large-issuer portfolios in the IG and HY markets. The small portfolio includes the bottom 30% of issuers when sorted on size, while the large portfolio includes the top 30%. The medium portfolio includes the middle 40%. Size portfolios are rebalanced at the beginning of each month when sorting is repeated.

Corporate bonds statistics (e.g., durations, spreads, and returns) are first aggregated at the issuer level using bond market capitalization weights

TABLE 17.2 Average Transition Probabilities Across Issuer Size Deciles over 12m Periods in US IG, January 1994 to May 2018

		Size at end of period (12 mths)									
		D1 = Small	D2	D3	D4	D5	D6	D7	D8	D9	D10 = Large
Size at beginning of period (12 mths)	D1 = Small	72%	10%	10%	6%	2%	1%	-	-	-	-
	D2	15%	59%	11%	8%	5%	2%	1%	-	-	-
	D3	7%	15%	53%	13%	8%	3%	1%	1%	-	-
	D4	2%	5%	18%	51%	15%	7%	2%	1%	-	-
	D5	1%	2%	5%	18%	47%	18%	6%	1%	1%	-
	D6	-	-	1%	4%	20%	50%	18%	4%	1%	-
	D7	-	-	-	1%	3%	18%	54%	20%	3%	-
	D8	-	-	-	-	-	2%	20%	59%	17%	1%
	D9	-	-	-	-	-	1%	1%	15%	71%	12%
	D10 = Large	-	-	-	-	-	-	-	-	10%	90%

Source: Barclays Research

TABLE 17.3 Average Transition Probabilities Across Issuer Size Deciles over 12m Periods in US HY, January 1994 to May 2018

		Size at end of period (12 mths)								
		D1 = Small	D2	D3	D4	D5	D6	D7	D8	D9	D10 = Large
Size at beginning of period (12 mths)	D1 = Small	86%	4%	3%	3%	2%	2%	0.01	0.01		
	D2	14%	71%	7%	3%	3%	2%	1%			
	D3	3%	18%	60%	7%	4%	4%	2%	1%		
	D4	3%	4%	16%	58%	9%	6%	3%	1%	0.01	
	D5	1%	2%	6%	15%	54%	11%	7%	3%	1%	
	D6	0.01	0.01	2%	5%	14%	55%	13%	6%	2%	
	D7			0.01	2%	5%	14%	55%	17%	5%	0.01
	D8					0.02	5%	15%	57%	19%	2%
	D9							3%	15%	68%	13%
	D10 = Large								0.01	10%	89%

Source: Barclays Research

and excluding subordinated issues. Individual issuers are then weighted by market capitalization to form size portfolios.

Figure 17.3 shows the historical average issuer sizes (in $MM) for the three size portfolios. The charts are plotted in logarithmic scale to accommodate the significant growth over time. Results for the IG and HY universes are reported in panels A and B. The sorting procedure clearly discriminates between small- and large-size issuers. For example, average issuer sizes in small and large portfolios in the IG universe were $0.65bn and $18.5bn, respectively, as of 31 May 2018. In contrast, these were $0.14bn and $4.0bn in December 1993. In the HY universe, average issuer sizes in small and large portfolios increased from $0.14bn and $1.92bn to $0.31bn and $3.64bn between December 1993 and May 2018, respectively.

Panels A and B of Figure 17.3 show jumps in average issuer sizes in 2000, which correspond to increases in the minimum amount outstanding for index-eligible bonds. These changes in index rules pushed bonds with small outstanding amounts out of the universe, which led to increases in the average size of issuers remaining in the index.

Table 17.4 compares performance and risk of our size portfolios in IG and HY markets over different periods. Average risk-adjusted returns (information ratios) of small-size portfolios are higher than those of large-size portfolios. This result holds both in the IG and HY markets in all periods: 1994 to 2006 and 2007 to 2018.

Portfolio statistics in Table 17.4 reveal that two factors contribute to the higher risk-adjusted returns of small-size portfolios. First, small-size IG

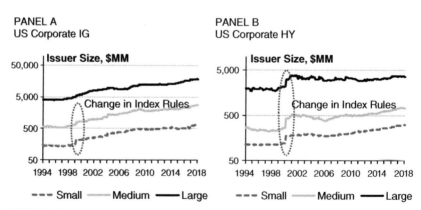

FIGURE 17.3 Average Issuer Size of Sorted Portfolios (log-scale)
Source: Barclays Research

portfolios have higher average excess returns than large-size portfolios. In HY, however, small-size portfolios had higher average excess return than large-size portfolios only in the period from 2007 to 2018.

The second factor contributing to the higher information ratios of small-size portfolios is the volatility of portfolio excess returns. Small-size portfolios, as shown in Table 17.4, have lower volatilities than large-size portfolios in both subperiods, in both IG and HY markets.

Ben Dor et al. (2007) have shown that volatility of portfolio excess returns is a liner function of credit exposure, Duration Times Spread (DTS), irrespective of sector or credit rating. So, in order to better understand the differences in volatilities of excess returns between small- and large-size portfolios, we provide average DTS along with return volatilities in Table 17.5. The table includes two time periods: 1994 to 2006 and 2007 to 2018. Surprisingly, we observe that small-size portfolios tend to be less volatile than large-size portfolios *despite* having higher average DTS.

Table 17.5 also reports volatilities of portfolio monthly excess returns *normalized* by beginning-of-month DTS. Volatilities of normalized excess returns usually tend to be invariant with respect to portfolio characteristics, such as duration, rating, or industry sector. This, however, does not seem to hold for portfolios sorted on issuer size. Indeed, volatilities per unit of DTS of small-size portfolios are roughly 30% lower than those of large-size portfolios in IG and 20% lower in HY. The differences are larger in the 2007 to 2018 period. Is there a plausible explanation for this anomaly?

One possible explanation for the lower excess return volatility of small-size portfolios is that bonds issued by small issuers tend to be less liquid than those issued by larger ones. We confirm this directly using average Liquidity Cost Scores (LCS) of size portfolios.[7] Figure 17.4 shows that the average LCS of small-size portfolios are more than 50% higher than the average LCS of large-size portfolios for both IG and HY issuers.

Illiquidity of smaller issuers is likely to manifest itself in less frequent trading and, as a result, in auto-correlated portfolio excess returns. This occurs because prices of less liquid bonds often adjust more slowly to new information than those of liquid ones. To verify this, we plot in Figure 17.5 the average autocorrelations of size portfolios returns for one- and two-month lags. Autocorrelations of excess returns are much higher for small-size portfolios than for large ones.

High positive autocorrelations of small-size portfolios suggest that their low return volatility could be an artifact of illiquidity. Volatilities measured over longer horizons could be more in line with the volatilities of large-size portfolios. In order to verify this, we report in Figure 17.6 annualized volatilities based on monthly, quarterly, and semiannual excess returns.[8]

TABLE 17.4 Performance of Size Portfolios

	US Corporate IG			US Corporate HY		
	Small	Medium	Large	Small	Medium	Large
January 1994–May 2018						
Avg. Exc. Ret., %/yr	1.12	0.66	0.68	2.6	2.21	2.61
Volatility, %/yr	3.48	3.91	4.2	7.82	9.14	10.63
Max. Drawdown, %	−25.5	−24.3	−22.8	−41.6	−45.8	−45.5
Information Ratio	0.32	0.17	0.16	0.33	0.24	0.25
January 1994–December 2006						
Avg. Exc. Ret., %/yr	0.72	0.25	0.34	1.19	0.71	1.70
Volatility, %/yr	1.69	2.19	2.35	5.95	7.35	9.33
Max. Drawdown, %	−7.0	−10.20	−9.40	−30.0	−38.9	−41.0
Information Ratio	0.43	0.11	0.15	0.20	0.10	0.18
January 2007–May 2018						
Avg. Exc. Ret., %/yr	1.58	1.13	1.08	4.21	3.92	3.65
Volatility, %/yr	4.77	5.23	5.63	9.52	10.85	11.97
Max. Drawdown, %	−25.5	−24.3	−22.6	−41.6	−43.0	−45.5
Information Ratio	0.33	0.22	0.19	0.44	0.36	0.30

Source: Barclays Research

TABLE 17.5 Spread Exposure and Excess Return Volatility of Size Portfolios

	US Corporate IG			US Corporate HY		
	Small	Medium	Large	Small	Medium	Large
January 1994–May 2018						
Volatility (%/y)	3.5	3.9	4.2	7.8	9.1	10.6
Avg. DTS (%×y)	10.8	9.8	9.0	23.4	21.7	21.3
Volatility per DTS, %/m	6.6	8.0	9.6	8.8	10.2	11.2
January 1994–December 2006						
Volatility (%/y)	1.7	2.2	2.3	6.0	7.3	9.3
Avg. DTS (%×y)	7.8	7.5	6.5	22.2	20.7	19.9
Volatility per DTS	5.8	7.0	8.4	8.9	10.0	11.1
January 2007–May 2018						
Volatility (%/y)	4.8	5.2	5.6	9.5	10.9	12.0
Avg. DTS (%×y)	14.3	12.4	12	24.7	22.9	22.9
Volatility per DTS	7.4	9.1	10.9	8.7	10.4	11.3

Source: Barclays Research

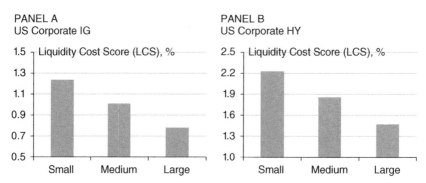

FIGURE 17.4   Average Liquidity Cost Scores of Size Portfolios, January 2007 to May 2018
Source: Barclays Research

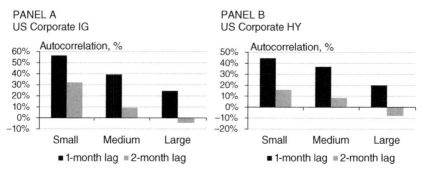

FIGURE 17.5   Autocorrelations in Excess Returns of Size Portfolios, January 1993 to May 2018
Source: Barclays Research

In IG, volatilities of small-size portfolios become higher than those of large-size portfolios when returns are measured over quarterly or semiannual periods. This finding clearly demonstrates that eliminating the effect of autocorrelation (due to stale pricing), by measuring returns over longer time intervals, makes volatility estimates more realistic. Panel B of Figure 17.6 shows that annualized volatilities of small-size portfolios in HY also increase proportionately more than those of large-size portfolios when returns are measured over longer time intervals, so that the difference between volatilities of small- and large-size portfolios declines. However, in contrast to our results in IG, small-size HY portfolios remain

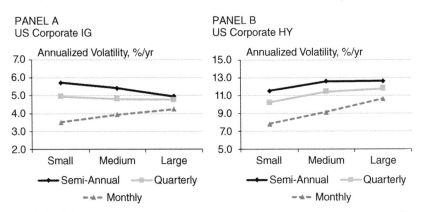

FIGURE 17.6 Size Portfolios' Excess Returns Volatilities Measured over Different Horizons, January 1993 to May 2018
Source: Barclays Research

slightly less volatile than large ones. We conclude that the benefits to risk-adjusted returns of smaller-size portfolios attributed to their seemingly low volatilities are induced by illiquidity and might be fictitious in reality.

Portfolios sorted on issuer size can have different characteristics or sector composition. Table 17.6 compares the characteristics of small- and large-size portfolios in the IG and HY corporate markets as of 31 May 2018. The small-size portfolio has higher spread and lower quality than the large-size portfolio. The spread differences between small- and large-size portfolios (SML) are 14bp in IG and 86bp in HY. The average differences in rating numbers are respectively 0.6 and 1.5.[9] The small-size portfolio is less liquid than the large one. Liquidity is measured using LCS. The differences in LCS between small- and large-size portfolios were 0.29% in IG and 0.45% in HY. Bonds in the small-size portfolio also experienced significantly lower trading volumes as a percentage of their amount outstanding compared to those in the large-size portfolio: 4.2%/month vs. 7.2%/month in IG and 11.7%/month vs. 13.9%/month in HY.

The lower panel of Table 17.6 shows that sector allocation in small- and large-size portfolios is quite different and is broadly consistent with average issuer sizes reported in Table 17.1.

In particular, the small- size portfolio in IG significantly overweights basic & capital goods and financial others but underweights communication & technology, transportation & energy, and banks & brokerage. Similarly,

TABLE 17.6 Comparing Characteristics and Allocations of Issuer Size Portfolios, 31 May 2018

	US Corporate IG				US Corporate HY			
	Small	Medium	Large	SML	Small	Medium	Large	SML
OAS, bp	126	118	112	14	434	378	348	86
OAD, yr	7.7	7.1	7.5	0.3	3.3	3.6	4.0	-0.8
DTS, % × yr	10.1	9.6	10.2	-0.1	13.4	13.4	14.7	-1.3
Rating No.	8.7	9.1	8.1	0.6	16.3	16.0	14.8	1.5
LCS, %	0.86	0.74	0.57	0.29	1.31	1.11	0.86	0.45
Monthly Volume, % Amount/m	4.20%	5.10%	7.20%	-3.00%	11.70%	13.50%	13.90%	-2.20%
Broad Sector Allocation								
Basic and Capital Goods	24%	19%	6%	18%	32%	26%	12%	20%
Cyclical	7%	9%	7%	0%	21%	17%	12%	9%
Noncyclical	18%	13%	20%	-2%	9%	15%	17%	-8%
Comm. & Technology	6%	14%	22%	-16%	14%	16%	28%	-14%
Transport. & Energy	6%	11%	12%	-6%	11%	16%	18%	-7%
Utilities	6%	5%	5%	1%	3%	1%	4%	0%
Banks & Brokerage	8%	6%	20%	-13%	2%	1%	1%	1%
Financial Others	25%	22%	7%	17%	7%	8%	7%	0%

Note: Option-adjusted spread (OAS), option-adjusted duration (OAD).
Source: Barclays Research

the small-size portfolio in HY overweights basic & capital goods and cyclical and underweights noncyclical, communication & technology, and transportation & energy.

The differences in characteristics of the small- and large-size portfolios have been persistent over time, as shown in Table 17.7, which covers different time periods: 1994 to 2006 and 2007 to 2018. Small-size portfolios have higher spreads, higher DTS, lower quality (higher rating number), lower liquidity (higher LCS) and lower trading volumes. Although the differences are more pronounced in the 2007–2018 period, they were also present from 1994 to 2006.

Differences in portfolio characteristics and sector allocations can affect spread premia as well as excess returns. Therefore, it is important to control for rating and sector allocations when attributing spread or returns due to a size factor.

ESTIMATING SIZE SPREAD PREMIUM

In order to measure the spread premium associated with size, we account for differences in sector, rating allocations, and liquidity between small- and large-size portfolios. We use a statistical technique[10] where spreads of individual issuers are attributed to their characteristics, including size, duration, sector, rating, and liquidity. We illustrate the incremental steps in spread attribution by using three regression models. Model 1 includes size dummy variables for small (bottom 30%) and large (top 30%) issuers while controlling for duration and sector allocation. Model 2 adds control variables for rating quality. Finally, Model 3 includes LCS per unit of duration in addition to the control variables used in model 2.

The spread difference between small and large issuers can be measured as the difference between spreads attributed to small and large issuers in the three models. This difference changes as we control for an increasingly larger set of issuer characteristics.

Table 17.8 shows the estimated spread difference between small and large issuers (SML) in US IG and HY as of 31 May 2018, using different sets of control variables. It also highlights control variables included into different models.[11]

According to Model 1, the spreads between small and large issuers are 17.2bp in IG and 69.1bp in HY. This does not account for the fact that small-size issuers tend to have lower credit ratings. Model 2 accounts for this by controlling for quality and reports a smaller spread difference

TABLE 17.7 Comparing Characteristics of Size Portfolios in Different Periods

	US Corporate IG				US Corporate HY			
	Small	Medium	Large	SML	Small	Medium	Large	SML
	January 1994–May 2018				January 1994–May 2018			
OAS, bp	172	151	133	39	656	554	483	174
OAD, yr	6.2	6.3	6.2	-0.1	3.8	4.1	4.7	-0.9
DTS, % × yr	10.8	9.8	9.0	1.8	23.4	21.7	21.3	2.1
Rating No.	8.8	8.5	7.4	1.4	16.2	15.8	14.9	1.3
	January 1994–December 2006				January 1994–December 2006			
OAS, bp	132	119	103	28	578	505	427	150
OAD, yr	5.7	6.1	5.7	0.0	4.1	4.2	4.9	-0.8
DTS, % × yr	7.8	7.5	6.5	1.3	22.2	20.7	19.9	2.4
Rating No.	8.6	8.1	7.3	1.3	15.8	15.5	14.7	1.2
	January 2007–May 2018				January 2007–May 2018			
OAS, bp	218	188	166	52	746	610	546	200
OAD, yr	6.7	6.5	6.9	-0.1	3.4	3.9	4.4	-0.9
DTS, % × yr	14.3	12.4	12	2.3	24.7	22.9	22.9	1.7
Rating No.	9.0	9.0	7.6	1.4	16.6	16.0	15.1	1.5
LCS, %	1.23	1.01	0.78	0.45	2.23	1.86	1.47	0.76
Monthly Volume, % Amount	5.00%	6.30%	7.60%	-2.60%	6.30%	8.20%	10.40%	-4.10%

Note: Option-adjusted spread (OAS), option-adjusted duration (OAD).
Source: Barclays Research

TABLE 17.8 Estimating Size Spread Premium, 31 May 2018

	US Corporate IG			US Corporate HY		
	Model 1	Model 2	Model 3	Model 1	Model 2	Model 3
SML	17.2	5.7	3.0	69.1	6.9	5.3
Control variables						
Duration	Y	Y	Y	Y	Y	Y
Sectors	Y	Y	Y	Y	Y	Y
Ratings	-	Y	Y	-	Y	Y
Liquidity	-	-	Y	-	-	Y
R^2	26%	72%	73%	4%	34%	35%

Source: Barclays Research

between small and large issuers: 5.7bp in IG and 6.9bp in HY. Controlling for liquidity, as done in Model 3, reduces SML spread difference further to 3.0bp in IG and 5.3bp in HY markets.

The regression analysis in Table 17.8 is run as of 31 May 2018. This analysis can be repeated each month in our sample, so that historical spread differences between small- and large-size issuers can be decomposed into size, liquidity, and rating components. The rating component reflects the spread due to differences in credit ratings between small and large issuers. The liquidity component is the spread portion attributed to differences in liquidity between small and large issuers. Finally, the size component reflects the spread differential between small and large issuers when controlling for sector, rating, duration, and liquidity.

Panels A and B of Figure 17.7 show the attribution results of historical spread differences between small and large issuers in IG and HY universes. Bond-level LCS are available only from 2007 so the results cover a relatively short period. Monthly results are aggregated to obtain yearly averages.

In the IG universe, the two most important factors affecting spread differences are rating and liquidity. Once they are taken into account, the remaining spread premium is relatively low. The size premium varied significantly over time: from –22bp in 2008, when smaller-size issuers had tighter spreads than large ones, to 24bp in 2012. The size premium has been small (3bp) in 2018, while the spread difference between small and large issuers attributed to differences in credit rating has been sizable (17bp). The spread premium attributed to differences in *liquidity* between small- and large-size IG issuers also varied significantly over time. It declined from 48–58bp in 2008–2009 to only 3bp in 2018.

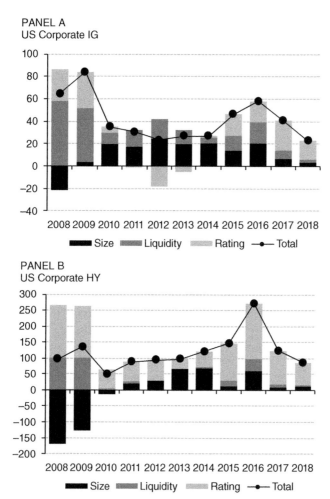

PANEL A
US Corporate IG

PANEL B
US Corporate HY

FIGURE 17.7   Attributing Spread Difference Between Small- and Large-Size Issuers
Source: Barclays Research

In the HY universe, differences in credit rating have been the most important contributor to the spread differential between small and large issuers: The rating spread premium has always been positive and varied in a range between 32bp (in 2013) and 175bp (in 2016). Differences in credit rating contributed 73bp to the spread differential between small and large issuers in 2018. Interestingly, the liquidity component seems to be less important in HY than in IG. It became sizable during market distress (e.g., during the financial crisis in 2008–2009 or the energy crisis in 2015–2016) but otherwise remained relatively low. In 2018 the spread premium attributed to liquidity was only 2bp. The size spread premium in HY has varied significantly over time. It was negative in 2008 to 2010, reached a maximum of 70bp in 2014, and was only 13bp in 2018.

Interestingly, the size spread premium is not necessarily a monotonic function of issuer size. Figure 17.8 plots average spread premium (controlling for sector, rating, duration, and liquidity) for size deciles in January–May 2018.[12] Both small and very large issuers in IG and HY seem to have a positive spread premium.

There could be several explanations for a positive spread premium of the largest issuers. One possibility is that very large issuers can create a significant risk concentration in credit portfolios benchmarked to the index. Investors may accordingly demand an additional spread premium for holding those names. Another explanation is that very large issuers have become large by issuing debt more aggressively than their peers. Since aggressive issuers tend to underperform moderate issuers, especially during market turmoil,[13] the market could demand extra spread premia as compensation. Spread premia for different issuer sizes can change over time according to the market environment.

PERFORMANCE OF EXPOSURE-MATCHED SIZE PORTFOLIOS

Using the analogy from equity markets, we call return differentials between small- and large-size portfolios the SML returns or SML factor. As shown in the previous analysis, portfolios sorted on issuer size can be very different in

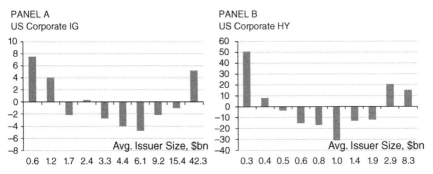

FIGURE 17.8 Average Size Spread Premium by Issuer-Size Deciles, January 2018 to May 2018
Source: Barclays Research

terms of their sector and rating allocations.[14] Such differences could have a large effect on performance and dwarf the effect of a pure SML return factor. To isolate the effects of issuer size on portfolio returns, we assemble two exposure-matched portfolios that have very similar allocations and systematic risk characteristics but different issuer sizes.

The portfolios are built by minimizing (small size) or maximizing (large size) issuer size subject to constraints that make portfolio exposures identical to the ones of the Bloomberg Barclays US Corporate IG or HY indices.

At the beginning of each month, the two portfolios are required to match OAS, OAD, and DTS of the index. In addition, the portfolios have identical weights, OAD and DTS contributions across 16 sector-maturity buckets, and identical weights and duration contributions across rating buckets. Finally, in order to ensure sufficient diversification, we impose strong restrictions on issuer concentration in terms of deviations from index weights and DTS contributions.

As a result, at the beginning of each month, we obtain two exposure-matched portfolios with very different issuer sizes but identical exposures to systematic risk. Figure 17.9 plots historical OAD, DTS (Panel A) and OAS (Panel B) of small- and large-size portfolios in the US IG universe. The two portfolios seem indistinguishable on any of these characteristics. Exposures are similarly matched for sector, maturity, and rating partitions.

We next verify that the two portfolios are sufficiently diversified to limit issuer-specific risk with a view to isolate the size factor. Table 17.9 shows the average number of bonds and issuers in each portfolio over different periods. Small-size portfolios included on average 500 bonds of 300 issuers, while large portfolios included around 400 bonds of 110 issuers. In both cases, size portfolios were sufficiently diversified. Large-size portfolios are more concentrated because concentration limits are anchored to issuer weights in the capitalization-weighted index. Table 17.9 also reports the large and intended differences between average issuer sizes in small- and large-size portfolios.

We next compare historical performance of small- and large-size portfolios in US IG and HY markets.[15] Table 17.10 summarizes performances in different periods. Small-size portfolios *underperformed* large-size portfolios by 67bp/yr and 32bp/yr in the US IG and HY markets respectively, with a stronger underperformance in the period from 2007 to 2018. In HY, small-size portfolios outperformed their large-size peers by 12bp/yr between 1994 and 2006, while in IG, small-size portfolios underperformed by 28bp/yr

PANEL A
OA duration (OAD) and duration times spread (DTS)

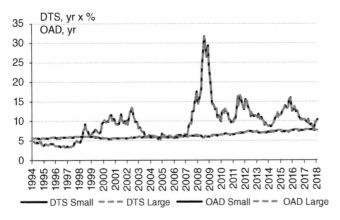

PANEL B
OA spread (OAS)

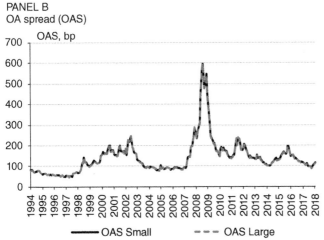

FIGURE 17.9 Historical Characteristics of Exposure-Matched Portfolios in US IG
Source: Barclays Research

over the same period. Given the fact that small- and large-size portfolios are
otherwise exposure-matched, the difference in their returns can be attributed to issuer size.

TABLE 17.9   Characteristics of Exposure-Matched Portfolios in US IG by Period

	# Bonds		# Issuers		Size in $bn	
Period	Small	Large	Small	Large	Small	Large
1994–1998	491	401	306	105	0.27	1.4
1999–2003	503	380	316	108	0.45	3.23
2004–2008	481	371	282	110	0.81	4.21
2009–2013	529	397	297	119	0.9	5.02
2014–2018	569	417	332	127	0.88	5.91

Source: Barclays Research

Consistent with Table 17.5, excess returns of small-size portfolios appear less volatile than those of large ones, despite the fact that systematic exposures are closely matched. Indeed, volatilities of excess returns of small- and large-size portfolios are respectively 3.37%/yr and 4.50%/yr in IG; and 8.06%/yr and 10.27%/yr in HY.

Cumulative SML returns are reported in Figure 17.10 and illustrate the performance dynamics of exposure-matched size portfolios in IG and HY markets.

Panel A shows that in IG, small-size portfolios consistently *underperformed* large-size portfolios. Panel B shows similar results for HY. In both cases, SML underperformed during benign environment but outperformed during the telecom (2001–2002) and the financial (2008) crises. Table 17.11 details SML performance during the crises across sectors.

Unsurprisingly, the strongest SML returns occurred in the communication & technology sector in 2001–2002. Indeed, small-size portfolios outperformed by 20.2% in IG and by 43.3% in HY in the communication & technology sector. Similarly, strong SML returns during the 2008 crisis were observed in the financial sector: 5.6% in IG and 38.7% in HY.[16]

Significant reversals of the SML factor during market distress can be explained by the fact that larger, potentially more aggressive and leveraged, debt issuers tend to suffer more during the crisis than their smaller, moderate, counterparts.[17] Additionally, bonds issued by small issuers tend to be illiquid during market distress, which can make the process of price discovery difficult.

PANEL A
US Corporate IG

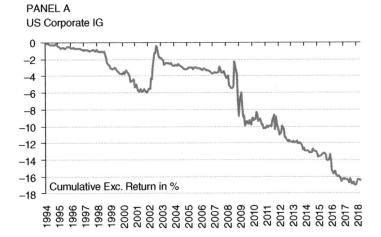

PANEL B
US Corporate HY

FIGURE 17.10 Cumulative SML Returns Obtained as Return Differentials Between Small and Large Exposure-Matched Portfolios
Source: Barclays Research

Results reported in Table 17.10 and Figure 17.10 indicate that SML credit factor tend to have a negative risk premium other things equal: Bonds issued by small issuers, with otherwise similar characteristics to those issued by large issuers, tend to *underperform*.[18] This is probably not surprising, as access to capital markets might be generally harder for smaller issuers.

TABLE 17.10 Performance of Exposure-Matched IG and HY Size Portfolios over Different Periods

	US Corp IG			US Corp HY		
	Small	Large	Diff (SML)	Small	Large	Diff (SML)
January 1994–May 2018						
Avg. Exc. Ret., %/yr	0.3	0.97	−0.67	2.62	2.93	−0.32
Volatility, %/yr	3.37	4.5	1.65	8.06	10.27	4.31
Information Ratio	0.09	0.22	−0.41	0.32	0.29	−0.07
Max. Drawdown, %	−24.6	−24.4	−15.9	−43	−46	−21
January 1994–December 2006						
Avg. Exc. Ret., %/yr	0.28	0.56	−0.28	1.64	1.53	0.12
Volatility, %/yr	1.73	2.36	1.02	6.25	8.29	3.54
Information Ratio	0.16	0.24	−0.27	0.26	0.18	0.03
Max. Drawdown, %	−7.5	−7.8	−5.8	−29.9	−40	−10.5
January 2007–May 2018						
Avg. Exc. Ret., %/yr	0.31	1.43	−1.12	3.72	4.53	−0.81
Volatility, %/yr	4.57	6.07	2.15	9.71	12.12	5.05
Information Ratio	0.07	0.24	−0.52	0.38	0.37	−0.16
Max. Drawdown, %	−24.3	−24.4	−13.8	−43	−45.9	−17.8

Source: Barclays Research

TABLE 17.11 SML Returns Across Industry Sectors During Market Distress

| | US Corporate IG | | | | | | US Corporate HY | | | | | |
| | Jan 2002–Sep 2002 | | | Jul 2008–Sep 2008 | | | Jan 2001–Jul 2002 | | | Apr 2008–Nov 2008 | | |
	Small	Large	SML	Small	Large	SML	Small	Large	SML	Small	Large	SML
Basic & Capital Goods	2.2	1.4	0.8	-3.2	-5.8	2.5	-1.4	2.0	-3.4	-27.3	-33.3	6.0
Cyclical	-0.2	-3.2	3.1	-4.3	-5.7	1.4	6.5	3.1	3.4	-37.8	-49.1	11.3
Noncyclical	1.2	0.8	0.4	-4.3	-4.4	0.0	8.8	18.9	-10.1	-22.4	-24.7	2.4
Energy	2.2	2.9	-0.7	-5.9	-9.2	3.3	2.5	5.8	-3.3	-33.3	-32.4	-0.9
Comm. & Technology	-3.9	-24.1	20.2	-4.7	-6.2	1.4	-20.6	-63.8	43.3	-33.8	-38.4	4.6
Utility	-3.5	-15.7	12.2	-6.0	-6.2	0.2	-21.8	-36.3	14.5	-29.5	-28.9	-0.6
Financial	0.2	-2.0	2.2	-13.1	-18.7	5.6	6.2	2.2	4.0	-31.8	-70.5	38.7
Total	-0.6	-6.1	5.6	-8.5	-11.7	3.2	-6.0	-20.2	14.2	-31.5	-39.1	7.6

Source: Barclays Research

CONCLUSION

We found that bonds issued by smaller issuers typically have higher spreads. However, a large portion of this spread premium is attributed to difference in sector and rating allocation between portfolios of small- and large-size issuers. When accounting for differences in sector allocation, credit rating, and liquidity, the average spread premium attributed to size was 3bp in IG and 5.3bp in HY in May 2018 but varied widely from –22bp to 24bp in IG and from –171bp to 70bp in HY.

Excess returns of small-issuer portfolios seem less volatile than those of their large-issuer counterparts. However, this phenomenon is likely related to the poor liquidity of bonds issued by small issuers.

When controlling for systematic risk exposures and characteristics, we find that portfolios of small issuers tend to underperform portfolios of large issuers. The annualized underperformance between 1994 and 2018 was –67bp/yr in US IG and –32bp/yr in US HY. A few episodes when small-issuer portfolios outperformed those of large issuers were associated with market distress.

Our findings generally do not support the existence of a size factor that could be exploited by credit investors the same way many equity investors systematically favor smaller-capitalization stocks with a view to enhance returns.

APPENDIX 17.1

Estimating SML Spread Premia

Tables 17.12 and 17.13 detail the estimation of size spread premia in the IG and HY markets using regression models similar to the Fama–MacBeth approach. As discussed in the text, we use three models, which sequentially add control variables to the analysis. Model 1 controls issuer spread for duration and sector. Spread premium (SML) is estimated as the difference between coefficient of size dummy variables for bottom and top 30% of issuers sorted on size. Estimated SML spread before controlling for ratings and liquidity is 17.2bp as of 31 May 2018. Table 17.12 also shows a significant variation in sector spreads.

Next, we add rating dummies to the set of explanatory variables in Model 2. As expected, credit ratings explain a large portion of SML spread estimated in Model 1: SML spread declines from 17.2 to 5.7bp when

TABLE 17.12 Size Premia in US Corporate IG, 31 May 2018

Category	Variable	Model 1: Sector		Model 2: Sector + Rating		Model 3: Sector + Rating + Liquidity	
		Coeff.	t-stat.	Coeff.	t-stat.	Coeff.	t-stat.
Size	**SML**	17.2		5.7		3	
	Small	11.8	3	8.1	3.3	6.6	2.6
	Large	−5.4	−1.4	2.3	0.9	3.6	1.4
OAD	OAD	4.8	8	6.8	17.9	7.2	18.2
Sector	BAS	105	24	37	5.1	37	5.2
	CYC	120	21.3	50	6.8	51	6.9
	NCY	117	24.7	46	6.5	47	6.7
	COT	123	24.6	55	7.8	55	7.9
	TRE	142	28.6	60	8.3	61	8.5
	UTI	105	16.5	40	5.1	39	5
	BAB	105	17.6	61	8	63	8.3
	FIO	127	29.4	63	8.9	62	8.8
Rating	A1	-	-	10	1.1	9	1
	A2	-	-	29	3.9	28	3.9
	A3	-	-	40	5.7	40	5.7
	BAA1	-	-	59	8.5	59	8.5
	BAA2	-	-	78	11.4	78	11.5
	BAA3	-	-	103	15.1	103	15.2
Bid-Ask	Liquidity	-	-	-	-	0.79	3.2
	R-sq	26%		72%		73%	

Source: Barclays Research

TABLE 17.13   Size Premia in US Corporate HY, 31 May 2018

Category	Variable	Model 1 Coeff.	Model 1 t-stat.	Model 2 Coeff.	Model 2 t-stat.	Model 3 Coeff.	Model 3 t-stat.
Size	SML	69.1		6.9		5.3	
	Small	56.8	2.1	18.1	0.8	19.5	0.9
	Large	-12.3	-0.5	11.2	0.5	14.2	0.7
OAD	OAD	-7.9	-1	19.9	3	25.9	3.7
Sector	BAS	316	11.6	149	3.5	145	3.5
	CYC	356	13.4	202	4.8	200	4.8
	NCY	402	17.3	201	4.7	198	4.7
	UAE	421	15.3	237	5.6	236	5.6
	FIN	281	6	156	3	150	2.9
Rating	BA2	-	-	33	0.7	35	0.7
	BA3	-	-	49	1.1	52	1.2
	B1	-	-	69	1.6	70	1.6
	B2	-	-	144	3.4	143	3.4
	B3	-	-	196	4.6	201	4.7
	CCC and below	-	-	445	10.4	445	10.5
Bid-Ask	Liquidity	-	-	-	-	0.21	2.9
	R-sq	4%		34%		35%	

Source: Barclays Research

controlling for rating quality. Finally, SML drops to only 3bp when controlling for liquidity.

Table 17.13 estimates SML spread premium in the US HY market as of 31 May 2018. It drops from 69.1bp in Model 1 (before controlling for rating and liquidity) to only 5.3bp in Model 3.

EXPOSURE-MATCHED PORTFOLIOS WITH RELAXED CONSTRAINTS

SML factor returns in this chapter are estimated by building exposure-matched portfolios of small and large issuers. Among other things, we required that the average spread and DTS of the small and large portfolios be identical.

However, investors who buy bonds issued by small issuers often wish to collect a positive spread premium (please see Table 17.8 and Figure 17.7). This additional spread carry can, at least partially, offset the underperformance of SML seen above. We therefore repeated our analysis of exposure-matched small- and large-size portfolios but this time allowed the portfolios to have slightly different spreads (OAS) and DTS exposures while keeping other constraints (sector, rating allocation, and duration contributions) unchanged. In particular, portfolio spreads and DTS exposures were allowed to deviate by 10% from the spread of the underlying index.

As before, the portfolios are built by minimizing (small size) or maximizing (large size) issuer size subject to remaining constraints.

Table 17.14 shows performance statistics for IG and HY exposure-matched size portfolios with relaxed spread and DTS constraints. Over the entire period, SML continues to underperform in IG (–16bp/yr) and has a negligible return in HY.

Finally, Figure 17.11 shows the cumulative return of the SML return factor obtained as return differentials between exposure-matched portfolios with relaxed spread and DTS constraints.

Overall, our findings do not support the existence of a size factor that could be systematically exploited by credit investors, even though opportunistic allocation to smaller-size issuers is possible on a tactical basis.

TABLE 17.14 Performance of Exposure-Matched Size Portfolios with Relaxed Spread and DTS Constraints

	US Corp IG			US Corp HY		
	Small	Large	Diff (SML)	Small	Large	Diff (SML)
January 1994–May 2018						
Avg. Exc. Ret., %/yr	0.52	0.68	-0.16	2.72	2.69	0.03
Volatility, %/yr	3.4	4.44	1.7	8.36	10.49	4.59
Information Ratio	0.15	0.15	-0.09	0.33	0.26	0.01
Max. Drawdown, %	-24.1	-24.6	-8	-43.8	-46.3	-17.2
January 1994–December 2006						
Avg. Exc. Ret., %/yr	0.38	0.4	-0.03	1.44	1.56	-0.12
Volatility, %/yr	1.71	2.34	1.08	6.38	8.61	3.92
Information Ratio	0.22	0.17	-0.02	0.23	0.18	-0.03
Max. Drawdown, %	-6.9	-9.1	-3.4	-32.4	-40	-11.6
January 2007–May 2018						
Avg. Exc. Ret., %/yr	0.69	1	-0.31	4.18	3.98	0.2
Volatility, %/yr	4.62	6	2.2	10.13	12.28	5.26
InformationRatio	0.15	0.17	-0.14	0.41	0.32	0.04
Max. Drawdown, %	-24	-24.5	-6.8	-43.8	-46.3	-13.3

Source: Bloomberg, Barclays Research

PANEL A
US Corporate IG

PANEL B
US Corporate HY

FIGURE 17.11 Cumulative SML Returns Obtained from Exposure-Matched Portfolios with Relaxed Spread and DTS Constraints
Source: Barclays Research

REFERENCES

Alquist, R., R. Israel, and T. J. Moskowitz. 2018. "Fact, Fiction, and the Size Effect." *Journal of Portfolio Management* 45(1): 34–61.

Asness, C., A. Frazzini, R. Israel, T. J. Moskowitz, and L. H. Pedersen. 2018. "Size Matter, If You Control Your Junk." *Journal of Financial Economics* 129(3): 479–509.

Ben Dor, A., L. Dynkin, J. Hyman, P. Houweling, E. Van Leeuwen, and O. Penninga. 2007. "DTS^{SM} (Duration Times Spread)." *Journal of Portfolio Management* 33(2): 77–100.

Fama, E., and D. MacBeth. 1973. "Risk, Return, and Equilibrium: Empirical Tests." *Journal of Political Economy* 81(3): 607–636.

Harri, A., and B. W. Brorsen. 2009. "The Overlapping Data Problem." *Quantitative and Qualitative Analysis in Social Sciences* 3(3): 78–115.

Houweling, P., and J. Zundert. 2017. "Factor Investing in the Corporate Bond Market." *Financial Analysts Journal* 73(2): 1–16.

Hyman, J., and S. Polbennikov. 2017, June 13. "Smart Beta in Credit." Barclays Research.

Konstantinovsky, V., K. Y. Ng, and B. D. Phelps. 2016. "Measuring Bond-Level Liquidity." *Journal of Portfolio Management* 42(4): 116–128.

NOTES

1. See, for example, Asness, Frazzini, Israel, Moskowitz, and Pedersen (2018).
2. Please note that Bloomberg Barclays US Corporate and US HY indices also include USD-denominated bonds issued by foreign companies. Such bonds are often called *Yankees*. We exclude them from our analysis because, in principle, a large foreign issuer can have a relatively small representation in the USD market.
3. This definition of issuer size is similar to the one used in Houweling and Van Zundert (2017), who used issuer index weights as the measure of size. Our motivation to consider issuer's outstanding amount rather than its market value is to make the size measure independent of bond pricing. We look at issuer's debt outstanding in both Bloomberg Barclays US IG and HY indices. Some issuers can appear in both universes—for example, if an issuer has both senior and lower-rated subordinated debt.
4. Bonds with amount outstanding below \$300m in US IG and \$250m in US HY are excluded according to the index rules. This could potentially eliminate some small issuers.
5. In cases when an issuer is a private subsidiary of a public company, we use financial data provided by the parent. Our methodology, therefore, implicitly assumes that a parent company would step in if its issuing subsidiary falls into distress. This might not always be the case. For example, a holding company can allow its subsidiary to fall.
6. Please see Hyman and Polbennikov (2017).
7. LCS are based on trader bid–offer quotes and measure a round-trip transaction cost in individual bonds. Higher LCS correspond to less liquid securities. Barclays Research makes regularly updated bond-level scores (LCS) available to investors. See Konstantinovsky, Ng, and Phelps (2016) for more details.

8. We annualize volatilities of monthly, quarterly, and semiannual returns by multiplying them by square roots of 12, 4, and 2, respectively. Volatilities of quarterly and semiannual returns are calculated from overlapping time-series sampled monthly. Even though the overlapping returns are auto-correlated, the resulting volatility estimates remain consistent and utilize available information more efficiently than would be the case with nonoverlapping quarterly or semiannual returns. Please see Harri and Brorsen (2009) for details.
9. Bond index rating numbers vary from 1 to 24 on a linear scale with a higher number representing a lower credit rating.
10. Our approach is similar to Fama–MacBeth cross-sectional regression; please see Fama and MacBeth (1973).
11. Model details including estimated coefficients and *t*-statistics are provided in Appendix 17.1.
12. The spread premium as function of issuer size is obtained by averaging regression residuals by issuer size deciles. Issuer spreads are regressed on: (a) sector dummies, (b) rating dummies, (c) duration, and (d) LCS normalized by the duration. Average spread premium across all issuer sizes is zero.
13. We discussed the effect of issuance dynamics on corporate bond returns in Chapter 5.
14. See Tables 17.6 and 17.7.
15. Small- and large-size exposure-matched HY portfolios are built using the methodology analogous to the one described for the IG market.
16. Please note the differences in respective periods for IG and HY markets. In both episodes, small-size portfolios started outperforming large-size portfolios earlier in HY than in IG markets.
17. See the discussion on issuance dynamics in Chapter 5.
18. At the same time, we recognize that investors usually receive a spread premium for investing into small issuers. This additional spread carry can, at least partially, offset the documented underperformance of smaller-size issuers. We repeated our analysis of exposure-matched small and large issuer size portfolios, where we allowed the portfolios to have slightly different OAS and DTS but left other exposure constraints (sector, rating allocation, and duration contributions) intact. As a result, small-size portfolios acquired additional spread premium related to size and liquidity. The performance results are reported in Table 17.14 and Figure 17.11 in Appendix 17.1.

Combining Factor Strategies

CHAPTER 18

Integrating Systematic Strategies into Credit Portfolio Construction

INTRODUCTION

Quantitative models and strategies are often used by institutional investors in liquid markets: Value, momentum, reversion, and sentiment signals[1] have been adopted by traders and portfolio managers in equity, rates, and foreign exchange markets.

Interest in systematic strategies has recently broadened to credit markets. Informative signals based on valuation, momentum and sentiment have been advocated in the industry as well as in academic literature.[2] In Chapters 13 to 16, we introduced systematic strategies based on value and stock-bond momentum. Based on this research, we have designed quantitative scorecards called the Excess Spread to Peers (ESP) and the Equity Momentum in Credit (EMC) scorecards. These scorecards provide security-level value and momentum signals in US and European corporate bond markets.

Implementing quantitative strategies in credit portfolio entails some unique challenges. In addition to quantitative signals that must be produced periodically for a broad universe, portfolio construction must be carefully designed to control turnover, prudently estimate transaction costs, and ensure that the portfolio structure conforms with the allocation of a market index.

These requirements contrasts with the much simpler approach commonly followed in equity markets. Stock-selection strategies often involve *percentile* portfolios, where individual names are sorted on an informative signal with the top percentile forming a strategy portfolio.

For example, individual stocks in an equity index can be sorted on a valuation measure into decile portfolios with the strategy portfolio represented by the top decile. The performance of this top-value portfolio, after estimated transaction costs, can be compared to that of a benchmark index in order to assess the usefulness of the signal.

In contrast to the equity market, similarly sorted bond *percentile* portfolios are unlikely to be practical for credit portfolio managers because they ignore turnover, transaction costs, bond liquidity, and the structure of an underlying benchmark index.

Transaction costs of corporate bonds can be high, so excessive turnover can create a significant drag on portfolio performance. Implementing a realistic strategy portfolio of corporate bonds requires turnover controls as well as a reliable way to measure transaction costs. In addition, liquidity of corporate bonds varies over time and across individual securities. A corporate bond included in a broad market index may often be unavailable to buy in the secondary market. A practical implementation of a strategy portfolio should therefore correctly identify and avoid highly illiquid securities. Doing this can be especially challenging in a back-test as historical liquidity characteristics of individual corporate bonds are required to make a portfolio simulation realistic.

We address these challenges by carefully building and back-testing strategy portfolios net of transaction costs between 2007 and 2019 using Barclays quantitative scorecards and analytics. In the absence of a long industry track record of managing actual credit portfolios according to systematic styles, our portfolio simulation can help inform investors about the performance and properties of systematic investing in corporate bond markets.

In our analysis we apply the ESP model of Chapter 13 and the EMC model of Chapter 15 to US corporate investment-grade (IG) bonds, and we explain how these relative value and equity momentum signals can be integrated into an actual investment portfolio while limiting turnover and respecting benchmark-related constraints.

Using Liquidity Cost Scores (LCS) as a conservative measure of bond-level trading costs, we confirm that strategy portfolios based on ESP and EMC signals delivered sizable returns over the Bloomberg Barclays US Corporate index *net of rebalancing costs*.

In this chapter, we first revisit the quantitative relative value (ESP) and equity momentum (EMC) strategies and provide the case for combining them in a strategy portfolio. We then review Barclays LCS and explain how they can be used to measure historical transaction costs and monitor security-level liquidity. Next we propose two alternative mechanisms for controlling turnover in the implementation of strategy portfolios. In the first, a turnover buffer precludes trading securities with intermediate signal levels; transactions are initiated only by a strong signal to either buy or sell. In the second, the portfolio is rebalanced monthly to maximize strategy scores subject to an explicit turnover budget and exposure constraints. In a case study of each approach, we demonstrate that strategy portfolios based on a combination of ESP and EMC signals can reduce rebalancing costs by including one of these two mechanisms for controlling turnover.

RELATIVE VALUE AND EQUITY MOMENTUM STRATEGIES IN CREDIT

Quantitative strategies based on relative value and equity momentum have gained prominence among corporate bond investors. In Chapters 13, 14, and 15, we documented the characteristics and performance of these strategies before transaction costs. We introduced quantitative scorecards that rank corporate bonds on relative value[3] and stock-bond momentum: excess spread to peers and equity momentum in credit. Security-level (ESP) or issuer-level (EMC) scores are updated monthly and cover corporate bonds included in major indices.[4]

As discussed in Chapter 13, the ESP scorecard assigns scores from 1 to 10 to bonds according to their relative valuation with a high score indicating attractiveness. The model is implemented in two steps, as outlined in Figure 18.1. First, peer groups are identified within the corporate bond universe. In this process, individual bonds are grouped based on rating, sector, and maturity to capture systematic credit risk. The ESP Scorecard calculates the excess spread of each bond over its peer group average. Bonds with *high* or *low* excess spreads over peers are deemed *undervalued* or *overvalued*, respectively.

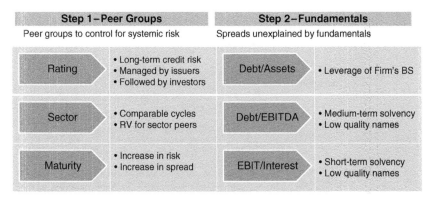

FIGURE 18.1 Excess Spread to Peers Scorecard Implementation
Source: Barclays Research

In the second step, the ESP Scorecard corrects excess spreads for differences in issuer fundamentals and bond characteristics using a regression analysis. Three fundamental ratios are used to capture variation in excess spreads: financial leverage, net debt to earnings before interest, tax, and depreciation (EBITDA), and interest coverage.[5] The *unexplained* part of excess spread over peers is translated into the ESP score by ranking all bonds in an index.[6] Securities with high *unexplained* spreads over peers are assigned high ESP scores and are deemed undervalued. Issues with *negative* unexplained spread over peers receive low ESP scores and are deemed overvalued.

As described in Chapter 15, EMC is designed to differentiate issuers by their stock price momentum. A schematic view of the algorithm is shown in Figure 18.2. EMC assigns scores from one to 10 to issuers, with a high score indicating strong equity momentum. In empirical studies, past equity returns have been found to be positively correlated with subsequent excess returns of corporate bonds.

The equity momentum of an issuer is measured as the equally weighted combination of stock price returns calculated over one-, three-, and six-month horizons and adjusted for the lengths of the signal formation periods. Doing this helps differentiate between trending stocks and stocks with short-term price volatility.

Bond- and issuer-level signals produced by ESP and EMC scorecards are informative of subsequent performance, as illustrated in Panels A and B of Figure 18.3. Corporate bonds are sorted by ESP and EMC scores into market-capitalization-weighted portfolios, whose subsequent excess returns are recorded.[7] This exercise is repeated for each month from 2007 to 2019. The results for portfolios sorted on ESP and EMC scores are shown in Panels A and B respectively.

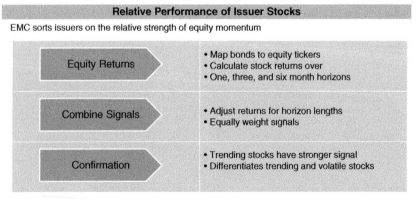

FIGURE 18.2 Equity Momentum in Credit Scorecard Implementation
Source: Barclays Research

Panel A shows that average excess returns of portfolios sorted on relative value (ESP score) increase as the score becomes larger. Portfolios of bonds with the lowest scores (ESP = 1, 2) have a negative realized average return of –0.74%/yr. In contrast, portfolios of bonds with the highest scores (ESP = 9, 10) have a positive average return of 3.39%/yr. Over the same period, the Bloomberg Barclays US Corporate IG index delivered an average excess return of 1.08%/yr.

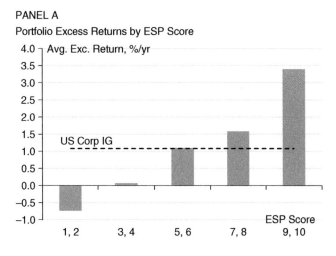

PANEL A
Portfolio Excess Returns by ESP Score

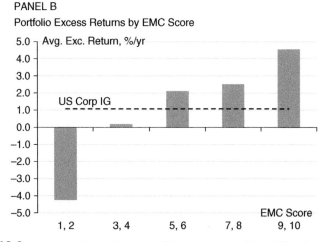

PANEL B
Portfolio Excess Returns by EMC Score

FIGURE 18.3 Average Excess Returns of Corporate Bond Portfolios Sorted on ESP and EMC Scores, March 2007 to July 2019
Source: Bloomberg, Barclays Research

Similarly, Panel B shows that average excess returns of bond portfolios sorted on equity momentum (EMC score) increase as the score becomes higher. Portfolios of bonds with the lowest scores (EMC = 1, 2) have an average return of –4.25%/yr. In contrast, portfolios of bonds with the highest scores (EMC = 9, 10) have an average return of +4.55%/yr.

These results clearly indicate that both ESP and EMC scores can add value in bond selection: Investors overweighting (underweighting) securities with high (low) scores could have outperformed the benchmark index. In addition, both scorecards can be utilized as quantitative filters to identify issues with attractive value and equity momentum characteristics in order to narrow the focus of subsequent fundamental analysis.

While ESP and EMC scores constitute informative signals for issuer selection in isolation, their combination could be even more appealing. Indeed, ESP and EMC signals can complement each other in an investment process, as shown by their low cross-sectional correlations[8] across index constituents.

Figure 18.4 shows that historical correlations between ESP and EMC scores remained low over time, oscillating around zero. Similar to other asset classes, value and momentum signals in credit tend to be uncorrelated.[9] Low correlations between ESP and EMC scores indicate that the signals are likely to complement each other without significantly reducing the investment opportunity set: There should always be a good chance to identify *undervalued* bonds with *strong issuer equity momentum*. In contrast, positive correlations between ESP and EMC would mean that the signals overlap in terms of their information content, while large negative correlations would make signals mutually exclusive because investors would be forced to trade one signal for the other.

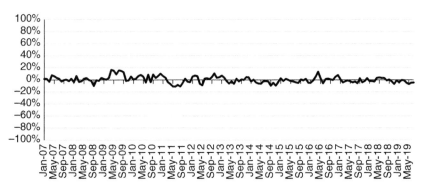

FIGURE 18.4   Monthly Cross-Sectional Rank Correlations Between ESP and EMC Scores
Source: Barclays Research

Another way to illustrate that ESP and EMC signals tend to work well in combination is to analyze the returns of top ESP and EMC portfolios[10] over the index during credit down-cycles. We define a credit down-cycle as a significant decline (top-to-trough) in cumulative excess returns of the Bloomberg Barclays US Corporate IG index in a rolling period of 12 months.

Figure 18.5 highlights seven such episodes associated with well-known market events: the 1998 Asian crisis, the 2001 telecom crisis, the 2008 financial crisis, the 2011 European Union sovereign crisis, the 2015 energy crisis, and the market decline of 2018.

Table 18.1 shows the annualized returns of the index and the top score-card portfolios during each of the market down-cycles. The first three columns report absolute average excess returns of the index and the strategy portfolios in each of the down-cycle episode. The last two columns report excess returns of the top EMC and top ESP portfolios over the index. The performance of the top ESP portfolios over the index tends to be pro-cyclical: They underperformed the index in each down-cycle except for the market decline of 1998. This should not be surprising as the ESP strategy typically selects higher-spread bonds in each rating-sector peer group, other things being equal. This often results in a positive net credit exposure (Duration Times Spread [DTS][11]) relative to the index. In contrast, the relative performance of the top EMC portfolios over the index tends to be contra-cyclical as they outperformed the index in each down-cycle. The different performance of top ESP and EMC portfolios in credit down-cycles suggests that using the two signals jointly can potentially improve risk-adjusted performance.

To illustrate the benefit of jointly utilizing ESP and EMC signals, we create two additional sets of strategy portfolios. First, we build a combined

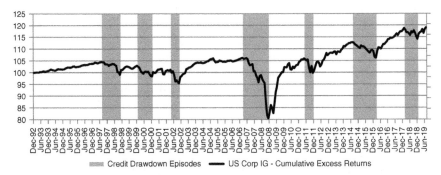

FIGURE 18.5 Drawdown Episodes in Cumulative Excess Returns of the US Corporate IG Index
Source: Bloomberg, Barclays Research

TABLE 18.1 Annualized Average Excess Returns of Top Scorecard Portfolios in Credit Down-Cycles Between January 1993 and July 2019, %/yr

Down-Cycle Episodes	Absolute			Over Index	
	US Corp	Top EMC	Top ESP	Top EMC	Top ESP
Aug 1997–Oct 1998	−4.2	−2.8	−3.8	1.4	0.4
Jan 2000–Dec 2000	−4.5	−2.0	−7.0	2.5	−2.5
Apr 2002–Oct 2002	−9.9	4.3	−19.8	14.2	−9.9
Mar 2007–Nov 2008	−15.4	−11.6	−15.6	3.8	−0.2
May 2011–Nov 2011	−9.9	−5.5	−12.5	4.5	−2.6
Aug 2014–Feb 2016	−3.8	−1.6	−4.2	2.2	−0.5
Feb 2018–Dec 2018	−4.3	−3.5	−4.4	0.8	−0.1
All Other Periods (71% of months)	*4.1*	*6.5*	*6.7*	*2.4*	*2.6*

Source: Bloomberg, Barclays Research

portfolio by equally weighting the top ESP and EMC portfolios. Combining the two portfolios should help diversify risk and smooth the performance of the two strategies taken in isolation. Second, we build a portfolio based on a combination of the ESP and EMC signals. We calculate the equally weighted ESP-EMC score for each bond in the index universe and then select bonds in the top quintile of the combined signal. Doing this ensures that the strategy portfolio invests into undervalued securities issued by names with strong equity momentum.

Table 18.2 reports the performance of the top ESP and top EMC portfolios, their equally weighted combination (*Combined Portfolios 50/50*), and the portfolios based on the combined ESP-EMC signal (*Combined Signals 50/50*).

The first three columns of Table 18.2 report absolute average excess returns of the index and the strategy portfolios. The last three columns report the relative performance of strategy portfolios over the index.

Top ESP and EMC portfolios outperformed the index between 2007 and 2019 by 2.31%/yr and 3.48%/yr, respectively. Despite higher tracking error volatility (TEV), the top EMC portfolios had a higher information ratio than the top ESP portfolios: 1.68 vs. 1.45.

As expected, combining top ESP and EMC portfolios with equal weights resulted in a strategy portfolio with a lower TEV (1.51%/yr) and a higher information ratio (1.92). The strategy portfolio based on the combined signal delivered a similar information ratio (2.06) but outperformed the index

TABLE 18.2 ESP and EMC Scorecards: Combining Signals vs. Combining Portfolios

Portfolios	Absolute			Over US Corp. Index		
	Avg. Exc. Ret., %/yr	Volatility, %/yr	Inf. Ratio	Avg. Exc. Ret., %/yr	Volatility, %/yr	Inf. Ratio
	March 2007–July 2019			March 2007–July 2019		
Bloomberg Barclays US Corp. IG	1.08	5.49	0.20	–	–	–
Top ESP (ESP = 9,10)	3.39	6.36	0.53	2.31	1.60	1.45
Top EMC (EMC = 9,10)	4.55	6.07	0.75	3.48	2.07	1.68
Combined Portfolios 50/50	3.97	6.13	0.65	2.89	1.51	1.92
Combined Signals 50/50	7.08	6.77	1.05	6.00	2.91	2.06
	March 2007–December 2012			March 2007–December 2012		
Bloomberg Barclays US Corp. IG	0.57	7.51	0.08	–	–	–
Combined Portfolios 50/50	4.81	8.31	0.58	4.24	2.02	2.10
Combined Signals 50/50	9.25	9.14	1.01	8.67	3.89	2.23
	January 2013–July 2019			January 2013–July 2019		
Bloomberg Barclays US Corp. IG	1.52	2.64	0.58	–	–	–
Combined Portfolios 50/50	3.23	3.08	1.05	1.7	0.67	2.54
Combined Signals 50/50	5.16	3.43	1.5	3.64	1.28	2.85

Source: Bloomberg, Barclays Research

by 6.00%/yr with a TEV of 2.91%/yr. The TEV of the strategy based on combined signals appears to be significantly higher than that based on combined strategies. This is because the former strategy is significantly less diversified than the latter strategy. Indeed, the number of bonds in a combined portfolio is by construction almost double that in a portfolio based on signal combination.

The strategy based on combining top portfolios and the one combining signals deliver similar information ratios. However, they differ in terms of return and risk. The outperformance of the combined portfolio over the index is always equal to the average outperformances of the top ESP and EMC portfolios in isolation, which limits the potential return upside of the strategy. In contrast, the strategy based on signal combination selects bonds that have attractive value and equity momentum characteristics. This boosts returns, as illustrated in Table 18.2. Combining signals also has a practical advantage because strategies based on signal combination are likely to have higher returns per unit of transaction cost than strategies based on portfolio combination.

Table 18.2 illustrates the benefits of combining value and momentum signals for credit selection. However, the strategies reported in the table are not practical, due to high turnover and rebalancing costs. Indeed, quintile portfolios may have high turnover as rebalancing is triggered every time a bond crosses the percentile threshold. In addition, the quintile portfolios in Table 18.2 might include highly illiquid bonds that were not available in the secondary market. Finally, most credit funds are designed to track a benchmark index. Therefore, broad alignment with index allocations and exposures might be required to limit portfolio TEV over the index.

In the next analysis, we explain how to integrate ESP and EMC signals into portfolio construction, taking into account turnover, liquidity, transaction costs, and the market structure of the underlying index.

MEASURING LIQUIDITY AND TRANSACTION COSTS WITH BARCLAYS LIQUIDITY COST SCORES

As mentioned at the beginning of this chapter, measuring rebalancing costs is crucial when implementing systematic credit strategies. However, doing this can be a challenging task in the absence of bond-level transaction costs. Liquidity can vary across individual securities according to broad patterns. For example, recent large size issues tend to be reasonably liquid, while small seasoned issues are often illiquid and sometimes even impossible to source. In any case, detailed security-level data on liquidity is required to estimate portfolio transaction costs.

In 2009, Barclays launched a bond-level liquidity measure called Liquidity Cost Score (LCS),[12] which focuses on cost of trading, arguably one of the most important dimensions of liquidity. More specifically, LCS measures the cost of an immediate round-trip transaction of a typical institutional size and is expressed as a percentage of a bond price. The LCS relies on simultaneous two-way quotes issued by Barclays traders to other market participants. Corporate bonds are quoted on either spread or price. For bonds quoted on spread, LCS is calculated as a product of bid–offer spread and spread duration. For lower-quality bonds traded on price, LCS is calculated as the difference between offer and bid prices divided by the bid price.

Currently Barclays computes LCS for more than 20,000 fixed income securities with a total amount outstanding of about $50trn, covering a very broad range of global fixed income markets.

Table 18.3 summarizes the LCS coverage universe as of 31 July 2019. Historical bond-level LCS are available for constituents of the Bloomberg

TABLE 18.3 LCS Market Coverage, 31 July 2019

Bloomberg Barclays Index	Inception Date	July 2019 LCS, %
USD Credit IG	Jan-07	0.608
USD Credit HY	Jan-07	0.941
USD IG Credit 144A (no registration rights)	Jan-07	0.583
USD Treasuries	Nov-09	0.028
USD TIPS	Jul-10	0.137
USD Fixed Rate Agency MBS	Mar-10	0.084
USD Emerging Markets	Feb-12	0.601
Pan Euro Credit IG	May-10	0.427
Pan Euro Credit HY	May-10	0.954
Pan Euro Credit FRN	May-10	0.187
GBP Corporate 100–200mm Amt Outstand	May-10	1.208
Pan Euro Agencies	May-10	0.364
Pan Euro Local Authorities	May-10	0.243
Pan Euro Treasuries	Feb-11	0.097
Pan Euro Inflation Linked	Mar-11	0.201
Global Covered Bonds	Sep-12	0.218
JPY Treasuries	Sep-13	0.177

Source: Barclays Research

Barclays US Corporate IG and US Corporate HY indices since January 2007. LCS for Pan-European credit are available since May 2010.

Liquidity of the US corporate market varies a lot over time. Panel A of Figure 18.6 shows the evolution of the average LCS of the US Corporate IG index from 2007 to 2019. The average LCS of the corporate market overall increased from 0.4% in 2007 to 2.8% in 2008 and then declined to 0.6% in 2018–2019. Arguably, this large variation in market liquidity over time would make it difficult for investors to estimate historical rebalancing costs of a corporate bond portfolio.

While index average LCS gives a broad indication of the evolution of market liquidity conditions over time, the LCS of individual bonds also tends to vary significantly across index constituents. Panel B of Figure 18.6 shows distributions of bond LCS in December 2008 and December 2018. It shows significant variation of transaction costs across corporate bonds even at a given point in time. This implies that rebalancing costs of a strategy portfolio greatly depend on its composition at a given time. Accurate modeling of transaction costs without access to historical quote data can be a difficult task.

Bond liquidity analytics provided by Barclays can also help identify corporate bonds that are actively traded at a particular point in time. It is important to avoid illiquid bonds with low trading volumes in a realistic portfolio simulation as those securities could be difficult or impossible to source.

In order to identify actively traded bonds with relatively low transaction cost, we use Trade Efficiency Scores (TES) published by Barclays alongside LCS. TES blend LCS[13] and trading volume of a bond into a single relative score that reflects both the cost and flow. Bonds with higher trading volume and lower LCS per unit of duration have lower TES. As a relative measure, TES can be used as a filter to help identify actively traded bonds available to investors at a given time and for a reasonably low bid–offer spread. Such a filter can help make a strategy portfolio more realistic and implementable in practice. Figure 18.7 shows cross-sectional distributions of monthly trading volumes as a percentage of amount outstanding and LCS adjusted for option-adjusted spread duration (OASD) for bonds falling into liquid (TES = 1–3) and illiquid (TES = 8–10) categories. The low-TES category includes liquid, frequently traded bonds while the high-TES category consists of illiquid, infrequently traded securities.

In subsequent sections, we explain how to use TES to design strategy portfolios of liquid bonds and estimate their rebalancing costs with LCS.

PANEL A
LCS of the US Corp. IG Index Over Time

PANEL B
LCS Distribution of Bonds in the US Corp. IG Index

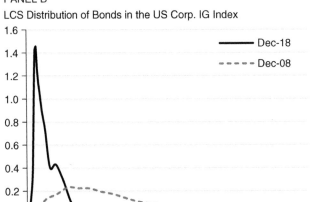

FIGURE 18.6   LCS of Corporate Bonds over Time and in the Cross-Section
Source: Barclays Research

PANEL A
Trading Volume as % of Notional

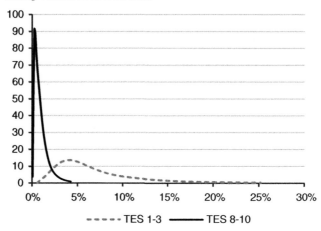

PANEL B
LCS per Unit of Duration

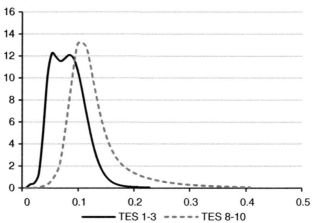

FIGURE 18.7   Volume and LCS Distributions of US IG Corporate Bonds, December 2018
Source: Barclays Research

STRATEGY PORTFOLIOS WITH TURNOVER BUFFERS

Our early results suggest that a combination of relative value (ESP) and equity momentum (EMC) scores can be an informative signal for corporate bond selection (see Table 18.2). Indeed, portfolios that include bonds with top combined scores have significantly outperformed the index before transaction costs. However, the sorted portfolios used to illustrate usefulness of the signal are not practical due to high turnover. They might also include securities not actively traded and hence difficult to source.

A realistic strategy portfolio should control for turnover and transaction costs. One way to achieve this is to avoid trading securities with intermediate signal values. This can be done by introducing *turnover buffers*: ranges of ESP and EMC signals where bonds would not be traded in or out of the portfolio. Figure 18.8 illustrates example implementations of a turnover buffer for ESP and EMC scores, two dimensions in which buy and sell rules can be specified.

PANEL A

Based on Combined Scores: "Relative Value and Momentum"

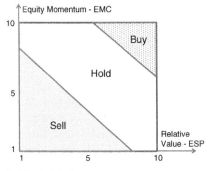

PANEL B

Based on Individual Scores: "Relative Value" Subject to Acceptable EMC Score

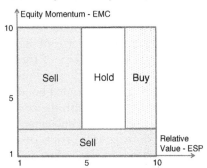

FIGURE 18.8 Strategy Rules Designed Using Individual or Combined ESP and EMC Scores
Source: Barclays Research

Panel A of Figure 18.8 shows a turnover buffer implemented using the combined equally weighted ESP–EMC signal. The strategy portfolio buys bonds with sufficiently strong signals, so buy candidates should have attractive relative value and equity momentum characteristics. The shaded area at the top right of Panel A highlights ranges of EMC and ESP scores corresponding to a buy decision. Similarly, the strategy sells bonds held in the portfolio when their combined ESP–EMC signal becomes sufficiently low. The shaded area at the bottom left highlights the region that corresponds to a sell decision. Bonds with intermediate signal values falling outside of buy and sell regions (the *turnover buffer*) are not traded but kept in the portfolio.

In the subsequent analysis, we use the implementation of the turnover buffer based on the combined equally weighted ESP–EMC signal as illustrated in Panel A. However, alternative implementations that define separate buy and sell regions for ESP and EMC signals are also possible. Panel B of Figure 18.8 provides an illustration of this, where the primary objective of the strategy is to implement a relative value style based on ESP while the EMC signal is used as a risk-control mechanism to avoid issuers with too negative equity momentum (deemed "value trap" risks). The strategy buys bonds with high ESP signals as long as they do not have very low EMC scores. Bonds with too-low ESP are sold from the portfolio. The shaded areas in Panel B represent buy and sell regions, respectively, while the remaining uncolored area represents the turnover buffer.

In the following analysis, we implement strategy portfolios based on the turnover buffer for the combined signal, as illustrated in Panel A. Before this, we filter the universe of index bonds by identifying liquid actively traded securities with TES of three and below. The filtered bonds should have relatively high trading volumes and low transaction costs.

From the actively traded bonds identified by the TES filter, our strategy portfolio buys bonds with the combined ESP–EMC signal in the top 20%. Positions are then kept unchanged unless the combined signal drops to or below the bottom 45%, triggering a sale. This separate implementation of buy and sell rules helps reduce portfolio turnover. Indeed, a bond added to the strategy portfolio can be kept for a number of months before its combined signal becomes sufficiently low to trigger its liquidation.

Figure 18.9 shows average monthly turnover of the strategy portfolio over 12-month rolling windows. Portfolio turnover varied significantly over time in the range between 7% and 14%, averaging at 10.4% for the entire period.

Strategy turnover cannot be controlled precisely as it is driven by the evolution of ESP and EMC signals. Relative value (ESP) scores typically change slowly because relative mispricing of corporate bonds tends to correct only gradually.[14] In contrast, EMC scores can be volatile and change significantly month on month.

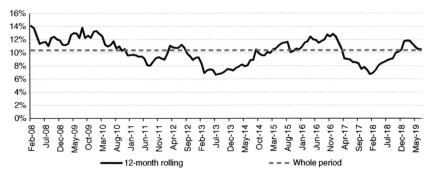

Figure 18.9   Average Turnover (in %/month) of the Strategy Portfolio with Turnover Buffer, 12 Months Rolling
Source: Barclays Research

Investors frequently use a lower rebalancing frequency to reduce portfolio turnover. For example, portfolio turnover can be reduced by moving from monthly to quarterly or semiannual rebalancing. In such an approach, quantitative signals are updated less frequently, leading to lower returns. Indeed, the speed of reversion of the combined ESP–EMC signal can vary across individual names. As a result, some bonds should be rebalanced faster than others. Imposing a low rebalancing frequency uniformly would prevent bonds with quickly reverting signals from being rebalanced in a timely manner, likely reducing strategy returns.

Figure 18.10 illustrates the variation in rebalancing speed across different bonds by plotting the distributions of time a bond spends in the strategy portfolio since its inclusion. The distributions, derived from portfolio compositions in 2007 to 2012 and 2013 to 2019, are remarkably similar. Positions are kept for 14 months on average. This is roughly consistent with the average portfolio turnover of 10.4% that we observe in the overall

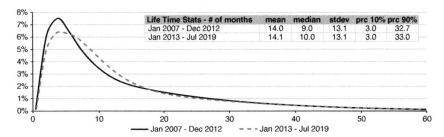

Figure 18.10   Distribution of Time (in Months) a Bond Spends in the Strategy Portfolio
Source: Barclays Research

sample.[15] At the same time, there is a significant portion of bonds that remain in the portfolio for less than six months, which illustrates that imposing a uniform rebalancing frequency for all bonds in the portfolio might be suboptimal because it would prevent more frequent rebalancing required by the evolution of signals for some securities.

As discussed previously, the strategy portfolio aims to buy only liquid actively traded corporate bonds by imposing a TES filter. Only bonds with TES of 3 or lower are eligible. However, while newly added bonds are liquid at the time of purchase, their liquidity tends to decline over time.

Figure 18.11 illustrates this by plotting the evolution of average liquidity characteristics as a function of time since inclusion. Panel A plots bonds' average TES against the number of months passed since inclusion. The average TES gradually increases from two to the index average of five as the holding period increases. This increase in average TES occurs faster in the first few months after inclusion and slower subsequently.

Panel B shows average monthly trading volume of portfolio bonds[16] as a function of their holding period. The average volume declines from 23% as bonds get included into the portfolio to 7% as the holding period increases to 24 months.

Using historical bond-level LCS as a measure of transaction costs, we can quantify performance of the strategy portfolio net of rebalancing costs. Table 18.4 shows the performance of the strategy portfolio *before* and *after* transaction costs. The strategy portfolio is likely to be investable, while transaction costs implied by LCS are likely to be conservative.[17]

The first three columns of the table report performance statistics of the strategy portfolio and the index in absolute terms. The last three columns report the relative performance of the strategy portfolio over the index. The strategy portfolio outperformed the index by 2.66%/yr before transaction costs between 2007 and 2019. Accounting for the rebalancing costs reduces relative returns from 2.66%/yr to 1.78%/yr, while the tracking error volatility remains virtually unchanged at 1.41%/yr. The impact of transaction costs is higher in the earlier period, which includes the 2008 crisis. Indeed, portfolio relative return declines by 1.15%/yr (from 3.94%/yr to 2.79%/yr) from 2007 to 2012. In comparison, the drag from transaction costs in the 2013 to 2019 period is only 0.64%/yr.

Figure 18.12 plots cumulative portfolio returns before and after transaction costs alongside the index cumulative returns. The portfolio outperformed the index over the past decade even net of conservatively measured rebalancing costs. This finding suggests that a style portfolio based on value and equity momentum factors could have been successfully implemented in practice.

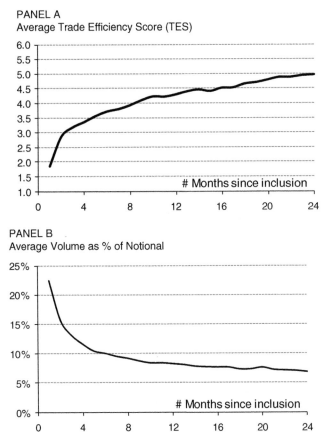

FIGURE 18.11   Evolution of Liquidity Characteristics of Bonds in the Strategy Portfolio over Holding Period, January 2007 to July 2019
Source: Barclays Research

Our portfolio performance is function of the evolution of the combined signal for each bond in the index universe. Whenever the signal is strong enough to trigger a buy order, a bond is added to the portfolio. If the signal of a portfolio bond becomes sufficiently negative, the bond is sold. In the strategy implementation via the turnover buffer, there is no explicit requirement to match index characteristics. Indeed, Figure 18.13 plots annual averages of the DTS of the portfolio and of the index.

DTS exposures of the portfolio significantly exceed those of the index in 2014 to 2019. This can lead to *unintended* systematic TEV relative to the

TABLE 18.4 Performance of the Strategy Portfolio with Turnover Buffer

Portfolios	Absolute			Over US Corp. Index		
	Avg. Exc. Ret., %/yr	Volatility, %/yr	Inf. Ratio	Avg. Exc. Ret., %/yr	TEV, %/yr	Inf. Ratio
	March 2007–July 2019			March 2007–July 2019		
Bloomberg Barclays US Corp. IG	1.08	5.49	0.2	-	-	-
Strategy w. Turn. Buffer before TC	3.74	6.1	0.61	2.66	1.48	1.8
Strategy w. Turn. Buffer after TC	2.85	6.08	0.47	1.78	1.41	1.26
	March 2007–December 2012			March 2007–December 2012		
Bloomberg Barclays US Corp. IG	0.57	7.51	0.08	-	-	-
Strategy w. Turn. Buffer before TC	4.52	8.13	0.56	3.94	1.85	2.14
Strategy w. Turn. Buffer after TC	3.37	8.1	0.42	2.79	1.75	1.59
	January 2013–July 2019			January 2013–July 2019		
Bloomberg Barclays US Corp. IG	1.52	2.64	0.58	-	-	-
Strategy w. Turn. Buffer before TC	3.04	3.41	0.89	1.52	0.94	1.62
Strategy w. Turn. Buffer after TC	2.4	3.4	0.71	0.88	0.92	0.95

Source: Bloomberg, Barclays Research

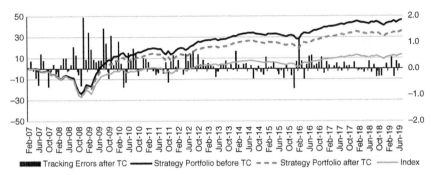

FIGURE 18.12 Cumulative Excess Returns of the Strategy Portfolio and of the US Corporate IG Index
Source: Bloomberg, Barclays Research

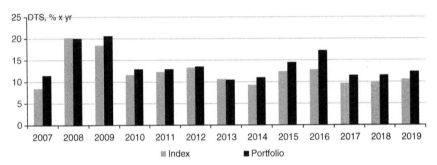

FIGURE 18.13 Average DTS Exposures of Strategy Portfolio and the US Corporate IG Index
Source: Bloomberg, Barclays Research

index. In practice, it might be desirable to avoid this and try to match index allocations and exposures explicitly.

In the next section, we introduce an alternative implementation of a strategy portfolio where we explicitly control exposures relative to the index by imposing broad allocation and exposure constraints.

STRATEGY PORTFOLIOS WITH TURNOVER BUDGETS

As shown in the previous section, a buffer based on the value taken by quantitative signals can be used to indirectly control turnover. The advantage of such an approach is that portfolio rebalancing is driven by changes in the underlying signals (a combination of ESP and EMC in our case).

At the same time, a turnover buffer does not impose any explicit turnover constraints, which leaves the possibility of large rebalancing events. For example, a large number of portfolio bonds could be sold if their combined ESP–EMC signals dropped sufficiently. Some investors might prefer to introduce a hard limit on portfolio turnover to avoid the risk of a very large rebalancing in a single month.

Another important limitation of the turnover buffer approach is that it makes it difficult to impose exposure and allocation constraints, either outright or relative to the index. As a result, a significant portion of TEV relative to the index can result from *unintended* systematic risk induced by mismatched exposures. It could be desirable to explicitly control portfolio exposures relative to the benchmark index.

To address these issues, we introduce a strategy portfolio with an explicit monthly turnover budget and exposure constraints relative to the index. As before, only sufficiently liquid bonds, with TES of 3 and below, are eligible to be included. The portfolio is built using a linear optimization program according to the methodology outlined in Figure 18.14.

Bonds included in a strategy portfolio are selected from index constituents subject to eligibility criteria. Bonds must be actively traded and sufficiently liquid: TES of three and below. In addition, the portfolio does not buy (but can keep) bonds with maturities below three years.

The bonds are selected to *maximize* an informative signal in the portfolio: the combined ESP–EMC signal. Exposure and sector allocation constraints relative to the index ensure that portfolio's risk characteristics broadly match those of the index. Specifically, portfolio option-adjusted

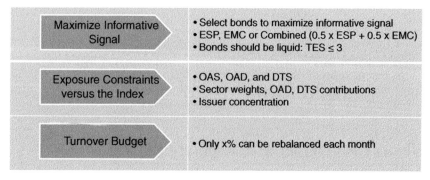

FIGURE 18.14 Building a Strategy Portfolio with an Explicit Turnover Budget and Exposure Constraints Relative to the Index
Source: Barclays Research

spread (OAS), option-adjusted duration (OAD), and DTS are required to be broadly consistent with those of the index. In addition, sector allocation and exposure constraints are used to emulate the index market structure, while issuer concentration limits make the portfolio sufficiently diversified.

Portfolio rebalancing is controlled by an explicit *turnover budget*. This budget is defined as the maximum percentage of portfolio market value that can be rebalanced in a given month. Generally, the rebalancing process should replace bonds with the lowest signal by liquid bonds with the highest signal subject to turnover, exposure, and issuer concentration constraints. Some rebalancing might also be required to ensure that portfolio allocation remains in line with that of the index as it changes over time due to new issuance, passage of time, or rating migration. The turnover required to passively track the index is usually low, so it consumes only a small portion of the turnover budget.

The optimization just outlined is repeated every month to obtain a realistic dynamic allocation. We can compare different strategies by varying the *turnover budget* while maximizing the combined ESP–EMC signal. The results for ESP and EMC signals in isolation are provided in Appendix 18.1.

Figure 18.15 reports the relative performance over the index alongside rebalancing costs as a function of turnover budget. Each point in the figure corresponds to a historical simulation with a given turnover budget.

Both average excess returns over the index and associated transaction costs increase as the turnover becomes larger. Outperformance increases faster than transaction costs for portfolios with moderate turnover, but the increase in transaction costs outpaces the increase in returns for high turnover budgets.

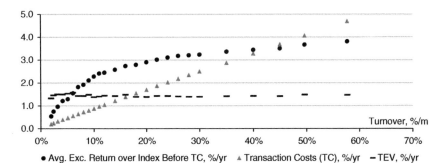

FIGURE 18.15 Average Returns of Strategy Portfolios over the US Corp. IG Index and Rebalancing Costs as a Function of Turnover, March 2007 to July 2019, %/yr
Source: Barclays Research

Figure 18.15 also shows annualized TEV of strategy portfolios over the index. TEV does not seem to vary significantly with turnover because all strategy portfolios remain subject to the same exposure and issuer concentration constraints irrespective of variations in turnover limits.

The transaction costs plotted in Figure 18.15 can be subtracted from returns to get portfolio average excess returns over the index *after* transaction costs. Figure 18.16 shows portfolio net performance over the index against turnover. Portfolio net returns remain low for small-turnover budgets because signals cannot be fully implemented. The outperformance increases and reaches a peak for moderate-turnover budgets. It then declines as turnover budget becomes so high that associated transaction costs outweigh the benefits of a more aggressive implementation of the strategy.

Figure 18.16 shows that, generally, *two* strategy portfolios with *low* and *high* turnover achieve the same net performance over the index. From a practical perspective, it is prudent for a portfolio manager to implement portfolios with lower turnover budgets.

For the purpose of our analysis, we chose (with hindsight) a strategy portfolio with 11% turnover budget and report its performance in Table 18.5.[18] The first three columns show absolute performance statistics of the portfolio and of the index. The last three columns report the relative performance of the strategy portfolio over the index.

The average portfolio return between 2007 and 2019 was 3.49%/yr, significantly higher than the average return of the index: 1.08%/yr. Transaction costs reduced portfolio average return by almost 1%/yr to 2.52%/yr, which is still significantly higher than that of the index.

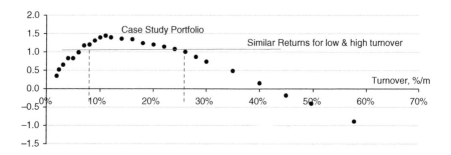

FIGURE 18.16   Average Excess Returns of Strategy Portfolios over the US Corp. IG Index After Transaction Costs as a Function of Turnover, March 2007 to July 2019, %/yr
Source: Barclays Research

TABLE 18.5 Performance of Strategy Portfolio with 11% Turnover Budget

Portfolios	Absolute			Over US Corp. Index		
	Avg. Exc. Ret., %/yr	Volatility, %/yr	Inf. Ratio	Avg. Exc. Ret., %/yr	TEV, %/yr	Inf. Ratio
March 2007–July 2019						
Bloomberg Barclays US Corp. IG	1.08	5.49	0.2	-	-	-
Strategy Portfolio *before* TC	3.49	5.17	0.68	2.41	1.41	1.72
Strategy Portfolio *after* TC	2.52	5.16	0.49	1.45	1.38	1.05
March 2007–December 2012						
Bloomberg Barclays US Corp. IG	0.57	7.51	0.08	-	-	-
Strategy Portfolio before TC	3.89	6.98	0.56	3.32	1.93	1.72
Strategy Portfolio after TC	2.69	6.98	0.39	2.12	1.9	1.12
January 2013–July 2019						
Bloomberg Barclays US Corp. IG	1.52	2.64	0.58	-	-	-
Strategy Portfolio before TC	3.14	2.67	1.17	1.61	0.57	2.81
Strategy Portfolio after TC	2.37	2.67	0.89	0.85	0.57	1.5

Source: Bloomberg, Barclays Research

After transaction costs, the information ratio was 1.05. The outperformance was stronger in 2007 to 2012 than in 2013 to 2019: 2.12%/yr vs. 0.85%/yr with respective information ratios of 1.12 and 1.50. Figure 18.17 shows that the strategy portfolio with a turnover budget of 11% persistently outperformed the index after rebalancing costs. Portfolio tracking errors and transaction costs were high in the 2008 crisis but declined considerably in the subsequent period as the market stabilized.

As in the case of the strategy portfolio with a turnover buffer, we can analyze portfolio dynamics, including the distribution of bond lifetime in the portfolio, as reported in Figure 18.18. The average time a bond spends in the portfolio is 9.8 months, which is roughly consistent with the turnover budget of 11%.

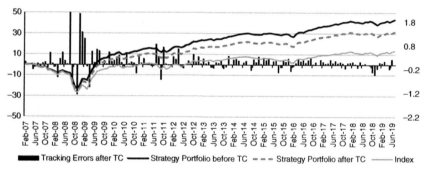

FIGURE 18.17   Cumulative Excess Returns of the Strategy Portfolio with 11% Turnover Budget
Source: Bloomberg, Barclays Research

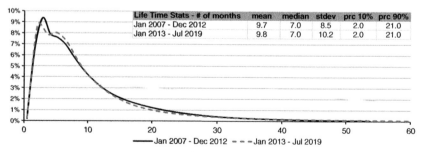

Life Time Stats - # of months	mean	median	stdev	prc 10%	prc 90%
Jan 2007 - Dec 2012	9.7	7.0	8.5	2.0	21.0
Jan 2013 - Jul 2019	9.8	7.0	10.2	2.0	21.0

FIGURE 18.18   Distribution of Time (in Months) a Bond Spends in the Strategy Portfolio
Source: Barclays Research

A significant portion of bonds remain in the strategy portfolio for more than six months. However, some bonds leave the portfolio relatively quickly. The average time spent in the portfolio is a function of the chosen turnover budget and of signal mean reversion. The latter can vary greatly across individual bonds

We can finally compare the performance of our strategy portfolio with turnover budget with that of the portfolio using turnover buffer. Table 18.6 summarizes the performance statistics of the two portfolios after transaction costs.

The two portfolios achieved qualitatively comparable results, outperforming the index by, respectively, 1.45%/yr and 1.78%/yr after transaction costs with information ratios above one. The portfolio with the turnover budget underperformed the portfolio with the buffer by 0.67%/yr in 2007 to 2012. In the second subperiod, 2013 to 2019, the average returns of the two portfolios were similar.

Although average portfolio turnovers of the two implementations are close (10.4% and 11%), the two approaches are materially different. First, the turnover of the strategy portfolio based on the turnover buffer is dynamic and is driven by the evolution of the underlying signals. The portfolio is likely to rebalance more in periods of large changes in the combined signal and less in periods of small changes. In contrast, the turnover of the portfolio with the turnover budget is constant over time, so that the portfolio is likely to be less opportunistic in volatile periods. This finding explains the relatively weak performance of the turnover budget portfolio in 2008–2009. Second, the portfolio with the turnover budget is subject to exposure constraints relative to the index. These constraints can also be costly in terms of performance because they limit the scope for opportunistic rebalancing across sectors. In Chapter 16, we showed that a significant part of added value of the EMC signal comes from timing sector allocation.

CONCLUSION

We find that systematic strategies that utilize relative value and equity momentum styles can be practically implemented in credit portfolios, but doing so requires addressing several challenges.

First, transaction costs in credit are high, so a turnover control mechanism is required. Second, liquidity of corporate bonds can vary substantially over time and across individual issues. A practical strategy should focus on bonds that are actively traded in the market. Finally, credit portfolios usually refer to a benchmark index, which means that the primary objective of

TABLE 18.6 Performance of Strategy Portfolios with Turnover Buffer and Turnover Budget

Portfolios	Absolute			Over US Corp. Index		
	Avg. Exc. Ret., %/yr	Volatility, %/yr	Inf. Ratio	Avg. Exc. Ret., %/yr	TEV, %/yr	Inf. Ratio
	March 2007–July 2019			*March 2007–July 2019*		
Bloomberg Barclays US Corp. IG	1.08	5.49	0.2	-	-	-
Strategy w. Turn. Budget after TC	2.52	5.16	0.49	1.45	1.38	1.05
Strategy w. Turn. Buffer after TC	2.85	6.08	0.47	1.78	1.41	1.26
	March 2007–December 2012			*March 2007–December 2012*		
Bloomberg Barclays US Corp. IG	0.57	7.51	0.08	-	-	-
Strategy w. Turn. Budget after TC	2.69	6.98	0.39	2.12	1.9	1.12
Strategy w. Turn. Buffer after TC	3.37	8.1	0.42	2.79	1.75	1.59
	January 2013–July 2019			*January 2013–July 2019*		
Bloomberg Barclays US Corp. IG	1.52	2.64	0.58	-	-	-
Strategy w. Turn. Budget after TC	2.37	2.67	0.89	0.85	0.57	1.5
Strategy w. Turn. Buffer after TC	2.4	3.4	0.71	0.88	0.92	0.95

Source: Bloomberg, Barclays Research

implementing informative signals should be balanced against the need to follow the benchmark index allocation and overall risk exposures.

We explain how to address these challenges through realistic case studies that leverage on two Barclays datasets: quantitative scorecards for selecting securities based on relative value (ESP) and EMC signals; and Barclays liquidity analytics—LCS and TES.

We explain how to build practical strategy portfolios while controlling turnover and investing in liquid, actively traded bonds, with positions rebalanced according to quantitative signals updated every month. The strategy portfolios are constructed using two separate approaches illustrated in two case studies.

The first approach utilizes a turnover buffer that avoids trading bonds with intermediate signal levels. Consequently, individual bond positions result from separate buy and sell decisions based on a combined ESP–EMC signal. Rebalancing volume changes over time based on signal dynamics.

The second methodology uses an explicit turnover budget to avoid excessive rebalancing and sets exposure constraints relative the index to control tracking error risk. The rebalancing volumes in this implementation are exogenous and remain constant over time.

We use the two approaches to simulate strategy portfolios historically and report performances over time *net* of conservatively measured transaction costs.

We find that realistic portfolio strategies, based on ESP and EMC scores and implemented with liquid securities, significantly outperformed the benchmark index *after* transaction costs, with information ratios above 1 since 2007. In the absence of a long track record of actual portfolio returns, our portfolio simulations support the case for systematic factor investing in credit markets.

APPENDIX 18.1

Strategy Portfolios Based on ESP and EMC Signals in Isolation

We implement strategy portfolios with turnover budget for EMC and ESP signals in isolation. All other constraints and portfolio construction rules, including the liquidity filter, remain the same as in the case of the implementation based on the combined signal.

Figure 18.19 shows average excess returns over the index of portfolios based on the EMC signal as a function of the turnover budget. The outperformance is reported before transaction costs, shown separately.

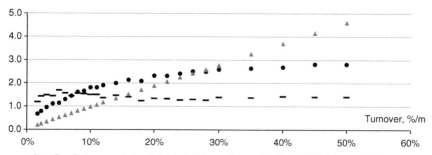

FIGURE 18.19 Average Excess Returns of EMC-Based Portfolios over the US Corporate IG Index and Transaction Costs as a Function Turnover, March 2007 to July 2019
Source: Barclays Research

We find that for a wide range of turnover budgets, EMC-based portfolios outperform the index net of conservatively measured transaction costs. However, the achievable net returns are significantly smaller than those of the strategy based on the combined signal discussed in the main text.

Figure 18.20 shows similar average excess returns over the index of portfolios based on the ESP signal as a function of the turnover budget. The outperformance is reported *before* transaction costs.

Table 18.7 reports the performance of the strategy portfolios with a turnover budget of 11%. The table shows the performance of portfolios based on isolated and combined ESP and EMC signals *after* transaction costs. Portfolios based on isolated signals have lower average returns than that of the strategy portfolio based on the equally weighted combination of the two signals.

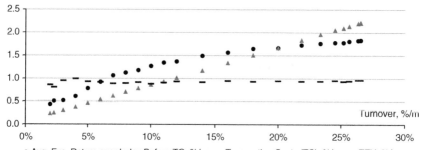

FIGURE 18.20 Average Excess Returns of ESP-Based Strategy Portfolios over the US Corporate IG Index and Transaction Costs as a Function Turnover, March 2007 to July 2019
Source: Barclays Research

TABLE 18.7 Performance of Strategy Portfolios with 11% Turnover Buffer after Transaction Costs

Portfolios	Absolute			Over US Corp. Index		
	Avg. Exc. Ret., %/yr	Volatility, %/yr	Inf. Ratio	Avg. Exc. Ret., %/yr	TEV, %/yr	Inf. Ratio
	March 2007–July 2019			March 2007–July 2019		
US Corp. IG Index	1.08	5.49	0.2	-	-	-
EMC w. Turn Budget after TC	1.83	5.12	0.36	0.75	1.5	0.5
ESP w. Turn Budget after TC	1.5	5.69	0.26	0.42	0.9	0.46
Combined w. Turn Budget after TC	2.52	5.16	0.49	1.45	1.38	1.05
	March 2007–December 2012			March 2007–December 2012		
US Corp. IG Index	0.57	7.51	0.08	-	-	-
EMC w. Turn Budget after TC	1.75	6.84	0.26	1.18	2.12	0.56
ESP w. Turn Budget after TC	0.9	7.81	0.11	0.32	1.19	0.27
Combined w. Turn Budget after TC	2.69	6.98	0.39	2.12	1.9	1.12
	January 2013–July 2019			January 2013–July 2019		
US Corp. IG Index	1.52	2.64	0.58	-	-	-
EMC w. Turn Budget after TC	1.9	2.83	0.67	0.37	0.49	0.76
ESP w. Turn Budget after TC	2.03	2.65	0.76	0.5	0.53	0.94
Combined w. Turn Budget after TC	2.37	2.67	0.89	0.85	0.57	1.5

Source: Bloomberg, Barclays Research

REFERENCES

Asness, C., T. Moskowitz, and L. H. Pedersen. 2013. "Value and Momentum Everywhere." *Journal of Finance* 68(3): 929–985.

Ben Dor, A., L. Dynkin, J. Hyman, P. Houweling, E. Van Leeuwen, and O. Penninga. 2007. "DTS^SM (Duration Times Spread)." *Journal of Portfolio Management* 33(2): 77–100.

Correia, M. M., S. A. Richardson, and A. I. Tuna. 2012. "Value Investing in Credit Markets." *Review of Accounting Studies* 17(3): 572–609.

Haesen, D., P. Houweling, and J. Van Zundert. 2017. "Momentum Spillover from Stocks to Corporate Bonds." *Journal of Banking and Finance* 79: 28–41.

Jegadeesh, N. 1990. "Evidence of Predictable Behavior of Security Returns." *Journal of Finance* 45(3): 881–898.

Konstantinovsky, V., K. Y. Ng, and B. D. Phelps. 2016. "Measuring Bond-Level Liquidity." *Journal of Portfolio Management* 42(4): 116–128.

Stambaugh, R., J. Yu, and Y. Yuan. 2012. "The Short of It: Investor Sentiment and Anomalies." *Journal of Financial Economics* 104(2): 288–302.

NOTES

1. See, for example, Asness, Moskowitz, and Pedersen (2013); Jegadeesh (1990); and Stambaugh, Yu, and Yuan (2012).
2. See, for example, Haesen, Houweling, and Van Zundert (2017); or Correia, Richardson, and Tuna (2012).
3. We have produced two relative value models in credit, called excess spread over peers (ESP) and spread per unit of debt to earnings ratio (SPiDER). ESP looks at relative spread within peer groups of issuers while controlling for issuer fundamentals and bond characteristics. ESP signals (scores) are updated monthly although the effective horizon of the strategy can be one to six months. SPiDER looks at issuer spread per unit of debt to earnings ratio as the valuation measure. The SPiDER investment horizon is six to 12 months. The two strategies are discussed in Chapters 13 and 14. In this chapter, we focus on ESP as a measure of relative value.
4. ESP and EMC scores are produced at the beginning of each month and are available to Barclays clients. Both ESP and EMC scorecards cover US IG, US HY, and Euro IG markets. EMC was extended to also cover the sterling corporate bond market. Monthly bulletins are published to document the performance of the scorecards before transaction costs.
5. These ratios apply to nonfinancial issuers. For financials, only the ratio of long-term debt over long-term assets is used in the second step.
6. The methodology is separately applied to constituents of the US Corporate IG, US HY Ba–B, and Euro Corporate Senior IG Indices.
7. In this analysis, all returns are excess returns over duration-matched Treasury portfolios, as published by the index provider. Excess returns isolate the credit

component of a bond return from the part associated with changes in Treasury yields. The duration exposure of a corporate bond portfolio can be managed separately using overlays of government bond futures or interest rate swaps.

8. We use Kendal tau rank correlation defined as the difference between concordant and discordant observation pairs normalized by the sample size. Like the conventional correlation coefficient, Kendall tau varies in the range between –1 and 1.

9. Please see Asness et al. (2013).

10. Top EMC and ESP score portfolios include bonds from the US Corporate IG index with respective scores nine and 10. The top ESP portfolio therefore includes top 20% of index bonds sorted on ESP. The top EMC portfolio includes top 20% of index issuers sorted on EMC.

11. DTS—Duration Times Spread—is a measure of exposure to credit spreads that was introduced by Barclays Quantitative Portfolio Strategy in collaboration with Robeco in 2005; see Ben Dor et al. (2007). DTS has been shown to track credit spread risk of corporate bond portfolios better than commonly used alternatives.

12. See Konstantinovsky, Ng, and Phelps (2016).

13. In this case, LCS is adjusted for duration.

14. There are several channels for ESP scores to change over time. First, excess spreads over peers can converge, resulting in outperformance of high-ESP names. This convergence would eventually occur in the absence of defaults as bond prices get pulled to par when a bond approaches maturity. Second, bonds can move to a different peer group over time as a result of a downgrade, so that the new excess spread to peers becomes low, which typically would lead to underperformance of the high-ESP name. Finally, issuer fundamental characteristics can change over time, which can lead to changes in ESP scores. Given the historical performance of top ESP portfolios, convergence in relative spreads is likely to be the dominant factor affecting changes in ESP scores.

15. An average holding period of 14 months would imply portfolio turnover of 7.14% (100%/14). However, since holding periods in a strategy portfolio vary significantly across individual bonds, the actual turnover is likely to be higher, as implied by Jensen's inequality: $E[100/T] \geq 100/E[T]$.

16. In this exercise we measure trading volume as percentage of a bond's outstanding amount, so trading volumes of large- and small-size issues could be compared or aggregated on a fair basis.

17. Liquidity cost scores are based on bid–offer quotes provided by Barclays trading desks and, therefore, represent a relatively conservative measure of transaction costs. In practice, investors face competing bid–offer quotes from several broker dealers, so effective market bid–offer spreads are usually tighter than those implied by LCS, resulting in lower costs. The ability to reduce transaction costs depends on the effectiveness of an investor's execution team. LCS can be used to benchmark costs incurred by an execution desk.

18. The selected turnover budget of 11% is also comparable to the average turnover of 10.4% achieved by the strategy portfolio with the turnover buffer in the previous section.

CHAPTER 19

OneScore: Combining Quantitative and Fundamental Views in Credit

INTRODUCTION

Our results in Chapters 13 to 16 show that style factors can help enhance returns of corporate bond portfolios. These style factors are represented by the excess spread to peers (ESP) and equity momentum in credit (EMC) quantitative scorecards designed to identify issuers with attractive value and momentum characteristics respectively. In Chapter 18, we showed that selecting issuers according to a combination of value and momentum signals, with appropriate turnover controls, significantly increased portfolio performance *after* conservatively estimated transaction costs.[1]

Chapter 18 illustrates a relatively simple approach to combining ESP and EMC signals by equally weighting them at the security level. However, analyst recommendations in investment-grade (IG) credit usually apply to issuers rather than to individual bonds. Therefore, in this chapter, we explore an alternative approach of combining relative value and equity momentum signals by first aggregating them at the issuer level.

Another important aspect of our approach is that we renormalize issuer-level ESP and EMC signals within individual industry sectors to ensure that companies with top and bottom scores can be identified at the sector level. Sector neutrality of overweight and underweight recommendations can be an important consideration for investors who want to separate issuer selection from sector allocation decisions. It also facilitates the task of comparing quantitative signals with the views of fundamental research analysts who typically are organized by industry.

The resulting issuer-level composite signal—OneScore—can be used to identify issuers that are undervalued relative to their peers and whose stock prices also exhibit strong equity momentum. The latter can add a significant advantage to credit investors because excluding issuers with negative equity momentum can potentially help avoid value traps—companies with continuously deteriorating business conditions.

In this chapter, we explain the methodology and provide a summary of OneScore performance. The OneScore framework is implemented to make the format of its output consistent with that provided by fundamental research.

The disciplined combination of quantitative and fundamental approaches is often called *quantamental* investing. While quantitative models can handle large data sets and cover a broad investment universe systematically, they are usually based on relatively simple analytical frameworks. Fundamental research, on the other hand, can provide more depth to the analysis of a given issuer and thereby help mitigate the selection risk inherent to a quantitative model. We strongly advocate applying quantitative and fundamental approaches together to enhance performance outcomes in actively managed portfolios.

ONESCORE METHODOLOGY

To construct OneScore, we first aggregate ESP and EMC signals at the issuer level by averaging the scores of bonds with maturities of more than three years using market weights. Bonds with maturities three years or below are excluded from the analysis because their contribution to performance is likely to be very low.[2] Issuer-level signals are then ranked (normalized) within individual industry sectors to ensure that each sector contains issuers with both strong and weak relative value (ESP) or equity momentum (EMC) scores. The normalized issuer-level ESP and EMC ranks are combined using equal weights. The resulting average ESP-EMC signals are then re-ranked within each sector. Final scores are assigned based on ranks falling into decile groups, ranging from one to 10. A higher OneScore indicates relative attractiveness of an issuer within a given sector.

Table 19.1 provides a sample snapshot of top and bottom OneScore issuers in the basic industry sector of the Bloomberg Barclays US Corporate IG Index as of 28 February 2020. The table shows issuer option-adjusted spread (OAS) as well as ESP, EMC, and OneScore values normalized within the basic industry sector. The last column includes issuer ratings assigned by fundamental analysts, whose views can either agree or disagree with quantitative scores.

Compared to a quantitative framework, fundamental analysts usually have access to more detailed information about underlying issuers. Providing fundamental views alongside quantitative scores can therefore be highly valuable to investors.

TABLE 19.1 Basic Industry: Top 10 and Bottom 10 Issuers Based on OneScore, 28 February 2020

Ticker	Issuer Name	OAS	ESP	EMC	OneScore	Analyst Rating
Top Scores						
SUZANO	SUZANO AUSTRIA GMBH	3.2	9.6	9.2	10	Overweight
FIBRBZ	FIBRIA OVERSEAS FINANCE	2.45	9.4	9	10	Overweight
BRASKM	BRASKEM FINANCE LTD	2.94	9.8	7.7	10	Underweight
KCN	KINROSS GOLD CORP	1.96	8.1	9.4	10	Overweight
ALB	ALBEMARLE CORP	1.72	7.3	10	10	-
CELARA	CELULOSA ARAUCO CONS.	2.56	9	7.9	9	-
SCCO	SOUTHERN COPPER CORP	2.46	8.7	6.7	9	Market Weight
CBT	CABOT CORP	1.65	8.5	5.8	9	-
HUN	HUNTSMAN INTERNATIONAL	2.2	8.3	6	9	Overweight
MTNA	ARCELORMITTAL	2.58	6.7	6.4	8	Underweight
Bottom Scores						
NUE	NUCOR CORP	1.51	2.7	1.8	1	Underweight
PKG	PACKAGING CORP OF AMERICA	1.04	2.5	3.9	1	Market Weight
EMN	EASTMAN CHEMICAL CO	1.69	4.3	2.3	1	Market Weight
WRK	WRKCO INC	1.21	3.9	2.9	1	Market Weight
CE	CELANESE US HOLDINGS LLC	1.19	5.2	2	2	-
DOW	DOW CHEMICAL CO/THE	1.79	5.4	2.5	2	Overweight
STLD	STEEL DYNAMICS INC	1.45	3.1	4.8	2	Market Weight
BHP	BHP BILLITON FINANCE	1.19	4.1	4.1	2	Underweight
IP	INTERNATIONAL PAPER CO	1.85	4.8	3.7	3	Market Weight
MOS	MOSAIC CO	2.04	5	3.5	3	Market Weight

Source: Barclays Research

In practice, research analysts would also write a commentary to explain their reasoning. For example, Table 19.1 shows that Kinross Gold Corp (KCN) was among the top OneScore picks as of 28 February 2020. Indeed, the issuer had both an attractive valuation over sector peers (ESP = 8.1) as well as a strong equity momentum (EMC = 9.4). Fundamental analysts assigned an "Overweight" rating to KCN, which agreed with OneScore in this case, stating that Kinross (KCN) is a primary beneficiary of the gold price environment, as excess cash flow provides flexibility to fund mine life extension and diversification capex while further strengthening its balance sheet. The company was recently upgraded to investment grade at Moody's, in line with the existing ratings from S&P and Fitch. With the removal of crossover status and a strong commodity, we think the credit can continue to compress toward its larger peers."

Investors are likely to benefit from an approach that allows comparing quantitative signals with recommendations of fundamental analysts. The systematic nature of quantitative models helps monitor large investment universes and focus the attention of fundamental analysts to issuers that score well relative to peers. At the same time, analyst commentaries can help investors form their views regarding the reasons that led to a particular recommendation.

PERFORMANCE OF ONESCORE

Has the OneScore framework been successful in capturing winners and losers? To verify this, we form equally weighted *top* and *bottom* OneScore portfolios at the beginning of each month by combining top and bottom issuers across all sectors. In each sector, the model selects a maximum of 10 issuers in the top and bottom sets. Fewer issuers are selected in more concentrated sectors, such as, for example, transportation.

Bonds representing individual issuers are market-weighted, while securities with maturities of three years and lower are excluded from the analysis because deploying them in an active strategy would be impractical. Indeed, while short-maturity bonds are likely to contribute little to portfolio returns, trading them as part of an active strategy could still incur significant transactions costs.

Figure 19.1 reports the cumulative excess returns[3] of top and bottom OneScore portfolios over a five-year period ending in February 2020 for the entire IG market. The issuers with top scores have persistently outperformed the issuers with bottom scores, confirming the relevance of the framework.

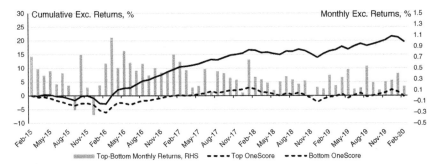

FIGURE 19.1 Cumulative Excess Returns of OneScore Top and Bottom Investment-Grade Portfolios
Source: Barclays Research

We can also validate the performance of OneScore portfolios in each industry sector. Table 19.2 reports the performance of top over bottom OneScore portfolios in different sectors over one-, three-, and five-year periods ending on 28 February 2020. Despite the fact that sector-level portfolios are quite concentrated, OneScore delivered high risk-adjusted returns in all sectors in 2016 to 2020. The framework demonstrated especially strong results in basic, cyclical, and technology sectors. The OneScore risk-adjusted returns over the different subperiods are broadly consistent.

ONESCORE AND SYSTEMATIC CREDIT FACTORS DURING MARKET DRAWDOWNS

As we discussed in Chapter 18, ESP and EMC strategies have performed differently during drawdown episodes in the credit market, which motivates combining the two signals into OneScore.

Following the same approach as in Figure 18.5 of Chapter 18, we identify periods that correspond to significant drawdowns in cumulative excess returns of the Bloomberg Barclays US IG Corporate Index. These drawdown periods correspond to well-known crises, such as the 2001 telecom or the 2008 financial crisis.

Table 19.3 reports the performance of the systematic factor strategies (OneScore, EMC, ESP) during these drawdown episodes. The strategies buy issuers with top scores and sell issuers with bottom scores. The ESP and EMC strategies shown in the table are constructed in a similar way as the OneScore strategy, by equally weighting top (bottom) issuers when sorted by normalized scores within individual industry sectors.

TABLE 19.2 Relative Performance of Top over Bottom OneScore Portfolios in Periods Ending on 28 February 2020

Top–Bottom (Long–Short)	Avg. Excess Returns, %/yr			Volatilities, %/yr			Information Ratios, %/yr		
	1y	3y	5y	1y	3y	5y	1y	3y	5y
Basic Industry	3.36	5.16	8.57	2.69	2.24	5.07	1.25	2.3	1.69
Capital Goods	3.49	2.44	2.47	1.28	1.22	1.48	2.72	2	1.67
Consumer Cyclical	4.51	4.77	4.91	1.29	1.17	1.36	3.49	4.09	3.61
Healthcare & Pharma	5.05	4.95	3.82	2.16	1.91	1.96	2.34	2.59	1.95
Noncyclical	3.7	2.28	3.00	1.34	1.4	1.43	2.75	1.62	2.09
Energy	0.27	2.24	4.73	3.31	2.49	5.06	0.08	0.9	0.93
Utility	1.94	2.76	3.6	1.69	1.64	1.72	1.15	1.69	2.09
Technology	3.47	3.09	4.22	1.54	1.44	1.82	2.26	2.14	2.33
Communication	3.28	2.56	3.03	1.7	1.53	1.78	1.93	1.67	1.7
Banking, Brokerage, Financing	3.45	2.75	3.57	1.65	1.3	1.23	2.09	2.12	2.91
Insurance	3.51	3.88	4.01	1.55	1.27	1.85	2.27	3.05	2.17
REITS	3.84	2.92	3.28	0.89	0.95	1.18	4.31	3.07	2.78
Transportation	1.53	1.65	2.03	1.11	1.13	2.22	1.38	1.46	0.92
ALL	3.24	3.24	4.00	0.49	0.52	0.83	6.58	6.23	4.84

Sources: Barclays Research

TABLE 19.3 Monthly Excess Returns of Systematic Strategies During Credit Drawdown Periods (bp/month)

Drawdown Episodes	# months	US Corp IG	Outright Sorted L/S Portfolios			DTS-Matched L/S Portfolios		
			EMC	ESP	OneScore	EMC	ESP	OneScore
Aug 1997–Oct 1998	15	-35	14	-3	10	18	44	52
Jan 2000–Dec 2000	12	-37	44	-3	24	39	17	34
Apr 2002–Oct 2002	7	-82	113	1	80	94	23	83
Mar 2007–Nov 2008	21	-128	88	24	67	53	17	43
May 2011–Nov 2011	7	-83	52	18	39	35	24	39
Aug 2014–Feb 2016	19	-31	38	1	30	28	11	30
Feb 2018–Dec 2018	11	-36	19	14	21	14	28	27
Jan 2020–Mar 2020	3	-432	175	-77	66	86	38	89
Other Periods	230	35	26	36	39	22	25	31

Source: Bloomberg, Barclays Research

The first block of data in Table 19.3 shows that EMC returns are contra-cyclical as the strategy tends to perform well during market down-cycles, while ESP returns are pro-cyclical as its returns are small or negative in down-cycles. The OneScore strategy, which uses the composite ESP-EMC signal and, therefore, benefits from signal diversification, has relatively stable returns during the drawdown episodes.

The observed directionality of strategy returns should not be surprising. Indeed, top and bottom picks do not take into account differences in credit risk exposures. The ESP model tends to select higher spread names within peer groups after controlling for issuer characteristics and fundamentals. As a result, the credit exposures (DTS) of top-ESP portfolios are likely to be systematically higher than those of the bottom ones.

In contrast, as discussed in Chapter 15, the contra-cyclical behavior of the EMC strategy in credit down-cycles seem to be caused by flight to quality. Indeed, as illustrated in Figure 15.5 and Table 15.4 of Chapter 15, top-EMC portfolios tend to have lower credit exposures than their bottom counterparts during volatile episodes when safer, low-OAS issuers tend to have less negative equity momentum.

We address potential exposure mismatches between the long and short legs of all strategies by normalizing the DTS exposures of each leg to a common target level of 12, the time average DTS of the credit index.[4] Specifically, we divide the excess returns of each strategy leg by its beginning-of-month DTS and then multiply by 12. As a result, the DTS exposures of long- and short-strategy portfolios become equal to 12 at the beginning of each month of the period considered.[5]

The rightmost block of data in Table 19.3 shows that, with this DTS adjustment, both the EMC and ESP long-short strategies delivered strong performance during all drawdown episodes. The apparent pro-cyclicality of ESP returns and the contra-cyclicality of EMC returns have, to a large extent, been caused by risk exposure biases and can be significantly reduced by neutralizing these biases in strategy portfolios. While their relative contributions vary over time, both ESP and EMC strategies tend to add value in volatile and in benign periods. Consequently, OneScore continues to benefit from signal diversification and exhibits stable performance in all regimes considered.

We further illustrate the importance of risk management when implementing systematic factors in credit in Table 19.4, which contrasts the correlation structure of factor returns with and without DTS matching of the long and short legs of strategy portfolios, in crisis and in "normal" periods. The left-hand side of the table relates to "raw" strategy returns, without controlling for differences in credit risk, while the right-hand part of the table relates to DTS-neutral strategies.

TABLE 19.4 Correlations of Strategy and Market Monthly (Excess) Returns, January 1993 to March 2020

	Outright Sorted L/S Portfolios					DTS-Matched L/S Portfolios				
	ESP	OneScore	US Corp	US Tsy	S&P 500	ESP	OneScore	US Corp	US Tsy	S&P 500
Credit Drawdown Periods										
EMC	-32%	67%	-64%	37%	-44%	-38%	41%	-50%	27%	-29%
ESP		43%	34%	-18%	23%		62%	-6%	0%	-2%
OneScore			-37%	21%	-24%			-48%	24%	-25%
US Corp				-39%	62%				-39%	62%
US Treasury					-38%					-38%
All Other Periods										
EMC	43%	81%	20%	-2%	-13%	11%	54%	-11%	2%	-15%
ESP		84%	44%	-28%	-2%		82%	-22%	-16%	-30%
OneScore			35%	-19%	-12%			-28%	-12%	-34%
US Corp				-28%	40%				-28%	40%
US Treasury					-5%					-5%

Source: Barclays Research

Without the DTS adjustment, the ESP and EMC strategies are negatively correlated during drawdown periods but positively correlated in benign environments. ESP is positively correlated with the market (represented as the excess return of the US IG Corporate Bond Index over duration-matched Treasuries) in both volatile and benign periods. In contrast, EMC is negatively correlated with the market in volatile periods but positively correlated in benign periods. OneScore exhibits a pattern of correlations similar to EMC.

When considering DTS-neutral strategies (right-hand side of Table 19.4), systematic factors appear to be generally less directional on market performance, in both crisis and noncrisis periods. In the case of ESP, adjusting for DTS reduces correlations with US Corporate Index excess returns from 34% to –6% in drawdown episodes and from 44% to –22% in other (benign) periods. For EMC, the changes in correlation are smaller but nonetheless significant: from –64% to –50% in crisis times and from +20% to –11% in normal times.

The effect of controlling risk is also reflected in OneScore diversification properties: DTS-neutral OneScore strategies are more defensive in drawdown periods (the correlation with index returns drops from –37% to –48%) and less market-directional in other periods when the correlation with index returns drops from +35% to –28%.

These results confirm our earlier conclusions that DTS adjustment eliminates exposure biases and makes strategy returns less directional so that both relative value and equity momentum strategies can consistently add value in most periods, including market turmoil.

CONCLUSION

OneScore is a quantitative framework that combines value and equity momentum characteristics of credit issuers within industry sectors. Its methodology is aligned with the typical way fundamental credit research teams are organized. OneScore can therefore support a quantamental investment process that combines quantitative signals and fundamental views. We showed an example detailing the top and bottom issuers by model scores alongside views from fundamental analysts.

The historical performance of OneScore strategies illustrates the benefits of combining value and momentum signals. We have found that the performance of the relative value (ESP) strategy has been pro-cyclical (positively correlated to the market) in volatile periods while that of the equity momentum (EMC) strategy has been contra-cyclical with respect to the market. For both strategies, market directionality can be significantly reduced by ensuring that the long and short legs of a strategy are matched in terms of risk exposure.

NOTES

1. The control of turnover and transaction cost is a critical element of strategy implementation and was the central focus of Chapter 18. In this chapter, however, our aim is to refine the combination of ESP and EMC scores to maximize the effectiveness of the combined score at the issuer level. Therefore, turnover and transaction costs are not explicitly reflected in this chapter. No constraints are placed on turnover, and all performance results are presented before transaction costs, as in earlier chapters. Investors wishing to use OneScore in portfolio construction could certainly incorporate either of the mechanisms described in Chapter 18 for controlling turnover.
2. The magnitude of portfolio excess returns is proportional to its spread duration for a given level of spread. As a result, contribution of short-maturity bonds is relatively low. We excluded bonds with maturities of three years and below from the analysis because trading these securities would still incur transaction costs while their contribution to excess returns of is small. From this perspective, deploying them in an active strategy would be impractical.
3. Portfolio performance is measured using excess returns over duration-matched Treasuries. Similar outperformance of top-over-bottom OneScore portfolios is observed when total returns are used instead.
4. The time-average DTS of the Bloomberg Barclays US Corporate IG index in the period 1993 to 2020 is close to 12.
5. Targeting DTS might require holding cash in volatile high-spread periods and leveraging in benign periods.

Five

Using Equity-Related Data, Dynamics, and Instruments

A firm's capital structure may consist of different securities that are broadly classified into two categories: debt and equity. Despite the difference in the way they are structured, all these securities represent claims to the same cash flow stream and therefore are impacted by the same set of fundamental drivers that influence the firm's activities. Merton (1974) formalized this idea and introduced a model that explicitly linked the valuation of debt and equity (represented by a corporate bond and a common stock) to a single common variable: the firm's total assets. This connectivity implies that stock price dynamics and more broadly information from equity markets can be useful to credit investors and allow them to more efficiently value and manage their investments.

There are several reasons why the information reflected in the pricing of bonds and stocks issued by the same company may not be identical. First, the institutional investor base in the two markets differs substantially, resulting in possibly different information sets. Furthermore, since the corporate bond market is almost exclusively an institutional market, it is less likely to be affected by market hype than equity markets, where various behavioral biases have been documented. Second, the valuation dispersion in the equity market is far greater than in the bond market since there is no uniformly accepted approach to pricing equities.[1] Moreover, equity valuations are highly sensitive to a number of input assumptions, such as future growth and payout ratios. The sensitivity arises both from stocks' payoff structure (i.e., call options on the firm's assets) and the need to extrapolate these inputs in time to infinity. In contrast, valuation models for bonds are based on pricing principles that are widely accepted among investors. These models are fairly insensitive to the above assumptions because of the limited maturity and limited upside of bonds. Third, with the exception of non-economically motivated trading, investors will participate in the secondary market when the value of the accumulated information they possess exceeds the marginal cost of trading (e.g., Lesmond, Ogden, and Trzcinka 1999). Because trading bonds is more costly than trading equities, new information may be reflected in equity prices faster.

In this part, we focus on an area that has received only limited attention so far: using equity-related data, dynamics, and instruments in credit markets. Research in this area can be classified into a number of categories.

The first category includes studies that examine whether various anomalies and behavioral biases that have been documented in equity markets are also evident in credit markets. The low volatility anomaly, for example, refers to the tendency of low-risk assets to outperform otherwise similar higher-risk assets on a risk-adjusted basis. Although this phenomenon has been extensively documented in equity markets, it also applies to credit markets. Short-dated corporate bonds deliver higher return per unit of risk on average than long-dated ones, as we illustrated in Chapter 11. Chapter 20 focuses on another anomaly: the post-earnings announcement drift (PEAD)—the tendency of stock prices to only gradually incorporate new information from earnings announcements. We study whether PEAD is also present in the price dynamics of credit securities. We employ several measures to capture the surprise component of earnings announcements and find evidence that supports the existence of the PEAD phenomenon in credit markets over the last two decades. Specifically, the bonds of issuers with more positive earnings surprises earned higher subsequent abnormal returns over the following several months relative to otherwise similar bonds of issuers with less positive earnings surprises. We illustrate how this anomaly can be exploited in practice in credit markets by constructing index-tracking portfolios that match the investment-grade (IG) and high-yield (HY) index key analytics but overweight issuers with positive earnings surprises. We then show that these portfolios outperformed both IG and HY indices.

The second category includes research that employs information from equity markets including pricing, financial reports, and other analytics directly in the construction of credit portfolios. One such analytic used in Chapter 21 is equity short interest (ESI)—the fraction of a company's outstanding equity that is being shorted by investors, an analytic that has been shown to be predictive of a firm's future equity returns. We investigate whether the negative views reflected in ESI levels are informative of other securities issued by the same firm, specifically corporate bonds. The results indicate that variations in the level of ESI are useful in identifying corporate bond issuers with an increased likelihood of future rating downgrades and subsequent low returns, after controlling for risk measures such as duration, spread, and rating. The use of position data from equity markets rather than fundamental data or pricing information makes ESI unique and complementary to other scorecards, such as excess spread to peers (Chapter 13) and equity momentum in credit (Chapter 15) discussed earlier in the book that also rely on equity data.

Some of our studies in this area that are not included in this book belong to two additional categories.

The first category consists of research focusing on the use of equity instruments as an integral part of the investment process in credit. For example, in 2015, Ben Dor and Guan published a study showing the greater efficacy of equity derivatives compared with credit default swaps in hedging the systematic risk of high-yield portfolios. They demonstrated that this is due to closer alignment between cash high yield and synthetic equity as opposed to credit instruments during crisis periods when hedging is needed most. Pricing of synthetic credit instruments can deviate significantly from corresponding cash bonds, creating basis risk that hurts their hedging properties.

The second category is comprised of integrated studies where the research hypothesis is examined simultaneously in both equity and credit markets. In 2018, for example, we applied natural language processing to examine whether sentiment extracted from earnings call transcripts is predictive of subsequent returns of stocks and corporate bonds. The analysis was applied to both bonds and stocks since if the natural language processing technique is truly able to uncover new information from the transcripts, it should have similar implications for both asset classes. These integrated studies can be very powerful because the use of a second asset class can be seen as offering an out-of-sample validation to the results produced for the first asset class. In contrast, the additional dimensions of the data used in most studies to perform robustness tests (such as expanding the universe of companies, number of geographies, and time periods) often are correlated and therefore not as effective in supporting or refuting the initial results. These types of studies are becoming much more mainstream, given the benefits they offer and the increased linkages between equity and credit markets.

Finally, it is worth mentioning that the benefits enjoyed by credit investors from using equity-related data, dynamics, and instruments also apply in the opposite direction. Systematic equity investors can exploit data from credit markets. Two examples of our research related to cross-market signals are BEAM and SPiDER for equities. The first, by Ben Dor and Xu (2015) is an equity momentum signal where stocks are ranked based on the relative performance of the bonds issued by the same companies rather than their stocks. The second is an application of the SPiDER measure presented in Chapter 14 to equities, based on the idea that different investors can make the same pricing errors when valuing different securities of the same firm. Specifically, we posit that credit and equity investors trying to price bonds and stocks of hard-to-value firms are likely to make the same pricing errors, which should lead to correlation in pricing errors across equity and credit markets. As a result, the same SPiDER signal used to identify companies with undervalued bonds can be used to identify value stocks.

REFERENCES

Ben Dor, A., and J. Guan. 2017. "Hedging Systematic Risk in High Yield Portfolios with a Synthetic Overlay: A Comparative Analysis of Equity Instruments vs. Credit Default Swaps." *Journal of Fixed Income* 26(4): 5–24.

Ben Dor, A., and J. Xu. 2015. "Should Equity Investors Care about Corporate Bond Prices? Using Bond Prices to Construct Equity Momentum Strategies." *Journal of Portfolio Management* 41 (4): 35–49.

Lesmond, D. A., Ogden, J. P. & Trzcinka, C. A. (1999). "A New Estimate of Transaction Costs." *Review of Financial Studies* 12:1113–1141.

Merton, R. C. 1974. "On the Pricing of Corporate Debt: The Risk Structure of Interest Rates." *Journal of Finance* 29(2): 449–470.

Miller, E. M. 1977. "Risk, Uncertainty, and Divergence of Opinion." *Journal of Finance* 32: 1151–1168.

NOTE

1. The degree of valuation dispersion may also affect the actual price level since, as Miller (1977) demonstrated, in the presence of short-sale constraints, dispersion would lead to overpricing.

CHAPTER 20

Does the Post-Earnings-Announcement-Drift Extend to Credit Markets?

INTRODUCTION

Post-earnings-announcement-drift (PEAD) refers to investors' tendency to under react to new information revealed publicly during earnings announcements. It is one of the earliest discovered and most researched anomalies in equity markets. Empirical studies as early as Ball and Brown (1968) find that stock prices drift in the same direction as the initial earnings surprises over the weeks and months subsequent to the announcements, a pattern that is difficult to reconcile with market efficiency but is consistent with markets' slow incorporation of information (Bernard and Thomas 1990; Chan, Jegadeesh, and Lakonishok 1996). Additional studies find that the PEAD phenomenon extends to international markets (for examples, see Gerard 2012; Griffin, Kelly, and Nardari 2010; and Liu, Strong, and Xu 2003) and that investors can exploit the phenomenon in practice. For example, Chordia and Shivakumar (2006) show that a long-short portfolio that buys stocks with positive earnings surprises and short sells those with negative surprises delivers a monthly alpha of almost 1%. Ben Dor and Guan (2017) find that although the magnitude of the phenomenon has declined since 2008, equity investors are still able to achieve economically significant returns.

Ex ante, it is not clear whether we should expect to find the existence of the PEAD phenomenon in credit markets. On one hand, the small presence of retail investors in credit markets implies that behavioral biases, such as underreaction, is less likely to affect corporate bond prices, limiting the PEAD effect. On the other hand, there is also evidence showing that credit and equity investors do share the similar behavior.[1] In addition, the lower liquidity of credit markets can contribute to the existence of the PEAD phenomenon (i.e., partial incorporation of information). The lower liquidity of credit markets also poses a separate yet perhaps more important question: Can credit investors actually benefit from the PEAD phenomenon in practice?

Despite the economic significance of the PEAD phenomenon and the fact that earnings information is equally applicable to credit and equity investors, there has been very little research looking at whether the PEAD exists in credit markets due to two data limitations. First, examining such a question requires daily high-quality and comprehensive corporate bond pricing and analytics data, which is crucial for studying the impact on corporate bonds from events like earnings announcements. Second, a mapping between bond and equity is needed to link bond data to earnings and other firm fundamental data.[2] Such mapping is not commercially available and is in fact very challenging to build.[3]

Using Bloomberg Barclays Corporate Bond Index database and a proprietary bond-to-equity mapping, we examine whether the PEAD phenomenon is also present in credit markets. Our analysis shows that the PEAD is present in corporate bonds. First, issuers that experienced positive (negative) surprises during earnings announcements have earned higher (lower) abnormal performance in the subsequent 60 to 70 trading days. Second, we find that the phenomenon is evident across all years, industries, and credit ratings. More important, the PEAD phenomenon is present in the most liquid bonds and is thus unlikely to be driven just by illiquidity. In order to evaluate the economic benefits of the phenomenon, we form several replicating portfolios with similar characteristics to the Bloomberg Barclays US Corporate and High Yield indices but with a tilt toward issuers with positive earnings surprises. These replicating portfolios outperformed the corresponding index in both investment grade (IG) and high yield (HY), showing that the PEAD phenomenon can be exploited by credit investors in practice.

This chapter is organized as follows. We begin with a discussion of sample construction and the measures we use to quantify earnings surprises. The next section presents an event study approach to analyze whether earnings surprises are predictive of subsequent bond performances. In the subsequent section, we further explore the consistency of the phenomenon across subsamples and investigate whether it is driven solely by illiquidity. The last section examines the economic implication for investors.

DATA AND METHODOLOGY

The starting universe for our sample consists of all bonds included in the Bloomberg Barclays US Corporate and High Yield indices between January 2001 and December 2017.[4] All bonds issued by companies for which we do not have equity data are removed from the sample since equity data is needed for our analysis.[5]

In addition, we have several filters to make sure that earnings surprise data is accurate and complete. First, if the mapped equities are American depositary receipts or traded over the counter, we remove bond issuers from the sample. This ensures that earnings data is available on a regular basis and avoids exchange rate dynamics from affecting stock returns, which will be used as one of the earnings surprise measures later. Second, we cross-check earnings announcement dates using Compustat and I/B/E/S. We remove the observations where the date difference from the two sources are more than two calendar days. Third, we also filter out companies that are not covered by analysts in the I/B/E/S database or do not have complete stock return data over the three-day window centered on the announcement dates in Compustat. These filters are imposed for the construction of earnings surprises, the details of which will be discussed later.

The final sample includes 1,929 unique firms over the entire sample period. There are, on average, 847 firms per quarter, and each firm reports an average of 30 quarterly earnings announcements. Table 20.1 reports the percentage of Bloomberg Barclays US Corporate and High Yield indices covered by the final sample. The coverage ratio by market value reaches 84% for the IG index and 70% for the HY index at the end of the sample. The coverage is lower for the HY index because there is a higher percentage of HY issuers that are private companies and are usually not required to report earnings data. The difference between the numbers in the rows of "Mapped" and "Included in Final Sample" are due to the three filters we mentioned above.

Despite the partial coverage of the two indices, the final sample is very similar to each respective index in terms of sector representation and key analytics. Figure 20.1 shows that the sector compositions are very similar between the sample and the index. In addition, Figure 20.2 shows that the time series of value-weighted averages of bond-level option-adjusted spreads (OAS) and option-adjusted spread durations (OASD) are very much aligned between the two datasets. Therefore, any dynamics we observe are unlikely to be driven by the sample differences.

TABLE 20.1 Percentage of Bloomberg Barclays US Indices Included in the Sample

Year-End Market Values ($bn)	Corporate Index						High-Yield Index					
	2001	2005	2009	2013	2017		2001	2005	2009	2013	2017	
Index Population	1,590	1,609	2,555	3,727	5,192		318	596	747	1,270	1,339	
Mapped	90%	95%	98%	97%	98%		80%	87%	82%	80%	85%	
Included in Sample	68%	77%	82%	81%	84%		64%	66%	58%	54%	70%	

Note: To calculate the index coverage, we look at the issuer constituents in the index statistics universe at the end of December and then report how many of them have earnings data in the final sample in October, November, and December.

Source: Bloomberg, Compustat, I/B/E/S, Barclays Research

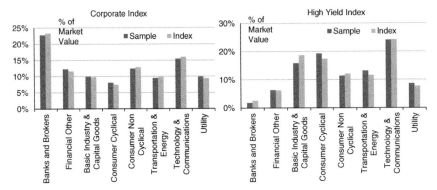

FIGURE 20.1 Sector Market Value Distribution in Sample vs. in the Corresponding Bloomberg Barclays US Index
Source: Bloomberg, Barclays Research

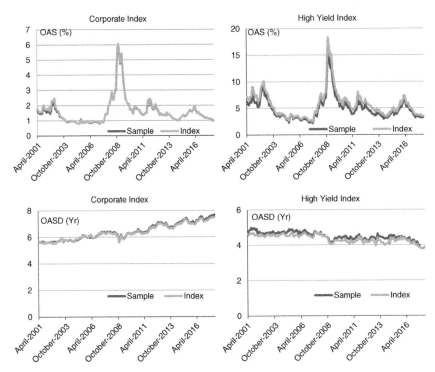

FIGURE 20.2 Characteristics of the Sample vs. the Corresponding Index
Note: OAS and OASD are aggregated bond-level averages weighted by a bond's market value from the previous month-end.
Source: Bloomberg, Barclays Research

Figure 20.3 plots the distribution of earnings announcements by reporting month and day of the week. The charts suggest that there is a cluster of announcements in February and March compared to other months that are quarters away (e.g., February vs. May, August, and November). This is because the announcements of annual reports usually overlap those of the fourth-quarter quarterly reports, so the announcements covering the fourth quarter tend to occur later and cluster in February and March instead of in January.

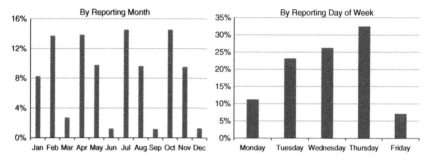

FIGURE 20.3   Percentage of Earnings Announcements by Month and Day of the Week
Note: The sample period is from January 2001 to December 2017.
Source: Bloomberg, Compustat, I/B/E/S, Barclays Research

Measures of Earnings Surprises

One key challenge in examining the PEAD phenomenon is how to quantify earnings surprises. The general method of calculating a firm's earnings surprise is to take its realized earnings-per-share number and subtract from it the expected level of earnings before the actual announcement, and then scale this difference by a form of company-specific scaler to standardize the magnitude of earnings surprises in the cross-section for easy comparisons.

One of the earliest measures that came to use is standardized unexpected earnings, also known as SUE (Bernard and Thomas 1989), which uses a time-series model (seasonal random walk) to proxy for the earnings expectations and uses the standard deviation of past earnings surprises as the scaler:

$$SUE_{i,q} = \frac{EPS_{i,q} - E\left(EPS_{i,q}\right)}{\sigma_{i,q}}$$

where $EPS_{i,q}$ is the realized earnings per share for firm i in quarter q, $E(EPS_{i,q})$ denotes the expected earnings per share, and $\sigma_{i,q}$ represents the standard deviation of earnings surprises over the last eight quarters.

A seasonal random walk with a drift is usually used to formulate the expected earnings per share, such as:

$$E(EPS_{i,q}) = EPS_{i,q-4} + \frac{\sum_{n=1}^{8}\left(EPS_{i,q-n} - EPS_{i,q-n-4}\right)}{8}$$

The SUE measure is appealing for its simplicity. However, the choice of a time-series model for the earnings expectation in this measure is inherently backward-looking as it is based solely on historical time-series averages and ignores other newly available information that is relevant for earnings and may have already been incorporated by the market. New measures were proposed to address this limitation (Doyle, Lundholm, and Soliman 2006; Livnat and Mendenhall 2006). The idea was to use earnings forecasts from analysts to model earnings expectations. This approach is intuitive because analysts can incorporate timelier and more comprehensive information into earnings forecasts and model more complex scenarios rather than simply following the pattern of historical earnings. This measure, denoted as consensus forecast error (CFE), is defined as:

$$CFE_{i,q} = \frac{EPS_{i,q} - Analyst\ Forecast\ Consesus_{i,q}}{p_{i,q}}$$

where $p_{i,q}$ is the stock close price as of the most recent month-end prior to the earnings announcement.

In addition to capturing surprises more accurately from a conceptual standpoint, using analysts' forecasts was found, in general, to be more effective than SUE in predicting future stock returns following earnings announcements (Ben Dor and Guan 2016; Doyle, Lundholm, and Soliman 2006; Livnat and Mendenhall 2006). Therefore, in the interest of brevity, we use only CFE instead of both.

One limitation of CFE is that it only captures the surprise on a company's bottom-line earnings figure. In reality, during the announcement, a firm may release information on many other aspects that are relevant for its valuation, such as changes in revenue/sales and net income, and others. Firm also frequently discuss forward-looking updates, such as future guidance and changes in dividend policy and business strategies. Similar to earnings, investors may only partially incorporate the surprises in these aspects at the time of the announcements and may slowly incorporate the rest over a longer window. For example, Jegadeesh and Livnat (2006) find that surprises in revenues also lead to a persistent post-announcement drift. To capture these surprises, stock returns around the time of the announcements are used as a composite measure to include both earnings and nonearnings surprises (Brandt, Kishore, Santa-Clara, and Venkatachalam 2008; Chan et al. 1996). Intuitively, if the released information is overall positive, the stock market reaction during the announcement should be positive as well. This all-inclusive measure, termed the earnings announcement returns (EAR), is defined as issuer i's cumulative abnormal return over the return of a benchmark portfolio of firms with similar risk exposures in a three-day window[6] centered on quarter q's announcement date q_t:

$$EAR_{i,q} = \prod_{j=q_t-1}^{q_t+1} \left(1 + R_{i,j}\right) - \prod_{j=q_t-1}^{q_t+1} \left(1 + FF_j\right)$$

where FF_j is the contemporaneous return of the size and book-to-market Fama-French portfolio to which stock i belongs.[7]

Using abnormal returns ensures that the EAR measure captures only the company-specific information, not the systematic market movements driven by other risk characteristics, such as size and value.

We further expand the set of surprise measures by including credit market reaction, a measure we term bond announcement returns (BAR). The idea is similar: All relevant information released during earnings announcements, earnings and nonearnings, could be reflected by the idiosyncratic bond price movements around earnings announcements.[8] More important, the measure might be complementary to EAR because equity and bond markets have varying clientele bases and different pricing models and focus on different maturities of firm cash flows. (See Ben Dor and Xu 2015.)

The construction of BAR is also similar to that of EAR. Specifically, we first calculate bond k's daily abnormal return on day j by subtracting its peer bonds' return ($R_{peers,j}$, value-weighted return of bond k's industry and credit-rating-matched peers in the index) from its own return ($R_{k,j}$), i.e., $R_{k,j} - R_{peers,j}$. The peer groups are formulated by dividing index bonds into four-by-eight ratings and industry buckets.[9] The daily abnormal returns of bonds are then aggregated to the issuer level using bonds' market values w_k^{MV}. In particular, BAR for issuer i in quarter q is the sum of issuer i's daily abnormal returns over the three-day window centered on the announcement date q_t:

$$BAR_{i,q} = \sum_{j=q_t-1}^{q_t+1} \left(\sum_{k=1}^{Total\,\#\,of\,Bonds_i} w_{k,j-1}^{MV} \left(R_{k,j} - R_{peers,j} \right) \right)$$

We also use the same abnormal return calculation and issuer-level aggregation method behind BAR to measure issuers' post-announcement returns. Specifically, we sum up each issuer's daily abnormal returns over a window of multiple days subsequent to the announcement (holding horizon) and report that as the issuer's post-earnings announcement drift. Excess returns are used for IG bonds while total returns are used for HY bonds.

Table 20.2 summarizes the definitions and information sources of the measures used in this chapter. The stock prices, returns, book-to-market ratios, and market values are from Compustat data, whereas the reported EPS values and analyst consensus are based on data from I/B/E/S. To formulate the analyst consensus, we utilize the most recent forecast of each analyst before a company's earnings announcement dates. Forecasts from analysts that have ceased their coverage by the time of a company's announcement dates are excluded.[10] We also remove estimates that are provided on an accounting basis different from the majority in I/B/E/S, which is flagged in the database's IBDSL table. The consensus is then defined as the average of all surviving analysts' forecasts.

TABLE 20.2 Earnings Surprise Measures

Measure	Surprise Source	Definition
Consensus Forecast Error (CFE)	Accounting measure	Earnings deviation from analyst consensus forecasts scaled by stock prices
Earnings Announcement Returns (EAR)	Equity market reaction	Stock's cumulative abnormal return over characteristics-matched benchmark portfolio during 3-day window centered on earnings announcement
Bond Announcement Returns (BAR)	Credit market reaction	Issuer's total abnormal return over industry- and rating-matched peers during 3-day window centered on earnings announcement

Source: Barclays Research

Table 20.3 reports various summary statistics of the three measures. The average surprises are all close to zero except those based on CFE, which are negative. CFE also have large standard deviations, consistent with

TABLE 20.3 Summary Statistics of Earnings Surprise Measures

Index	Surprise	Mean	Std Deviation	Percentiles					Pairwise Correlation	
				5th	25th	50th	75th	95th	CFE	EAR
IG	CFE (%)	-0.39	38.40	-0.38	-0.01	0.05	0.17	0.66		
	EAR (%)	0.06	5.20	-7.44	-2.34	0.07	2.50	7.52	0.28	
	BAR (%)	0.01	1.06	-0.64	-0.13	0.00	0.12	0.71	0.02	0.05
HY	CFE (%)	-3.28	219.59	-3.28	-0.19	0.06	0.32	1.85		
	EAR (%)	0.01	9.44	-13.63	-4.13	-0.03	4.16	13.43	0.32	
	BAR (%)	0.02	2.23	-1.72	-0.34	0.01	0.41	1.86	0.11	0.18

Note: The sample period is from January 2001 to December 2017. Pairwise correlations are rank correlations.
Source: Bloomberg, Compustat, I/B/E/S, Barclays Research

Lermann, Livnat, and Mendenhall (2008) and many other studies. Unreported results also indicate that CFE has the largest kurtosis and a negative skewness among the three measures, which suggests large outliers, especially negative ones. A further inspection shows that these outliers are mainly driven by firms that were close to bankruptcy with low stock prices. Nevertheless, the median of each surprise measure is close to zero, indicating that surprises are mostly free from directional biases. Hence, nonparametric methods, such as bucketing, are unlikely to be affected by the outliers.

The table also indicates that surprises tend to be larger in magnitude in HY names, suggested by their wider percentiles and larger standard deviations. Several factors could lead to this observed pattern. First, HY issuers tend to be small in size and therefore usually are covered by fewer analysts and receive less investor attention, leading to bigger surprises. Second, HY names are more leveraged and are hence inherently riskier and more difficult to value. Both can contribute to HY issuers' bigger surprises. Table 20.3 also lists the pairwise correlations of the three measures. Overall, the correlation varies from low to medium, showing that the three measures are capturing different aspects of information from earnings announcement events. In particular, CFE and EAR have a positive correlation, but not very high, confirming the intuition that EAR captures additional information besides CFE. In addition, the pairwise correlations between CFE and BAR and between EAR and BAR are very low, highlighting the differences among the three measures, indicating that even though EAR and BAR are constructed using the same intuition and for the same firm, bonds and stock behavior around earnings announcements can be very different.

In the next section, we investigate whether these surprise measures are predictive of subsequent bond performance.

IS PEAD PRESENT IN CORPORATE BONDS?

Given that reported earnings and returns are public information, market efficiency would imply that they should not be predictive of a security's future performance, especially at medium- to long-term horizons. To investigate the existence of PEAD in credit, we examine the existence of such predictability in an event-study setting by assigning each issuer announcement in the sample into one of five buckets based on their earnings surprise measures. The assignment is done within each sector separately, and the breakpoints are the previous quarter's quintile cut-offs from each sector. Using cut-offs from the previous quarter allows the bucket assignment to be implementable in practice while grouping issuers by sectors neutralizes the possible impact of sector effects on performance. We then track the subsequent performance of each issuer following its announcements over various holding horizons, starting from the second trading day after the earnings announcement date.[11] If the earnings surprise measures have no predictability (i.e., the PEAD phenomenon is absent), the subsequent performance of each bucket should be similar on average.

Table 20.4 reports the average abnormal returns of each earnings surprise bucket over different holding horizons, ranging from 30 trading days to 120 trading days. Panel A reports the results for IG with excess returns, and Panel B for HY with total returns. The choice of return units for the two indices follows the market convention. To allow comparison across IG and HY, we also report HY results in excess returns in Panel C. All the results reported in this section start from April 2001, because breakpoints from the previous quarter are needed for bucket assignment.

Several observations emerge from the table regarding the performance of the different PEAD quintile buckets. Panel A shows that a larger positive surprise is generally associated with higher subsequent returns both across different earnings surprise measures and across different holding horizons. This effect is particularly evident when issuers are ranked by EAR. The return difference between issuers with the biggest EAR (Q5, the most positive surprises) and those with the smallest EAR (Q1, the most negative surprises) is always positive and significant. The return difference gradually increases when the holding horizon lengthens and the difference stops increasing at roughly 90 trading days. Although there is also some predictability associated with CFE, the magnitude and strength is smaller than that of EAR. BAR seems to have the weakest predictability as it has the smaller Q5–Q1 differences in subsequent abnormal returns across all horizons.

The results in Panel B for HY names are broadly similar. Regardless of the surprise measure, more positive earnings surprises are followed by higher average subsequent abnormal returns. EAR remains the most effective measure in predicting future performance, CFE the second, while BAR is the weakest predictor.

Third, a cross-panel comparison shows that the Q5–Q1 difference in subsequent abnormal returns in HY are always larger than the corresponding number in IG. This pattern persists regardless of the measure used for ranking the issuers. The smallest return difference between Q5 and Q1 in HY based on BAR is similar to the biggest Q5–Q1 return difference in IG based on EAR. One possible reason for the variation between IG and HY is the different types of returns used for reporting. However, Panel C shows that the return differences between Q5 and Q1 in the HY universe barely changed when switching to excess returns. Another possible explanation for seeing the bigger Q5–Q1 return difference in HY is that HY-rated issuers are more likely to experience larger surprises in earnings than IG issuers. HY

TABLE 20.4 Cumulative Abnormal Returns Following Earnings Announcements by Ranking Measure and Subsequent Holding Horizon

Ranking Measure	CFE				EAR				BAR			
Holding Horizon (Trading Days)	30	60	90	120	30	60	90	120	30	60	90	120
					Panel A: Investment Grade (Excess Returns, %)							
Q1	-0.06	-0.03	0.06	0.08	-0.17	-0.24	-0.17	-0.18	0.00	0.05	0.13	0.20
Q2	0.05	0.01	0.07	0.06	0.09	0.15	0.15	0.18	0.05	0.03	0.05	0.03
Q3	0.06	0.07	0.15	0.14	0.10	0.11	0.21	0.26	0.11	0.09	0.12	0.10
Q4	0.14	0.12	0.17	0.21	0.15	0.18	0.24	0.27	0.10	0.10	0.17	0.17
Q5	0.16	0.29	0.37	0.40	0.20	0.29	0.42	0.39	0.09	0.18	0.33	0.35
Q5-Q1	0.22***	0.32***	0.31***	0.32***	0.37***	0.53***	0.59***	0.57***	0.09**	0.13**	0.20***	0.15**
					Panel B: High Yield (Total Returns, %)							
Q1	-0.29	-0.45	-0.59	-0.69	-0.56	-0.82	-1.00	-1.24	-0.03	-0.20	-0.31	-0.50
Q2	0.06	0.10	0.06	-0.21	-0.06	-0.33	-0.41	-0.33	0.10	0.14	0.13	0.05
Q3	0.02	0.03	0.18	0.14	0.14	0.25	0.37	0.32	0.03	0.07	0.11	0.11
Q4	0.24	0.21	0.25	0.20	0.25	0.32	0.51	0.37	0.12	0.14	0.18	0.18
Q5	0.47	0.45	0.55	0.53	0.74	0.90	0.96	0.86	0.29	0.17	0.31	0.12
Q5-Q1	0.76***	0.90***	1.14***	1.22***	1.30***	1.72***	1.96***	2.10***	0.32***	0.37**	0.62***	0.62**

(Continued)

TABLE 20.4 (*Continued*)

Ranking Measure	CFE				EAR				BAR			
Holding Horizon (Trading Days)	30	60	90	120	30	60	90	120	30	60	90	120
					Panel C: High Yield (Excess Returns, %)							
Q1	−0.28	−0.45	−0.59	−0.68	−0.57	−0.84	−1.02	−1.27	−0.03	−0.21	−0.36	−0.56
Q5	0.47	0.45	0.54	0.55	0.75	0.90	0.96	0.89	0.32	0.19	0.36	0.19
Q5–Q1	0.75***	0.90***	1.13***	1.23***	1.32***	1.74***	1.99***	2.15***	0.35***	0.41**	0.72***	0.75**

Note: The sample period is from April 2001 to December 2017. The holding horizon tracks the performance from trading day $t+2$, where t represents the earnings announcement date. When reporting cumulative abnormal total (excess) returns for HY names, the ranking measure BAR is computed in the same way, using total (excess) returns. The superscripts *** , ** , and * indicate statistical significance of Q5–Q1 return difference at the 1%, 5%, and 10% level respectively. The statistical significances for individual quintile portfolio returns are not reported to avoid overly cluttered tables.

Source: Bloomberg, Compustat, I/B/E/S, Barclays Research

bonds are usually more difficult to value because of their higher risk. The wider percentiles and larger standard deviation of CFE, EAR, and BAR in Table 20.3 support this observation empirically. One last explanation is that, controlling for the magnitude of the surprises, prices of HY bonds are more sensitive to earnings news since they are closer to defaults. For example, a 1-standard deviation change in earnings surprises may lead to a much larger overall price impact in HY than in IG bonds. In the next section, we show that in a parametric regression analysis, HY names still earn higher abnormal returns even after controlling for the magnitude of the surprises.

Overall, the results in Table 20.4 are consistent with the existence of the PEAD in credit markets. However, this observation may be driven by our benchmark construction methodology, in particular, the use of sector- and credit-rating-matched peer groups in calculating bond abnormal returns. Indeed, when risks between an issuer and its underlying benchmark are not matched sufficiently close, the subsequent return difference could be a result of other unintended risks instead of a delayed reaction to earnings surprises. Although this partition captures two major sources of risk in corporate bonds, it does not address the differences of spread and duration among bonds.[12]

To neutralize possible differences in spread and duration among bonds, we adjust the peer returns by the difference between a bond's and its peer group's Duration Times Spread (DTS), which measures the expected volatility of a bond's excess returns (Ben Dor et al. 2007). Since bonds with higher DTS carry more risk, they should be compensated for by a higher expected return. Specifically, before subtracting the value-weighted return of a bond's industry and credit-rating-matched peers, we first multiply the peer group return by the ratio of the bond's DTS to the market value weighted DTS of its peer group. The DTS-adjusted abnormal return of bond k, $R_{k,t}^{\text{DTS-adj.abn}}$ is computed as:

$$R_{k,t}^{\text{DTS-adj.abn}} = R_{k,t} - \frac{DTS_{k,t}}{DTS_{peers,t}} R_{peers,t}$$

where $DTS_{k,t}$ is bond k's DTS as of day t and
$DTS_{peers,t}$ is the market-value-weighted average DTS of all peers as of day t.

As before, excess returns are used when bonds are IG and total returns are used when bonds are HY. To compute cumulative returns, we first aggregate daily DTS-adjusted bond abnormal returns to the issuer level and then sum over the respective evaluation window.

Table 20.5 reports the results when both subsequent abnormal returns and BAR are adjusted by DTS ratios. First, the return differences between

TABLE 20.5 Cumulative Abnormal Returns Following Earnings Announcements with DTS Adjustments to Benchmark Returns

Ranking Measure	CFE				EAR				BAR			
Holding Horizon	30	60	90	120	30	60	90	120	30	60	90	120
Panel A: Investment Grade (DTS Adjusted Excess Returns, %)												
Q1	−0.03	−0.01	0.10	0.14	−0.16	−0.24	−0.17	−0.15	0.02	0.00	0.13	0.19
Q5	0.10	0.22	0.27	0.27	0.19	0.34	0.46	0.43	0.06	0.14	0.25	0.25
Q5–Q1	0.13***	0.23***	0.17***	0.13*	0.35***	0.58***	0.63***	0.58***	0.04	0.13**	0.12*	0.06
Panel B: Investment Grade (Non-DTS-Adjusted Excess Returns, %)												
Q1	−0.06	−0.03	0.06	0.08	−0.17	−0.24	−0.17	−0.18	0.00	0.05	0.13	0.20
Q5	0.16	0.29	0.37	0.40	0.20	0.29	0.42	0.39	0.09	0.18	0.33	0.35
Q5–Q1	0.22***	0.32***	0.31***	0.32***	0.37***	0.53***	0.59***	0.57***	0.09**	0.13**	0.20***	0.15**
Panel C: High Yield (DTS-Adjusted Total Returns, %)												
Q1	−0.50	−0.84	−1.08	−1.38	−0.67	−1.07	−1.32	−1.67	−0.02	−0.32	−0.50	−0.89
Q5	0.42	0.44	0.50	0.46	0.69	0.87	0.96	0.91	0.18	0.03	0.12	−0.04
Q5–Q1	0.92***	1.28***	1.58***	1.83***	1.36***	1.94***	2.28***	2.58***	0.21*	0.34**	0.61***	0.85***

TABLE 20.5 (*Continued*)

Ranking Measure	CFE				EAR				BAR			
Holding Horizon	30	60	90	120	30	60	90	120	30	60	90	120
Panel D: High Yield (Non-DTS-Adjusted Total Returns, %)												
Q1	-0.29	-0.45	-0.59	-0.69	-0.56	-0.82	-1.00	-1.24	-0.03	-0.20	-0.31	-0.50
Q5	0.47	0.45	0.55	0.53	0.74	0.90	0.96	0.86	0.29	0.17	0.31	0.12
Q5–Q1	0.76***	0.90***	1.14***	1.22***	1.30***	1.72***	1.96***	2.10***	0.32***	0.37**	0.62***	0.62**

Note: The sample period is from April 2001 to December 2017. The holding horizon tracks the performance from trading day $t+2$, where t represents the earnings announcement date. The computation of BAR is always consistent with the way that abnormal return is reported. For example, when reporting cumulative DTS-adjusted abnormal excess returns for IG bonds, BAR is also computed with DTS-adjusted abnormal excess returns. The superscripts ***, **, and * indicate statistical significance of Q5–Q1 return difference at the 1%, 5%, and 10% level respectively. The statistical significances for individual quintile portfolio returns are not reported to avoid overly cluttered tables.

Source: Bloomberg, Compustat, I/B/E/S, Barclays Research

Q5 and Q1 are very similar for both CFE and EAR, and some even become larger when spread and duration differences are controlled for, ruling out the hypothesis that the Q5–Q1 return differences were driven by spread and duration differences. This holds up in both IG and HY universes. Second, when we adjust for DTS in both BAR and subsequent returns, the performance was very similar to before, indicating that controlling for the spread and duration differences in the predictor (BAR) would not improve its predictive power.[13]

UNDERSTANDING PEAD DYNAMICS

The key result we established in the previous section was that, on average, there is a statistically significant predictive relationship between earnings surprises and subsequent bond returns over the following 60 to 70 trading days. In this section, we take a detailed look at the dynamics of the phenomenon and examine PEAD in various subsamples and subperiods. As EAR proved to be the most effective measure, we focus our discussion on PEAD portfolios that are ranked by EAR. In addition, all results are based on DTS-adjusted abnormal returns.

Calendar Time Effects

First, we examine the subsequent bond returns on a daily basis and examine its decays over the days after the announcements. Panels A and B of Figure 20.4 plot the daily average abnormal excess returns of top- and bottom-ranked IG issuers. In addition, the charts also display the cumulative daily average abnormal returns (shown in solid lines). Panel A suggests that the top-ranked issuers have a steady upward trend in their cumulative abnormal returns for 60 to 70 trading days. The bars show that the daily average abnormal excess returns for the top-ranked issuers are highly positive in the beginning and become less consistent as they move farther away from the initial announcements. Panel B shows a similar pattern for the bottom-ranked issuers with an opposite trend. These patterns show that the predictability of surprises post-announcement span a good number of days instead of concentrating just in a few days. Panels C and D of Figure 20.4 show similar daily dynamics of PEAD among HY issuers, although the bottom-ranked EAR quintile does exhibit a stronger downward trend that continues beyond 70 trading days.

Collectively, the results in Figure 20.4 confirm that the post-earnings announcement drift in corporate bonds persists steadily after the earnings announcements for about 70 days, after which the effect dissipates with no subsequent mean reversion. This is similar to the PEAD dynamics in the

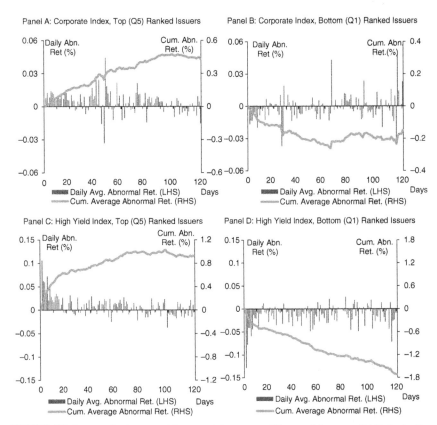

FIGURE 20.4 Daily Average Abnormal Returns of Top and Bottom EAR Quintiles Following Earnings Announcements

Note: The sample period is from April 2001 to December 2017. The horizontal axis is the number of trading days since trading day *t*+2, where *t* represents the earnings announcement date. The daily average abnormal returns (bar) are computed as the average of all issuers' DTS-adjusted abnormal excess (total) returns on the "-ith" trading day for the IG (HY) universe. The cumulative (line) is the cumulative sum of the daily average abnormal returns. Issuers are assigned to Bottom (Q1) and Top (Q5) buckets using same universe and same sector's EAR quintile cut-offs from the previous quarter.

Source: Bloomberg, Compustat, I/B/E/S, Barclays Research

equity market and is consistent with the market slowly incorporating the earnings surprises information into prices.

Next we examine whether the results are consistent over time or driven by a limited number of years. Figure 20.5 reports the differences in average abnormal returns between top- and bottom-ranked EAR quintiles grouped by year.[14] The charts suggest that the return difference is positive in all years for both IG and HY universes. The difference generally increases from 30 trading days to 60 trading days, and for the majority of years the increment continues up to 90 trading days, with a similar pattern to the aggregate results in Tables 20.4 and 20.5. As before, we observe a larger top-bottom return difference in HY compared with IG in all years.

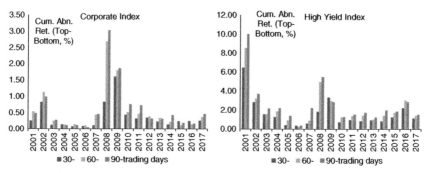

FIGURE 20.5 Corporate Abnormal Return Differences Between Top and Bottom EAR Quintiles, by Year and Holding Horizon
Note: The sample period is from April 2001 to December 2017. Issuers are assigned to bottom (Q1) and top (Q5) buckets using same universe and same sector's EAR quintile cut-offs from the previous quarter. For issuers in the IG universe, reported return differences are based on DTS-adjusted abnormal excess returns; in the HY universe, they are based on DTS-adjusted abnormal total returns. Year is based on the earnings announcement date.
Source: Bloomberg, Compustat, I/B/E/S, Barclays Research

Industry and Rating Effects

Next, we investigate whether the PEAD is specific to certain industries and whether it is affected by ratings. Table 20.6 reports the differences in average abnormal returns between top- and bottom-ranked EAR quintiles grouped by different industries. Ranking issuers by EAR leads to positive return differences between top and bottom buckets in all industries, showing that the phenomenon is not industry specific. Most patterns we observed in the aggregate performance, such as the increase in the top-bottom difference in abnormal performance for longer holding horizons and the differences between IG and HY bonds, are still present at the industry level.

TABLE 20.6 Cumulative Abnormal Return Differences Between Top and Bottom EAR Quintiles, by Industry and Holding Horizon

Sector	Corporate Index (%) Trading Days			High-Yield Index (%) Trading Days		
	30	60	90	30	60	90
Financials	0.56	1.08	1.18	1.69	2.12	2.28
Basic Industry	0.47	0.49	0.43	0.82	1.49	1.64
Capital Goods	0.18	0.15	0.40	0.92	1.43	1.68
Consumer Cyclical	0.32	0.51	0.71	0.85	1.64	1.95
Consumer Noncyclical	0.12	0.22	0.22	1.53	2.15	2.79
Transportation & Energy	0.40	0.49	0.60	2.24	2.90	3.33
Technology & Communications	0.20	0.40	0.46	1.92	2.34	2.73
Utility	0.26	0.36	0.27	0.51	0.87	1.19

Note: The sample period is from April 2001 to December 2017. Issuers are assigned to top (Q1) and bottom (Q5) buckets using same universe and same sector's EAR quintile cut-offs from the previous quarter. For issuers in IG universe, reported return differences (%) are based on DTS-adjusted abnormal excess returns; in HY universe, they are based on DTS-adjusted abnormal total returns (%).
Source: Bloomberg, Compustat, I/B/E/S, Barclays Research

Table 20.7 shows that the difference in abnormal returns between top- and bottom-ranked EAR quintiles are positive for all rating buckets with an inverse relation between the rating and the difference: The lower the credit rating, the larger the difference in subsequent abnormal returns. This is consistent with the performance difference between IG and HY indices. As discussed earlier, one possible contributing factor to the phenomenon is that lower-rated issuers usually experience larger surprises. Table 20.7 is consistent with this hypothesis as the median EAR between top- and bottom-ranked issuers increases as the rating deteriorates.

Taken together, Figures 20.4 and 20.5 as well as Tables 20.6 and 20.7 show that the PEAD effect as represented by the outperformance of Q5 over Q1 is not limited to a specific day after the announcement, a specific year, an industry, or a rating bucket.

TABLE 20.7 Cumulative Abnormal Return Differences Between Top and Bottom EAR Quintiles, by Credit Rating and Holding Horizon

	Differences in Cumulative Abnormal Returns Subsequent to Announcements (Top-Bottom, %) Trading Days			Median EAR Value (Around Announcements) of Bottom- and Top-Ranked Issuers (%)	
Rating Bucket	30	60	90	Q1	Q5
A or higher	0.28	0.64	0.74	−4.22	4.61
BBB	0.41	0.53	0.55	−4.89	5.02
BB	0.80	1.10	1.18	−7.56	7.60
B or lower	1.66	2.40	2.88	−9.31	9.27

Note: Issuers are assigned to bottom (Q1) and top (Q5) buckets using same universe and same sector's EAR quintile cut-offs from the previous quarter. For issuers rated with Baa and above, reported return differences are based on DTS-adjusted abnormal excess returns; issuers rated with Ba or lower are based on DTS-adjusted abnormal total returns. The holding horizon tracks the performance starting from trading day t+2, where t represents the earnings announcement date, for the next 30, 60 and 90 trading days.
Source: Bloomberg, Compustat, I/B/E/S, Barclays Research

Are Our Results Simply a Reflection of Illiquidity?

Credit markets are known to be relatively illiquid. The PEAD phenomenon reflects the gradual incorporation of information by investors. Hence, is it possible that our results are, to a large extent, driven by the lower liquidity in the credit market that prevents investors from trading quickly and acting on all the information revealed in the earnings announcements? To address this question, Table 20.8 examines the differences in cumulative abnormal returns in top-over-bottom EAR quintile as a function of liquidity. We use two measures as proxies of bond liquidity. The first is Trade Efficiency Scores (TES), that combines information on Liquidity Cost Scores (LCS bid–offer spreads) and trading volumes at the security-level (see Konstantinovsky, Ng, and Phelps 2016 for more details).[15] We group bonds into three TES buckets: liquid, actively traded bonds with TES between one and three, moderately liquid bonds with TES between four and seven, and illiquid less-frequently traded bonds with TES between eight and 10. The second liquidity measure is based on autocorrelation of bonds' daily excess returns. Autocorrelation is seen as a proxy for illiquidity because investors tend to break trades in less liquid securities into multiple transactions in order to limit market impact, leading to positive autocorrelation. In addition, the prices of illiquid bonds may be less frequently updated and would therefore be subject to "stale" pricing, contributing to return autocorrelation.

TABLE 20.8 Differences in Cumulative Abnormal Returns Between Top and Bottom EAR Quintiles, by Liquidity and Holding Horizon

Liquidity Proxy	Proxy Buckets	Liquidity	Corporate Index (%) Trading Days			HY Index (%) Trading Days		
			30	60	90	30	60	90
TES (starting from 2007)	1–3	Liquid	0.33	0.68	0.75	0.77	1.53	2.00
	4–6	Medium	0.41	0.55	0.64	1.29	2.12	2.51
	7–10	Illiquid	0.52	0.89	1.09	1.53	1.97	1.90
Auto-Correlation in Daily Excess Return	Low	Liquid	0.43	0.68	0.78	1.86	2.35	2.97
	Medium	Medium	0.34	0.49	0.56	1.38	1.98	2.32
	High	Illiquid	0.28	0.52	0.51	0.83	1.44	1.24

Note: The sample period is from April 2001 to December 2017. Issuers are assigned to bottom (Q1) and top (Q5) buckets using same universe and same sector's EAR quintile cut-offs from the previous quarter. For issuers in the IG universe, reported return differences are based on DTS-adjusted abnormal excess returns; in the HY universe, they are based on DTS-adjusted abnormal total returns. Issuer-level TES ranks are market-value-weighted bond-level TES ranks (rounded to the nearest integer) from the most recent month-end before earnings announcement. Because TES is available only since 2007, results in TES rows are based on a subperiod starting from 2007. We compute auto-correlation using issuers' daily excess returns over[t−121, t−2] trading day window, where t represents the earnings announcement day and requires at least 60 daily observations. In each quarter, issuers in each bond universe are ranked into terciles using auto-correlation values.

Source: Bloomberg, Compustat, I/B/E/S, Barclays Research

The results in Table 20.8 suggest that the PEAD effect is evident for all liquidity buckets for both measures. More important, if the PEAD effect was entirely driven by illiquidity, the phenomenon should have been stronger among bonds with lower liquidity. The table indicates that the difference in cumulative abnormal returns increases as liquidity (TES) deteriorates in the first 30 trading days. However, the monotonicity breaks up when the holding horizon extends to 60 and 90 trading days for both IG and HY universes. When issuers are grouped by autocorrelation, the return difference is actually larger among liquid issuers than illiquid issuers. Overall, the results in Table 20.8 do not support the notion that the PEAD phenomenon observed in the credit market is just an artifact of illiquidity.

Understanding the Drivers of Cross-Sectional Variation in PEAD

In this section, we analyze the PEAD effects in a regression setting with two objectives: (1) to quantify the relative predictive power of the three earnings surprise measures we looked at and (2) to examine whether their effects are subsumed by other possible predictors of bond returns. To understand the decay in predictability over time, we use three dependent variables, each representing subsequent cumulative abnormal bond returns over a different nonoverlapping 20-trading-day holding horizon: [2d,21d], [22d, 41d], and [42d, 61d].[16]

We begin with univariate regressions where we regress the subsequent cumulative abnormal returns on each of the three earnings surprise measures in isolation. Table 20.9 reports the regression results, with Panel A for the IG universe and Panel B for the HY universe. The table shows that EAR is the only measure that is statistically significant in predicting bond abnormal returns over all three holding horizons, and the coefficients on EAR have the largest magnitude among the three measures. CFE demonstrates significant predictive power over the first two holding horizons but not for the 42–61d horizon. BAR demonstrates no predictive power as it has the smallest coefficients, which are either insignificant or have the wrong sign.

Panel B of Table 20.9 reports the results for the same univariate regressions in the HY universe. The table shows that all three surprise measures in isolation exhibit significant predictive power over the three holding horizons, consistent with the results in Table 20.4. Similar to the results in the IG universe, the coefficients on EAR have the largest magnitude, CFE the second, and BAR the smallest. As found previously, the effect in the HY universe is larger than that in the IG universe. This can be partially explained by the larger surprises experienced by HY issuers, as shown in Table 20.7. Table 20.9 provides further evidence that even after controlling for the magnitude of

TABLE 20.9 Cross-Sectional Univariate Regressions of Cumulative Abnormal Returns on Earnings Surprises

		Dependent Variable: Cumulative Abnormal Bond Returns over Subsequent $[t_1,t_2]$-Day Holding Horizon					
		Panel A: Corporate Index			Panel B: High-Yield Index		
Univariate Predictor		[2,21]	[22,41]	[42,61]	[2,21]	[22,41]	[42,61]
EAR	Coef.	0.06	0.05	0.02	0.15	0.06	0.05
	t-stat.	(9.26)	(6.73)	(2.51)	(5.93)	(7.62)	(5.38)
	Adj. R^2	0.50%	0.20%	0.10%	2.20%	0.40%	0.30%
CFE	Coef.	0.02	0.02	0.01	0.07	0.04	0.03
	t-stat.	(2.63)	(1.98)	(1.19)	(4.06)	(2.95)	(2.22)
	Adj. R^2	0.20%	0.00%	0.10%	0.50%	0.20%	0.20%
BAR	Coef.	−0.04	0.01	0.01	0.03	0.03	0.02
	t-stat.	(−3.22)	(0.60)	(1.11)	(1.91)	(2.38)	(1.81)
	Adj. R^2	0.30%	0.00%	0.10%	0.20%	0.10%	0.20%

Note: The sample period is from April 2001 and December 2017. The notation for holding horizon $[t1, t2]$ is always relative to the earnings announcement date, which is represented by $t=0$. Stock return $[−250, −21]$ and stock return $[−20, −2]$ are both adjusted by the contemporaneous return of the Fama–French size- and book-to-market-matched portfolio, similar to the construction of EAR. The numbers in parentheses are t-statistics and are computed with errors clustered at year-quarter level. Explanatory variables that are continuous and dependent variables are all standardized to have mean 0 and standard deviation of 1.
Source: Bloomberg, Compustat, I/B/E/S, Barclays Research

surprises, HG bonds are still more likely to display larger effects as the coefficients on the surprises in HY are larger than those in IG.[17]

For the second objective, to examine whether the effects of the earnings surprise measures are subsumed by other predictors of bond returns, we move to multivariate regressions and include four additional predictor variables. The first two predictors are past returns of stocks issued by the same company. We use the *stock return momentum over the intermediate term* (250 trading days preceding the announcement skipping the most recent 20 trading days) and the *stock return reversal over the short term* (20 trading days preceding the announcement skipping the most recent trading day). Prior research finds a positive empirical relationship between past equity returns and subsequent returns of corporate bonds. (See Chapter 15 for the equity momentum phenomenon in credit.) Including past stock returns in the regression tests whether the PEAD in credit is a distinct phenomenon from the equity momentum phenomenon in credit. In the equity market, there is mixed evidence of whether the PEAD is subsumed by momentum.[18] We separate past stock returns over the intermediate and short terms because returns over the two look-back windows are found to predict future stock returns in opposite directions: At the intermediate term, a continuation of momentum (past winners continue to be winners; Jegadeesh and Titman 1993) is present, and at the short term, a price reversal (past winners become losers; Lo and MacKinlay 1990) is present. The third predictor is *past bond returns* (DTS-adjusted abnormal bond return over the same window as short-term stock return) to capture the general trend in bond prices that may be unrelated to the announcements themselves but potentially have predictive power of future returns. The last predictor is the *lagged EAR* (EAR from the previous quarter) to control for any spillover effect from the previous quarter. We include the lagged term only on EAR because it is the most significant surprise measure. We also include sector dummies and rating dummies in the regressions as control variables. Continuous explanatory variables and dependent variables are all trimmed at 0.5 and 99.5 percentiles and then standardized to have mean zero and standard deviation of 1 within each year-quarter for easy interpretation. We cluster errors at the year-quarter level.

Table 20.10 reports the results for the multivariate regressions, with Panel A for the IG universe and Panel B for the HY universe. Although the predictability of CFE is no longer significant in the multivariate regressions, EAR continues to be a statistically significant predictor with the presence of past intermediate stock return, past short-term stock return, past short-term bond return, and lagged EAR. This demonstrates that the PEAD is a distinct phenomenon and is not subsumed by other bond price predictors. In fact, the coefficients on EAR have larger magnitude than the other predictors

TABLE 20.10 Cross-Sectional Multivariate Regressions of Cumulative Abnormal Returns

Dependent Variable: Cumulative Abnormal Bond Returns over Subsequent $[t_1, t_2]$-Day Holding Horizon

Multivariate Predictors	Panel A: Corporate Index			Panel B: High-Yield Index		
	[2,21]	[22,41]	[42,61]	[2,21]	[22,41]	[42,61]
EAR	0.06	0.05	0.01	0.14	0.05	0.04
	(8.84)	(6.32)	(2.07)	(3.73)	(6.23)	(4.98)
CFE	0.01	0.00	0.00	0.04	0.02	0.02
	(0.69)	(0.42)	(0.36)	(2.25)	(1.49)	(1.14)
BAR	−0.05	0.00	0.01	−0.02	0.01	0.01
	(−3.74)	(0.19)	(1.01)	(−1.10)	(0.59)	(0.79)
Stock Ret [−250,21]	0.01	0.01	0.01	0.02	0.03	0.04
	(1.53)	(2.06)	(1.76)	(2.21)	(3.12)	(4.02)
Stock Ret [−20,−2]	0.04	0.03	0.02	0.07	0.04	0.03
	(5.94)	(2.87)	(2.34)	(7.02)	(3.77)	(3.43)
Bond Ret [−20,−2]	−0.06	−0.02	0.00	−0.05	0.04	0.05
	(−3.33)	(−1.36)	(−0.14)	(−2.49)	(1.73)	(3.48)

(Continued)

TABLE 20.10 (*Continued*)

	Dependent Variable: Cumulative Abnormal Bond Returns over Subsequent $[t_1,t_2]$-Day Holding Horizon					
lag(EAR)	0.01	0.00	-0.01	0.00	0.00	0.00
	(2.38)	(-0.04)	(-0.75)	(-0.18)	(0.39)	(0.26)
Adj. R^2	1.20%	0.30%	0.10%	2.90%	0.90%	1.10%

Note: The sample is from April 2001 to December 2017. The notation for holding horizon $[t_1,t_2]$ is always relative to the earnings announcement date, which is represented by $t=0$. Stock return $[-250,-21]$ and stock return $[-20,-2]$ are both adjusted by the contemporaneous return of the Fama–French size and book-to-market matched portfolio, similar to the construction of EAR. The bond return $[-20,-2]$ is adjusted by the DTS-inflated contemporaneous return of industry and credit-rating matched issuers, similar to the construction of BAR. The lag(EAR) represents the EAR from the previous quarter. The column header $[t_1,t_2]$ represents the DTS-adjusted abnormal excess return. The numbers in parentheses are t-statistics and are computed with errors clustered at year-quarter level. Continuous explanatory variables and dependent variables are all standardized to have mean 0 and standard deviation of 1.
Source: Bloomberg, Compustat, I/B/E/S, Barclays Research

considered. Since the independent variables have been standardized to have mean zero and a standard deviation of 1, this observation means that a 1-standard-deviation change in EAR has a bigger impact on future bond returns than a 1-standard-deviation change in other predictors. Unlike EAR and CFE, BAR appears to have little predictability after the first 20 trading days, and its slope is significantly negative in the first 20 trading days. One more observation worth noting is that the predictability (coefficients) of EAR decays when the holding horizon is farther away from the announcement date in both the univariate and the multivariate regressions, consistent with investors slowly incorporating new information at a decreasing rate.

The results for the HY universe in Panel B of Table 20.10 are broadly similar to the IG universe. As found in the univariate regressions, the coefficients on EAR in HY are larger than those in IG. As discussed earlier, it suggests that the overall PEAD effects are larger in HY not only because the surprises are larger, as suggested in Table 20.7, but also because the reactions to the surprises are larger, as shown in the comparison of EAR coefficients between Panel A and Panel B of Table 20.10. The regression results in Tables 20.9 and 20.10 are based on the full sample. Although we have looked at the PEAD across different years, we are interested to see if regression results would remain similar across different subperiods. We focus on two subperiods, one prior to the financial crisis and one after the crisis. Excluding the financial crisis from the analysis also helps to prevent drawing conclusions driven by extreme yet rare economic environments. We run the same sets of multivariate regressions for both subperiods in both IG and HY. Overall, results are very similar across subperiods (not reported for brevity). For example, the magnitude of the EAR coefficients varies little between the two sample periods, and the coefficients on EAR in HY continue to be larger than those of IG.

CAN INVESTORS BENEFIT FROM PEAD DYNAMIC IN PRACTICE?

As discussed at the beginning of this chapter, the existence of PEAD does not necessarily mean that investors can profit from the phenomenon. This is especially true in credit markets, given the high transaction costs and low liquidity of corporate bonds. Our previous analysis helps understand the dynamics of the phenomenon but does not address its practical relevance. First, performance numbers in Tables 20.4 and 20.5 are obtained by transacting thousands of bonds, which is unrealistic for a credit portfolio manager. Second, earning the performance difference between Q5 and Q1 requires shorting thousands of corporate bonds, which is even more challenging. Third, issuers do not release earnings all on the same day each quarter. Instead, announcements are made sporadically and in an unsynchronized way. Therefore, continuously establishing positions immediately after an announcement is very difficult from a practical stand point of portfolio rebalancing.

To address all these practical concerns, we consider a more realistic portfolio formulation. In particular, we build a tracking portfolio for the Bloomberg Barclays US indices while tilting toward bonds with positive earnings surprises. We then examine PEAD's economic value by inspecting the tracking portfolio's performance. Next, we provide details on how to build the tracking portfolio.

The portfolio is constructed on a monthly basis with two steps. In the first step, we form a universe of liquid bonds as candidates for index tracking. The tracking universe starts with bonds that satisfy this set of eligibility criteria:

- Senior bonds;
- Time to maturity is more than three years;
- Notional is greater than the 25th percentile of the notional amounts of all bonds in the corresponding Bloomberg Barclays US index.

After that, if an issuer has multiple eligible bonds, we select one bond to represent the issuer and remove the others based on this rule: If an issuer has any eligible bonds with ages less than two years, we remove the bonds with age more than two years. If there are still multiple eligible bonds for the issuer, we select the one with duration closest to the industry average. As a result, the final tracking universe consists at most of one bond per issuer in the index representing only liquid names.

In the second step, we build well-diversified bond portfolios to track Bloomberg Barclays US indices, using bonds from the tracking universe. We constrain the tracking portfolio to match the risk profiles of the index while tilting the portfolio toward issuers with more positive surprises by maximizing portfolio's weighted average of EAR. An issuer's EAR is from its most recent announcement in the past three months. Specifically, we implemented these constraints on the tracking portfolios: We cap the weight on each bond in the portfolio at 1% to ensure that the tracking portfolios are highly diversified and idiosyncratic risks are minimized. Also, to match the risk profile of the index and eliminate unintended risk exposures, we require the tracking portfolio to have the exact same characteristics as the index across these dimensions of risks: sector weights, index-OAS and index-DTS exposures. Such matching is implemented on a monthly basis.

Table 20.11 shows the characteristics of the tracking portfolio, tracking universe, and the index. First, due to the 1% cap imposed on issuer weights,

TABLE 20.11 Characteristics of Bonds in the Index, Tracking Universe, and Tracking Portfolio

		# Bonds	Quality	OAS(bps)	OASD (yr)	DTS	LCS	Avg. Bond Market Value ($MM)	Avg. Ret (%/Yr)	Vol. (%/Yr)	Inf. Ratio (ann.)	Worst Ret. (%/m)	Corr. w. Index
									Excess Returns				
IG	Index	3890	3.21	162	6.38	10.85	0.88	691	1.11	4.86	0.23	-8.38	
	Tracking Universe	690	3.36	167	6.59	11.04	0.89	703	1.23	4.75	0.26	-8.25	0.98
	Tracking Portfolio	105	3.34	162	6.73	10.85	0.95	735					
HY	Index	1755	5.78	566	4.36	23.12	1.68	452	3.98	10.86	0.37	-16.50	
	Tracking Universe	681	5.86	564	4.37	23.78	1.73	485	3.68	11.06	0.33	-18.87	0.99
	Tracking Portfolio	100	5.73	566	4.37	23.12	1.78	521					

Note: The sample period is from April 2001 to December 2017. The tracking portfolio has a tilt on EAR while matching index DTS, OAS, and industry weights and subject to bond weights no more than 1%. The numeric values of quality ratings are converted by following scale AAA=1, AA=2, A=3, BAA=4, BA=5, B=6, CAA=7, C/CA=8 and D=9. The reported LCS numbers use the sample starting only from 2007 because that is when LCS became available. Quality, OAS, spread duration, DTS, and LCS are all first aggregated by the market value weight across issuers on a monthly basis. The reported value is the average of the monthly time series.
Source: Bloomberg, Barclays Research

the number of bonds in the tracking portfolio is about 100. Second, the characteristics and performances of the tracking universe are similar to those of the index, ensuring that any performance difference between the tracking portfolio and the index is unlikely to be driven by the universe difference. Third, the table confirms that OAS and DTS of the tracking portfolio is the same as the index, showing successes in matching the risk profiles.

Table 20.12 reports the performance of the tracking portfolios. Apart from the portfolio construction specifications discussed earlier, we also consider several alternative specifications. One is to drop the restriction on matching index OAS. The other is to relax the cap on the weight of each bond from 1% to 2%. First, as shown in Table 20.12, tracking portfolios with EAR tilt are able to outperform the index regardless of the specification. Second, when a portfolio's OAS is matched to the index besides the other risk characteristics, the tracking error is generally reduced, as the tracking portfolio becomes more similar to the index. The performance is also reduced in IG, whereas it does not change much in HY. Third, having a more concentrated portfolio (2% cap) increases the tracking error but returns also go up. As a result, the direction of change in the information ratio of the tracking portfolio over the index is less clear. It increases for HY and remains almost unchanged for IG. Fourth, in addition to constructing a tracking portfolio using issuers with positive earnings surprises, we construct another portfolio in the exact same way except minimizing rather than maximizing a portfolio's weighted average of EAR. To distinguish between the two portfolios, we denote the former as Max-EAR and the latter as Min-EAR. The Min-EAR portfolio tilts toward issuers with negative earnings surprises while matching the major risk characteristics of the index. The performance of a long-short portfolio between Max-EAR and Min-EAR demonstrates the benefits of PEAD when shorting or avoiding negative surprise names is possible. Table 20.12 reports performances of the long-short portfolio in the "Max-EAR over Min-EAR" column. Returns and information ratios of the long-short portfolio increase by two to four times compared to those of Max-EAR over index, indicating considerable benefits of screening out issuers with negative earnings surprises.

Figure 20.6 plots the cumulative outperformance of the tracking portfolios (Max-EAR) over the index and over Min-EAR. Both Max-EAR and Min-EAR portfolios are formed by matching index DTS, OAS, and sector weights on a monthly basis, subject to a 1% cap on each bond. In the IG universe, the outperformance of Max-EAR over index is restricted to the beginning of the sample as well as months between late 2008 and early 2011. However, Max-EAR consistently outperforms Min-EAR with outperformance built gradually over the entire sample. These results indicate that there is a consistent benefit in avoiding the issuers with low EAR rankings.

TABLE 20.12 Performance Summary Statistics of Index-Tracking Portfolios with EAR Tilts

Issuer Cap	Constraints	Matched Index DTS + Sector Weight			Matched Index DTS + OAS + Sector Weight		
		Tracking Portfolio (Max-EAR)	Max-EAR over Index	Max-EAR over Min-EAR	Tracking Portfolio (Max-EAR)	Max-EAR over Index	Max-EAR over Min-EAR
		Panel A: Corporate Index					
1%	Avg. Ex. Ret. (%/Yr)	1.98	0.87	1.74	1.51	0.40	1.48
	Vol. (%/Yr)	4.31	1.17	1.20	4.32	1.10	1.10
	Inf. Ratio (ann.)	0.46	0.74	1.45	0.35	0.36	1.35
	Worst Ret. (%/m)	−6.49	−1.56	−0.83	−6.56	−1.67	−0.79
	Corr. w. Index	0.97	−0.56	−0.15	0.98	−0.58	−0.12
2%	Avg. Ex. Ret. (%/Yr)	2.23	1.12	2.45	1.71	0.60	2.01
	Vol. (%/Yr)	4.18	1.54	1.85	4.25	1.33	1.68
	Inf. Ratio (ann.)	0.53	0.73	1.32	0.40	0.45	1.20
	Worst Ret. (%/m)	−5.47	−2.38	−1.62	−5.74	−2.25	−1.52
	Corr. w. Index	0.95	−0.57	−0.16	0.97	−0.57	−0.07

(Continued)

TABLE 20.12 (Continued)

Constraints		Matched Index DTS + Sector Weight			Matched Index DTS + OAS + Sector Weight		
		Panel B: High-Yield Index					
1%	Avg. Ret. (%/Yr)	10.00	1.97	3.06	9.99	1.96	3.04
	Vol. (%/Yr)	9.07	2.65	2.41	9.30	2.88	2.37
	Sharpe (Inf.) Ratio (ann.)	0.91	0.74	1.27	0.89	0.68	1.29
	Worst Ret. (%/m)	−16.75	−4.39	−2.41	−17.70	−6.06	−2.40
	Corr. w. Index	0.96	−0.27	−0.15	0.95	−0.20	−0.18
2%	Avg. Ret. (%/Yr)	10.76	2.73	5.02	10.51	2.48	4.72
	Vol. (%/Yr)	9.06	3.15	3.51	9.15	3.14	3.56
	Sharpe (Inf.) Ratio (ann.)	1.00	0.87	1.43	0.96	0.79	1.33
	Worst Ret. (%/m)	−16.90	−3.35	−3.72	−17.18	−4.30	−3.43
	Corr. w. Index	0.94	−0.28	−0.22	0.94	−0.25	−0.15

Note: The sample period is from April 2001 to December 2017. Tracking portfolio (Max-EAR) is formulated by tracking the index while tilting toward bonds with positive earnings surprise (EAR). The Min-EAR portfolio is constructed in the same way as the Max-EAR portfolio with only one exception of tilting toward issuers with negative earnings surprises. Sharpe Ratios are computed using one-month Libor rate.

Source: Bloomberg, Compustat, I/B/E/S, Barclays Research

The outperformance of Max-over-Min EAR has not waned in recent years. Instead, it becomes stronger, having a steeper slope post-2010 compared to that prior to 2008. In the HY universe, unlike the IG universe, the cumulative performance of Max-EAR over the index has been trending upward more uniformly over the entire sample. Max-EAR also beats Min-EAR consistently throughout the sample, which suggests that in HY, there is both consistent benefit from holding the high-EAR issuers as well as avoiding low-EAR issuers. Similar to the IG index, we also do not see any deterioration of performance in recent years.

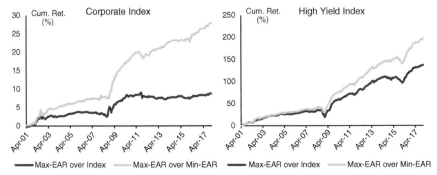

FIGURE 20.6 Cumulative Performance of the Tracking Portfolio (Max-EAR) over the Corresponding Index and Min-EAR Portfolio

Note: The sample period is from April 2001 to December 2017. Tracking portfolio (Max-EAR) is formed by tracking the index while tilting toward bonds with positive earnings surprise (EAR). The tracking portfolio matches index sector weights, OAS and DTS on a monthly basis, and has a cap of 1% on bond weight in the portfolio. The Min-EAR portfolio is constructed in the same way as the Max-EAR portfolio except for tilting toward issuers with negative earnings surprises.

Source: Bloomberg, Compustat, I/B/E/S, Barclays Research

It is worth highlighting that the tracking portfolios are rebalanced on a monthly basis and maximize EAR values from the past three-month window. This means that some surprises are fresher and some are from the more distant past. The current portfolio construction treats them equally, which we acknowledge might not be the most efficient way to use the EAR information. In fact, one challenge in exploiting PEAD in credit, where constantly positioning after announcement is almost infeasible, is how to make a trade-off between issuers with weaker but more recent surprises vs. those with stronger but less recent surprises.

To differentiate bonds with different levels of informativeness in the earnings surprise measures, we use the relative value score proposed in Chapter 13 to filter out bonds that are already "expensive", surprises of which may have already been picked up by the market. The idea is simple. What matters most is how much of the initial surprise is left to be exploited rather than how far back the announcement is. We use excess spread to peers (ESP) to measure the cheapness of the bond. ESP is bond-level score (1–10) that measures a bond's relative value as its spread over peers unexplained by issuer characteristics and fundamentals (see Chapter 13 for details.) A high ESP score indicates that a bond is cheap relative to its peers.

Table 20.13 reports performances of the tracking portfolios using bonds from the tracking universe with ESP scores greater than or equal to five (bonds that are still cheap relative to peers). The tracking portfolios are formed by matching index DTS, OAS, and sector weights on a monthly basis, subject to a 2% cap on each bond. The index tracked by HY bonds is a subset of the standard index with ratings B/Ba because ESP is available only for bonds rated B and above. A 2% cap is imposed instead of 1% because there are fewer HY names in the intersected universe back in the early years, and using the 1% cap would be too restrictive.

As shown in Table 20.13, PEAD performance strengthens among issuers with high ESP scores. The tracking portfolios with an ESP>= 5 filter deliver higher returns, lower volatilities, and higher information ratios than those without the filter. The outperformance is present regardless of the index that is being tracked. Some may argue that the performance we see in the tracking portfolios with an ESP filter is completely driven by ESP. To test whether that is the case, we form a tracking portfolio with minimum EAR using high-ESP bonds. If ESP can fully explain the performance, we should see no difference between such portfolio and the Max-EAR portfolio with the ESP filter. However, this hypothesis is not supported by the evidence. We find that a similar tracking portfolio that minimizes the portfolio EAR with an ESP filter (last column in Table 20.13) produces much lower returns and information (Sharpe) ratios than the Max-EAR portfolio with the ESP filter (column 4) in both IG and HY. In sum, our results show that a relative value measure is complementary to the earnings surprise measure in exploiting the PEAD phenomenon in credit. This is especially valuable given that credit investors might be unable to exploit PEAD immediately after the announcements and have to decide when it is too late to enter the game.

TABLE 20.13 Performance Summary Statistics of Tracking Portfolios with an ESP Filter

	Tracking Portfolio (Max-EAR)	Max-EAR over Index	Min-EAR	Tracking Portfolio (Max-EAR)	Max-EAR over Index	Min-EAR
	Without ESP Filter			ESP>= 5		
	Panel A: Tracking the Corporate Index					
Avg. Ex. Ret. (%/Yr)	1.71	0.60	-0.30	2.17	1.06	0.34
Vol. (%/Yr)	4.25	1.33	4.50	4.25	1.26	4.66
Inf. Ratio (ann.)	0.40	0.45	-0.07	0.51	0.84	0.07
Worst Ret. (%/m)	-5.74	-2.25	-5.71	-6.67	-1.46	-7.72
Corr. w. Index	0.97	-0.57	0.94	0.97	-0.58	0.95
	Panel B: Tracking the HY B/Ba Index					
Avg. Ret. (%/Yr)	9.20	1.78	5.68	10.67	3.25	7.95
Vol. (%/Yr)	8.19	2.27	8.67	8.20	2.87	8.47
Sharpe/Inf. Ratio (ann.)	0.91	0.79	0.46	1.09	1.14	0.74
Worst Ret. (%/m)	-15.80	-1.81	-16.82	-15.74	-3.64	-17.53
Corr. w. Index	0.96	-0.18	0.96	0.94	-0.20	0.93

Note: The sample period is from April 2001 to December 2017. Tracking portfolio (Max-EAR) is formulated by tracking the index while tilting toward bonds with positive earnings surprises (EAR). The Min-EAR portfolio is constructed in the same way as the Max-EAR portfolio with only one exception of tilting toward issuers with negative earnings surprises. Sharpe ratios are computed using one-month Libor rate.

Source: Bloomberg, Compustat, I/B/E/S, Barclays Research

650 USING EQUITY-RELATED DATA, DYNAMICS, AND INSTRUMENTS

CONCLUSION

We find that the phenomenon of post-earnings announcement drift is present in corporate bonds. Issuers that are associated with more positive earnings surprises had higher subsequent abnormal bond returns than issuers with more negative earnings surprises. Furthermore, our study shows that PEAD is not driven by liquidity and is a distinct phenomenon from other bond price behaviors, such as equity momentum in corporate bonds.

We have also investigated the economic value embedded in PEAD by examining the performance of an index-tracking portfolio with a tilt toward issuers with positive earnings surprises. Such tilted portfolios have outperformed the indices.

REFERENCES

Ball, R., and P. Brown. 1968. "An Empirical Evaluation of Accounting Numbers." *Journal of Accounting Research* 6 (2): 159–178.
Ben Dor, A., L. Dynkin, J. Hyman, P. Houweling, E. Van Leeuwen, and O. Penninga. 2007. "DTS^{SM} (Duration Times Spread)." *Journal of Portfolio Management* 33(2): 77–100.
Ben Dor, A., and J. Guan. 2016, May 11. "Using Credit Signals to Enhance Equity 'Value' Strategies." Barclays Research.
Ben Dor, A., and J. Guan. 2017, May 10. "The Post-Earnings-Announcement Drift (PEAD): Has the Market Finally Caught Up." Barclays Research.
Ben Dor, A., and J. Xu. 2015. "Should Equity Investors Care about Corporate Bond Prices? Using Bond Prices to Construct Equity Momentum Strategies." *Journal of Portfolio Management* 41 (4): 35–49.
Bernard, V. L., and J. K. Thomas. 1989. "Post-Earnings-Announcement Drift: Delayed Price Response or Risk Premium." *Journal of Accounting Research* 27: 1–36.
Bernard, V. L., and J. K. Thomas. 1990. "Evidence that Stock Prices Do Not Fully Reflect the Implications of Current Earnings for Future Earnings." *Journal of Accounting and Economics* 13(4): 305–340.
Brandt, M. W., R. Kishore, P. Santa-Clara, and M. Venkatachalam. 2008. "Earnings Announcements Are Full of Surprises." SSRN Working paper.
Chan, L. K. C., N. Jegadeesh, and J. Lakonishok. 1996. "Momentum Strategies." *Journal of Finance* 51(5): 1681–1713.
Chordia, T., and L. Shivakumar. 2006. "Earnings and Price Momentum." *Journal of Financial Economics* 80(3): 627–656.
Doyle, J. T., R. J. Lundholm, and M. T. Soliman, 2006. "The Extreme Future Stock Returns Following I/B/E/S Earnings Surprises." *Journal of Accounting Research* 44 (5): 849–887.

Even-Tov, O. 2017. "When Does the Bond Price Reaction to Earnings Announcements Predict Future Stock Returns." *Journal of Accounting and Economics* 64 (1): 167–182.

Gerard, X. 2012. "Information Uncertainty and the Post-Earnings Announcement Drift in Europe." *Financial Analysts Journal* 68(2): 51–69.

Griffin, J. M., P. J. Kelly, and F. Nardari. 2010. "Do Market Efficiency Measure Yield Correct Inferences? A Comparison of Developed and Emerging Markets." *Review of Financial Studies* 23(8): 3225–3277.

Jegadeesh, N., and S. Titman. 1993. "Returns to Buying Winners and Selling Losers: Implications for Stock Market Efficiency." *Journal of Finance* 48(1): 65–91.

Jegadeesh, N., J. Livnat. 2006. "Revenue Surprises and Stock Returns." *Journal of Accounting and Economics* 41(1–2): 147–171.

Konstantinovsky, V., K. Y. Ng, and B. D. Phelps. 2016. "Measuring Bond-Level Liquidity." *Journal of Portfolio Management* 42(4): 116–128.

Lerman A., J. Livnat, and R. R. Mendenhall. 2008, April 18. "The High-Volume Return Premium and Post-Earnings Announcement Drift." Working paper. https://papers.ssrn.com/sol3/papers.cfm?abstract_id=1122463

Liu, W., N. Strong, and X. Xu. 2003. "Post-Earnings-Announcement Drift in the UK." *European Financial Management* 9(1): 89–116.

Journal of Accounting Research 44(1): 177–205. Lo, A. W., and A. C. MacKinlay, 1990. "When Are Contrarian Profits Due to Stock Market Overreaction?" *Review of Financial Studies* 3(2): 175–205.

Novy-Marx, R., 2015, February. "Fundamentally, Momentum Is Fundamental Momentum." NBER Working Paper No. 20984.

NOTES

1. For example, Ben Dor and Guan (2016) find that companies mispriced by credit investors (in terms of bond prices) tend also to be mispriced by equity investors (in terms of stock prices) in the same direction.

2. Earnings data is usually labeled with equity identifiers because earnings announcements are part of the regulatory requirement for companies with publicly traded stocks.

3. Mapping bonds to equities issued by the same firm is challenging for a number of reasons. First, there are no common firm-level identifiers across equity and bond markets. Second, corporate actions have different impacts on trading activities of bonds and equities. For example, bonds issued by the acquired company often continue to trade after the acquisition whereas equities cease to do so. Last but not least, firms usually have a single class of common shares but may have multiple bonds outstanding, sometimes issued by more than one entity associated with the same firm.

4. The sample begins in year 2001 due to data availability at the daily frequency, which is necessary to track bond returns immediately following the earnings announcements.

5. The process of creating the bond-equity mapping is discussed in great detail in Ben Dor and Xu (2015).

6. We accumulate returns until one day after the announcement date because sometimes earnings announcements are made after market close, so market reaction will be captured in the following day (q_t+1).

7. We use 25 portfolios based on the intersection of five size-based cut-offs and five book-to-market-based cut-offs as the benchmark portfolios. The cut-offs and portfolio returns are from Kenneth French's website https://mba.tuck.dartmouth.edu/pages/faculty/ken.french/data_library.html.

8. For example, Even-Tov (2017) finds that the credit market reaction during the announcement predicts the PEAD in equity markets.

9. The four rating buckets are A+/A, Baa, Ba, and B/B–. The eight industry buckets are financials, basic industry, capital goods, consumer cyclical, consumer non-cyclical, transportation & energy, technology & communications, and utility.

10. To avoid any look-ahead bias, we only use real-time information that was available at each point in time in applying this exclusion rule. For example, if an analyst stopped coverage on a company before one of its earnings announcement, but such termination of coverage was not announced until after the earnings announcement, we still keep this particular analyst's estimate in the calculation of analyst consensus.

11. We exclude the first day after the earnings date because announcements can be released either intraday or overnight, and Compustat data does not provide the exact timing of the announcement. This also ensures that the subsequent holding horizon we use to measure post-announcement drift is not overlapped with the window used for constructing EAR and BAR.

12. For example, if the bonds in Q5 have higher spreads than those in Q1, it could potentially explain why Q5 bonds have higher subsequent returns.

13. If we adjust for DTS only in the subsequent returns and not in the BAR measure, the results are very similar to those using nonadjusted returns in both measures (Panel B and D). Results are not reported for brevity.

14. The year refers to the time when the earnings announcements were released. The subsequent holding horizon could extend to the following year.

15. LCS measures the cost of an immediate, institution-sized, round-trip transaction and is expressed as a percentage of the corporate bond's price. LCS relies on simultaneous, bond-level, bid–ask quotes issued by Barclays traders.

16. The numbers represent the number of trading days following the earnings announcement date, defined as day 0.

17. In alternative regressions (not reported for brevity), we include both IG and HY issuers in a pooled regression allowing different slopes for IG and HY issuers while the variables were standardized over the same mean and standard deviation. HY issuers still have larger slopes on EAR, indicating that, controlling for the actual size of surprises, HY issuers still have a larger drift.

18. For example, Chan, Jegadeesh, and Lakonishok (1996) find that both earnings surprises and past intermediate equity returns contributed significantly to the predictability of future equity returns even after controlling for each other, whereas Chordia and Shivakumar (2006) and Novy-Marx (2015) find that equity momentum is subsumed by the equity PEAD effects.

CHAPTER 21

Equity Short Interest as a Signal for Credit Investing

INTRODUCTION

Short selling of securities is widely recognized as beneficial to market liquidity and price efficiency. Market makers, for example, can use short selling to provide liquidity if a client order cannot be filled from their inventory. Short selling also allows investors to hedge their positions and manage certain risks, and it allows informed investors to position themselves according to their negative views on a company. A large body of empirical evidence documents that stock market short sellers indeed have informational advantages and earn significant returns over relatively short horizons.[1]

Negative views on a company's prospects apply to the company's equity and also to its corporate bonds, as the value of both assets is tied to the company's future performance. Short selling in a company's equities, if associated with negative views among informed traders, might therefore have return-relevant information for the company's corporate bonds too. Yet we find few studies on this relationship.[2]

In this chapter, we investigate whether equity short interest (ESI) has return-relevant information for corporate bonds. We define a company's ESI as the ratio between the number of shares on loan and total shares outstanding. The more a company's shares are in outstanding stock loans, the higher is its ESI. Shorting is associated with high risk and involves an ongoing cost for borrowing the shares; thus, increased lending activity in a company's stock is likely to come from investors with strong convictions in their negative information. Intuitively, we expect high values of ESI to be followed by low future returns.

We find that ESI is predictive of future corporate bond returns and rating downgrades. For the Bloomberg Barclays US Corporate and High Yield indices, we show that issuers with the highest level of ESI within their rating category are the most likely issuers to be downgraded over the next three to 12 months. This finding suggests that ESI contains information about the quality of a company's corporate bonds.

ESI correlates positively with several bond risk measures. To correctly assess the efficacy of ESI as a signal for future issuer returns, we account for different risk measures and form tradable index-tracking portfolios from a universe of liquid bonds. These portfolios are formed separately for high-yield (HY) and investment-grade (IG) issuers, with a tilt toward issuers with high ESI values. The tilted portfolios consistently underperform the index.

ESI is an addition to a growing suite of signals that use equity market information and help differentiate among corporate bond issuers. Another notable example is equity momentum in credit (EMC), which differentiates issuers based on their stock price momentum. Chapter 15 documents the positive empirical relationship between past equity returns and subsequent corporate bond returns of the same company.[3] Another example is the equity market's reaction around earnings announcements documented in Chapter 20.

We further investigate bond short interest as an additional measure to identify future underperformance and find that its predictive information is subsumed by information in ESI. Both signals lead to similar portfolios in the HY space, and bond short interest is not a useful indicator in the IG space as IG bonds are likely shorted as part of market-making activity.

We also explore whether ESI is subsumed by relative value measures. We measure a bond's relative value by its excess spread to peers (ESP), documented in Chapter 13. We find that ESI is useful to identify future underperformance among both cheap and expensive bonds and that both signals complement each other. A portfolio formed on a combination of both signals achieves almost twice the risk-adjusted return of portfolios formed on the individual signals.

The remainder of this chapter is organized as follows. We begin with a description of securities lending data and our bond and equity universe. We then assess the performance of a long-short strategy in quintile portfolios formulated on ESI values and discuss risk characteristics of the different portfolios. In the subsequent section, we take account of many practical considerations for implementing the ESI strategy in reality and present a use case of exploiting ESI in index tracking portfolios. We discuss the benefits of combining ESI with two intuitively related signals—bond short interest and relative value among corporate bonds—before we conclude the chapter.

LENDING DATA AND SAMPLE CONSTRUCTION

A central part of our analysis is the mapping between corporate bonds and equity short interest of the same company. We leverage Ben Dor and Xu (2015) in order to map corporate bonds and equities at the security level. This section briefly describes our data sources and the filters we apply to obtain our corporate bond sample.

Stock Lending Activity

All data on equity and bond lending activity in this study is obtained from FIS Astec Analytics, a commercial provider of security lending market information. The data is collected from security lenders and borrowers who rely on FIS Astec's information service to receive timely updates on current lending fees and lending volumes. In exchange for this information, security lenders and borrowers have to submit all their lending and borrowing data, such as fees and volumes to FIS Astec, which then matches and aggregates transaction-level data to the security level and returns it to the end users.

The securities lending data files have historical position data at daily frequency and are updated each morning with the latest data for the previous trading day. The files cover several thousand equity and fixed income securities at each point in time, domiciled in more than 100 countries. Securities are identified by CUSIP or ISIN as of the day the data are reported.

Two other features of this dataset are important to highlight. First, the lending activity reported by FIS Astec Analytics does not cover all lending transactions that took place. Some lenders or borrowers do not rely on FIS Astec's service and hence have no incentive to report their lending transactions. All data regarding shares on loan are, therefore, to be taken as a lower bound, likely underestimating the total lending volume in a security. Second, securities are reported only if at least one lending transaction is currently open. Thus, a security can be missing in the database either because there is no lending transaction involving this security or because the lenders and borrowers transacting this security do not report to FIS Astec Analytics.

In Table 21.1, we briefly describe selected variables reported in the lending data files. We broadly group them into two categories. The first category contains variables to filter for the date, security, and characteristics of the loan. The "Contract Type" can either be specified as overnight (O) or any (A), which includes overnight and long term. The "Loan Stage" differentiates between new (N), returned (R), and recalled (L) loans, and (A) summarizes all loans open at business close. The "Collateral Type" for a loan can be cash (C) or noncash (N), both included in any (A). We also find a

"Collateral Currency" code to identify the currency of all cash collateral, which determines the respective overnight rate paid on the collateral. The second category of variables is quantifying the lending activity. "Tickets" represents the number of lending transactions for every date, security, and all of the previously specified loan characteristics. "Units" has two interpretations, depending on the type of the transacted security. For equity securities, it represents the number of shares lent in transactions. For bonds, it represents the par value. To measure the average rate paid by the borrower to the lender for a particular security on a particular date, the variable "Retail Loan Rate Average" summarizes the costs across all tickets and hence types of loans, considering overnight rates and rebate rates where applicable.

TABLE 21.1   Selected Variables in FIS Astec Analytics Security Lending Files

Aggregation Levels	Description
Date, CUSIP, ISIN	Date and security Identifiers
Contract Type ID	Loan contract type: A (any), O (overnight)
Loan Stage ID	Loan stages: A (any outstanding at business close), N (new), R (returned), L (recalled)
Collateral Type ID	Type of collateral for this loan: A (any), C (cash), N (noncash)
Collateral Currency ID	ISO code for currency of the cash loan's collateral (e.g., EUR, USD, XXX for noncash)
Measures of Lending Activity	**Description**
Tickets	Number of transactions
Units	Number of units—shares (equity) or par value (bonds)—lent in transactions
Retail Loan Rate Average	Weighted average retail loan rate for all transactions of this security and date

Source: FIS Astec Analytics, Barclays Research

The main part of our study relies on units in equity securities, for which we consider all contract types and any loan outstanding at business close with any type of collateral. To illustrate the calculation of ESI from FIS Astec Analytics data, we provide an example in Table 21.2. For a particular security, we find 2,000,000 shares across all lending transactions outstanding at business close on January 28, 2020. Based on a total of 100,000,000 shares outstanding, for which we consult Compustat North America, we obtain a 2% ESI for this security on this date. The retail loan rate average, an estimate of the annualized cost the average investor faces when borrowing this security, is 3.55%.

TABLE 21.2   Illustrative Data

Field Name	Value
Date	20200128
Contract Type ID	A
Loan Stage ID	A
Collateral Type ID	A
Tickets	10
Units	2,000,000
Retail Loan Rate Average	3.55

Source: FIS Astec Analytics, Barclays Research

Corporate Bond Universe

The corporate bond universe for this chapter comprises the Bloomberg Barclays US Corporate and High Yield indices between January 2007 and December 2019. For every corporate bond issuer, we check for each month separately whether the parent company has common stock listed on a US exchange that is part of at least one lending transaction. If this is the case, we include the issuer with all of its index bonds in our sample. We exclude American depositary receipts (ADRs) from our sample because we find ESI in ADRs to be materially different from ESI in common stock.

Table 21.3 lists the year-end market value of all bonds in the respective index that have been successfully mapped to equity securities (Compustat) and equity lending transactions (FIS Astec Analytics). From the start of our sample in 2007, the mapping has improved steadily for both the IG and HY index. In 2007 already, we can map 76% (in terms of market value) of the IG index to a company with common stock in lending transactions; this value increases to 84% at the end of 2019. For HY, the percentage increases from 57% to 75% over the same period. The main reason for the lower mapping rate in HY is the larger share of private issuers, the equity of which is not listed on a stock exchange.

TABLE 21.3 Bond Mapping to Equity Short Interest

Market Value and Percentage Mapped with Compustat and FIS Astec Analytics

		2007	2010	2013	2016	2019
IG	Index ($bn)	1,978	2,843	3,727	4,907	5,809
	Mapped to ESI	76%	80%	82%	82%	84%
HY	Index ($bn)	629	930	1,270	1,334	1,277
	Mapped to ESI	57%	57%	58%	66%	75%

Note: The indices are the Bloomberg Barclays US Corporate and High Yield indices. Numbers are year-end statistics.
Source: Bloomberg, Compustat, FIS Astec Analytics, Barclays Research

How similar are the final samples to their respective index in terms of characteristics and performance? Our IG sample has a similar rating, spread, duration, and information ratio to the index on average, as can be seen in Table 21.4. Our HY sample has a slightly better average rating, higher spread duration, lower spread, and Duration Times Spread (DTS) than the HY index.[4] This finding is intuitive, given that we exclude all private issuers. Despite these differences, our sample and the index share almost the same information ratios. Dynamics in the strategies discussed later are thus unlikely to be driven by sample differences.

TIME-SERIES AND CROSS-SECTIONAL CHARACTERISTICS OF ESI

Equity short interest is defined as the ratio between shares in outstanding stock loans and total shares outstanding:

$$\text{ESI}_{i,t} = \frac{Shares\ Lent_{i,t}}{Shares\ Outstanding_{i,t}}.$$

Figure 21.1 illustrates the time series of average ESI values for the companies in our IG and HY sample. In order to obtain the value-weighted estimates, we weight each company's ESI value by the company's equity market value. Two features are particularly noteworthy. First, ESI is, on average, significantly larger for companies whose bonds are classified as HY—the value-weighted average in the IG sample is 1.28%, less than half of the 3.27% in the HY sample. One potential reason is that HY companies are perceived as more volatile, such that returns from successful speculative

TABLE 21.4 Characteristics of Bonds in the Samples and Their Respective Index

		Characteristics						Return Statistics					
		Avg. # Bonds	Quality	OAS (bps)	OASD (yr)	DTS (%*yr)	MV ($MM)	Ex. Ret. (%/yr)	Vol. (%/yr)	Inf. Ratio	Min. Ret. (%/m)	Max. DD (%)	Index Corr.
IG	Index	4,557	3.30	153	6.98	11.52	811	1.18	5.41	0.22	−8.38	−20.05	
	Sample	3,856	3.33	150	7.09	11.59	784	1.04	4.71	0.22	−7.42	−17.74	99%
HY	Index	1,905	5.78	503	4.10	20.20	552	3.81	10.89	0.35	−16.50	−44.76	
	Sample	1,213	5.62	442	4.17	18.52	559	3.26	9.80	0.33	−15.02	−40.63	99%

Note: The indices are the Bloomberg Barclays US Corporate and High Yield indices. The numeric values of quality are converted from ratings by the following scale: Aaa=1, Aa=2, A=3, Baa=4, Ba=5, B=6, Caa=7, Ca=8, C=9, D=10. OAS: option-adjusted spread, OASD: option-adjusted spread duration, MV: market value, Max. DD: maximum drawdown.
Source: Bloomberg, Compustat, FIS Astec Analytics, Barclays Research

short positions are potentially larger. Second, the value-weighted estimates are significantly lower than the equal-weighted estimates of ESI. This implies that ESI is, on average, larger for smaller companies within the respective index. One potential reason is that smaller companies are less well researched and short sellers might find more opportunities to trade on their informational advantages.

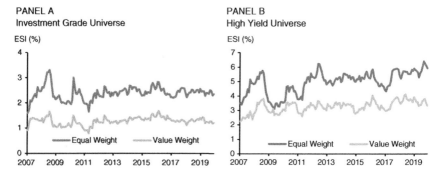

FIGURE 21.1   Estimates of Average ESI for US IG and HY Issuers
Source: Bloomberg, Compustat, FIS Astec Analytics, Barclays Research

Variation of ESI Across Sectors

Are certain sectors more shorted than others? There are several reasons why the average level of ESI across sectors might differ–industrials, for example, are more cyclical than consumer staples, and energy or financial companies might be shorted in expectation of sector-specific regulatory changes. For this, we group issuers into one of eight bond index sectors[5]. These sectors have been chosen to ensure that they include a sufficiently large number of issuers during the period of our study.

Figure 21.2 displays the value-weighted averages of ESI and the respective lending fees for each sector. Across all sectors, companies in the HY sample have been more shorted on average than companies in the IG sample. In addition, we find that lending fees have been larger for HY bonds. Industrials have been the cheapest to short in HY with 0.77%/yr, still more expensive than the most expensive sector in IG, utilities with 0.64%/yr. Variation across sectors has also been stronger in the HY sample, in both ESI and lending fees–energy companies have been 2.4 times more shorted than utility companies on average. Based on this evidence, we argue for sector-neutrality in portfolios formed on ESI to not falsely attribute sector performance to the efficacy of ESI as a signal, and to assess whether the efficacy holds within sectors. For the strategies discussed in this study, we will explicitly state the respective approach to neutralize sector effects.

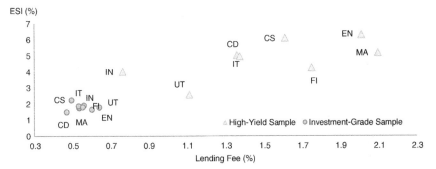

FIGURE 21.2 Value-weighted ESI and Lending Fees across Sectors

Note: We report average ESI and lending fees for these eight sectors: consumer discretionary (CD), consumer staples (CS), energy and transport (EN), financials and real estate (FI), industrials (IN), communications and information technology (IT), materials (MA), and utilities (UT). The sample period covers January 2007 to December 2019.

Source: Bloomberg, Compustat, FIS Astec Analytics, Barclays Research

Relationship Between ESI and Fundamental Risk

If short sellers have an informational advantage on the quality of a company, we expect ESI to predict future changes in the company's creditworthiness beyond its current rating. Every month we sort bond issuers into quintile portfolios within each rating bucket according to their ESI value from the previous month-end. We then track the rating changes of these issuers over the subsequent three-, six-, nine-, and 12-month horizons. Table 21.5 shows that, after controlling for issuers' initial ratings, issuers with high ESI values (Q5) have realized larger or more downgrades than issuers with lower ESI values (Q1) over horizons up to one year. The pattern exists in all rating buckets and is more pronounced with an increasing horizon. This finding indicates that ESI predicts future downgrades and supports the hypothesis that equity short sellers possess information about the future quality of a company's corporate bonds which is not yet reflected in its current ratings.

TABLE 21.5 Rating Notch Changes by ESI Quintile Portfolios, Rating, and Horizon

Panel A. Investment-Grade Universe

	Aaa/Aa						A						Baa					
Horizon	Q1	Q2	Q3	Q4	Q5	Q1–Q5	Q1	Q2	Q3	Q4	Q5	Q1–Q5	Q1	Q2	Q3	Q4	Q5	Q1–Q5
3m	.00	.06	.04	.09	.10	.10	.00	.01	.03	.04	.06	.06	-.01	-.01	-.01	.01	.04	.05
6m	.06	.11	.11	.20	.20	.14	.00	.03	.07	.08	.12	.12	-.02	-.02	-.01	.01	.09	.11
9m	.12	.21	.18	.28	.30	.18	.01	.06	.10	.13	.18	.17	-.04	-.03	-.02	.03	.13	.17
12m	.21	.30	.27	.40	.40	.19	.02	.09	.13	.16	.24	.22	-.05	-.04	-.02	.04	.17	.22

Panel B. High-Yield Universe

	Ba						B						Caa/Ca/C					
Horizon	Q1	Q2	Q3	Q4	Q5	Q1–Q5	Q1	Q2	Q3	Q4	Q5	Q1–Q5	Q1	Q2	Q3	Q4	Q5	Q1–Q5
3m	-.01	-.03	.00	.02	.11	.12	-.04	-.04	-.02	.00	.09	.13	-.01	-.03	.03	-.02	.13	.14
6m	-.02	-.06	.00	.03	.22	.24	-.06	-.07	-.02	.01	.17	.24	-.06	-.03	.02	-.02	.22	.28
9m	-.02	-.09	-.02	.05	.33	.35	-.08	-.10	-.02	.02	.24	.32	-.08	-.04	-.01	-.01	.29	.38
12m	-.02	-.11	-.02	.08	.41	.43	-.10	-.12	-.02	.05	.29	.39	-.10	-.05	-.06	-.04	.35	.45

Note: Each rating notch is assigned a numerical value. A better rating is assigned to a lower value: Aaa=1, Aa1=2, . . ., C=21, D=22. One represents one notch down. Each month we sort issuers into quintile portfolios based on their ESI value from the end of the previous month. The ranking is done within each of the six rating buckets (Aaa/Aa, A, Baa, Ba, B, Caa/Ca/C). For each issuer, we then track its rating changes in the subsequent three, six, nine and 12 months. The rating change is calculated as the difference between the end rating (last available rating at the earlier of the issuer exiting the index or the end of the evaluation window) and the rating at the beginning of the evaluation window. Individual bond ratings of an issuer are value-weighted to obtain the average issuer rating. All issuer rating changes are equally weighted within each quintile portfolio. The sample period covers January 2007 to December 2019.
Source: Bloomberg, Compustat, FIS Astec Analytics, Barclays Research.

Performance and Characteristics of ESI Quintile Portfolios

If it were true that short sellers trade on information which is not yet reflected in current valuations, we would expect bonds of issuers with high ESI values to underperform bonds of issuers with low ESI values. In this case, ESI should be useful in differentiating bond issuers with respect to their subsequent returns. In this section, we examine the existence of a stable relationship between ESI and corporate bond returns.

On the last trading day of each month, we sort issuers within their sectors into quintile portfolios based on their most recent ESI value. We value-weight issuers at portfolio formation and keep the portfolios unchanged for one month, then rebalance again according to updated ESI values. Figure 21.3 contains the returns, volatilities, and Sharpe ratios for each quintile portfolio in the IG sample (Panel A and C) and the HY sample (Panel B and D). For the IG sample, excess returns over duration-matched Treasury portfolios are reported in order to focus on the credit component of performance. For the HY sample, total returns are used. The ESI strategy, which consists of buying the least shorted issuers (Q1) and selling short the most shorted issuers (Q5), is reported by Q1–Q5.

Surprisingly, the ESI strategy has delivered a negative information ratio of –0.08 between 2007 and 2019 for IG issuers and an information ratio of 0.16 for HY issuers. While return volatility is increasing with ESI in both samples, we find no stable relationship with future returns. A long-only position in the least shorted issuers, Q1, has delivered identical risk-adjusted returns as the entire index for IG issuers; both have yielded a Sharpe ratio of 0.22. For HY issuers, being long Q1 has resulted in a Sharpe ratio of 0.82, close to the index at 0.77. The one significant difference to the index is in HY portfolio Q5, the Sharpe ratio of which is half as large at 0.38. A closer look at portfolio characteristics might help us to interpret these results.

We provide different characteristics of ESI quintile portfolios in Table 21.6. For several risk measures, we find that high-ESI issuers are riskier. First, we find that issuer quality deteriorates with increasing ESI. Second, we find widening credit spreads as we move from Q1 to Q5, resulting in higher DTS, which measures the expected volatility of a bond's excess return. This finding suggests that the ESI strategy might be subject to market directionality. For IG issuers, we document a decrease in issuer size and mild deterioration of liquidity, as measured by the increase in Liquidity Cost Scores (LCS),[6] meaning the ESI strategy might pick up a liquidity premium. All of these findings provide a potential reason for the low performance of the ESI strategy, as it has a negative exposure to certain risk measures with a long position in Q1 and a short position in Q5, thus reducing the expected returns of the strategy.

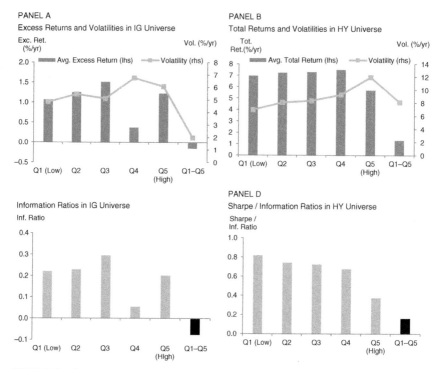

FIGURE 21.3   Average Excess Returns, Volatilities, and Information Ratios in ESI Quintile Portfolios
Note: We use 1-month Libor as funding rate to compute Sharpe ratios in HY portfolios. The sample period covers January 2007 to December 2019.
Source: Bloomberg, Compustat, FIS Astec Analytics, Barclays Research

In the next section, we disentangle the contributions of ESI and other risk characteristics to portfolio performance and thus evaluate ESI's efficacy more accurately. Instead of investing in several hundred bonds based on univariate quintile sorts, we apply ESI to a concentrated universe of liquid bonds and match the indices' key risk characteristics.

INDEX-REPLICATING PORTFOLIOS WITH AN ESI TILT

Index-replicating portfolios have two noteworthy advantages over univariate quintile sorts. First, an index-replicating portfolio matches the key characteristics of an index, allowing for a clearer attribution of performance

TABLE 21.6 Average Issuer Characteristics in ESI Quintile Portfolios

Metric	Investment Grade					High Yield				
	Q1	Q2	Q3	Q4	Q5	Q1	Q2	Q3	Q4	Q5
Quality	3.05	3.25	3.42	3.52	3.65	5.55	5.53	5.56	5.62	5.84
OAS (bps)	1.44	1.62	1.69	1.78	2.11	4.38	4.32	4.61	4.87	6.29
DTS	11.17	11.86	12.19	12.64	14.11	17.94	18.68	19.45	20.59	24.95
Size ($MM)	5.18	4.54	3.60	2.66	2.10	1.04	1.21	1.21	1.09	1.08
LCS (%)	0.19	0.20	0.22	0.27	0.33	0.83	0.72	0.71	0.78	0.79
ESI (%)	0.31	0.64	1.13	2.10	5.98	0.54	1.51	2.96	5.71	14.09

Note: The numeric values of quality are converted from ratings by the following scale: Aaa=1, Aa=2, A=3, Baa=4, Ba=5, B=6, Caa=7, Ca=8, C=9, D=10. OAS, DTS, LCS, and ESI are aggregated by issuer bond market value weight across issuers. The market-value-weighted statistics are later averaged across all months. The sample period covers January 2007 to December 2019.
Source: Bloomberg, Compustat, FIS Astec Analytics, Barclays Research

to isolated risk measures. Second, the construction aims at a reasonably sized portfolio of liquid securities, meeting important constraints that credit portfolio managers usually face in practice. In this study, the corporate bond indices we replicate are the Bloomberg Barclays US Corporate and Bloomberg Barclays US High Yield indices.

The monthly portfolio construction is split into two steps. In the first step, we decide on a set of liquid bonds that are suitable for index replication, the replication universe. In the second step, we create an index-replicating portfolio from these bonds.

To enter the replication universe, a bond must be senior, with a time to maturity beyond three years and an outstanding notional that exceeds the 25th percentile of all outstanding bonds' notional in the index at month-end. If an issuer has several bonds in the index that meet the criteria, of which at least one bond was issued less than two years ago, we discard all the bonds issued longer than two years ago. If there are still several bonds for an issuer to choose from, we choose the bond whose duration is closest to the average duration of its industry. The replication universe will thus consist of liquid senior bonds, with at most one bond per issuer.

We select and weigh bonds to match the risk profile of the index and at the same time maximize the portfolio's average ESI, limiting idiosyncratic risks. These constraints are in place to find such a portfolio on a monthly basis:

Each issuer (or bond) can account for up to 2% of the portfolio, which means that we have at least 50 different issuers to avoid a high concentration. In order to not load on sector effects, the portfolio sector allocation mimics the allocation in the index. In addition, the portfolio OAS and DTS must be the same as those of the index to eliminate undesired risk exposures. From all the possible combinations within these constraints, we pick the one that maximizes the portfolio's ESI.

Key analytics for the respective index, replication universe, and tilted portfolio can be found in Table 21.7. The weight limit of 2% at the issuer level results in portfolios with 55 issuers on average in both IG and HY. While OAS and DTS are the same in the indices and portfolios as intended, the average ESI in the tilted portfolios is about five (IG) and three (HY) times larger than the average ESI in the index or replication universe. This tilt does not materially affect the average rating and leads to only modest increases in LCS.

Performance Statistics

Table 21.8 reports the performance of the replicating portfolios. In addition to the portfolio that maximizes ESI, which we expect to underperform the

TABLE 21.7 Bond Characteristics in Index, Replication Universe, and Tilted Portfolio

		Avg. # Bonds/m	Quality	OAS (bps)	OASD (yr)	DTS (%*yr)	LCS (%)	ESI (%)	Bond MV ($MM)
IG	Index	4547	3.26	170	6.81	12.27	0.84	1.39	809
	Repl. Universe	546	3.45	174	6.72	11.79	0.84	1.80	803
	Repl. Portfolio (Max. ESI)	55	3.39	170	7.25	12.27	0.96	6.94	730
HY	Index	1897	5.79	551	4.14	22.09	1.56	4.56	552
	Repl. Universe	400	5.71	493	4.17	20.59	1.43	4.78	602
	Repl. Portfolio (Max. ESI)	55	5.75	551	4.03	22.09	1.67	15.90	554

Note: The indices are the Bloomberg Barclays US Corporate and High Yield indices. The reported ESI for the respective index ignores all issuers without ESI values. The tracking portfolio has a tilt toward high ESI and matches index DTS, OAS, and sector weights, with no bond assuming more than 2% of the portfolio weight. The numeric values of quality are converted from ratings by the following scale: Aaa=1, Aa=2, A=3, Baa=4, Ba=5, B=6, Caa=7, Ca=8, C=9, D=10. We report returns in excess of a duration-matched Treasury portfolio for IG bonds and total returns for HY bonds. The market-value-weighted statistics are later averaged across all months. The sample period covers January 2007 to December 2019.
Source: Bloomberg, Compustat, FIS Astec Analytics, Barclays Research

TABLE 21.8   ESI: Performance of Replicating Portfolios and Long-Short Strategies

		Index	Min. ESI	Max. ESI	Min.–Max.	Index–Max.	Min.–Index
IG	Avg. Ex. Ret. (%/yr)	1.18	1.64	-0.42	2.06	1.61	0.45
	Vol. (%/yr)	5.41	4.81	5.13	1.61	2.20	1.63
	Inf. Ratio	0.22	0.34	-0.08	1.28	0.73	0.28
	Min. Ex. Ret. (%/m)	-8.38	-6.70	-10.36	-0.77	-3.55	-2.11
	Corr. w. Index		0.95	0.91	-0.06	0.33	-0.50
HY	Avg. Tot. Ret. (%/yr)	7.41	7.04	5.44	1.61	1.97	-0.37
	Vol. (%/yr)	10.89	9.22	10.22	3.02	2.66	3.01
	Sharpe / Inf. Ratio	0.63	0.63	0.40	0.53	0.75	-0.12
	Min. Tot. Ret. (%/m)	-15.91	-17.20	-18.84	-2.77	-4.40	-3.55
	Corr. w. Index		0.95	0.96	-0.35	-0.08	-0.13

Note: The indices are the Bloomberg Barclays US Corporate and High Yield indices. Min. and Max. ESI are the replicating portfolios that minimize and maximize portfolio ESI, at the same time matching the index OAS, DTS, and sector weights. Index–Max. describes the return series of the index over the Max. ESI portfolio, and Min.–Max. describes the return series of the Min. ESI over the Max. ESI portfolio. The sample period covers January 2007 to December 2019.
Source: Bloomberg, Compustat, FIS Astec Analytics, Barclays Research

index, we compute the performance of a portfolio that minimizes ESI. While our sample does not include issuers with zero ESI, it is worth investigating if issuers with low ESI outperform the index.

In the IG universe, we find that bonds from issuers with high ESI tend to have low future returns. The index outperforms the Max. ESI portfolio in 104 out of 155 months and by 1.61% on average per year. The Min. ESI portfolio outperforms the Max. ESI portfolio by 2.06%. This long-short strategy, which we call "ESI strategy" going forward, achieves an information ratio of 1.28 in our sample. The significant return differences between the portfolios cannot be explained by DTS, carry, or sector imbalances, as those are matched in the construction process. The cumulative performance of the different strategies shown in Panel A brings us two insights. First, the index outperforms the Max. ESI portfolio consistently throughout our sample, as can be seen in Figure 21.4, and is not driven by events. Second, the on-average higher return of low-ESI issuers relative to the index comes most of all from the outperformance during the financial crisis in 2008 and 2009.

Our findings in the HY universe are similar to the findings in the IG universe. ESI is useful to identify bonds with future underperformance but not outperformance. The index return has been 1.97% per year larger on

PANEL A
Investment Grade Universe

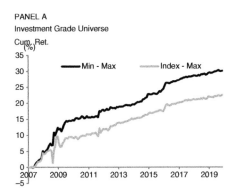

PANEL B
High Yield Universe

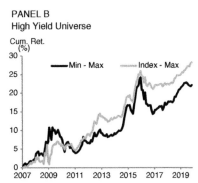

FIGURE 21.4 ESI: Cumulative Strategy Returns

Note: The indices are the Bloomberg Barclays US Corporate and High Yield indices. Min. and Max. ESI are the replicating portfolios that minimize and maximize portfolio ESI, at the same time matching the index OAS, DTS, and sector weights. Index–Max. describes the return series of the index over the Max. ESI portfolio, and Min.–Max. describes the return series of the Min. ESI over the Max. ESI portfolio. The sample period covers January 2007 to December 2019.

Source: Bloomberg, Compustat, FIS Astec Analytics, Barclays Research

average than the Max. ESI portfolio return, which it outperformed in 100 out of 155 months. Unlike in the IG universe, the average annualized return of the Min. ESI portfolio has been 0.37% lower on average than the return of the index. We interpret this as evidence that ESI is a one-sided signal, useful for the identification of low future performance.

We conclude that ESI is an effective signal to identify corporate bond issuers with subsequent low returns in both indices—once we account for relevant risk measures in the portfolio construction. A univariate sort of bonds or issuers into low- and high-ESI portfolios ignores the fact that high-ESI issuers, on average, tend to have higher spreads and DTS exposure. Accounting for these risk characteristics allows us to estimate a signal's efficacy more accurately.

INCORPORATING SHORT INTEREST FROM THE CORPORATE BOND MARKET

Investors can also implement their negative views through short selling in the bond market. In this section, we investigate whether bond short interest is predictive of corporate bond returns and whether its information is complementary to information in ESI.

The data on bond short interest comes from FIS Astec Analytics at the security level. To differentiate issuers based on bond short interest, it is important to incorporate the available information across all their bonds and aggregate the data from the security level to the issuer level. We define issuer-level bond short interest (BSI) as the average short interest in all of their bonds for which we find at least one outstanding lending transaction in the current month.[7]

How different are BSI and ESI as predictive variables in the bond cross-section? Before we can answer this question, we have to add one additional filter to our IG and HY bond samples from the previous analysis—for a bond to be included, the issuer must have a value for both ESI and BSI. This ensures that we evaluate the efficacy of the signals in the same bond universe. We find that the sample is almost identical to the previous one. The average coverage of index market value is about one percentage point lower once we add the BSI requirement: from 81% to 80% in the IG universe and 63% to 62% in the HY universe.

Performance and Characteristics of BSI Quintile Portfolios

We sort issuers into quintile portfolios according to their BSI value the same way we did according to their ESI value. On the last trading day of each month, we rank issuers within sectors based on their most recent BSI value, then sort them into value-weighted quintile portfolios. Table 21.9 summarizes the results.

Although high values of ESI correspond to an increased likelihood of being downgraded over the next three to 12 months in every rating class, BSI does not differentiate IG issuers in this regard. We find a positive relationship between BSI and the likelihood of being downgraded in the HY universe, but the relationship is weaker than for ESI. This can be seen from the difference in future rating notch changes between low- and high-BSI issuers (Q1–Q5), which is smaller than for ESI in every rating class.

We present average risk characteristics and return performance for each quintile portfolio in Table 21.10. A few points are worth highlighting. In both the IG and HY universes, issuers with the lowest BSI values yield the highest Sharpe (information) ratios. In the HY universe, the level of ESI increases with the level of BSI, and intuitively issuers in Q5 underperform issuers in Q1 to Q4. Yet, for IG issuers, Q5 has the second highest average return. This observation in the IG universe is at odds with the hypothesis of informed short sellers who implement their negative views, just as the previous results are on the predictability of downgrades.

Although we do not know the purpose of the individual lending transactions, it is likely that lending activity in IG bonds is driven by very different motives. First, there are opportunistic traders implementing their negative views, which also applies to HY bonds. Second, market makers might borrow bonds in order to provide liquidity to investors with positive views. If a market maker cannot meet the demand of one client from inventory or purchase the relevant bond in the market, the market maker might borrow the bond from another client instead and later net the short position. As soon as the latter scenario accounts for a significant share of lending activity, BSI is no longer as effective in differentiating bond issuers because it is not directly related to issuer-level information.

Index-Replicating Portfolios with a BSI Tilt

As with ESI, we form index-replicating portfolios tilted toward high and low BSI issuers to assess the efficacy of BSI as a signal for future corporate bond returns. We apply the exact same constraints to form our replication universe from each index as with ESI,[8] adding the constraint that issuers must have both an ESI and BSI value. Then we form our replicating portfolios by maximizing or minimizing BSI, matching index DTS and OAS, matching index sector weights, and capping issuer weights at 2%.

The strategy performance is summarized in Table 21.11 and Figure 21.5. Consistent with previous findings, BSI is not informative about future

TABLE 21.9 Rating Notch Changes by BSI Quintile Portfolios, Rating, and Horizon

Panel A: Investment-Grade Universe

	Aaa/Aa						A						Baa					
Horizon	Q1	Q2	Q3	Q4	Q5	Q1–Q5	Q1	Q2	Q3	Q4	Q5	Q1–Q5	Q1	Q2	Q3	Q4	Q5	Q1–Q5
3m	.07	.08	.07	.07	.07	.00	.04	.03	.03	.02	.04	−.01	.00	.00	.00	.00	.03	.04
6m	.14	.19	.14	.16	.15	.01	.09	.07	.06	.05	.07	−.02	−.01	−.01	.01	.00	.06	.07
9m	.23	.30	.21	.24	.24	.02	.14	.12	.09	.08	.11	−.03	−.01	−.02	.01	.01	.09	.10
12m	.32	.40	.31	.35	.35	.03	.18	.16	.12	.11	.15	−.03	−.01	−.02	.01	.01	.12	.14

Panel B: High-Yield Universe

	Ba						B						Caa/Ca/C					
Horizon	Q1	Q2	Q3	Q4	Q5	Q1–Q5	Q1	Q2	Q3	Q4	Q5	Q1–Q5	Q1	Q2	Q3	Q4	Q5	Q1–Q5
3m	.00	.00	.01	.00	.09	.09	−.04	−.03	−.01	−.01	.07	.11	−.02	−.01	.04	.04	.04	.06
6m	−.01	.01	.01	.00	.17	.18	−.07	−.04	−.02	.00	.14	.21	−.04	−.04	.06	.06	.08	.12
9m	−.02	.02	.01	.01	.24	.26	−.09	−.05	−.03	.00	.19	.28	−.05	−.06	.05	.08	.10	.15
12m	−.02	.03	.02	.03	.30	.31	−.11	−.05	−.04	.02	.24	.34	−.07	−.07	.03	.07	.10	.17

Note: Each rating notch is assigned a numerical value. A better rating is assigned to a lower value: Aaa=1, Aa1=2, . . ., C=21, D=22. 1 represents one notch down. Each month we sort issuers into quintile portfolios based on their BSI value from the end of the previous month. The ranking is done within each of the six rating buckets (Aaa/Aa, A, Baa, Ba, B, Caa/Ca/C). For each issuer, we then track its rating changes in the subsequent three, six, nine, and 12 months. The rating change is calculated as the difference between the end rating (last available rating at the earlier of the issuer exiting the index or the end of the evaluation window) and the rating at the beginning of the evaluation window. Individual bond ratings of an issuer are value-weighted to obtain the average issuer rating. All issuer rating changes are equally weighted within each quintile portfolio. The sample period covers January 2007 to December 2019.

Source: Bloomberg, Compustat, FIS Astec Analytics, Barclays Research.

TABLE 21.10 Issuer Characteristics and Performance of BSI Quintile Portfolios

Metric	Investment Grade					High Yield				
	Q1	Q2	Q3	Q4	Q5	Q1	Q2	Q3	Q4	Q5
Avg. Ret. (%/yr)	1.99	1.03	1.22	0.95	1.32	8.76	6.42	8.67	6.50	4.67
Vol. (%/yr)	4.50	5.89	5.04	5.47	5.53	8.41	8.54	9.48	9.24	10.03
Inf. (Sharpe) Ratio	0.44	0.17	0.24	0.17	0.24	0.90	0.61	0.80	0.57	0.36
Quality	3.54	3.39	3.25	3.28	3.40	5.55	5.53	5.56	5.62	5.84
OAS (bps)	193	171	161	162	170	498	468	462	479	542
DTS (%*yr)	12.48	11.68	11.55	12.04	13.15	19.59	19.32	19.63	20.18	22.55
Size ($MM)	1.00	2.46	4.63	6.91	4.30	0.51	1.00	1.51	1.68	1.36
LCS (%)	0.60	0.30	0.19	0.16	0.23	1.34	0.81	0.62	0.58	0.69
ESI (%)	1.88	1.61	1.40	1.31	1.82	3.95	4.16	4.17	4.54	6.50

Note: We use one-month Libor as funding rate to compute Sharpe ratios for HY portfolios. The numeric values of quality are converted from ratings by the following scale: Aaa=1, Aa=2, A=3, Baa=4, Ba=5, B=6, Caa=7, Ca=8, C=9, D=10. OAS, DTS, LCS, and ESI are aggregated by issuer bond market value weight across issuers. The market-value-weighted statistics are later averaged across all months. The sample period covers January 2007 to December 2019.

Source: Bloomberg, Compustat, FIS Astec Analytics, Barclays Research

TABLE 21.11 BSI: Performance Statistics of Replicating Portfolios and Long-Short Strategies

		Index	Min. BSI	Max. BSI	Min.–Max.	Index–Max.	Min.–Index
IG	Avg. Ex. Ret. (%/yr)	1.18	0.40	1.13	-0.73	0.05	-0.78
	Vol. (%/yr)	5.41	4.81	4.64	1.61	1.75	2.07
	Inf. Ratio	0.22	0.08	0.24	-0.45	0.03	-0.37
	Min. Ex. Ret. (%/m)	-8.38	-9.06	-5.07	-3.99	-4.19	-2.82
	Corr. w. Index		0.92	0.95	0.02	0.57	-0.46
HY	Avg. Tot. Ret. (%/yr)	7.41	8.66	6.15	2.52	1.26	1.26
	Vol. (%/yr)	10.89	9.59	9.72	3.96	2.67	4.08
	Sharpe / Inf. Ratio	0.63	0.90	0.63	0.64	0.47	0.31
	Min. Tot. Ret. (%/m)	-15.91	-19.40	-17.59	-2.74	-4.00	-5.93
	Corr. w. Index		0.80	0.83	-0.09	0.03	0.11

Note: The indices are the Bloomberg Barclays US Corporate and High Yield indices. Min. and Max. BSI are the replicating portfolios that minimize and maximize portfolio BSI, at the same time matching the index OAS, DTS, and sector weights. Index–Max. describes the return series of the index over the Max. BSI portfolio, and Min.–Max. describes the return series of the Min. BSI over the Max. BSI portfolio. The sample period covers January 2007 to December 2019.
Source: Bloomberg, Compustat, FIS Astec Analytics, Barclays Research

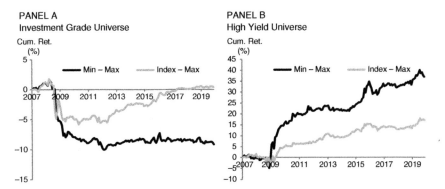

FIGURE 21.5   BSI: Cumulative Strategy Returns
Note: The indices are the Bloomberg Barclays US Corporate and High Yield indices. Min. and Max. BSI are the replicating portfolios that minimize and maximize portfolio BSI, at the same time matching the index OAS, DTS, and sector weights. Index–Max. describes the return series of the index over the Max. BSI portfolio, and Min.–Max. the return series of the Min. BSI over the Max. BSI portfolio. The sample period covers January 2007 to December 2019.
Source: Bloomberg, Compustat, FIS Astec Analytics, Barclays Research

returns in the IG universe. Since the end of the financial crisis in June 2009, the return of the Min. BSI over the Max. BSI portfolio was close to zero, at –0.15% per year. In addition, the Min. BSI portfolio consistently underperforms the index, and the index yielded a cumulative return of only 0.43% over the Max. BSI portfolio during the 13-year period.

The performance of BSI-tilted portfolios in the HY space is qualitatively similar to the performance of ESI-tilted portfolios. The Min. BSI portfolio outperforms the index by 1.26% per year, just as much as the index outperforms the Max. BSI portfolio. All long-short strategies have a close to zero correlation with the HY index, and the highest information ratio is obtained in the BSI strategy (Min. BSI–Max. BSI). A notable difference to ESI-tilted portfolios is the slightly improved return profile of the Min. BSI portfolio over the index.

Can We Benefit from a Combination of BSI and ESI in High Yield?

Before we discuss and explore possible combinations of ESI and BSI for an improved portfolio allocation, we discuss why a combination might actually be beneficial in the HY universe.

First, both signals are informative on their own. Our previous analysis documents that, while BSI is not an effective signal in the IG universe, both signals are predictive of future returns among HY issuers.

Second, the signals share a low correlation in the cross-section. For each month and index, we compute the Pearson and Spearman correlation coefficients between BSI and ESI in the cross-section. As a company can have several issuing entities present in the index, we aggregate issuer-level short interest to the company level, value-weighting individual BSI by the market value of an issuer's bonds in the respective index. The average cross-sectional correlation coefficients are 0.20 (Pearson) and 0.18 (Spearman) for HY issuers and 0.14 (Pearson) and 0.01 (Spearman) for IG issuers.

In order to assign the same importance to both measures within a combined signal, we standardize both BSI and ESI to have a mean of zero and standard deviation of 1 on a monthly basis. The combined signal is then the sum of both standardized measures at the issuer level:

$$CSI_{i,t} = standardized\ ESI_{i,t} + standardized\ BSI_{i,t}.$$

Despite the low cross-sectional correlation between ESI and BSI and their individual predictive power, the CSI-tilted portfolio does not offer an improved performance over the ESI-tilted portfolio. Table 21.12 compares the performance of the different portfolios in our HY sample of issuers with values on both BSI and ESI. The performance in the two long portfolios (Min. ESI, Min. CSI) is almost identical in terms of returns and volatility, just as in the two short portfolios (Max. ESI, Max. CSI).

Explanation for the Similarity Between the Combined Signal and ESI

In order to better understand the surprising result that the combined signal does not improve upon ESI, we rank issuers twice into quintile portfolios— once according to BSI, once according to ESI. This independent double sort offers additional insights about the correlation results obtained from the cross-section. We compute the average number of issuers in each of the 25 rank combinations, the average ESI, BSI, and next month's total return.

The matrix in Panel A of Table 21.13 shows that issuers with high (low) ESI values tend to have high (low) BSI values, as the buckets with most issuers are located at both ends of the main diagonal. The return matrix in Panel B illustrates that the issuers which rank highest in both ESI and BSI have significantly lower returns (–2.12%) than issuers that rank high in only one of the measures (on average 6.67% for the remaining ESI 5 issuers and 5.93% for the remaining BSI 5 issuers). This observation adds to the puzzle why the combination of ESI and BSI does not improve upon ESI as a standalone signal.

TABLE 21.12 Performance Comparison of Replicating Portfolios and Long-Short Strategies in the HY Universe

		Min. CSI	Min. ESI	Max. CSI	Max. ESI	Index–Max. CSI	Index–Max. ESI
HY	Avg. Tot. Ret. (%/yr)	7.11	7.03	5.54	5.31	1.97	2.19
	Vol. (%/yr)	9.08	9.22	10.10	10.22	2.59	2.78
	Sharpe / Inf. Ratio	0.64	0.63	0.43	0.40	0.76	0.79
	Min. Tot. Ret. (%/m)	–18.16	–17.21	–18.80	–18.84	–2.43	–4.40
	Corr. w. Index	0.95	0.95	0.96	0.96	–0.06	–0.07

Note: Index refers to the Bloomberg Barclays US High Yield Index. Min. and Max. CSI are the replicating portfolios that minimize and maximize portfolio CSI, at the same time matching the index OAS, DTS, and sector weights. Index–Max. CSI describes the return series of the index over the Max. CSI portfolio. The sample period covers January 2007 to December 2019.
Source: Bloomberg, Compustat, FIS Astec Analytics, Barclays Research

TABLE 21.18 Statistics from ESI and BSI Double Sorts in the HY Universe

Panel A: Average Number of Issuers

	BSI 1	BSI 2	BSI 3	BSI 4	BSI 5
ESI 1	20.73	18.83	17.14	14.12	10.08
ESI 2	17.29	18.06	17.02	15.63	12.03
ESI 3	16.12	16.12	17.05	16.03	14.88
ESI 4	14.81	14.82	15.45	17.38	17.71
ESI 5	11.72	12.26	13.45	16.95	25.81

Panel B: Average Annualized Total Return (%)

	BSI 1	BSI 2	BSI 3	BSI 4	BSI 5
ESI 1	7.67	5.94	6.05	7.76	6.30
ESI 2	7.52	9.01	7.86	6.40	6.48
ESI 3	7.66	6.74	6.89	5.36	5.50
ESI 4	11.62	5.99	5.62	4.03	5.42
ESI 5	8.95	6.94	5.91	4.90	-2.12

Panel C: Average ESI (%)

	BSI 1	BSI 2	BSI 3	BSI 4	BSI 5
ESI 1	0.46	0.48	0.49	0.49	0.48
ESI 2	1.45	1.45	1.43	1.46	1.50
ESI 3	2.92	2.92	2.93	2.97	2.99
ESI 4	5.77	5.87	5.90	5.91	6.08
ESI 5	13.87	14.36	14.63	15.59	17.03

Panel D: Average BSI (%)

	BSI 1	BSI 2	BSI 3	BSI 4	BSI 5
ESI 1	0.18	0.74	1.51	2.77	6.95
ESI 2	0.19	0.73	1.51	2.79	7.11
ESI 3	0.18	0.75	1.51	2.82	7.45
ESI 4	0.17	0.73	1.53	2.83	7.76
ESI 5	0.17	0.73	1.54	2.91	8.53

Note: Each month HY issuers are ranked according to their ESI and BSI values independently and sorted into 25 portfolios. For example, ESI 1 contains the 20% of issuers with the lowest ESI values, ESI 2 the next 20% of issuers, and so on. Issuer-level returns, ESI, and BSI are equally weighted within the quintile and then averaged across time. The sample period covers January 2007 to December 2019.
Source: Bloomberg, Compustat, FIS Astec Analytics, Barclays Research

A potential resolution can be found in Panels C and D. In Panel C, we document the average ESI value for each one of the 25 rank combinations. Within a particular ESI rank, ESI is almost the same across the different levels of BSI, except for within ESI 5. In Panel D, we observe the same for BSI. Within a particular BSI rank, ESI seems to be uncorrelated with BSI, except for within BSI 5. In addition, the highest values for ESI and BSI can be found in the same bucket. An allocation strategy that maximizes the combination of ESI and BSI will invest in several bonds that are part of a strategy that maximizes ESI alone.

This leads us to an important question: Do the tilted portfolios with maximized short interest have a significant overlap? On average, we find that 22% of the bonds in the Max. ESI and Max. BSI portfolios are the same. Between the portfolios formed on ESI and the combined signal CSI, the overlap is even at 57%, and at 62% between portfolios formed on BSI and CSI.

Although the combination of the two predictive signals BSI and ESI appeared promising due to their low average cross-sectional correlation, it did not improve upon ESI as a stand-alone signal. A closer look at the portfolio compositions and the distribution of returns across the different values of ESI and BSI suggests that ESI and BSI share similar information in the tail of the distribution.

We formally evaluate the interaction between ESI and BSI with a set of regressions of total returns within our HY replication universe on ESI, BSI, and an interaction term:

$$r_{i,t+1} = a + b\,BSI_{i,t} + c\,BSI_{i,t} + d\,BSI_{i,t} * ESI_{i,t} + \varepsilon_{i,t}.$$

The coefficient estimates documented in the first three columns of Table 21.14 suggest that both ESI and BSI are, alone and jointly, predictive of future corporate bond returns. The introduction of an interaction term, although only weakly significant, brings the coefficient estimates for both ESI and BSI closer to zero, indicating that bonds with high ESI and BSI values perform worse than the average bond in the sample. In addition, the coefficient estimate on BSI becomes less significant while the estimate for ESI remains significant at the 1% level. This supports our finding that part of the predictive information in BSI can be attributed to its interaction with ESI.

TABLE 21.14 Regression Coefficient Estimates

	BSI	ESI	BSI and ESI	With Interaction
Intercept (a)	0.6135***	0.7005***	0.7513***	0.7333***
ESI (b)	−0.0392***		−0.0329***	−0.0298***
BSI (c)		−0.0359***	−0.0249***	−0.0188*
ESI * BSI (d)				−0.0008*

Note: All estimates are for the period January 2007 to December 2019 and all bonds within the HY replication universe. The econometric method used ordinary least squares. The superscripts ***, **, and * indicate statistical significance at the 1%, 5%, and 10% level, respectively, and are based on autocorrelation-consistent Newey-West standard errors.
Source: Bloomberg, Compustat, FIS Astec Analytics, Barclays Research

ESI AND RELATIVE VALUE IN CREDIT

We have documented that bonds of issuers associated with high ESI values tend to be overpriced and perform significantly worse than bonds with similar risk characteristics but lower ESI values. In light of this evidence, one might wonder whether the informational content in ESI is subsumed by measures of relative value in credit.

To investigate whether ESI becomes redundant once we account for relative value, we rely on excess spread to peers, discussed in Chapter 13. ESP is a quantitative filter designed to measure a bond's relative value. ESP ranks bonds (from one to 10) within their peer group according to their relative value, derived from a bond's spread over peers unexplained by issuer characteristics and fundamentals. A high ESP score is an indication that a bond is relatively undervalued.

We first estimate the cross-sectional correlation between the two signals. This time, for a bond to be included in our sample, the bond must have a value for both ESI and ESP. We find that the IG sample is almost identical to the initial sample based on ESI alone. With few exceptions, all bonds with an ESI value also have an ESP score, such that the index coverage stays at 81% on average across the sample. For HY issuers, the ESP score is available for all issuers with a rating of single B and above, which reduces our sample from 63% to 54% in terms of index coverage.

At the company level,[9] the average cross-sectional Spearman correlation coefficient between ESP and ESI is 0.08 in the IG sample and −0.04 in the HY sample. To further understand the correlation between the two

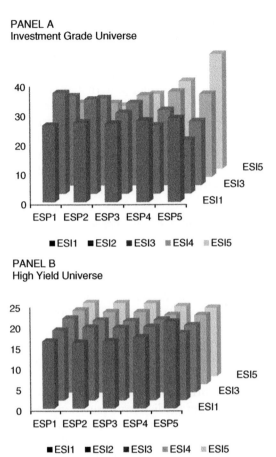

PANEL A
Investment Grade Universe

■ESI1 ■ESI2 ■ESI3 ▥ESI4 ▨ESI5

PANEL B
High Yield Universe

■ESI1 ■ESI2 ■ESI3 ▥ESI4 ▨ESI5

FIGURE 21.6   Average Number of Companies per ESI and ESP Quintile
Combination
Note: Each month companies are ranked according to their ESI value and ESP
score independently and sorted into 25 portfolios. For example, ESI 1 contains the
20% of issuers with the lowest ESI values, ESI 2 the next 20% of issuers, and so
on. The sample period covers January 2007 to December 2019.
Source: Bloomberg, Compustat, FIS Astec Analytics, Barclays Research

signals, we sort companies twice independently into quintile portfolios:
once according to their ESP scores and once according to their ESI values.
The resulting double-sort matrix will allow us to see whether particular
combinations of ESI and ESP are dominant in our sample.

Figure 21.6 illustrates the average number of companies per ESP and ESI combination in our sample. The result for IG companies in Panel A suggests that the most shorted companies (ESI 5) tend to have more relatively cheap bonds than expensive ones, as the number of bonds increases with the ESP score. We do not find a consistent pattern across other quintile combinations. We can see in Panel B that there is no particular relationship between ESI and ESP for HY companies: We find a very similar number of bonds for all signal combinations but one. The combination of cheapest (ESP 5) and least shorted (ESI 1) is the one combination that stands out, which is plausible as the equity corresponding to these bonds might also be considered cheap and less worth shorting.

Does ESI Predict Returns Within Bonds of Similar ESP Scores?

If ESI were subsumed by relative value measures, we would expect the ESI strategy to not work for bonds with similar ESP scores. To see whether ESI has predictive information beyond the information in ESP scores, we split both the IG and HY replication universe into two universes each. One universe contains "expensive" bonds with an ESP score of one to five; the other universe contains "cheap" bonds with an ESP score of six to 10. For each of these universes, we form our index-replicating portfolios according to the same criteria we used for the entire replication universe. We are then going to compare the return characteristics of the Max. ESI and Min. ESI portfolio. If ESI were without predictive information beyond ESP, we would expect the Min. ESI portfolio to not outperform the Max. ESI portfolio.

Table 21.15 documents the outperformance of the Min. ESI portfolio over the Max. ESI portfolio, which is significant regardless of the index and the ESP filter. An index-replicating portfolio that minimizes ESI achieves larger returns and better Sharpe ratios than a similar portfolio that maximizes ESI, among both relatively cheap and expensive HY and IG bonds. Our results show that a relative value measure is complementary to the return-relevant information in equity short interest.

Our analysis shows that ESI and ESP share a low cross-sectional correlation and have different informational content regarding future corporate bond returns. Over a pure ESI strategy, it seems preferable to hold relatively cheap bonds with low ESI values and to short expensive bonds with high ESI values. The same applies to a relative value strategy. It appears preferable to differentiate cheap bonds by those with low and high ESI values; the same holds for expensive bonds.

We provide evidence on the relationship between ESI and equity momentum with a similar analysis. For brevity, this analysis can be found in

TABLE 21.15 Performance Statistics of Replicating Portfolios with an ESI Tilt, Universe Split into Expensive and Cheap Bonds

		Entire Replicating Universe			Expensive Bonds			Cheap Bonds		
		Min.	Max.	Min.–Max.	Min.	Max.	Min.–Max.	Min.	Max.	Min.–Max.
IG	Avg. Ex. Ret. (%/yr)	1.64	−0.42	2.05	0.61	−0.65	1.25	2.33	1.25	1.08
	Vol. (%/yr)	4.81	5.13	1.61	4.86	5.10	1.25	4.85	5.03	1.37
	Inf. Ratio	0.34	−0.08	1.27	0.12	−0.13	1.00	0.48	0.25	0.79
	Min. Ex. Ret. (%/m)	−6.7	−10.36	−0.76	−8.44	−9.17	−1.19	−6.01	−6.83	−1.94
	Corr. w. Index	0.96	0.92	−0.06	0.95	0.91	−0.05	0.97	0.95	−0.08
HY	Avg. Tot. Ret. (%/yr)	7.04	5.44	1.60	3.13	2.19	0.93	5.71	3.84	1.86
	Vol. (%/yr)	9.22	10.21	3.02	4.61	4.7	0.98	8.29	8.85	2.14
	Sharpe / Inf. Ratio	0.76	0.53	0.53	0.41	0.21	0.95	0.54	0.30	0.87
	Min. Tot. Ret. (%/m)	−17.21	−18.85	−2.77	−4.44	−3.89	−0.58	−18.47	−17.79	2.62
	Corr. w. Index	0.84	0.82	−0.21	0.44	0.44	−0.06	0.82	0.83	−0.27

Note: The indices are the Bloomberg Barclays US Corporate and High Yield indices. Expensive bonds are bonds within the replication universe that have an ESP score from one to five, and cheap bonds are those within the replication universe that have an ESP score from six to 10. Min. and Max. replicating portfolios minimize and maximize the portfolio's overall ESI value, at the same time matching the index OAS, DTS, and sector weights. Min.–Max. represents the return series of the Min. over the Max. portfolio. The sample period covers January 2007 to December 2019. We use one-month Libor to compute Sharpe ratios from total returns.
Source: Bloomberg, Compustat, FIS Astec Analytics, Barclays Research

Appendix 21.1. In the next section, we illustrate the improved performance of a replicating portfolio from a combination of the signals over the signals on their own with an intuitive example.

Index-Replicating Portfolios with a Tilt Toward ESI and ESP

We compute and compare the performance of an ESI-tilted portfolio, an ESP-tilted portfolio, and a portfolio tilted toward a combination of ESP and ESI (ESIvalue). As before with ESI and BSI, we combine both standardized signals on an equal-weight basis:

$$ESIvalue_{i,t} = standardized\ ESI_{i,t} - standardized\ ESP_{i,t}.$$

The standardization computes both signals with a mean of zero and standard deviation of one. Instead of adding the standardized signals, we subtract the standardized ESP score from the standardized ESI value. ESIvalue is aimed at identifying potential underperformers. Intuitively, we would like to avoid issuers that trade relatively expensive to their peers (low ESP) and whose parent companies are shorted to a relatively large extent (high ESI); thus we flip the sign of the ESP score in order to maximize the ESIvalue signal.

We apply the same filters to our IG and HY samples as with ESI to identify the respective replication universes. We find that the replication universe in the IG space is almost unchanged and so are the average characteristics, as almost all bonds have an ESP score. Once we exclude issuers in the HY sample that do not have an ESP score, the average number of bonds in the HY replication universe decreases from 400 to 337. The average DTS and OAS in the HY replication universe slightly decrease and average quality slightly improves.

The performance of the different portfolios is summarized in Table 21.16. For IG issuers, the ESIvalue signal is superior to the single signals in both the long and short portfolios. While the ESP strategy (Max. ESP–Min. ESP) and the ESI strategy (Min. ESI–Max. ESI) achieve information ratios of 1.40 and 1.27, respectively, the ESIvalue strategy achieves an information ratio of 2.42, with higher average returns and lower average volatility. The consistent improvement in both legs of the strategy is reflected in the cumulative returns in Figure 21.7 and makes this signal combination interesting to both long-only and long-short investors. In HY, results are mixed, with ESI being the superior signal in the short portfolio and ESP being the superior signal in the long portfolio. The combination of both signals is in all three cases slightly inferior to one of the other signals on their own.

TABLE 21.16 ESI + ESP: Performance Statistics of Replicating Portfolios and Long-Short Strategies

		Index	Min. ESI	Max. ESP	Min. ESI Value	Max. ESI	Min. ESP	Max. ESIvalue	ESI Strategy	ESP Strategy	ESIvalue Strategy
IG	Avg. Ex. Ret. (%/yr)	1.18	1.64	1.79	2.45	-0.42	-0.27	-0.92	2.05	2.06	3.37
	Vol. (%/yr)	5.41	4.81	5.23	4.93	5.13	4.69	4.77	1.61	1.47	1.39
	Inf. Ratio	0.22	0.34	0.34	0.50	-0.08	-0.06	-0.19	1.27	1.40	2.42
	Min. Ex. Ret. (%/m)	-8.38	-6.70	-9.12	-7.47	-10.36	-5.68	-7.41	-0.76	-3.44	-0.65
	Corr. w. Index		0.96	0.96	0.96	0.92	0.97	0.94	-0.06	0.31	0.18
HY	Avg. Tot. Ret. (%/yr)	7.41	7.04	10.38	9.91	5.44	4.67	4.78	1.60	5.70	5.13
	Vol. (%/yr)	9.61	9.22	9.45	9.43	10.21	10.44	10.67	3.02	2.91	2.83
	Sharpe / Inf. Ratio	0.77	0.76	1.10	1.05	0.53	0.45	0.45	0.53	1.96	1.81
	Min. Tot. Ret. (%/m)	-15.91	-17.21	-17.10	-18.26	-18.85	-20.90	-20.68	-2.77	-2.23	-2.80
	Corr. w. Index		0.84	0.83	0.83	0.82	0.81	0.81	-0.21	-0.21	-0.30

Note: The indices are the Bloomberg Barclays US Corporate and High Yield indices. Min. and Max. ESI are the replicating portfolios that minimize and maximize portfolio ESI, at the same time matching the index OAS, DTS, and sector weights. The Strategy statistics are for the return series of the Min. over the Max. portfolio for each respective signal. The sample period covers January 2007 to December 2019.
Source: Bloomberg, Compustat, FIS Astec Analytics, Barclays Research

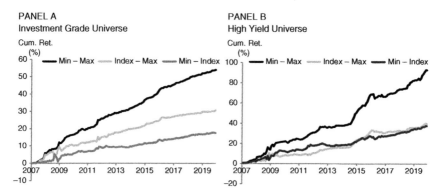

FIGURE 21.7 ESI + ESP: Cumulative Strategy Returns
Note: The indices are the Bloomberg Barclays US Corporate and High Yield indices. Min. and Max. replicating portfolios minimize and maximize the portfolios signal value, at the same time matching the index OAS, DTS, and sector weights. Min.–Max. represents the return series of the Min. over the Max. portfolio.
Source: Bloomberg, Compustat, FIS Astec Analytics, Barclays Research

CONCLUSION

We document the efficacy of equity short interest, a well-documented indicator of low returns in the cross-section of equity, as a signal for corporate bond returns. ESI consistently identifies issuers with an increased likelihood of rating downgrades and low corporate bond returns in both the HY and IG universe. An index-replicating portfolio with a tilt toward high ESI consistently underperforms its respective index over the next month.

ESI is a measure based on position data in the equity market. This feature distinguishes ESI from traditional bond risk measures based on fundamental data, prices or ratings, and makes it a promising candidate to combine with pure bond market signals. We include two such signals in our study to further understand the informational content in ESI. We find that the return-relevant information in bond short interest is subsumed by information in ESI. In addition, we find that ESI is only weakly correlated with relative value in credit and has complementary information regarding future returns.

APPENDIX 21.1

ESI and Equity Momentum in Credit

Companies with high values of ESI tend to have low subsequent equity returns and might therefore be associated with low equity price momentum. Introducing equity momentum in credit, Chapter 15 shows that equity momentum has a strong positive relationship with future corporate bond returns of the same company. As a consequence, ESI and EMC might overlap in their informational content regarding future corporate bond returns. Here we provide a brief analysis of the relationship between the two measures.

First, we keep all bonds of our mapped universe for which we have an EMC score. Not surprisingly, the sample is largely unchanged, since it is a prerequisite to have listed equity for an issuer to be included. In both the HY and IG universes, the index coverage decreases by less than half a percentage point on average in terms of market value once we exclude bonds without an EMC score. Next, we look at the average cross-sectional Spearman correlation between EMC and ESI at the company level. We find average correlation coefficients of -0.01 in the IG sample and -0.09 in the HY sample. Figure 21.8 illustrates the average number of companies for different ESI and EMC quintile portfolio combinations. Both the IG and HY universes share a relatively flat distribution of companies in the different quintile combinations. Intuitively, we find a slightly increased number of companies in the lowest EMC quintile that are at the same time among the most shorted.

We test whether ESI is predictive of corporate bond returns for companies with either low or high equity momentum. Similar to our analysis with ESP, we divide our IG and HY universes into bonds with low and bonds with high equity momentum, based on their EMC score. The EMC score is a bond-level metric ranging from one (lowest equity momentum) to 10 (highest equity momentum). All bonds with an EMC score above five are considered to have high equity momentum; the remaining bonds are considered to have low equity momentum. We then form replicating portfolios in the different universes and again compare the return characteristics of the Max. ESI and Min. ESI portfolio. If ESI were without predictive information beyond EMC, we would expect the Min. ESI portfolio to not outperform the Max. ESI portfolio.

Table 22.17 documents the outperformance of the Min. ESI portfolio over the Max. ESI portfolio, which is significant regardless of the index and the EMC filter. Our results suggest that information in equity short interest is complementary to the return-relevant information in equity momentum, as ESI is useful to differentiate among issuers with high and low equity momentum.

PANEL A
Investment Grade Universe

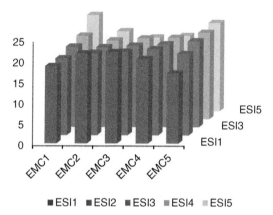

■ ESI1 ■ ESI2 ■ ESI3 ■ ESI4 ■ ESI5

PANEL B
High Yield Universe

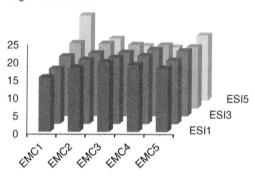

■ ESI1 ■ ESI2 ■ ESI3 ■ ESI4 ■ ESI5

FIGURE 21.8   Average Number of Companies per ESI and EMC Quintile Combination

Note: Each month companies are ranked according to their ESI value and EMC score independently and sorted into 25 portfolios. For example, ESI 1 contains the 20% of issuers with the lowest ESI values, ESI 2 the next 20% of issuers, and so on. The sample period covers January 2007 to December 2019.

Source: Bloomberg, Compustat, FIS Astec Analytics, Barclays Research

TABLE 21.17 Performance Statistics of Replicating Portfolios with an ESI Tilt, Universe Split into Low and High Equity Momentum Bonds

	Entire Replicating Universe			Low Equity Momentum Bonds			High Equity Momentum Bonds		
	Min.	Max.	Min.–Max.	Min.	Max.	Min.–Max.	Min.	Max.	Min.–Max.
IG Avg. Ex. Ret. (%/yr)	1.64	−0.42	2.05	1.00	−0.33	1.33	2.47	1.19	1.28
Vol. (%/yr)	4.81	5.13	1.61	4.21	4.25	1.16	4.41	4.69	1.21
Inf. Ratio	0.34	−0.08	1.27	0.23	−0.07	1.14	0.56	0.25	1.05
Min. Ex. Ret. (%/m)	−6.7	−10.36	−0.76	−4.99	−5.61	−1.67	−5.21	−7.89	−0.63
Corr. w. Index	0.96	0.92	−0.06	0.85	0.84	0.02	0.91	0.90	−0.20
HY Avg. Tot. Ret. (%/yr)	7.04	5.44	1.60	0.87	−0.65	1.52	7.10	6.65	0.46
Vol. (%/yr)	9.22	10.21	3.02	7.58	7.88	1.66	4.15	4.34	1.23
Sharpe / Inf. Ratio	0.76	0.53	0.53	−0.04	−0.23	0.91	1.40	1.23	0.37
Min. Tot. Ret. (%/m)	−17.21	−18.85	−2.77	−20.04	−20.08	−1.49	−3.06	−3.81	−2.36
Corr. w. Index	0.84	0.82	−0.21	0.68	0.69	−0.16	0.36	0.37	−0.07

Note: The indices are the Bloomberg Barclays US Corporate and High Yield indices. Low equity momentum bonds are those within the replication universe that have an EMC score from one to five, and high equity momentum bonds are bonds within the replication universe that have an EMC score from six to ten. Min. and Max. replicating portfolios minimize and maximize the portfolio's overall ESI value, at the same time matching the index OAS, DTS, and sector weights. Min.–Max. represents the return series of the Min. over the Max. portfolio. The sample period covers January 2007 to December 2019. We use 1-month Libor to compute Sharpe ratios from total returns.
Source: Bloomberg, Compustat, FIS Astec Analytics, Barclays Research

REFERENCES

Ben Dor, A., L. Dynkin, J. Hyman, P. Houweling, E. Van Leeuwen, and O. Penninga. 2007. "DTS^SM (Duration Times Spread)." *Journal of Portfolio Management* 33(2): 77–100.

Ben Dor, A., and J. Xu. 2015. "Should Equity Investors Care about Corporate Bond Prices? Using Bond Prices to Construct Equity Momentum Strategies." *Journal of Portfolio Management* 41 (4): 35–49.

Boehmer, E., C. Jones, and X. Zhang. 2008. "Which Shorts Are Informed?" *Journal of Finance* 63(2): 491–527.

Christophe, S., M. Ferri, J. Hsieh, and T.-H. D. King. 2016. "Short Selling and the Cross-Section of Corporate Bond Returns." *Journal of Fixed Income* 26 (2): 54–77.

Hendershott, T., R. Kozhan, and V. Raman. 2020. "Short Selling and Price Discovery in Corporate Bonds." *Journal of Financial and Quantitative Analysis* 55(1): 77–115.

Konstantinovsky, V., K. Y. Ng, and B. D. Phelps. 2016. "Measuring Bond-Level Liquidity." *Journal of Portfolio Management* 42(4): 116–128.

NOTES

1. See Boehmer, Jones, and Zhang (2008) for a study on the US stock market.
2. Christophe, Ferri, Hsieh, and King (2016) find that stock shorting activity is informative about subsequent corporate bond returns. Hendershott, Kozhan, and Raman (2020) confirm this finding and conclude that short sellers' information flows from stocks to bonds but not from bonds to stocks.
3. We discuss the relationship between ESI and EMC in Appendix 21.1.
4. See Ben Dor et al. (2007) for details about DTS.
5. We group issuers into sectors according to the Bloomberg sector classification of their largest bond in the respective index. We aggregate the different sectors into these eight categories: consumer discretionary, consumer staples, energy and transport, financials and real estate, industrials, communications and information technology, materials, and utilities.
6. Liquidity cost scores (LCS) is a bond-level metric that measures the cost of an immediate, institutional-size, round-trip transaction, and is expressed as a percentage of the corporate bond's price. See Konstantinovsky, Ng, and Phelps (2016) for details about LCS.
7. Different from equity short interest, which is defined by the amount of shares in lending transactions vs. shares outstanding, short interest at the bond level is defined by bond notional in lending transaction vs. notional outstanding.
8 Qualifying bonds are senior bonds with at least three years to maturity, a notional above the 25th percentile, if available issued less than two years ago, and with a duration closest to the sector average.
9. We aggregate bond-level ESP scores to the company level by taking the value-weighted average of all of the ESP scores of the company's bonds that are part of the respective index.

Index

Printed and bound by CPI Group (UK) Ltd, Croydon, CR0 4YY

23/04/2025

14660920-0001
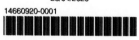